SONS OF THE BRAVE
Volume One

The Old Boys of the Duke of York's Royal Military School who fell in the Great War

Including the "Lost Boys" missing from the school memorial at the Duke of York's Royal Military School, Dover, Kent

Richard Watt, Andy Benns & Chris Tomlinson

Sons of the Brave

Copyright © Richard Watt, Andy Benns & Chris Tomlinson 2023

All rights reserved. This book or any portion thereof may not be reproduced or used in any manner whatsoever without the express written permission of the Authors except for the use of brief quotations in a book review or scholarly journal.

ISBN: 9781399951685
Imprint: Guston Gate Publishing

First published 2023

Various: the black and white images of the former school site in Chelsea throughout the book, are taken from *An Album of Views of Duke of York's Royal Military School, Chelsea, Centenary of the Foundation 1801-1901*, by Gale & Polden. The images from the current school site in Guston are a second Album of Views, published in 1910, also by Gale & Polden. They both likely show, sadly unnamed, some of the boys who would go on to lose their lives in the First World War

Contents

Introduction & Glossary	*Page 7*
The School Song	*Page 16*
The School Memorial	*Page 19*
The Fallen, by Service, Regiment & Corps	*Page 28*
Those Recorded in Error	*Page 611*
Burial & Memorial Locations	*Page 615*
Index, by Service, Regiment & Corps	*Page 637*
Appendix I – the unveiling of the war memorial	*Page 641*
Appendix II – account of the death of Harold Kenney	*Page 647*
In Memoriam – Richard Hill Watt	*Page 650*

Sons of the Brave

Sons of the Brave

Introduction & Glossary

Introduction

The Duke of York's Royal Military School can trace its history back more than two hundred years, to 1801, and the foundation by Royal Warrant of the Royal Military Asylum for the Children of Soldiers of the Regular Army[1] by Frederick, Duke of York, Commander-in-Chief of the British Army and second son of King George III. The first meeting of the Board of Commissioners took place on 18 April 1801. The idea of an institution to provide support and education to the orphans of fallen service personnel in Britain was not new. The first of these institutions was the Royal Hospital School, which was founded by Royal Charter in 1712 and co-located with the Greenwich Hospital in London. The school had been founded to provide assistance and education to the orphans of seafarers in the Royal and Merchant Navies. It remained in Greenwich until it was relocated to Holbrook, on the northern shore of the estuary of the River Stour in Suffolk in 1933.

The second institution was the Royal Hibernian Military School, located in Phoenix Park in Dublin, also founded by Royal Charter, in 1769. This establishment was intended to educate orphaned children of members of the British armed forces in Ireland. The last of the institutions was the infant establishment. This orphanage was located on the Isle of Wight in a rented farmhouse and run by General Sir George Hewett[2], the funding from this establishment being raised by Hewett from fellow officers and influential friends.

The Royal Military Asylum was to be located near the end of the King's private road in Chelsea and the regulations for the school were to be based upon those of the Royal Hibernian Military School. The buildings for the school were designed by John Sanders[3], and although there were some delays and problems with the construction, the first children arrived on 29 August 1803, 43 girls and 17 boys, who had been living in General Hewett's institution on the Isle of Wight. Children also arrived from the Paddington (Naval) Asylum on 06 September as well as from the York Military Hospital, Chelsea,

---

[1] The definition of Asylum being *"an institution providing care and protection to needy individuals"*
[2] General Sir George Hewett, 1st Baronet GCB PC (Ire) was Commander-in-Chief, India and then Commander-in-Chief, Ireland for the British Army
[3] John Sanders was the first pupil of Sir John Soane and as well as designing the Royal Military Asylum (1801-1803), he is also known for designing the Royal Military College, Sandhurst (1808-1812)

so that in total there were 130 admissions, 52 of them girls and 78 boys.

Admission to the school was by a parent or guardian of the child petitioning the Governors for the child to be admitted. The Petition Documents for each child asked questions about the father's service, his name, rank and regimental number, as well as the regiment in which he had served and any medals that he had been awarded. The mother's name was also recorded, as was the date of marriage. Along with the Petition Document, the parent or guardian was also expected to submit the parents' marriage certificate as well as the child's birth and baptism certificates.

If the application was successful, the child could be admitted to the school from the age of seven, where, as well as receiving lessons based on the Madras System[4], the students were also taught a trade. At the age of fourteen, the children were discharged from the school. Many embarked on a four-year indentured apprenticeship, completion of which, accompanied by a good behaviour certificate provided by the person to whom they were apprenticed, resulted in the award of a five Guinea bonus[5]. However, in the case of many of the boys, they followed in their father's footsteps by enlisting in the military, predominantly the army.

Due to overcrowding in the school in Chelsea, a branch of the Royal Military Asylum was opened in 1816, located in the old Cavalry Barracks on London Road, Southampton, Hampshire. These buildings were enlarged in order to accommodate 400 boys, but in 1823 the boys were returned to Chelsea and their place was taken by orphaned daughters of the rank-and-file soldiers. However, over the next seventeen years, the number of girls at this location lessened, with the last of them being moved back to Chelsea in 1840 and the buildings being taken over by the Ordnance Survey. Once the girls who had been returned to Chelsea left the school, the last to do so being in 1845, for a century and a half the school became a boys' only school.

The school remained in Chelsea for more than one hundred years, its name changing in 1892 to the Duke of York's Royal Military School, but in 1909 it moved to new, purpose-built premises, a stone's throw from Dover Castle and a quarter of a mile south of

---

[4] So called because it originated at the Military Male Orphan Asylum, Egmore, near Madras, India, where education was imparted by senior pupils who educated juniors
[5] Approximately £250 in 2021, but 35 days wages for a skilled tradesman in 1810 (*The National Archives*)

the village of Guston in Kent, where the school remains to this day. The school did see the boys evacuated during both the First and Second World Wars. During the First World War, the evacuation was to Hutton, near Brentwood in Essex, the reason for this being to provide a transit point at the school site for the troops who were passing through the port of Dover heading to or returning from the Western Front.

In the aftermath of the war and following the end of the Anglo-Irish War of 1919-21, the Royal Hibernian Military School closed its site in Dublin and relocated to Shorncliffe, near Folkestone, Kent, in 1922. After two years in this location, the school was then merged with the Duke of York's, many of the boys who were originally "Hibs", as the boys of that school were known, becoming "Dukies", as the Duke of York's boys were known, in September 1924. During the Second World War, the boys were evacuated in 1940, this time to the Saunton Sands Hotel, near Braunton, Devon, and they were not moved back to Dover until 1946. The school saw the reintroduction of girls as students in 1994, as well as becoming tri-service, also in the 1990s[6], and in 1999 the school saw its first civilian Headmaster, all of the previous Headmasters being army officers of at least Lieutenant-Colonel rank. The school was also granted Academy status in 2010, which saw the admission of non-military children for the first time in its long history.

There have been several extensive histories of the school written in the past, but this is not a history of the school, but a history of some of the boys who attended the school. Most of the boys followed in their fathers' footsteps and enlisted in the British Army, with many of those who did so making the ultimate sacrifice, the first of these being four Dukies who gave their lives during the Peninsula Campaign of 1808-1814, and two who died at the Battle of Waterloo in 1815. It is the successors of these boys, who lost their lives whilst serving their country a century later, that this book is produced to remember.

The boys who have given their lives in the service of their country are commemorated on a series of memorial tablets that are located within the school chapel, The Chapel of St. Michael and St. George, which were erected *"In Memory of OLD BOYS of the DUKE OF YORK'S SCHOOL who fell in BATTLE or died on ACTIVE SERVICE for SOVEREIGN and COUNTRY".*

---

[6] Prior to this, the school was purely for the sons of soldiers

The first of these tablets records those that fell in the Peninsula Campaign (1808-14) and the Crimean War (1854-6) and the last tablet records some of those who fell during the Second World War and continues until the present time, the last person commemorated being Rodney Wilson, who was killed in Iraq in 2007. In 2014, with the centenary of the outbreak of the First World War approaching, it was decided by some of the Old Boys of the school that they would produce rugby shirts commemorating the event, with each person who purchased a rugby shirt choosing a name from the war memorial of a boy who had been killed in that conflict and for it to be displayed on the back of the shirt.

During the choosing of the names, it was discovered that there were several errors made in the names of the boys recorded on the memorial tablets. In addition, whilst there are 231 names on the memorial tablets for the First World War, with a further two added in recent years, a newspaper report at the time of the unveiling of the school's war memorial in 1922 stated that there had been 247 Old Boys who had given their lives during the conflict[7]. Six years after the 2014 commemoration, during the Covid-19 pandemic, the authors were each individually researching the names of the boys recorded on the tablets commemorating those who fell during the First World War. Once it was discovered that we were all working on a similar project, the three of us "pooled resources".

The idea of the project was therefore to establish how many of the names recorded had errors and also to locate the "Lost Boys" who had not been recorded, as well as documenting those whose names were recorded without error. All who took part in the project were surprised by the findings. Of the 231 boys named on the memorial, only 144 were recorded without error, including two who had only been recognised in recent years with the addition of an additional, smaller, plaque next to the main memorial tablet. Of the 88 errors found, these included incorrect spelling of names, incorrectly recorded regiments in which the boys had served and four names that should not have been recorded on the memorial. However, the biggest surprise was the number of "Lost Boys" found. Rather than the 16 that were initially sought, there are actually 181 Old Boys who gave their lives in the Great War and who are not commemorated on the memorial tablets in the school chapel. They are now included,

---

[7] *Dover Express*, Friday 30 June 1922, see Appendix I for the full article

but any further boys "found" will be included in later editions of the book.

This book contains the biographies of all the 409 Dukies, recorded in order of precedence of their service, regiment and corps, who died during the First World War, either in action, as a result of action, due to an accident or by disease, and who have been commemorated by the Commonwealth War Graves Commission, which includes deaths up to the date of the official end of the conflict, 31 August 1921. The biographies of the four names incorrectly commemorated are also included, with as much detail about them as it has been possible to ascertain. No fallen servicemen have been included without a corresponding admission record or Petition Document and a number of "claimed" Dukies have been disregarded on that basis, including Lance Corporal, 556040, Walter Coombes, Royal Engineers, listed by the Commonwealth War Graves Commission as having been *"Educated at Duke of York's Royal Mil' School"*, but no boy of that name was ever admitted to the school. With the publication of this book, the aim is that any funds that are raised will be used to make corrections to those who have been recorded with errors and, more importantly, have the names of the "Lost Boys" commemorated in the chapel of the school which they attended, in some cases more than a century and a half ago.

Attribution has been given where we have relied on specific sources, particularly local newspaper publications and sincere apologies are offered for any inadvertent breach of copyright. This will be willingly rectified in future editions should you make your concerns known to us via Facebook, at "DYRMS & RHMS History Research Group". We are very grateful for the photographs shared with us either directly or via Ancestry.co.uk. We have not sought permission to use all of the images from the latter, but our sincerest thanks are offered to family members/picture holders for uploading the images and the inclusion of them adds an additional layer of interest to this Roll of Honour. Members of Greatwarforum.org were very generous with their time and knowledge, and the Longlongtrail.co.uk was a great resource for 1914 troop movements in particular. Finally, please note that towns, counties and countries have been included in their contemporary usage, with an accompanying footnote where required, but the anglicised graveyard names have been used, consistent with the Commonwealth War Graves Commission.

The school has an extensive archive, including holding almost all of the Petition Documents dating back to the first admissions in 1803, and this resource has made it possible to confirm that those "Lost Boys" were in fact Dukies. However, possibly the biggest resource has been the Archive Lead, Mr Andrew Nunn, former teacher and now a Governor of the school, whose help has been invaluable, particularly in granting access to the Petition Documents that have been scanned for The Ogilby Muster[8], a First World War Digitisation Project which is being undertaken by the Army Museums Ogilby Trust, as well as the thousands that have not been scanned and are stored in the Archive Centre within the school.

This is a companion book to another volume which documents the boys from The Royal Hibernian Military School who fell during the First World War, *Fear God Honour The King*[9], using the motto of that school as its title, in the same way that the motto of the Duke of York's Royal Military School – *Sons Of The Brave* – has been used as the title for this book. During the project, it was discovered that it was not just the fact that the Royal Military Asylum regulations were to be based on those of the older establishment, nor that the two schools became one in 1924, but that many of the Dukies had brothers, fathers or uncles who were Hibs. In addition, Dukies and Hibs fell alongside each other on a number of occasions, with at least two instances of nearly adjacent burials.

In addition, this book is the first volume documenting the fallen who had attended the Royal Military Asylum and Duke of York's Royal Military School, as during the course of the research it has been discovered that in addition to those recorded "error free", there are also errors and omissions relating to Dukies who fell during the Second World War, which will be published in a later volume. In the future, it is also planned to produce a third volume documenting those Dukies who fell during both the conflicts of the nineteenth century and the conflicts that have taken place since the Second World War, as errors and omissions have also been discovered from these conflicts during the course of the research for this book.

Richard Watt, August 2022

---

[8] www.theogilbymuster.com
[9] Benns, A., Tomlinson, C. & Watt, R. (2021). *Fear God Honour The King*, Guston Gate Publishing

Glossary

Corps
: a battlefield formation of the British Army; contained two or more divisions and c. 50,000 men. One step below an army group and normally commanded by a Lieutenant General.

Division
: a large military formation of the British Army; at the start of the war a British infantry division comprised three brigades and supporting arms such as artillery and engineers. They were often numbered and with regional affiliations, especially those that were formed from volunteers rather than the Regular Army.

Brigade
: the major tactical formation of the British Army; at the start of the war, a brigade comprised four infantry battalions along with a small headquarters, but by 1918 this was reduced to three battalions due to casualties. Also commonly used by the Royal Artillery at that time for a battalion sized unit, normally comprising three batteries.

Battalion
: the standard operational unit of the British infantry; normally comprised of around 1000 men (at full establishment), including four fighting companies, a headquarters and support. British county infantry regiments generally had two regular service infantry battalions (normally one on Home Service and one posted overseas) and several Territorial Force and Reserve battalions at the start of the Great War (see below).

Company
: the smallest complete tactical unit of the British Army; divided into four platoons of around 50 men. The rough equivalent sub-unit in cavalry regiments was the squadron.

Battery
: the standard operational unit of the British and Empire artillery; normally comprised of around 200 men plus guns, limbers, horses and other wheeled transport.

War Diary	the official unit war record of the British Army in the Great War and all successive wars and campaigns.
Commemorated	used where a fallen serviceman has no known grave and is commemorated on a memorial such as the Menin Gate, rather than buried within a graveyard.
Reserve	most infantry regiments had a number of Reserve battalions during the war, where recruits were trained and men passed through when returning from a period away due to wounds or other reasons. They performed the function of a home depot.
Service	an infantry battalion raised after the outbreak of hostilities for war service only; most commonly associated with the so-called Pals' battalions of the New Army recruited by Lord Kitchener with his famous posters.
Territorial Force	an infantry battalion that was part of the Territorial Force, which came into being in 1908 as part of the Haldane Reforms. These units were intended for home defence and as a second line reinforcement for an expeditionary force in future conflicts; pre-war some would have enlisted in the TF as it had a lower minimum age at 17.

Sons of the Brave

The School Song

Play up, Dukies!

Words by G. C. Nugent MVO[10]
Music by M. A. C. Salmond

Verse 1

We're drilled and dressed and disciplined, and taught to play the game,
Play up, Dukies! Play up, Dukies!
We'll take you on at anything and beat you at the same,
Play up, Dukies! Play up, Dukies!
The spirit of our soldier sires is round about us still,
And everything we've got to do we work at with a will;
Oh! We've got no use for slackers at the School on Lone Tree Hill,
Play up Dukies! Play up Dukies!

Chorus

Be it Peace or be it War, Play up, Dukies!
As your Fathers did before, Play up, Dukies!
For the honour of your name,
Take the torch and fan the flame,
Play the game, Play the game, Play up, Dukies!

Verse 2

And when we join our regiments and we march and ride and shoot,
Play up, Dukies! Play up, Dukies!
You'll recognise the Dukie as the very best recruit,
Play up, Dukies! Play up, Dukies!
For when the British soldier marches forth to right the wrong,
And work is at its hardest and the fight is fierce and long,
Then the old White Rose shall lead us, and the Dukie shall be strong.
Play up, Dukies! Play up, Dukies!

---

[10] George Colborne Nugent MVO was Commandant of the school from July 1913 until August 1914, when he was recalled to command 5th London Brigade. He was killed in action as a Brigadier-General in France on 31 May 1915

Sons of the Brave

Chorus

Be it Peace or be it War, Play up, Dukies!
As your Fathers did before, Play up, Dukies!
For the honour of your name,
Take the torch and fan the flame,
Play the game, Play the game, Play up, Dukies!

Verse 3

When veterans and pensioners we're drifting down the hill,
Play up, Dukies! Play up, Dukies!
Though Death be in the valley, we will face him, Dukies still,
Play up, Dukies! Play up, Dukies!
And though our lonely graves be dug in some far distant land,
Our spirits coming back again will hover near at hand,
And the boys will hear us whisper and the boys will understand,
Play up, Dukies! Play up, Dukies!

Chorus

Be it Peace or be it War, Play up, Dukies!
As your Fathers did before, Play up, Dukies!
For the honour of your name,
Take the torch and fan the flame,
Play the game, Play the game, Play up, Dukies!

Sons of the Brave

The School Memorial

The war memorial of the Duke of York's Royal Military School

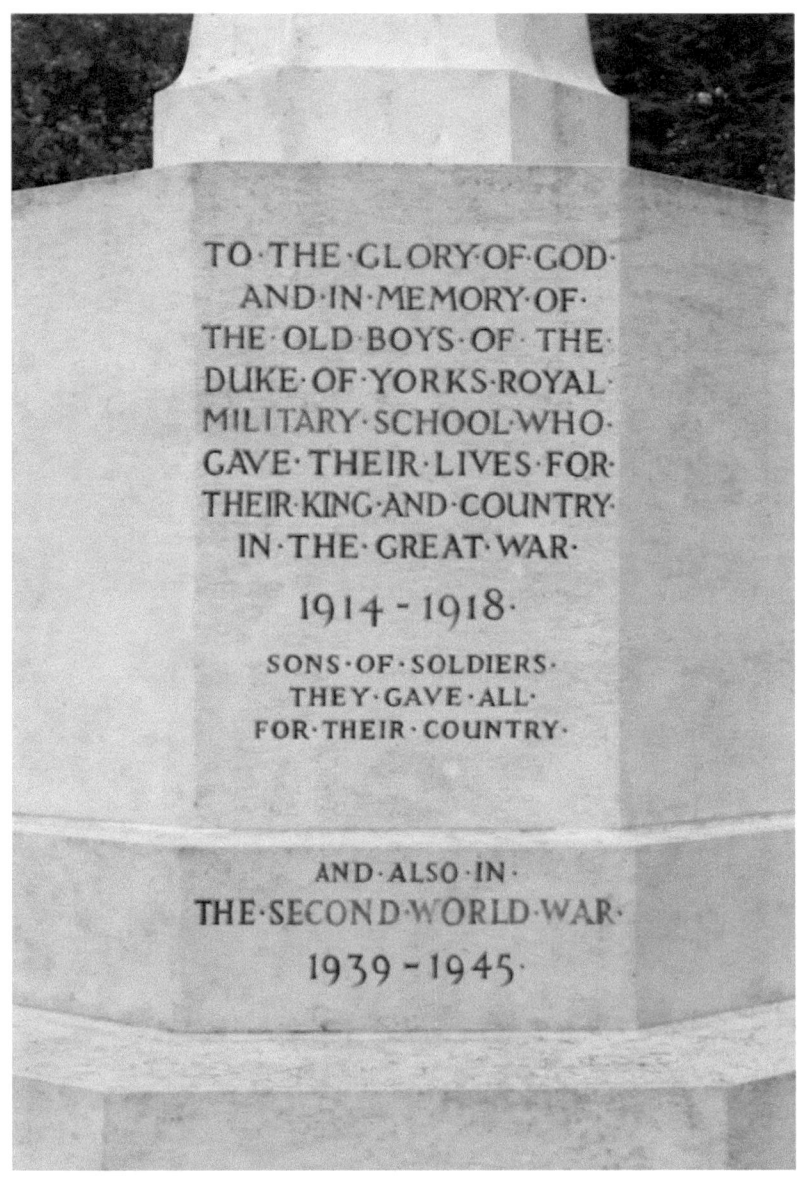

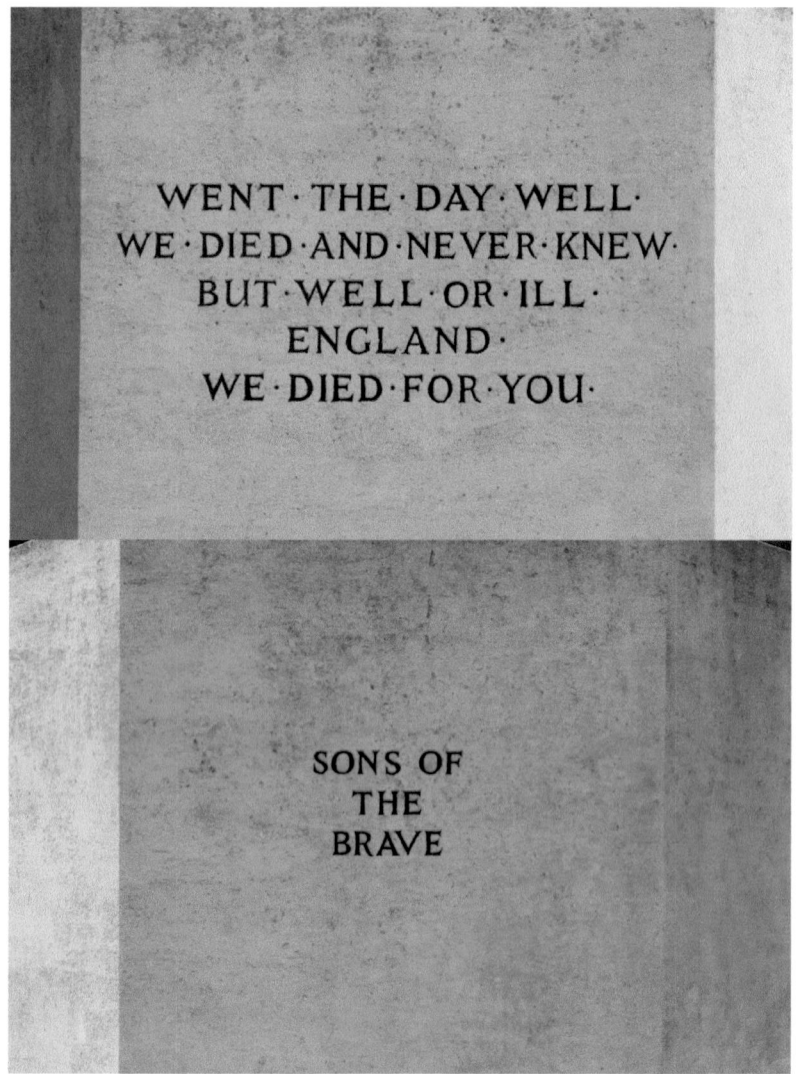

The school chapel, now dedicated as "The Royal Military Chapel of Saint Michael and Saint George". The following pages show the First World War memorial tablets, which hang in the chapel.

THE EAST WINDOW
OF
THIS CHAPEL
WAS ERECTED TO THE
GLORY OF GOD AND IN MEMORY
OF OLD BOYS OF THE DUKE OF YORKS
SCHOOL WHO FELL IN BATTLE OR DIED
ON ACTIVE SERVICE
FOR SOVEREIGN AND COUNTRY

SOUTH AFRICA
CONTINUED

J. ELLICOT — MIDDLESEX REGT
HENRY WALKER — 13TH HUSSARS
J. J. ROWLEY — 5TH FUSILIERS
G. WHEELER — ROYAL ARTILLERY
D. R. MACKIE
CECIL KEMPSTER
H. E. MARTIN
G. T. McGARAGLE
F. BAMFORD — ROYAL ARTILLERY
W. H. GRACEY
S. SMYTH — EAST SURREY REGT
W. GOWARD
H. P. TIMLOCK

THE GREAT WAR
1914-1918

A. H. SCOTT — ROYAL HORSE GUARDS
G. WEBB — THE QUEEN'S BAYS
E. R. BATES
L. D. S. S. SENIOR — CARABINIERS
P. W. A. HAVILAND — THE SCOTS GREYS
E. ELLIOTT — 5TH HUSSARS
T. J. FULLER
T. MAXTED — 5TH LANCERS
S. E. BENNETT — 9TH LANCERS
S. H. ALLEN — 12TH LANCERS
D. PITMAN — 15TH HUSSARS
F. M. WREN
A. G. CHESHIRE — 15TH HUSSARS
A. J. LUTON — 16TH LANCERS
G. H. HARGROVE
R. E. SLADON — 17TH LANCERS
H. W. KENNY — 19TH HUSSARS
W. KENNEDY — KING EDWARD'S HORSE
J. V. NICHOLSON — YEOMANRY

THE GREAT WAR
CONTINUED

C. S. SINCLAIR
T. E. CHERRY
T. JAMES — ROYAL FIELD ARTILLERY
R. T. PATTERSON
L. CROSS
D. HURLEY
W. M. COLLINS
A. BELCHER
W. L. RAGIN
A. W. LAWRIE
C. CORBIN
A. J. CARNE
C. H. POLLARD
R. GWYTHER
A. W. GANLEY
T. M. BRYAN
G. E. FUNNELL
R. B. P. JOHNSON, M.C.
W. A. McKENZIE
R. BEESTON
E. RUST — ROYAL ARTILLERY
H. G. SMITH
C. WHITE
A. W. PORTER — ROYAL ENGINEERS
A. REES
J. C. ATKEY
L. A. HOWELL
R. J. DAVIES
W. J. CURTISS, M.M.
A. W. ROMAINE
H. E. ELWICK — COLDSTREAM GUARDS
T. DRAKE — SCOTS GUARDS
P. PITMAN — IRISH GUARDS
J. D. LAKE — THE QUEENS REGT
J. W. POPE
A. V. HUNGERFORD
F. R. ROUTLEY

THE EAST WINDOW
of
THIS CHAPEL
WAS ERECTED TO THE
GLORY OF GOD AND IN MEMORY
OF OLD BOYS OF THE DUKE OF YORKS
SCHOOL WHO FELL IN BATTLE OR DIED
ON ACTIVE SERVICE
FOR SOVEREIGN AND COUNTRY

THE GREAT WAR 1914-1918 CONTINUED

A. CARTER	G. CATER
C. COCKRAINE THE QUEENS REGT	W. B. DICKS
H. J. SEYMOUR	R. F. FERGUSON
H. R. SOMERS THE BUFFS	W. E. DAYMOND
W. L. DONELAN	J. W. TALO
G. T. WILSON	J. P. PAGE
R. W. WINTER NORTHAMPTON	H. W. MUDDLE
W. M. ROUTLEDGE	G. E. SIMPSON
G. T. MAYCOCK	E. R. HUMPHREY
T. ANGEL	S. WALKER
S. D. W. COOPER ROYAL FUSILIERS	G. BOOTH
H. W. KING	J. A. COLLINS
G. S. MATHEWS	F. W. H. BLANE
A. E. NORRINGTON	A. J. HUMPHRIES
E. G. GAVEN	W. F. FROST
G. LANGDON	J. MELVILLE
H. KENNY	S. MERRIOTT
S. J. YATES	A. F. MERRIOTT
F. WILSON	T. G. GOLDING
J. BRIGHTY	B. J. GRAY M.M.
W. H. P. TOOMEY THE NORFOLK REGT	W. E. FOX
K. A. WHITE	J. W. FORREST
W. P. CLARKIN	S. BRIGHTMORE
H. L. W. FREEMAN	A. DONNELLY
W. STROHM	A. A. TAYLOR
W. T. CARR THE DEVONSHIRE REGT	S. G. SANDERS
J. H. ELLIS	C. G. PEARCE
N. J. BATTERS	W. FITZGERALD
L. E. HILL THE SUFFOLK REGT	E. CHURCH
F. E. C. HALL	A. T. CLEAR
W. L. HARDY	S. G. MERRIOTT
J. SPIERS THE SOMERSET LIGHT INFANTRY	J. W. LEWIS
J. BARCLAY WEST YORKSHIRE REGT	F. BROOKER
H. BOOTH	W. B. LATHOM
C. PYE	H. B. EDNEY
J. W. KAVENY EAST YORKS THIRD REGT	J. W. CROSS
J. E. WOOD D.C.M.	E. W. CATHCART

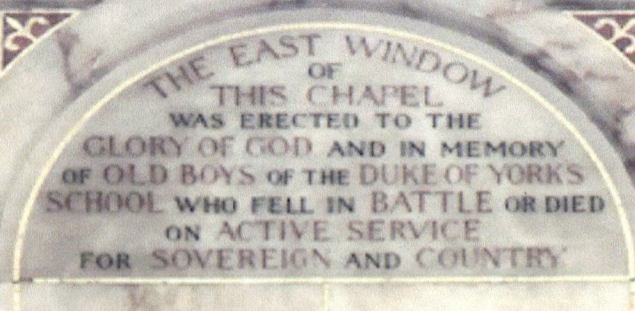

THE EAST WINDOW
OF
THIS CHAPEL
WAS ERECTED TO THE
GLORY OF GOD AND IN MEMORY
OF OLD BOYS OF THE DUKE OF YORK'S
SCHOOL WHO FELL IN BATTLE OR DIED
ON ACTIVE SERVICE
FOR SOVEREIGN AND COUNTRY

THE GREAT WAR 1914-1918 CONTINUED

W. R. JAMES	THE DORSETSHIRE REGT	
F. T. HARNET		
E. G. MASSIE		
A. MOFFATT		
C. BLUNDELL	PRINCE OF WALES	
H. GREGSON		
H. E. J. HAYES	THE WELSH REGT	
F. S. PEOPLES		
G. E. JOHNSON		
E. J. ANDREWS		
C. L. PALMER		
J. G. JOSEPH	THE BLACK WATCH	
C. MELDUM		
S. H. BISHOP		
J. J. PEGRAM	OXFORD & BUCKS LIGHT INFANTRY	
W. H. SMITH		
J. SOUGHAN	THE ESSEX REGT	
E. P. F. FIG		
C. D. RANDALL	SHERWOOD FORESTERS	
H. MEYNOE		
T. ENNIS		
G. DARCY	THE LOYAL REGT	
G. A. HAYMAN	NORTHAMPTON REGT	
S. W. LENNON		
W. BRINDALL	ROYAL WEST SURREY	
B. KNIGHT		
F. H. WAY		
W. RYAN		
L. G. FALKNER	WEST RIDING REGT	
L. J. H. FALKNER		
T. A. J. GREEN	MIDDLESEX REGT	
W. T. VAUSE. D.C.M.		
S. W. HALLETT		
E. J. H. BROMWICH		
H. H. ADSHEAD	ROYAL SUSSEX	
H. F. P. CARTER		
G. A. HOOKER		

W. R. KING	KING'S ROYAL RIFLE CORPS	
A. V. SOMERSET		
W. P. McCARRAGHER	WILTSHIRE REGT	
W. J. LEWIS		
A. BABBINGTON		
R. G. SMITH	MANCHESTER REGT	
A. J. RUTLEDGE	NORTH STAFFORD LIGHT INFY	
H. S. BOOTH	YORK & LANCS REGT	
R. SCOTT	DURHAM LIGHT INFANTRY	
R. DOUGLAS		
L. MONGER		
J. B. RYAN	HIGHLAND LIGHT INFANTRY	
W. ANDERSON		
J. FINDLAY		
F. M. HUSHER	SEAFORTH HIGHLANDERS	
W. H. BARRETT		
W. CHILTON. M.M.		
J. A. HUME		
R. F. WILLIAMS		
A. V. HARBER		
R. W. ELDER	GORDON HIGHLANDERS	
P. HYDE		
W. MILNE		
W. G. TAYLOR	CAMERON HIGHLANDERS	
W. A. ROWE		
W. G. PROSSER		
H. G. RAWLINSON	ROYAL ULSTER	
W. A. B. CLARK		
H. HARDWICK	ROYAL IRISH RIFLES	
F. W. CORRY	CONNAUGHT RANGERS	
A. G. RATTRAY	ARGYLL & SUTHERLAND HIGHLANDERS	
H. T. BUNNETT		
C. W. THOMAS		
J. CHILTON		
T. R. R. COTCHERZ		
F. R. WALKER. M.C.		
W. CHUDLEY		

THE EAST WINDOW of
THIS CHAPEL
WAS ERECTED TO THE
GLORY OF GOD AND IN MEMORY
OF OLD BOYS OF THE DUKE OF YORK'S
SCHOOL WHO FELL IN BATTLE OR DIED
ON ACTIVE SERVICE
FOR SOVEREIGN AND COUNTRY

THE GREAT WAR
CONTINUED

A.H. ROBERTSON — ARGYLL & SUTHERLAND HIGHLANDERS
V.H. WATERFORD
G.A. AXON
H.A. MILLER
G.E. ROBERTS — THE LEINSTER REGT / ROYAL MUNSTER FUSILIERS
A.G. KELLEY — THE RIFLE BRIGADE
L.J. RICKWOOD — CORPS OF ARMY SCHOOLMASTERS
F.J.A. CROWE — ROYAL ARMY MEDICAL CORPS
J.C. VICKERS
A. GRIEVE — ROYAL ARMY ORDNANCE CORPS
H. HORNER
J. ELDRIDGE
A.B. SMITH — ROYAL ARMY SERVICE CORPS
H.H.J. SAINTY
G.W. WHEELHOUSE
C. MARS
C.N. MATHIESON — MACHINE GUN CORPS
A.E. ANDERSON
W.J. BURTENSHAW — ROYAL FLYING CORPS
F.G. HALL — AUSTRALIAN LIGHT HORSE
J.T. TOOHEY — AUSTRALIAN LIGHT INFANTRY
H.G. ANDREWS — CANADIANS
W.C.T. KNIGHT — ROYAL IRISH FUSILIERS
H. BARRATT M.C. — ROYAL ARTILLERY
A.R. TOWELLS
E. TOWELLS

THE SECOND WORLD WAR
1939-45

F. CANNON — 3RD THE KING'S
J. FORRISTER — 12TH ROYAL L
T.C. COLE
H.A. BLEACH O.B.E. M.C. — GRENADIER GU
L.E. MAYNARD
H.A. CHEESEMAN
E.M. KEHOE — ROYAL EN
F.J. POPE
S. BENNETT — ROYAL COR
J. DUNNING
G. DUNNING
S. GRAVER
F. WILLIS
M.G. DUNKELD
S.H.L. LYNWOOD
J. GOBLE — THE ROYAL LIN
M. ST. J. RICHARDS
W. LANE — THE BEDFORD HERTFORDSH
B.R.T. McLEAN
R. BANKS — THE ROYAL LI
K.A. GUTTERIDGE
C.C. BEDWELL
R. DENNIS — THE EAST
B.F. GOOSEY — THE NOR
E.H. CRANE
E.A. EDGEWORTH

Sons of the Brave

The Fallen, by Service, Regiment & Corps

F R P Gerkins	*Royal Naval Volunteer Reserve*
G H Holmes	*Royal Marines*
A F Richards	*Royal Marine Light Infantry*
A H W G C Scott	*Royal Horse Guards (The Blues)*
N W Fielding	*Royal Horse Artillery*
R M Hume	" "
E Rust	" "
H G Smith	" "
A E Stone	" "
E Towells	" "
C J White	" "
R J Meredith	*1st (King's) Dragoon Guards*
C F Bartholomew	*2nd Dragoon Guards (Queen's Bays)*
E R Bates	" "
G Webb	" "
F Cooney	*3rd (Prince of Wales's) Dragoon Guards*
E W Roake	*4th (Royal Irish) Dragoon Guards*
L D S S Senior	*6th Dragoon Guards (Carabiniers)*
R A Grizzell MM	*1st (Royal) Dragoons*
P W A Haviland	*2nd Dragoons (Royal Scots Greys)*
E Elliott	*3rd (The King's Own) Hussars*
T J Fuller	" "
L R Lewry	*8th (The King's Royal Irish) Hussars*
S E Bennett	*9th (The Queen's Royal) Lancers*
S H Allen	*12th (The Prince of Wales's Royal) Lancers*
W F Quigley	" "
D Pitman	*13th Hussars*
F M Wren	" "
A G Cheshire	*15th (The King's) Hussars*
C H Hargrove	*16th (The Queen's) Lancers*
A J Luton	" "
R E Sladden	*17th (Duke of Cambridge's Own) Lancers*
F D Maxted	*5th (Royal Irish) Lancers*
H W Kenney	*19th (Queen Alexandra's Own Royal) Hussars*
J C Bullen	*20th Hussars*
H C Watsham	" "
J V Nicholson	*Berkshire (Hungerford) Yeomanry*

W Kennedy	**King Edward's Horse (The King's Oversea Dominions Regiment)**
J May	**Reserve Cavalry Regiment**
J R Beavers	**Royal Regiment of Field Artillery**
J W Butts	" "
T E Cherry	" "
W G Cowley	" "
L C F Cross	" "
A T Crouch	" "
R J S Crowe	" "
C W Curling	" "
F T Frith	" "
F C Hilliard	" "
J L C Hirst	" "
F J Hodgkins	" "
C S Holmes	" "
W R Hope	" "
D Hurley	" "
A T James	" "
I James	" "
A H King	" "
H McNally	" "
E N Monger DSO	" "
R R Patterson	" "
P Potter	" "
H W Pridgeon	" "
C S Sinclair	" "
A R Towells	" "
J C Turner	" "
J E Williams	" "
R C Beeston	**Royal Regiment of Garrison Artillery**
A Belcher	" "
A C Browning	" "
A J Carne	" "
C J Corbin	" "
P D Donovan	" "
R C Duggan	" "
A E Freeborn	" "
G E Funnell	" "
A W Ganley	" "
E Gascoyne	" "

A E Gee	**_Royal Regiment of Garrison Artillery_**
R Gwyther	" "
R B P Johnson MC	" "
A W Laurie	" "
J E Maddocks	" "
A F McFarlane	" "
W A McKenzie	" "
W G Newland	" "
J E E Parker	" "
C H Pollard	" "
A L Ragin	" "
T M Ryan	" "
E P Sadler	" "
G Truett	" "
A E E Urell	" "
J C Atkey	**_Corps of Royal Engineers_**
A Barber DCM	" "
T J Briggs	" "
H C Caston	" "
W J Curtis MM & Bar	" "
R J Davis	" "
T W Goodall	" "
F M Graydon	" "
L A Howell	" "
A Lunn	" "
J W Maycock	" "
A W Porter	" "
A C Rees	" "
A W Romain	" "
M H Scarff	" "
V E A Stimpson	" "
W J Burtenshaw	**_Royal Flying Corps_**
J C McNamara	" "
H H Elwick	**_Coldstream Guards_**
H Gratton	" "
T Drake	**_Scots Guards_**
P Pitman	**_Irish Guards_**
G J L Ellis	**_The Royal Scots (Lothian Regiment)_**
G R Simpson	" "
A Carter	**_The Queen's (Royal West Surrey Regiment)_**

31

G Cochrane	**The Queen's (Royal West Surrey Regiment)**
A V Hungerford	" "
J D Lake	" "
J R N Pope	" "
F R Routley	" "
J J Coughlan	**The Buffs (East Kent Regiment)**
A B Davis	" "
W L Donelan	" "
H J Seymour	" "
H R Summers	" "
G T Wilson	" "
E Jepson	**The King's Own (Royal Lancaster Regiment)**
H E Pack	" "
W M Rutledge	**The Northumberland Fusiliers**
R W D Winter	" "
G T Maycock	**The Royal Warwickshire Regiment**
J J Waring	" "
T Angell	**The Royal Fusiliers (City of London Regiment)**
S D W Cooper	" "
F C Ellery	" "
A Harrison	" "
H W King	" "
J A Kirtland	" "
G P Langdon	" "
A E R Norrington	" "
A Peet	" "
W J Pepler	" "
W J Kearney	**The King's (Liverpool Regiment)**
H Kenny	" "
F Wilson	" "
S J Yates	" "
J A Yorke	" "
J H Brighty	**The Norfolk Regiment**
J S Ellard	" "
B R Hungerford	" "
T W O'Hara	" "
W S Reynolds	" "
W E Baldwin	**The Lincolnshire Regiment**
T Brown	" "
W P Clarkin	" "

H L W Freeman	**The Lincolnshire Regiment**
J T Nokes	" "
W H Strohm	" "
W H P Toomey	" "
A A White	" "
N J Batters	**The Devonshire Regiment**
W F J Carr	" "
J H Ellis	" "
B T Smith	" "
T A Coleman	**The Suffolk Regiment**
R Dean	" "
F E C Hall	" "
W L Hardy	" "
L C Hill	" "
F C Spiers	**Prince Albert's (Somerset Light Infantry)**
W E Whall MC	" "
T J Barclay	**The Prince of Wales's Own (West Yorkshire Regiment)**
H Booth	" "
C Pye	" "
W S Wade	" "
J W Kaveney	**The East Yorkshire Regiment**
S C Larkin	" "
J E Wood DCM	" "
G A Bigsby	**The Bedfordshire Regiment**
J E D Caney	" "
G Carter	" "
W B Dicks	" "
W E Daymond	**The Leicestershire Regiment**
R F Ferguson	" "
J F C Kifford	" "
J W Talo	" "
J R Christie	**The Royal Irish Regiment**
J T Toohey	" "
A A E Williams	" "
J P Page	**Alexandra, Princess of Wales's Own (Yorkshire Regiment)**
R Webb	" "
W F Bond	**The Lancashire Fusiliers**
W G Brown	" "
E R Humphrey	" "

W Muddle	**The Lancashire Fusiliers**
G E Simpson	" "
S C Walker MM	**The Royal Scots Fusiliers**
W H Grant	**The Cheshire Regiment**
A G Booth	**The Royal Welsh Fusiliers**
G W Howell	" "
F W H Blane	**The South Wales Borderers**
A J Humphries	" "
A J Thurston	" "
J H Roberts	**The Kings Own Scottish Borderers**
W F Frost	**The Cameronians (Scottish Rifles)**
A J R McKay	**The Royal Inniskilling Fusiliers**
F Adcock	" "
G W Durham	" "
J Melville	" "
J C Case	**The Gloucestershire Regiment**
W E Fox	" "
T G Golding	" "
B J Gray MM	" "
A F Merriott	" "
S Merritt	" "
J W Forrest DCM	**The Worcestershire Regiment**
C E Jelley	" "
S Brightmore	**The East Lancashire Regiment**
A C A Richmond	" "
A T Donnelly	**The East Surrey Regiment**
J T Edgar	" "
A A Taylor	" "
J W Robinson	" "
J Sparks	" "
C F A West	" "
W Fitzgerald	**The Duke of Cornwall's Light Infantry**
C G Pearce	" "
S G Saunders	" "
E W Church	**The Duke of Wellington's (West Riding Regiment)**
W A Springett	" "
A T Cleare	**The Royal Sussex Regiment**
S G Merritt	" "
F Brooker	**The Hampshire Regiment**
H A F Eade	" "

W B Latham	**The Hampshire Regiment**
J W Lewis	" "
J D H Marlow	" "
H G Marquiss	" "
G W Marshall	" "
H B Edney	**The South Staffordshire Regiment**
E W Cathcart	**The Dorsetshire Regiment**
F G Clarke	" "
J W M Cross	" "
F T Harnett	" "
W R James	" "
E G Massie	" "
A E Moffatt	" "
E B Tristram	" "
C H Blundell	**The Prince of Wales's Volunteers (South Lancashire Regiment)**
H Gregson	" "
T E Pett	" "
E J Andrews	**The Welsh Regiment**
J A Collins	" "
H J Hayes	" "
G E Johnston	" "
C L Palmer	" "
A W Payne	" "
F S Peoples	" "
W A Spong	" "
S H Bishop	**The Black Watch (Royal Highlanders)**
G A Joseph	" "
C Meldrum	" "
C J Robertson	" "
W C Critcher	**The Oxfordshire and Buckinghamshire Light Infantry**
P Hawkins	" "
J J Pegram	" "
W H Smith	" "
E P T Figg	**The Essex Regiment**
J C Onn	" "
J L Soughan	" "
W J Tipper	" "
A C Vile	" "
E J Wise	" "

T Ennis	**The Sherwood Foresters (Nottinghamshire and Derbyshire Regiment)**
H Neynoe	" "
C D Randall DCM	" "
G P Darcey	**The Loyal North Lancashire Regiment**
E J C H Bromwich	**The Northamptonshire Regiment**
G A Hayman	" "
H E C Kendall	" "
S W Lennon	" "
W Brindle	**The Princess Charlotte of Wales's (Royal Berkshire Regiment)**
B Knight	" "
A H Main	" "
W K Ryan	" "
J E Smith	" "
F H Way	" "
T M Croft	**The Queen's Own (Royal West Kent Regiment)**
J L H Falkner	" "
R G G Falkner	" "
E P Ryan	" "
H J Allen	**The (Duke of Cambridge's Own) Middlesex Regiment**
F A J Green	" "
S W Hallett	" "
H H Toomey	" "
W T Vause DCM	" "
H H Adshead	**The King's Royal Rifle Corps**
W J Harman	" "
G A Hooker	" "
W R King	" "
F A McManus	" "
A V Somerset	" "
A W Trickey	" "
A Babbington	**The (Duke of Edinburgh's) Wiltshire Regiment**
E V Davies	" "
W J Lewis	" "
W R McCarragher	" "
B C L Joyce	**The Manchester Regiment**
C J Peat	" "
R G Smith	" "

A J Rutledge	**The (Prince of Wales's) North Staffordshire Regiment**
H S Booth	**The York and Lancaster Regiment**
A G W O'Leary	" "
F H G Woolgar	" "
R D Douglas	**The Durham Light Infantry**
L W Monger	" "
R Scott	" "
W Smith	" "
W Anderson	**The Highland Light Infantry**
J Findlay DCM	" "
J B Ryan	" "
W R Barrett	**Seaforth Highlanders (Ross-shire Buffs, The Duke of Albany's)**
J Chilton MM	" "
A V Harber	" "
J A Hume	" "
F M Usher	" "
C H Walker	" "
R F Williams	" "
R W Elder	**The Gordon Highlanders**
J W Gibbon	" "
J Hawtin	" "
P Hyde	" "
W Milne	" "
A D Ramsay	" "
W J Prosser	**The Queen's Own Cameron Highlanders**
W A Rowe	" "
J G Taylor	" "
W A B Clark	**The Royal Irish Rifles**
H G A Rawlinson	" "
H E Hardwick	**The Princess Victoria's (Royal Irish Fusiliers)**
A Knight	" "
F W Corry	**The Connaught Rangers**
G A Axon	**Princess Louise's (Argyll and Sutherland Highlanders)**
H T Bunnett	" "
W Chudley	" "
T R D Cotcher	" "
G Counter	" "

A G Rattray	***Princess Louise's (Argyll and Sutherland Highlanders)***
A R R Robertson	" "
C W Thomas	" "
F R Walker MC	" "
V H Waterfield	" "
H A Millar	***The Prince of Wales's Leinster Regiment (Royal Canadians)***
A E Douch	***The Royal Munster Fusiliers***
G E Roberts	" "
J E Helson	***The Prince Consort's Own (Rifle Brigade)***
A G Kelly	" "
J W Monger	" "
J Murphy	" "
J F Wood	" "
A E Anderson	***Machine Gun Corps***
H B Grayham	" "
H Ollerton	" "
C M Matheson	***Tank Corps***
C E Gass	***Royal Defence Corps***
E T Hayes	" "
C Amos	***Army Service Corps***
A T Ashton	" "
W H Gould	" "
J W H Howard	" "
C E Mars	" "
F McVicar	" "
H St. J Sainty	" "
A B B Smith	" "
G W Wheelhouse	" "
S J Wilson	" "
W J Adds	***Army Ordnance Corps***
J E Eldridge	" "
A S Grieve	" "
H J Horner	" "
T R C Redford	" "
B D Conolly	***Royal Army Medical Corps***
F J A Crowe	" "
J H Kay	" "
J C Vickers	" "
C V Agate	***Army Pay Corps***

L J Rickwood	***Corps of Army Schoolmasters***
W A Avis	***The London Regiment***
E G Gavin	" "
M Joyce	" "
G P Langdon	" "
G S Matthews	" "
A H Nichols	" "
E T Wall	" "
W J Werry	" "
C Crissall	***The Cambridgeshire Regiment***
J W E Woods	***Royal Air Force***
F G Hall	***Australian Light Horse***
A R Matthews	" "
B Booth	***Australian Infantry***
D E Docwra	" "
A E Webber	" "
H G T Andrews	***Canadian Mounted Rifles***
P J Ford	***Canadian Infantry***
T D Rouse	" "
P T Furnish	***New Zealand Infantry***
F Walters	***South African Infantry***
J E Nichols	***South African Native Labour Corps***

Royal Naval Volunteer Reserve

Frederick Reginald Pretoria GERKINS
Ordinary Seaman, Z/9936, Royal Navy Depot (Crystal Palace), Royal Naval Volunteer Reserve who died on 12 October 1918, aged 18. Commemorated in Beckenham Crematorium and Cemetery, Kent, United Kingdom

Born on 15 September 1900 in Peckham, London, the only child of Frederick William Gerkins and Kate Emma née Hancock, his father was a Private in The Buffs (East Kent Regiment) who died of disease whilst on active service in Pretoria, South Africa, on 05 May 1902 during the Second Boer War.

Frederick was admitted to the school on 09 November 1909 (Petition No. 12697) and remained until he was withdrawn on 27 October 1914, two months after the start of the war. From correspondence between his mother and the school, it appears that the reason for the withdrawal was medical.

After leaving the school, Frederick was employed as a Laboratory Assistant (Chemical), but enlisted into the Royal Naval Volunteer Reserve a month before his eighteenth birthday, on 21 August 1918.

He was posted to the Royal Navy training establishment that had been set up at Crystal Palace, London, known as HMS[11] *Victory VI*, or more informally as HMS Crystal Palace, on 09 September and whilst there he developed pneumonia, dying in Davidson Road War Hospital, Croydon, on 12 October 1918. He is also the first of the "Lost Boys" here recorded whose name has been omitted from the memorial tablets in the school chapel.

---

[11] His Majesty's Ship, the prefix by which all ships and certain shore establishments were known in the Royal Navy at the time

Royal Marines

George Henry HOLMES
Musician, RMB/1458, H.M.S. Monmouth, Royal Marine Band who died on 01 November 1914, aged 34. Commemorated on the Portsmouth Naval Memorial, Hampshire, United Kingdom

Born on 26 October 1880 in St. Thomas' Mount, India, the only child of Samuel Holmes and Lucy Emma née Randall, his father was a Sergeant in the Royal Artillery, who was discharged from the army on 01 April 1889 and died in Uppingham, Rutland, on 03 August 1889. His mother died, also in Uppingham, on 09 October 1889, and George's Petition Document was submitted by his aunt, Anne Elizabeth Holmes, on 26 October 1889, his ninth birthday.

George was admitted to the school on 26 December 1889 (Petition No. 9942) and was discharged on 03 November 1894, enlisting into The Duke of Wellington's (West Riding Regiment). Following his attestation, George was posted to the 1st Battalion, where almost a year later, on 03 August 1895, he was appointed as a Drummer. A month later, on 30 September 1895, he was posted with the battalion to Malta, remaining there until it returned to Britain on 14 September 1898.

However, six months after returning to Britain, on 16 February 1899, George was in trouble for the first time when he was convicted by the Civil Power of *"Attempting to have carnal knowledge of a girl under the age of 13 years"* and was sentenced to six months' imprisonment. Despite the serious nature of his offence, when he was released from prison on 15 August 1899, he was able to return to duty.

Four months after he returned to the battalion, he was posted to South Africa during the Second Boer War. However, whilst serving there, on 01 January 1902, he was sentenced by Field Courts Martial to 168 days' detention for *"an act to the prejudice of good order and military discipline"*, although this sentence was halved by the General Officer Commanding, Pretoria District, and George again returned to duty.

George returned to Britain on 06 October 1902 before he was posted three years later, on 05 October 1905, to India. A year after being posted there, he returned to Britain on 07 October 1906 and was discharged from the army on 02 November 1906 having completed 12 years' service.

There is limited information available about George following his discharge from the army, but it is known that he married Elizabeth Jarvis in York, Yorkshire North Riding, on 29 December 1907.

On 12 August 1908, George enlisted into the Royal Marine Artillery, but on the same day was transferred to the Royal Marine Band as a Musician. George spent the first two years of his service at the Royal Marine School of Music in Eastney, Hampshire, before he embarked on HMS *Prince of Wales* on 15 December 1910, remaining on this ship until he was posted to HMS *King Edward VII* on 17 May 1912.

George was only on this ship for five months before he returned to the Royal Marine School of Music on 26 October 1912. Again, this was only a short posting, as on 15 January 1913, he was posted to HMS *Vivid*, which was the Devonport base ship in Devonshire.

Just prior to the outbreak of war, on 02 August 1914, George was posted to HMS *Monmouth*. The ship was mobilised on 04 August and was sent to join the 5th Cruiser Squadron that was based on the Cape Verde–Canary Islands station. However, when the ship arrived on 13 August 1914, Rear Admiral Archibald Stoddart, the Squadron Commander, detached *Monmouth* and it was sent to the Brazilian coast to search for German light cruisers that were known to be in the area. It arrived in September 1914 and came under the command of Rear Admiral Christopher Craddock.

On 31 October 1914, HMS *Glasgow* entered Coronel Harbour, Chile, and discovered the German supply ship, *Göttingen*, and intercepted radio messages that it sent, suggesting that there were other German warships close by.

Glasgow left Coronel on 01 November and met with the remainder of Craddock's squadron, *Monmouth*, HMS *Good Hope* and HMS *Otranto*, 40 miles west of the port at midday, but it was not until later that afternoon that these ships came into contact with the German ships *Leipzig*, *Scharnhorst*, *Gneisenau*, *Dresden* and *Nürnberg*. During the course of the ensuing Battle of Coronel, *Scharnhorst* fired on *Good Hope* and *Gneisenau* fired on *Monmouth*, blowing the roof off *Monmouth*'s forward turret and starting a fire, which caused an ammunition explosion that completely blew the turret off the ship and causing it to veer out of the line.

At 2035hrs, *Nürnberg* spotted *Monmouth* listing to port and unable to fire its guns on that side. *Nürnberg* then approached *Monmouth* and illuminated its flag in the hope that the British ship would surrender, but when there was no response, *Nürnberg* opened fire at 2120hrs, although it aimed high. Again, the British did not respond, so the

Germans fired a torpedo, which missed its target. Following this, *Monmouth* increased speed and turned toward the German ship, which caused the latter to again open fire. At 2158hrs, *Monmouth* capsized and sank with the loss of all 734 members of its crew, including George, with the seas too rough to attempt any rescue effort.

Due to being lost at sea, George has no grave, and is commemorated on the Portsmouth Naval Memorial. He is also a "Lost Boy" whose name has been omitted from the memorial tablets in the school chapel.

Royal Marine Light Infantry

Albert Francis RICHARDS

Bugler, PO/15949, Portsmouth Division, Royal Marine Light Infantry who died on 11 August 1920, aged 23. Buried in Portsmouth (Kingston) Cemetery, Hampshire, United Kingdom

Born on 17 December 1897 in Ryde, Isle of Wight, the youngest of ten children of Edward Richards and Ellen née Silk, his father had been a Serjeant Drummer in The Connaught Rangers who had been discharged from the army on 06 June 1882 and died in Ryde on 05 January 1900.

Albert was admitted to the school on 25 February 1909 (Petition No. 12569) and having moved from Chelsea to Guston, was discharged on 03 January 1912, enlisting into the Royal Marine Light Infantry, unusual for a Dukie at the time, with the vast majority joining the army.

His first year of service was spent in Portsmouth, Hampshire, but on 27 March 1913 he embarked on HMS *Liverpool* as a Bugler, remaining on this ship until after the outbreak of war, returning to Portsmouth on 15 November 1914[12].

Alfred was only to spend a further six months in the military before he was invalided out of the Royal Marines, although the reason for this is not given in his service record.

Following his discharge, Alfred remained in Portsmouth, marrying Kathleen Essie Banks in the town in 1916. He was still in Portsmouth four years later, when he died of tuberculosis on 11 August 1920. Following his death, his widow was denied a pension as he had been discharged before their marriage.

The fact that Alfred is commemorated by the Commonwealth War Graves Commission[13] suggests that his death was attributable to his time in the service. He is also a "Lost Boy" whose name has not been recorded on the memorial tablets in the school chapel.

---

[12] On 28 August 1914, *Liverpool* was serving with the 5th Light Cruiser Squadron and participated in the Battle of Heligoland Bight, the first naval engagement of the war

[13] the first war graves organisation, founded in 1917 as the Imperial War Graves Commission; an inter-governmental organisation, responsible for commemorating all Commonwealth war dead to this day

Royal Horse Guards (The Blues)

Arthur Henry William George Christopher SCOTT

Trumpeter, 1357, Royal Horse Guards (The Blues) who died on 02 November 1914, aged 20. Commemorated on the Ypres (Menin Gate) Memorial, West-Vlaanderen, Belgium

Born on 13 December 1893 in Windsor, Berkshire, the eldest son of George Frederick Scott and Jane née Bull, his father had been the Regimental Corporal Major in the Royal Horse Guards (The Blues) who had been discharged from the army on 21 November 1901 and died in Windsor on 06 November 1904.

Arthur was admitted to the school three months after his father's death, on 24 February 1905 (Petition No. 12087) and was discharged into his father's old regiment on 22 December 1908. The 1911 Census records him as a Musician with the regiment in Windsor.

At the outbreak of war, the Royal Horse Guards were still stationed in Combermere Barracks in Windsor and on mobilisation one squadron left and came under orders of the Household Cavalry Composite Regiment. The remainder of the regiment moved to Ludgershall, Wiltshire, before embarking at Southampton, Hampshire on 05 October and landing at Ostend and Zeebrugge on 08 October 1914.

The regiment's first action occurred five days later when, near Ypres, it fired on a Taube monoplane which subsequently came to the ground and was captured by the Army Service Corps, but its first "ground" action occurred on 18 October when "D" Squadron, whilst reconnoitring, came across a considerable force of enemy cyclists. As the ground was unsuitable for cavalry, the troopers dismounted and attacked, killing 11 Germans as well as capturing one enemy soldier and fourteen bicycles, before firing a house in which the Germans were sheltering whilst continuing to shoot at the troopers. The regiment was then engaged for the remainder of the month as infantry, rather than in a cavalry role, including manning the trenches.

At the beginning of November, the regiment was located in woods near Hooge as support for the Guards Brigade. On 02 November, it was ordered to move up to fill a gap near Gheluvelt, but as it neared the front, the German guns found the range of the rear squadron on the road, which suffered four killed, seventeen wounded and three missing.

Arthur Scott was one of the four killed, dying on 02 November 1914. He may have had a grave, but if so, its location was lost during the fighting of the next four years and he is therefore commemorated on the Menin Gate Memorial.

Royal Horse Artillery

Nelson Willie FIELDING
Bombardier, 56825, "V" Battery, Royal Horse Artillery who died on 02 March 1915, aged 19. Buried in Aire Communal Cemetery, Pas de Calais, France

Born on 11 June 1895 in Norwich, Norfolk, one of three children of Percival Thorne Fielding and Margaret Ellen née Nelson, his father had been a Squadron Serjeant Major in the 1st (King's) Dragoon Guards, but had retired from the army on 27 March 1897. The family had then settled in Cambridge, Cambridgeshire, where Margaret died on 06 February 1904.

Nelson and his twin brother, Percival Thorne Fielding, were admitted to the school nine months after their mother's death, on 04 November 1904 (Nelson's Petition No. 12033, Percival's Petition No. 12034), with Nelson being discharged from the school on 30 June 1909 and enlisting into the Royal Horse Artillery.

Although his service record is no longer available[14], the 1911 Census shows that he was a Boy serving at the Royal Horse Artillery Depot in the Royal Artillery Barracks (East Side) in Woolwich. His brother appears in the same census, the name immediately below his.

At the outbreak of war, "V" Battery was stationed in Meerut, India, as part of XII Brigade, Royal Horse Artillery, which was part of the 7th (Meerut) Division. However, on 17 November, the battery embarked on the SS[15] *Huntsman* at Bombay, departing two days later and landing at Marseille on 14 December 1914.

However, Nelson had landed in France on 15 August 1914 as part of III Brigade, Royal Horse Artillery, which was part of the Cavalry Division, and it is not certain at which point that he, by now a Bombardier, was posted to "V" Battery.

---

[14] Although the service records of First World War soldiers were kept at the War Office Record store in Arnside Street, London, a German incendiary bomb during the Blitz in September 1940, resulted in a fire that destroyed two thirds of these records, with the remainder largely charred or water-damaged

[15] Screw Steamer

This battery spent the majority of its time following its arrival in France training, either as a battery or as part of the Cavalry Brigade, having transferred from the Indian to the Home Establishment on 15 January 1915. On 02 March 1915, troops from the battery were practicing firing trench mortars at Serny, when there was an accident that resulted in seven soldiers being killed and two officers and 39 men being wounded.

One of those killed was Nelson Fielding. He was buried in Aire Communal Cemetery in the town that was the location of the Corps Headquarters and his death was reported in the local newspaper of the time:

> "Mr. P. Fielding, Lensfield-road, has been officially informed that his son, Nelson Willie Fielding, of the Royal Horse Artillery, was killed in action on March 2nd. He had lately been transferred from "J" Battery to "V" Battery, attached to the Indian Expeditionary Force, and promoted from Bombardier to Corporal. His twin brother, Percy, is still in "J" Battery. Both boys joined the R.H.A. from the Duke of York's School at 14 years of age, and not yet 20. They went out to France with the original Expeditionary Force, and had been through
> every engagement since the commencement of the war. Nelson had never once been off duty. He was a fine specimen of manhood, standing over 6ft. in height, and was well known in Cambridge. Mr. Fielding, the bereaved father, himself an old soldier, with 29 years' service to his credit. He left the Army Squadron-Sergt.- Major the King's Dragoon Guards in 1897. He joined the Loyal Suffolk Hussars coming to Cambridge, and held the position of Regimental Quartermaster-Sergt. At the time of his retirement"[16].

Although definitely a Dukie, and commemorated by the Commonwealth War Graves Commission, Nelson is one of the "Lost Boys" whose name has been omitted from the memorial tablets in the school chapel.

Percival was discharged from the school two months after Nelson, on 09 August 1909, also enlisting into the Royal Horse Artillery. He survived the war, the medal records showing that by the end of the conflict he was an Acting Battery Serjeant Major. He died in Bromley, Kent, in July 1961, having been appointed as a Member of the Victorian Order 5th Class on 08 June 1944 and Member of the

---

[16] *The Cambridge Independent Press*, 19 March 1915

Victorian Order 4th Class on 01 June 1953, although the reason for these appointments is not known.

Ronald Malcolm HUME
Trumpeter, 65863, "J" Battery, Royal Horse Artillery who died on 24 March 1918, aged 20. Commemorated on the Pozieres Memorial, Somme, France

Born on 10 April 1897 in Gosport, Hampshire, the third of four sons of James Hume and Mary née McSweeney, his father had been a Serjeant in the 78th (Highlanders) Regiment of Foot (The Ross-shire Buffs)[17], and had been discharged from the army on 02 July 1867. He died in Gosport on 20 October 1905.

Ronald was admitted to the school on 30 May 1907 (Petition No. 12381), a year after his older brother, John Alexander Hume, had been admitted on 16 February 1906 (Petition No. 12195). Having made the transition from Chelsea to Guston, Ronald was discharged from the school on 29 June 1911, enlisting into the Royal Horse Artillery.

He disembarked in France with "L" Battery, Royal Horse Artillery, on 15 August 1914, aged 17. Less than two weeks later, it is possible that he took part in the famous action at Néry, on 01 September 1914, when the 1st Cavalry Brigade defeated the German 4th Cavalry Division. Although the British artillery was mostly put out of action in the first few minutes, a gun of "L" Battery kept up a steady fire for two and a half hours against a full battery of German artillery, earning 3 men in the battery the Victoria Cross.

At the outbreak of the war, the battery which Ronald was serving with in 1918, "J" Battery, Royal Horse Artillery, was stationed in Aldershot and, having been brought up to strength by men from "C" Battery, Royal Horse Artillery, landed at Rouen on 18 August 1914, coming into action for the first time on 24 August and participating in the British Expeditionary Force's Retreat from Mons.

The battery participated in the First Battle of Ypres and then spent much of January and February 1915 in billets, going into action during the Battle of Neuve Chapelle and the Second Battle of Ypres, before being in action again during the Battle of Loos in September 1915.

---

[17] Amalgamated with the 72nd (Duke of Albany's Own Highlanders) Regiment of Foot on 01 July 1881 to become Seaforth Highlanders (Ross-shire Buffs), renamed Seaforth Highlanders (Ross-shire Buffs, The Duke of Albany's) on 22 November 1881

During 1916, the battery again spent much of its time in billets, including during the start of the Somme Offensive, when it was at Borre, and then Wallon-Cappel, on six hours' notice move, its next major action being in 1917 during the Third Battle of Ypres.

In March 1918, the battery was in action as a result of the German Spring Offensive. On 24 March 1918, its war diary entry states that it *"Fired early but withdrew in morning and marched through Béthencourt- Caillouël-Crepigny to an orchard near Grandrue from where we covered the Caillouël Ridge. Wagon line in field near battery was shelled during night. Tptr Hume killed, horses killed and wounded"*[18].

Ronald Hume was killed on 24 March 1918 and as the battery was forced to withdraw early the following morning, it is possible that his grave was not adequately marked. He therefore has no known grave and is commemorated on the Pozieres Memorial, although he is also a "Lost Boy" whose name has been omitted from the memorial tablets in the school chapel.

John was discharged from the school on 23 November 1908 and enlisted into the Seaforth Highlanders (Ross-shire Buffs, The Duke of Albany's). He was serving as a Lance Corporal in the 2nd Battalion of that regiment when he was killed on 01 July 1916, but unlike Ronald, he is commemorated in the school chapel.

Ronald's eldest brother, James Arthur Hume, who was not a Dukie, served in the Royal Marine Artillery from 1906 until 1916 before he was discharged as medically unfit. He died as a result of tuberculosis on 05 May 1920 and is also commemorated by the Commonwealth War Graves Commission.

Edgar RUST

Bombardier, 37785, "Y" Battery, Royal Horse Artillery who died on 19 May 1915, aged 24. Buried in Alexandria (Chatby) Military and War Memorial Cemetery, Egypt

Born on 25 November 1890 in Woolwich, London, the eldest of three children of Edgar Rust and Minnie née Gilpin, his father had been a Serjeant in the Royal Horse Artillery, but had been medically discharged from the army on 09 October 1894 and died in Teignmouth, Devonshire, on 11 February 1895.

Edgar was admitted to the school on 12 July 1900 (Petition No. 11444) and discharged to the Royal Horse Artillery on 26 July 1905,

---

[18] WO 95/1135/2: "J" Battery Royal Horse Artillery, 1914 Aug. - 1918 Aug., The National Archives, Kew

although his service record is not available and so his postings pre-war are unknown, although according to the 1911 Census, he was serving with "Y" Battery, Royal Horse Artillery and stationed in Mhow, India.

At the outbreak of war, the battery was still stationed in Mhow, but returned to Britain in November 1914, before sailing for the Mediterranean in 1915. Prior to departing, Edgar had married Elizabeth Ann Nason in Warwick, Warwickshire, in January 1915, but it appears that they had less than two months together, as Edgar's medal index card[19] shows his date of his entry into theatre, in Egypt, as 03 March 1915.

The battery re-embarked at Alexandria on 07 April, arriving at Lemnos on 18 April and landing at Cape Helles on the Gallipoli Peninsula on 27 April 1915, where it participated in the First and Second Battles of Krithia on 28 April and 06–08 May respectively. It appears that during one of these actions, Edgar was wounded and evacuated to Egypt, where he died of wounds on 19 May 1915, likely in the 21st General Hospital in Alexandria, being interred in the nearby cemetery.

Edgar is commemorated on the memorial tablets in the school chapel, but his regiment is recorded as Royal Artillery. Whilst the Royal Field Artillery, Royal Garrison Artillery and Royal Horse Artillery were all part of the Royal Regiment of Artillery, at the time that he was serving, each of these was a separate entity.

Despite being married for less than two months, when Edgar departed for the Dardanelles, Elizabeth was pregnant. Their daughter, Edwina Rust, was born in October 1915 in Stratford-upon-Avon, Warwickshire, five months after her father's death.

Hubert George SMITH
Corporal, 33818, "S" Battery, Royal Horse Artillery who died on 22 November 1915, aged 25. Commemorated on the Basra Memorial, Iraq

Born on 18 February 1890 in Little Hallingbury, Essex, the fourth of five children of Charles Smith and Hannah née Johnson, his father had been a Private in The King's Royal Rifle Corps, but had retired from the army on 07 March 1882.

---

[19] More correctly the Medal Rolls Index Card, created by the Army Medal Office towards the end of the war and recording an individual's medal entitlement, including first entry in a theatre of war

Hubert was admitted to the school on 16 October 1899 (Petition No. 11351), joining his older brothers, Charles Perkins Smith and Joseph Johnson Smith, both of whom had been admitted to the school on 15 July 1898 (Charles' Petition No. 11185, Joseph's Petition No. 11186).

Hubert was discharged from the school to the Royal Horse Artillery as a Musician on 05 March 1904, initially being posted to "B" Depot at Larkhill, Wiltshire, where he was to spend the next three years, during which time he was also given fourteen days' detention in June 1906 for presenting a forged letter for leave and making a false statement. He was also confined to barracks for eight days in December 1906 for gambling.

On 23 May 1907, he was posted as a Trumpeter to "Q" Battery, stationed in St John's Wood, London, being appointed a Gunner in August 1908 and an Acting Bombardier in December 1909, before being posted to "X" Battery in India on 05 March 1910.

Hubert was promoted to Bombardier on 03 September 1911 whilst stationed in Mhow, India, and was transferred to "S" Battery in Bangalore on 31 October 1914, after the war had broken out. Hubert was then promoted to Corporal on 26 July 1915, and posted with his battery to Mesopotamia[20] two weeks later, on 14 August.

In November 1915 the battery was in the area of Ctesiphon, and on 17 November it was in bivouacs when the picquet line was attacked and the gun park was shelled. The battery suffered nine killed and *"many"*[21] wounded.

It appears that Hubert was one of those wounded, dying from those wounds on 22 November 1915, and it then appears that his grave was subsequently lost, so he is commemorated on the Basra Memorial.

Although commemorated on the memorial tablets in the school chapel, his regiment is recorded as Royal Artillery, rather than Royal Horse Artillery.

Charles was discharged from the school on 31 August 1901, enlisting into The King's Royal Rifle Corps. He served during the war and survived, dying in Chelmsford, Essex, in 1971.

---

[20] Modern-day Iraq
[21] WO 95/5087/5: 6 Indian Cavalry Brigade: Patiala Lancers; S Battery Royal Horse Artillery, Patiala Lancers 1918 Sept - 1918 Dec, S Battery Royal Horse Artillery 1915 Feb - 1916 Dec; 1918 April - 1919 Feb, 1915 Feb - 1919 Feb, The National Archives, Kew

Joseph was discharged from the school to the 17th (Duke of Cambridge's Own) Lancers on 03 January 1903. He also served during the war and survived, dying in Hatfield Heath, Essex, in 1974.

Archibald Ernest STONE
Trumpeter, 1035807, "C" Battery, Royal Horse Artillery (Formerly 126521) who died on 01 December 1920, aged 19. Buried in Meerut Cantonment Cemetery, India

Archibald Ernest Stone was born on 23 January 1901 in Melksham, Wiltshire, the fourth of six children of Edwin Stone and Kate née Pady, his father had been a Lance Corporal in The Hampshire Regiment who had been discharged from the army on 25 April 1901 and died in Melksham in November 1905.

Archibald was admitted to the school on 06 January 1912 (Petition No. 12938), and would have made the transition to Hutton, Essex, where the school was evacuated during the First World War, before he was discharged to the Royal Horse Artillery on 21 December 1915.

Due to his age, it is unlikely that Archibald saw active service during the war, although his service record is not available to confirm this. What is known is that in 1920 he was a Trumpeter, posted to "C" Battery, Royal Horse Artillery, which was stationed in India. It was whilst here that he developed a liver abscess that led to his death on 01 December 1920.

Archibald was buried in Meerut Cantonment Cemetery and commemorated by the Commonwealth War Graves Commission, but despite this, his name has been omitted from the memorial tablets in the school chapel, making him another of the "Lost Boys".

Edward TOWELLS
Lance Bombardier, 61746, "F" Battery, Royal Horse Artillery who died on 24 August 1918, aged 27. Buried in Mory Abbey Military Cemetery, Pas de Calais, France

Born on 12 January 1891 in West Hartlepool, County Durham, the sixth of eight children of Robert Moss Towells and Mary née Mitchell, his father had been a Company Serjeant Major in the Royal Artillery, but retired from the army on 31 January 1895, dying four months later on 12 May 1895 in West Hartlepool.

Edward was admitted to the school, on 06 March 1902 (Petition No. 11661), and was joined a year later by his younger brother,

Arthur Thomas Towells, who was admitted on 12 February 1903 (Petition No. 11799). Their older brother, Alexander Robert Towells, had also been at the school, having been admitted on 07 August 1896 (Petition No. 10920), but was no longer at the school when his younger brothers were admitted.

Edward was discharged from the school to the Royal Garrison Artillery on 21 January 1905, although he was discharged seven months later, on 28 August 1905 *"Services no longer required"*[22].

Edward must have re-enlisted in the next six years, although there is no service record available for this second period of service, as in 1911 the census shows that he was a Driver with "U" Battery, Royal Horse Artillery and stationed in Dilkusha Barracks, Lucknow, India, although he must have been posted back to Britain during the course of the next three years.

At the outbreak of war, Edward was serving with III Brigade, Royal Horse Artillery, which was stationed in Newbridge, County Kildare. After mobilisation, the brigade landed in France on 15 August 1914, coming into action for the first time during the Battle of Mons. Fellow Dukie Nelson Fielding was in the same brigade at that stage.

It seems that Edward continued to serve on the Western Front throughout the next four years, although his postings during this period are not known. However by August 1918, he was a Lance Bombardier serving with "F" Battery, Royal Horse Artillery, which was part of XIV Brigade, Royal Horse Artillery and was in the vicinity of Courcelles.

On 21 August, the battery supported an attack on the German positions, which were taken and held, despite a German counterattack the following day, going on to support an attack on the village of Mory on 23 August, which was also successful. The next attack that the battery supported was on Ervillers, which again was successful, the battery moving forward in the evening. However, during that last attack, on 24 August 1918, "F" Battery suffered one officer and eight other ranks killed, one of whom was Edward Towells.

Edward is commemorated on the memorial tablets in the school chapel, but his regiment is incorrectly recorded as Royal Artillery.

---

[22] WO 97: Royal Hospital Chelsea: Soldiers Service Documents, 1760-1913, The National Archives, Kew

Alexander was dismissed from the school less than a month after being admitted, on 04 September 1896, although the reason for this is not known. Like his brother, he also enlisted in the army, serving in the Royal Field Artillery. He died of wounds on 12 June 1917 and is commemorated with his brother on the memorial tablets in the school chapel.

It would appear that both of their names were added some time later than most of the other casualties, possibly after 1923, as they appear alongside Henry Barratt who died that year.

The youngest Dukie brother, Arthur, also served in the Royal Horse Artillery, surviving the war and dying in London in 1980.

Charles James WHITE

Bombardier, 61464, "H" Battery, Royal Horse Artillery who died on 15 December 1915, aged 19. Buried in Noeux-Les-Mines Communal Cemetery, Pas de Calais, France

Born on 17 February 1896 in Islington, London, the tenth of twelve children of Thomas White and Louisa née Brown, his father had served as a Gunner in the Royal Artillery, and had retired from the army on 06 January 1891, dying in London on 28 July 1905.

Charles was admitted to the school on 25 July 1907 (Petition No. 12316) and having moved from Chelsea to Guston, was discharged to the Royal Horse Artillery on 06 April 1910. His service record is no longer available, but the 1911 Census records him as a Boy, serving in the Depot of the Royal Horse Artillery and stationed in the Royal Artillery Barracks (East Side) in Woolwich.

The battery with which he would go on to serve, "H" Battery, was stationed in Trowbridge, Wiltshire, at the outbreak of war, but after mobilisation, it landed in France on 28 September 1914, replacing "L" Battery in VII Brigade, Royal Horse Artillery, as this unit had been almost completely wiped out during the action at Néry on 01 September.

The battery was in action during the Second Battle of Ypres in 1915, particularly the Battle of Frezenberg, which was fought between 09–13 May and the Battle of Bellewaarde Ridge on 24 May.

By December, the unit was in action at Vermelles between 05 and 31 December, the battery diary stating that, on 15 December 1915, *"No 61464 A/Bdr C. J. White severely wounded. Died of his wounds same evening. Buried at Noeux-Les-Mines"*[23].

---

[23] WO 95/1111/2: `H' Battery Royal Horse Artillery, 1914 Sept. 1919 Mar., The National

Charles is also commemorated on the memorial tablets in the school chapel, but his regiment is recorded as Royal Artillery.

Archives, Kew

1st (King's) Dragoon Guards

Robert James MEREDITH
Lance Sergeant, 4403, 1st (King's) Dragoon Guards who died on 17 November 1918, aged 34. Buried in York Cemetery, Yorkshire, United Kingdom

Born on 20 February 1884 in Hong Kong, China, the third of four children of Joseph Meredith and Catherine Elizabeth née Mortimer, his father had served in The Buffs (East Kent Regiment), but was on the General Staff as a Garrison Sergeant Major when he died at sea on board HMS *Himalaya* on 09 December 1892 when returning to Britain from Hong Kong.

Robert was admitted to the school on 29 December 1893 (Petition No. 10558) and was joined by his younger brother, George Mortimer Meredith, on 20 August 1897 (Petition No. 11057). Robert was discharged from the school on 01 March 1899 and enlisted into the 1st (King's) Dragoon Guards three days later.

Robert spent the first three and a half years of his service in Britain before he was posted to South Africa on 04 November 1902, remaining there for a year and returning to Britain on 14 November 1903.

After four years in Britain, during which time he married Elsie Croft in London on 08 November 1904, Robert was posted with his regiment to India on 05 November 1907. He was appointed as a Lance Corporal on 05 April 1910 and a year after the birth of his first child, promoted to Corporal on 21 June 1913.

When the war commenced, the regiment was still stationed in Lucknow, India, as part of the 8th (Lucknow) Cavalry Brigade, but in October 1914 it returned to Europe, the brigade forming part of the 1st Indian Cavalry Division, Robert disembarking at Marseille on 11 November 1914.

Although the regiment did not fight in its traditional cavalry role due to the nature of the static warfare, it did participate in the Battle of Festubert and the Second Battle of Ypres in May 1915.

The following year, during the Somme Offensive, the regiment was holding the line near Trones Wood on 31 July when a high-explosive shell burst above the position and Robert was hit by pieces of the shell, which resulted in several wounds to his back and complete paralysis of both of his legs.

Robert was returned to Britain, where he underwent surgery to remove some of the shell fragments from his spine, however, even after the surgery, his right leg remained completely paralysed and his left leg was partially paralysed. He was also left doubly incontinent.

As a result of his injuries, he was discharged from the army on 21 May 1917, but never recovered from his wounds, dying in York, Yorkshire North Riding, eighteen months later. He is also a "Lost Boy" whose name has been omitted from the memorial tablets in the school chapel.

George was *"Detained off pass"* on 11 August 1900. Not a lot is known of his life after this, although he married Elizabeth Swinton in Scoonie, Fife, in 1911. It is unclear whether he served during the war, but he did emigrate to New York, United States, in 1923, although it appears that he and Elizabeth divorced and he returned to Britain in 1928. He re-married to Helen Welsh in 1933 and died in Wemyss, Fife, in 1966.

2nd Dragoon Guards (Queen's Bays)

Charles Frederick BARTHOLOMEW
Corporal, 2641, 2nd Dragoon Guards (Queens Bays) who died on 11 February 1919, aged 24. Buried in Les Baraques Military Cemetery, Sangatte, Pas de Calais, France

Born on 30 September 1894 in Kilkenny, County Kilkenny, the eldest of three children of Charles Frederick Bartholomew and Mary née Burke, his father was a Serjeant Major in The Royal Sussex Regiment who died in Chichester, Sussex, on 21 June 1904 whilst still serving.

Charles was admitted to the school on 16 December 1904 (Petition No. 12052) and was discharged on 16 October 1908, enlisting into the 2nd Dragoon Guards (Queen's Bays).

Charles's service record is no longer available, so his pre-war postings are not known, but he is recorded in the 1911 Census as a Musician in that regiment and stationed in Badajos Barracks, Wellington Lines, Aldershot, Hampshire, serving alongside Eustace Bates and George Webb.

Following the outbreak of war, Charles deployed with the regiment and his medal index card records that he disembarked in theatre on 15 August 1914 as a Trumpeter, likely spending the next four years serving on the Western Front.

On the day of the Armistice, 11 November 1918, the regiment was located in the town of Basecles, Belgium, and at 0700hrs marched out of the town, with patrols from "B" and "C" Squadrons, Charles serving in "C" Squadron, encountering Uhlan patrols east of Montignies-lez-Lens, taking approximately twelve prisoners without suffering any casualties. It was not until 1630hrs that the regiment was informed of the Armistice, spending its first night of peace billeted in the town of Montignies-lez-Lens.

The remainder of the month was spent billeted in various towns in Belgium, but on 01 December 1918, it crossed the frontier into Germany where it was to spend the remainder of its time prior to being repatriated to Britain. However, at some point, Charles caught influenza and was evacuated back to one of the five Allied and Red Cross hospitals located in Calais, France. Having survived the entire war, Charles died of influenza on 11 February 1919, although this is recorded by the Commonwealth War Graves Commission as 10 February 1919, and he was buried in Sangatte. He is also a "Lost Boy" whose name has been omitted from the memorial tablets in the school chapel.

Eustace Robinson BATES
Private, 6328, 2nd Dragoon Guards (Queen's Bays) who died on 01 September 1914, aged 25. Buried in Verberie French National Cemetery, Oise, France

Born on 22 October 1888 in Bengal, India, the youngest of eight children of Robert David Bates and Jane née Fletcher, his father was a Serjeant and a musician in the 100th (Prince of Wales's Royal Canadian) Regiment of Foot[24], appropriate as he was born in Canada himself.

In 1881, the family were living in the hamlet of Whitton, Twickenham, the home of Kneller Hall, the Royal Military School of Music, Robert becoming the Bandmaster of 2nd Battalion, The Wiltshire Regiment. He had been discharged from the army on 11 June 1889, but then served as the Bandmaster of the 6th Regiment of Bengal Native (Light) Infantry from 12 June 1889 until his death in India on 05 June 1890.

Eustace was admitted to the school on 08 September 1899 (Petition No. 11337), the third Bates brother to attend the school. Robert Thomas John Bates had been admitted on 29 May 1891 (Petition No. 10168), and George Fletcher Bates had been admitted on 25 May 1894 (Petition No. 10615), although both had been discharged to the army by the time Eustace was admitted.

Eustace was discharged to the army on 08 November 1902, enlisting into the 2nd Dragoon Guards (Queen's Bays). He is recorded in the 1911 Census as a Private in the regiment and stationed in Badajos Barracks, Wellington Lines, Aldershot.

When war broke out, the regiment was still stationed in Aldershot, but quickly mobilised and landed at Le Havre on 16 August 1914 as part of 1st Cavalry Brigade, participating in the early battles of the war, prior to the Retreat from Mons.

Eustace was killed in action on 01 September 1914 during the Néry encounter. Although it was a minor affair in the scheme of what was to follow, it was a brilliant feat of arms, achieved when defeat was imminent and against a much superior force. It was a true cavalry versus cavalry action, but the 2nd Dragoon Guards fought the battle dismounted, with their horses either killed or stampeded

---

[24] Amalgamated with the 109th Regiment of Foot (Bombay Infantry) on 01 July 1881 to become The Prince of Wales's Leinster Regiment (Royal Canadians)

due to the artillery bombardment at the start of the action. He is buried in Verberie French National Cemetery, along with nine other soldiers from his regiment who were killed at Néry in 1914.

When Robert was discharged from the school on 09 February 1895, he enlisted in The King's Royal Rifle Corps. Although discharged from the army in 1913, it appears that he was recalled to the Colours at the outbreak of war, enlisting on 19 October 1914. However, he was discharged five days later as medically unfit. He died in York in 1942.

George also enlisted in The King's Royal Rifle Corps when he was discharged on 19 January 1899. He had also been discharged from the army prior to the war and also appears to have been recalled, re-enlisting on 28 August 1914 and serving throughout. Having survived the war, he was discharged from the army in March 1919. He died in Grimsby, Lincolnshire, in 1923.

George WEBB

Trumpeter, 6453, 2nd Dragoon Guards (Queen's Bays) who died on 13 October 1914, aged 25. Buried in Terlincthun British Cemetery, Wimille, Pas de Calais, France

Born on 07 September 1889 in Shorncliffe, Kent, the eldest of five children of Henry Webb and Frances Rose née West, his father was a Lance Corporal in The Lincolnshire Regiment, but died whilst serving in Sheffield, Yorkshire West Riding, on 29 July 1898.

George was admitted to the school on 13 January 1899 (Petition No. 11251) and discharged on 16 September 1903, enlisting into the 2nd Dragoon Guards (Queen's Bays), although his service record is no longer available and his career prior to the war is not known.

At the outbreak of war, George would have been stationed in Aldershot, Hampshire, and the actions that he participated in until 01 September 1914, would have been the same as those of fellow Dukie Eustace Bates.

Once the retreat had finished and as the front line stabilised, the cavalry found itself employed in an infantry role manning the trenches, although during the latter part of September the regiment was in billets for much of the time, it being noted that *"The horses and men are getting very fat. Horses look really well"*[25]. However, this was to change at the start of October, as the regiment was back on horseback and advancing north at the head of the 1st Cavalry Brigade.

On 13 October, the regiment was in the area of Vieux-Berquin in northern France when there was heavy firing to the right of its "B"

---

[25] WO 95/1109/1: 2 Dragoon Guards, 1914 Aug. - 1918 Dec., The National Archives, Kew

Squadron, which forced the French cavalry in this position to retire. The brigade then concentrated at Flêtre, and as it advanced into Belgium, two German shells fell among the regiment's "A" Squadron, causing the death of George Webb, wounding four others and killing four horses.

George died on 13 October 1914, and it is likely that he was buried close to where he was killed, but that his body was moved to Terlincthun British Cemetery, Wimille, when many of the isolated cemeteries elsewhere in the location were "brought in" to the larger ones after the war.

George's younger brother, Frederick Webb, was not a Dukie, but died of wounds on 22 February 1915 in Flanders, whilst serving as a Private with The Northumberland Fusiliers.

3rd (Prince of Wales's) Dragoon Guards

Frank COONEY
Serjeant, 390425, 3rd (Prince of Wales's) Dragoon Guards who died on 07 September 1920, aged 34. Buried in Jutogh New Cemetery, India

Born on 26 January 1886 in West Ham, Essex, the fifth of seven children of John Cooney and Elizabeth née Lambert, his father was a Serjeant in the 57th (the West Middlesex) Regiment of Foot[26] who was discharged to pension on 01 August 1876.

Frank was admitted to the school on 29 May 1896 (Petition No. 10892) and joined by his younger brother, Percy Cooney, on 07 April 1899 (Petition No. 11285). Frank was discharged from the school on 04 February 1901 and enlisted into the 1st (King's) Dragoon Guards as a Musician on the same day.

After almost two years in Britain, Frank was posted with the regiment to South Africa on 04 November 1902, returning to Britain a year later, on 14 November 1903. His next posting overseas was four years later, when he was posted to India on 07 November 1907, appearing in the 1911 Census as a Private and stationed in Ambala, India.

At the outbreak of war, 1st Dragoon Guards was stationed in Lucknow, India, part of the Lucknow Cavalry Brigade, but was mobilised and returned to Europe as part of the 1st Indian Cavalry Division, which landed at Marseille on 07 November, although it seems that Frank did not disembark until four days later.

Due to the nature of the warfare, the regiment spent much of its time on the Western Front serving in an infantry role, seeing action at the Battle of Festubert in May 1915, the Second Battle of Ypres also in May 1915 and the Battle of Morval in September 1916. However, it then returned to India on 26 October 1917.

At some point after returning to India, Frank transferred to the 3rd (Prince of Wales's) Dragoon Guards, although it appears he never actually served with the regiment itself.

The 3rd Dragoon Guards had returned from Egypt at the outbreak of war and having landed in France on 04 November 1914,

---

[26] Amalgamated with the 77th (East Middlesex, Duke of Cambridge's Own) Regiment of Foot to become The Duke of Cambridge's Own (Middlesex Regiment)

it spent the entire war on the Western Front, before, in 1919, it was deployed to Ireland for two years during the Anglo-Irish War. During this deployment, Frank was in India, attached to His Excellency The Viceroy's Band.

In the autumn of 1920, it seems that Frank succumbed to disease, dying in Simla in the north of India on 07 September. He is buried in Jutogh New Cemetery, one of sixteen British soldiers who died between November 1914 and July 1921 to be interred there and commemorated by the Commonwealth War Graves Commission. However, he is another "Lost Boy" whose name has been omitted from the memorial tablets in the school chapel.

Percy was discharged from the school to *"Civil Life"* on 20 July 1904. He does not appear in the 1911 Census, but it does seem that he served during the war, disembarking in France in September 1915 as a Driver in the Royal Field Artillery. However, in June 1916, he was discharged from the army due to illness. It is known that he married in 1919 and he appears in the 1939 England and Wales Register, living in Bath, Somerset, and employed as a Civil Servant for the Admiralty. Nothing more is known about him following this.

Their youngest brother, Arthur Patrick Cooney, who was not a Dukie, was also a casualty of the war. He died of wounds in Palestine on 10 April 1917 whilst serving with the 1/6th Battalion, The Essex Regiment and is buried in Jerusalem War Cemetery.

4th (Royal Irish) Dragoon Guards

Ernest William ROAKE
Private, 2770, 4th (Royal Irish) Dragoon Guards who died on 10 October 1914, aged 33. Commemorated on the Ploegsteert Memorial, Hainaut, Belgium

Born on 23 June 1881 in Shepperton, Middlesex, the youngest of four sons of William Roake and Mary née Page, his father was Private in the 48th (the Northamptonshire) Regiment of Foot[27] who had been discharged from the army on 07 September 1875 and died in Shepperton on 28 December 1890. His mother also died in Shepperton on 13 June 1889.

Ernest was admitted to the school on 24 September 1891 (Petition No. 10198) and was discharged on 29 August 1896, enlisting into the 20th Hussars.

Ernest spent the first two years of his service in the Regimental Depot before he was posted to India on 07 December 1898, where he remained for three years before the regiment was posted to South Africa on 13 December 1901 during the Second Boer War, by which time Ernest had been appointed as a Bandsman, becoming a Trumpeter.

Ernest spent eighteen months in South Africa, during which time he was awarded the Queen's and King's South Africa Medals with the clasps *Orange Free State* and *Transvaal*, before he was posted to Egypt on 18 March 1903.

After serving in Egypt for almost two years, Ernest was then posted back to Britain, reverting from Bandsman to Private on 01 November 1905, before he was discharged from the army at the end of his first period of service on 28 August 1908.

Three months after being discharged from the army, on 24 November 1908, Ernest re-enlisted into the army, joining the 4th (Royal Irish) Dragoon Guards, his previous 12 years' service in the 20th Hussars being taken into consideration. On 31 August 1909, he was appointed as a Bandsman, and two years later, on 21 June 1911, he married Ellen Martha Price in Steyning, Sussex.

---

[27] Amalgamated with the 58th (the Rutlandshire) Regiment of Foot on 01 July 1881 to become The Northamptonshire Regiment

At the outbreak of war, 4th (Royal Irish) Dragoon Guards was stationed in Tidworth, Wiltshire, part of the 2nd Cavalry Brigade of the Cavalry Division, but quickly mobilised and landed in France on 16 August 1914.

Six days after landing, two of the squadrons of the regiment became the first members of the British Expeditionary Force to engage the enemy, when Drummer Edward Thomas is reputed to have fired the first British shots of the war in Europe and Captain Charles Hornby is reputed to have been the first British soldier to have killed a German, with his sword, when they came across a patrol of four German cavalryman of the 2nd Kuirassiers at Casteau, near Mons.

The regiment participated in the Battles of Mons and Le Cateau, as well as being part of the retreat from Mons, and it would appear that during the retreat, Ernest was captured, reported missing on 01 September 1914. There is then some confusion, as his service record states that he re-joined as a reinforcement, before he was again reported missing on 01 November 1914. There is then a further entry dated 04 June 1915, stating that Ernest was a prisoner of war at Munster, Germany, the next entry stating *"To be regarded for official purposes as having DIED on or since 10.10.14"*[28]. However, the International Committee of the Red Cross records show him as being captured on 11 October 1914 and being held in Lager III in Munster, although there is no date of death in these records, which is why it is likely that the Commonwealth War Graves Commission has recorded it as 10 October 1914.

As well as having no known grave and so being commemorated on the Ploegsteert Memorial, Ernest is also a "Lost Boy" whose name has been omitted from the memorial tablets in the school chapel.

---

[28] WO 363: First World War Service Records 'Burnt Documents'

6th Dragoon Guards (Carabiniers)

Leonard Dalziel Sharpe Smith SENIOR
Corporal, 1436, 6th Dragoon Guards (Carabiniers) who died on 26 April 1915, aged 22. Commemorated in Wandsworth (Earlsfield) Cemetery, London, United Kingdom

Born on 27 December 1892 in Edinburgh, Midlothian, the eldest of four children of Geoffrey Gilbert Smith Senior and Jane Russell née Sharpe, his father had served in The Royal Sussex Regiment from 1884 until 1887 before transferring to the 6th Dragoon Guards (Carabiniers). He was a Staff Quartermaster Serjeant in this regiment when he was killed in action at Boschbult River, South Africa, on 31 March 1902 during the Second Boer War.

Leonard was admitted to the school on 10 September 1903 (Petition No. 11875), a year after his father's death, being joined by his younger brother, Gilbert Russell Smith Senior on 05 October 1906 (Petition No. 12280). Leonard was discharged to his father's old regiment on 19 December 1907, a year before his youngest brother, Geoffrey John Senior, was admitted to the school on 08 September 1908 (Petition No. 12545).

Leonard's service record is not available, so his pre-war postings are not known, but at the outbreak of war 6th Dragoon Guards was stationed in Canterbury, Kent, although following mobilisation the regiment embarked on 15 August and landed at Le Havre on 16 August 1914.

During 1914, the regiment participated in the Battle of Mons and the subsequent retreat, the Battle of the Marne and the First Battle of Ypres, the latter in an infantry role as the static nature of the war reduced the effectiveness of cavalry in their traditional role.

The regiment also participated in the Second Battle of Ypres in April 1915. However, it is likely that Leonard had been wounded prior to this and been evacuated back to Britain.

Leonard died of wounds in No. 3 London General Hospital, which was located in the Royal Victoria Patriotic School in Wandsworth, London, on 26 April 1915. It appears that, for whatever reason, he was not buried, and is commemorated on the Screen Wall in Wandsworth Cemetery.

Leonard is also commemorated on the memorial tablets in the school chapel, but his regiment is recorded as The Carabiniers, rather than its correct title.

Leonard's brother, Gilbert, moved with the school from Chelsea to Guston and also enlisted when he was discharged from the school on 17 October 1910, the 1911 Census showing that he was serving in the 3rd (Prince of Wales's) Dragoon Guards. However, he must have transferred prior to the outbreak of war, as his medal index card for the conflict states that he was in the same regiment as his older brother. He survived the war, dying in Southend-on-Sea, Essex, in 1969.

The youngest brother, Geoffrey, also enlisted into the 6th Dragoon Guards when he was discharged from the school on 01 April 1913. According to medal records, he served overseas at some point, likely after he turned eighteen in March 1917. He survived the war and died in Westcliff-on-Sea, Essex, in 1979.

1st (Royal) Dragoons

Richard Arthur GRIZZELL MM
Private, 911, 1st (Royal) Dragoons who died on 25 June 1917, aged 28. Commemorated on the Thiepval Memorial, Somme, France

Born on 01 September 1888 in Aldershot, Hampshire, the third of four children of Richard Grizzell and Annie née Mayne, his father had been a Private in the 1st (Royal) Dragoons, but had retired from the army on 01 December 1896 and died in Lewisham, London, on 08 August 1897.

Richard was admitted to the school on 03 January 1899 (Petition No. 11256), but was only at the school for two years before being *"returned to mother – dirty habits"*[29].

It is known that after leaving school, Richard had joined the Royal Navy on 7 March 1905 and his service record includes an absence in April 1907. He was discharged on 01 September 1907 with character described as "fair". Interestingly, at the time that he was absent from the Royal Navy, he enlisted in the Royal Field Artillery, on 10 April 1907, but *"absconded on route to join"*[30] on 18 April 1907.

At some point following his discharge from the Royal Navy, Richard enlisted in the army and was serving with the 1st (Royal) Dragoons at the outbreak of war. In August 1914, the regiment was serving in Potchefstroom, South Africa, but quickly embarked on the SSs *Dunluce Castle* and *Guildford Castle*, landing at Southampton, Hampshire on 19 September. After a brief period for training and in order to be made up to strength, 1st Dragoons re-embarked at Southampton and sailed, via Deal, to Belgium, landing at Zeebrugge on 08 and 09 September 1914.

Over the course of the next three years, the regiment took part in the First Battle of Ypres, which commenced in October 1914, and the Second Battle of Ypres, which commenced in April 1915, during which Richard was wounded on 13 May.

---

[29] "Dirty habits" covered a multitude of things, from poor hygiene to enuresis (bed-wetting)
[30] WO 97: Royal Hospital Chelsea: Soldiers Service Documents, 1760-1913, The National Archives, Kew

The regiment also participated in the Battle of Loos, which commenced in September 1915, and it is possibly during this battle that Richard was recommended for the award of a Military Medal, although this was not Gazetted until the following year[31].

Although 1st Dragoons were prepared to exploit the expected breakthrough that was anticipated with the commencement of the Somme Offensive in the summer of 1916, it was not until the following year that it was involved in any major actions.

Richard Grizzell MM was killed during a raid on enemy trenches on the night of 24/25 June 1917, in the sector near Épehy. Two parties comprising 100 men crossed 750 metres of No Man's Land through five feet high thistles and, after cutting the wire, were successful in identifying the opposing troops. Second Lieutenant John Spencer Dunville of the regiment was awarded a posthumous Victoria Cross for his actions in shielding the engineers working to cut the wire, but the casualties suffered were 6 killed, 9 wounded and 2 missing, both later discovered to have been killed. Richard was one of the missing. He is also another of the "Lost Boys" whose name has been omitted from the memorial tablets in the school chapel.

Richard's youngest brother, Robert James Grizzell, had been admitted to the Royal Hibernian Military School. He served in the Royal Army Medical Corps during the war and died in London in 1957.

---

[31] *The London Gazette*, 2 June 1916, Supplement:29608

2nd Dragoons (Royal Scots Greys)

Percy Walter Ambrose HAVILAND
Private, D/4037, 2nd Dragoons (Royal Scots Greys) who died on 08 October 1918, aged 22. Buried in Bellicourt British Cemetery, Aisne, France

Born on 22 October 1895 in Warley, Essex, the fourth of five sons of John Henry Haviland and Ellen Louisa née Saywood, his father was a Private in The Essex Regiment and died of disease in Bloemfontein, South Africa on 10 June 1900 whilst on active service.

Percy was admitted to the school on 03 February 1905 (Petition No. 12081), joining his older brother, Basil Arthur Frederick Haviland, who had been admitted on 06 March 1902 (Petition No. 11663). He would have made the transition from Chelsea to Guston, as he was discharged on 29 November 1909, five months after his younger brother, Cyril George Haviland, was admitted to the school on 30 June 1909 (Petition No. 12623).

When he was discharged, Percy enlisted into the 2nd Dragoons (Royal Scots Greys) and the 1911 Census shows him as a Boy Musician in that regiment, stationed in Cavalry Barracks, Fulford, York, Yorkshire North Riding.

At the outbreak of war, the regiment was still stationed in York, but landed in France on 17 August 1914. Soon after arriving in France, the regiment was ordered to dye their horses, partly because the grey mounts made conspicuous targets, but also partly based on making the regiment less easy to identify. For the rest of the war, the grey horses of the regiment would be dyed a dark chestnut.

The 2nd Dragoons' first action was on 22 August near Mons, where, dismounted, it fought off a detachment from the German 13th Division, which reported that it had encountered a brigade. However, by the end of 1914, the regiment, along with the other cavalry regiments, was dismounted and fighting in the trenches.

Although Percy's service record is not available, there are records that show that during the spring of 1915 he was a patient in No. 14 General Hospital in Rouen on the 28 May and No. 11 Stationery

Hospital in Wimereux on 29 May, although the records do not state whether this was as a result of a wound or disease.

It was not until August 1918 that the regiment returned to its traditional cavalry role. During this time, it rarely operated as a unit. Instead, detachments were engaged in a variety of traditional cavalry duties. As the British approached the Sambre river, elements of the regiment were used to probe the available river crossings. However, just as it did, many soldiers of the 2nd Dragoons began to fall ill from influenza. Within a few days, due almost solely to the influenza outbreak, the regiment could muster only one composite company of men healthy enough to fight.

At the beginning of October, the regiment was in the area of Belle-Église, providing the advance guard for the brigade on 08 October 1918. This advanced guard was harassed by the Germans all day, which resulted in Percy being killed.

When Basil was discharged from the school on 08 November 1906, he enlisted into the Royal Garrison Artillery, but was discharged from the army on 20 July 1909 as medically unfit due to a ruptured eardrum. The 1911 Census shows him employed as an Engine Cleaner and living in Stratford Essex. It is not known whether he served during the war, but if he did, he survived, dying in Romford, Essex, in 1960.

Cyril enlisted into The Lincolnshire Regiment when he was discharged from the school on 25 June 1912. He survived the war, dying in Colchester, Essex, in 1975.

3rd (The King's Own) Hussars

Edward ELLIOTT
Corporal, 10035, 3rd (The King's Own) Hussars who died on 05 November 1914, aged 23. Buried in Wimereux Communal Cemetery, Pas de Calais, France

Born on 21 November 1890 in Kingston, Surrey, the sixth of seven children of James William Elliott and Phillis Ann née Anderson, his father had been a Colour Serjeant in The East Surrey Regiment, being discharged to pension on 18 May 1898.

Edward was admitted to the school on 09 February 1900 (Petition No. 11398), remaining at the school for four years and being discharged on 08 November 1904. According to the school records, when Edward was discharged from the school, he enlisted into the Royal Horse Artillery and was recorded as a Gunner in "C" Battery, Royal Horse Artillery, stationed in Christchurch Barracks, Dorsetshire, in the 1911 Census.

At some point prior to the outbreak of war, Edward transferred to the 3rd (The King's Own) Hussars, but as his service record is no longer available, it is not possible to ascertain exactly when this transfer occurred. When war was declared, 3rd Hussars was stationed in Shorncliffe, as part of IV Cavalry Brigade. However, it was quickly deployed to France, landing at Rouen on 17 August 1914, with the formation to which the regiment belonged changing from "The" Cavalry Division to the 1st Cavalry Division in September 1914, before the brigade of which the regiment was part was transferred to the 2nd Cavalry Division on 14 October 1914.

Due to the nature of the conflict, most of the troopers fought as dismounted infantry and participated in the First Battle of Ypres, which commenced in October 1914. On one day alone, the regiment suffered 50% casualties and it is likely that Edward was wounded and evacuated to the medical facilities in the town of Wimereux as a consequence of one of these battles, quite possibly on 02 November when the regiment suffered six casualties killed and wounded due to German shelling close to its billets near Mont Kemmel.

Edward died on 05 November 1914 and is buried in Wimereux Communal Cemetery.

Thomas John FULLER
Trumpeter, 116, 3rd (The King's Own) Hussars who died on 26 March 1918, aged 25. Commemorated on the Pozieres Memorial, Somme, France

Born on 31 December 1892 in Dublin, County Dublin, the eldest of the five children of Thomas Edward Fuller and Amy Annie Florence née Baldwin, his father had been a Colour Serjeant in The Duke of Cornwall's Light Infantry, but had been discharged to pension on 14 November 1891 and by the time of the 1901 Census was working as a factory storekeeper, the family living in West Ham, London, which was where Amy died in 1905.

By the time of his mother's death, Thomas had been at the school for two years, having been admitted on 08 January 1903 (Petition No. 11778) and remaining there for two more years, before being discharged to the 3rd (The King's Own) Hussars on 07 February 1907.

Although his service record is not available, Thomas was shown in the 1911 Census as a Private in that regiment and stationed at Roberts Heights, Transvaal, South Africa, although by August 1914, the regiment had returned to Britain. In the lead up to the outbreak of war and for the first three months, Thomas' history would have been the same as that of fellow Dukie Edward Elliott.

The regiment was to spend the rest of the war after November 1914 in the various sectors of the Western Front in France and Flanders, mostly fighting as dismounted soldiers in the trenches, alongside its infantry colleagues. During a period of home leave, in 1915, Thomas married Margaret Wood in Bethnal Green, London and twin daughters Emily and Margaret were born in May 1918.

The German Army launched the "Kaiserschlacht"[32], its Spring Offensive, on 21 March 1918 and the soldiers of the 3rd Hussars were rushed into the line in order to try to prevent the advance. On the morning of 26 March 1918, it was reinforced by the 6th Dragoon Guards (Carabiniers), 4th (Queen's Own) Hussars and the Oxfordshire Yeomanry (Queen's Own Oxfordshire Hussars), before attempting to stop the German advance in the area of Dive Le Franc. The action was to last all day, with Thomas being one of the seventeen soldiers killed or wounded that day. His body was never recovered and he is commemorated on the Pozieres Memorial on the Somme.

---

[32] "Kaiser's Battle"

8th (The King's Royal Irish) Hussars

Leonard Robert LEWRY
Trumpeter, H/4530, 8th (The King's Royal Irish) Hussars who died on 16 November 1918, aged 23. Buried in Brighton City (Bear Road) Cemetery, Sussex, United Kingdom

Born on 12 July 1895 in Jubbulpore, India, the third of four children of James Robert Lewry and Rosa Jane née Honeysett, his father was a Quartermaster Serjeant in The Royal Irish Regiment who died from tuberculosis in Woolwich, London, on 19 February 1901.

Leonard was admitted to the school on 27 January 1905 (Petition No. 12070), joining his older brother, Walter Herbert Lewry, who had been admitted to the school on 12 August 1903 (Petition No. 11834). Leonard was joined by his youngest brother, Albert Ernest Lewry, on 08 September 1908 (Petition No. 12538).

Leonard was discharged from the school on 22 July 1909 and enlisted into the 8th (The King's Royal Irish) Hussars, joining that regiment in India on 08 October 1910.

When war was declared, 8th Hussars was stationed in Ambala, India, as part of the Ambala Cavalry Brigade, although it was quickly mobilised for Europe with the rest of the 1st Indian Cavalry Division, landing at Marseille on 10 November 1914, its first experiences of the trenches being in December 1914, although it was in billets for Christmas.

The regiment spent the majority of the war digging trenches, although "D" Squadron took part in the regiment's last mounted charge, at Villers-Faucon on 27 March 1917, Leonard's discharge documents confirming that he was in that squadron.

Leonard remained on the Western Front until 21 December 1917, before he was discharged from the army as no longer physically fit for war service due to tubercle of lung, which was recorded to have originated in France in October 1917. He died in Brighton, Sussex, as a result of this disease, five days after the Armistice.

Leonard's brother Walter was discharged from the school on 27 February 1902, enlisting into The Royal Irish Fusiliers. He was captured at Caudry, France, on 27 August 1914, spending the remainder of the war as a prisoner. He died in Southwark, London, in 1973.

Albert was only at the school for a month before he was discharged from the school on 13 October 1908 as *"medically unfit for army life"*. He died in Birmingham, West Midlands, in 1984.

9th (The Queen's Royal) Lancers

Sydney Ernest BENNETT
Private, 4794, 9th (The Queen's Royal) Lancers who died on 22 March 1918, aged 19. Commemorated on the Pozieres Memorial, Somme, France

Born on 05 June 1898 in Walthamstow, Essex, the youngest child of George Henry Bennett and Alice Evana née Tucker, his father had been a Drummer in The Royal Fusiliers (City of London Regiment) and had been discharged from the army on 03 October 1893, the 1901 Census showing that he was working as a Gatekeeper to the Honourable Artillery Company in City Road, London. He died in Walthamstow on 02 August 1902.

Sydney was admitted to the school on 31 October 1907 (Petition No. 12441), just over a year after his older brother, Percy Bennett, was discharged. Percy had been admitted on 05 March 1903 (Petition No. 11805).

Sydney remained at the school for six years, making the transition from Chelsea to Guston and was discharged to the 9th (The Queen's Royal) Lancers on 24 June 1913. His service record is no longer available, and there is no disembarkation date recorded on his medal index card, which suggests that he did not serve overseas until after 1916. The regiment remained on the Western Front for the duration of the war, although it seems likely that, due to the nature of the conflict, the majority of that time would have been spent as dismounted troops and manning the trenches alongside their infantry colleagues.

When the German Army launched its Spring Offensive on 21 March 1918, the 9th Lancers were used to support the hard-pressed infantry. The regiment had been located in the vicinity of Le Mesnil, but was forced to retire. On 22 March, a mounted party moved, with extra horses, to Buire to fetch a dismounted party, which it managed to do, returning at about noon. However, the regiment also suffered three other ranks killed, four officers and eighteen other ranks wounded and five other ranks unaccounted for.

It is likely that Sydney Bennett was one of those unaccounted for, killed on 22 March 1918, as he has no known grave, but is commemorated along with 29 of his comrades from the 9th Lancers on the Pozieres Memorial.

When Percy was discharged from the school on 05 April 1906, he enlisted in the Royal Garrison Artillery. He survived the war and appeared to have continued in the army, reaching the rank of Battery Serjeant Major. He died in Rodmell, East Sussex, in 1970.

Percy's twin sons, Percy and Sidney Bennett, born in 1919, were both Dukies. They were admitted to the school on 09 January 1930 (Percy's Petition No. 15160, Sidney's Petition No. 15161). Percy was discharged from the school, enlisting into the Royal Regiment of Artillery on 26 July 1934, which was three months after Sidney had been discharged to the Royal Corps of Signals on 05 April 1934. Sidney, like his uncle, is recorded on the memorial tablets in the school chapel, having died in Japanese captivity in Osaka on 17 February 1943.

12th (The Prince of Wales's Royal) Lancers

Stuart Henry ALLEN
Lance Corporal, L/5807, 12th (The Prince of Wales's Royal) Lancers who died on 26 September 1914, aged 26. Buried in Aldershot Military Cemetery, Hampshire, United Kingdom

Born on 24 March 1888 in Chelsea, Middlesex, the eldest son of James Allen and Annie née Belsham, his father had been born in Canada and served in the 71st (Highland) Regiment of Foot[33], but had left the Army on 20 October 1879, the 1891 Census showing that he was working as a Butler in Chelsea. He died on 14 December 1898.

James was also a Dukie, having been admitted to the school on 05 January 1861 (Petition No. 6602) and discharged to the 71st Foot on 17 November 1865, which was his thirteenth birthday.

Stuart was admitted to the school at Chelsea on 14 July 1899 (Petition No. 11304) and was discharged four years later on 24 July 1903, enlisting into the 12th (The Prince of Wales's Royal) Lancers. Although his service record is not available, the 1911 Census shows that Stuart was a Private in that regiment and stationed in the Cantonments in Pretoria, South Africa, although by the time that war was declared, the regiment was back in Britain and stationed in Norwich, Norfolk. It left Norwich on 16 August, embarking on the SSs *African Prince* and *Manchester Importer* at Southampton, Hampshire, in the early hours of the following morning, landing at Le Havre on the same day, 17 August 1914.

Records show that the 12th Lancers deployed to France as part of V Cavalry Brigade, becoming part of General Hubert Gough's 2nd Cavalry Division on 13 September 1914. It was involved in the early battles of the war prior to moving into billets on 15 September. During one of these battles, Stuart was wounded.

Following wounding, Stuart was evacuated back to Britain, where he died of wounds in the Cambridge Military Hospital,

---

[33] Amalgamated with the 74th (Highlanders) Regiment of Foot on 01 July 1881 to become The Highland Light Infantry

Aldershot, on 26 September 1914 and was subsequently buried in Aldershot Military Cemetery.

William Francis QUIGLEY

Lance Corporal, L/1283, 12th (The Prince of Wales's Royal) Lancers who died on 31 May 1916, aged 28. Buried in Plumstead Cemetery, London, United Kingdom

Born on 02 January 1888 in Woolwich, Kent, the eldest of three children of Edward Quigley and Minnie Elizabeth née Lockyer, his father was a Corporal in the Royal Artillery who had been discharged to pension on 06 June 1882 and died in Woolwich on 29 May 1894.

William was admitted to the school on 11 August 1898 (Petition No. 11198) and was discharged five years later on 29 August 1903, enlisting into the 5th (Royal Irish) Lancers, spending the first five years of his service with this regiment before transferring to the 12th (The Prince of Wales's Royal) Lancers and being posted to India on 05 September 1908.

After spending just over two years in India, the regiment was posted to South Africa, remaining there until 30 December 1912 before returning to Norwich, Norfolk.

William landed in France on 17 August 1914 and it is possible that he would have taken part in the famous action at Moÿ-de-l'Aisne twelve days later, when a squadron of the 12th Lancers made a successful charge against a dismounted squadron of Prussian Dragoons during the Great Retreat.

The regiment also participated in the Second Battle of Ypres and William's service record states that he was *"On active service 30 April 1915 at Ypres. Whilst in trenches a percussion shell burst just in front of him and shattered the right foot... Permanent. Capacity lessened by ½"*[34]. During surgery that was performed on the same day, William had all of his toes amputated, in addition to two metacarpal bones, which ultimately resulted in his discharge from the army on 06 February 1916.

He died, likely as a result of complications from these wounds, three months after discharge, on 31 May 1916, and is another of the "Lost Boys" whose name has been omitted from the memorial tablets in the school chapel.

---

[34] WO 363: War Office: Soldiers' Documents, First World War 'Burnt Documents' (Microfilm Copies), 1914-1920, The National Archives, Kew - First World War Service Records 'Burnt Documents'

13th Hussars

Denis PITMAN
Private, 1201, 13th Hussars who died on 12 July 1915, aged 24. Buried in Cabaret-Rouge British Cemetery, Souchez, Pas de Calais, France

Born on 01 October 1890 in Beaconsfield, Buckinghamshire, the second of four children of James Pitman and Gertrude née Rolfe, his father was a Dukie, having been at the Royal Military Asylum between 1879 and 1883 (Petition No. 8401). Following his discharge from the school, he served first in the Grenadier Guards and then The Royal Sussex Regiment, which was the regiment in which he was serving in South Africa at the time that Denis was admitted to the school.

Denis was admitted on 06 December 1901 (Petition No. 11637) and discharged to the 13th Hussars on 15 October 1904. His younger brother, Percy Pitman, was admitted to the school four months after his discharge, on 03 February 1905 (Petition No. 12080).

The service record for Denis is no longer available, but the 1911 Census shows him as a Private in the 13th Hussars stationed in Meerut, India. At the outbreak of war, the regiment was still stationed in Meerut, sailing from Bombay on 19 November and landing at Marseille on 14 December 1914. However, rather than being used in its cavalry role, due to the way in which the fighting had degenerated to trench warfare, the regiment was used to supplement the infantry, moving into the trenches for the first time on 13 January 1915 near Festubert.

After a brief spell in the trenches, the regiment spent the rest of January-April in billets, although it did move from the vicinity of Béthune to Witternesse in the April, and was still there in July 1915, providing working parties in the rear areas as well as in support of the units that were rotating through the front-line.

On 12 July 1915, the regimental diary reports *"2 men of working party killed by shell fire near VERMELLES"*[35]. One of these two men was

---

[35] WO 95/1186/3: 13 Hussars, 1914 Oct. - 1916 June, The National Archives, Kew

Denis Pitman, the other being Private J. Tracey. They were buried adjacent to each other in Cabaret-Rouge British Cemetery, Souchez.

Denis's brother Percy was discharged from the school on 20 February 1908, enlisting into the Irish Guards. He was killed in action on the 01 November 1914 and is commemorated on the Menin Gate Memorial, as well as being recorded with his brother on the memorial tablets in the school chapel.

Frank Martin WREN
Private, 7003, 13th Hussars who died on 05 March 1917, aged 25. Commemorated on the Basra Memorial, Iraq

Born on 03 September 1891 in Guernsey, Channel Islands, the eldest son of David MacMurdo Wren and Mary Jane née Burns, his father had been a Serjeant in The King's Own (Yorkshire Light Infantry) who had been discharged to pension on 16 November 1897.

Frank was admitted to the school on 10 October 1902 (Petition No. 11743) and discharged to the 13th Hussars on 28 September 1905.

His service record is no longer available, but his history until July 1915 would have been the same as fellow Dukie, Denis Pitman. With the regiment spending much of 1915 in billets, with occasional stints in the trenches and carrying out a few reconnaissance tasks as well as providing working parties, this enabled soldiers to take home leave in Britain and during one of these Frank married Emily Margaret Porter in Walthamstow, Essex, on 23 November 1915.

The first half of 1916 was much the same as 1915, but on 04 June 1916 the regiment received orders that, along with the rest of the Meerut Brigade, it was to be prepared to move to Marseille and return to India, embarking at the port on 26 June and landing at Bombay on 07 July 1916. It re-embarked at Bombay twelve days later, heading for Mesopotamia, where it landed at Basra on 25 July.

Once it had arrived, the regiment then remained in Makina Masus Camp in Basra until November, when it relocated to Amarah, prior to moving further north.

By the beginning of March 1917, the regiment was in the area of Aziziyah when armoured cars and aircraft reported the presence of scattered patrols of Ottoman infantry, and it was ordered to support Watson's Horse (6th Duke of Connaught's Own Lancers), an Indian Army unit, which was under attack. Initially the attack was launched mounted, but when it was realised that it could not be forced home on horseback, the squadrons involved retired, dismounted, and returned to the attack.

The attack was not a success and the regiment was forced to retire by the evening. Frank was killed during this action and it is likely that his was one of the bodies that it was not possible to recover, as he has no known grave and is commemorated on the Basra Memorial.

15th (The King's) Hussars

Alfred George CHESHIRE
Trumpeter, 10337, 15th (The King's) Hussars who died on 30 March 1918, aged 18. Commemorated on the Pozieres Memorial, Somme, France

Born on 31 May 1899 in Frimley, Surrey, the youngest of five children of James Cheshire and Agnes née Lampard, his father had been a Private in the 15th (The King's) Hussars, but had retired from the army on 17 April 1888. He died in Frimley on 16 August 1904.

Alfred was admitted to the school on 01 September 1910 (Petition No. 12639), a year after it had relocated from Chelsea to Guston, remaining there for three years before being discharged on 12 July 1913 and enlisting in his father's old regiment.

At the outbreak of war, the 15th Hussars was stationed in Longmoor, Hampshire, rapidly mobilising and landing at Rouen on 18 August 1914. The squadrons of the regiment were then each sent to a different division to form the divisional reconnaissance element, "A" Squadron to the 3rd Division, "B" Squadron to the 2nd Division and C Squadron to the 1st Division, and it was not until 14 April 1915 that the regiment was reconstituted, joining IX Cavalry Brigade, part of the 1st Cavalry Division.

However, it is unlikely that Alfred would have deployed with the regiment in 1914 due to his age, and although his medal index card has no date for entry into theatre, it does show that he was not entitled to the award of the 1914-15 Star. It is likely that it was not until he was at least seventeen, in May 1916, that he was able to deploy.

The regiment did participate in cavalry actions whilst serving on the Western Front, but, due to the nature of the warfare, it also spent much time either providing working parties or manning the trenches alongside the infantry units.

On 21 March 1918, the German Army launched its Spring Offensive, a series of attacks along the Western Front as a last-ditch attempt to defeat the Triple Entente prior to the influx of American soldiers being able to turn the tide completely in favour of the Allies.

On 30 March 1918, the 15th (The King's) Hussars and 19th (Queen Alexandra's Own Royal) Hussars stopped the Germans from advancing down the Amiens Road in the vicinity of Warfusée-Abancourt during the late afternoon. The manner of Alfred's death was conveyed to his mother in a letter sent by one of his comrades:

> *"He, together with six more of a party were sent out at dawn to reinforce a part of the line that had been reported by our officers to be a weak salient. It was while in the open that we unfortunately came under observation from a Bosch machine gun which accounted for four other fellows. Captain Arnett (killed later that day) and I managed to get your son under cover of the trench and although every endeavour was made to keep life going we failed and your son died a short while after being hit. His last words to my knowledge were 'mother, mother'. One consolation, if consolation it can be called, was that he died peacefully and without any pain or disfigurement. It was not until darkness set in that I buried him just over from where he had been killed. Ever since the offensive commenced I had your son alongside of me and to be so young was a credit to his regiment, knowing no fear, resourceful and tactful in critical moments and it affected me more than I like to admit when he got killed. His death left me practically without a pal, more so when I found myself the only survivor"*[36]

Despite being buried by his comrade, it would appear that the location of the grave was lost during the subsequent fighting, as Alfred has no known grave and is commemorated on the Pozieres Memorial.

---

[36] https://sites.google.com/site/frimleyandcamberley/lest-weforget-my-family-s-military-memorial/a-list-of-the-menincluding-military-details

16th (The Queen's) Lancers

Charles Henry HARGROVE
Private, 3591, 16th (The Queen's) Lancers who died on 11 November 1918, aged 21. Buried in Valenciennes (St. Roch) Communal Cemetery, Nord, France

Born in on 14 July 1897 in Gibraltar, the eldest of five children of Frederick Reginald Hargrove and Kate Emily née Burbridge, his father was a Private in The Northumberland Fusiliers who had retired from the army on 19 July 1904.

Charles was admitted to the school on 08 September 1908 (Petition No. 12542), and having moved from Chelsea to Guston, he was discharged to the 16th (The Queen's) Lancers on 05 September 1911.

His service record is no longer available, but at the outbreak of war, the regiment was stationed at Curragh Camp, Newbridge, County Kildare, embarking on the SS *Indian* at Dublin on 15 August and landing at Le Havre on 18 August 1914.

The regiment fought on the Western Front throughout the war, initially in its cavalry role, but, due to the nature of the static warfare, more so in an infantry role, manning the trenches. It did not return to its cavalry role until the Hundred Days Offensive in the aftermath of the early-1918 German Spring Offensive, when there was a return to the war of movement that had not been seen for almost four years.

On 10 November 1918, the regiment was tasked with capturing the high ground around the village of Villers St. Ghislain. Whilst the objectives were achieved, it suffered sixteen other ranks casualties.

It is likely that Charles Hargrove was one of these casualties, and although he was evacuated to No.4 Canadian Casualty Clearing Station, he died of his wounds the following day, 11 November 1918, the day that the guns fell silent at the end of the war. He was buried in Valenciennes, the town where the Casualty Clearing Station in which he died was located.

Whilst Charles is commemorated on the tablets in the school chapel, he is incorrectly recorded as G H Hargrove.

Arthur John LUTON
Private, 13210, 16th (The Queen's) Lancers who died on 23 March 1918, aged 40. Commemorated on the Pozieres Memorial, Somme, France

Born on 28 December 1877 in Ballincollig, County Cork, the fifth of seven children of William Luton and Rebecca Mary née Toole, his father had been a Serjeant in the 2nd Dragoon Guards (Queen's Bays), but had been discharged from the army on 19 February 1884, dying in Bath, Somersetshire, on 11 March 1885.

Arthur was admitted to the school on 25 August 1888 (Petition No. 9688) and was discharged on 05 March 1892, enlisting straight into The Northumberland Fusiliers.

Just over a month after enlisting, Arthur transferred to his father's old regiment in which his older brother was already serving, being posted to India seven months later. After two years in India, the regiment was then posted to Egypt, for a further two years, before returning home in 1896.

During this time, Arthur seems to have been a "disciplinary problem", as he was regularly granted and then forfeited his good conduct pay. He was shown in the 1901 Census as being stationed with the 2nd Dragoon Guards (Queen's Bays) in the West Cavalry Barracks, Aldershot, Hampshire.

After five years at home, Arthur was deployed with his regiment to South Africa during the Second Boer War, where he was briefly a Lance Corporal before losing his tape for drunkenness, and on 07 March 1903 Arthur was discharged as a Trumpeter, having completed his first term of service.

How long Arthur was out of the army for is unknown, as he re-enlisted at some point, although there is no service record available to confirm when, but he is recorded in the 1911 Census as a Private in the 16th (The Queen's) Lancers and stationed in Shrapnel Barracks, Woolwich, London. After the outbreak of war, Arthur's history would have been the same as fellow Dukie Charles Hargrove, serving in the same regiment.

Following the launch of the Spring Offensive by the German Army, which initially met with such success, all available troops were utilised in an effort to stop the advance. It is likely that it was during this German offensive that Arthur Luton was killed, *"on or since"* 23 March 1918. His body was never recovered and he is remembered on the Pozieres memorial.

His older brother, Frederick, with whom he served in the 2nd Dragoon Guards, was shown as still with this regiment and stationed in Aldershot in the 1911 Census. He died in Bath, Somerset, at the age of 45, in 1917, but it is likely that his death was not related to his military service as he is not commemorated by the Commonwealth War Graves Commission.

17th (Duke of Cambridge's Own) Lancers

Richard Edward SLADDEN
Private, 72692, 17th (Duke of Cambridge's Own) Lancers who died on 11 August 1918, aged 22. Buried in Mezieres Communal Cemetery Extension, Somme, France

Born on 18 February 1896 in Newry, County Down, the sixth of ten children of Thomas Sladden and Emma née Williams, his father was a Colour Serjeant in The Duke of Cornwall's Light Infantry and died whilst serving in Falmouth, Cornwall on 23 December 1904.

Richard was admitted to the school on 30 March 1906 (Petition No. 12215), joining his older brother, Thomas Sladden, who had been admitted on 09 June 1905 (Petition No. 12111).

After making the move from Chelsea to Guston, Richard was discharged to the 17th (Duke of Cambridge's Own) Lancers on 03 May 1910, but not before being joined at the school by his younger brother, Jeffrey Royston Williams Sladden, who was admitted on 09 November 1909 (Petition No. 12694).

Richard's service record is no longer available, but at the outbreak of war, the 17th Lancers was stationed in Sialkot, India, as part of the Sialkot Cavalry Brigade. However, it was soon mobilised, embarking at Karachi on 16 October and landing at Marseille on 07 November 1914.

Due to the static nature that the war had developed into, it was not until three years later that the regiment reverted to its traditional cavalry role in November 1917, during the Battle of Cambrai. In the intervening three years, the soldiers from the regiment were employed in manning the trenches as well as providing working parties.

Following the launch of the German Spring Offensive in March 1918, the regiment was employed in both a cavalry and mobile infantry role, used to plug gaps as needed. However, it reverted back to its traditional role again during the Hundred Days Offensive.

This offensive was launched with the Battle of Amiens on 08 August 1918, with the regiment in action from the first day and suffering casualties from the start. On the 10 August, it was fighting in the area of Foquescourt, and during that day suffered one other rank killed, one who died of wounds and one wounded, in addition to ten horses killed. It is likely that the soldier wounded on 10 August was Richard, who died of wounds on 11 August 1918[37] and was buried in Mezieres, close to where he died.

Although Richard is commemorated on the memorial tablets in the school chapel, he is incorrectly recorded as R E *Sladon*.

Thomas was discharged from the school on 02 February 1909, enlisting into the band of the 17th (Duke of Cambridge's Own) Lancers, the 1911 Census showing him as a Musician at the Royal Military School of Music at Kneller Hall. He survived the war, dying in Watford, Hertfordshire, in 1975.

Jeffrey was discharged from the school to the Royal Engineers on 01 April 1913, transferring to the Royal Air Force in 1918. He died in Fife, Scotland, in 1960.

---

[37] The Commonwealth War Graves Commission incorrectly records his date of death as 12 August 1918

5th (Royal Irish) Lancers

Frank David MAXTED
Lance Corporal, 6694, 5th (Royal Irish) Lancers who died on 30 October 1914, aged 27. Commemorated on the Ypres (Menin Gate) Memorial, West-Vlaanderen, Belgium

Born on 31 July 1887 in Frimley, Surrey, the eldest of two children of Frank Maxted and Alice née Wood, his father was a Corporal in the 5th (Royal Irish) Lancers who was discharged from the army on 04 January 1895 and died in Whitechapel, London, on 20 July 1896.

Frank was admitted to the school on 13 July 1897 (Petition No. 11030), a year after his father died, and was discharged to his father's regiment on 12 July 1902.

Frank's service record is no longer available, nor can he be found in the 1911 Census, but at the outbreak of war, his regiment was stationed in Marlborough Barracks, Dublin. Eleven days after the start of the war, it embarked on the SS *Kingstonian* at Dublin North Wall and landed at Le Havre on 17 August 1914.

It then participated in the Battles of Mons and Le Cateau in its cavalry role, but as the war became more stagnant and both sides dug-in, it was employed more in an infantry role manning the trenches.

The regiment was in the area of Ypres during the first of the battles that took their name from the town, and which had commenced on 19 October, entrenching near Berthen on 20 October.

The 5th Lancers then remained in this area, relieving the 129th Baluchis of the Indian Army in the trenches at 0530hrs on 30 October. Once there, it was subjected to heavy shelling from 0700hrs until 1200hrs, after which it was forced to retire, with the loss of 2 officers killed or missing and 26 other ranks killed, wounded or missing. Frank was one of those who was killed on 30 October 1914. His body was not recovered and he is commemorated on the Menin Gate Memorial.

Frank is also commemorated on the tablets in the school chapel, although he is incorrectly named as T Maxted.

19th (Queen Alexandra's Own Royal) Hussars

Harold William KENNEY
Private, 37, 19th (Queen Alexandra's Own Royal) Hussars who died on 17 October 1914, aged 22. Commemorated on the Ypres (Menin Gate) Memorial, West-Vlaanderen, Belgium

Born on 15 December 1892 in Bangalore, India, one of nine children of Edmund Kenney and Elizabeth née Luckie, his father was the Farrier Quartermaster Serjeant in the 19th (Queen Alexandra's Own Royal) Hussars.

Harold was admitted to the school on 12 November 1903 (Petition No. 11901), the same day as his twin brother, Herbert John Kenney (Petition No. 11902). Both boys remained in the school for four years and were discharged on 11 January 1907. On discharge from the school, Harold enlisted into his father's old regiment.

Although his service record is no longer available, the 1911 Census shows him serving with the regiment as a Private and stationed in Wellington Lines, Aldershot.

By the time war broke out, the regiment was stationed in Hounslow, Middlesex. "A" and "B" Squadrons deploying to France and landing at Le Havre on 24 August 1914, with "C" Squadron, of which Harold was part, deploying a month later, moving first to Cambridge and landing at St. Nazaire on 11 & 12 September 1914.

For the first month that "C" Squadron was in France and Flanders, it was deployed to various places, but it was not until the 13 October, near Borre, France, that it saw action when it was *"shrapnelled"*[38], the only casualties being two horses hit.

On the 17 October 1914, the squadron *"marched at dawn as advanced guard to 17th Brigade to Rue du Bois. Here sent out three patrols under Sgts toward PERENCHIES, PREMESQUES and CAPINGHEM: these patrols reported Germans in considerable force & apparently entrenched on high ground just w. of the latter named place. Had two Corporals and one man hit whilst making these reconnaissances, the latter being, it is feared, badly wounded: it was impossible to get near him to bring him in. We were relieved by the infantry about*

---

[38] WO 95/1596/2: "C" Squadron 19 Hussars, 1914 Aug. - 1915 Jan., The National Archives, Kew

3pm when we returned to FLEURBAIX & billeted"[39].

It is almost certain that the badly wounded soldier that it was not possible to *"get in"* was Harold. He died on 17 October 1914 and his body was never recovered. As a result, he is commemorated on the Menin Gate Memorial. He is also commemorated on the memorial tablets in the school chapel, but his name is incorrectly recorded as H W Kenny.

When Herbert was discharged from the school on 11 January 1907, he, like his brother, enlisted in the 19th Hussars, receiving the consecutive service number. He survived the war and died in Sparsholt, Hampshire in 1963.

---

[39] Ibid

20th Hussars

James Charles BULLEN
Boy, 70169, 20th Hussars who died on 31 December 1919, aged 15. Buried in Ismailia War Memorial Cemetery, Egypt

Born on 07 January 1904 in Canterbury, Kent, the second of four children of James Bullen and Jennie née le Marquand, his father had been a Private in the 20th Hussars who was discharged from the army on 31 January 1907 and died in Brighton, Sussex, on 09 July 1913.

James was admitted to the school on 30 December 1913 and would have moved to Warley, Essex, when the school was evacuated during the war, before he was discharged on 16 January 1919, enlisting into the 20th Hussars.

Although James's service record is no longer available, it appears that after enlisting, he went to Egypt with his regiment in July 1919. Sadly, his was not to be a long army career, dying of enteric fever[40] in the Military Hospital on 31 December 1919.

James is another "Lost Boy" whose name has been omitted from the memorial tablets in the school chapel.

Harold Claude WATSHAM
Private, 11857, 20th Hussars who died on 01 December 1917, aged 28. Buried in Rocquigny-Equancourt Road British Cemetery, Manancourt, Somme, France

Born on 16 October 1889 in West Ham, Essex, the fourth of five children of Edmund Watsham and Eliza née Miller, his father had been a 3rd Class Staff Sergeant in The Commissariat and Transport Corps[41] who was discharged from the army on 13 April 1886 and died in Colchester, Essex, on 04 March 1897.

Harold was admitted to the school on 05 October 1900 (Petition No. 11494) and discharged to the Army Service Corps on 24 October 1903.

Harold spent all of his service in Britain, appointed as a Trumpeter on 21 December 1903, but after he had turned eighteen, he transferred to the ranks as a Driver on 02 May 1905.

---

[40] Another name for Typhoid fever
[41] Amalgamated with the Commissariat and Transport Staff in December 1888 to become the Army Service Corps

On 04 October 1910, he was tried and convicted of disobeying a lawful command given by his superior officer and sentenced to detention, being released on 29 October 1910. However, this conviction was quashed on 26 October 1910, which may be the reason for his release, but despite this, he was discharged from the army for misconduct on the day that he was released from detention.

Following his discharge from the army, Harold appears to have moved back to his mother's home in Colchester, Essex, and is recorded in the 1911 Census as being employed as a Groom. A year later, it appears that Harold was living in Birkenhead, Cheshire, as he married Florence Large in the town on 06 November 1912. Their first child, Harold William Watsham, was born in Birkenhead eleven months later.

Following the outbreak of war, Harold re-enlisted at York, Yorkshire North Riding, on 17 August 1914, joining the 20th Hussars, although he did not disembark in theatre until 21 December 1915. It is likely that the lateness of his arrival was that he was again tried for insubordination, in Colchester on 14 September 1915, and sentenced to 84 days' detention, although 42 days were remitted. By the time of his disembarkation in France, he and his wife were expecting their second child, Leslie Thomas Watsham, who was born a month later, in January 1916.

Due to the nature of the war, the cavalry was not employed in its traditional role, but instead provided working parties or fulfilled an infantry role by manning the trenches, and this would have been the role that Harold carried out whilst he was in theatre.

At 1100hrs on 30 November 1917, the regiment was in the vicinity of Flesquières, when a message was received that it was seize and hold a ridge to the south of the Fins-Gouzeaucourt road, approximately one mile west of the town of Gouzeaucourt itself. Patrols reported that to the west of the regiment's objective, there was a line of trenches that were being very thinly held by a company of Royal Engineers and that the Germans were 300 yards beyond that position.

Having ridden to the area, the regiment dismounted and reinforced the Royal Engineers, but after half an hour, it received orders that it was to advance, which it did.

Having advanced approximately 1000 yards, it was joined in the attack by the 2nd Battalion, Coldstream Guards and the line was further advanced to the ridge south of Gouzeaucourt. However, heavy enfilade machine-gun fire prevented any further advance.

Once darkness fell, efforts were made to consolidate the gains made and to plug the gap that had developed between the Coldstream Guards and the 20th Hussars, this being filled by companies of infantry. During this consolidation process, the regiment suffered 25 soldiers killed, wounded or missing, Harold being one of those wounded, dying from his wounds the following day.

Although he has a marked grave, he is another of the "Lost Boys" whose name has been omitted from the memorial tablets in the school chapel.

His youngest son, Gordon Dennis Watsham, was born three months after Harold's death, in March 1918.

Berkshire (Hungerford) Yeomanry

James Victor NICHOLSON
Lance Corporal, 18094, 1/1st, Berkshire (Hungerford) Yeomanry who died on 27 November 1917, aged 30. Buried in Jerusalem War Cemetery, Israel

Born on 26 August 1887 in South Leith, Midlothian, the second of six children of James Saunderson Nicholson and Julia Charlotte née Smith, his father was a Band Serjeant in the 15th (The King's) Hussars.

James was admitted to the school on 07 May 1897 (Petition No. 11027) and was discharged to the 5th (Royal Irish) Lancers on 14 February 1903.

After enlisting, James remained with the regiment on the mainland and in Ireland, but not without incident, his first offence being in August 1908 (disobedience of a regimental order and improperly dressed in Market Lavington), with a further two offences that year, and a further three in 1910, 1911 and 1912, the last three all being as a result of drunkenness.

James was still serving with the 5th Lancers at the outbreak of war, stationed in Marlborough Barracks, Dublin, embarking on the SS *Kingstonian* on 15 August and landing at Le Havre on 17 August 1914, before coming into action for the first time at 0430hrs on 24 August near Angre, Belgium, south-west of Mons. At this stage he would have been serving with fellow Dukie Frank Maxted.

The regiment then retired with the remainder of the British Expeditionary Force, fighting at Le Cateau, before turning to advance on the Germans on 06 September.

As with all other cavalry units, the 5th Lancers spent almost the whole of the next four years in an infantry role as the war settled into trench stalemate. However, on 01 February 1916, James was transferred to Rouen and then England, where he was discharged from the army on 11 February having completed his period of service.

At some point after discharge, James re-enlisted into the 1/1st Berkshire Yeomanry, a Territorial Force unit. This regiment had been mobilised at the outbreak of war and served at Gallipoli before being transferred to Egypt. It is unclear at what point James joined this regiment, as his second service record is unavailable, but it is known that he was with it in late-1917.

From 31 October 1917, the regiment took part in the Third Battle of Gaza, including the Battle of Beersheba and the Capture of the Sheria Position, as well as taking part in the Battle of Mughar Ridge on 13 and 14 November and the Battle of Nebi Samwil from 17 to 24 November. From 27 to 29 November, it then withstood the Turkish counterattacks during the Capture of Jerusalem. It is likely that it was during these counterattacks that James was killed in action on 27 November 1917.

James younger brother, Albert Henry Nicholson, who was not a Dukie, also lost his life during the war. He was a Bandsman in the 6th (Inniskilling) Dragoons when he was killed on 07 September 1915 and is buried in Authuille Military Cemetery, Authuille, Somme, France.

King Edward's Horse
(The King's Overseas Dominions Regiment)

William KENNEDY
Major, 1st King Edward's Horse (The King's Overseas Dominions Regiment) who died on 29 May 1915, aged 61. Buried in Streatham Cemetery, London, United Kingdom

Born on 17 October 1853 in Hounslow, Middlesex, the son of Michael Kennedy and Ann née Nixon, his father was a Lance Serjeant in the 17th Regiment of (Light) Dragoons (Lancers).

William was admitted to the school on 03 September 1860 (Petition No. 6572) and was discharged on 19 October 1867 into his father's old regiment, by now renamed the 17th Regiment of Lancers.

William spent the first 12 years of his service in Britain and was a Serjeant when, in 1879, the regiment, which had been renamed the 17th (The Duke of Cambridge's Own) Lancers in 1876, was sent to Natal Colony, south-eastern Africa, during the Anglo-Zulu War.

The regiment then returned to India in October 1879, William having been promoted to Squadron Serjeant Major, where he married Jessie Catherine Hart on 08 March 1881, their only child, Charles Kennedy, being born in Mhow, India, in 1882.

William returned home for five years in 1884, before returning to India. He was then posted to Egypt in October 1890, returning to Britain thirteen months later and promoting to Regimental Serjeant Major on 21 December 1892, the rank at which he was discharged from the army on 19 October 1898 *"having reached the age for discharge"*[42].

William re-enlisted into the Imperial Yeomanry on 21 February 1900, and was immediately promoted to his old rank of Regimental Serjeant Major, serving in South Africa from 13 March 1900 until 20 March 1901, before being Commissioned as an Honorary Lieutenant and appointed as Quartermaster to the 6th Battalion, Imperial Yeomanry, on 30 March 1901[43]. That same year, on 18

---
[42] WO 97 - Chelsea Pensioners British Army Service Records 1760-1913
[43] *The London Gazette*, 10 May 1901, Issue:27312

September, his son Charles was killed whilst serving as a Private in the 17th Lancers, his old regiment, at Modderfontein, South Africa, during the Second Boer War.

The Imperial Yeomanry was a volunteer mounted force, formed in 1900 for service during the Second Boer War. It existed until it was incorporated into the Territorial Force, and was eventually renamed King Edward's Horse (The King's Overseas Dominions Regiment) in 1910. In 1911, William was still the Quartermaster of that regiment, but had been promoted to the rank of Honorary Major.

The regiment became part of the Special Reserve in 1913, a reservoir of manpower for the army, training replacement drafts in times of war, and in 1914 it was mobilised at the Duke of York's Headquarters in Chelsea, William's old school site.

William did not see service overseas and provided support from home to those deploying. He died whilst serving in Wandsworth Summers Town, London, on 29 May 1915 and was buried in Streatham Cemetery with full military honours on 03 June 1915.

William is the oldest of the Dukies to have died in uniform during the war and to have been commemorated by the Commonwealth War Graves Commission, as well as on the memorial tablets in the school chapel.

The Reserve Regiments of Cavalry

John MAY
Private D/29671, 4th Reserve Cavalry Regiment who died on 16 November 1918, aged 19. Buried in Aldershot Military Cemetery, Hampshire, United Kingdom

Born on 02 October 1899 in Newbridge, County Kildare, the third of six children of George May and Marion née Palmer, his father was a 1st Class Staff Sergeant Major in the Army Service Corps and died in the Archcliffe Military Hospital, Dover, whilst still serving, on 31 January 1908.

John was admitted to the school on 23 September 1909 (Petition No. 12676) and was discharged to the army on 23 September 1914, just over a month after war had broken out.

The school records state that when he was discharged, John enlisted into the Army Service Corps, but there is no service record available to confirm this. It also appears that John never served overseas, probably due to his age, as there are no records for him in the medal rolls.

It is known that at some point, John transferred to the cavalry, the D-prefix at the beginning of his service number indicating that he joined the Dragoon Guards, and he was serving with the 4th Reserve Cavalry Regiment in 1918.

John died from influenza and pneumonia on 16 November 1918, five days after the Armistice ending the war came into effect. He was buried in Aldershot Military Cemetery.

Whilst he is commemorated by the Commonwealth War Graves Commission, for many years he was a Dukie "Lost Boy". However, a supplementary tablet with his name and that of Joseph Hawtin has been added to those already in place in the school chapel in recent years.

Royal Regiment of Field Artillery

James Robert BEAVERS
Acting Serjeant, 69470, British Military Mission, Royal Field Artillery, who died on or after 01 February 1920, aged 21. Commemorated on the Haidar Pasha Memorial, Turkey

Born on 05 May 1898 in Bangalore, India, the eldest of four children and only son of Edis Beavers and Margaret née Barry, his father was a Battery Serjeant Major in the Royal Artillery who died whilst serving in Colchester, Essex, on 07 January 1908.

James was admitted to the school on 18 March 1909 (Petition No. 12582) and having moved from Chelsea to Guston, he was discharged on 25 June 1912, enlisting into the Royal Artillery. A year after his discharge from the school, his mother re-married, to Walter Harrison, in Staines, Middlesex.

James's service record survives, although it has been very badly damaged, but it would appear that when he enlisted in the army he gave his name as John Robert Beavers, although the reason for this is not known[44].

Nine months after enlisting, James was appointed as a Trumpeter on 04 March 1913 and was posted to 124 Battery, XVII Brigade, Royal Field Artillery, which was stationed in Dundalk, County Louth.

Following the outbreak of war, the brigade was mobilised and James's medal index card shows that he disembarked in France on 19 August 1914, being posted to the ammunition column of this brigade on 06 October 1914. However, he was only with the ammunition column for one week prior to being posted back to 124 Battery, with which he remained for a year before he was posted back to Britain on 03 November 1915, now underage for active service once the regulations changed, joining No. 4 Depot in Woolwich, London.

Five days after returning to Britain, James was posted to 56 Reserve Battery, Royal Field Artillery, remaining with this battery

---

[44] James is the name given on his birth record and all of the school records. Only one Beavers attended the school and the service record for John Robert Beavers confirms that he was a Dukie.

for just over two years, appointed as a paid Acting Bombardier on 23 November 1916. However, by 13 December 1917, he had reverted to Gunner and was then appointed as a paid Acting Lance Bombardier, although he again reverted to Gunner on 02 April 1918.

On the same day that he reverted to Gunner, James was posted back to France, joining 126 Battery, XXIX Brigade, Royal Field Artillery and being appointed as a Bombardier on 15 June 1918. On 05 September 1918, it appears that James was wounded by gas and following treatment he returned to duty on 10 October 1918, being posted to CLIII (Empire) Brigade, Royal Field Artillery.

Following the Armistice, James returned to No. 4 Depot at Woolwich, London, on 29 February 1919, but three months later on 21 May 1919, he was posted to the British Military Mission[45] in Southern Russia, attached to the Ural Army.

Little is known about James's time in Russia, but there is correspondence from the War Office to The Officer in Charge of Records of the Royal Artillery within his service record[46], dated 02 March 1920, asking that following the receipt of a telegram from the Chief of the General Staff at Petrovsk, his next of kin be informed that he was safe. However, there are later letters stating that he was last heard of serving with his unit in January 1920 and that there were investigations into his fate still being carried out in December 1920. His next of kin had been informed on 15 October 1920 that he was feared dead and subsequent to his death, he was awarded the Silver Medal on the Ribbon of St. Stanislas by the White Russian Government in 1921.

It seems that it was not until 07 January 1921 that the army finally recorded him as having *"Died (cause not stated)"*. However he died, his body does not appear to have been recovered, or if it was, the location of his grave is not recorded, and he is therefore commemorated on the Haidar Pasha Memorial in a suburb of Istanbul, Turkey. The addenda panel on which he is commemorated was added to the original memorial in order to record the Commonwealth casualties who are buried in cemeteries in South Russia and Transcaucasia, whose graves can no longer be maintained by the Commonwealth War Graves Commission.

---

[45] The British Military Mission in Russia initially began following the Russian withdrawal from the war in the aftermath of the Russian Revolution and was aimed at limiting the German expansion east, but following the Armistice the British remained in support of the White Russians, who were involved in a civil war against the Bolsheviks

[46] WO 363-First World War Service Records 'Burnt Documents'

James is also a "Lost Boy" whose name has been omitted from the memorial tablets in the school chapel.

James William BUTTS

Gunner, 6055, 1/5th Hampshire Howitzer Battery, Royal Field Artillery who died on 04 September 1916, aged 35. Buried in Baghdad (North Gate) War Cemetery, Iraq

Born on 18 September 1880 in Weedon, Northamptonshire, the youngest of two sons of James Butts and Ellen née Andrews, his father was a Gunner in the Royal Artillery who had been discharged from the army on 20 February 1883 and died in Woolwich, Kent, on 21 August 1889.

James was admitted to the school on 25 September 1891 (Petition No. 10203) and was discharged on 29 September 1894, enlisting into the Royal Artillery.

James's service record is no longer available, so his pre-war career is unknown, but he is recorded in the 1901 Census as serving in the Royal Field Artillery in Fulwood Barracks, Preston, Lancashire, and in the 1911 Census he was a Gunner with 4 Battery, Royal Field Artillery in Rawalpindi, India.

The unit with which he served during the war, 1/5th Hampshire Howitzer Battery, Royal Field Artillery, was a Territorial Force unit located on the Isle of Wight and was posted to India following the commencement of hostilities. It then landed at Basra, Mesopotamia, with the 12th Indian Division on 23 March 1915, joining Indian Expeditionary Force "D", although it was quickly transferred to the 6th (Poona) Division.

The battery was part of the column under the command of Major-General Charles Townsend that advanced up the River Tigris, taking part in the Battle of Amara on 31 May 1915. However, according to his medal index card, James did not arrive in theatre until 16 August 1915, with this likely to have been Gallipoli, and it is probable that he was one of the Regular Army replacements to the battery[47] at a later date.

Following James's arrival in theatre, the battery took part in the Battles of Es Sinn and Ctesiphon, and was one of the British and Indian units that surrendered in April 1916 at the end of the Siege of Kut.

It appears that James was a Prisoner of War held at Bagtche, Turkey, and that he died of enteric fever on 04 September 1916. In

---

[47] This is likely as James's name does not appear on the memorial tablet commemorating the members of the battery who were killed in Mesopotamia, but there is an inscription on the tablet which states *"Also in memory of 25 regular soldiers attached to the battery in Mesopotamia"*

the aftermath of the war, his body was moved to Baghdad (North Gate) War Cemetery, but he is another "Lost Boy" whose name has been omitted from the memorial tablets in the school chapel.

Thomas Edward CHERRY
Corporal, 74712, CLXXXI Brigade, Royal Field Artillery who died on 21 February 1917, aged 19. Buried in Peronne Communal Cemetery Extension, Somme, France

Born on 29 November 1897 in Newbridge, County Kildare, the youngest son of John Cherry and Emily née Stark, his father was a Serjeant in the Royal Artillery who died of wounds near Bothaville, South Africa, on 06 November 1900 during the Second Boer War.

It would appear that following John's death, the family fell on hard times, as the 1901 Census records Thomas's older brother, Albert John Cherry, resident in the All Saints Boys Orphanage in Lewisham, London. However, Emily remarried in Bermuda on 17 November 1903, to John Henry Knight, a Serjeant in 4th Battalion, The Worcestershire Regiment. Just over two years later, Albert was admitted to the school, on 16 January 1906 (Petition No. 12181).

Thomas joined Albert at the school on 09 October 1908 (Petition No. 12559), making the transition from Chelsea to Guston before he was discharged on 02 December 1913, enlisting into the Royal Horse Artillery in which his father had also served.

There is also no service record available for Thomas, so it has not been possible to determine with which units he served from leaving school until 1917, but at some point, he transferred to the Royal Field Artillery, and in that year, he was serving with CLXXXI Brigade of that regiment.

The brigade had been formed in November 1915 as part of the New Army[48], joining the 40th Division and arriving on the Western Front in June 1916, where it participated in the Battle of Ancre, part of the larger Somme Offensive.

In early-1917, the brigade was still located on the Somme and on 21 February 1917 it responded to an SOS from the front-line trenches. No casualties are recorded in the brigade diary, but the Registers of Soldiers' Effects[49] records Thomas as having been killed in action on that day, likely during a retaliatory barrage by the German artillery.

---

[48] Also known as Kitchener's army, it referred to the all-volunteer part of the British Army that was formed in the period following the outbreak of war in August 1914

[49] UK, Army Registers of Soldiers' Effects, 1914-1915, Woolwich and Blackheath, 430001-431500; these registers included details of the money owed to soldiers of the British Army, who died in service 1901-29 and are useful for next of kin information in particular

Thomas is buried in Peronne Communal Cemetery Extension, along with two other soldiers from his battery who died on the same day as him. He is buried in Grave I. B. 39, with a comrade either side of him in Graves I. B. 38 and I. B. 40.

Albert was discharged from the school to the Royal Garrison Artillery on 04 February 1909. Having survived the war, he married in 1921 and seems to have emigrated to the United States after he was widowed in 1963, dying in Columbus, Ohio, in 1974.

William Godfrey COWLEY
Gunner, 68247, Royal Field Artillery who died on 31 August 1916, aged 23. Commemorated on the Islahie Memorial 199, Baghdad (North Gate) War Cemetery, Iraq

Born on 28 May 1893 in Portsmouth, Hampshire, the seventh of nine children of John Robert Cowley and Jane née Foley, his father had been a Regimental Quartermaster Serjeant in the Royal Artillery who had been discharged from the army on 10 October 1895 and died in Portsmouth on 01 January 1901.

William was admitted to the school on 20 November 1902 (Petition No. 11759) and was discharged on 12 June 1907, enlisting into the Royal Garrison Artillery.

William's service record is no longer available, but at some point, he transferred to the Royal Field Artillery and at the outbreak of war it would appear that he was serving in India with 63 Battery, Royal Field Artillery.

In September 1914, 63 Battery replaced 81 Battery in the 6th (Poona) Division of the Indian Army, embarking at Bombay on 08 November and landing as part of Indian Expeditionary Force "D" at Abadan, Mesopotamia, on 16 November, coming into action for the first time the following day.

The division and its artillery were involved in the Battle of Shaiba, which lasted from 12 to 14 April 1915, and during which William was wounded on 12 April. It was also involved in the Tigris Campaigns, before it was besieged by the Ottoman Army in the town of Kut al Amara on 07 December 1915, a siege that was to last until 29 April 1916 and resulted in the surrender of the surviving besieged troops.

However, by the time the remainder of the garrison surrendered, William's medal records confirm that he had already been captured, on 26 March, a month prior to the final surrender. Those that were captured were forced to march into captivity and experienced brutal treatment from their Ottoman captors. It is recorded that those who were sick were left at Islahie with little medical treatment and it is also reported that there was an outbreak of cholera in the camp in which they were held in June 1916.

The circumstances of William's death are unknown, but it is likely that he succumbed to disease, dying in Islahie on 31 August 1916, five months after he had been captured, although this may not be the exact date, more so an indication of the month in which he died.

Although commemorated in Baghdad (North Gate) Cemetery and by the Commonwealth War Graves Commission, William is another of the "Lost Boys" whose name has been omitted from the memorial tablets in the school chapel.

William's older, non-Dukie, brother also gave his life during the war. Serjeant Albert Edward Handscombe Cowley died on 04 July 1915 in Aden, Arabia, whilst serving with the Royal Garrison Artillery, likely during the disastrous attempt to defend Lahej from the Turks.

Leslie Cuthbert Frederick CROSS
Second Lieutenant, 44 Battery, Royal Field Artillery who died on 30 September 1915, aged 23. Buried in Merville Communal Cemetery, Nord, France

Born on 24 March 1892 in Rawalpindi, India, the second child of John Thomas Cross and Sarah Lily née Collis, his father had been a Farrier Serjeant in the Royal Artillery, who died at sea on 06 February 1900 during passage to South Africa.

Leslie was admitted to the school on 06 March 1902 (Petition No. 11664), joining his older brother, John William Montague Cross, who had been admitted on 13 July 1900 (Petition No. 11452).

Leslie was discharged from the school on 05 April 1906, enlisting into the Royal Horse Artillery, and although his service record is not easily available as an officer, it is known that he remained in the Royal Horse Artillery, reaching the rank of Bombardier.

One month after the outbreak of war, on 15 September 1914, Leslie was Commissioned as a Second Lieutenant into 7th (The Princess Royal's) Dragoon Guards[50], which at the outbreak of war was stationed in Secunderabad, India, part of the Secunderabad Cavalry Brigade. The regiment was moved to France as part of the 1st Indian Cavalry Division, landing at Marseille on 13 October 1914 and it is likely that Leslie joined the regiment here.

Although cavalry, due to the nature of the conflict the 7th Dragoon Guards spent much of its time fighting as dismounted

---

[50] *The London Gazette*, 6 October 1914, Supplement:28930

troops in the various battles at the end of 1914 and beginning of 1915.

On 07 March 1915, Leslie transferred back to his old regiment[51], although it is not documented whether he went straight to 44 Battery, Royal Field Artillery, or whether he joined this unit later. However, by September 1915, he was serving with this battery, which was under the command of the 7th (Meerut) Division of the Indian Army.

The division participated in the Battle of Loos which commenced on 25 September 1915, and although the main attack was unsuccessful, with the British troops being back at their starting line by the time there was a lull in the battle on 28 September, the artillery on both sides continued to ply their trade, and it is likely during this time that Leslie was killed, although there is no mention of his death in the battery war diary.

Leslie died on 30 September 1915 and is buried in Merville Communal Cemetery in the town that was the Headquarters of the Indian Corps. However, although he is commemorated as a Lieutenant by the Commonwealth War Graves Commission, there is no evidence that he was ever promoted beyond Second Lieutenant.

Leslie's older brother, John, also served in the First World War, and like Leslie, he too was killed. Both brothers are commemorated on the memorial tablets in the school chapel.

Archibald Thomas CROUCH
Corporal, 45272, V Reserve Brigade, Royal Field Artillery who died on 23 October 1918, aged 25. Buried in Heavitree (St. Michael) Churchyard Extension, Devon, United Kingdom

Born on 13 December 1892 in Trimulgherry, India, the oldest of eight sons of William Frank Crouch and Harriet née Kent, his father was a Battery Serjeant Major in the Royal Artillery and had been Mentioned in Despatches during the defence of Ladysmith in South Africa, during the Second Boer War.

Archibald was admitted to the school on 07 February 1902 (Petition No. 11658) and was discharged to the Royal Field Artillery almost five years later, on 20 December 1906. His service record is no longer available, so it is not possible to determine his career prior to the outbreak of war, but it is known that he was serving with 89 Battery, Royal Field Artillery, in XVI Brigade, 1st (Peshawar) Division of the Indian Army and based at Nowshera, India when war did break out.

---

[51] *The London Gazette*, 5 March 1915, Supplement:29092

Archibald was discharged from the army on 23 August 1916 having been diagnosed with tuberculosis and died two years later in Exeter, Devonshire, as a result of this disease. This is confirmed by the Registers of Soldiers' Effects[52], although his date of death is recorded as 21 October 1918.

Despite being commemorated by the Commonwealth War Graves Commission, Archibald is another of the "Lost Boys" whose name has been omitted from the memorial tablets in the school chapel.

Two of Archibald's younger brothers, neither of whom were Dukies, also died due to their war service. Second Lieutenant Clarence Cecil Crouch MC, who served in the Royal Field Artillery, died in Exeter of wounds received in action on 22 October 1917, and Bombardier Ralph Joseph Crouch, also of the Royal Field Artillery, was discharged from the army on 11 July 1917 as a result of disease and died in Exeter on 06 April 1920.

Robert John Spencer CROWE
Corporal, 43079, XLV Brigade, Royal Field Artillery who died on 11 November 1916, aged 25. Commemorated on the Thiepval Memorial, Somme, France

Born on 14 April 1891 in Bermuda, West Indies, the fourth of six children of William John Crowe and Sarah Jane née Fowler, his father and uncle, Robert John Crowe, had both attended the Royal Hibernian Military School in Dublin, and William had been a 1st Class Master Gunner in the Royal Artillery. His father was in the London Hospital with an incurable disease at the time of Robert's admission to the school and he died two weeks later on 23 May 1902.

Robert was admitted to the school on 09 May 1902 (Petition No. 11694) and was joined by his younger brother, Alfred Edward Charles Crowe, on 06 March 1903 (Petition No. 11822). Robert was discharged to the Royal Field Artillery on 26 April 1906, but because his service record is no longer available, his pre-war postings are not known, although he is recorded as a Bombardier in the 1911 Census, visiting an uncle, Walter Crowe and his family in Norwich.

At the outbreak of war, XLV Brigade, Royal Field Artillery[53], in which Robert served, was stationed in Chapeltown Barracks, Leeds, comprising of 1, 3 and 5 Batteries, Royal Field Artillery. It was quickly mobilised and placed under the command of the 8th

---

[52] UK, Army Registers of Soldiers' Effects, 1914-1915, War Gratuity of Soldiers Dying After Discharge, 958001-959500
[53] Incorrectly recorded by the Commonwealth War Graves Commission as 145th Brigade

Division, sailing from Southampton, Hampshire on the SS *Armenian* on 04 November and landing at Le Havre on 05 November 1914, coming into action ten days later east of Estaires.

The brigade remained under the command of the 8th Division throughout the remainder of 1914 and into 1915, taking part in the Battles of Neuve Chapelle and Aubers as well as the action at Bois-Grenier, which was a diversionary attack launched by the division at the same time as the commencement of the Battle of Loos.

During 1916, XLV Brigade participated in the bombardment that preceded the commencement of the Somme Offensive on 01 July, continuing to support the battle in the days after it was launched, although at some point after the commencement of the offensive, Robert must have been granted home leave, as he married Margaret Murty in Preston, Lancashire, during the second quarter of 1916.

By November 1916, the brigade was located near Ginchy-les-Boeufs in support of the French attack on Le Transloy and on 11 November its diary records that it was a *"quiet day"*[54], even though 1,115 rounds were fired. It also records that 1 Battery suffered one Corporal killed, one Gunner wounded, one Gunner gassed and one Battery Serjeant Major gassed.

The Corporal who was killed on 11 November 1916 was Robert Crowe. It is likely that his being a member of 1 Battery was the cause of the error by Commonwealth War Graves Commission, as the Record of Soldiers' Effects[55] records him as being *"1/45th Bde. RFA."* So, it appears that there has been an error in the transcription.

Robert name has been omitted from the memorial tablets in the school chapel, so he is another of the "Lost Boys". However, there is correspondence between the school and Robert's mother in 1929 in which the school claims that there is no record of a Robert Spencer John Crowe having ever been a pupil at the school. The existence of his Petition Document within the school records proves this to have been an error on the part of the then School Secretary.

Alfred did not finish his time at the school, as he was expelled for theft on 12 November 1907, the entry in his disciplinary record stating that his offence was *"Being in possession of, and changing a Postal Order, not his own"*. Alfred, like his brother, served in the Royal Field Artillery during the war, marrying Margaret, his brother's widow, in Woolwich, London, in July 1917, eight months after Robert's death.

---

[54] WO 95/1694/2: 45 Brigade Royal Field Artillery, 1914 Oct. - 1919 Apr., The National Archives, Kew
[55] UK, Army Registers of Soldiers' Effects, 1914-1915, Woolwich and Blackheath, 811001-812500

Their eldest brother, William Herbert Crowe, who was not a Dukie, died of sunstroke on 24 June 1920 in India, whilst serving with the Indian Ordnance Department and is also commemorated by the Commonwealth War Graves Commission as a casualty of the Great War.

Cecil Winfred CURLING
Gunner, 68003, 87th Battery, Royal Field Artillery who died on 14 March 1915, aged 21. Buried in Bois-Guillaume Communal Cemetery, Seine-Maritime, France

Born on 07 December 1893 in Woolwich, London, the fourth of five children of James Curling and Alice Mary née Lightbourn, his father had been in Gunner in the Royal Artillery who was discharged from the army to pension on 19 July 1894.

Cecil was admitted to the school on 13 January 1905 (Petition No. 12063), joining his older brother, Richard James Curling, who had been admitted on 12 July 1902 (Petition No. 11708). Cecil was then discharged from the school on 13 March 1908 and marked as *"Educationally unfit for the army"*. However, there is no explanation as to what this actually meant.

It is known that Cecil joined the army after leaving the school, although his service record is no longer available to confirm when this was. However, the 1911 Census records him as being employed as a Shop Assistant in a Greengrocers in Southsea, Hampshire, so it was after April 1911 that he enlisted, but he was clearly serving prior to the outbreak of the war in XII (Howitzer) Brigade, Royal Field Artillery.

At the outbreak of war, XII Brigade was stationed in Queenstown, County Cork, but moved initially to Liverpool, Lancashire, on 15 August and then Cambridge, Cambridgeshire, prior to embarking at Southampton, Hampshire, on 07 September and landing at St. Nazaire on 10 and 11 September 1914, Cecil disembarking on the latter date. The brigade fired its first rounds of the war six days later when it shelled the vicinity of the village of Chivres, setting the village on fire. It also fought during the First Battle of the Aisne and the First Battle of Ypres.

In early-1915, Cecil became unwell and required hospitalisation, although the exact date of Cecil's admission to hospital is not known. However, we do know that he was a patient in No. 8 General Hospital, Rouen, during March 1915, as he died of pneumonia on 14 March and was buried in Bois-Guillaume Communal Cemetery on the outskirts of the town. He is also a "Lost Boy" whose name has been omitted from the memorial tablets in the school chapel.

Robert was discharged from the school on 25 May 1905, but was considered *"unfit for army service"*. However, despite this, he enlisted into the Royal Field Artillery in 1908. He also served during the war, married in 1917 and died in Samford, Suffolk, in 1961.

Frederick Thomas FRITH
Gunner, 940126, CCLXXX (1st City of London) Brigade, Royal Field Artillery who died on 25 November 1917, aged 21. Buried in Lebucquiere Communal Cemetery Extension, Pas de Calais, France

Born on 27 February 1896 in Plaistow, Essex, the seventh of eight children of William John Frith and Annie née Savage, his father had been a Serjeant in The Essex Regiment who was discharged from the army after 21 years' service on 20 May 1889 and died in Leyton, Essex, on 27 November 1898.

Frederick was admitted to the school on 01 September 1905 (Petition No. 12131) and was *"detained on leave"* on 02 September 1910. He was recorded in the 1911 Census living in Forest Hill, London, with his mother and three of his siblings, employed as a Junior Clerk in an insurance office.

Frederick enlisted into the Territorial Force on 08 May 1913, joining the Royal Field Artillery and giving his occupation as a Clerk in the British Crown Assurance Corporation. It is likely that when he enlisted, he would have joined the 1st (City of London) Brigade, Royal Field Artillery, which was a Territorial Force unit.

At the outbreak of war, the brigade came under orders of the 1st (London) Division which was later renamed as the 56th (1st London) Division. Having been mobilised in August 1914, the brigade landed in France on 04 and 05 October 1915, Frederick's medal index card recording his date of disembarkation as 04 October, and coming under orders of the 36th (Ulster) Division.

For the next two months, the brigade was transferred between the 38th (Welsh), 16th (Irish), 47th (2nd London) Divisions and then 56th (1st London) Division, which had been broken up during 1915 and was re-assembled in February 1916, providing divisional artillery support. From then, he would have been serving in the re-named CCLXXX Brigade, with its first major action being during the Somme Offensive.

In November 1917, the brigade was in the vicinity of Demicourt and supporting an Allied attack on Bourlon Wood, including bombarding the enemy trenches between the Moeuvres-Demicourt and Inchy-Louverval roads on 22 November. The attack was unsuccessful due to a German counterattack that evening, and for the next two days, the brigade supported repeated attacks on the German positions, which were also unsuccessful.

At midday on 25 November another attack was made, this one proving successful, but the Germans again counter-attacked and the brigade was employed until late evening firing on the SOS lines and experiencing counter-battery fire from the German guns. It was on this day that Frederick was killed in action.

It is likely that he was buried close to where he fell, being moved to Lebucquiere Communal Cemetery Extension when surrounding smaller cemeteries were *"brought in"* after the war. However, he is another "Lost Boy" whose name has been omitted from the memorial tablets in the school chapel.

Frederick Charles HILLIARD
Battery Sergeant Major, 94231, Royal Field Artillery who died on 21 November 1919, aged 41. Buried in Croydon (Mitcham Road) Cemetery, Surrey, United Kingdom

Born on 11 November 1878 in Neemuch, India, the youngest of six children of James Hilliard and Elizabeth Jane née Roberts, his father had been a Serjeant in the Royal Artillery who was discharged after 21 years' service on 18 May 1880.

Frederick was admitted to the school on 21 June 1889 (Petition No. 9866) and was discharged on 12 November 1892, enlisting into the Royal Artillery.

Frederick's service record is no longer available, so his movements after he joined the army are unknown, but it is known that he was serving in India in 1902, as he married Violet Anne Clarke in Dinapore. However, by the following year, he had returned to Britain, as his first child, also called Frederick Charles Hilliard, was born in Lichfield, Staffordshire.

Two years later, Frederick was in Ireland, as his second child, Irene Hilda Hilliard, was born in Athlone, County Westmeath, although it would appear that he was then posted back to India, as his next two children, Violet Ann Hilliard and William George Hilliard, were born in Jubbulpore and Bangalore in 1907 and 1909 respectively. Frederick was also recorded in the 1911 Census as a Sergeant serving in No. 10 Ammunition Column, Royal Field Artillery, stationed in Bangalore.

It also appears that at the outbreak of war, Frederick was still serving in India, as part of IV Brigade, Royal Field Artillery. This brigade came under the command of the 7th (Meerut) Division on the outbreak of war and was sent to the Western Front, Frederick's medal index card showing that he arrived in theatre on 14 October 1914.

Again, the lack of service record means that it is not possible to follow Frederick's movements whilst he was in France, or whether he was still serving with that brigade when it was transferred to the 3rd (Lahore) Division for service in Mesopotamia and Palestine. Furthermore, all his medal records refer to his rank as Battery Quartermaster Serjeant rather than the Battery Serjeant Major on his headstone.

What is known is that following the end of the war, Frederick was back in Britain, where he died on 21 November 1919 at the Grove Military Hospital, Tooting, of *"dropsy of the peritoneum"*[56]. Sadly, at the time of his death, his wife was an inmate of an asylum in Wolverhampton, Staffordshire.

Frederick is also another of the "Lost Boys" whose name has been omitted from the memorial tablets in the school chapel.

James Louis Clifford HIRST
Gunner, 71172, II Reserve Brigade, Royal Field Artillery who died on 29 September 1918, aged 19. Buried in Terlincthun British Cemetery, Wimille, Pas de Calais, France

Born on 16 October 1898 in Islington, London, the only child of James John Hirst and Florence Paulina née White, his father was a Driver in the Royal Artillery when he died of disease on 08 January 1900 at Bloemfontein, South Africa, during the Second Boer War.

James was admitted to the school on 04 November 1909 (Petition No. 12674) and was discharged on 07 November 1912, enlisting into the Royal Field Artillery in Dover on the same day.

He was initially posted to CXLI Brigade, Royal Field Artillery, as a Boy, prior to being posted to II Reserve Brigade on 01 August 1913, the unit with which he was serving when he landed in France on 20 December 1914, aged sixteen.

After serving in France and Flanders for just over nine months, James was posted back to Britain on 28 September 1915, likely when the age regulations changed, remaining there until 08 November 1917, when he was posted back to France and appointed as a Gunner.

He was initially serving with LXV (Howitzer) Brigade, Royal Field Artillery, a New Army Brigade, but on 11 August 1918 he was posted to "D" Battery, CLXXIV (Howitzer) Brigade, Royal Field

---

[56] Ascites, which is an abnormal collection of fluid in the abdomen, likely as a result of cirrhosis, tuberculosis or cancer

114

Hibernian Military School in Dublin and served in the Highland Light Infantry following his discharge.

Although Charles did not enlist into the army straight from school, he did so five months later, on 10 December 1892, enlisting into the Royal Field Artillery, his occupation given as Errand Boy. During the time that he served, until his discharge at the end of his service, he served in India and Gibraltar as well as Britain. During one of his postings to Britain, he married Ada Thompson in Woolwich, on 31 March 1902, their only son, Harry Walter Holmes being born two years later in Shoreham, Sussex, on 08 February 1904.

At the outbreak of war, Charles was no longer serving, but his service record for the period shows that he re-enlisted as a Special Reservist in Woolwich on 28 September 1914. He was immediately promoted to his previous rank of Serjeant and employed as an instructor.

Charles spent all of his wartime service in Britain and he was promoted to Acting Battery Serjeant Major on 01 May 1915. He was serving with No 6 Territorial Force Artillery Training School when he died from a duodenal ulcer at the Royal Herbert Hospital, Woolwich on 31 March 1916. Although commemorated by the Commonwealth War Graves Commission, he is another "Lost Boy" whose name has been omitted from the memorial tablets in the school chapel.

Charles's brother, Harry, survived the war, dying in Southport, Lancashire in 1936, but another older brother, Thomas Arthur Holmes, died on 13 October 1915 from a gastrointestinal perforation whilst serving on the Isle of Wight as a Serjeant in the Royal Garrison Artillery

William Robert HOPE

Gunner, 50327, 60 Battery, Royal Field Artillery who died on 22 September 1914, aged 20. Buried in Maintenon Communal Cemetery, Eure-et-Loire, France

Born on 17 March 1894 in Templemore, County Tipperary, the second of seven children of John Hope and Annie née Peters, his father had been a Gunner in the Royal Artillery who had been discharged to pension after 21 years' service on 16 October 1895.

William was admitted to the school on 02 September 1904 (Petition No. 11998) and discharged on 02 April 1908, enlisting into the Royal Field Artillery as a Tailor.

Although William's service record is no longer available, he is recorded in the 1911 Census as a Boy stationed in No. 3 Depot, Royal Field Artillery, in Seaforth, Lancashire.

By the outbreak of war, William had been posted to 60 (Howitzer) Battery which was one of the batteries of XLIV (Howitzer) Brigade, which was placed under the command of the 2nd Division. The battery received orders on 04 August 1914 to mobilise at Brighton, Sussex, this mobilisation being completed on 13 August. The battery then left Brighton on 18 August and embarked for Boulogne, landing on 19 August. However, William's medal index card records that he disembarked in theatre on 16 August 1914.

The battery came into action for the first time on 24 August 1914 prior to participating in the long retreat that was to last until September, during which it was in action most days. Although there is nothing recorded in the battery diary[60] as to when William was wounded, we know that he died of wounds.

William was buried in Maintenon Communal Cemetery, in the town south-west of Paris and is another "Lost Boy" whose name has been omitted from the memorial tablets in the school chapel.

Daniel HURLEY
Serjeant, 46847, XCI Brigade, Royal Field Artillery who died on 10 October 1916, aged 24. Buried in Guards' Cemetery, Lesboeufs, Pas de Calais, France

Born on 16 May 1892 in Deptford, Kent, the eldest son of Daniel Hurley and Ellen née Mallon, his father had been a Corporal in The Border Regiment, but had been discharged on 22 May 1888. He died in Hammersmith, London, ten years later, on 30 June 1898.

Daniel was admitted to the school on 07 February 1902 (Petition No. 11655), being joined by his younger brother, Timothy Hurley, on 02 December 1904 (Petition No. 12046). Daniel was discharged from the school on 29 August 1908, enlisting into the Royal Field Artillery, although his service record is no longer available, so it is not possible to follow his career prior to the outbreak of the war, or even during the early years of that conflict.

What is known is that XCI Brigade, Royal Field Artillery, originally comprised of 283, 284 and 285 Batteries, Royal Field Artillery, and the Brigade Ammunition Column. It was placed under command of the 20th (Light) Division, remaining with that formation for the remainder of the war.

---

[60] WO 95/1327/2: 44 Brigade Royal Field Artillery (1914 Aug – Dec, 1915 Feb, Apr), Also includes diaries of 2 Division Ammunition Column (1914 Aug – Dec), 56 Battery Royal Field Artillery (1914 Aug – Dec), 47 Battery Royal Field Artillery (1914 Aug – Nov), 60 Battery Royal Field Artillery (1914 Aug – Nov)., 1914 Aug - 1915 Apr, The National Archives, Kew

On 15 February 1915, the three six-gun batteries were reorganised to become four four-gun batteries and were re-titled as "A", "B", "C" and "D" Batteries. However, "D" Battery left on 12 May 1915, to go to XCII Brigade, and became that formation's "B" Battery, being replaced by "C" (Howitzer) Battery from XCII Brigade, which was renamed as "D" (Howitzer) Battery.

The division to which the brigade belonged did not arrive in France until July 1915, following which it participated in the battles of the Somme Offensive in 1916. October 1916 saw the third phase of the offensive with the launching of the Battle of Ancre Heights on 01 October, a battle that was to last until 11 November 1916 and it is likely during this battle that Daniel was killed. He is buried in the Guards Cemetery, which had been started in September 1916, but was enlarged after the Armistice when bodies were *"brought in"* from other cemeteries.

Daniel's younger brother, Timothy, was discharged from the school on 24 July 1908, enlisting into The King's Royal Rifle Corps. He served during the war before being discharged in August 1918 due to malaria. He died in Woolwich, London, in 1965.

Archibald Thomas JAMES
Serjeant, 74355, XIV Brigade, Royal Field Artillery who died on 25 November 1917, aged 26. Buried in Kemmel Chateau Military Cemetery, West-Vlaanderen, Belgium

Born on 15 April 1891 in Colchester, Essex, the third of six children of Thomas George James and Alice née Penny, his father had been a Band Serjeant in the 1st (Royal) Dragoons and died whilst serving in Dundalk, County Louth, on 16 April 1897.

Archibald was admitted to the school three years after his father's death, on 10 August 1900 (Petition No. 11463). He, unusually, remained at the school until he was almost sixteen, being discharged to the 21st (Empress of India's) Lancers on 20 March 1907.

Archibald's service record is no longer available, so his pre-war career is unknown, including when he transferred to the Royal Artillery. However, the 1911 Census shows him as a Private, serving with the 21st Lancers and stationed in Abbassia, Cairo, Egypt, so it was clearly after this date.

At the outbreak of war, Archibald was a Gunner serving with "V" Battery, Royal Horse Artillery, the Commonwealth War Graves Commission information suggesting that he was serving with this unit prior to his disembarkation in France on 18 December 1914.

It is not possible to establish with which units he served prior to 1917, nor at which point he transferred to the Royal Field Artillery, but by November 1917, Archibald was a Serjeant and serving in "A" Battery, XIV Brigade, Royal Field Artillery. The brigade was in the Ypres Salient at this time, firing from Dormy House near Zillebeke, and on 25 November 1917, Archibald was one of two killed in action by German artillery early in the morning.

Archibald was buried in Kemmel Chateau Military Cemetery, some distance from the place where he was killed, so it is possible that his body was relocated to this cemetery following the cessation of hostilities. He is also another of the "Lost Boys" whose name has been omitted from the memorial tablets in the school chapel.

Ivor JAMES
Trumpeter, 70984, XXX Brigade, Royal Field Artillery who died on 16 September 1914, aged 15. Buried in Vailly British Cemetery, Aisne, France

Born on 23 September 1898 in Athlone, County Roscommon, the second, and youngest child of Ivor Treherne James and Rosina Frances née Dunlop, his father had been a Corporal in the Royal Artillery and was killed in action on 10 March 1900 at Driefontein, South Africa, during the Second Boer War.

Ivor was admitted to the school on 31 March 1908 (Petition No. 12493), making the move from Chelsea to Guston and was discharged to the Royal Field Artillery on 07 November 1912.

He was originally posted to XLIII Brigade, Royal Field Artillery Headquarters, before being posted to No.4 Reserve Brigade on 01 August 1912 and finally being appointed as a Trumpeter and posted to 128 Battery, XXX Brigade, Royal Field Artillery, on 25 February 1914.

At the outbreak of war, the brigade was stationed in Bulford, Wiltshire, embarking at Southampton, Hampshire, on the SS *Honorius* on 18 August and landing at Rouen on 21 August 1914.

Ivor's battery went into action three days later at Ciply, but was forced to retire as part of the Retreat from Mons. For the rest of the month, although all three batteries of the brigade came into action more than once during the retreat, 128 Battery did not fire.

The brigade participated in the Battle of the Marne and the Battle of the Aisne in September 1914 and on 16 September, 128 Battery had moved to a position just north of Brenelle. Although nothing is recorded in the brigade diary, it would appear that either during or after this move, Ivor was killed in action, exactly a week before his sixteenth birthday, and making him the youngest Dukie to have been killed in action during the First World War, and possibly the youngest soldier to die in the 1914 Campaign. His body was recovered and he is buried in Vailly-sur-Aisne, three miles from the place where he died.

Ivor is also commemorated on the memorial tablets in the school chapel, but he is incorrectly recorded on these as T James.

Alfred Henry KING
Shoeing Smith, 50778, LXXI Brigade, Royal Field Artillery who died on 07 July 1917, aged 23. Buried in Lijssenthoek Military Cemetery, West-Vlaanderen, Belgium

Born on 21 April 1894 in Woolwich, London, the second of three children of Alfred Henry King and Emma Mary née Lawless, his father was a Battery Serjeant Major in the Royal Artillery. His mother died in Jullundur, India, on 01 May 1898.

Alfred was admitted to the school on 26 May 1905 (Petition No. 12105) and was discharged on 25 June 1908, enlisting into the Royal Field Artillery.

Alfred's service record is no longer available, so his postings prior to the war are unknown, although he is recorded in the 1911 Census as a Boy in the Royal Artillery and stationed in Woolwich, London. The lack of service record also means that his posting's during the early part of the war also cannot be ascertained, although his medal index card states that he disembarked in France on 09 July 1915.

At the outbreak of war, LXXI Brigade was placed under the command of the 15th (Scottish) Division, which had been established by the Scottish Command in September 1914, and moved with that division to France in July 1915, following which it participated in the Battle of Loos and many of the battles of the Somme Offensive in 1916.

Although the brigade diary is available, the months of July, August and September 1917 are missing. It is known that on 21 June 1917 the brigade arrived in the village of Watou, near Poperinghe, Belgium, where it was to be at rest for the remainder of the month. However, on 24 June, an officer from "B" Battery, in which Alfred was serving, moved forward to prepare positions near Ypres.

The circumstances surrounding Alfred being wounded are unknown, but it is known that following his injury he was evacuated to the 3rd Canadian Casualty Clearing Station, located in Lijssenthoek, where he died of wounds on 07 July 1917.

Alfred was buried in the military cemetery in the town, but he is a "Lost Boy" whose name has been omitted from the memorial tablets in the school chapel.

Herbert McNALLY

Serjeant, 16531, 51 Battery, Royal Field Artillery who died on 11 November 1914, aged 32. Commemorated on the Ypres (Menin Gate) Memorial, West-Vlaanderen, Belgium

Born on 06 September 1882 in Atcham, Shropshire, the youngest of eight children of Henry McNally and Elizabeth née Phillips, his father had been a Battery Serjeant Major in the Royal Artillery who was discharged from the army on 05 August 1884 and died in Atcham on 24 January 1886.

Herbert was admitted to the school on 28 July 1893 (Petition No. 10493). Both of his older brothers were also Dukies. Walter McNally had been admitted on 22 February 1889 (Petition No. 9761) but was discharged six months prior to Herbert's admission and Charles McNally had been admitted on 30 January 1891 (Petition No. 10113), overlapping with Herbert's time at the school by two years.

Herbert was discharged from the school on 19 September 1896 and enlisted into the Royal Artillery, but as his service record is no longer available, it is not possible to follow his career prior to the outbreak of war, although it is known that he was serving in India between 1909 and 1912, as he married Marie Annie Theresa Beesty in Bombay on 23 August 1909, and their first daughter, Eileen Margaret Joan McNally was born in Ferozepore on 13 September 1912.

By the outbreak of war, Herbert was a Serjeant and serving with 51 Battery, Royal Field Artillery, which was part of XXXIX Brigade, 1st Division. The formation was stationed in Bordon, Hampshire, but was quickly mobilised, embarking at Southampton, Hampshire, on the SS *Winifredian* on 19 August 1914, and landing at Le Havre the following day. Herbert's battery came into action for the first time near Rouveroy at 0300hrs on 24 August.

The brigade took part in the Great Retreat in August and September of 1914, before the British Expeditionary Force turned and advanced on the German Army, moving into Flanders and participating in the First Battle of Ypres.

At the beginning November, 51 Battery was deployed near Veldhoek and working in co-operation with the 6th Cavalry Brigade. The entry in the brigade diary[61] for 11 November states that it was subjected to a German bombardment and that enemy infantry also infiltrated a wood to the west of its position, from which snipers were able to kill all of the horses pulling two wagons from the ammunition column that were in the process of replenishing 54 Battery.

---

[61] WO 95/1249/1: Divisional Troops: 39 Brigade Royal Field Artillery, 1914 Aug 1 - 1914 Dec 31, The National Archives, Kew

This was the last major German offensive of the battle and Herbert either died from shellfire or his burial location was subsequently lost, as all records state he was killed in action on that date, but he has no identified grave. The British artillery was initially held in reserve, but due to the gains made by the numerically superior Germans against British forces, low on numbers and supplies after the Battle of the Marne, it was pressed into action along with cooks, drivers and clerks, in a ferocious defensive action.

His only daughter, Mabel Immaculata McNally, was born in Shropshire a month after his death, on 10 December 1914.

As well as having no known grave, Herbert is another of the "Lost Boys" whose name has been omitted from the memorial tablets in the school chapel.

Herbert's brother Walter was discharged from the school on 07 January 1893 and enlisted into the Royal Artillery as a Drummer. He was discharged from the army as medically unfit on 26 May 1903 and died in Portsmouth in 1954.

Charles was discharged from the school on 23 November 1895 and enlisted into the Royal Artillery. He served during the war in the Royal Garrison Artillery and emigrated to Canada in later life, dying in White Rock, British Columbia, in 1964

Edwin Newton MONGER DSO (served as Bill STUART)
Major, Royal Field Artillery, who died on 03 June 1920, aged 31. Buried in Baghdad (North Gate) War Cemetery, Iraq

Born on 22 September 1888 in Reading, Berkshire, the fifth of eight children of Edwin Henry Monger and Annie née Orstridge, his father had been a Serjeant in the 60th (The King's Royal Rifle Corps) Regiment of Foot[62] and had been discharged to pension on 28 October 1879. Following his discharge from the army, it would appear that he worked in Africa, although it is not recorded in what capacity. What is known is that he was killed on 07 May 1898 in Freetown, Sierra Leone, during the Hut Tax War[63].

Edwin was admitted to the school on 03 February 1899 (Petition No. 11264), being joined by his younger brother, Llewellyn William Monger, on 10 August 1900 (Petition No. 11465). Edwin was at the school for three years before he, along with his brother, were *"Detained on pass"*[64] on 23 August 1902.

---

[62] Renamed The King's Royal Rifle Corps on 01 July 1881

[63] An insurrection by Sierra Leoneans as resistance to a new tax that had been imposed by the colonial Governor in the newly annexed British Protectorate

[64] This likely means that he and Llewellyn returned home on leave and were not returned to

Little is known of Edwin for the next four years, but in 1906 he enlisted into the Royal Artillery using the name Bill/William Stuart. Edwin disembarked in France on 06 October 1914 as a Serjeant with XXII Brigade, Royal Field Artillery, having returned from South Africa. On 14 January 1915 he was commissioned as a Second Lieutenant *"for service in the field"* and returned to the Western Front, although this does not appear to have been Gazetted.

He had an eventful war, serving on the Western Front in 1915-16 and in the invasion of Palestine in 1917-18. On 13 December 1917 he was sent to a field hospital suffering from neurasthenia and after recovery, was posted to 424 Battery, Royal Field Artillery on 16 February 1918, nine days later suffering a gunshot wound to the head at Kantara which resulted in his being invalided back to Britain.

By August 1918, Edwin was Acting Major and commanding "D" Battery, LXXVII Brigade, Royal Field Artillery at Morlancourt, France, when he earnt the Distinguished Service Order for bringing in a wounded officer and then a 77mm gun from no-man's land[65]. He was then wounded again in October 1918 and was also Mentioned in Despatches on 07 July 1919.

Edwin served in Iraq from December 1919 to March 1920 with 8 Battery, Royal Field Artillery, before being posted to the Civil Authorities and appointed Commandant of the Gendarmerie at Tel-a-Far. Concern grew amongst the political officers that a rebellion was imminent and Edwin was shot by one of his own men as he was making his rounds on 03 June 1920.

It is not known why Edwin adopted the name Bill Stuart when he enlisted and his officer's service record from that time does not provide any real clues. He provided two differing birth dates to the army and stated his mother was 'Mrs E Stuart', but birth records confirm that the date in the school register is correct. His Officers' Statement of Services records that he went to the school, but the final confirmation that Bill Stuart was Edwin Monger comes via probate records, with the connection explicitly stated and his mother Annie Monger the legatee.

His date of death is recorded as 03 June 1920 by Commonwealth War Graves Commission and on his medal index card, although probate and written accounts of his death state 04 June 1920.

Despite being killed in Iraq as a civilian administrator, he is still commemorated as a Great War casualty by the Commonwealth War Graves Commission, although he is a "Lost Boy" whose name has been omitted from the memorial tablets in the school chapel.

---

the school by their mother, although there is no confirmation of this within the school records for either brother

[65] *The Edinburgh Gazette*, 5 June 1919, Issue:13453

However, as he served under a different name to the one under which he was at the school, this is perhaps understandable.

Llewellyn was detained on pass at the same time as Edwin. There is no service record available for Llewellyn either, but it is known that he joined the army at some point after leaving the school and served during the war. He was a Serjeant in 11th Battalion, The Durham Light Infantry, when he was killed in action in March 1918. Unlike Edwin, he is commemorated on the memorial tablets in the chapel.

Robert Reilly PATTERSON
Corporal, 33737, 47 Battery, Royal Field Artillery who died on 24 October 1914, aged 26. Commemorated on the Ypres (Menin Gate) Memorial, West-Vlaanderen, Belgium

Born on 09 June 1888 in Ipswich, Suffolk, the second of five children of William John Patterson and Letitia née Reilly, his father was a Dukie, having been admitted to the Royal Military Asylum on 26 May 1866 (Petition No. 7079) and discharged to the Royal Artillery on 21 June 1873. At the time of Robert's birth, William was a Superintendent Clerk, Serjeant Major, in the Royal Artillery, but was discharged from the army as medically unfit on 31 May 1896[66] and died in Wandsworth Infirmary, London on 07 May 1897.

Robert was admitted to the school on 05 November 1897 (Petition No. 11090), joining his older brother, Frank Patterson, who had been admitted eight months before him, on 05 March 1897 (Petition No. 11001). Robert was discharged *"to mother-dirty habits"* on 04 December 1901.

However, when he was sixteen, Robert enlisted into the Royal Artillery, on 12 August 1904, initially being posted to No. 7 Depot in Preston, Lancashire. Although Robert was posted a further three times prior to the outbreak of war, his service record is damaged, so none of the locations of these postings can be properly ascertained, although it is known that between 10 November 1908 and 14 March 1914, he was posted to 47 Battery, Royal Field Artillery, stationed in Multan, Punjab, India.

At the outbreak of war, he was still serving with 47 Battery, now stationed in Brighton, Sussex, before embarking on the SS *Armenian* at Southampton, Hampshire, on 18 August and landing at Boulogne on 19 August 1914 as part of XLIV Brigade. The battery crossed the Belgian frontier on 23 August, and after entrenching north of Givry, came into action for the first time against the German guns, after

---

[66] The Petition Document for Frank Patterson, dated 26 May 1896, states *"Father about to be discharged, medically unfit (insane)"*

which it was forced into the long retreat, before being in action again during the Battles of the Marne and of the Aisne.

During October 1914, 47 Battery was involved in the various actions that constituted the First Battle of Ypres, often in close proximity to the enemy. On 24 October 1914, the battery diary reports *"Rifle fire on Battery all the morning. Corpl Patterson killed"*[67].

Having been killed on 24 October 1914, it is likely that Robert Patterson was buried close to where he fell. It is also likely that the fighting in this area during the next four years resulted in the location of his grave being lost and he is therefore commemorated on the Menin Gate Memorial. He is also commemorated on the tablets in the school chapel, but he is incorrectly recorded as R T Patterson.

Frank was discharged to The Leicestershire Regiment on 01 December 1900 and was recorded as a Corporal stationed in Glen Parva Barracks, Leicestershire, in the 1911 Census. His service record shows that he was promoted to Serjeant in January 1913 the same year in which he was diagnosed with disease of his cardiac valves. Despite being a champion army runner and gymnast, this condition resulted in his death in the military hospital in Fermoy, County Cork, on 10 November 1913 at the age of only 26.

Robert's medals were auctioned during 2021 and these are now in the possession of one of the authors.

Percival POTTER

Gunner, 55143, XXII Brigade, Royal Field Artillery who died on 12 October 1917, aged 22. Commemorated on the Tyne Cot Memorial, West-Vlaanderen, Belgium

Born on 17 March 1895 in Plymouth, Devonshire, the third of five children of Charles Edward Potter and Henrietta Annie née Mills, his father had been a Quartermaster Serjeant in the Royal Artillery who had been discharged from the army after 21 years' service on 28 January 1901. Percival's mother had died in Islington, London, on 26 October 1905.

Percival was admitted to the school on 23 February 1906 (Petition No. 12199) and was discharged on 07 April 1909, enlisting into the Royal Field Artillery.

Percival's service record is no longer available, so his pre-war postings are not known, but he is recorded in the 1911 Census as a Trumpeter in the Royal Field Artillery and stationed in Newfoundland Farm, Salisbury Plain, Wiltshire.

---

[67] WO 95/1327/2: 44 Brigade Royal Field Artillery (1914 Aug – Dec, 1915 Feb, Apr). Also includes diaries of 2 Division Ammunition Column (1914 Aug – Dec), 56 Battery Royal Field Artillery (1914 Aug – Dec), 47 Battery Royal Field Artillery (1914 Aug – Nov), 60 Battery Royal Field Artillery (1914 Aug – Nov)., 1914 Aug - 1915 Apr, The National Archives, Kew

By the outbreak of war, it appears that Percival had been posted to XXXV Brigade, Royal Field Artillery, stationed in Woolwich, London. In September 1914, the brigade was placed under the command of the new 7th Division and landed in France the following month, Percival's medal index card recording that he disembarked in theatre on 06 October 1914.

Because his service record is not available, it is not possible to ascertain Percival's movements during the war, nor to establish at what point he was posted to XXII Brigade, Royal Field Artillery. However, it is recorded in his medal index card that he had been a Bombardier when he disembarked in France, and was later promoted to Corporal, although he then reverted to Gunner at his own request on 16 August 1916.

The brigade with which he was serving at the time of his death had also joined the 7th Division at the start of the war and had landed in Zeebrugge in October 1914, remaining as part of the 7th Division throughout the war.

In October 1917, the brigade was located in the area of Dickebusch near Ypres and in action east of Chateau Wood during the Third Battle of Ypres. On 11 October 1917, it was out of action for 24 hours rest, but work commenced on forward positions near Glencourse Wood. However, on that day the brigade diary[68] reported that the batteries of the brigade had been steadily shelled during the last ten days, causing 100 casualties among the men and slight casualties among the horses.

The following day, 12 October 1917, although all of the batteries remained at rest around Dickebusch, work continued on the forward positions, and it is likely that the German shelling also continued. It was also on this day that Percival was killed. The fact that his body was not recovered and he is commemorated on the Tyne Cot Memorial suggests that he was killed by the German shelling. He is also a "Lost Boy" whose name has been omitted from the memorial tablets in the school chapel.

Henry William PRIDGEON
Serjeant, 15091, Royal Field Artillery who died on 03 May 1915, aged 51. Buried in Guildford (Stoke) Old Cemetery, Surrey, United Kingdom

Born on 09 December 1863 in Devonport, Devonshire, one of five children of William Henry Pridgeon and Ellen née Mahoney, his father had been a Corporal in the Royal Artillery, but by the time Henry was admitted to the school, his father had been discharged

---
[68] WO 95/1643/1: 22 Brigade Royal Field Artillery, 1914 Oct. - 1917 Nov., The National Archives, Kew

from the army and transferred to the Lunatic Asylum at Grove Hall, London.

Henry was admitted to the school on 20 August 1875 (Petition No. 7894) and was discharged to the Royal Artillery on 08 December 1877 as a Musician. He served for 12 years before being discharged from the army on 02 May 1890, although he re-enlisted three months later, on 21 August, being discharged for a second time on 14 December 1902 as a Serjeant Telegraphist. During his second period of service, he married Mary Ann Eastham in Guildford in 1894 and also served in South Africa.

Following this second discharge, it is not known what Henry was employed as, but the 1911 Census records him as living in Guildford, Surrey, with his wife and three daughters, his occupation recorded as Army Pensioner (Friary Brewery).

It appears that when the war commenced in August 1914, Henry again volunteered for service, this being recorded in a local newspaper at the time of his death:

"A SOLDIER'S DEATH. MILITARY FUNERAL YESTERDAY.

An old soldier with a long military record died in the Surrey County Hospital on Monday in the person of Henry William Pridgeon, of the 120th Brigade, R.F.A., who resided at 4, Leapale-road, Guildford.

He was 51 years of age, and over half of these years had been spent in the service of his country. He entered the R.F.A. from the Duke of York's School[69], and spent fifteen years in India. He served through the South African War, and was awarded the Queen's and King's medals. He left the Army after the war, and kept the Lion beerhouse at Ash for two years. Subsequently he became caretaker at the Hog's Back Forts, and latterly had been employed in the stores department at Messrs. Billing and Sons' Printing Works.

When the present war broke out he volunteered for service, and had been with the Artillery since September. At about Christmas time he had the misfortune to fall from his horse, and after that his health seemed to give away. He was sent home towards the end of January on sick leave, and entered the County Hospital, where he stayed five weeks. He had, however, to return to the institution, and on Thursday of last week he underwent an operation, which was successfully performed. Pneumonia developed, and he died as stated. He leaves a widow and three daughters, for whom much sympathy is felt.

Sergeant Pridgeon's family and that of his wife have had a very long connection with the services. His father was a master tailor in the Artillery, and of his three brothers in the service one is Regimental-Quartermaster-

---

[69] Still the Royal Military Asylum when Henry was both admitted and discharged

Sergt. Charles Pridgeon, R.G.A., who resides at 20, Leapale-road. All four brothers were in the South African War, and at one period of the campaign accidentally met…"[70]

Henry's cause of death on 03 May 1915 was recorded as stricture of the oesophagus and he was buried in Guildford (Stoke) Old Cemetery. His brother, Charles, who had attended the Royal Hibernian Military School and who was a Regimental Quartermaster Serjeant in the Royal Garrison Artillery, died from pneumonia in Southampton, Hampshire, on 22 June 1918, aged 50. He was buried in the same graveyard as Henry, along with Charles's son, also Charles, who had been a Corporal in the Royal Garrison Artillery and who died in his sleep at home on 18 January 1919.

Cecil Stanley SINCLAIR
Serjeant, 32759, 126 Battery, Royal Field Artillery who died on 29 June 1916, aged 26. Buried in Sucrerie Military Cemetery, Colincamps, Somme, France

Born on 03 November 1889 in Woolwich, London, the second of six children of James Wood Sinclair and Elizabeth Louisa née Plank, his father was a 3rd Class Master Gunner in the Royal Artillery. His mother died in Allahabad, India, on 19 June 1896.

Cecil was admitted to the school on 10 August 1899 (Petition No. 11317) and was discharged to the Royal Field Artillery on 14 November 1903.

Cecil's service record is no longer available, so his pre-war postings are unknown, although the 1911 Census records that he was serving as a Driver with 127 Battery, Royal Field Artillery and stationed in Louisburg Barracks, Bordon, Hampshire. This was also the year that Cecil married Mildred Lillian Owen in St Martin's Church, Cheriton, Kent, the pair going on to have three children, Cecil Vernon Sinclair, born July 1912, Constance Lillian Sinclair, born August 1913, and Harold Victor Sinclair, born September 1914.

At the outbreak of war, XXIX Brigade, Royal Field Artillery, of which 127 Battery was part, quickly mobilised, embarking at Southampton, Hampshire, on 22 August and landing at Le Havre on 23 August 1914.

The brigade participated in the Battles of the Marne, of the Aisne and of Messines during 1914, remaining in the area of Ypres during 1915 and participating in the Second Battle of Ypres. However, by

---

[70] *Surrey Advertiser* 8 May 1915

June 1916, it had moved south and was engaged in the preliminary bombardment prior to the launching of the Somme Offensive on 01 July.

According to the brigade war diary[71], on 29 June 1916, it was targeting the neighbourhood of Sucrerie when a gun from 126 Battery was hit by one shell and completely destroyed, three men at the gun also being killed.

The Commonwealth War Graves Commission records Cecil's date of death as 29 June 1916, suggesting that he was one of the soldiers that was killed by the enemy counter-battery fire that destroyed the gun, but the brigade medal records[72] state that Cecil died of wounds the following day, 30 June 1916, although the records for the award of the British War Medal and Victory Medal[73] state his death was 29 June 1916.

Cecil was buried close to where he died, in Sucrerie Military Cemetery and although he is commemorated on the memorial tablets in the school chapel, his regiment is incorrectly recorded as Royal Horse Artillery.

Alexander Robert TOWELLS

Serjeant, 90613, CLXXXIX Brigade, Royal Field Artillery who died on 12 June 1917, aged 30. Buried in Hop Store Cemetery, West-Vlaanderen, Belgium

Born on 11 March 1887 in West Hartlepool, County Durham, the fifth of eight children of Robert Moss Towells and Mary née Mitchell, his father had been a Company Serjeant Major in the Royal Artillery who was discharged from the army on 31 January 1895 and died in West Hartlepool four months later, on 12 May 1895.

Alexander was admitted to the school on 07 August 1896 (Petition No. 10920), the year after his father's death, but was at the school for less than a month before he was dismissed on 04 September 1896. However, the reason for his dismissal is not known.

Six years after Alexander's dismissal, his younger brother, Edward Towells, was admitted to the school, on 06 March 1902 (Petition No. 11661), followed a year later by another brother, Arthur Thomas Towells, on 12 February 1903 (Petition No. 11799).

Little is known of Alexander's life after he left the school and prior to the outbreak of war, although it is known that his mother was

---

[71] WO 95/1466/5: 29 Brigade Royal Field Artillery, 1914 Aug. - 1919 Feb., The National Archives, Kew
[72] UK, World War I Service Medal and Award Rolls, 1914-1920: 1914 Star, Royal Field Artillery, Piece 2406: Royal Field Artillery
[73] UK, World War I Service Medal and Award Rolls, 1914-1920: British War Medal and Victory Medal, Royal Field Artillery, Piece 0071: Royal Field Artillery

remarried to Charles Coad in 1896 and that he was living with his mother, four of his siblings and a half-sister in Darlington, County Durham, in 1901.

According to the 1911 Census, Alexander was a Labourer and living with the parents of Elsie May Guthrie, whom he had married in January of that year, still in Darlington. He and Elsie had two children, Arthur Edward, born in 1913 and Josephine, born in 1915.

It is also unknown when Alexander enlisted and his service record is no longer available, but it could well have been at the start of the war, although according to his medal index card it was not until 07 September 1915 that he first entered theatre. It is not known with which units he served after arriving in theatre, although it is known that in 1917, he was an Acting Battery Serjeant Major in CLXXXIX Brigade, Royal Field Artillery.

The circumstances of his death are also not known, but Alexander Towells died of wounds on 12 June 1917 and is buried in Hop Store Cemetery, to the west of the village of Vlamertinghe. Although he is commemorated on the memorial tablets in the school chapel, his regiment is recorded as Royal Artillery.

Alexander's brother, Edward, was discharged from the school to the Royal Garrison Artillery on 21 January 1905, but was serving in the Royal Horse Artillery when he was killed in action on 24 August 1918. He is also commemorated on the memorial tablets in the school chapel and he is documented earlier in this book.

Arthur was discharged from the school to the Royal Horse Artillery on 14 February 1907. He survived the war, living until he was 88 and died in London in 1980. His oldest son, born in 1930, was named Alexander Robert.

Alexander's son, Arthur Edward, also served in the Royal Artillery during the Second World War. He died in captivity in Stalag 344 in Kędzierzyn-Koźle, Poland, on 11 April 1945 and is commemorated on the Dunkirk Memorial.

James Clifford TURNER
Acting Bombardier, 69471, XXVIII Brigade, Royal Field Artillery who died on 02 May 1917, aged 19. Buried in Vimy Communal Cemetery, Farbus, Pas de Calais, France

Born on 28 April 1898 in Horfield, Gloucestershire, the eldest of two children of John Turner and Miriam née Case, his father had been a Bombardier Collar Maker in the Royal Artillery who had died of disease at Bloemfontein, South Africa, on 10 April 1900. His mother had remarried Albert Ernest Wright in 1905 and by the time that James entered the school, he had a 3-year-old half-brother.

James was admitted to the school on 28 May 1909 (Petition No. 12599) and was discharged on 25 June 1912, enlisting into the Royal Field Artillery.

James's service record is no longer available, but it is known that at the outbreak of war he was serving in VIII (Howitzer) Brigade which was stationed in Ireland. It came under the orders of the 5th Division and landed at Le Havre on 19 August 1914, the date of disembarkation that is shown on James's medal index card.

Because there is no service record available, James's movements once he had arrived on the Western Front are unknown, but it is known that on 21 May 1916, VIII Brigade was broken up and the batteries were re-assigned to other brigades of the Royal Field Artillery. It is likely that James was serving with 65 (Howitzer) Battery, which was re-assigned to XXVIII Brigade, as although the Commonwealth War Graves Commission records his unit as 6 Battery, Royal Field Artillery, the Registers of Soldiers' Effects[74] records that he was serving with 65 Battery, XXVIII Brigade at the time of his death.

The brigade war diary after December 1916 is also not available, so the circumstances surrounding James's death are unknown, however it was likely that the brigade was in the vicinity of Arras in order to provide support for the British attack that became known as the Battle of Arras, launched on 09 April 1917.

Part of this offensive was a flanking assault on the town of Bullecourt, the first attack being launched the day before the main offensive, on 08 April 1917. This attack had been unsuccessful, but a second attack was scheduled to commence on 03 May 1917 and it is likely that it was during the preparations for this attack that James was killed in action on 02 May 1917.

Following his death, James was buried in Vimy Communal Cemetery, Farbus, approximately ten kilometres north-north-east of Arras. However, he is a "Lost Boy" whose name has been omitted from the memorial tablets in the school chapel.

John Edward WILLIAMS
Gunner, 41455, CXXXIV Brigade Ammunition Column, Royal Field Artillery who died on 07 March 1917, aged 25. Commemorated on the Basra Memorial, Iraq

Born on 15 December 1891 in Landport, Hampshire, the youngest of two children of Peter Williams and Mary Maria née Craggs, his father had been a Private in The Hampshire Regiment

---

[74] UK, Army Registers of Soldiers' Effects, 1901-1929, 1914-1915, Woolwich and Blackheath, 475001-476500

who had been discharged to pension on 28 February 1888. His mother died in Portsmouth, Hampshire, on 18 August 1896.

John was admitted to the school on 10 January 1902 (Petition No. 11651) and was discharged on 15 January 1906, enlisting into the Royal Field Artillery.

Because his service record is no longer available, it is not possible to follow John's career prior to the outbreak of war in 1914, although the 1911 Census records that he was a Driver serving with 135 Battery, Royal Field Artillery, and stationed in Louisburg Barracks, Bordon, Hampshire.

The battery with which John was serving in 1911 was part of XXXII Brigade, Royal Field Artillery, which deployed to France in August 1914, spending the entire war on the Western Front, so it is not known when John was posted to the Middle East.

The brigade with which he was initially serving, 4.5 Howitzer Brigade, Royal Field Artillery, was formed on 02 May 1916 from LX and LXI Brigades, Royal Field Artillery, which were New Army Brigades that had been formed in the regiment's No.3 Depot in Hilsea, Hampshire.

The brigade took part in the ultimately successful advance on Baghdad in the aftermath of the disaster at Kut al Amara, being renamed CXXXIV Brigade, Royal Field Artillery, in November 1916.

In March 1917, the brigade was accompanying the 14th Division in its pursuit of the Ottoman Army on the left bank of the Tigris. The brigade diary shows that it had marched to Ctesiphon on 06 March 1917, the entry for the following day stating that the march continued, and that *"During this march a wagon of the Brigade Ammunition Column was blown up by an aeroplane bomb, 2 British & 3 Indian ranks being killed & 10 others wounded"*[75].

One of the British soldiers killed was John, the nature or location of his death meaning that rather than having a grave, he is commemorated on the Basra Memorial. He is also another of the "Lost Boys" whose name has been omitted from the memorial tablets in the school chapel.

---

[75] WO 95/5078/1: Corps Troops: 134 Brigade Royal Field Artillery, 1916 May - 1917 June, The National Archives, Kew

Royal Regiment of Garrison Artillery

Reginald Clifford BEESTON
Trumpeter, 125197, 13th Fire Command, Royal Garrison Artillery who died on 09 November 1918, aged 16. Buried in Dover (Buckland) Cemetery, Kent, United Kingdom

Born on 22 September 1902 in Dover, Kent, the third of four children of Clifford Dundas Beeston and Maude née Cox, his father had been a Quartermaster Serjeant (Artillery Clerk) on the District Staff of the Royal Garrison Artillery who had been discharged from the army on 13 August 1908 and who died in Dover on 17 June 1909.

Clifford had originally enlisted into the Royal Marines in 1887, however, four months later he enlisted into the Royal Artillery, giving his name as Charles Best, possibly because he was Absent Without Leave from the Royal Marines.

Four years after his father's death, Reginald was admitted to the school on 21 August 1913 (Petition No. 13141), joining his older brother Leslie Phillip Edward Beeston, who had been admitted on 04 February 1910 (Petition No. 12730).

Reginald remained at the school until he was discharged to the army on 14 July 1916, enlisting into the Royal Garrison Artillery in Warley, Essex, close to Hutton, where the school had been evacuated at the start of the war. He was posted to 13th Fire Command, stationed in Shoeburyness, also in Essex, part of the Eastern Coast Defences, where he died, in Shoeburyness Military Hospital, on 09 November 1918. His cause of death is not known.

When Leslie was discharged from the school on 18 November 1913, he enlisted in the Royal Garrison Artillery. He survived the war and emigrated to Canada, where he died in 1964.

Arthur BELCHER
Bombardier, 29704, 115 Heavy Battery, Royal Garrison Artillery who died on 13 November 1914, aged 24. Commemorated on the Ypres (Menin Gate) Memorial, West-Vlaanderen, Belgium

Born on 12 August 1890 in Abingdon, Berkshire, the youngest of five children of William Belcher and Charlotte Moona née Anderson, his father had been a Colour Serjeant in The Princess

Charlotte of Wales's (Royal Berkshire Regiment) who had been discharged from the army on 26 August 1895 and died in Moulsford, Berkshire, on 18 November 1895.

Arthur was admitted to the school on 12 January 1900 (Petition No. 11392), joining his older brother, Charles Thomas Belcher, who had been admitted on 09 July 1896 (Petition No. 10899). Arthur was discharged *"To Mother-Dirty habits"* just over a year after admission, on 13 April 1901, two months after his brother had been discharged.

Although Arthur's service record is no longer, it is known that he joined the army, as the 1911 Census shows that he was a Bombardier in No. 21 Company, Royal Garrison Artillery, and stationed in Shoeburyness, Essex.

The unit which Arthur was serving with at the start of the war was 115 Battery, Royal Garrison Artillery, which had been formed at Woolwich on 28 September 1914 from No. 5 Company, Royal Garrison Artillery. It embarked at Southampton, Hampshire, on 04 October and landed at Le Havre on 05 October 1914.

In November, the battery was involved in the First Battle of Ypres, the battery diary reporting that it delivered an abnormally large amount of ammunition during the early days of the month, including 240 rounds on 13 November.

Although there is no record of casualties on 13 November 1914, it is known that Arthur Belcher died of wounds on that day. It is possible that he was wounded when supply lorries were hit when passing through Ypres on 09 November, the last time before 13 November that casualties were reported by the battery, dying as a result of those wounds four days later. He may have been buried close to where he died, or he may have "vanished" in the explosion of these shells, but he has no known grave and is commemorated on the Menin Gate.

When Charles was discharged from the school on 23 February 1901, he enlisted into the Army Service Corps. He was discharged from the army on 12 February 1913, but appears to have re-enlisted when war broke out, serving in the 8th Battalion, London Regiment (Post Office Rifles), a Territorial Force unit, which landed in France in March 1915. He is recorded on the Honours Board in the school as having been awarded the Meritorious Service Medal. He died in Middlesex in 1932.

Arthur's older brother, Frederick Belcher, and younger brothers, Frank Herbert Belcher and Stanley Oswald Belcher, all attended the Royal Hibernian Military School in Dublin, Frederick being admitted on 05 June 1897, Frank on 29 July 1902 and Stanley on 18 December 1902.

Frederick was serving in the 1st Battalion, Royal Berkshire Regiment, when he was killed on 26 October 1914, whilst assisting a wounded officer at Zonnebeke during the First Battle of Ypres. Like Arthur, he has no known grave and is commemorated with his brother on the Menin Gate Memorial.

Both Frank and Stanley also served during the war, Frank in the Army Service Corps and Stanley in the 5th Battalion, Royal Berkshire Regiment, with both surviving. Frank died in London in 1955 and Stanley in Aldershot in 1963.

Arthur Charles BROWNING
Serjeant, 40186, 1st Siege Artillery Reserve Brigade, Royal Garrison Artillery who died on 05 August 1920, aged 31. Buried in Charlton Cemetery, Greenwich, London, United Kingdom

Born on 21 July 1889 in New Charlton, Kent, the eighth of nine children of George Browning and Mary Ann née Hook, his father had been a Serjeant Saddler in the 19th Hussars who had been discharged to pension after 21 years' service on 13 August 1888 and who died in Woolwich, London, on 10 October 1896. Arthur's mother had died in Charlton, London, three months before his father, on 01 July 1896.

Arthur was admitted to the school on 10 March 1899 (Petition No. 11275), joining his older brother, Percy Browning, who had been admitted on 05 March 1897 (Petition No. 11004). Arthur was discharged *"To Civil Life"* on 08 July 1903.

Although Arthur did not enlist in the army when he was discharged from the school, it would appear that he did enlist into the Militia, as when he enlisted in the Royal Artillery on 08 November 1907, he stated that he was still serving in the 3rd Battalion, Queen's Own (Royal West Kent Regiment), a Militia battalion of that regiment.

Arthur served for five years, but this time was not without incident, as he spent 56 days in detention between enlisting and 17 August 1910.

He is recorded in the 1911 Census as a Gunner in 132 Battery, Royal Field Artillery, stationed in Ewshot Barracks, Farnham, Hampshire, but is then recorded as having deserted from here on 14 August 1912. This seems to have been the final straw for the army, as he returned to duty on 09 October 1912, but was tried and convicted of desertion ten days later and discharged from the army for misconduct when that period of detention ended on 07 November 1912.

Following his discharge from the army, Arthur was a civilian for just over a year, before he re-enlisted into the army on 25 February 1914, although he did not mention his previous service, did not use his middle name and changed his date of birth. However, for some reason, his accredited date of service for this period is recorded as 03 August 1914 even though he is recorded as being posted to 38 Battery, Royal Garrison Artillery, on 18 May.

Again, his service was not without incident, and he was awarded another period of detention on 24 September 1914, but following his return to duty on 18 October, he seems to have settled down.

On 01 December 1914, Arthur was posted to 11 (Siege) Battery, Royal Garrison Artillery, deploying to France with this unit on 21 April 1915, remaining in theatre until 07 December 1916 when he returned to Britain as a Corporal and during a period of home leave in 1916, he married Ada Frances Horne in London.

He only remained in Britain for two weeks before he was posted back to 11 (Siege) Battery, promoted to Serjeant on 30 May 1917 and then posted to No 2 Reserve Brigade (Siege) in Catterick, Yorkshire North Riding, on 01 January 1918.

Two months later, on 11 March 1918, Arthur was posted to the 1st Siege Artillery Reserve Brigade, Royal Garrison Artillery, and was still serving with this battery when he was seen by a medical board on 19 December 1918 and diagnosed with a tubercle of his lung that was deemed *"caused by service"* and led to his discharge from the army two days later, on 21 December 1918.

Arthur died as a result of the tuberculosis eighteen months after his discharge from the army on 05 August 1920, two weeks before his daughter's first birthday. He was buried in his hometown and commemorated by the Commonwealth War Graves Commission, but is another "Lost Boy" whose name has been omitted from the memorial tablets in the school chapel.

Percy was discharged from the school on 27 January 1902 and *"returned to brother"*, the brother being George, the fourth of the nine children and aged 20 in 1902. He enlisted into the Royal Garrison Artillery in December 1915 and served for two years, including overseas, before he was discharged due to disability. He died in London in 1957.

Alfred James CARNE

Gunner, 31734, 71 Heavy Battery, Royal Garrison Artillery who died on 25 June 1917, aged 22. Buried in Kemmel Chateau Military Cemetery, West-Vlaanderen, Belgium

Born on 02 April 1895 in Landport, Hampshire, the eldest son of Alfred Francis Carne and Ada Lilly née Blake, his father had been a Gunner in the Royal Artillery who was discharged from the army on 15 December 1898, being employed as a railway policeman, and died in Southsea, Hampshire on 20 December 1901.

Alfred was admitted to the school on 10 July 1906 (Petition No. 12244) and was discharged to the Royal Garrison Artillery on 28 May 1909. Although Alfred's service record is no longer available, and therefore his pre-war postings cannot be confirmed, the 1911 Census records that he was a Trumpeter serving with No. 46 Company, Royal Garrison Artillery, and stationed in Dover Castle.

It is also not known with which other units that he served, but it can be said with certainty that in 1917 he was serving with 71 Heavy Battery, Royal Garrison Artillery in Belgium. This battery had been in France and Flanders since 14 February 1915, Alfred's medal index card showing that this was the date on which he entered theatre, and it is likely that it provided artillery support to the Battle of Messines, which was fought between 07 and 14 June 1917. It is not known whether he was wounded during this battle and later died of wounds or if was killed after the battle, but Alfred died on 25 June 1917.

His younger brother, Charles Frederick Carne, who was not a Dukie, also died during the war. He was serving as a Private in 15th Battalion, The Hampshire Regiment, when he was killed on 15 September 1916. He is buried in Guards' Cemetery, Lesboeufs, Somme, France.

Christopher Joseph CORBIN

Second Lieutenant, 141 Heavy Battery, Royal Garrison Artillery who died on 05 June 1917, aged 37. Buried in Hop Store Cemetery, West-Vlaanderen, Belgium

Born on 23 December 1879 in Dublin, County Dublin, the eldest son of Frederick Corbin and Honoria née Stephens, his father was a Farrier Serjeant in the 7th (The Princess Royal's) Dragoon Guards who died in service in India on 05 June 1889. At the time of Christopher's Petition Document being completed, his widowed mother was still in India and awaiting embarkation on a troopship on 12 December 1889.

Christopher was admitted to the school on 27 December 1889 (Petition No. 9945), being joined by his younger brother, Frank Corbin, who was admitted to the school on 26 September 1890

(Petition No. 10061). Christopher was discharged to the Royal Artillery on 05 January 1895 and although his service record is not easily accessed as an officer, it is known that he was a Serjeant in July 1914, as he was a witness at the Courts Martial of a soldier who was absent from No. 4 Depot, Royal Garrison Artillery, which was located in Great Yarmouth, Norfolk.

Because his service record is not readily available, it is not possible to ascertain with which units Christopher served pre-war, but at the outbreak of war, he was serving with 109 Heavy Battery, Royal Garrison Artillery and entered theatre on 22 September 1914.

Again, little is known about the units with which he served during the first two years of the war, but it is known that he was on leave in early-1916, as he and Annie Charlotte Elizabeth Doe married in Great Yarmouth.

In early-1917, Christopher was an Acting Serjeant Major and recommended for a Commission for service in the field, being appointed as a Second Lieutenant on 30 April 1917[76].

By June of that year, he was serving with 141 Heavy Battery, Royal Garrison Artillery, and located near Ypres. The battery was involved in the preparation for the Battle of Messines, which was due to commence at 0310hrs on 07 June with the detonation of a series of mines that had been dug under the German positions.

Christopher did not live to see the start of the battle as he died two days before on 05 June 1917, although the circumstances of his death, like so much of his time after he joined the army, are unknown. He is buried in Hop Store Cemetery, just outside the town of Vlamertinghe.

Frank was discharged from the school on 02 February 1895 and enlisted into The Duke of Wellington's (West Riding Regiment) as a Bugler. He died of disease in Dinapore, India, on 02 December 1904.

Phillip Daniel DONOVAN
Gunner, 33930, No. 1 Mountain Battery, Royal Garrison Artillery who died on 22 April 1916, aged 32. Buried in Nairobi South Cemetery, Kenya

Born on 18 April 1884 in Secunderabad, India, the second of six children of Daniel Donovan and Bessie Maud née Jerrard, his father was a Gunner in the Royal Artillery who died in Plumstead, London, on 28 August 1898. His mother had died four years earlier, on 17 September 1894, in Woolwich, London.

Phillip was admitted to the school on 26 July 1895 (Petition No. 10766) and discharged to The Lincolnshire Regiment on 31 May

---

[76] *The London Gazette*, 27 April 1917, Supplement:30040

1898, going on to serve in South Africa and India, confirmation of this being in the service record of his brother, Henry John Donovan, who gives his next of kin as *"Phillip Daniel Donovan 1st Lincolnshire Regt, Jubbulpore"* although above this, and crossed through is *"D. of York's Roy. Mil. School"*[77].

Phillip's service record is no longer available, so the rest of his career until the outbreak of war is unknown, and it is not possible to establish at which point he transferred to the Royal Garrison Artillery. It is possible that he was discharged in 1910, having completed 12 years' service and then re-enlisted or been recalled at the outbreak of war.

No. 1 Mountain Battery, Royal Garrison Artillery, was part of the 2nd (Rawalpindi) Division of the Indian Army and stationed in India. It is possible that elements from this division were posted to East Africa to reinforce Indian Expeditionary Force "B" in its fight against the German colonies, which could explain Phillip's arrival in that theatre of war on 05 September 1915.

It is not possible to ascertain what part Phillip played in the fighting, but it would appear that he contracted malaria and died in Nairobi, British East Africa[78], seven months after arrival in theatre.

Phillip is another of the "Lost Boys" whose name has been omitted from the memorial tablets in the school chapel.

Robert Charles DUGGAN

Boy, 41128, No. 3 Depot, Royal Garrison Artillery who died on 31 August 1915, aged 15. Buried in Plymouth (Old Park) Cemetery, Devon, United Kingdom

Born on 20 June 1900 in Plymouth, Devonshire, the youngest of eight children of John Duggan and Elizabeth née Nicholson, his father had been a Serjeant in the Royal Artillery who had been discharged from the army after 21 years' service on 13 September 1891 and died in Plymouth on 08 June 1901.

Robert was admitted to the school on 20 October 1910 (Petition No. 12817)[79] and was discharged on 30 June 1914, enlisting into the Royal Garrison Artillery on the same day. He was posted to No 3 Depot (Heavy and Siege) in Plymouth, and whilst there he developed

---

[77] WO 363: War Office: Soldiers' Documents, First World War 'Burnt Documents' (Microfilm Copies), 1914-1920, The National Archives, Kew - First World War Service Records 'Burnt Documents'

[78] Modern-day Kenya

[79] His Petition Document incorrectly records his name as Charles Robert

tibial periostitis[80]. This worsened and became osteomyelitis[81], which resulted on him undergoing surgery on 08 May 1915.

Although he was discharged from Devonport Hospital, Plymouth, on 31 May 1915, it appears that the infection worsened, with Robert developing generalised septicaemia which resulted in his death from peritonitis in Devonport Hospital three months later and two months after his fifteenth birthday.

Robert was buried in his hometown, and because he died in service, he is commemorated by the Commonwealth War Graves Commission, although he is another "Lost Boy" whose name has been omitted from the memorial tablets in the school chapel.

Albert Edward FREEBORN

Corporal, 30843, 4 Siege Battery, Royal Garrison Artillery who died on 13 October 1916, aged 21. Buried in Boulogne Eastern Cemetery, Pas de Calais, France

Born on 07 February 1895 in Whitstable, Kent, the eldest of five children of Sydney James Freeborn and Eva Sarah née Belsey, his father was a Serjeant in the Royal Artillery and was still serving when he died on St. Lucia, West Indies, on 24 July 1903.

Albert was admitted to the school on 06 May 1904 (Petition No. 11971) and was discharged to the Royal Garrison Artillery on 16 February 1909. Just over a year after Albert had been discharged, his younger brother, Cecil George Freeborn, was admitted to the school on 01 June 1910 (Petition No. 12763).

Albert's service record is no longer available, so there is limited information on his pre-war career, but the 1911 Census records him as a Boy serving in No. 4 Depot, Royal Garrison Artillery, in the Royal Artillery Barracks, Great Yarmouth, Norfolk.

According to Albert's medal index card, he arrived in theatre on 17 September 1916, a Corporal in 4 Siege Battery, Royal Garrison Artillery. Just over a month later, the battery, which was in the area of Poperinghe, received orders to change with 6 Siege Battery, Royal Garrison Artillery, on the Somme, travelling by train to Calais on 11 October. The following day, the battery *"Left Calais 7.30am. Cpl Freeborn fell off train in Boulogne tunnel"*[82]. His death the following day was recorded as being from accidental injuries and he was buried in Boulogne. He is not recorded on the memorial tablets in the school chapel and is another of the "Lost Boys".

---

[80] Inflammation of the periosteum if the tibia, also known as shin splints
[81] An infection of the bone
[82] WO 95/543/4: Army Troops. 4 Siege Battery Royal Garrison Artillery, 1914 Sept - 1918 Jan, The National Archives, Kew

Cecil was discharged from the school on 14 April 1914 and like his older brother, enlisted into the Royal Garrison Artillery. He survived the war, married Lillian Brooker in Canterbury, Kent, in 1936 and was recorded in the 1939 England and Wales Register as living in Canterbury and being employed as a Crossing Keeper (Railway). He died in Canterbury in 1951.

His younger brother, Owen James Freeborn, was admitted to the Royal Hibernian Military School and served in The Lancashire Fusiliers.

George Edgar FUNNELL
Gunner, 38968, 239 Siege Battery, Royal Garrison Artillery who died on 28 June 1918, aged 19. Buried in Faubourg d'Amiens Cemetery, Arras, Pas-de-Calais, France

Born on 12 January 1899 in Swansea, Glamorganshire, the eldest son of James Funnell and Lillian Maud née Voisey, his father was a Serjeant in the Royal Artillery who died whilst still serving in Swansea on 30 March 1903.

George was admitted to the school on 04 November 1909 (Petition No. 12687), appearing in the 1911 Census, although incorrectly recorded as George Hector. He was discharged on 17 March 1913, enlisting into the Royal Garrison Artillery.

His service record is no longer available, so it is not possible to establish the batteries with which George served, nor is it possible to establish when he first deployed overseas, although the medal rolls record that he was entitled only to the British War and Victory medals, suggesting that he did not enter theatre until 1916 at the earliest. What is known is that in 1918 he was serving with 239 Siege Battery, Royal Garrison Artillery, which had deployed to France in January 1917.

By June 1918, the German Spring Offensive that had been launched in the March was reaching the limit of its advance, with the Allies being pushed back toward their supplies and the Germans extending their own supply lines. It is likely that it was during the latter stages of the German offensive, at a time when the Allied Armies were preparing to launch the counterattack that came to be known as the Hundred Days Offensive, that George was killed, on 28 June 1918. He is buried in Faubourg d'Amiens Cemetery in the western part of the town of Arras.

Alfred William GANLEY
Battery Serjeant Major, 16716, 146 Siege Battery, Royal Garrison Artillery who died on 23 March 1918, aged 37. Commemorated on the Arras Memorial, Pas-de-Calais, France

Born on 26 December 1880 in Vauxhall, Surrey, the sixth of eight children of James Ganley and Ann Sophia née Norgrove, his father had served in the Royal Artillery, his trade given as Tailor, with the rank of Gunner. He had been discharged from the army on 24 February 1876 and died in Lambeth, Surrey on 21 January 1888.

Although not the only boy in the family, Alfred was the only one to attend the school, being admitted on 24 February 1893 (Petition No. 10435) and discharged on 10 October 1896, enlisting into the Royal Artillery.

Alfred's service record is no longer available, but he is shown in the 1901 Census as a Gunner in the Royal Artillery, although he was obviously on leave, as he was staying at his uncle's house in Lambeth.

It is also likely that he was then posted to the Channel Islands as he married Annie Louise Austin in Guernsey in 1904, their only child, Dorothy Louisa Ganley, being born on the island on 19 December that year. By 1911, Alfred was a Corporal and serving with No. 56 Company, Royal Garrison Artillery, stationed in Royal Artillery Curepipe, Mauritius.

The lack of service record also means that it is not possible to establish with which batteries he served, nor when he arrived in France, but by 1918 Alfred was the Battery Serjeant Major of 146 Siege Battery, which had been in France since 16 August 1916. In March 1918 it is likely that the battery was located in the area of Arras when the German Spring Offensive commenced on 21 March. Two days into this assault, Alfred was killed, on 23 March. He has no known grave and is commemorated on the Arras Memorial, which is located in Faubourg d'Amiens Cemetery in the western part of the town of Arras.

Edward GASCOYNE
Serjeant, 6825, 70 Siege Battery, Royal Garrison Artillery who died on 15 January 1916, aged 38. Buried in Lydd Cemetery, Kent, United Kingdom

Born on 28 August 1877 in Portsmouth, Hampshire, the fifth of seven children of Richard Gascoyne and Elizabeth née Brereton, his father had been a Serjeant in the 87th (or Royal Irish Fusiliers) Regiment of Foot[83]. He was discharged from the army on 15 March

---
[83] Amalgamated with the 89th (The Princess Victoria's) Regiment of Foot on 01 July 1881 to become The Princess Victoria's (Royal Irish Fusiliers)

1870 and was employed as a Barrack Serjeant until his death in Alverstoke, Hampshire, on 10 December 1884.

Edward was admitted to the school on 23 March 1888 (Petition No. 9638), joining his older brother, Frederick Charles Gascoyne, who had been admitted on 11 December 1885 (Petition No. 9298). Edward was discharged from the school to the Royal Artillery on 05 September 1891. He then had a 22-year career before he was discharged as a Serjeant in Dover on 13 September 1913, during which time he served in South Africa (1894), Mauritius (1894-1897), Malta (1897-1901) and Hong Kong (1905-1908). When he retired, his behaviour was noted as exemplary, having committed no offenses during his career.

It would appear that following the outbreak of war, Edward was recalled to the Colours, immediately restored to the rank of Serjeant, but his service record for his war service is no longer available. However, 70 Siege Battery, Royal Garrison Artillery, to which Edward had been posted, was formed at Dover in 1915, deploying to France on 26 March 1916.

Edward did not see the deployment because he died in Lydd, Kent, on 15 January 1916. There is no record of the cause of Edward's death and he is buried in the town where he died. However, his name was omitted from the memorial tablets in the school chapel and is another of the "Lost Boys".

Frederick was discharged from the school on 28 September 1889 and also enlisted into the Royal Artillery. He was recorded in the 1911 Census as a Company Quartermaster Serjeant serving in No. 66 Company, Royal Garrison Artillery, and stationed in Bermuda, West Indies.

By the outbreak of the war, Frederick had been discharged from the army, but was recalled to the Colours from the reserve on 28 July 1916, re-enlisting into the Royal Garrison Artillery as a Battery Quartermaster Serjeant. He survived the war, being discharged in 1919 and died in Portsmouth, Hampshire, in 1956.

Albert Edwin GEE

Second Lieutenant, Royal Garrison Artillery who died on 14 December 1917, aged 39. Buried in Plumstead Cemetery, London, United Kingdom

Born on 30 March 1878 in Woolwich, Kent, the eldest of six children of Albert Benjamin Gee and Eliza née Church, his father was a Serjeant in the Royal Artillery, who was commissioned in 1896.

Albert was admitted to the school on 06 January 1890 (Petition No. 9954), being joined by his younger brother, Ernest Godfrey Gee, on 29 April 1902 (Petition No. 10326). Albert was *"withdrawn by father"* on 21 May 1892, although the reason for the withdrawal is not known.

Albert's life is a bit of mystery following his withdrawal from the school, although it is known that he enlisted into the army, joining the Royal Garrison Artillery. However, because his service record is not easily accessible, the date of his enlistment is not known, and he does not appear to be in the 1901 Census.

It is also known that he married Eva Florence Winifred Patterson in Woolwich in July 1906, their only child, Ronald Ivor Leslie Gee, being born in Milford Haven, Pembrokeshire, the following year. It is likely that Eva was also a military child, as she had been born in Gibraltar in 1877.

Albert is recorded in the 1911 Census as a 3rd Class Master Gunner serving with No. 54 Company, Royal Garrison Artillery, and stationed in the Casemates, Gibraltar. By the start of the war, Albert was a 2nd Class Master Gunner, and although it is not known with which unit he was serving, or where he was stationed, it is known that he disembarked in France on 17 July 1915. However, by the time that he did land in France, he was a Second Lieutenant, having been Commissioned four months earlier[84].

Albert's movements, and the units with which he served are not known, but almost two years after he arrived in theatre, on 22 June 1917, he retired from the army on account of ill-health[85]. Although the nature of this ill-health is not known, he died in Dartford, Kent, six months after retiring from the army, on 14 December 1917 and was buried in Plumstead Cemetery, London. He was commemorated by the Commonwealth War Graves Commission, but his name was omitted from the memorial tablets in the school chapel, so is another of the "Lost Boys".

Ernest was withdrawn from the school on the same day as Albert, and also enlisted into the Royal Artillery, recorded in the 1901 Census as a Corporal in the Royal Field Artillery, stationed in Colchester, Essex, and in the 1911 Census as Battery Quartermaster Serjeant in 144 Battery, Royal Field Artillery, stationed in Aldershot, Hampshire. He was Commissioned as a Second Lieutenant in October 1914, surviving the war and retiring as a Captain, having been Mentioned in Despatches. He served in the Second World War as a Squadron Leader in the Royal Air Force Volunteer Reserve and died in Colchester in 1961.

---

[84] *The London Gazette*, 5 March 1915, Issue:29091
[85] *The London Gazette*, 19 June 1917, Supplement:30143

Ralph GWYTHER
Serjeant, 101312, 217 Siege Battery, Royal Garrison Artillery who died on 30 August 1917, aged 20. Buried in Vlamertinghe New Military Cemetery, West-Vlaanderen, Belgium

Born on 25 May 1897 in Ferozepore, India, the eldest son of Percy James Philipps Gwyther and Letitia Louisa née Ellis, his father was a 2nd Class Master Gunner in the Royal Artillery and was still serving when he died in Hurst Castle, Hampshire, on 28 October 1903.

Ralph was admitted to the school on 31 March 1908 (Petition No. 12495), almost a year before his younger brother Ronald Ellis Gwyther was admitted on 18 March 1909 (Petition No. 12573), both making the transition from Chelsea to Guston, and both boys appearing in the 1911 Census, Ralph ten names above Ronald.

Ralph was discharged as a boy to become a Student at the school on 25 August 1913, but it is likely that he was conscripted into the army following the passing of the Military Service Act in January 1916, having been employed as a Schoolmaster. He enlisted into the Royal Garrison Artillery, in which his brother was already serving, on 24 January 1916.

Ralph was immediately put into the Army Reserve and was not mobilised until 24 August 1916, posted to No. 1 Depot in Newcastle upon Tyne, to 47 Battery, Royal Garrison Artillery, at Tynemouth Garrison a month later and to 217 Siege Battery, Royal Garrison Artillery in August 1916. He was promoted to Bombardier three days after joining this battery, and by September he had been promoted to Corporal.

The battery deployed to France on 20 January 1917 and by March was in positions near Arras, where on 03 March, Ralph was promoted to Acting Serjeant. The unit remained in France until the start of July 1917, when it was transferred to Belgium in preparation for the Third Battle of Ypres, which commenced on the last day of that month and in which it was used to support the battle throughout August, Ralph being promoted to Serjeant on the 24 August.

Six days after his promotion, Ralph was killed in action, one of four men from his battery killed that day. He was buried in Vlamertinghe New Military Cemetery, in the town of the same name and which had been used as a location for both artillery and field ambulance units for much of the war, as it was just outside the normal range of German shell fire.

Ronald was discharged from the school on 24 June 1913 and enlisted into the Royal Garrison Artillery. He survived the war, marrying in 1923 and having two children. He died in Southall, Middlesex, a month after his 61st birthday in 1960.

Robert Blissett Powell JOHNSON MC
Lieutenant, 109 Heavy Battery, Royal Garrison Artillery who died on 19 September 1918, aged 31. Buried in Westoutre British Cemetery, West-Vlaanderen, Belgium

Born on 12 February 1887 in Westminster, Middlesex, the second of four children of William Joseph Powell Johnson and Catherine Isabella née Wooton, his father had been a Private in the 6th Dragoon Guards (Carabiniers), but had been medically discharged from the army on 31 October 1872. He died in Westminster on 25 April 1895.

Robert was admitted to the school a year after his father's death, on 24 September 1896 (Petition No. 10937) and was discharged on 02 March 1901, enlisting into the Royal Garrison Artillery on the same day.

He was initially posted to the Depot at Woolwich, where he was appointed as a Gunner in July 1903, before being posted to Glasgow two years later and appointed Acting Bombardier fifteen months later.

In July 1910, Robert married Lilian May Pye, and this is the first occasion on which his name appears as the hyphenated Powell-Johnson. Their daughter was born a year later when Robert was an Acting Bombardier stationed in the Royal Artillery Barracks (East Side) in Woolwich, again appearing as Powell-Johnson.

Robert was discharged from the army at the end of his period of service on 10 January 1913 and joined the Metropolitan Police on 24 February 1913 as a Police Constable. It appears that he was either recalled from the Reserve, or re-enlisted at the start of the war, although this information is in his officer record, which is not easily accessed, but it is known that he was Commissioned as a Temporary Second Lieutenant on 08 November 1916[86].

Little is known of his service in France, but on 30 July 1917 he was awarded the Military Cross for conspicuous gallantry[87]. It does not state the battery with which he was serving at that time, but it is known that in 1918 Robert was serving with 109 Heavy Battery, Royal Garrison Artillery, in Flanders, a battery that had been on the Western Front since 23 September 1914.

It appears that this battery was heavily involved in the battles of the Hundred Days Offensive in and around the Ypres Salient.

---

[86] *The London Gazette*, 7 November 1916, Issue:29815
[87] *The London Gazette*, 24 July 1917, Supplement:30204: *"Temp. 2nd Lt. Robert Blissett Powell Johnson, R.G.A. For conspicuous gallantry and devotion to duty in rescuing wounded men who had been buried in a dug-out by hostile shell fire. He was aided in this by four of his men, two of whom were wounded severely during their efforts to save their comrades. All were got clear and taken to the dressing station, although the shelling was heavy and continuous all the time"*

Robert Powell-Johnson MC[88] died on 19 September 1918 and is buried in Westoutre British Cemetery, although whether his was one of the 50 graves *"brought in"* from other sites on the Ypres battlefield in the aftermath of the war is not known.

Alfred William LAURIE

Second Lieutenant, 42 Siege Battery, Royal Garrison Artillery who died on 22 November 1916, aged 26. Buried in Bazentin-le-Petit Military Cemetery, Somme, France

Born on 25 June 1890 in Belfast, County Antrim, the third of seven children of Frederick Horace Laurie and Bessie Bath née Banks, his father was a Colour Serjeant in The East Lancashire Regiment and died in St Bartholomew's Hospital, London, on 06 January 1899, although the cause of death is not known.

Alfred was admitted to the school on 13 October 1899 (Petition No. 11354), three months after his older brother, Frederick Horace Laurie, had been admitted on 14 July 1899 (Petition No. 11311). A third brother, Charles James Laurie, was also admitted to the school on 31 August 1907 (Petition No. 12415).

Alfred was discharged on 19 July 1904, not to the army but to *"Civil Life Unfit for the Army"*. However, he clearly did enlist into the Royal Garrison Artillery, but his service record is not readily available, so it is not known when, but the 1911 Census records that he was an Acting Bombardier, serving with No. 7 Company, Royal Garrison Artillery, stationed in Shoeburyness, Essex.

Alfred's medal index card shows that at the outbreak of war, he was serving with 1 Siege Battery, Royal Garrison Artillery and entered theatre on 17 September 1914, although it is not known with which batteries he served during his service in France.

On 06 October 1915 Alfred was a Corporal and Commissioned as a Second Lieutenant[89]. He was clearly on home leave at about this time as well, as he married Florence Rhoda Whitehouse in Tynemouth in September of that year.

In November 1916, Alfred was serving with 42 Siege Battery on the Somme. The battery was employed in bombarding the German front-line trenches near Bazentin-le-Petit and on 22 November 1916 Alfred was making his way from the observation post when he was dangerously wounded in the head by a high explosive shell. He died on his way to the main dressing station at Bazentin-Le-Petit at about 1700hrs and was interred in the cemetery in that village. Although

---

[88] The name by which he is commemorated by the Commonwealth War Graves Commission
[89] *The London Gazette*, 5 October 1915, Issue:29316

he is commemorated on the memorial tablets in the school chapel, his surname is misspelled as Lawrie.

Frederick was *"Returned to mother"* on 02 May 1902 and died five years later on 29 March 1907.

Charles also served in the Royal Garrison Artillery during the war, enlisting when he was discharged from the school on 23 June 1913. He entered theatre on 30 August 1915 and had reached the rank of Serjeant when he was Commissioned in August 1917, subsequently being awarded the Military Cross[90]. He survived the war and died in Carnoustie, Scotland, in 1995.

Joseph Edward MADDOCKS

Bombardier, 63383, 242 Siege Battery, Royal Garrison Artillery who died on 19 July 1917, aged 27. Buried in Spoilbank Cemetery, West-Vlaanderen, Belgium

Born on 30 November 1889 in Meerut, India, the second of three children of Edward William Maddocks and Jane née Davies, his father had been a Corporal in The King's Own Scottish Borderers who had been discharged as medically unfit on 09 August 1892 and died in Peckham, London, on 12 July 1893.

Joseph was admitted to the school on 03 February 1899 (Petition No. 11266), but only remained at the school for seventeen days before he was detained on pass on 20 February 1899.

Between leaving the school and the outbreak of the First World War, little is known of Joseph, although the 1901 Census shows him as living with his widowed mother and sisters in Westminster, London, and the 1911 Census shows him as still living with his mother and sisters, now in Brixton, London, and employed as a Relief Stamper[91].

Joseph's service record shows that he enlisted into the Royal Garrison Artillery on 03 November 1915, the question regarding attendance at the Duke of York's having been left blank as he joined as an adult and he was posted three days later to No. 4 Depot, Royal Garrison Artillery, located in Great Yarmouth, Norfolk.

He then spent the next fourteen months being posted between various Royal Garrison Artillery batteries in Britain before he was posted to 242 Siege Battery, Royal Garrison Artillery and deployed to France with this unit on 27 January 1917.

---

[90] *The London Gazette*, 31 January 1919, Supplement:31158: *"2nd Lt. Charles James Laurie, 12th Hy. Bty., R.G.A. For conspicuous gallantry and devotion to duty on 7th September, 1918, near Villers-Cognicourt, in keeping his battery in action under heavy shelling. He was cheerful and cool, and carried one of his men who had been wounded to a place of safety"*

[91] A person who stamps engraved or embossed designs on stationary

Two months after arriving in France, Joseph was promoted to Acting Bombardier, being confirmed in the rank a month after that on 29 April 1917. The circumstances surrounding Joseph's death on 19 July 1917 are not known, but his service record confirms that he was killed in action on that date and that he was buried in Spoilbank Cemetery.

The fact that Joseph was at the school for such a short time may be the reason that he is one of the "Lost Boys" whose name has been omitted from the memorial tablets in the school chapel, but he does deserve to be remembered at the school.

Archibald Ferguson McFARLANE

Lance Bombardier, 40429, 113 Siege Battery, Royal Garrison Artillery who died on 01 February 1919, aged 31. Buried in Portsmouth (Kingston) Cemetery, Hampshire, United Kingdom

Born on 21 January 1888 in Portsmouth, Hampshire, the fourth of seven children of Alexander McFarlane and Elizabeth Louisa née Arbuckle, his father had been a Serjeant in the 77th (East Middlesex, Duke of Cambridge's Own) Regiment of Foot[92] who had been discharged from the army after 26 years' service on 09 July 1878.

Archibald was admitted to the school on 10 March 1899 (Petition No. 11276), joining his older brother, Albert Charles McFarlane, who had been admitted on 31 January 1896 (Petition No. 10862). Their eldest brother, William John McFarlane attended the Royal Hibernian Military School. Archibald was discharged from the school on 21 May 1902 and enlisted into the Alexandra, Princess of Wales's Own (Yorkshire Regiment).

Once he had enlisted, Archibald spent the first six years of his service in Britain, being appointed as a Bandsman on 05 August 1904. His first overseas posting was to Egypt on 16 January 1908, where he was to spend three years before he was posted to Sudan on 30 January 1911. After a year in that country, he was then posted to India, on 29 January 1912, returning to Britain two years later on 09 January 1914.

Once he was back in Britain, Archibald re-engaged to complete 21 years' service in the army on 13 January 1914, but at the same time he transferred to the Royal Garrison Artillery. As with his time in his previous regiment, Archibald was a musician and spent the first three years of his service in Britain, even after the outbreak of war, disembarking in France for the first time on 27 July 1917.

---

[92] Amalgamated with 57th (West Middlesex) Regiment of Foot on 01 July 1881 to become The Duke of Cambridge's Own (Middlesex Regiment)

After four months in France, Archibald returned to Britain on 17 November 1917, but was again posted to France on 31 March 1918, joining 113 Siege Battery. Almost a year later, Archibald was on leave in Portsmouth when he developed septic pneumonia, dying on 01 February 1919. He was buried in the town where he was born and commemorated by the Commonwealth War Graves Commission, but he is another "Lost Boy" whose name has been omitted from the memorial tablets in the school chapel.

Albert was discharged from the school on 15 September 1900 and enlisted into The Princess Louise's (Argyll and Sutherland Highlanders) as a Bandsman. He also served during the war, but unlike Archibald, he survived. He died in Bridgenorth, Shropshire, in 1973.

William served in the Alexandra, Princess of Wales's Own (Yorkshire Regiment) during the war. It is known that he survived the war, but nothing is known of him after this.

William Alfred McKENZIE
Musician, 28257, Band, Royal Garrison Artillery who died on 24 October 1918, aged 25. Buried in Gibraltar (North Front) Cemetery, Gibraltar

Born on 29 June 1893 in Aldershot, Hampshire, the eldest of four children of William McKenzie and Kate Ellen née Winser, his father was a Serjeant in the Royal Artillery and was still serving when he died in Aldershot on 22 November 1901.

William was admitted to the school eighteen months after his father's death, on 06 June 1903 (Petition No. 11817), remaining there for almost five years before being discharged on 23 January 1908 and enlisting into the Royal Garrison Artillery as a Musician.

As William's service record is no longer available, it is extremely difficult to find any information about his service, or which Royal Garrison Artillery Band he was serving in. However, it is known that in 1918 he was stationed in Gibraltar. According to the Registers of Soldiers' Effects[93], William was attached to No. 55 Company, Royal Garrison Artillery, a Coastal Defence battery.

William died on 24 October 1918 and although there is no cause of death documented, there is a distinct possibility that he died as a result of Influenza. This had first appeared in the spring of 1918 and by the end of the year had reached pandemic status and spread to the Straits of Gibraltar, Algeria, Britain, Ireland and other European countries.

---

[93] UK, Army Registers of Soldiers' Effects, 1901-1929, 1914-1915, Miscellaneous, 760001-761500

Neither of William's brothers attended the school, but it is known that both did serve during the war. His oldest brother, George, served in 15th Battalion, The Hampshire Regiment and was killed in Belgium in 1917. He has no known grave and is commemorated on the Menin Gate.

William George NEWLAND
Bombardier 1402391, 10 Medium Battery, Royal Garrison Artillery who died on 23 June 1921, aged 30. Commemorated on the Delhi Memorial (India Gate), India

Born on 12 January 1891 in Cairo, Egypt, the youngest of two sons of William Newland and Giuseppa Margherita Irene née Corti, his father had served in the 20th Hussars, but transferred to the Military Mounted Police and was a Sergeant at the time of his death in Cairo on 12 July 1890, six months prior to William's birth. His mother also died in Cairo, on 07 October 1895.

William was admitted to the school on 10 February 1900 (Petition No. 11410) and discharged to the Royal Garrison Artillery on 21 January 1905, although his service record is no longer available.

Due to the lack of service record, it is not possible to establish where, or with which batteries, William served, although it is known that during the war he served as a Gunner with 304 Siege Battery, Royal Garrison Artillery and that he was a Corporal by the time of the Armistice.

Once William had returned to Britain, he married Mary Louisa Gardiner in Govanhill, Glasgow on 01 March 1919, the following year being posted to India, with his wife accompanying him. Their only child, Irene Marie Newland, was born in Mooltan, India, on 09 July 1920.

Between 1919 and 1921, the Muslim tribesmen of Waziristan, in the border region between British India and Afghanistan, rebelled against the British Indian Army, encouraged by the Afghan invasion of British India in 1919. Although peace was quickly achieved with the Afghans, it was a different story with the Waziris, who continued the fight. It was during this conflict that William was killed, dying on 23 June 1921. He was buried in Ladha Cemetery, but when all of the cemeteries to the west of the River Indus were abandoned as maintenance was no longer possible, his name was added to the Delhi Memorial.

It is possible that, because he was killed almost two years after the signing of the Treaty of Versailles, William is one of the "Lost Boys" whose name has been omitted from the memorial tablets in the school chapel, despite being commemorated by the Commonwealth War Graves Commission.

John Edward Ernest PARKER
Bombardier, 16525, No. 8 Company, Royal Garrison Artillery who died on 21 June 1920, aged 30. Buried in Gibraltar (North Front) Cemetery, Gibraltar

Born on 10 July 1889 in Newbridge, County Kildare, the fourth of eight children of Thomas Parker and Annie née Clinton, his father had been a Farrier Staff Serjeant in the 5th (Princess Charlotte of Wales's) Dragoon Guards who had died of enteric fever on 07 February 1900, at the Siege of Ladysmith during the Second Boer War.

John was admitted to the school six months after his father's death on 10 August 1900 (Petition No. 11461) and was discharged on 05 September 1903, enlisting into the Royal Garrison Artillery. Following his attestation, John spent the first four years of his service in Britain, during which time he was appointed as a Trumpeter on 08 December 1905 and posted to No. 44 Company, Royal Garrison Artillery, stationed in Pembroke Dock, Pembrokeshire, part of the Western Coast Defences, on 14 December 1905.

On 25 September 1907, he was posted to No. 4 Company, Royal Garrison Artillery, located in the Southern Section of Gibraltar, remaining here for five years before returning home on 30 March 1912.

A month before the outbreak of war, on 01 July 1914, John was posted to No. 50 Company, Royal Garrison Artillery in Sierra Leone, although he was to be there for just over a year before he returned to Britain on 31 July 1915, arriving on 13 November 1915.

After spending a month at the B Depot, Siege Artillery, in Bexhill, Sussex, John was posted to the newly formed 93 (Siege) Battery, Royal Garrison Artillery, stationed in Plymouth, Devonshire, deploying with the battery when it landed in France on 05 May 1916 and being appointed as an Acting Bombardier on 23 July.

After spending eighteen months on the Western Front, during which time he is likely to have taken part with his battery in the fighting at Gommecourt in 1916 and the Battle of Passchendaele in 1917, he was then posted back to Britain on 26 October 1917 and was still in Britain when the Armistice was signed in November 1918.

Two years after the end of the war, on 08 March 1920, John was posted to No. 8 Company, Royal Garrison Artillery, again in the Southern Section of Gibraltar. However, three months after arrival, he died as a result of *"dilatation and stenosis, double aortic"* at the Military

Hospital in Gibraltar and was buried in Gibraltar (North Front) Cemetery.

Despite his commemoration by the Commonwealth War Graves Commission, he is another "Lost Boy" whose name has been omitted from the memorial tablets in the school chapel.

Charles Henry POLLARD

Battery Serjeant Major, 327 Siege Battery, Royal Garrison Artillery who died on 16 August 1917, aged 35. Buried in Tilloy British Cemetery, Tilloy-Les-Mofflaines, Pas-de-Calais, France

Born on 07 April 1882 in Paignton, Devonshire, the sixth of ten children of John Smith Pollard and Charlotte née German, his father had been a Battery Serjeant Major in the Royal Artillery, but had left the army on 10 June 1884 and is shown in the 1891 Census as being employed as a Gymnastic Instructor, the family living in Accrington, Lancashire. He died in Haslingden, Lancashire, on 07 November 1891.

Charles was admitted to the school a year after his father's death, on 25 November 1892 (Petition No. 10388). He was joined by his younger brother, Gordon Havelock Pollard, the following year on 29 September 1893 (Petition No. 10523).

Charles was discharged from the school *"To mother"* on 07 April 1897 and because there is no service record available for him, it is not possible to ascertain when he joined the army. He did enlist into the Royal Garrison Artillery and seems to have spent a lot of his pre-war career in Gibraltar, as he married Beatrice Caroline Taylor there in 1906 and their son, Charles Gordon Pollard was born there in the same year. The 1911 Census also shows him as a Band Corporal stationed in Grand Casemate Barracks, Gibraltar. By 1914, Charles was stationed in Plymouth, Devonshire, as his daughter, Margaret Beatrice Pollard, was born there that year.

It is also unsure at what point Charles entered theatre during the war, although it could be speculated that it was not until August 1916 as his medal index card shows that he was not eligible for the 1914-15 Star, but it does show his unit as 135 Siege Battery, which did not arrive in France until that time.

Again, little is known about Charles' movements during the next year, but it is known that in August 1917 he was the Battery Serjeant Major of 327 Siege Battery, Royal Garrison Artillery, of which it is very difficult to find any information (there is no war diary in the National Archives). However, in August 1917, the battery was in action during the Battle of Langemarck, part of the Third Battle of Ypres. Charles died on 16 August 1917 and is buried in Tilloy British

Cemetery, two miles south-east of the town of Arras, suggesting that he may have been wounded and evacuated to that town.

Gordon also served throughout the war, initially in the Royal Field Artillery and then the Army Service Corps. He survived, emigrating to Canada in 1924 and dying there in 1966.

Albert Lingard RAGIN
Trumpeter, 33821, 86 Heavy Battery, Royal Garrison Artillery who died on 21 August 1916, aged 19. Buried in Baghdad (North Gate) War Cemetery, Iraq

Born on 04 September 1896 in Portsmouth, Hampshire, the youngest of three children of John Edward Ragin and Louisa Patty Ann née Lingard, his father had been a Band Lance Corporal in The Princess Charlotte of Wales's (Royal Berkshire Regiment), having previously served in The King's Own (Royal Lancaster Regiment), although he had retired from the army on 27 January 1885 and died in Portsmouth on 01 September 1904.

At the time that Albert's Petition Document was completed by his mother, on 16 November 1904, his older brother, Edward Louis Ragin, was serving as a Private in The Hampshire Regiment.

Albert was admitted to the school on 01 December 1905 (Petition No. 12167) and having made the transition from Chelsea to Guston, was discharged to the Royal Garrison Artillery on 23 September 1910.

Albert's service record is no longer available, although he is shown in the 1911 Census as a Boy stationed in No.4 Depot of the Royal Garrison Artillery in the Royal Artillery Barracks, Great Yarmouth, Norfolk. The lack of service record also means that it is not known with which units Albert served prior to being posted to 86 Heavy Battery, Royal Garrison Artillery, although his medal index card states that his first entry to theatre was when he entered the Asiatic Theatre on 10 March 1915.

At the outbreak of war, 86 Heavy Battery was stationed in Multan, India, as part of the 3rd (Lahore) Division, but was mobilised and sent to Europe as part of Indian Expeditionary Force "A", arriving in September 1914.

The division fought on the Western Front during 1915, participating in the Battles of Neuve Chapelle, St. Julien, Aubers and Festubert, but beginning in December 1915, the division was withdrawn from France and relocated to Mesopotamia, the Headquarters being established in January 1916 and the division coming under the command of the Tigris Corps, whose aim was to relieve the troops besieged at Kut al Amara.

At some point during the advance to relieve the siege at Kut al Amara, Albert was captured by the Ottoman Forces and transported to a prisoner of war camp in Turkey.

Albert died in captivity, likely from enteric fever at Yarbaschi Hospital, on 21 August 1916. He is buried in Baghdad (North Gate) War Cemetery, but this would have happened post-war, when this cemetery was enlarged with the addition of those who were buried in cemeteries in Anatolia, where Commonwealth prisoners of war were buried by the Turks.

Albert is commemorated on the memorial tablets in the school chapel, but he is incorrectly recorded as W L Ragin.

Thomas Martin RYAN

Battery Serjeant Major, 604, Ammunition Sub Park, 327 Siege Battery, Royal Garrison Artillery who died on 04 April 1918, aged 32. Commemorated on the Pozieres Memorial, Somme, France

Born on 31 July 1885 in Aldershot, Hampshire, the second of eleven children of John Joseph Ryan and Agnes Annie née Wilson, his father was a Staff Quartermaster Serjeant in the Army Service Corps.

Thomas was admitted to the school on 24 September 1896 (Petition No. 10939), and despite being one of five sons, appears to be the only one to have attended the school. He was discharged to the Royal Artillery on 29 July 1899.

Thomas's service record is no longer available, so his career from 1899 to 1911 is unknown, but the 1911 Census shows that he was a Bombardier with No. 93 Company, Royal Garrison Artillery, stationed in Echelon Barracks, Colombo, Ceylon[94].

It is also not known when Thomas entered theatre after the commencement of the war, but as his medal index card shows that he was not entitled to the award of a 1914-15 Star, it must have been 1916 at the earliest. Records do show that his Military Service Region prior to deployment was Ireland, but it is not known with which unit he was serving.

By April 1918, Thomas was the Battery Serjeant Major of 327 Siege Battery's Ammunition Sub Park, where ammunition was stored prior to it being supplied to the guns. The battery had landed at Le Havre on 13 May 1917, but there is no diary available to enable its movements and actions to be followed.

It is also not known for certain whether Thomas's death was the result of an accident, disease or due to action during the German Spring Offensive, which had been launched fourteen days earlier, but

---

[94] Modern-day Sri Lanka

he died on 04 April 1918. The Registers of Soldiers' Effects[95] does record his death as *"in action"* and it would appear that his body was lost, as he is commemorated on the Pozieres Memorial.

Although commemorated on the memorial tablets in the school chapel, he is incorrectly commemorated as T M Bryan.

Ernest Percival SADLER
Staff Serjeant, 5871, Royal Garrison Artillery attached Indian Ordnance Department who died on 24 November 1919, aged 33. Commemorated on the Delhi Memorial (India Gate), India

Born on 17 September 1886 in Thayetmyo, Burma, the eldest of five children of Frederick Sadler and Ellen née Gilbert, his father was a Company Serjeant Major in the Royal Artillery and was serving in Seaforth, Lancashire, when he died on 25 July 1895.

Ernest was admitted to the school six months later, on 31 January 1896 (Petition No. 10854), being joined two years later by one of his younger brothers, Horace Cecil Sadler, on 04 March 1898 (Petition No. 11133) and by his youngest brother, Eustace Reginald Sadler, on 08 September 1899 (Petition No. 11339).

Ernest was discharged from the school on 22 September 1900, enlisting into the Royal Garrison Artillery on the same day, spending his first two years of service in Britain, and appearing in the 1901 Census as a Boy in the Royal Garrison Artillery, stationed in Dover Castle. Ernest's first overseas posting was to St. Helena, in the South Atlantic in December 1902, the same month that he was appointed as a Trumpeter, and where he remained for just over a year, before being posted to South Africa in January 1904, then appointed as an acting Bombardier the following year.

After five years in South Africa, during which he was promoted to Bombardier in 1908, Ernest returned to Britain in April 1909. He completed his 12 years of service in 1912, but re-engaged to complete 21 years and was then posted to India. Once in India, Ernest was attached to the Indian Ordnance Department on 28 March 1914, being promoted first to Serjeant and then Staff Serjeant two years later on 28 March 1916.

Ernest's service record shows that he served with the Mesopotamia Expeditionary Force from 05 July 1916 until 11 December 1918, suggesting that he would have been involved in the capture of Baghdad in March 1917 and the Battle of Sharqat in October 1918, which forced the Ottoman surrender.

He then returned to India, and was part of the North-West Frontier Force from 06 May 1919, participating in the conflict in

---

[95] UK, Army Registers of Soldiers' Effects, 1901-1929, 1914-1915, Dover, 670001-671500

Waziristan and qualifying for that clasp on his India General Service Medal.

Ernest died of bronchopneumonia in Dardoni Hospital in the north-west of British India[96] and was buried in Bannu Cemetery. This cemetery was abandoned by the Commonwealth War Graves Commission in the 1950s[97] and so he is now commemorated on the Delhi Memorial.

The Commonwealth War Graves Commission Certificate of Commemoration for Ernest[98] states that he was twice Mentioned in Despatches, however, there is no record of this within his service record and it has only been possible to find a Gazette entry for one of these[99].

Although it clearly states in his service record that Ernest attended the school, he is another of the "Lost Boys" whose name has been omitted from the memorial tablets in the school chapel.

Both of Ernest's brothers enlisted into the Royal Garrison Artillery when they were discharged from the school, Horace on 01 March 1902 and Eustace on 30 July 1903, and both boys served on the Western Front.

Horace deployed to France on 08 March 1915 and finished the war as a Warrant Officer Class II. According to one school history[100], he was also Mentioned in Despatches, although the Gazette entry cannot be found. After the war, he married Catherine Alice Forrest in 1920 and in 1939 he was recorded as living in Chislehurst, Kent, employed as a Railway Police Passenger Inspector & Special Constable for the London Midland & Scottish Railway. He died in Bromley, Kent, on 23 August 1957.

Eustace deployed to France on 14 October 1914 and finished the war as a Serjeant. He married Ethel Mary Bury in 1919 and was recorded in 1939 as living in Lewisham and employed as a Second Keeper for London County Council. He died in Christchurch, Hampshire, in 1973.

---

[96] Now Pakistan
[97] CWGC - Records of the Commonwealth War Graves Commission, Governance and Corporate Planning, Commission Meeting Minutes, Commission Meeting Minute Files: CWGC/2/2/1/320, WG 1831/262, Commission Meeting No.320 - November 1949
[98] Incorrectly recording his name as Ernest Perceval Sadler
[99] *The London Gazette*, 30 July 1920, Supplement:32002
[100] Rudd, L. (1935). *The Duke of York's Royal Military School 1801-1934: Its History, Aims and Associations.* Dover: G. W. Grigg and Son, St. George's Press

Gordon TRUETT

Trumpeter, 37577, No. 32 Company, Royal Garrison Artillery who died on 21 May 1915, aged 16. Buried in Sandown (Christ Church) Churchyard, Isle of Wight, United Kingdom

Born on 18 July 1898 in Gibraltar, the fourth of six children of William Joseph Robert Truett and Mary Ann Hester née Clamp, his father was a Bombardier in the Royal Artillery and was serving at Parkhurst Camp, Isle of Wight, when he died on 12 February 1907.

Gordon was admitted to the school six months after his father's death, on 31 August 1907 (Petition No. 12389) and having moved from Chelsea to Guston and appearing in the 1911 Census at the school, he was discharged into the Royal Garrison Artillery on 16 August 1912.

Gordon's service record is no longer available, so his army career prior to 1915 is not known. However, in that year, he was part of No. 32 Company, Royal Garrison Artillery, which was stationed in Culver (Sandown), Isle of Wight, as part of the Southern Coast Defences.

Gordon Truett died on 21 May 1915 in Parkhurst Military Hospital, Isle of Wight. His cause of death is not known, but it does not appear to be service-related as he did not deploy overseas. He is also another "Lost Boy" whose name is omitted from the memorial tablets in the school chapel.

Albert Edward Easter URELL

Boy, 101758, No. 1 Depot, Royal Garrison Artillery who died on 16 August 1918, aged 16. Buried in Cannock Chase War Cemetery, Staffordshire, United Kingdom

Born on 23 May 1902 in Hythe, Kent, the second of four children of Henry James Albert Urell and Laura Catherine Eliza née White, his father had been a Bandsman in both the 14th (King's) Hussars and 7th (Queen's Own) Hussars, but had left the army and was unemployed at the time of Albert's admission to the school.

Albert was admitted to the school on 08 January 1913 (Petition No. 13081) and having moved to Hutton when the school was evacuated, was discharged to the Royal Garrison Artillery on 04 July 1916, being posted to No 1 Depot (Heavy and Siege) in Derby, Derbyshire. However, he was only there for eight months before he was admitted to the military hospital in Rugeley, Staffordshire, on 31 March 1917, with pain and swelling of his left thigh. This was later diagnosed as osteomyelitis, and in the days prior to antibiotics, was difficult to treat. Albert never left hospital and died as a result of the infection more than a year later.

Although commemorated by the Commonwealth War Graves Commission and buried in Cannock Chase War Cemetery, Albert is a "Lost Boy" whose name has been omitted from the memorial tablets in the school chapel.

Corps of Royal Engineers

John Charles ATKEY
2nd Corporal, 7648, 15 Field Company, Royal Engineers who died on 25 October 1915, aged 28. Buried in Sailly-Sur-La-Lys Canadian Cemetery, Pas de Calais, France

Born on 29 January 1887 in Sheffield, Yorkshire West Riding, the third child of John Charles Atkey, and his second wife, Harriet née Long, his father had been a Corporal Collar Maker in the Royal Artillery, but died from an aortic aneurysm whilst serving in Aldershot, Hampshire, on 03 April 1890 and it then appears that John, his mother and two sisters returned to Sheffield.

John was admitted to the school on 07 January 1898 (Petition No. 11118), remaining there until 04 February 1901, when he enlisted into the Royal Engineers. John served the first four years as a Bugler, mostly in Malta, before returning to Chatham, Kent, in December 1904 and being promoted to Sapper in January 1905.

Later that year he was stationed in Gosport, Hampshire, and seemed to be doing well with his trade training, receiving regular increases in his Good Conduct pay. However, in August of that year, John was arrested and subsequently convicted of stealing a live lame duck, which resulted in a ten shilling fine from the magistrates, and, within the army, the loss of one Good Conduct Badge and forfeiture of his Good Conduct pay.

Despite this, John continued to pass his various trade courses, and in 1912, whilst stationed in Edinburgh and a year before the end of his initial 12 years of service was completed, he was re-engaged for a further nine years' service, being appointed to Lance Corporal in November 1913, and Acting Corporal in September 1914.

Unlike many soldiers, when war broke out John was not immediately posted to France, remaining in Britain until April 1915, when he was posted from 49 (Fortress) Company, Royal Engineers to 15 (Field) Company, reverting to Lance Corporal when he did so.

Two months after arrival in France, John was promoted to Acting 2nd Corporal[101], being made substantive just under a month later.

---

[101] Second Corporal was a rank within the Royal Engineers and Army Ordnance Corps. The insignia was one chevron, like Lance Corporal, but was considered full Non-Commissioned

Despite being given a severe reprimand for neglect of duty in September 1915, John did not suffer a demotion, and was still a 2nd Corporal when he died of wounds in 26 Field Ambulance on 25 October 1915.

John is buried in Sailly-Sur-La-Lys Canadian Cemetery, so called because it was begun by Canadian units in March 1915 and was used as a front-line cemetery until July 1916.

Arthur BARBER DCM

Serjeant, 7602, 3 Field Squadron, Royal Engineers who died on 15 May 1915, aged 28. Commemorated on the Ypres (Menin Gate) Memorial, West-Vlaanderen, Belgium

Born on 20 January 1887 in Lambeth, Surrey, the youngest of five children of John Barber and Sarah née Turner, his father had been a Corporal in the Royal Engineers who had been discharged from the army on 23 September 1885. He died in Farnham, Surrey, on 10 December 1894, which was ten days after Arthur's mother had died.

Arthur was admitted to the school eighteen months after he had been orphaned, on 09 July 1896 (Petition No. 10903), remaining there for five years, until 29 January 1901. Three days prior to discharge, on 26 January 1901, Arthur enlisted into the Royal Engineers, where he was to become a skilled carpenter.

In March 1902, Arthur was posted to Gibraltar, remaining there for eighteen months, returning to Britain in December 1903, where he remained until the start of the war and marrying Beatrice Elizabeth Perkins in Hartley Wintney, Hampshire, on 24 December 1910. His son Arthur Frederick John Barber was born almost a year later on 12 November 1911 and by this stage Arthur was a 2nd Corporal.

Arthur completed his first period of service on 25 January 1913 and was discharged in Aldershot, although he signed on again the following day for a further four years' service.

A month after the outbreak of war, Arthur was promoted to Corporal, deploying to France a month after that, on 04 October 1914 and serving with 3 Field Squadron, Royal Engineers, with whom he served for the remainder of his war.

The day after arriving in France, he was appointed an Acting Serjeant, although a month later he reverted to Corporal at his own request, before being appointed again to Acting Serjeant in February 1915. It was also in 1915 that Arthur's actions resulted in his being

---

Officer rank, unlike Lance Corporal, which was an appointment, and therefore the equivalent of a Bombardier in the Royal Regiment of Artillery

awarded the Distinguished Conduct Medal[102], during which he was wounded.

It is unlikely that Arthur was aware of the award of the Distinguished Conduct Medal as, two days after the actions for which it was awarded, the Adjutant of 4th Battalion, The East Yorkshire Regiment, reported that he had died of wounds and had been *"buried in a field near the road at Wittepoort Farm"*[103].

Sadly, the site of this was lost and he has no known grave, being one of more than 54,000 remembered on the Menin Gate. Arthur is also one of the "Lost Boys" whose name has been omitted from the memorial tablets in the school chapel.

Terence John BRIGGS

2nd Corporal, 29916, 2 (Independent) Field Squadron, Royal Engineers who died on 13 October 1916, aged 30. Buried in A.I.F. Burial Ground, Flers, Somme, France

Born on 10 April 1886 in Grantham, Lincolnshire, the youngest of three children of John Briggs and Mary Elizabeth née Matthews, his mother died when he was less than two years old, on 04 December 1887, in Skillington, Lincolnshire. His father had been a Private in the 22nd (the Cheshire) Regiment of Foot[104] who had been discharged to pension after 21 years' service on 30 May 1881 and who also died in Skillington, on 11 January 1897.

Terence was admitted to the school on 13 July 1897 (Petition No. 11041) and was discharged on 21 April 1900, enlisting into the Royal Engineers on the same day. Terence was appointed as a Trumpeter on 13 December 1901, but once he was eighteen, he was posted the ranks as a Driver in 57 Company, Royal Engineers, on 21 April 1904.

On 14 October 1905, he was posted to South Africa with that company, but was posted to 55 Field Company, Royal Engineers on 21 April 1906 and was still serving in this unit when he was recorded in the 1911 Census as a Driver, stationed in Roberts Heights, Transvaal, South Africa.

Terence was then transferred to 9 Field Company, Royal Engineers, on 25 December 1911, although he did not join that unit until 16 January 1912, four days before he returned to Britain, where

---

[102] *The London Gazette*, 3 August 1915, Supplement:29252: *"For great gallantry and resource on the night of 12th-13th May, 1915, near Ypres. Corporal Barber handled his working parties with great ability and courage when digging a communication trench from the firing line to the rear under heavy fire"*.

[103] WO 363: War Office: Soldiers' Documents, First World War 'Burnt Documents' (Microfilm Copies), 1914-1920, The National Archives, Kew - First World War Service Records 'Burnt Documents'

[104] Renamed The Cheshire Regiment on 01 July 1881

he spent the last four months of this period of service before he was discharged from the army having completed 12 years' service on 22 May 1912.

Following his discharge from the army, little is known about Terence, but it would appear that following the outbreak of war, he was either recalled to the Colours or re-enlisted. However, there is no service record available for this second period of service, so it is not possible to follow his movements in the early years of the war.

By October 1916, he was an Acting 2nd Corporal and serving with "C" Troop, 2 (Independent) Field Squadron, Royal Engineers, and located in the area of Fricourt, Somme. At 0830hrs on 13 October 1916, "C" Troop was tasked to work on dugouts for 76th Brigade, Royal Field Artillery. The squadron diary[105] records that *"a/2nd Cpl Briggs C Troop killed by shell in trench near 76th Bde HQ"*.

Although his body was recovered and he was buried in a marked grave, Terence is another "Lost Boy" whose name has been omitted from the memorial tablets in the school chapel.

Hugh Charles CASTON
Company Serjeant Major, 231, Kent Fortress Company, Royal Engineers who died on 18 June 1917, aged 35. Buried in Gillingham (Grange Road) Cemetery, Kent, United Kingdom

Born on 18 August 1881 in Chelsea, London, the son of Hugh Edwin Caston and Emily née Evans, his father was a Corporal in the Royal Engineers, but died whilst still serving in Portsmouth, Hampshire, on 02 August 1885.

Hugh was admitted to the school on 25 March 1892 (Petition No. 10310) and discharged to his father's old corps on 01 August 1896, being appointed as a Bugler on 01 June 1897 and posted to the ranks as a Sapper on 01 August 1899.

Hugh spent the majority of his army career stationed in Britain, although in May 1902 he was posted to Malta, by which time he was a 2nd Corporal, returning to Britain in February 1904. Three years later on 25 September 1907, he married Mary May Coast in Hollingbourne, Kent, by this time being a Serjeant Instructor. This was also the same year that he re-engaged in the army to complete 21 years' service.

By the following year he and his wife were living in Smethwick, Staffordshire, their first child, Hubert Charles Edwin Caston, being born there in 1908. Sadly, Hubert died in infancy. Their second child, Joan Caston, was also born in Smethwick in 1910.

---

[105] WO 95/1182/4: 2 Field Squadron Royal Engineers, 1915 Feb. - 1916 Dec., The National Archives, Kew

Two months after the outbreak of war, on 01 October 1914, Hugh was promoted to Acting Company Sergeant Major and posted to the Kent Fortress Company, Royal Engineers, stationed in Chatham, Kent.

However, on 12 January 1915, Hugh had a breakdown. According to a local newspaper[106], he had gone to a house to pay the owner some billeting money, but when he had found the house unoccupied, he ransacked it and stole items, offering the police who arrested him a sovereign[107] to let him off.

Hugh was admitted to the Royal Victoria Hospital, Netley, on 20 January 1915, where he was diagnosed as "insane", his medical notes describing a "total incapacity" and recording delusions that he was about to be promoted to the rank of Major and wanted to provide Egyptian cigarettes to all the other patients. Although his behaviour whilst serving had been "Exemplary", Hugh was discharged from the army as permanently unfit on 02 February 1915 and he died in Dartford, Kent, on 18 June 1917.

It is possible that Hugh is a "Lost Boy" whose name has been omitted from the memorial tablets in the school chapel because of the fact that he had been discharged from the army by the time of his death, but he has been commemorated by the Commonwealth War Graves Commission, and therefore should be commemorated in the school.

William John CURTIS MM & Bar

Serjeant, 112222, "H" Special Company, Royal Engineers who died on 07 June 1918, aged 23. Buried in Etretat Churchyard Extension, Seine-Maritime, France

Born on 11 May 1895 in Shoreham, Sussex, the third of nine children of William John Curtis and his second wife, Janet Mercy née Ballantyne, his father also had three children from his first marriage. He had been a Serjeant Major in The Prince Consort's Own Rifle Brigade and the 87th (Royal Irish Fusiliers) Regiment of Foot, and had been discharged to pension on 31 March 1874.

William, known as Jack, was admitted to the school on 07 April 1905 (Petition No. 12096) and discharged to The Princess Victoria's (Royal Irish Fusiliers) on 22 February 1909, the 1911 Census showing that he was serving with the 1st Battalion of that regiment and stationed in St. Lucia Barracks, Bordon, Hampshire.

---

[106] *Kent Messenger & Gravesend Telegraph*, Saturday 23 January 1915
[107] Worth £1 in 1915, approximately £65.00 in modern money

At the outbreak of war, the battalion was stationed in Shorncliffe, Kent, moving first to York, Yorkshire North Riding, and then Harrow, Middlesex, before embarking on the SS *Lake Michigan* at Southampton, Hampshire, on 22 August and landing at Boulogne on 23 August 1914.

The battalion was then moved to Le Cateau, where it participated in that battle, suffering heavy losses, as well as participating in the Battles of the Marne, the Aisne and Messines. By November, the battalion was in the area of Armentières and on the 28 November it was in trenches. Its support line was shelled by the Germans and Jack was one of those wounded, suffering a chest injury that damaged his lungs.

After a period of recuperation, in June 1915 Jack transferred to the Royal Engineers. It is not known with which units he served between his transfer and 1917, but by the latter year he was serving with "H" Special Company, Royal Engineers.

The Special Companies had been formed in July 1915 and employed technically skilled men who would deal with the new British weapon, poison gas. These men would handle gas discharged from cylinders as well as firing gas shells from Stokes mortars[108]. Four special sections were also formed to use flamethrowers.

On 07 October 1917, Jack was appointed as a Serjeant and two days later, although the reason is not stated, he was awarded a Military Medal[109].

It is not documented when the award was made, or the reason for it, but during 1918 Jack was awarded a Bar to his Military Medal[110], although it is not known whether William was aware of this award.

On 28 May, the billets in which the company was stationed were shelled. William was one of the two other ranks wounded, sustaining a back injury and was evacuated to No. 1 General Hospital in Étretat, twenty miles north-east of Le Havre, where he died of his wounds on 07 June 1918 and was buried in the town. Although he is commemorated in the school chapel, he is incorrectly named as Curtiss.

Jack's younger brother, Douglas Ivo, was also a Dukie, admitted to the school on 27 October 1915 (Petition No. 13436) and discharged to the Royal Engineers on 08 April 1920. He died in Manitoba, Canada in 1976.

---

[108] A British trench mortar designed by Sir Wilfred Stokes KBE
[109] *The London Gazette*, 11 December 1917, Supplement:30424
[110] *The London Gazette*, 4 October 1918, Supplement:30940

Rupert John DAVIS
Quartermaster Serjeant, 1308, Establishment for Engineers' Service, Royal Engineers who died on 25 September 1917, aged 33. Buried in Plymouth (Ford Park) Cemetery, Devon, United Kingdom

Born on 16 October 1883 in Plymouth, Devonshire, the youngest of four children of James Davis and Jane Elizabeth née Matthews, his father was a Gunner in the Royal Artillery who was still serving when he died in Plymouth on 25 September 1890.

Rupert was admitted to the school on 06 July 1894 (Petition No. 10620) and was discharged to the Royal Engineers on 15 October 1897. A year after enlisting, he was appointed as a Bugler, being sent to South Africa for service during the Second Boer War in 1899, and although it is not certain where he served on his return from that country, he was appointed as a Lance Corporal on 11 January 1903.

Four years later, Rupert was promoted to Engineering Clerk Sergeant, and was again promoted on 16 September 1910, to Engineering Clerk Staff Serjeant. In 1911, Rupert was stationed in the British Headquarters in Alexandria, Egypt, but it appears that he was posted back to Britain prior to the outbreak of the war, being promoted to Engineering Clerk Quartermaster Serjeant on 16 September 1913 and spending the first two years of the war in that role.

On 12 September 1916, Rupert was posted to Sierra Leone, arriving twelve days later. At the time that Rupert was posted to Sierra Leone, the conflict between the British and German Colonial troops in West Africa had ended, but it is likely that, due to his trade, he was part of a unit that was carrying out engineering tasks to improve infrastructure in the difficult terrain of this area.

It seems likely that Rupert succumbed to disease whilst in Sierra Leone, as he was sent back to Britain on 03 September 1917 and it also seems probable that on arrival on 15 September he was admitted to hospital.

Rupert died from tuberculosis in the Seaforth Auxiliary Hospital, Dingle, Merseyside, ten days after returning, on 25 September 1917. His body was returned to the city of his birth and he was interred in Ford Park Cemetery in Plymouth.

Whilst Rupert is commemorated on the memorial tablets in the school chapel, he is incorrectly commemorated as R J Davies.

Thomas William GOODALL

Trumpeter, 25598, Training Depot Royal Engineers who died on 26 September 1916, aged 16. Buried in Fort Pitt Military Cemetery, Kent, United Kingdom

Born on 31 October 1899 in Warwick, Warwickshire, the second of three children of Thomas William Goodall and Clara Emma née Snelling, his father had been a Private in The Royal Warwickshire Regiment who was discharged from the army at the end of his period of engagement on 20 August 1897. He died in Warwick on 17 September 1901.

Thomas was admitted to the school on 16 November 1910 (Petition No. 12829) and after three years, was discharged to the Royal Engineers on 28 November 1913. Thomas spent his first year of service in Britain, but following the outbreak of war, he deployed to France, arriving in theatre on 20 August 1914, although his service record does not state with which unit he was serving.

Again, there is limited information on his movements during 1914, but it is recorded that in January 1915 he was on horseback when his right knee was caught between his horse and a stretcher that was protruding from an ambulance wagon, which resulted in an injury severe enough that he was evacuated back to Britain.

He was admitted to North Easington War Hospital, Leicester, Leicestershire, on 20 May 1915 with *"synovitis[111] of knee"* and was discharged from the army as no longer physically fit for service two months later, on 03 July 1915. He was not yet sixteen years old.

Thomas underwent an amputation of his right leg and never fully recovered from the infection, dying on 26 September 1916. A contemporary report[112] recorded the occasion of his funeral:

"*A TRUMPETER'S FUNERAL.*

LAD WHO WENT THROUGH MONS RETREAT.

A pathetic funeral was witnessed at Chatham yesterday, when a party of forty young trumpeters of the R.E. attended the interment of the remains of a comrade, Trumpeter T. W. Goodall. The lad passed from the Duke of York's School at the age of fourteen, and joined the R.E. in November 1913. He went out with the original Expeditionary Force, and met with an accident in the retreat from Mons. He was invalided home, and had his right leg amputated, and he died after a lingering illness. He was not quite seventeen years of age. The trumpeters sounded "The Last Post" over the grave of their comrade."

---

[111] Inflammation
[112] *Pall Mall Gazette,* 5 October 1916

Thomas was interred in Fort Pitt Military Cemetery in Rochester, Kent, and despite his discharge from the army more than a year previously, he has been commemorated by the Commonwealth War Graves Commission. However, he is one of the "Lost Boys" whose name has been omitted from the memorial tablets in the school chapel.

Frederick Martin GRAYDON
Captain, Headquarters Staff, Inland Water Transport, Royal Engineers who died on 18 September 1920, aged 29. Buried in Basra War Cemetery, Iraq

Born on 31 January 1891 in Exeter, Devonshire, the third of five children of Henry Richard Graydon and Rosa Ann née McConville, his father was a Private in The Devonshire Regiment who died of enteric fever whilst on active service at Chieveley, Natal, South Africa, during the Second Boer War.

Frederick was admitted to the school on 09 May 1901 (Petition No. 11538) and was *"Struck off strength"* having been detained on pass on 03 February 1905.

Little is known about Frederick after he left the school, although he is recorded in the 1911 Census as living in Devonport, Devonshire, with his mother and sister, Maude Lavinia Graydon, and employed as an Electrical Engineer's Labourer in the Devonport Dockyard.

Frederick's service record is not easily accessible, but it possible that he was at some point Commissioned into the Royal Indian Marine[113], as a Sub-Lieutenant Frederick Grayson was promoted to Temporary Lieutenant in this service[114], stating that this was for service in the Inland Water Transport, Grayson being corrected to Graydon in a later publication[115]. However, his original Commission information cannot be found in *The London Gazette*.

It is also known that he was promoted from Temporary Lieutenant to Temporary Captain on 01 April 1918[116] and Mentioned in Despatches in 1919[117].

His medal index card is also unavailable, so it is not possible to ascertain at what point Frederick entered theatre, or whether he actually did see any active service during the First World War, but what is known is that after the war, he was located in Mesopotamia and serving with the Inland Water Transport, Royal Engineers,

---

[113] The precursor to the Royal India Navy which was led by British Officers
[114] *The London Gazette*, 16 October 1917, Supplement: 30339
[115] *The London Gazette*, 5 April 1918, Supplement:30617
[116] *The London Gazette*, 21 June 1918, Supplement:30763
[117] *The London Gazette*, 18 February 1919, Supplement:31195

when he contracted malaria, which resulted in his death in the Officers' Hospital at Basra in September 1920.

Frederick was buried in Basra War Cemetery and commemorated by the Commonwealth War Graves Commission, but he is another of the "Lost Boys" whose name has been omitted from the memorial tablets in the school chapel.

Lewis Albert HOWELL

Serjeant, 14422, "B" Reserve Company, Special Brigade Depot, Royal Engineers who died on 25 July 1917, aged 27. Buried in Southampton (Hollybrook) Cemetery, Hampshire, United Kingdom

Born on 09 January 1890 in Netley, Hampshire, the son of William Howell and Elizabeth Eliza née Casey. His mother died in Jersey, Channel Islands on 08 September 1898, and his father, who was a Private in the Royal Army Medical Corps, died on active service in Wynberg, South Africa, which was where the Field Hospital was located during the Second Boer War, on 03 October 1900.

Prior to his death, William had petitioned for Lewis to be admitted to the school, which he was, a month after his father's death, on 09 November 1900 (Petition No. 11499), remaining at the school until he was discharged to the Royal Engineers on 21 January 1905.

Lewis's service record has not survived, nor does he appear in the 1911 Census. However, it is known that he served in France during the war as he is recorded as being a Serjeant in 59 Field Company, Royal Engineers and an in-patient in No. 11 General Hospital in Boulogne. The cause of this admission is not given.

In 1917, Lewis was located on Salisbury Plain, Wiltshire, with "B" Reserve Company, Special Brigade Depot, Royal Engineers. Late on the evening of 24 July 1917, he was admitted to Salisbury Infirmary, where he died just over an hour later. An inquest at Larkhill, Wiltshire, two days later was recorded in *The Salisbury Times*:

> *"In this case the unfortunate victim was Sergt. Louis Albert Howell, of the Royal Engineers, aged 27, and engaged at an experimental ground in the district in the work of destroying unexploded bombs and explosives. From the evidence of his officer, Lieut J Macleish, RE, it appeared that the sergeant was missed on Tuesday evening and a search party found him practically unconscious huddled up in a "crater." He was terribly injured. Witness thought he was dead but he moved slightly when spoken to.*
> *Subsequently he was taken to the Infirmary. He must have been close to the explosion which occurred and which was probably of a number of bags of explosives, but no one heard or saw anything of it.*

Miss D'Abreu, the house surgeon at the Infirmary, said the sergeant was admitted about 11.30 on Tuesday night and died about 12.45. She detailed his terrible injuries, which included the loss of both hands, damage to the sight, chest and legs.

The jury returned a verdict of "death from an explosion, probably the result of an accident".

Lewis Howell is buried in Southampton (Hollybrook) Cemetery, although he does not have a "traditional" Commonwealth War Graves Commission headstone and is commemorated on the memorial tablets in the school chapel.

Alfred LUNN

2nd Corporal, 13867, 7 Signal Company, Royal Engineers who died on 08 October 1917, aged 28. Buried in Bletchley Cemetery, Buckinghamshire, United Kingdom

Born on 02 June 1889 in Greenwich, Kent, the fifth of nine children of John Cocker Lunn and Eliza née Hyde, his father had been a Farrier Sergeant in the Army Service Corps and was discharged to pension on 05 December 1888.

Alfred was admitted to the school on 13 January 1899 (Petition No. 11258), joining his older brother, Herbert James Lunn, who had been admitted on 09 July 1896 (Petition No. 10902). Alfred remained in the school until 13 June 1904, when he was discharged to the Royal Engineers. A year after Herbert was discharged, their younger brother, Frank Lunn, was also admitted to the school, on 10 October 1902 (Petition No. 11745).

The 1911 Census records Alfred was a 2nd Corporal serving with 7 Division Telegraph Company, Royal Engineers and stationed in Roberts Heights, Transvaal, South Africa. He was a Telegraphist by trade, although his place of birth in the census is incorrectly recorded as Colchester, Essex.

Due to his service record being unavailable, Alfred's wartime movements are unknown, but his medal index card shows that at the outbreak of war he was a Lance Corporal with 7 Signal Company, Royal Engineers, and that he entered theatre on 04 October 1914.

In 1916, he was serving in the Fenny Stratford Signal Depot Royal Engineers in Buckinghamshire and married Laura May Souster in the town in September 1916. However, in 1917 he became ill and was admitted to Murthly Hospital in Perthshire. During the First World War, Perth District Asylum was used as a war hospital, offering beds for 350 other ranks. It was also used as a Military Psychiatric Hospital from 1917 to 1919.

Alfred Lunn died in the hospital of "Exhaustion from stupor", likely a form of Post-Traumatic Stress Disorder, on 08 October 1917, and was buried in Bletchley, Buckinghamshire, not far from where he had married in Fenny Stratford.

Alfred is another "Lost Boy" whose name has been omitted from the memorial tablets in the school chapel, even though he is recorded on the Roll of Honour published in the school magazine[118].

Herbert was discharged from the school on 13 July 1901 and joined the 6th (Inniskilling) Dragoons. He survived the war, dying in Stratford-upon-Avon in 1972.

Frank was discharged from the school on 26 July 1906, joining the Army Service Corps. He also survived the war, but died on 28 October 1923 in Bletchley, Buckinghamshire.

Joseph William MAYCOCK
Sapper, WR/504200, No. 1 Mechanical Unit Inland Water Transport, Royal Engineers who died on 27 June 1918, aged 30. Buried in Bleue-Maison Military Cemetery, Eperlecques, Pas-de-Calais, France

Born on 16 January 1888 in Warwick, Warwickshire, the eighth of nine children of George Maycock and Catherine Charlotte née Dyke, his father had been a Serjeant Major in The Queen's (Royal West Surrey Regiment) who had served for 21 years before he was discharged on 13 July 1888. He died in Southwark, London on 15 May 1891.

Joseph was admitted to the school on 06 March 1897 (Petition No. 11008), a year after his older brother, George Trevor Maycock, who had been admitted on 27 November 1891 (Petition No. 10238), had been discharged. He was joined by his younger brother, Richard Arthur Maycock, on 19 July 1901 (Petition No. 11581). Joseph was discharged on 07 January 1902, but unlike many of his peers, it appears that he did not join the army on discharge, entering service in the East India Club.

Little is known of Joseph's life pre-war, but he is recorded in the 1911 Census living in Coventry and employed as an Engine Tester (motor). It appears that he joined the army after the outbreak of war, by which stage he was living in Partick, Lanarkshire, enlisting in Glasgow on 21 November 1914 into 1 Battery, Motor Machine Gun Service, Royal Field Artillery, giving his occupation as Engineering Fitter. He was then transferred to the Army Service Corps on 19 December 1914 and served in France from 17 February 1915 to 26 July 1915 in a Mechanical Transport Section, before he was discharged on 12 January 1916 as *"no longer physically fit for war service"*

---

[118] *The Chronicle of the Duke of York's Royal Military School*, Vol. VII, No. 12, July 1918

due to defective vision aggravated by the strain of driving on active service. He re-enlisted on 27 November 1916, joining the Inland Water Transport section of the Royal Engineers, which was founded in 1915 to operate barges on the canals of France and Mesopotamia. It was originally stationed in Longmoor Camp, Hampshire, but relocated to Richborough, Kent, in January 1916.

By 1918, the need to transport vast quantities of supplies to the Western Front saw three ferries constantly travelling between Richborough, Calais and Dunkirk. During that year, 4,000 tons of ammunition, 17,818 guns and over 14 million tons of other stores were transported from Britain to France by ferry.

It was soon discovered at Richborough that Joseph had re-enlisted following his previous discharge and a subsequent medical board found in February 1918 that the *"aggravation has now quite passed away"*, but in June 1918 he was admitted to No. 36 Casualty Clearing Station at Watten, reported as being there on 21 June 1918. He died six days later, on 27 June 1918 and was buried in Bleue-Maison Military Cemetery, less than two miles from the site where the Casualty Clearing Station was located.

George had been discharged from the school on 22 February 1896, enlisting into The Royal Warwickshire Regiment. He was killed in action in September 1916, but unlike Joseph, who is a "Lost Boy", George is commemorated on the memorial tablets in the school chapel.

Richard was discharged from the school on 16 March 1906, also entering service. He married in 1916, at which time he was employed as a Red Cross chauffeur. He had disembarked in France on 30 October 1914 with Motor Ambulance Unit No. 2, served in France until 13 October 1915 and again from 15 January 1917 until 04 April 1918. Following the war, nothing more is known of him.

Alexander William PORTER

Sapper, 11676, 11 Field Company, Royal Engineers who died on 16 May 1915, aged 26. Commemorated on the Le Touret Memorial, Pas de Calais, France

Born on 07 September 1888 in Chatham, Kent, the youngest child of William Porter and Minnie Agnes née Wood, his father had been a Colour Serjeant in the 83rd (County of Dublin) Regiment of Foot[119], but was discharged from the army on 10 June 1873. He died in Chatham, Kent, on 12 April 1897.

---

[119] Amalgamated with the 86th (Royal County Down) Regiment of Foot on 01 July 1881 to become The Royal Irish Rifles

173

Alexander was admitted to the school on 12 August 1898 (Petition No. 11204), the second of William's sons to attend, Arthur Charles Mestyr Porter being admitted on 28 November 1884 (Petition No. 9152).

Alexander was discharged from the school on 20 September 1902, enlisting into the Royal Engineers. The 1911 Census shows him as a Sapper, serving with 44 Company, Royal Engineers, and stationed in Jamaica, West Indies. It is likely that by the time war was declared, Alexander had been posted to 11 Field Company, which was stationed in Aldershot, Hampshire, moving to Southampton, Hampshire, on 15 August and landing at Rouen on 16 August 1914.

The company was employed by 23 August in clearing areas and preparing entrenchments, but this work was interrupted with the Engineers reverting to an infantry role, assisting The Princess Charlotte of Wales's (Royal Berkshire Regiment) in the defence of the village of Harmignies and losing three of their pack horses with all the equipment that these were carrying during this action.

As with the rest of the British Expeditionary Force, the company was involved in the long retreat south, often fighting as infantry, and once the British and French forces began to advance on the Germans, it was used to improve the ground on which the British positions were based, as well as improving the trenches.

During the First Battle of Ypres, 11 Field Company was employed in the Ypres Salient and appears to have been the one that prepared dugouts in the front-line positions. By May, it was in the area of La Couture, north-east of Béthune, with sections of the company located in the front-line trenches in order to accompany the attacking infantry and work to "reverse" the captured German trenches during the Battle of Festubert.

On 15 May 1915, these sections accompanied the third wave of the assaulting infantry at 2330hrs, with two lines of German trenches being captured and the company commenced digging communication trenches to the old British front line by midnight. This work continued the following day despite heavy German fire, and it is likely that Alexander Porter was killed by machine-gun fire on 16 May 1915. If his body was recovered and buried, the location of the grave was subsequently lost and he is remembered on the Le Touret Memorial.

Arthur was discharged from the school on 29 January 1887, enlisting into The Northamptonshire Regiment, although he had retired from the army by the time war commenced and did not take part in the conflict.

Albert Charles REES
Sapper, 15195, 55 Company, Royal Engineers who died 03 June 1915, aged 23. Buried at Guards Cemetery, Windy Corner, Cuinchy, Pas de Calais, France

Born on 29 November 1891 in Swindon, Wiltshire, the second of five children of Charles Edward Rees and Eleanor Elizabeth née Ridley, his father had been a Sapper in the Royal Engineers, but had been discharged from the army on 23 November 1895. He died on 09 September 1901 in Kroonstad, Orange Free State, South Africa and his mother died five days later.

Albert was admitted to the school on 06 June 1902 (Petition No. 11702) and discharged on 07 December 1906, enlisting straight into the Royal Engineers, although his service record is no longer available.

When war did break out, 55 Company, Royal Engineers, was stationed in Pretoria, South Africa, but left Cape Town on 27 August, arriving at Southampton, Hampshire, on 20 September. After preparations, including ensuring that it was up to war strength, the company re-embarked on 05 October, landing at Zeebrugge on 07 October 1914.

It was then employed in the Ypres Salient in the build-up to, and during, the First Battle of Ypres, entrenching and improving the front-line positions, as well as improving the barbed wire defences, something that was often difficult due to the proximity of the German trenches.

By January 1915, it was in France, near Fromelles, where it was employed in improving the trenches and defences, digging dug outs and roofing "funk holes", as well as attempting to improve the drainage of the front-line trenches. It was also employed in assisting the "miners" who were digging out into "No-Man's Land" in order to place mines under the German positions.

The company remained in this location during the Battle of Neuve Chapelle, prior to returning to Belgium for the Second Battle of Ypres, and then back to France for the Battles of St. Julien, Aubers and Festubert.

At the beginning of June, 55 Company, Royal Engineers, was sent to Windy Corner, Cuinchy. On the evening of 03 June, it was again at Windy Corner, marching to the location at 1900hrs with orders to improve the communication trenches. However, by the time that it arrived at 2300hrs, 6th Battalion, The Gordon Highlanders, had captured German trenches in front of their position and the orders changed, as the company was now to consolidate the newly captured trenches. One section was sent to wire the new front and with another two sections also employed in improving the new position, one strengthening the captured trench and the other digging a communication trench from the old British front-line. This work continued until dawn, which at that time of the year was 0300hrs. During the course of the night, the company suffered two killed and six wounded, although how these men became casualties is not recorded.

Albert was one of the two killed, dying overnight on 03/04 June 1915. He is buried in the cemetery that is located close to where he was killed.

Albert William ROMAINE
Serjeant, 10151, 1st Reserve Battalion, Royal Engineers who died on 08 November 1918, aged 30. Commemorated on the Special Memorial, Gillingham (Woodlands) Cemetery, Kent, United Kingdom

Born on 11 December 1887 in New Brompton, Kent, the second child of Henry Romaine and Florence Martha née Maynard, his father was a Company Serjeant Major in the Royal Engineers, and died whilst still serving in Devizes, Wiltshire, on 09 March 1896.

Albert was admitted to the school 07 May 1897 (Petition No. 11024) and discharged to the Royal Engineers on 14 December 1901. His service record is no longer available, so it is not possible to follow his postings during his time as a Sapper, other than knowing that he is recorded in the 1911 Census in Tempe, near Bloemfontein, South Africa, as a Draughtsman in 5 Company, Royal Engineers.

It is known that Albert served on the Western Front during the war, as his medal index card shows that, as a 2nd Corporal, he qualified for the 1914 Star on 20 November 1914. Which units he served with whilst in France and Flanders and where he served is not known, but by 1918 he was back in Britain with the rank of Serjeant.

The 1st Reserve Battalion, Royal Engineers, was co-located with the Depot Battalion in Chatham, Kent. It had been organised in August 1914 in order to train new recruits for service overseas and it is likely that Albert was employed as an instructor.

Albert died of illness in Fort Pitt Military Hospital on 08 November 1918, three days before the end of the First World War and is commemorated in Gillingham (Woodlands) Cemetery.

Matthew Henry SCARFF
Sapper, 16336, 5 Field Company, Royal Engineers who died on 14 June 1915, aged 22. Buried in Boulogne Eastern Cemetery, Pas de Calais, France

Born on 12 September 1892 in Chatham, Kent, the third of four children of Matthew Scarff and Charlotte Sarah née Fox, his father was a Mechanical Quartermaster Serjeant in the Royal Engineers who died of pneumonia on 14 July 1903 in Pretoria, South Africa.

Matthew was admitted to the school on 04 December 1903 (Petition No. 11916) and was discharged on 21 September 1906, enlisting into the Royal Engineers[120].

Having been attested as a Boy, Matthew was promoted to Bugler on 22 March 1907 before he was posted to the ranks as a Sapper on 21 September 1910 after he had turned eighteen, at which point he was transferred to the training battalion at Chatham, where he was recorded in the 1911 Census as a Draughtsman. On 06 May 1911 Matthew was posted to 19 Company, Royal Engineers and five months later, on 31 October 1911, to 13 Company, Royal Engineers, with which he was still serving at the outbreak of war.

Seven months after the war commenced, Matthew was posted to 5 Field Company, Royal Engineers, disembarking in France on 21 March 1915, although there is no record in the company diary[121] as to when he actually joined the unit. There is also no record of when he was wounded, although it is possible that he was one of the sixteen Sappers wounded when the company's positions were shelled on 16 May 1915.

What is known is that by the middle of June, Matthew had been evacuated to No. 11 General Hospital in Boulogne, where he died as a result of wounds on 14 June 1915. He is also a "Lost Boy" whose name has been omitted from the memorial tablets in the school chapel.

Victor Edward Alexander STIMPSON
Bugler, 37591, 3rd Hampshire Fortress Company, Royal Engineers who died on 09 August 1918, aged 17. Buried in Portsmouth (Kingston) Cemetery, Hampshire, United Kingdom

Born on 08 July 1901 in Calbourne, Isle of Wight, the youngest of two children of John Edward Stimpson and May Ann née Williams, his father had been a Serjeant in the Royal Engineers who was discharged from the army after 29 years' service on 17 September 1903.

Victor was admitted to the school on 28 June 1912 (Petition No. 12981) and would have moved to Warley, Essex, when the school was evacuated there after the outbreak of war. He was discharged on 30 July 1915 and enlisted into the Royal Engineers.

---

[120] Despite both his birth record and his petition document giving his name as Matthew Henry Scarff, his service record gives his name as Harry Matthew Scarff. However, the service record also confirms that he was a Dukie, and no other Scarff had attended the school before.

[121] WO 95/1330/2: Divisional Troops: 5 Field Company Royal Engineers, 1915 Jan 1 - 1915 Dec 31, The National Archives, Kew

177

Victor's service record is no longer available, so his movements after he enlisted are unknown, but because he was not seventeen until July 1918 and with no medal entitlement, he did not serve overseas during the war. What is known is that in 1918 he was serving with 3rd Hampshire Fortress Company, Royal Engineers and stationed in St. Margaret's Bay, Kent. The Fortress Companies, Royal Engineers, were all employed on coastal defence duties, both in Britain and abroad, some operating searchlights and some having works responsibilities.

Victor was found drowned at St. Margaret's Bay on 09 August 1918, whilst working on a breakwater. His body was returned to Portsmouth for interment and he is commemorated by the Commonwealth War Graves Commission, but he is another "Lost Boy" whose name has been omitted from the memorial tablets in the school chapel.

Royal Flying Corps

William John BURTENSHAW
Serjeant, 239, No. 25 Squadron, Royal Flying Corps who died on 28 April 1917, aged 23. Buried in Lapugnoy Military Cemetery, Pas de Calais, France

Born on 03 August 1893 in Aldershot, Hampshire, the second of three children of William John Burtenshaw and Louisa née Baxter, his father had been a Serjeant in the Royal Engineers and deployed to South Africa with 2 Balloon Section of that corps on 10 June 1899, arriving at Ladysmith on 27 October 1899 and remaining within the besieged town for the next four months. He died of enteric fever on 09 March 1900.

Following William's death, Louisa remarried in 1904, to Sidney Augustus Ridgwell, another Non-Commissioned Officer in the Royal Engineers and also a Dukie, having been at the Royal Military Asylum from 19 November 1880 until 13 January 1883 (Petition No. 8573), so it may have been his idea for William to attend the school.

William was admitted to the school on 05 March 1903 (Petition No. 11806) and was discharged on 03 October 1907, enlisting into the Royal Engineers, and although his service record is no longer available, the 1911 Census records him as a Sapper stationed in the Royal Engineer training establishment at Shornemead Fort, near Gravesend, Kent.

Sometime in 1911 or 1912, William was posted to the Air Battalion, Royal Engineers, which was Britain's fledgling military aircraft unit and on 13 May 1912 he was recorded as an Air Mechanic 1st Class, transferring to the newly formed Royal Flying Corps.

At the outbreak of war, on 06 August 1914, William who was now a Corporal, deployed as an air mechanic to the Aircraft Park, Royal Flying Corps, in Northern France. This was a logistics and repair base configured to provide second-line support to British military aircraft deployed in Royal Flying Corps squadrons in France.

Eighteen months later, on 02 February 1916, he was posted to one of the front-line squadrons, 24 Squadron, Royal Flying Corps, as a mechanic and six months after that, on 27 August 1916, he returned to Britain to undertake pilot training.

He completed his pilot training at the Brooklands Military Pilot Training Centre in Surrey and qualified as a Sergeant Pilot on 24 November 1916. According to his Royal Aero Club Aviator's Certificate, he left Brooklands qualified on the Maurice Farman biplane, also known as the Farman Experimental 2 (FE 2) fighter. This was a twin-seat aircraft, employing a pusher propeller arrangement behind the pilot and the observer gunner was in the forward crew station equipped with two machine-guns.

After his flight training, he was posted to 25 Squadron, Royal Flying Corps and was based at the Lozinghem aerodrome in the Pas de Calais region, where he flew the FE 2b aircraft and he is believed to have claimed two victories from March 1917. His casualty card records that on 28 April 1917 he took an FE 2b for a test flight after some engine servicing and that there was a collision with the topmost branch of a tree on landing, causing him to crash. William died as a result of his injuries in No. 18 Casualty Clearing Station and he was buried in the cemetery at Lapugnoy.

Joseph Charles McNAMARA
Second Lieutenant, No. 4 Squadron, Royal Flying Corps who died on 02 June 1917, aged 30. Commemorated on the Arras Flying Services Memorial, Pas de Calais, France

Born on 31 October 1886 in Pietermaritzburg, South Africa, the second of four children of James O'Reilly Patrick McNamara and Henrietta née Betjeman, his father had been a Colour Serjeant in The Prince of Wales's Volunteers (South Lancashire Regiment) and had been discharged after 18 years' service on 04 September 1888. Following his discharge, his father had been appointed as Inspector of the 1st Perak Sikhs[122] and died in Taiping, China, on 18 June 1894.

Joseph was admitted to the school on 31 January 1896 and *"Detained on Pass"* on 11 August 1900. He is recorded in the 1901 Census as living with his mother and older brother, James John Henry McNamara, in Plymouth, Devonshire, employed as an Errand Boy, although a local newspaper in February of that year reported him on remand for stealing items whilst working at the Army & Navy Stores in Plymouth, employment he had commenced

---

[122] This unit was formed in 1885 from the paramilitary Perak Armed Police and recruited mostly Sikhs and Pashtuns in the Malay State. It was used as a policing and security unit in Perak and was also used to quell civil unrest, suppress criminal activity and combat the violent feuding of Chinese secret societies

in September 1900; he was lectured by the Magistrate and the charges were dropped, on condition of a six-month good behaviour bond with his mother[123]. Little is known about Joseph for the next few years, but on 11 July 1910 he enlisted into the Royal Engineers in Devonport, Devonshire and is recorded in the 1911 Census as a Sapper, employed as an Engine Driver and stationed in Brompton Barracks, Chatham, Kent.

On 26 June 1912, Joseph transferred to the Royal Flying Corps and was appointed as a 1st Class Air Mechanic, obtaining his Royal Aero Club Certificate a year later on 13 March 1913, which enabled him to fly, being graded as a 2nd Class Flyer. He was promoted to Serjeant soon after, on 07 July 1913.

Prior to the outbreak of war, Joseph married Lillian Rosa Mullins, on 04 April 1914 in Newton Abbot, Devonshire and their only child, Joan Gladys McNamara, was born in Pewsey, Wiltshire, in May 1915, by which stage Joseph was a Flight Serjeant, having been promoted on 01 March 1915. Nine months after his daughter's birth, Joseph was deployed to France, disembarking on 19 December 1915 and serving with No. 15 Squadron, Royal Flying Corps.

Eight months after his arrival in France, he was appointed as an acting Warrant Officer on 01 August 1916, prior to returning to Britain on 13 December 1916 in order to undertake the Commissioning course. Having Commissioned, he was appointed as a Flying Officer[124] on 13 April 1917 and returned to France, joining No. 4 Squadron, Royal Flying Corps.

Two months after he joined the squadron on 02 June 1917, he was flying a Royal Aircraft Factory RE8 biplane on a photo-reconnaissance mission with Second Lieutenant George Herbert Fletcher in the Messines area, when their plane suffered a direct hit from German anti-aircraft fire and was seen to fall in flames, the two men being killed. Both Joseph and George are commemorated on the Arras Flying Services Memorial, but Joseph is another "Lost Boy" whose name has been omitted from the memorial tablets in the school chapel.

---

[123] *Western Evening Herald*, 11 February 1901
[124] *The London Gazette*, 4 May 1917, Supplement:30051

Coldstream Guards

Harry Herbert ELWICK
Corporal, 9385, 2nd Battalion, Coldstream Guards who died on 27 August 1918, aged 22. Buried in Croisilles British Cemetery, Pas de Calais, France

Born on 09 November 1895 in Chelsea, London, the third of five children of Henry Elwick and Gertude Marion née Cubis, his father was a Quartermaster Serjeant in the Coldstream Guards who died whilst serving in Pirbright Camp, Surrey, on 15 April 1905.

Harry was admitted to the school the year after his father died, on 16 March 1906 (Petition No. 12210). He was discharged, having moved from Chelsea to Guston, on 04 January 1912, enlisting into his father's old regiment.

Harry's service record is no longer available, but at the start of the war, the 2nd Battalion, Coldstream Guards was stationed in Windsor, Berkshire. On 12 August it embarked on the SSs *Olympia* and *Novara* at Southampton, Hampshire, landing at Le Havre on 13 August 1914. Although Harry was eighteen, it appears that he did not deploy with the battalion as, although his medal index card has no date of entry into theatre, he did not qualify for the award of the 1914-15 Star, suggesting that he did not enter theatre until 1916 or later.

During 1914, the battalion participated in the Battle of Mons and the subsequent retreat, and then the Battles of the Marne, of the Aisne and the First Battle of Ypres. Unlike many units, the battalion did not fraternise on Christmas Day, reporting that *"snipers caused a few casualties, otherwise quiet"*[125]. After participating in the winter operations of 1914-15, the battalion then took part in the Battles of Festubert and Loos, transferring to the 1st (Guards) Brigade in August 1915. At the start of the Somme Offensive, the battalion was in reserve in the Ypres sector, although it did participate in the later Battles of Delville Wood, of the Ancre and the Operations on the Ancre.

The battalion was not in the line of advance when the Germans launched their Spring Offensive in March 1918, but did pursue the

---

[125] WO 95/1342/2: 2 Battalion Coldstream Guards, 1914 Aug. - 1915 July, The National Archives, Kew

Germans during their retreat to the Hindenburg Line, as well as taking part in the First Battle of the Scarpe, the Battle of Arleux, the Second Battle of the Scarpe and the Battle of Cambrai.

On 26 August 1918, the battalion relieved the 1st Battalion, Welsh Guards, in trenches at St. Leger, attacking the German positions on a 500-yard front in conjunction with the 2nd Battalion, Grenadier Guards at 0700hrs the following morning. Although the attack was ultimately successful, it was described as difficult due to Croisilles being strongly occupied by German machine-guns. During this attack, the 2nd Battalion, Coldstream Guards, suffered 11 officers and 314 other ranks killed, wounded and missing. Harry was one of those killed on 27 August 1918, being interred in the cemetery in the town that had been so strongly defended by the Germans.

Although commemorated on the memorial tablets in the school chapel, he is incorrectly commemorated as H E Elwick.

Henry GRATTON
Private, 13240, 2nd Battalion, Coldstream Guards who died on 24 March 1918, aged 24. Buried in Bucquoy Road Cemetery, Ficheux, Pas de Calais, France

Born on 25 January 1894 in Walthamstow, Essex, the youngest of two children of Henry Gratton and Elizabeth née Richardson, his father was a Corporal in the Royal Engineers who died of disease on 02 February 1901, whilst on active service in South Africa during the Second Boer War.

Henry was admitted to the school on 01 September 1905 (Petition No. 12128) and was discharged home on 01 February 1908 *"unfit for army service"*. However, it appears that eighteen months later on 17 August 1909, he enlisted into the Royal Engineers, although he only served for eighteen months before he was discharged for misconduct on 31 March 1911, although the nature of the misconduct is not recorded in his service record.

Following the outbreak of war, Henry re-enlisted into the army, joining the Coldstream Guards. Although his service record for this period of service is no longer available, his service number suggests that he enlisted between 05 October and 09 November 1914. The battalion to which Henry was posted, the 2nd Battalion, had been stationed in Windsor, Berkshire, in August 1914, but had quickly mobilised, landing at Le Havre on 13 August 1914. However, Henry's medal index card records that he did not disembark in theatre until 27 April 1915.

The battalion had initially been part of the 4th (Guards) Brigade, 2nd Division, but in August 1915 it was transferred to the 1st

(Guards) Brigade, 2nd Division, subsequently participating in the Battle of Loos in 1915 as well as various battles of the Somme Offensive the following year.

In mid-March 1918, the battalion was located in support trenches near Arras, France, but was relieved by 1st Battalion, The Hampshire Regiment and moved into billets at Schramm Barracks, Arras, as the Corps Reserve. Following the launch of the German Spring Offensive on 21 March 1918, on 22 March the battalion marched to Boisleux-au-Mont and dug-in in support, remaining in this position for two days until it withdrew to a new support line near Boiry-St. Martin.

During the withdrawal on 24 March, the battalion suffered 4 other ranks killed and 13 other ranks wounded, Henry being one of those who was killed. It is likely that he was buried close to where he fell, as nine smaller cemeteries were concentrated into Bucquoy Road Cemetery after the war, where he is now interred.

Henry is another of the "Lost Boys" whose name has been omitted from the memorial tablets in the school chapel.

Scots Guards

Tom DRAKE
Boy, 17089, 3rd (Reserve) Battalion, Scots Guards who died on 08 March 1918, aged 15. Buried in Brompton Cemetery, London, United Kingdom

Born on 07 March 1903 in Woking, Surrey, the fourth of seven children of George Drake and Emily née Reeks, his father had served in the Scots Guards, but at the time of his death in London on 30 September 1912, he was a Colour Serjeant in the Irish Guards. Tom's Petition Document, dated 01 November 1912, states that his mother was being supported by the officers of 13th (Princess Louise's Kensington) (County of London) Battalion, The London Regiment, to *"prevent her starving until she can find work"*.

Tom was admitted to the school on 20 March 1913 (Petition No. 13096) and was at the school when it was relocated in December 1914 from Guston to Hutton, near Brentwood in Essex, via Tonbridge School in Tonbridge, Kent. It was from Hutton that Tom was discharged on 29 October 1917, enlisting into the Scots Guards the same day and being posted to the 3rd (Reserve) Battalion at Chelsea Barracks in London.

Unfortunately for Tom, in March 1918, he was admitted to the King George Hospital, Stamford Street, Waterloo. This was a Red Cross Hospital that had been set up in a newly built five-storey warehouse for His Majesty's Stationery Office. He underwent an appendicectomy in the hospital, but developed peritonitis after the surgery, from which he died on 08 March 1918, the day after his fifteenth birthday.

He is buried in Brompton Cemetery in London and is the youngest Dukie to have died whilst serving during the First World War and to be commemorated on the memorial tablets in the school chapel.

Irish Guards

Percy PITMAN
Drummer, 2972, 1st Battalion, Irish Guards who died on 01 November 1914, aged 20. Commemorated on the Ypres (Menin Gate) Memorial, West-Vlaanderen, Belgium

Born on 28 January 1894, in Westminster, London, the youngest of four children of James Pitman and Gertrude née Rolfe, his father was also a Dukie, having been at the Royal Military Asylum between 1879 and 1883 (Petition No. 8401), serving first in the Grenadier Guards and then The Royal Sussex Regiment. He was a Serjeant Drummer on the Permanent Staff with 3rd (Reserve) Battalion, The Royal Sussex Regiment, at the time that Percy was admitted.

Percy was admitted to the school on 03 February 1905 (Petition No. 12080), which was four months after his older brother, Denis, who had been admitted on 06 December 1901 (Petition No. 11637), had been discharged. Percy was discharged to the Irish Guards on 02 February 1908.

The service record for Percy is no longer available, but it is known from the 1911 Census that he was a Drummer in the 1st Battalion and stationed in Chelsea Barracks, London. At the outbreak of war, the battalion was still in London, although now stationed in Wellington Barracks, then departing Southampton, Hampshire, on the SS *Novara* on 12 August and landing at Le Havre on 13 August 1914.

The battalion crossed the frontier into Belgium on 23 August and was initially ordered to take up positions at Bois La Haut on the outskirts of Mons. However, when it was found that this area was already occupied by another unit, it was ordered to take up positions just north of the Harmignies-Mons road. As the German forces advanced, the battalion acted as rear-guard for the retiring British forces, taking part in the small-scale action at Landrecies and the action at Villers-Cotterêts on 01 September during the Battle of Le Cateau.

By the end of October, the unit was within the Ypres Salient and in trenches defending the village of Zillebeke, destined to play a major part in stopping the German breakthrough to the Channel

Ports. On 01 November, the trenches which it occupied were subjected to sustained bombardment and repeated attacks, suffering 3 officers and 95 other ranks killed, including Percy Pitman, killed during the defence of Zillebeke. His body was never recovered or lost during the course of the war and he is commemorated on the Menin Gate.

Denis was discharged from the school on 15 October 1904, enlisting into the 13th Hussars. He was killed eight months after Percy, in July 1915. Both Percy and Denis are commemorated on the memorial tablets in the school chapel and Denis is documented earlier in this book.

The Royal Scots (Lothian Regiment)

George John Leonard ELLIS
Serjeant, 3564, 11th (Service) Battalion, The Royal Scots (Lothian Regiment) who died on 13 December 1915, aged 39. Commemorated in Kensal Green (All Souls') Cemetery, London, United Kingdom

Born on 03 March 1876 in Devonport, Devonshire, the second of three children of David Ellis and Mary née Byrne, his father had been a Private in the 36th (the Herefordshire) Regiment of Foot[126] who was discharged from the army on 19 April 1881 and died in Handsworth, Staffordshire, on 25 January 1887.

George was admitted to the school on 06 April 1888 (Petition No. 9644) and was discharged on 08 March 1890, enlisting into The Royal Scots (Lothian Regiment). A year after George's discharge from the school, his younger brother, John Ellis, was admitted on 29 May 1891 (Petition No. 10161).

On enlistment, George was posted to the 2nd Battalion, which was stationed in Malta, where he was appointed as a Drummer on 22 July 1891 and after almost a year he was then posted to the East Indies, likely Borneo, on 07 March 1892.

Once in the East Indies, George reverted to Private at his own request, but was appointed as a Lance Corporal three years later, on 08 October 1895, and promoted to Corporal on 29 March 1898. However, a year later, on 08 May 1899, George was tried and convicted by General Courts Martial of *"Conduct to the prejudice of good order and military discipline"* and was reduced to the ranks, although a month later, he re-engaged to complete 21 years' service.

Despite this, on 08 January 1901, George was appointed as a Lance Serjeant, and promoted to Serjeant four months later, on 12 May 1901, although his time in this rank was to only last a year. On 16 June 1902, George was again Courts Martialled, this time for drunkenness, and was reduced to the rank of Corporal.

On 29 November 1903, George returned to Britain on furlough, marrying Ellen Elizabeth Mills in Richmond, Surrey, on 13 April 1903, before being posted to India on 09 May 1903, where two

---

[126] Amalgamated with the 29th (the Worcestershire) Regiment of Foot on 01 July 1881 to become The Worcestershire Regiment

children were born, Ivy May Ellis in 1904 and Frederick George Leonard Ellis in 1907.

George was again promoted to Serjeant on 05 December 1907, spending the next eighteen months in India before he was posted to Britain on 09 March 1909 and then being posted to the Regimental Depot at Glencourse Barracks, Penicuik, Lothian, on 15 October 1909. He was then discharged from the army at his own request after 18 years' service on 17 April 1910.

Two months after his discharge, George's third child, Gladys Ellen Elizabeth Ellis, was born and the family were recorded in the 1911 Census as living in Shepherd's Bush, London, with George employed as a Railway Conductor.

When war broke out, George was still in the same employment, but was recalled to the Colours on 28 August 1914. He was returned to his previous rank of Serjeant on the same day and joined the 11th (Service) Battalion of his old regiment.

This battalion had been formed at Edinburgh, Midlothian, in August 1914, coming under the command of the 27th Brigade, 9th (Scottish) Division, quickly moving to Bordon, Hampshire. It is possible that the battalion's last move was to Holybourne, Hampshire, in December 1914 before it landed in France on 11 May 1915, the date shown on George's medal index card for his entry into theatre.

Whilst in France, George was classified as unfit for front-line service, being employed in the Serjeants' Mess as a caterer. However, on 27 September 1915, he wrenched his knee whilst stepping out of a bath, the pain and swelling from this leading to his being admitted to No. 24 General Hospital, Étaples, with a diagnosis of synovitis.

George was returned to Britain and admitted to Fulham Military Hospital, not far from where he lived and on 28 October 1915, at his own request, George underwent surgery to repair the damage that he had done to his knee. Unfortunately, post-operatively, the knee became septic and despite being drained, the sepsis spread, leading to George's death on 13 December 1915.

Although commemorated by the Commonwealth War Graves Commission, George is another "Lost Boy" whose name has been omitted from the memorial tablets in the school chapel.

John was discharged from the school on 22 April 1893 and enlisted into the Army Service Corps. He was transferred to the Army Reserve as a Lance Corporal on 01 June 1899, but was recalled on 01 January 1900, reverting to the rank of Driver on 21 April 1900, three days prior to being deployed to South Africa during the Second Boer War. John returned to Britain on 30 August 1903, having been transferred to the Army Reserve again on 02 June 1903. He was then

189

discharged from the army on 21 April 1905, having completed his first period of service.

Following his discharge, apart from the fact that he is possibly the John Ellis who was recorded in the 1911 Census as married and working as a Hotel Barman in West Derby, Lancashire, nothing else is known about him.

George Riddle SIMPSON

Private, 354, 7th (Leith) Battalion, The Royal Scots (Lothian Regiment) who died on 22 May 1915, aged 25. Buried in Edinburgh (Rosebank) Cemetery, Edinburgh, United Kingdom

Born on 09 April 1890 in Gibraltar, the second of six children of George Simpson and Ellen née Riddle, his father was a Colour Serjeant in The Black Watch (Royal Highlanders) who died whilst serving in Perth, Perthshire on 18 July 1899.

George was admitted to the school on 11 January 1900 (Petition No. 11386) and was discharged home as unfit for army service on 06 April 1904, after which very little is known about him prior to the outbreak of war, although he is recorded in the 1911 Census as living with his mother and four of his siblings in Canongate, Edinburgh, Midlothian, and employed as a Colourman, working for an Oil Colour Merchant.

It is not known at what point he enlisted, as his service record is no longer available, but it is known that by 1915 he was a Private serving in 7th (Leith) Battalion, The Royal Scots (Lothian Regiment). This was a Territorial Force battalion that had been formed in Dalmeny Street, Leith, Midlothian, in August 1914 as part of the Lothian Brigade, Scottish Coast Defences, although on 24 April 1915 it was transferred to the 156th (Scottish Rifles) Brigade, 52nd (Lowland) Division.

A month after this transfer, the battalion was mobilised for service in Gallipoli, "A" and "D" Companies leaving Stirling for Liverpool by rail. At 0649hrs on 22 May 1915, the train on which these troops were travelling was involved in a head-on collision with a local passenger train at Quintinshill, just north of Gretna, Dumfries-shire. The local train would normally have been held in one of the loops at Quintinshill, but both of these were occupied by goods trains, and so it had been "parked" on the south-bound main line.

The troop train containing the Royal Scots overturned, falling mostly onto the north-bound main line, where a minute later, the wreckage was hit by the Glasgow-bound express, causing it to burst into flames. As a result of the crash and the fire, 216 all ranks from the battalion were killed, including George, in what remains Britain's worst railway disaster. Only 62 all ranks from the half-battalion were uninjured.

The survivors, including the Commanding Officer, continued their journey to Liverpool, where they were joined by the other half of the battalion, sailing on 24 May 1915 on board HMT[127] *Empress of Britain*, arriving on Gallipoli in June.

On the same day that the battalion sailed, there was a funeral in which 101 of those killed were buried in a mass grave in Edinburgh's Rosebank Cemetery, the route that the procession took being lined by an estimated 3,150 soldiers.

George is also another of the "Lost Boys" whose name has been omitted from the memorial tablets in the school chapel.

George's younger brother, David Riddle Simpson, who was not a Dukie, also gave his life during the war. He was serving in Mesopotamia with 2nd Battalion, The Black Watch (Royal Highlanders), when he was killed on 14 March 1917. He is commemorated on the Basra Memorial.

---

[127] His Majesty's Transport

The Queen's (Royal West Surrey Regiment)

Arthur CARTER

Private, G/3046, 2nd Battalion, The Queen's (Royal West Surrey Regiment) who died on 12 May 1917, aged 23. Commemorated on the Arras Memorial, Pas de Calais, France

Born on 27 October 1893 in Shorncliffe, Kent, the fifth of six children of George Carter and Elizabeth née Elliott, his father had originally served in The Duke of Cornwall's Light Infantry, before joining the Army Gymnastic Staff, but at the time of Arthur's birth, he was a Quartermaster Sergeant on the Garrison Staff at Shorncliffe. His mother died in Shorncliffe on 05 May 1901.

Arthur was admitted to the school on 08 April 1904 (Petition No. 11952), remaining there for four years before being discharged on 17 February 1908, *"unfit for army service"*, with the 1911 Census recording Arthur employed as a Fitter in Shorncliffe Camp.

Little is known about his army career as his service record is no longer available, but Arthur must have enlisted prior to 1917 as in that year it is known that he was serving in 2nd Battalion, The Queen's (Royal West Surrey Regiment).

At the outbreak of war, this battalion was stationed in Pretoria, South Africa, but was quickly transferred back to Britain, arriving on 19 September 1914, before landing at Zeebrugge on 06 October, although Arthur is recorded as disembarking in theatre on 31 August 1915, likely as a replacement. The battalion was then involved in most of the major battles of the early years of the war, including the Battle of Ypres, Battle of Aubers Ridge, Battle of Festubert, Battle of Loos and the Battle of the Somme.

On 10 May 1917, it moved into trenches opposite Bullecourt in preparation for an attack on 12 May, in which it was to support the Australian Division's attempt to capture that town. In turn, it was supported by 21st (Service) Battalion, The Manchester Regiment and assigned to capture support positions.

The success or otherwise of the attack is not documented in the battalion war diary, but it did report *"hostile artillery very active"*[128] and

---

[128] WO 95/1670/1: 2 Battalion Queen's (Royal West Surrey Regiment), 1916 Jan. - 1917 Nov., The National Archives, Kew

it may be this that caused Arthur's death, particularly as it appears that his body was never recovered. He is one of almost 35,000 British servicemen commemorated on the Arras Memorial.

George COCHRANE
Private, 9691, 10th (Service) Battalion (Battersea), The Queen's (Royal West Surrey Regiment) who died on 07 November 1918, aged 22. Buried in Écuélin Churchyard, Nord, France

Born on 21 April 1896 in Tenterden, Kent, the second of two children of George Cochrane and his second wife, Mary Jane née Holyer, his father had been a Serjeant in The Prince of Wales's Volunteers (South Lancashire Regiment) who had been discharged to pension on 16 June 1885 and died in Lydd, Kent on 10 May 1903. His mother was widowed when she married his father and so George had nine half-siblings from his mother's first marriage, and one from his father's first marriage.

George was admitted to the school on 13 June 1907 (Petition No. 12383), and having moved from Chelsea to Guston, he was discharged to The Queen's (Royal West Surrey Regiment) on 12 July 1910.

George's service record is no longer available, so his pre-war career is unknown. However, his medal index card shows that he was serving in the 2nd Battalion, which was stationed in Pretoria, South Africa, at the start of the war, returning to Britain on 19 September and landing at Zeebrugge on 04 October 1914. It is not known at what point he was posted to the 10th Battalion, but a local newspaper reported he was wounded *"through the knee"* [129] in September 1914 and gassed the following August.

10th (Service) Battalion (Battersea), was formed by the Mayor and Borough of Battersea on 03 June 1915. It moved to Stanhope Lines in Aldershot, Hampshire, in February 1916, before embarking at Southampton, Hampshire, on 05 May and landing at Le Havre on 06 May 1916.

At the commencement of the Somme Offensive, the battalion was located in the Ypres sector, although it was moved to the Somme and participated in the Battles of Flers-Courcelette and the Transloy Ridges, although George may have been in Britain at this stage, as he married Sabrina Grace Holyer in Staple, Kent, on 14 November 1916. She died on 01 February 1917.

During 1917, the battalion fought in the Third Battle of Ypres, as well as taking part in operations on the Flanders coast. However, in

---

[129] *The Kentish Express*, 14 December 1918

November, following the disaster at Caporetto, it was sent to the Italian Front to support the Italians, being deployed along the River Piave.

By March 1918, it had been posted back to the Western Front, involved not only in the battles of the German Spring Offensive, but also those of the Hundred Days Offensive that led to the end of the war.

In November 1918 it was in the vicinity of Coutrai in Belgium, moving into the trenches on 02 November and remaining there until the night of 04-05 November, when it was relieved. Although the war diary reported that *"enemy infantry and artillery inactive during the tour"*[130], during the relief one other rank was killed and three were wounded.

It seems likely that George was one of those wounded, dying of those wounds two days later, on 07 November 1918, just four days before the war ended. He is one of eight British soldiers buried in Ecuelin Churchyard, two of whom died at Christmas 1918.

Whilst George is commemorated on the memorial tablets in the school chapel, he is incorrectly commemorated as C Cockraine.

Albert Victor HUNGERFORD

Lance Corporal, L/8965, 2nd Battalion, The Queen's (Royal West Surrey Regiment) who died on 02 November 1914, aged 22. Commemorated on the Ypres (Menin Gate) Memorial, West-Vlaanderen, Belgium

Born on 01 May 1892 in Upper Holloway, London, the youngest of eight children of Thomas Christopher Hungerford and Mary Jane née Gamble, his father had been a Staff Serjeant serving in both the 26th (Cameronian) Regiment of Foot[131] and the Army Service Corps, but had been discharged to pension on 15 February 1878. He died in Wandsworth, London, on 30 June 1900, five months after Albert's mother, who had died in Islington, London, on 22 January 1900.

Albert was admitted to the school on 16 August 1901 (Petition No. 11595), a year after his older brother, Beecher Reginald Hungerford, who was admitted on 07 December 1900 (Petition No. 11503). Albert was discharged on 24 May 1906, enlisting into The Queen's (Royal West Surrey Regiment) and although his service record is no longer available, he is recorded in the 1911 Census as a Private in the 2nd Battalion, stationed in Gibraltar, but when war broke out, like fellow Dukie George Cochrane, he was stationed in

---

[130] WO 95/2643/2: 10 Battalion Queen's (Royal West Surrey Regiment), 1918 Mar - 1919 Jan, The National Archives, Kew
[131] Amalgamated with the 90th Regiment of Foot (Perthshire Volunteers) (Light Infantry) on 01 July 1881 to become The Cameronians (Scottish Rifles)

Pretoria, South Africa and his history is the same as George's until November 1914.

After landing at Zeebrugge on 06 October 1914, the battalion marched into Bruges two days later, before being ordered to return to Ostend, it was then deployed in various parts of Western Belgium before arriving in Ypres on 14 October, taking up positions to the east of the city near Zonnebeke.

It remained in positions east of Ypres, where it was frequently used to plug gaps in the line during what became the First Battle of Ypres and by the end of October it was located in trenches near Gheluvelt, where on 31 October, it was subjected to very heavy shellfire and a German attack which resulted in the unit suffering 99 killed, wounded and missing, before the remnants were combined with those of The Royal Welsh Fusiliers, to form a scratch battalion. This new unit was then placed in reserve.

Albert Hungerford died on 02 November 1914. As the battalion was not in action that day and reports no shelling, it is likely that he had been one of the wounded from the attack of 31 October, dying of wounds two days later. It is also likely that he was buried near where he died, but due to fighting that took place in this area over the course of the next four years, his grave was lost. This would explain why he has no known grave and is commemorated on the Menin Gate Memorial.

Albert's older brother, Beecher, was discharged from the school on 23 March 1904 to *"Civil Life"*. However, at some point he enlisted in the army and also served during the war, in 2nd Battalion, The Norfolk Regiment. He was to die almost two years after Albert, on 26 September 1916, in captivity in Mesopotamia. He is commemorated on the Angora Memorial located in Baghdad (North Gate) Cemetery. However, although a Dukie, unlike his younger brother he is one of the "Lost Boys" whose name had been omitted from the memorial tablets in the school chapel.

Joseph Downing LAKE

Private, L/9095, 2nd Battalion, The Queen's (Royal West Surrey Regiment) who died on 21 October 1914, aged 21. Commemorated on the Ypres (Menin Gate) Memorial, West-Vlaanderen, Belgium

Born on 04 May 1893 in Shorncliffe, Kent, the second of three sons of James Lake and Rosa Alice née Tribe, his father was a Serjeant in the Military Foot Police, who died in Cairo, Egypt, on 20 November 1899.

Joseph was admitted to the school on 03 June 1904 (Petition No. 11987), almost three years after his older brother, George William

Henry Lake, who had been admitted on 12 September 1901 (Petition No. 11598). Joseph was discharged from the school on 22 May 1907, enlisting into The Queen's (Royal West Surrey Regiment), and although his service record is no longer available, the 1911 Census records him as serving in the 2nd Battalion, stationed in Gibraltar, the name immediately above his in the census of that year being that of fellow Dukie, Albert Hungerford.

The battalion was stationed in Roberts Heights, Pretoria, South Africa when war was declared in August 1914, leaving Cape Town aboard HMT *Kenilworth Castle* on 23 August and arriving at Southampton, Hampshire, on 19 September, from where it deployed to carry out training in preparation for deployment to France and Flanders.

Alongside George Cochrane and Albert Hungerford, Joseph embarked at Southampton on 05 October, landing at Zeebrugge the following day and by the middle of the month was in Ypres, marching out on 15 October and taking up positions along the Dickebusch road. However, that afternoon, the battalion moved to the east of the town and into billets.

The following day, the battalion again marched out of Ypres, this time to Zonnebeke and took up positions covering the Zonnebeke to Langemarck road, where it began entrenching, although it then received intelligence that the Germans were entrenching near Menin, having its baptism of fire on 18 October, attacking this German position on the outskirts of that town.

On 20 October, it was ordered to entrench between Zonnebeke and Passchendaele, where it came under heavy shell fire at approximately 0800hrs the following morning, before the Germans launched an attack at 1000hrs.

Joseph was one of the eighteen members of the battalion killed during the attack on 21 October 1914. His body was never recovered and he is commemorated on the same panel of the Menin Gate as Albert Hungerford, who outlived him by a fortnight. He is incorrectly remembered by the Commonwealth War Graves Commission as Joseph *Dowing* Lake.

George was discharged from the school on 03 May 1906, enlisting in the Royal Engineers. He survived the war, dying in Folkestone, Kent, in 1965. However, their younger brother, James Arthur, who was not a Dukie, enlisted in The Buffs (East Kent Regiment) and was killed the day before Joseph in 1914. Like his brother, his body was also lost and he is commemorated on the Ploegsteert Memorial.

John Robert Nelson POPE
Drummer, 8970, 2nd Battalion, The Queen's (Royal West Surrey Regiment) who died on 24 October 1914, aged 22. Buried in Ledeghem Military Cemetery, West-Vlaanderen, Belgium

Born on 10 September 1892 in Roorkee, India, the second of three children of James Pope and Beatrice née Stratton, his father had been a Serjeant in the Royal Artillery, but had been medically discharged from the army with a pension on 21 November 1900 and died in Manchester, Lancashire, on 04 May 1901.

John was admitted to the school on 14 November 1901 (Petition No. 11619) and was discharged to The Queen's (Royal West Surrey Regiment) on 21 September 1906.

John spent the first three years of his service in Britain, being appointed as a Drummer on 01 October 1906, before being posted to Gibraltar. After two years in Gibraltar, John was then posted to Bermuda, West Indies, on 03 January 1912, before, on 21 January 1914, he was posted to Pretoria, South Africa, which is where the battalion was stationed at the outbreak of war.

John's history following the outbreak of war is the same as his three fellow Dukies, George Cochrane, Albert Hungerford and Joseph Lake, until the battalion attacked the German positions on the outskirts of Menin. According to his service record, John was reported missing the day after the attack and his death was confirmed on 24 October 1914. His body was recovered and he is buried in Ledeghem Military Cemetery, four miles north of the town of Menin.

Whilst John is commemorated on the memorial tablets in the school chapel, he is incorrectly named as J W Pope.

Francis Robert ROUTLEY
Lance Corporal, L/9513, 6th (Service) Battalion, The Queen's (Royal West Surrey Regiment) who died on 03 May 1917, aged 23. Buried in Arras Road Cemetery, Roclincourt, Pas de Calais, France

Born on 28 February 1894 in Aldershot, Hampshire, the eldest of two children of Robert Routley and his first wife, Alice née O'Sullivan, his father was a Quartermaster Serjeant in The Queen's (Royal West Surrey Regiment) and divorced from Alice at the time of Francis's Petition Document being completed, Francis then living with his father.

Francis was admitted to the school on 05 May 1905 (Petition No. 12102) and was discharged to his father's regiment on 30 December 1908, initially posted to the 2nd Battalion in Colchester, Essex, where he spent a year before being posted with it to Gibraltar, being appointed as a bandsman with the rank of Boy on 09 May 1911.

On 02 January 1912 the battalion was posted to Bermuda, West Indies, spending two years there before then being posted to Pretoria, South Africa, on 20 January 1914.

At the start of the war, he was still in Pretoria, returning to Britain on 19 September and landing at Zeebrugge on 06 October 1914. However, Francis did not land with that battalion as he was posted to the Regimental Depot at Stoughton Barracks, Guildford, Surrey.

It was not until 23 March 1916 that Francis was posted to the 6th (Service) Battalion, which had been formed in Guildford in August 1914 and landed at Le Havre on 02 June 1915. Within two months of joining the battalion, Francis was appointed as an unpaid Lance Corporal. This was made a paid appointment on 03 July 1916, two days after the Somme Offensive had commenced and during which the battalion had been in reserve, although it did enter the front-line trenches on the evening of 01 July. It attacked on 03 July at Ovillers and Francis's appointment may have been because it had suffered 294 other ranks killed, wounded and missing during that failed assault. The battalion remained in the sector for the rest of the offensive and was still there in May 1917, near Arras.

On 03 May it was in the support line and sent forward two companies to support The Queen's Own (Royal West Kent Regiment) during its attack on the German trenches. The attack failed, but the 6th Battalion suffered relatively light casualties, with only one officer wounded, three other ranks killed and 32 wounded.

One of those other ranks killed on 03 May 1917 was Francis. Although he is now buried in Arras Road Cemetery, it is likely that he was originally buried elsewhere, as until 1926 this was an exclusively Canadian cemetery. It was enlarged between 1926 and 1929, when 993 soldiers were *"brought in"* from seventeen other cemeteries, to the north and east of Arras.

The Buffs (East Kent Regiment)

James Job COUGHLAN
Private G/4606, 2nd Battalion, The Buffs (East Kent Regiment) who died on 14 October 1915, aged 31. Buried in Phalempin Communal Cemetery, Nord, France

Born on 25 November 1883 in Woolwich, Kent, the second of four children of James Coughlan and Ellen née Franks, his father had been a Gunner in the Royal Artillery who was discharged from the army on 23 January 1883 and died in Woolwich on 11 November 1888. Following his death, Ellen remarried, to Richard Power, in Plumstead in 1889.

James was admitted to the school on 30 November 1893 (Petition No. 10686) and was *"detained on pass"* on 05 March 1895. The 1901 Census shows him living in Plumstead and employed as a Bullet Case Trimmer, likely at the Royal Arsenal, Woolwich.

At the outbreak of war, 2nd Battalion, The Buffs (East Kent Regiment), was stationed in Madras, India, but quickly mobilised and returned to Britain, landing on 23 December 1914, before joining the 75th Brigade, 28th Division, and moving to Winchester, Hampshire, where it was made up to full strength.

On 17 January 1915, the battalion embarked on the SS *Inventor* at Southampton, Hampshire, landing at Le Havre the following day. The rest of January and the early part of February was spent carrying out training and tactical exercises before it moved to the area of Ypres, having its first experience in the trenches when it relieved 1st Battalion, The York and Lancaster Regiment, near Ypres on the evening of 06 February.

However, James enlisted in the army for war-time service only, denoted by the G/ prefix to his service number and he did not disembark in France until 12 May 1915, four months after the battalion had arrived in theatre.

In September 1915, the battalion participated in the Battle of Loos, which lasted from 25 September until 18 October, and it is likely that it was during this battle that James died.

There is a discrepancy regarding his date of death, as it is recorded by the Commonwealth War Graves Commission as being 04 November 1915, but all other records record it as 14 October 1915.

Due to the location in which he is buried, Phalempin, it is likely that he died of wounds having been captured, as the town was in German hands for most of the war. It is possible that James was wounded and taken prisoner during the battalion's attack on Fosse 8 on the morning of 28 September 1915, which is recorded in the battalion war diary[132] as *"Other Ranks. Killed 57. Wounded. 168. Missing 133. The majority of the latter are believed to have been killed or wounded on the Dump[133]"*.

James is another of the "Lost Boys" whose name has been omitted from the memorial tablets in the school chapel.

Alfred Benjamin DAVIS
Private, G/7681, 3rd (Reserve) Battalion, The Buffs (East Kent Regiment) who died on 06 March 1919, aged 43. Buried in Kingston-upon-Thames Cemetery, Surrey, United Kingdom

Born on 02 March 1876 in Dover, Kent, the third of five children of Maurice Robert Davis and Sarah Botwright née Tooke, his father had been a Private in the 28th (North Gloucestershire) Regiment of Foot[134] who had been discharged from the army on 11 November 1864 and was employed as a South Eastern Railway Constable at the time of Alfred's birth.

Alfred was admitted to the school on 17 December 1886 (Petition No. 9452) and was discharged 23 October 1890, taking up an apprenticeship, the 1891 Census recording him apprenticed to John Dennis, a Tailor in Hammersmith, London.

By the beginning of the 1900s, Alfred had moved back to Dover and was recorded in the 1901 Census as living in the town with his now widowed mother and younger brother Charles, being employed as a Railway Porter.

By the time of the 1911 Census, it would appear that Alfred was married and living in West Kensington, employed as a Tailor. It also appears that his wife had been married before, as there were two children with the surname Williams living with them, in addition to Alfred's own son, William, who was born in 1910. A second son Robert followed in 1915.

---

[132] WO 95/2279/2: 2 Battalion Buffs (East Kent Regiment), 1914 Dec. - 1915 Oct., The National Archives, Kew
[133] The slag heap at Fosse 8
[134] Amalgamated with the 61st (South Gloucestershire) Regiment of Foot on 01 July 1881 to become The Gloucestershire Regiment

Following the outbreak of war, Alfred enlisted into The Buffs (East Kent Regiment). However, his service record is no longer available, so it is not possible to ascertain which battalion he joined or what his movements were during the course of the war, although it is recorded in his medal index card that he landed in France on 25 November 1915 and served with the 6th (Service) Battalion of his regiment.

How long Alfred was on active service for is not known, but it seems likely that he only served on the Western Front. Following the end of the war, he was admitted to Kingston War Hospital in Surrey, probably due to disease, where he died on 06 March 1919 and was commemorated by the Commonwealth War Graves Commission.

Alfred was buried in the cemetery nearest the hospital, but he is also a "Lost Boy" whose name has been omitted from the memorial tablets in the school chapel.

William Lawrence DONELAN
Second Lieutenant, 8th (Service) Battalion, The Buffs (East Kent Regiment) who died on 05 April 1917, aged 36. Buried in Bully-Grenay Communal Cemetery, British Extension, Pas de Calais, France

Born on 19 July 1880 in Hampstead, Middlesex, the second son of James Donelan and Emma Mary Ann née Denbow, his father had been a Serjeant Major in the 44th (East Essex) Regiment of Foot[135] and had been Mentioned in Despatches by General Sir William Eyre KCB, Brigade Commander for the attack on Sebastopol on 18 June 1855 during the Crimean War. He had been discharged from the army on 12 April 1864.

William's mother died on 20 February 1890 and he was admitted to the school six months later, on 29 August 1890 (Petition No. 10050). After being at the school for four years, he was discharged on 19 July 1894, *"To Father"*. This followed an appeal to the school by his father, who wanted William to be returned after his other seven children had left home.

According to the 1901 Census, William was employed as a Clerk, and it is known that he married Susannah Hargreaves in Kingston, Surrey, in 1904. They then moved to Sandgate, near Folkestone, Kent, where they had four children. It is also known that he continued to be employed as a Clerk, as the 1911 Census showed that he was employed as such in Lord Radnor's Folkestone Estate Office.

William was also a Territorial, serving with the Kent Cyclist Battalion, which had originally been formed in 1908 at Tonbridge as 6th Battalion, The Queen's Own (Royal West Kent Regiment), but

---
[135] Amalgamated with the 56th (West Essex) Regiment of Foot on 01 July 1881 to become the Essex Regiment

separated from this regiment in 1910. He was a Serjeant in "H" Company which was located in Sandgate.

At the outbreak of war, he immediately volunteered for service overseas, joining The Buffs (East Kent Regiment). However, there was a delay in his deployment as he was selected for officer training and Commissioned as a Temporary Second Lieutenant on 19 December 1916[136], being transferred to the 8th (Service) Battalion on the same day[137]. It was to be another two months before he arrived in France, joining the battalion on 10 February 1917.

His obituary in one newspaper[138] states that William had been suffering from dysentery and been hospitalised, returning to the battalion two days before his death. However, other than an entry in the war diary dated 05 March 1917, stating *"Our signalling officer was evacuated sick. He is expected to return in a few days as he is not very ill really"*[139], there is no other mention of an officer being evacuated, or returning, even the evacuated signalling officer.

At the beginning of April, the battalion had been in the trenches, returning to billets in Bully-Grenay on 03 April. On 05 April 1917, it is reported that the Germans were heavily shelling the village to the extent that cellars were sought for all of the men, *"Matters were, however, brought to head about tea-time, when the enemy obtained a direct hit on the billet occupied by 2nd Lieut. W. L. Donelan, killing him instantaneously"*[140].

William is buried in Bully-Grenay Communal Cemetery, British Extension, the name being taken from the name of the railway station that serves both the villages of Bully-les-Mines and Grenay.

Henry John SEYMOUR

Private, L/8461, 2nd Battalion, The Buffs (East Kent Regiment) who died on 28 September 1915, aged 22. Commemorated on the Loos Memorial, Pas de Calais, France

Born on 08 May 1893 in Bethnal Green, London, the third of six children of Henry Seymour and Eliza née Macey, his father had been a Serjeant in The Prince Consort's Own (Rifle Brigade) who had been discharged from the army on 21 January 1896. He died in Mile End, London, on 01 May 1903, which was three years after Henry's mother, who had died on 24 October 1900, also in Mile End.

Henry was admitted to the school four months after his father's death, on 11 September 1903 (Petition No. 11879) and was

---

[136] *The London Gazette*, 9 January 1917, Supplement:29899
[137] *The London Gazette*, 11 May 1917, Supplement:30065
[138] *Folkestone Express, Sandgate, Shorncliffe & Hythe Advertiser*, Saturday 14 April 1917
[139] WO 95/2207/1: 8 Battalion Buffs (East Kent Regiment), 1915 Aug. - 1918 Jan., The National Archives, Kew
[140] Ibid.

discharged to The Buffs (East Kent Regiment) on 15 May 1907. On enlistment, his service record shows his brother, George, was at the Royal Hibernian Military School in Dublin, with his youngest siblings, Albert and Ada, at the Astley Orphanage in Bristol.

He was initially posted to the 1st Battalion, spending the first sixteen months of his service in Britain, before being posted to Hong Kong. After two years there, he was then posted to Singapore, before returning to Britain two months later on 22 December 1912.

When the war commenced, the battalion was stationed in Fermoy, County Cork, but was quickly moved to Cambridge, Cambridgeshire, before embarking at Southampton, Hampshire, and landing in France on 08 September 1914.

The battalion participated in the early battles of the war, and on 20 October, while in trenches at Radinghem in France, Henry received a gunshot wound to his buttock. However, this does not seem to have been too serious and he was back on duty by 22 December 1914.

He was wounded again on 08 March 1915, when in trenches at Rue du Bois, but more seriously on this occasion, as he sustained a gunshot wound to the neck which resulted in his evacuation back to Britain and hospitalisation.

On 03 June 1915, Henry was discharged from hospital and posted to the 3rd (Reserve) Battalion, located in Canterbury. However, he was only there for nine days before being posted back to France, joining the 2nd Battalion.

By the end of September, this battalion was located in trenches near Fosse 8, a German strongpoint near the Hohenzollern Redoubt, which had been captured and then lost by the British during the Battle of Loos. The battalion had been brought up from reserve in order, with the rest of 28th Division, to recapture this strategic point.

As the battalion made its way forward in the trenches, it suffered numerous casualties due to shell fire, so it did not launch the attack until 1000hrs, managing to capture the 30-foot-high dump. However, this feature was then plastered with shell fire from both sides and more casualties were suffered, so although the attack was mostly successful, the losses were high.

Henry was killed during this attack on 28 September 1915. As his brother, Albert, was informed in a letter of January 1921[141], when he enquired about Henry's grave, this was never located and he is therefore commemorated on the Loos memorial.

---

[141] WO 363: War Office: Soldiers' Documents, First World War 'Burnt Documents' (Microfilm Copies), 1914-1920, The National Archives, Kew - First World War Service Records 'Burnt Documents'

Herbert Richard SUMMERS

Drummer, 9136, 1st Battalion, The Buffs (East Kent Regiment) who died on 26 April 1916, aged 21. Buried in Poperinghe New Military Cemetery, West-Vlaanderen, Belgium

Born on 16 March 1895 in Bristol, Gloucestershire, the third of five children of Ralph Ernest Summers and Louisa née Brookman, his father was a Serjeant in The Buffs (East Kent Regiment) who died whilst serving in Bristol on 14 October 1905.

Herbert was admitted to the school on 22 August 1906 (Petition No. 12253), a year after his father had died and was discharged to his father's old regiment as a Musician on 14 April 1909, five months after his mother had died on 15 November 1908.

Herbert was posted to the 1st Battalion and would have had the same experience as Henry Seymour subsequent to landing in France on 07 September 1914, including participating in the Battle of the Aisne, and continuing to be engaged during the "Race to the Sea"[142]. By December, the battalion was in the area of Croix du Bac, south-east of Bailleul in Northern France, but as it was not in the trenches over Christmas it did not participate in the Christmas Truce.

During 1915, the only major action in which the battalion participated was the Battle of Hooge, during the Second Battle of Ypres.

A year later, it was again in the vicinity of Ypres, moving into the front-line trenches on 24 April in the Morteldje sector and relieving 2nd Battalion, The York and Lancaster Regiment, for a six-day tour, suffering two other ranks wounded on 25 April and three wounded and one killed the following day, Herbert being the soldier killed on 26 April 1916. He was buried in the cemetery in the town of Poperinghe, close to where he fell and although he is commemorated on the memorial tablets in the school chapel, his name is incorrectly recorded as H R Somers.

George Thomas WILSON

Company Quartermaster Serjeant, G/8058, 1st Battalion, The Buffs (East Kent Regiment) who died on 29 July 1918, aged 25. Buried in Abeele Aerodrome Military Cemetery, West-Vlaanderen, Belgium

Born on 08 October 1892 in Canterbury, Kent, the youngest of three children of William Wilson and Eliza Ellen née Filmer, his father had served in The Buffs (East Kent Regiment), but was a Staff Serjeant on the Army Gymnastic Staff when he died in Portsmouth,

---

[142] The Race to the Sea took place between 17 September and 19 October 1914 and referred to the attempts of the Franco-British and German armies to envelop the northern flank of the opposing army through the provinces of Picardy, Artois and Flanders

Hampshire, on 14 October 1898. George's mother also died in Portsmouth, on 25 July 1900.

George was admitted to the school sixteen months after his mother's death, on 14 November 1901 (Petition No. 11617), joining his older brother William Littser Wilson, who had been admitted on 07 April 1899 (Petition No. 11289). George was discharged three years later on 25 October 1906, enlisting into The Buffs (East Kent Regiment) on the same day.

Very little remains of George's service record, so it is not possible to follow his career. However, at the outbreak of war, he was stationed with fellow Dukies Henry Seymour and Herbert Summers in Fermoy, County Cork, his movements prior to landing in France in September 1914 being the same as theirs.

The battalion's first action was an attack on the village of Radinghem, near Armentières on 18 October, gaining the village but losing the chateau after some fierce fighting.

During 1915, it fought at Hooge and in 1916 was on the Somme, participating in the attack on Flers on 15 September, and suffering heavily along with the newly introduced tanks.

In March 1918, when the Germans launched their Spring Offensive, the battalion was in reserve, but suffered severe casualties as it was forced to withdraw, although it did in turn manage to inflict severe casualties on the enemy.

By July, it was in the area of Dickebusch, moving into the trenches on 27 July. Although it appears to have been a relatively quiet spell of duty, it was reported on 29 July that it had suffered three other ranks killed, one of whom was George. He is buried in Abeele Aerodrome Military Cemetery, eight miles west of Dickebusch.

The school records state that William was discharged to *"Mother Civil Life"* on 02 September 1903, although this was likely to be to his guardian, due to the death of his mother three years prior. By the outbreak of the war, he had emigrated to New Zealand, as he appears in George's service record as next-of-kin and living in that country, but nothing further is known of him.

The King's Own (Royal Lancaster Regiment)

Edwin JEPSON

Company Serjeant Major, 4735, 8th (Service) Battalion, The King's Own (Royal Lancaster Regiment) who died on 02 March 1916, aged 42. Commemorated on the Ypres (Menin Gate) Memorial, West-Vlaanderen, Belgium

Born on 19 February 1874 in Portsmouth, Hampshire, the sixth of seven children of Joseph Jepson and Elizabeth née Castles, his father had been a Serjeant Major in the 4th (The King's Own Royal) Regiment of Foot[143] who was discharged from the army after 12 years' service on 13 February 1877 and died in Tideswell, Derbyshire, on 12 June 1880.

Edwin was admitted to the school on 15 August 1884 (Petition No. 9110) and was discharged on 09 March 1889, enlisting into the 7th (The Queen's Own) Hussars. Two years after he had been discharged, his younger brother, Joseph John Jepson, was admitted to the school, on 27 November 1891 (Petition No. 10249).

Six months after joining the 7th Hussars, on 03 September 1889, Edwin was posted to India. Six years later, on 31 July 1895 and whilst still serving in India, he transferred to The King's Own (Royal Lancaster Regiment), being posted to the 2nd Battalion, and was appointed as a Lance Corporal on 04 December 1895.

On 25 February 1896, the battalion was posted back to Britain and nine months later, on 15 November 1896, Edwin was promoted to Corporal. He remained in Britain for the next three years, being promoted to Serjeant on 13 November 1899, before the battalion was posted to South Africa during the Second Boer War on 02 December 1899.

Three years later, having been awarded both the Queen's and the King's South Africa Medals, Edwin was posted to the Regimental Depot in Bowerham Barracks, Lancaster, Lancashire, on 18 January 1902. He then re-engaged to complete 21 years' service, but only served for another eight years before he was discharged on 26 February 1910 *"having been found medically unfit for further service"*, although the cause of this is not recorded. By the time of his

---

[143] Renamed The King's Own (Royal Lancaster Regiment) on 01 July 1881

discharge, he had married Katherine Skladnikiewicz in Colchester, Essex, in 1908, their eldest child, Mavis Euginie Victoria Jepson, being born the following year in Jersey, Channel Islands.

Following his discharge from the army, it appears that Edwin settled in Jersey and was recorded in the 1911 Census as an Army Pensioner, living in St. Helier with his wife, daughter, sister-in-law and niece, and it is known that he was the Deputy Bandmaster of the Jersey Musical Union. His two sons, James Edwin Carleton Jepson, born in 1911 and Wilfred Henry Hudson Jepson, born in 1913, were also both born in Jersey.

Following the outbreak of war, Edwin re-enlisted into his old regiment in Jersey on 02 October 1914, joining the 8th (Service) Battalion, which had been formed at Lancaster in October 1914 as part of K3[144]. It had come under the command of the 76th Brigade, 25th Division and landed in France of 27 September 1915, the date shown on Edwin's medal index card for his entry into theatre. A month after arriving in theatre, on 15 October 1915, the battalion became part of the 3rd Division.

On the evening of 01 March 1916, Edwin and his battalion moved from their billets and took over the trenches at Verbrande Molen, 3 miles south-east of Ypres. At 0430hrs on 02 March 1916, the battalion launched an assault on the German trenches opposite, during which it lost one officer and 104 other ranks killed, including Edwin.

Edwin's body was not recovered, and so he is commemorated on the Menin Gate Memorial, although the Commonwealth War Graves Commission has recorded his service number as 4135. However, he is another "Lost Boy" whose name has been omitted from the memorial tablets in the school chapel.

Joseph was discharged from the school to *"Civil Life"* on 24 August 1895. He was recorded in the 1911 Census as a Boarder living in Waltham Abbey, Essex, and employed as a Worker Royal Gun Powder Factory. It is likely that due to this profession, he was not conscripted into the military during the war, as he was still a civilian and living in Waltham Abbey when he married Henrietta Rose Smith in Edmonton, Middlesex, in 1917. He died in Battle, Sussex, in 1957.

Edwin's youngest son, Wilfred, was a Serjeant in the 14th/20th King's Hussars when he died on active service in Cyprus on 28 September 1956.

---

[144] Field Marshall Lord Kitchener, appointed Secretary of State for War in August 1914, appealed for large numbers of recruits. So many men joined the army that each 100,000 recruits were formed into an Army Group of six Divisions and designated K1, K2, K3, etc.

Henry Edward PACK
Corporal 4592, 2nd Battalion, The King's Own (Royal Lancaster Regiment) who died on 27 March 1917, aged 39. Buried in Sarigol Military Cemetery, Kriston, Greece

Born on 06 August 1877 in Gibraltar, the third of six children of William Pack and Hannah née Dear, his father had been a Private in the 4th (The King's Own Royal) Regiment of Foot, although by the time that Henry was admitted to the school, he had left the army and was employed as a Night Watchman.

Henry was admitted to the school on 16 March 1888 (Petition No. 9634), being joined by his younger brother, Albert John Pack, on 29 November 1889 (Petition No. 9940). Edward was discharged *"To mother"* on 27 August 1891 and it was not until five years later, on 27 January 1896, that he enlisted into his father's old regiment.

After four months in the Regimental Depot in Bowerham Barracks, Lancaster, Lancashire, Henry was posted to the 2nd Battalion, spending eighteen months with this battalion, prior to being posted to Malta where he joined the 1st Battalion. However, Henry was only to be in Malta for a fortnight before the battalion was posted to Hong Kong, where he was appointed as a Lance Corporal on 22 August 1898. He was then posted to Singapore for fourteen months, before he returned to Britain on 27 March 1900, during which time, he reverted to Private due to misconduct.

Henry's next posting was on 19 November 1901, when he was again posted to Malta, where he was to remain for two years, prior to returning to Britain on 11 November 1903 and being transferred to the Army Reserve the following day.

He was re-engaged in his old regiment on 20 January 1908, by which time he had married Mildred Harper Hodgetts on 15 January 1905 and they had had two children, Henry Edward Pack, born in Canning Town, Essex, on 28 April 1906, and Alfred William Pack, also born in Canning Town, on 16 August 1907. During the four years that Henry served on this occasion, prior to his discharge and the end of his term of engagement on 26 January 1912, he and Mildred had a third son, Albert John Pack, again born in Canning Town, on 08 February 1909, but he died in infancy.

Following the outbreak of war, it appears that Henry was recalled to the Colours as a Special Reservist, enlisting again at Canning Town on 17 September 1914, aged 37, with his occupation given as Lavatory Attendant. He had also had another child, Mildred Emily Pack, who was born on 06 January 1913 and Mildred was pregnant with their fifth child, George Albert Edward Pack, who was born on 23 May 1915.

On enlistment, Henry was posted to the 3rd (Reserve) Battalion, a month later being appointed as an unpaid Lance Corporal on 24 October. However, six months after re-enlisting, he was posted to the 2nd Battalion, arriving in France on 18 March 1915. It is possible that he took part in the Battle of Frezenberg in May 1915 when the battalion suffered heavy casualties.

On 18 October 1915, the battalion embarked at Marseille and landed at Alexandria, Egypt, on 02 November, prior to moving to Salonika as part of the Mediterranean Expeditionary Force. Henry remained in Salonika, being appointed as a paid Lance Corporal on 08 January 1916 and Acting Corporal on 30 July 1916.

Eight months later, Henry was killed, possibly in an air raid, on 27 March 1917 and post-war he was one of 560 graves *"brought in"* and re-buried in Sarigol Military Cemetery, Kriston. Henry is also another "Lost Boy" whose name has been omitted from the memorial tablets in the school chapel.

Albert was discharged from the school *"To father"* on 02 October 1893. It appears that he did not join the army, as the 1901 Census records him as a General Labourer, living in West Ham, Essex, and the 1911 Census records him as married with five children, still living in West Ham and employed as a Market Porter. It is not known if he served during the war, but he died in Hackney, London, on 01 November 1955.

The Northumberland Fusiliers

William Martin RUTLEDGE
Private, 7734, 2nd Battalion, The Northumberland Fusiliers who died on 07 October 1918, aged 30. Buried in St. Sever Cemetery Extension, Rouen, Seine-Maritime, France

Born on 08 March 1888 in Colchester, Essex, the eldest of two sons of William Rutledge and Elizabeth née Murphy, his father was a Private in The Northumberland Fusiliers who died whilst serving at Tynemouth Castle, Northumberland, on 17 July 1897.

William was admitted to the school on 06 January 1898 (Petition No. 11111) and discharged to The Northumberland Fusiliers on 22 March 1902, which was four months before his younger brother, Alfred John Rutledge, was admitted to the school on 12 July 1902 (Petition No. 11720).

William's service record is no longer available, which means that it is difficult to ascertain his career pre-war, but it is known that he married Ada Florence Voce in Nottingham, Nottinghamshire, in 1909 and the 1911 Census records that he was Drummer in The Northumberland Fusiliers, living in Newcastle on Tyne, Northumberland. This makes it likely that he was posted to the 3rd (Reserve) Battalion at that time.

By the outbreak of war, it would appear that he had been posted to the 1st Battalion, which was stationed in Portsmouth, Hampshire, landing at Le Havre on 13 August 1914, the date shown on his medal index card for his entry into theatre, with the battalion participating in the early battles of the war.

It is not known when William joined the 2nd Battalion, which was stationed in India at the start of the war and did not land at Le Havre until 18 January 1915. It is also not known if he was posted to this battalion when it was transferred to Egypt on 29 October 1915, or whether he served with the battalion when it landed at Salonika.

However, it is known that he was with the battalion in October 1918, after it had returned to the Western Front from Salonika in June 1918. On 06 October, it was in the line near Le Catelet and was instructed to attack trenches in the Beaurevoir Line. The attack was successful, with very little resistance, however, the Germans occupied high ground and were able to bring machine-gun fire to bear on the newly captured positions, which forced the battalion to withdraw to a sunken road to the rear of the position. The battalion war diary[145] records one officer and five other ranks killed during this action, as well as 12 other ranks wounded.

William was one of the five other ranks killed on 07 October 1918 and he is buried in St. Sever Cemetery Extension, Rouen. He is commemorated on the memorial tablets in the school chapel, although he is incorrectly commemorated as Routledge.

His younger brother is also commemorated on the memorial tablets. Alfred was discharged from the school on 07 February 1907, enlisting into The Prince of Wales's (North Staffordshire Regiment) and was killed on 19 May 1915. Unlike his brother, his name is correctly spelt on the memorial tablets in the school chapel and he is documented later in this book.

Richard William Dunnett WINTER
Private, 615, 2nd Battalion, The Northumberland Fusiliers who died 25 May 1915, aged 24. Commemorated on the Ypres (Menin Gate) Memorial, West-Vlaanderen, Belgium

Born on 09 September 1890 in Southwark, London, the youngest child of William Frederick Dunnett Winter and Margaret Lucy née Hare, his father was a Serjeant in The Prince Consort's Own (Rifle Brigade) and was still serving when he died in London on 06 January 1893.

Richard was admitted to the school on 12 January 1900 (Petition No. 11396) and was discharged four years later, on 17 September 1904, enlisting into The Northumberland Fusiliers.

Richard's service record is no longer available, so his pre-war career is not known, but at the outbreak of war, 2nd Battalion, The Northumberland Fusiliers was stationed in Sabathu, India, returning to Britain on 22 December 1914 and landing at Le Havre on 15 January 1915. Its first experience in the trenches was on 02 February when it relieved the French 95th Infantry Regiment in the front line near Zillebeke.

In May 1915, the battalion was still in Flanders and participating in the Second Battle of Ypres when, on 24 May, it was ordered out to support the attack on Wittepoort Farm, west of Ypres, initially taking up positions at the point where the railway line crossed the Menin Road. The attack on this farm was successful and led to a second attack on Bellewaarde Farm, which was also successful and

---

[145] WO 95/2836/1: 2 Battalion Northumberland Fusiliers, 1918 July - 1919 June, The National Archives, Kew

enabled the battalion to strengthen its positions on the ridge on which these farms stood.

During these attacks, it suffered 2 officers and 29 other ranks killed, 10 officers and 133 other ranks wounded and 1 officer (the Battalion Medical Officer) and 183 other ranks reported as missing.

It is likely that one of the missing was Richard, whose death is recorded as the day after these attacks, on 25 May 1915. His body was never recovered and he is one of the 17,756 soldiers from all battalions of The Northumberland Fusiliers killed during the war to be commemorated on the Menin Gate.

The Royal Warwickshire Regiment

George Trevor MAYCOCK
Serjeant, 16/1371, 16th (Service) Battalion (3rd Birmingham), The Royal Warwickshire Regiment who died on 26 September 1916, aged 34. Commemorated on the Thiepval Memorial, Somme, France

Born on 18 February 1882 in Peshawar, India, the fourth of eight children of George Maycock and Catherine Charlotte née Dyke, his father had been a Serjeant Major in The Queen's (Royal West Surrey Regiment) who had served for 21 years before he was discharged on 13 July 1888. He died in Southwark, London on 15 May 1891.

George was admitted to the school on 27 November 1891 (Petition No. 10238), being discharged on 22 February 1896 and enlisting into The Royal Warwickshire Regiment on the same day. George's younger brothers, Joseph William Maycock and Richard Arthur Maycock, were also admitted to the school, on 06 March 1897 (Petition No. 11008) and 19 July 1901 (Petition No. 11581) respectively.

It seems that George spent the majority of his service at home, as in 1901 he was stationed in Colchester Garrison, Essex, and the 1911 Census records him at Budbroke Barracks, near Warwick, Warwickshire, the Regimental Depot. He also married Catherine Hudson in Leamington, Warwickshire, in July 1904 and they had two children.

George rose steadily through the ranks and was promoted to Colour Serjeant on 01 April 1911. It appears, however, that his time in this rank was short-lived, as on 21 October 1912 he was reduced to the rank of Serjeant following trial by District Courts Martial. The offense that led to the trial is not documented. On 03 September 1913, he was posted to the 2nd Battalion in Malta, but was only there for five months before returning to Britain and being discharged from the army at his own request, on 07 March 1914, after eighteen years' service.

There is no service record for George following his re-enlistment, but it appears that after the outbreak of war he joined 16th (Service) Battalion (3rd Birmingham), The Royal Warwickshire Regiment, a

New Army battalion also known as the 3rd Birmingham Battalion, part of the "Birmingham Pals".

This battalion had been formed in Birmingham in September 1914 and after training, landed at Boulogne on 21 November 1915, moving into the frontline for the first time near Arras in March 1916, before moving to the Somme as reinforcements after the initial attack in July, where it participated in the Battles of High Wood, Guillemont and Flers Courcelette between July and September 1916.

On 26 September, George's battalion was part of the attack that became the Battle of Thiepval Ridge. It is likely that it was during this action that he was killed. He has no known grave and is commemorated on the Thiepval Memorial.

Joseph also gave his life during the war, in June 1918, whilst a Sapper in the Royal Engineers, although his name has been omitted from the memorial tablets in the school chapel, unlike that of his brother. He is documented earlier in this book.

Richard was discharged from the school on 16 March 1906, entering service. He married in 1916, at which time he was employed as a Red Cross chauffeur. He had disembarked in France on 30 October 1914 with Motor Ambulance Unit No. 2, served in France until 13 October 1915 and again from 15 January 1917 until 04 April 1918. Following the war, nothing more is known of him.

James John WARING
Private 266460, 1/7th Battalion, The Royal Warwickshire Regiment who died on 07 March 1917, aged 29. Buried in Bray Military Cemetery, Somme, France

Born on 17 August 1887 in Barford, Warwickshire, the fifth of six children of George John Waring and Annie née Cleaver, his father had served in the 1st, or The Royal Scots Regiment[146], 96th Regiment of Foot[147] and lastly the 67th (the South Hampshire) Regiment of Foot[148]. He was discharged from the army on 04 June 1878 and died in Leamington, Warwickshire, on 05 July 1897.

James was admitted to the school on 05 March 1898 (Petition No. 11146), which was the same day as his younger brother, Thomas Edward Waring (Petition No. 11147). James was expelled from the school for misconduct on 10 May 1900, although what form this misconduct took is not documented. However, it may have been an

---

[146] Renamed The Royal Scots (Lothian Regiment) on 01 July 1881
[147] Amalgamated with the 63rd (West Suffolk) Regiment of Foot on 01 July 1881 to become The Manchester Regiment
[148] Amalgamated with the 37th (North Hampshire) Regiment of Foot on 01 July 1881 to become The Hampshire Regiment

accumulation of "crimes", as his conduct sheet has a high number of entries.

James joined the army on 24 February 1902, enlisting into 3rd Battalion, The Manchester Regiment and served in St. Helena and South Africa. He was discharged on 17 December 1903 under King's Regulations, having been sentenced to 21 days' hard labour for desertion in June 1903 and then 42 days' hard labour for being absent without leave within three months of the first sentence, both offences occurring whilst he was serving in South Africa.

It is not known when James enlisted during the Great War, as his second service record has not survived, but he was serving with a Territorial Force battalion at the time of his death. 1/7th Battalion, The Royal Warwickshire Regiment, had been formed in Coventry, Warwickshire, in August 1914, landing at Le Havre on 23 March 1915. However, it is unlikely that James landed with the battalion, as although his medal index card does not record when he entered theatre, it is likely that this was in 1916 at the earliest, as he was not awarded the 1914-15 Star. In addition, he married Emma Dodd in Coventry in July 1915.

James died of wounds on 07 March 1917, likely during the Operations on the Ancre, which took place between 11 January and 13 March 1917. The battalion war diary[149] records two incidents in which he may have been wounded, the first being when a shell landed on a defensive post on 01 March and the second during an unsuccessful raid on the night of 02-03 March, in which one other rank was killed and four others wounded.

James is another "Lost Boy" whose name has been omitted from the memorial tablets in the school chapel. This may be because he had been expelled from the school for misconduct, or it may be because he is incorrectly commemorated by the Commonwealth War Graves Commission as *John* James Waring.

Thomas was discharged from the school to *"Civil Life"* on 10 December 1902. He enlisted into The Royal Warwickshire Regiment on 27 June 1906, serving for only two months before he transferred to the Royal Navy on 29 August 1908. It is not known how long he served in the Royal Navy, but the 1911 Census records him as living with his mother in Warwick and employed as a Groom. It is also not known if he served during the war, but if he did, he survived, dying in Coventry in 1948.

---

[149] WO 95/2756/1: 1/7 Battalion Royal Warwickshire Regiment, 1915 Mar. - 1917 Oct., The National Archives, Kew

The Royal Fusiliers (City of London Regiment)

Thomas ANGELL
Private, L/8136, 4th Battalion, The Royal Fusiliers (City of London Regiment) who died on 14 September 1914, aged 28. Commemorated on the La Ferte-Sous-Jouarre Memorial, Seine-et-Marne, France

Born on 26 June 1886 in Hounslow, Middlesex, the youngest of three children of Samuel Angell and Elizabeth née Syer, his father had been a Private in The King's (Liverpool Regiment) and The Royal Fusiliers (City of London Regiment). He had been discharged on 13 September 1887 and died in Hounslow on 05 July 1899.

Thomas was admitted to the school on 05 January 1897 (Petition No. 10970) and discharged to the last of his father's old regiments on 07 July 1900, a year after his father had died. His service record is no longer available, so his pre-war career and which battalions he served with are unknown. However, what is known that he married Rose Jackson in Depwade, Norfolk, on 24 March 1913.

At the outbreak of war 4th Battalion, The Royal Fusiliers, was stationed in Parkhurst, Isle of Wight, embarking at Southampton, Hampshire, on 13 August and landing at Le Havre on 14 August 1914.

On 22 August, the battalion was located in positions at Nimy, just north of Mons, where at 1100hrs on 23 August, the Germans began attacking its positions. The following day, at 1310hrs, the battalion received the order to retire, a retirement that was to last until 05 September, prior to the battalion beginning to advance north again on 06 September.

By the 13 September, it was in the vicinity of Vailly and had taken up positions near La Rouge Maison Farm. Despite it being foggy and very wet the following morning, it was attacked by the enemy, which had strong artillery and machine-gun support, and although the battalion was able to hold its ground initially, the withdrawal of the regiment to its right meant that it too had to withdraw to a sunken road approximately 200 yards south of its initial position. During this action, the battalion suffered 5 officers and about 200 other ranks killed, wounded or missing.

Thomas was one of those killed, dying on 14 September 1914. His body was not recovered, or if it was, his grave was lost during the course of the next four years of fighting and so he is commemorated on the La Ferte-Sous-Jouarre Memorial.

Whilst Thomas is commemorated on the memorial tablets in the school chapel, his surname is incorrectly recorded as Angel.

On 14 March 1915, six months after Thomas was killed, his only son, Samuel Thomas William Angell, was born. He too was a Dukie, admitted to the school on 30 April 1926 (Petition No. 14780) and discharged to the Royal Engineers on 01 May 1930. He died in Hounslow, in 1989.

Sidney Douglas William COOPER
Private, L/13777, 4th Battalion, The Royal Fusiliers (City of London Regiment) who died on 26 October 1914, aged 19. Commemorated on the Le Touret Memorial, Pas de Calais, France

Born on 04 October 1895 in Lucknow, India, the third of four children of William Douglas Cooper and Rachel Mabel Blanche née Cross, his father was a Schoolmaster (Warrant Officer) in the Corps of Army Schoolmasters. He appears as a scholar at the school in the 1881 Census, but he was not a Dukie and it is more likely that he was at the school whilst undergoing his Schoolmaster training. He was discharged from the army on 03 January 1904, but died in Aldershot, Hampshire, on 07 August 1904.

Sidney was admitted to the school on 27 January 1905 (Petition No. 12075) and would have made the move from Chelsea to Guston, before being discharged just after his fourteenth birthday, on 18 October 1909. Although his service record is no longer available, it is known that Sidney enlisted in The Royal Fusiliers (City of London Regiment) when he was discharged from the school and appears in the 1911 Census as a Boy in the 4th Battalion, stationed in Corunna Barracks, Stanhope Lines, Aldershot.

When war was declared, Sidney was stationed in Parkhurst, Isle of Wight, serving with fellow Dukie, Thomas Angell, mobilising and landing in France on the same day as Thomas.

The battalion first saw action during the Battle of Mons, during which two members, Lieutenant Maurice Dease and Private Sidney Godley, were awarded the first Victoria Crosses of the war, before it took part in the Retreat from Mons and the various battles that occurred during this period. It then went onto the offensive during the Battle of La Bassée. During this "Race to the Sea", the British attacks lasted from 14 until 20 October 1914, before the Germans began their counterattacks on 20 October.

On 26 October, the battalion was in billets, having moved out of the trenches at dawn that day. However, at about 1400hrs, it was called out to support the units that were in the firing line to the west of Neuve Chapelle and was immediately in the thick of the action, as the Germans had occupied some of its trenches. A night attack was made in order to recapture these, but it failed and the battalion suffered heavy casualties.

Sidney died during this action, on 26 October 1914, three weeks after his nineteenth birthday. He has no known grave and is remembered on the Le Touret Memorial, alongside 155 other members of his battalion who died during this period.

Frederick Charles ELLERY
Private, S/8231, 2nd Battalion, The Royal Fusiliers (City of London Regiment) who died on 24 April 1917, aged 30. Commemorated on the Arras Memorial, Pas de Calais, France

Born on 04 July 1886 in Liverpool, Lancashire, the third of four children of Augustus Harold Ellery and Emily née Garrard, his father had been a Serjeant in the 18th Hussars, but had been discharged from the army on 27 November 1883. His mother died in Camberwell, London, on 03 December 1889 and his father died in Kentish Town, London, on 15 November 1894, so Frederick's Petition Document for admission to the school was completed by his uncle, Alpha Ellery, who was a Serjeant Major in the Suffolk Yeomanry Cavalry (The Duke of York's Own Loyal Suffolk Hussars).

Frederick was admitted to the school on 02 September 1895 (Petition No. 10798), which was three days after his older brother, Harold Augustus Ellery, had been admitted on 30 August 1895 (Petition No. 10785). After almost five years at the school, Frederick was discharged on 07 July 1900 and enlisted into The East Yorkshire Regiment, initially joining the 2nd Battalion as a Boy.

He was to serve with this regiment for thirteen years, either as a Bandsman or Private, almost all of this time with the 2nd Battalion and stationed in India from 28 December 1905 until he returned to Britain on 04 April 1913, being discharged from the army at the end of his term of engagement the following day.

Nothing is known of Frederick from the time that he was discharged from the army until the outbreak of war sixteen months later, but it can be surmised from the prefix in his service number that he was recalled to the Colours at the outbreak of war as a Special Reservist, although why he enlisted into The Royal Fusiliers rather than his old regiment is not known.

It is also not known when he disembarked in France, but with no record of a 1914-15 Star it would suggest that it would have been from 1916 onwards. Furthermore, 2nd Battalion, The Royal Fusiliers was fighting in Gallipoli from 25 April 1915 and so it would have been recorded in his medal index card had he been in theatre at that time.

Because Frederick's wartime service record is not available, his movements between re-enlistment and April 1917 are unknown, however, between 9 April and 16 May 1917, the British Army attacked near Arras in a plan to engage the Germans on open ground. The initial advances were significant, but the battle became a costly stalemate for both sides. On 24 April 1917, Frederick's battalion attacked the second-line German trenches during the Second Battle of the Scarpe (23-24 August 1917), succinctly recorded in the battalion war diary as *"Attack on Blue line (Casualties 190)"*[150].

Frederick was likely one of those casualties, presumed dead on or since that date and his body was not recovered. Additionally, he is another "Lost Boy" whose name has been omitted from the memorial tablets in the school chapel.

Harold, was discharged from the school on 04 June 1898, enlisting into The East Yorkshire Regiment, although it appears that he, too, had been discharged prior to the outbreak of war, as the 1911 Census records him employed as an Asylum Attendant in Whittingham, Lancashire. He did see wartime service, but like his brother he served in a different regiment, in his case The Prince of Wales's (North Staffordshire Regiment), entering theatre on 23 March 1915. He survived the war, dying in Wandsworth, London, in 1964.

Andrew HARRISON

Lance Corporal, 13009, 25th (Service) Battalion (Frontiersmen), The Royal Fusiliers (City of London Regiment) who died on 21 March 1916, aged 39. Buried in Moshi Cemetery, Tanzania

Born on 06 December 1876 in Holborn, Middlesex, the third of four children of John Harrison and Emma née Hughes, his father had been a Private in the 3rd (King's Own) Hussars who had been discharged from the army on 22 March 1867 and died in Westminster, Middlesex in July 1886.

Andrew was admitted to the school on 12 August 1887 (Petition No. 9549) and was discharged on 03 January 1891, enlisting into The Northumberland Fusiliers. Once he was attested, Andrew was

---

[150] WO 95/2301/3: 2 Battalion Royal Fusiliers, 1916 Feb. - 1919 Mar., The National Archives, Kew

posted to the 1st Battalion and spent the first five years of his service in Britain, but 04 October 1896, he was posted to Gibraltar, remaining there for just over a year before he was posted to Egypt on 17 January 1898.

Nine months after this posting, on 03 October 1898, Andrew was posted to Crete as part of the occupation[151], remaining on the island for almost a year before he was posted back to Britain on 19 April 1899, but not before he had been imprisoned for two weeks with hard labour on 03 March 1899 for *"using threatening and obscene language to an NCO and drunk"*.

Five months after returning to Britain, on 02 September 1899, Andrew was posted to the 2nd Battalion, moving with that battalion to South Africa on 04 November 1899 during the Second Boer War.

Andrew remained in South Africa for just over three years, but was again in trouble when he was convicted by Regimental Courts Martial on 09 December 1902 of drunkenness and again confined for fourteen days.

Three months after this conviction, on 11 February 1903, Andrew returned to Britain, where he was discharged from the army the following day, having completed his first period of service.

Information following his discharge is scant, but it is known that on 18 December 1904, Andrew married Olive Florence Linstead in Rotherhithe, Surrey, his occupation given as Carman. Their first child, Elsie Olive Harrison, was born two years later.

Andrew and his family were also recorded in the 1911 Census, his occupation being given as Carter, with the family living in Finsbury, London. However, a year after the census, in April 1912, Andrew became a single father when his wife died, with his second child, Doris Winifred Harrison, having been born in January of that year.

Following the outbreak of war, and despite having two young daughters, Andrew re-enlisted into the army in Finsbury, Lily Wise becoming the Guardian to his children. However, it has not been possible to establish the relationship between Lily and Andrew, and his service record for this period of service is no longer available.

The battalion that Andrew joined, 25th (Service) Battalion (Frontiersmen), The Royal Fusiliers (City of London Regiment), had been formed in London on 12 February 1915 by the Legion of Frontiersmen[152]. Two months after its formation, on 10 April 1915,

---

[151] Following the Cretan Revolt (1897-1898), which was an insurrection of the Greek population of Crete against the rule of the Ottoman Empire, which resulted in the formation of an autonomous Crete. The insurrection also led to the Ottoman Empire declaring war on Greece, which led to intervention by Britain, France, Italy and Russia on the grounds that the Ottomans could no longer maintain control. This ultimately led to the final annexation of Crete to the Kingdom of Greece in 1908

[152] An Empire-wide civilian organisation formed in 1905 to be a field intelligence corps to

it embarked at Plymouth, Devonshire, arriving at Mombasa, British East Africa, on 04 May 1915, the date shown on Andrew's medal index card for his arrival in theatre.

From its arrival in theatre, the battalion fought in East Africa in the largely guerrilla campaign that was carried out by German forces and their colonial allies under the command of Lieutenant Colonel Paul von Lettow-Vorbeck, and by March 1916, it was in the territory of modern-day Tanzania, moving into positions at Store on 19 March 1916.

Overnight on the 20-21 March 1916, the formation came under heavy attack from the German and Colonial troops, although this was repulsed by the 129th Baluchis, an Indian Army regiment serving alongside the British, and the following morning The Royal Fusiliers were withdrawn from the trenches as part of the divisional reserve.

However, by 1600 hours that afternoon, the battalion was required to move forward again and came under fire once more at 1800hrs for an hour, before it was able to dig into these positions. During the firefight, two soldiers were killed and 12 wounded, one of those killed being Andrew.

Although Andrew is buried in the cemetery in Moshi, Tanzania, sixteen miles from where he was killed, he is another "Lost Boy" whose name has been omitted from the memorial tablets in the school chapel.

Herbert Wilfred KING

Drummer, 12704, 3rd Battalion, The Royal Fusiliers (City of London Regiment) who died 03 May 1915, aged 21. Commemorated on the Ypres (Menin Gate) Memorial, West-Vlaanderen, Belgium

Born on 24 May 1893 in Chatham, Kent, the eighth of nine children of Charles Henry King and Elizabeth née Clare, his father had been a Staff Quartermaster Serjeant in the Army Service Corps, but had been discharged from the army on 04 March 1898 and died in Peckham, London, on 01 February 1902.

Two years after his father's death, Herbert was admitted to the school, on 04 March 1904 (Petition No. 11941) and was discharged to The Royal Fusiliers (City of London Regiment) on 29 May 1907, however, his service record is no longer available and his pre-war postings are unknown.

At the outbreak of war, 3rd Battalion, The Royal Fusiliers, was stationed in Lucknow, India, quickly mobilising and returning to

---

protect the borders of the Empire, although never officially recognised as such

Britain, landing at Plymouth, Devonshire, on 22 December 1914, before moving to Winchester, Hampshire, two days later.

After being brought up to strength, the battalion re-embarked at Southampton, Hampshire, on 18 January and landed at Le Havre on 19 January 1915. It then moved to Hazebrouck on 21 January, where it is reported that approximately a quarter of the battalion were ill, which resulted in 48 men being admitted to hospital by the end of the month.

Despite this, the battalion's first experience of the front line was on 04 February, when it moved into trenches in support of The King's Own Yorkshire Light Infantry, which had launched a counterattack in order to recapture trenches that had been lost earlier that day. However, the first major battle in which the battalion was involved was the Second Battle of Ypres, which commenced on 22 April.

At the beginning of May, the battalion was in the vicinity of the village of Passchendaele where, on the morning of 03 May, the Germans attempted to capture a trench that it was holding, although the attack was repulsed by rifle fire.

In the afternoon the battalion was not only shelled, but the Germans opened fire on it from a wood that they had occupied to the left of the battalion's positions, blowing part of one trench to pieces and causing it to be evacuated.

At some point during this German attack, Herbert was reported "wounded or missing". When he did not reappear, he was presumed to have died on 03 May 1915. His body was never recovered and so he is commemorated on the Menin Gate.

John Almond KIRTLAND

Private, 35642, The Royal Fusiliers (City of London Regiment) who died on 24 August 1919, aged 32. Commemorated in West Norwood Cemetery and Crematorium, London, United Kingdom

Born on 26 December 1886 in Fulham, Middlesex, the eldest of four children of James Kirtland and Elizabeth née Almond, his father had served for eighteen years, firstly in the 105th Regiment of Foot (Madras Light Infantry)[153] before transferring to The Royal Scots Fusiliers. He was discharged from the army on 14 August 1883 and died in Clapham, London, on 21 July 1891.

John was admitted to the school on 05 March 1897 and discharged to *"Civil Life"* on 26 December 1900. It appears that he

---

[153] Amalgamated with the 51st (2nd Yorkshire West Riding) Regiment of Foot on 01 July 1881 to become The King's Own Light Infantry (South Yorkshire Regiment), renamed The King's Own Yorkshire Light Infantry in 1887 and further renamed The King's Own (Yorkshire Light Infantry) in 1902

remained a civilian until the outbreak of war, as there is no service record available for him prior to that time and he is recorded in the 1911 Census as living with his mother and sister in Westminster, London, being employed as a Chemist Porter.

Although his service record was badly damaged, it is known that John attested on 03 December 1915 into 15th (Reserve) Battalion, The Duke of Cambridge's Own (Middlesex Regiment) and was then mobilised into The Royal Fusiliers (City of London Regiment) the following April. He was subsequently transferred to 29th (Works) Battalion, The Middlesex Regiment and finally to the Labour Corps, where he was stationed in Edinburgh for a period.

It is likely that he was unfit for active service, with his medical records stating that he had a disability due to deformed feet, but other information in this regard is limited.

John's service record states that he served at home from 29 April 1916 to 21 August 1919, when he was discharged from the 6th Labour Battalion as *"being surplus to military requirements (Not having suffered impairment since entry into the Service)"*[154].

Sadly, John died three days after being discharged, having been admitted to the Queen Alexandra Military Hospital at Millbank, London, on 23 August 1919. His cause of death was recorded as nephritis and uraemia (kidney failure). The time of death was given as 1.20am, so death followed quickly after his admission.

John Kirtland is another of the "Lost Boys" who has been commemorated by the Commonwealth War Graves Commission and whose name has been omitted from the memorial tablets in the school chapel.

George Percival LANGDON
Private, 17242, The Royal Fusiliers (City of London Regiment) posted to 2/4th (City of London) Battalion (Royal Fusiliers), The London Regiment who died on 26 October 1917, aged 19. Commemorated on the Tyne Cot Memorial, West-Vlaanderen, Belgium

Born on 21 July 1898 in Greenwich, London, the youngest of two children of George Alfred Langdon and Esther Elizabeth née Jagot, his father had served in the Army Service Corps, although he did so using the alias George Watson and died of enteric fever whilst on active service in South Africa on 03 March 1900.

George was admitted to the school on 01 September 1909 (Petition No. 12642), at the time that the school was transitioning

---

[154] WO 363: War Office: Soldiers' Documents, First World War 'Burnt Documents' (Microfilm Copies), 1914-1920, The National Archives, Kew - First World War Service Records 'Burnt Documents'

from Chelsea to Guston. He was discharged on 22 October 1914 and enlisted into the Army Ordnance Corps. His service record for this time is no longer available, so it is not known for how long he served, but by 1917 he was serving in The Royal Fusiliers (City of London Regiment) and had been posted to a Territorial Force infantry battalion.

The original 2/4th (City of London) Battalion (Royal Fusiliers) had been formed in London in September 1914, before moving to Folly Farm, New Barnet, London, and then, on 14 December to Maidstone, Kent. It relieved the 1/4th (City of London) Battalion (Royal Fusiliers) in Malta on 31 December, moving to Egypt on 25 August 1915, from where, two months later, on 15 October, it landed at Cape Helles, Gallipoli, remaining there for three months before being evacuated to Egypt in January 1916. It then moved to France in April 1916 and was disbanded at Rouen in June 1916, after which the 3/4th Battalion was renamed the 2/4th Battalion.

The reconstituted 2/4th Battalion arrived at Le Havre on 24 January 1917 and was in action throughout the year. However, probably due to his age, it was not until later in the year that George joined them, his medal index card showing that he did not actually arrive in theatre until 05 October 1917, at which time, the battalion was engaged in training near Zouafques for an upcoming attack and George was one of a draft of 129 other ranks that joined it from base. The training was to continue until 23 October, when it moved into position for an attack, which was to be launched on 26 October.

When the attack was launched, the weather and ground was described as "absolutely filthy" and as a result the battalion did not take its objectives. During that day, it suffered eleven officers and 368 other ranks killed, wounded and missing, prior to being relieved at 2215hrs by the 2/7th (City of London) Battalion and returning to billets in Siege Camp. Among the missing on that day was George, the Registers of Soldiers' Effects[155] recording that he was presumed killed on or since 26 October 1917. His body was never recovered and he is commemorated on the Tyne Cot Memorial. At the time of his death, George had been in theatre for only three weeks.

Arthur Edmund Randolph NORRINGTON

Corporal, 1111, 17th (Service) Battalion (Empire), The Royal Fusiliers (City of London Regiment) who died on 04 June 1918, aged 35. Buried in Wallington (Bandon Hill) Cemetery, Surrey, United Kingdom

Born on 07 May 1883 in Dublin, County Dublin, the second of three sons of Walter Frederick Norrington and Abigail née Doray,

---

[155] UK, Army Registers of Soldiers' Effects, 1901-1929, 1914-1915, Hounslow, 749501-751000

his father had been a Musician in The Queen's Own (Royal West Kent Regiment) and was discharged from the army on 05 August 1890. He had also been a Dukie, having been admitted to the school on 08 August 1859 (Petition No. 6495) and was *"Delivered to his mother"* on 22 July 1865. Eleven days later, on 02 August 1865, he enlisted into one of the constituent regiments of what would become The Royal West Kent Regiment, the 97th (The Earl of Ulster's) Regiment of Foot, at Colchester, Essex. Arthur's mother died in Weymouth, Dorsetshire, on 16 May 1888.

Arthur was admitted to the school on 30 March 1894 (Petition No. 10587), joining his older brother Walter Frederick Norrington, who had been admitted on 29 April 1891 (Petition No. 10163). Arthur was discharged from the school on 08 July 1898, enlisting into The Royal Warwickshire Regiment as a Musician, and was posted to Malta in June 1899.

After three years' service in The Royal Warwickshire Regiment, Arthur was posted to the Regimental Depot in Budbrooke Barracks, Warwick, Warwickshire, on 02 June and discharged from the army on 26 June 1901 as *"not likely to become an efficient soldier"*[156].

Little is known of Arthur's life following his discharge, other than on 23 December 1906 he was working as a Caterer and married Sarah Ann (Minnie) Turner in East Dulwich, London, and that his son, Arthur Edmund Randolph Norrington, was born on 27 February 1911, the census of that year showing that the family were living in South Croydon, Surrey. At that time Arthur was employed as a Private Messenger by the Buenos Aires Pacific Railway.

Following the outbreak of war, Arthur re-joined the army, enlisting into 17th Battalion, The Royal Fusiliers on 09 October 1914. This battalion had been formed by the British Empire Committee on 31 August 1914 and landed at Le Havre on 17 November 1915, but did not have its first experience of the front line until early-1916. Later that year, although it did not attack on the first day of the Somme Offensive, it did participate in the later battles.

Whilst in the trenches near Bernafay Wood on 28 August 1916, Arthur sustained a gunshot wound that severely fractured his right tibia and fibula. This was operated on at the casualty clearing station, before he was evacuated to Britain, ending up eventually in the Royal National Orthopaedic Hospital in London.

Following his injury, it was deemed that Arthur was unfit for further military service and he was discharged from the army on 06 August 1917. He died almost a year later, on 04 June 1918, possibly

---

[156] WO 363: War Office: Soldiers' Documents, First World War 'Burnt Documents' (Microfilm Copies), 1914-1920, The National Archives, Kew - First World War Service Records 'Burnt Documents'

as a result of complications of the injury that he had sustained in France, as his Commonwealth War Graves Commission grave marker in Wallington (Bandon Hill) Cemetery is inscribed with the words *"First to the call, He made the great sacrifice"*.

Walter was discharged from the school on 13 July 1895 and enlisted into the Royal Engineers. He served throughout the war and was discharged from the army on 23 September 1919, having been Mentioned in Despatches on 18 December 1914. He died in Lewes, Sussex in, 1949.

Arthur PEET
Private, 1356, 8th (Service) Battalion, The Royal Fusiliers (City of London Regiment) who died on 07 July 1916, aged 34. Commemorated on the Thiepval Memorial, Somme, France

Born on 20 June 1882 in Hounslow, Middlesex, the sixth of seven children of Michael Peet and Mary née Hedges, his father had served in the Grenadier Guards for 21 years, being discharged from the army on 21 August 1876. He was then employed as permanent staff of 5th Battalion, The Royal Fusiliers (City of London Regiment), dying in Brentford, Middlesex, on 09 October 1890.

Arthur was admitted to the school on 07 January 1892 (Petition No. 10258) and was discharged on 08 August 1896, enlisting into the Grenadier Guards as a Musician the same day. Having been appointed as a Drummer on 06 December 1897, Arthur was then posted to Gibraltar on 13 July 1898, spending just over a year there before he was posted back to Britain on 03 October 1899.

Eight months after returning to Britain, Arthur was discharged from the army, on 02 June 1900, as unfit for further military service, following which little is known about him. However, he is recorded in the 1911 Census as a Kitchen Man employed by Frederick Barnett, a Coffee House Keeper and Tattooist in Commercial Road, Portsmouth, Hampshire.

Following the outbreak of war, it appears that Arthur re-enlisted, joining 8th (Service) Battalion, The Royal Fusiliers (City of London Regiment). This battalion had been formed on 21 August 1914 at Hounslow, Middlesex, coming under the command of the 36th Brigade, 12th (Eastern) Division and landing in France between 29 May and 01 June 1915, Arthur's medal index card recording that he landed on the latter date.

After training, the battalion had its first experiences in the trenches at Ploegsteert Wood on 23 June 1915, but was then moved from Belgium to France to participate in the Battle of Loos. The following year, the battalion moved into reserve positions at

Millencourt and Hencourt, reaching these positions by mid-morning on 01 July 1916, before relieving units of the 8th Division at Ovillers-la-Boiselle that night and attacking at 0315hrs the following morning, although this attack had limited success.

Five days after this first attack, the battalion launched a second attack, on 07 July, which resulted in the capture of the first and second lines near Ovillers, but also resulted in heavy casualties, one of whom was Arthur. His body was not recovered and he is commemorated on the Thiepval Memorial, as well as being another "Lost Boy" whose name has been omitted from the memorial tablets in the school chapel.

William John PEPLER

Corporal, 14140, Depot, The Royal Fusiliers (City of London Regiment) who died on 08 February 1917, aged 36. Buried in Twickenham Cemetery, Middlesex, United Kingdom

Born on 25 September 1880 in Salford, Lancashire, the eldest of four children of John Pepler and Annie Ellen née Godfray, his father had been a Sergeant in The King's (Shropshire Light Infantry) who was discharged from the army on 13 April 1889 and died in Cripplegate, London, on 14 April 1892.

William was admitted to the school on 26 August 1892 (Petition No. 10359) and was joined by his younger brother, Ernest Walter Pepler, on 26 May 1893 (Petition No. 10482). William was discharged from the school on 31 October 1894 and enlisted into The Welsh Regiment.

William spent all of this period of service in Britain, before he was discharged from the army having been found medically unfit for further service on 12 April 1901, although the reason for this is not given. A year after his discharge, in April 1902, William married Myra Beatrice Branch in Chertsey, Surrey, their oldest child, Myra Beatrice Pepler, being born on 19 September 1902.

Little is known about William following his marriage, and he does not seem to appear in the 1911 Census, but he does appear in the 1914 Electoral Register, living in Twickenham, Middlesex. By this time, he and Myra had six children.

Following the outbreak of war, William, who was serving in the National Reserve, was recalled and re-enlisted into The Welsh Regiment on 05 September 1914. However, he was again medically discharged just over a month later, on 26 October 1914, the reason being that he had varicose veins.

Following this second discharge, it appears that he was either conscripted or re-enlisted into the army, although it is not known when this happened, joining The Royal Fusiliers (City of London Regiment) and being posted to the Regimental Depot in Hounslow Barracks, Middlesex, serving as a Clerk on Home Service only.

It was from here that William was admitted to the military hospital in Hounslow with acute bronchitis and emphysema, where he died on 08 February 1917. Following his death, he was interred in Twickenham, the town where he and his family, by now seven children following the birth of his youngest daughter in 1916, were living. However, he is a "Lost Boy" whose name has been omitted from the memorial tablets in the school chapel.

Ernest was *"Detained on pass"* on 21 August 1897, but it appears that he subsequently joined the army, as he is recorded in the 1911 Census as a Lance Corporal in 2nd Battalion, The Welsh Regiment and stationed in Llanion Barracks, Pembroke Dock, Pembrokeshire. He survived the war and is recorded in the 1939 England and Wales Register as a Coal Merchant and Haulage Contractor, living in Battle, Sussex, the town in which he died in 1949.

The King's (Liverpool Regiment)

William James KEARNEY
Serjeant, 30084, 14th (Service) Battalion, The King's (Liverpool Regiment) who died on 14 September 1915, aged 40. Buried in Millencourt Communal Cemetery Extension, Somme, France

Born on 26 February 1875 in Rawalpindi, India, son of John Kearney and Catherine née Salvage, his father had been a Private in the 19th Hussars prior to transferring to the 4th (Queen's Own) Hussars. He had been discharged from the army on 04 September 1883 and died in Liverpool, Lancashire, on 03 April 1884.

William was admitted to the school on 08 May 1885 (Petition No. 9225) and discharged on 16 March 1889, enlisting into The Princess Charlotte of Wales's (Royal Berkshire Regiment) as a Boy on the same day and appointed as a Drummer seven months later on 29 October 1889.

William spent the first nine years of his career in Britain with the 2nd Battalion, being appointed as a Lance Corporal on 25 January 1897 and being promoted to Corporal on 12 February 1898, the day before he was posted to South Africa.

He then spent four years serving in South Africa, including during the time of the Second Boer War, being awarded the clasps *Cape Colony*, *Orange Free State* and *Transvaal* to his South Africa medal, appointed as a Lance Serjeant on 08 August 1901 and Serjeant on 08 October 1901.

William was posted back to the depot of The Royal Berkshire Regiment at Brock Barracks, Reading, Berkshire, on 02 April 1902 and discharged from the army at the end of his first period of service three days later, on 05 April 1902.

There is little information available about William following his discharge from the army, but it is known that he married Emily Jane Bateman in Shepherds Bush, London, on 21 December 1907 and that their daughter, Olive Eileen Kearney, was born in 1911. In that same year, William is recorded in the census living with his wife and child in West Kensington, London, and employed as a Housekeeper in company offices.

It is unknown when William re-enlisted, or why he enlisted into The King's (Liverpool Regiment), as his service record for this time is no longer available, but it is likely that he was one of the Kitchener volunteers and that he was quickly promoted to Serjeant due to his previous service. The battalion that he joined, 14th (Service) Battalion, had been formed at Seaforth, Lancashire, in October 1914, coming under the orders of the 75th Brigade, 22nd Division. After training, it landed at Boulogne almost a year later, on 05 September 1915.

There is a brief mention of William's death in a Regimental history that was written ten years after the war:

"The 14th King's of the 66th Brigade, 22nd Division, did not arrive in France until 5th September. The division proceeded direct to the Somme area, the King's men reaching Raineville on the following morning. They received their introduction into trench warfare in the trenches of the 18th and 51st Divisions. On 14th they suffered the first casualty, a sergeant dying of wounds received in action".[157]

It is likely that this was William, as he was the only Serjeant from the battalion to die that day. He is also another "Lost Boy" whose name has been omitted from the memorial tablets in the school chapel.

Hubert KENNY

Private, 9423, 1st Battalion, The King's (Liverpool Regiment) who died on 15 September 1914, aged 23. Commemorated on the La Ferte-Sous-Jouarre Memorial, Seine-et-Marne, France

Born on 06 September 1891 in Warrington, Lancashire, the youngest child of John Kenny and Catherine née Warburton, his father had been a Private in The Prince of Wales's Volunteers (South Lancashire Regiment). Further information regarding his father's service is unavailable, as Hubert's Petition Document is missing. However, it is known that his mother died in Warrington in 1895 and that it is likely that by 1901, his father had also died, as the census of that year records Hubert and his older sister, Sophia, living with their maternal grandparents, and Sophia was named as co-beneficiary in the Registers of Soldiers' Effects[158] when Hubert was later killed.

Hubert was admitted to the school on 21 November 1902 (Petition No. 11762) and was discharged to the army on 15 January

---

[157] Everard Wyrall, A., (1929). *The History of The King's Regiment (Liverpool) 1914-1919 Volume I.* London: Edward Arnold

[158] UK, Army Registers of Soldiers' Effects, 1901-1929, 1914-1915, Exeter, Preston, Shrewsbury, Warwick, Winchester, 142501-144500

1906, enlisting into The King's (Liverpool Regiment), the census of 1911 recording him as a Private in that regiment, although it is not known where he was stationed, the record showing that he was staying with his cousin and her husband in Horwich, Lancashire. Lily, his cousin, was the second co-beneficiary named in the Registers of Soldiers' Effects on Hubert's death.

When war broke out, 1st Battalion, The King's (Liverpool Regiment) was stationed in Talavera Barracks, Aldershot, Hampshire, but was quickly deployed, landing at Le Havre on 13 August 1914 and having its baptism of fire ten days later, when it was shelled in its positions between Harmignies and Givry. Between 24 August and 05 September, the battalion was constantly retiring, but on the 06 September, it found itself advancing against the now-retiring Germans in the area of Chaumes.

Although in reserve for much of this time, the battalion was placed into the front line at Chevillon on 10 September, with the advance continuing and the battalion reaching Moussy, where it dug in overnight on 14 September. The battalion war diary[159] reports that it stood to arms at 0300hrs on 15 September and experienced heavy shelling throughout the day, suffering five killed and the same number wounded.

One of those killed was Hubert, who died on 15 September 1914. It is possible that he was buried and that the location of the grave was lost, as he no longer has a known grave, and is commemorated on the La Ferte-Sous-Jouarre Memorial.

Frederick WILSON
Serjeant, 9956, 1st Battalion, The King's (Liverpool Regiment) who died on 14 October 1916, aged 23. Buried in Fort Pitt Military Cemetery, Kent, United Kingdom

Born on 13 May 1893 in Warrington, Lancashire, the third of five children of Ralph Wilson and Mary Ann née Cunningham, his father had been a Colour Serjeant in The King's (Liverpool Regiment) who had been discharged to pension on 31 January 1894.

Frederick was the first and only one of Ralph and Mary's sons to join the school, being admitted on 11 December 1902 (Petition No. 11766). He remained at the school for almost five years before being discharged to his father's old regiment on 22 May 1907.

His service record is no longer available, so it is not possible to determine with which battalions Frederick served prior to the war,

---

[159] WO 95/1359/1: 6 Infantry Brigade: 1 Battalion King's Liverpool Regiment., 1914 Aug 1 - 1914 Dec 31, The National Archives, Kew

but at the outbreak of war, he was serving with the 1st Battalion and stationed in Aldershot, Hampshire, quickly mobilising and landing at Le Havre on 13 August 1914.

The battalion first engaged the Germans at Mons after which it went into a retreat that was sustained until 05 September. Having acted as a rear-guard to the 2nd Division, the battalion and its brigade prevented a German force cutting off the 4th (Guards) Brigade and 70th Battery, Royal Field Artillery. It then moved north to Ypres, during the "Race to the Sea" and went on to fight at Langemarck during the First Battle of Ypres.

However, Frederick missed these battles as he did not arrive in theatre until 16 March 1915, just after the battalion had participated in the holding attack at Givenchy in support of the Battle of Neuve Chapelle, actually joining the battalion at Béthune on 20 March.

By mid-1916 the battalion was located in the Somme sector, and at some point, Frederick was wounded severely enough for him to be evacuated back to Britain and admitted to Fort Pitt Military Hospital in Chatham, Kent, where he died of wounds on 14 October 1916.

Samuel John YATES

Lance Serjeant, 9600, 1st Battalion, The King's (Liverpool Regiment) who died on 19 May 1915, aged 22. Commemorated on the Le Touret Memorial, Pas de Calais, France

Born on 04 August 1892 in Prescot, Lancashire, the only child of Thomas Yates and Sarah Jane née Knight, his father was a Company Quartermaster Serjeant in The King's (Liverpool Regiment) who died in 1894. Samuel's mother remarried, to William Hampson, in 1895 and by the time Samuel was admitted to the school 05 February 1904 (Petition No. 11929), he had two half-siblings, William, born in 1897 and Margaret Ann, born in 1900. His mother died in 1900, the year that her youngest child was born.

Samuel was discharged from the school to his father's old regiment on 30 August 1906, although his service record is no longer available, but it is known that at the outbreak of war he was serving in the 1st Battalion and stationed in Aldershot, Hampshire, alongside Dukie Hubert Kenny.

The battalion left Aldershot on 12 August, embarking on HMT *Irrawaddy* at Southampton, Hampshire, on the same day and landing at Le Havre on 13 August 1914, its baptism of fire being on 23 August when it was shelled in the positions that it occupied between Harmignies and Givry. The following day, 24 August, was the start of the long retirement that was to last until 05 September, before the battalion then turned and began to pursue the retiring Germans, participating in the First Battle of Ypres in the October.

By December, it was in the area of Cuinchy, and although it was in the front line on Christmas Day, it does not appear that there was any fraternisation in this sector, the battalion war diary for that day simply stating, *"Trenches very good, bricked on bottom. These trenches were dug by French sappers and are quite the best trenches that we have been in"*[160].

In March 1915, the battalion, along with the Territorial Force 1/5th Battalion, participated in a holding attack at Givenchy in support of the main offensive at Neuve Chapelle. However, an ineffectual preliminary bombardment failed to destroy much of the wire, fatally impeding the assault and resulting in heavy casualties.

In May, the battalion was in the area of Richebourg and on 17 May it launched an attack on the German positions, capturing an enemy trench and 200 prisoners, as well as forcing another 200 Germans to retire. It was still in these positions on 19 May when, at 1300hrs, a staff officer and several officers from the relieving battalion visited their trenches. For the relieving officers this was their first visit to the front line and their movements, which could be observed by the Germans, drew both rifle and artillery fire.

During the course of that day, 19 May 1915, Samuel was killed. It is possible that he was killed by a shell, as his body does not appear to have been recovered and he is commemorated on the Le Touret Memorial.

John Alfred YORKE
Private, 11329, 13th (Service) Battalion, The King's (Liverpool Regiment) who died on 03 May 1917, aged 21. Commemorated on the Arras Memorial, Pas de Calais, France

Born on 20 November 1895 in Cardiff, Glamorganshire, the eldest of two children of Alfred Yorke and Ellen née Droncy, his father was a Private in The Welsh Regiment who was discharged from the army at his own request on 25 January 1898. John's mother died in Bristol, Gloucestershire, on 01 October 1903 and his father died there on 08 February 1904.

John was admitted to the school on 02 December 1904 and transferred to the Gordon Boys' Home[161] on 19 March 1910. He

---

[160] WO 95/1359/2: 6 Infantry Brigade: 1 Battalion King's Liverpool Regiment, 1915 Jan 1 - 1915 Dec 31, The National Archives, Kew

[161] Founded in 1885 for *"necessitous boys"* and named as a memorial to Major-General Charles George Gordon who had been killed on 26 January 1885 in Khartoum, Mahdist Sudan. A small number of Dukies in this era had a place found for them at the Gordon Boys' Home when they were unfit for the army and had need for further education, likely due to them being orphans such as John

was discharged from the Gordon Boys' Home in 1912 and enlisted into The King's (Liverpool Regiment) in nearby Woking, Surrey.

It is not known to which battalion John was posted as his service record is no longer available, but his medal index card shows that he was not entitled to the award of the 1914-15 Star, showing that he did not enter theatre until at least 1916, although there is no date of disembarkation recorded.

The battalion with which he was serving, 13th (Service) Battalion, was formed at Seaforth, Lancashire, in September 1914 as part of K3 and attached as Army Troops to the 25th Division. In February 1915 it was transferred to the 76th Brigade, 25th Division and landed at Le Havre on 27 September 1915.

On 01 May 1917, the battalion entered the front-line trenches in preparation for an attack on 03 May, which was launched at 0345hrs that morning. Although it was still dark, the battalion advanced behind a creeping barrage, coming under heavy machine-gun fire but taking its objective. However, it was subjected to two strong German counterattacks, the first of which depleted the battalion to such an extent that it was forced to withdraw as a result of the second.

The battalion suffered 73 officers and other ranks killed during the day of the attack, including John. His body was not recovered, and so he is commemorated on the Arras Memorial. He is also another "Lost Boy" whose name has been omitted from the memorial tablets in the school chapel, although he is commemorated as one of the 156 boys from the now Gordon's School to have fallen in the First World War.

The Norfolk Regiment

James Harry BRIGHTY
Drummer, 8218, 2nd Battalion, The Norfolk Regiment who died on 15 October 1916, aged 20. Buried in Baghdad (North Gate) War Cemetery, Iraq

Born on 22 June 1896 in Aldershot, Hampshire, the second of four children of Charles William Brighty and Louisa née Howard, his father was a Private in The Norfolk Regiment who died of enteric fever on 08 March 1902 whilst on active service in South Africa.

James was admitted to the school on 11 January 1907 (Petition No. 12309) and after making the transition from Chelsea to Guston, he was discharged on 06 September 1910, enlisting into The Norfolk Regiment. His service record is unavailable, but the 1911 Census shows him as a Private in the 1st Battalion stationed in Malplaquet Barracks, Wellington Lines, Aldershot, Hampshire.

At some point, James was posted to the 2nd Battalion and this is likely to have happened pre-war, his first entry into theatre in the war being Mesopotamia in November 1914. In August 1914, the 2nd Battalion was stationed in Bombay, India, but was deployed to Mesopotamia as part of the protection force for the Persian oilfields, landing at Basra on 15 November 1914, part of the 6th (Poona) Division, which was pursuing the Ottomans gradually northward. However, after the inconclusive Battle of Ctesiphon in November 1915, the division was ordered to retire to the town of Kut al Amara.

By December, the Ottomans had arrived in such numbers that they were able to besiege the town, and, despite the launching of several relief forces from Basra, the division was forced to surrender on 29 April 1916, with around 13,000 British and Indian troops becoming prisoners, approximately 2,600 of whom were British.

On 06 May 1916, the Ottomans began the 1,200-mile forced march of the British and Indian prisoners across the Syrian Desert from Kut al Amara, with mounted Arab and Kurdish guards prodding the British soldiers with rifle butts and whips, on the long death march. Starvation, thirst, disease and exhaustion thinned out the British column, with only 837 soldiers surviving the march and the years of captivity that were to follow. James is recorded as having "died of sickness" on 15 October 1916 at Afion Karahissar camp, one of 1,700 British soldiers who died in captivity in this theatre.

The cemetery in which James is buried, Baghdad (North Gate) War Cemetery, was begun in April 1917 and has been greatly enlarged since the end of the First World War, with graves *"brought in"* from other burial grounds in Baghdad and Northern Iraq, and from battlefields and cemeteries in Anatolia where Commonwealth prisoners of war were buried by the Turks.

James Samuel ELLARD
Serjeant, 7473, 1st Battalion, The Norfolk Regiment who died on 24 August 1914, aged 31. Buried in Hautrage Military Cemetery, Hainaut, Belgium

Born on 28 October 1882 in Pimlico, London, the third of four children of Michael Francis Ellard and Mary née Hallett, his father had been a Private in The Queen's Own Cameron Highlanders who had been discharged from the army on 26 July 1881 and died in Westminster, Middlesex, on 24 June 1886.

James was admitted to the school on 27 May 1892 (Petition No. 10336), joining his older brother, Michael Henry Ellard, who had been admitted to the school on 28 February 1890 (Petition No. 9981). James was discharged on 23 October 1897 and enlisted into Princess Louise's (Argyll and Sutherland Highlanders).

James spent all of his service with this regiment in Britain, but on 13 June 1900 he was tried by Regimental Courts Martial for failing to comply with an order, was convicted, and sentenced to 28 days' imprisonment. At the end of his sentence, James was discharged from the army on 13 July 1900, *"Services no longer required"*.

Eight months after he was discharged from the army, James entered service with the London, Brighton and South Coast Railway, where he was employed as a Porter at Battersea Wharf Station. However, on 23 October 1905, he re-enlisted into the army, joining The Norfolk Regiment and being posted to the 1st Battalion.

James spent all of his service from enlistment in Britain and at the outbreak of war the battalion was stationed in Holywood, Belfast, County Antrim, part of the 15th Brigade, 5th Division. It was quickly mobilised and the battalion landed at Le Havre on 14 August 1914, by which time, James was a Serjeant.

The battalion diary for the initial weeks of the war is missing, but it is known that the 1st Battalion was located in the area of Mons when the German Army launched its offensive on 24 August.

There is some confusion as to James's fate. The Commonwealth War Graves Commission records his date of death as 24 August 1914, which if correct would make him the first Dukie killed in action in the First World War, sharing that sad date distinction with John Edgar, although the graves registration documents for James record the date as 24 September 1914. However, within his service record, he was initially reported as wounded in action and missing on 24 August 1914, followed by another entry stating that there was an unofficial report that he was killed in action on that date, as well as a another that states that he died of tetanus as a result of his wounds.

There is also an entry dated January 1915 that states that he was cared for in a Belgian Hospital and then taken to Germany as a Prisoner of War, but also an entry after this, but dated 26 October 1914, which stated that the Foreign Office had received a report from the International Committee of the Red Cross that he was treated in Field Hospital No. 8 at Thulin and buried at the cemetery at Boussu, Hainaut, Belgium.

Communication with the family continued until after the war, despite the report of his death being accepted in 1915 and there is also a letter in 1922 from a "great chum" who had served with him for six years and was wishing to reconnect with James.

Despite the confusion and debate, it seems likely that James died of wounds whilst in captivity on 24 August 1914, as the cemetery in which he is interred, Hautrage Military Cemetery, is located in a village that was in German hands for almost the entire war and the cemetery had been begun by the Germans in August and September of 1914.

James is also another of the "Lost Boys" whose name has been omitted from the memorial tablets in the school chapel.

Michael was discharged from the school on 21 April 1894 and enlisted into the Coldstream Guards, although he was discharged as medically unfit for further service nine months later, on 11 January 1895. It appears that following his discharge from the army, Michael married and moved to Canada, as he appears in the 1911 Canadian Census, but it is not known when he moved to that country, or when he returned, as he was in Britain when he was communicating with the authorities following his brother's death. He remained in Britain, dying in Islington, London, in 1949.

Beecher Reginald HUNGERFORD
Private, 8079, 2nd Battalion, The Norfolk Regiment, who died on 26 September 1916, aged 26. Commemorated on the Angora Memorial, Baghdad (North Gate) War Cemetery, Iraq

Born on 23 March 1890 in Kentish Town, London, the sixth of seven children of Thomas Christopher Hungerford and Mary Jane née Gamble, his father had been a Staff Serjeant serving in both the

26th (The Cameronian) Regiment of Foot and the Army Service Corps, but had been discharged to pension on 15 February 1878. He died in Wandsworth, London, on 30 June 1900, five months after Albert's mother, who had died in Islington, London, on 22 January 1900.

Beecher was admitted to the school on 07 December 1900 (Petition No. 11503), joined by his younger brother Albert Victor Hungerford on 16 August 1901 (Petition No. 11595). This was three days before their elder, non-Dukie brother, Augustus Morton Hungerford, died of enteric fever whilst serving with the 24th Battalion, Imperial Yeomanry, in South Africa, during the Second Boer War. Beecher was discharged from the school to *"Civil Life"* on 23 March 1904.

It is not known at what point Beecher joined the army, but his service number suggests that it was sometime between 11 February 1909 and 18 January 1910, enlisting into The Norfolk Regiment.

At the outbreak of war, 2nd Battalion, The Norfolk Regiment, was stationed in Bombay, India, but landed at Basra, Mesopotamia, on 15 November 1914. The history for Beecher is very similar to that of James Brighty, another fallen Dukie who served in the same battalion and it would appear that like James, Beecher was captured at the fall of Kut al Amara and would have made the same long march into captivity, being held in a camp near the city of Angora[162].

As with so many of the prisoners who were captured by the Ottoman forces, Beecher died of disease. He has no known grave and is commemorated on the Angora Memorial within Baghdad (North Gate) War Cemetery, Iraq.

The Commonwealth War Graves Commission has incorrectly recorded his name as *Belcher*, which is a possible explanation as to why he is a "Lost Boy" whose name has been omitted from the memorial tablets in the school chapel.

Albert was discharged from the school on 24 May 1906, enlisting into The Queen's (Royal West Surrey Regiment). He died in Belgium on 02 November 1914 and sadly like his brother has no known grave, being commemorated on the Ypres (Menin Gate) Memorial. However, unlike Beecher, he is commemorated on the memorial tablets in the school chapel.

---

[162] Modern-day Ankara

Thomas William O'HARA
Serjeant, 37287, 9th (Service) Battalion, The Norfolk Regiment who died on 17 February 1919, aged 45. Buried in Bois-Guillaume Communal Cemetery Extension, Seine-Maritime, France

Born on 18 June 1873 in Portsmouth, Hampshire, the second of four children of Thomas O'Hara and Emily Alice née Popplestone, his father had been a Serjeant in the 4th (The King's Own Royal) Regiment of Foot who had been discharged from the army on 18 May 1876 and died in Woodilee Asylum in Glasgow, Lanarkshire, on 02 February 1881.

Thomas was admitted to the school on 14 September 1883 (Petition No. 8994) and was discharged on 02 July 1887, enlisting into The King's Own (Royal Lancaster Regiment). He was posted to the 2nd Battalion and spent the first eighteen months of his service in Britain before he was posted to India on 04 December 1888. Thomas spent eight years in India, during which time he was appointed as a Bandsman on 23 May 1892 and as a Lance Corporal on 27 June 1893, although he reverted to Private on 04 May 1894. However, eight months later, on 05 January 1895, he was again appointed as a Lance Corporal, although he then reverted, at his own request to Bandsman, on 07 December 1895.

Thomas was posted back to Britain on 25 February 1896 and was promoted to Corporal on 05 December of the same year. Nine months later, on 28 September 1897, he was tried by Regimental Courts Martial and convicted of drunkenness on duty, his sentence being a fine of £1, although he did retain his rank.

Thomas then re-engaged to complete 21 years' service on 03 May 1899 and was promoted to Lance Serjeant the following day. He was then promoted to Serjeant on 13 November 1899 before he was posted to South Africa during the Second Boer War on 02 December 1899.

After eight months in South Africa, Thomas was posted to the 1st Battalion and returned to Britain on 21 August 1900, but three months after this posting, he was again posted to South Africa, on 26 November 1900, where he remained until 12 September 1902 before being posted back to Britain. Thomas spent the last three years of his service in Britain, promoted to Colour Serjeant on 03 June 1903, before he was discharged from the army on 30 November 1905.

Little is known about Thomas's life following his discharge from the army, although he is recorded in the 1911 Census, living in Dover, Kent, with his mother and stepfather, his occupation given as Retired Army Pensioner – Musician.

Following the outbreak of war, it appears that Thomas re-enlisted, joining The Norfolk Regiment, although the date of his enlistment is unknown as the service record for this period of service has not survived.

The battalion with which Thomas served, 9th (Service) Battalion, had been formed at Norwich, Norfolk, in September 1914 as part of K3, coming under the orders of the 71st Brigade, 24th Division and landing at Boulogne on 30 July 1915. The 71st Brigade was then transferred to the 6th Division on 15 October 1915.

It is not known when Thomas arrived in theatre, as there is no date of disembarkation recorded in his medal index card, but he did not qualify for the award of the 1914-15 Star, indicating that it was not until 1916 at the earliest. It is also not possible to confirm Thomas's movements once he did arrive in theatre, but it is known that at some point he was transferred to the 287th Area Employment Company, Labour Corps.

The Area Employment Companies were formed in 1917 for salvage work and it is possible that this work was the reason that he was still in theatre in 1919, following the cessation of hostilities. It is known that he was admitted to No. 8 General Hospital in Rouen and that he died there of influenza on 17 February 1919.

Thomas was buried in Bois-Guillaume Communal Cemetery Extension, most of the burials for this cemetery coming from No. 8 General Hospital. However, despite being commemorated by the Commonwealth War Graves Commission, he is another "Lost Boy" whose name has been omitted from the memorial tablets in the school chapel.

Walter Sibley REYNOLDS

Private, 242486, 1/5th Battalion, The Norfolk Regiment who died on 17 September 1917, aged 39. Buried in Baghdad (North Gate) War Cemetery, Iraq

Born on 09 January 1878 in Sunnyside, Lanarkshire, a son of Walter Reynolds and Elizabeth née Sibley, his father was a Serjeant Major in the 63rd (West Suffolk) Regiment of Foot[163], but died nine days after his son's birth, on 18 January 1878.

Walter was admitted to the school on 26 October 1888 (Petition No. 9706), ten months after his brother, Alfred Sibley Reynolds, had been admitted on 09 December 1887 (Petition No. 9590). Their elder brother, William John Reynolds, had been admitted to the school six months after Walter was born, on 05 July 1878 (Petition

---

[163] Amalgamated with the 96th Regiment of Foot on 01 July 1881 to become The Manchester Regiment

No. 8239). Walter was discharged from the school on 30 January 1892, enlisting into The Norfolk Regiment the same day and spending the first six years of his service in Britain, before being posted to India with the 2nd Battalion on 13 December 1898.

After sixteen months in India, he was then posted to South Africa for a year, returning to Britain on 11 February 1903 and re-engaging on 11 January 1904 to complete 21 years' service, before again being posted to South Africa on 12 October 1905.

During this second period of service in South Africa, Walter was appointed as a paid Lance Corporal on 12 October 1905. However, this elevation was short-lived, as he was posted as absent without leave on 23 November 1905, confined the following day and tried by District Courts Martial two days after that, being sentenced to 21 days' confinement and reduced to Private.

Walter was discharged from the army on 04 May 1906 and returned to Britain two days later, after which his life is something of a mystery, as he does not appear in the 1911 Census, next appearing in records when he re-enlisted into the army on 04 March 1916, recorded as living in Coventry, Warwickshire and employed as a Fitter's Mate.

He was initially posted to 3rd (Reserve) Battalion, The Norfolk Regiment in Felixstowe, Suffolk, before he was posted to the 7th (Service) Battalion in France on 06 June 1916. However, he was only in France for two months before he was wounded, on 20 August 1916, during the Somme Offensive, when he received gunshot wounds to the back and both legs, returning initially to the Regimental Depot before re-joining the 3rd (Reserve) Battalion on 11 December 1916.

Walter spent the next year in Felixstowe, Suffolk, and was then posted to the 1/5th Battalion on 12 February 1917. This battalion was a Territorial Force battalion, located in East Dereham, Norfolk, at the outbreak of war and had fought at Gallipoli from August to December 1915, before it was evacuated to Egypt, where Walter joined as a replacement.

On 17 April 1917, the Allied Egyptian Expeditionary Force launched the Second Battle of Gaza, which was to last until 19 April and resulted in an Ottoman victory, as had the first battle. Walter was captured on the last day of the battle and was interned in a work camp in Yarbaschi, Asia Minor[164], a work camp for the construction, or running, of the Baghdad Railway with deaths being high amongst prisoners held there, including Walter, who died as a result of dysentery and tropical malaria five months later. He was buried in

---

[164] Modern-day Turkey

the cemetery near to Bagtche in the Amanus Mountains[165] before his body was relocated to Baghdad following the Armistice. Walter is also another "Lost Boy" whose name has been omitted from the memorial tablets in the school chapel.

William was discharged from the school on 09 November 1881 and enlisted into The Black Watch (Royal Highlanders) as a Musician. He transferred to the Coldstream Guards on 10 August 1894 and was discharged from that regiment as a Band Serjeant on 29 July 1912. It is not known when he died.

When Alfred was discharged from the school on 31 August 1889, he enlisted into The King's Royal Rifle Corps. He was discharged a year later, on 18 July 1890, although he must have re-enlisted as he is shown in the 1911 Census as a 35-year-old Private in 1st Battalion, The South Wales Borderers and stationed in Chatham Barracks, Kent. He survived the war, dying in London on 25 November 1942.

---

[165] Now Nur Mountains

The Lincolnshire Regiment

Walter Edwin BALDWIN
Lance Corporal, 9436, 1st Battalion, The Lincolnshire Regiment who died on 16 June 1915, aged 22. Commemorated on the Ypres (Menin Gate) Memorial, West-Vlaanderen, Belgium

Born on 03 June 1893 in Woolwich, London, the eldest of two children of William Baldwin and Ada née Hood, his father was a Staff Sergeant Major in the Army Service Corps who died on active service from a self-inflicted gunshot wound to his head at Bloemfontein, South Africa, on 26 April 1900.

Walter was admitted to the school on 12 August 1903 (Petition No. 11836) and was joined by his younger brother, Archibald Harry Baldwin, on 29 June 1909 (Petition No. 12607). Walter was discharged from the school on 12 June 1907 and enlisted into the Army Service Corps.

The service record for this period of Walter's service is no longer available, so it is not known for how long he served, but he is recorded in the 1911 Census living in his mother's home in Plumstead, Kent, and employed as a Labourer in Woolwich Dockyard.

However, in the year after the census, it appears that Walter re-enlisted into the army, his service number in The Lincolnshire Regiment suggesting an enlistment date between 09 August 1911 and 12 October 1912, although there is again no service record available for this period of service.

At the outbreak of war, 1st Battalion, The Lincolnshire Regiment, was located in Portsmouth, Hampshire, and Walter would have been serving alongside fellow Dukie William Clarkin. However, the battalion was quickly mobilised, Walter's medal index card showing that he disembarked in France on 13 August 1914. Walter would also have participated in the early battles of the war, including the Battle of Mons and the subsequent retreat, as well as the First Battle of Ypres.

In 1915, the battalion took part of the Second Battle of Ypres and, in early-June, the Battle of Bellewaarde which was an effort to push the Germans off Bellewaarde Ridge, which was giving them good observation over all of the British positions. This attack was unsuccessful, and so on 16 June, the battalion participated in a second attempt to take the ridge, which was also unsuccessful and resulted in 1 officer and 25 other ranks killed, 4 officers and 265 other ranks wounded, and 3 officers and 76 other ranks missing.

Walter was one of the missing, who was *"regarded as dead"* and is commemorated on the Menin Gate Memorial. He is also a "Lost Boy" whose name has been omitted from the memorial tablets in the school chapel.

Archibald was discharged from the school having made the transition from Chelsea to Guston, on 05 September 1911, also enlisting into the Army Service Corps, serving throughout the war. He is recorded in the 1939 England and Wales Register as an Examiner of Ammunition and Chief Inspector of Armaments, living in Woolwich, London. He died in Lewisham, London, in 1971.

Thomas BROWN
Private, 21271, 1st Battalion, The Lincolnshire Regiment who died on 23 April 1917, aged 38. Commemorated in Nunhead (All Saints) Cemetery, London, United Kingdom

Born on 12 January 1879 in Lincoln, Lincolnshire, the second of seven children of William Brown and Jane née Salvage, his father had been a Private in the 72nd (or Duke of Albany's Own Highlanders) Regiment of Foot[166] who had fought during the Crimean War and had been discharged from the army on 18 March 1856, later being admitted to the Royal Hospital, Chelsea.

Thomas was admitted to the school on 29 November 1889 (Petition No. 9928) and discharged on 28 January 1893, enlisting into the Royal Artillery.

Thomas spent the first five years of his service in Britain before he was posted to Malta on 05 May 1898. He was to spend six years in Malta, during which time he married Alice Maud James on 05 November 1901, with three of their children being born on the island, twins Thomas and Alice Brown, born on 15 August 1902, although they both died within 90 minutes of birth and Gladys May Brown, born on 21 January 1904.

Thomas was appointed as a Bombardier on 05 September 1903 and posted back to Britain on 20 January 1904, where he re-engaged to complete 21 years' service on 15 November 1904. It appears that he was stationed in Plymouth, Devonshire, as the family was living in the St. Budeaux area of the city when daughter Alice Maud Brown

---

[166]Amalgamated with the 78th (Highlanders) Regiment of Foot (The Ross-shire Buffs) on 01 July 1881 to become the Seaforth Highlanders (Ross-shire Buffs), renamed the Seaforth Highlanders (Ross-shire Buffs, The Duke of Albany's) on 22 November 1881

was born on 09 May 1906. Sadly, she also died, on 19 December 1906.

Their next child, Walter Evan Brown, was also born in St. Budeaux on 12 August 1908, three years before Thomas was discharged from the army at his own request, having completed 18 years' service, on 17 March 1911. The family then moved to London, as they appear in the 1911 Census living in Low Leyton, Thomas's occupation given as *"Late Royal Garrison Artillery – no occupation"*.

Following the outbreak of war, by which time he and Alice had another child, Maud Mary Brown, born in 1912 and were expecting the birth of their sixth, Lilian Rose Brown, who was born in December 1914, Thomas was either recalled to the Colours or re-enlisted voluntarily. However, little is known of this period of service as his service record is no longer available, although it is known that he served in 1st Battalion, The Lincolnshire Regiment and that he re-enlisted at Greenwich, London.

In August 1914, the battalion was stationed in Portsmouth, Hampshire, but quickly mobilised and landed at Le Havre on 14 August 1914. There is also no date of entry into theatre recorded on Thomas's medal index card, but the fact that he was not entitled to the award of the 1914-15 Star suggests that any overseas service occurred after 1916.

The circumstances that resulted in Thomas being admitted to The King George Hospital in London are not known, but it is known that he died there on 23 April 1917, from wounds received in action. Although commemorated in Nunhead (All Saints) Cemetery and by the Commonwealth War Graves Commission, Thomas is another "Lost Boy" whose name has been omitted from the memorial tablets in the school chapel.

William Percy CLARKIN
Bandsman, 4926, 1st Battalion, The Lincolnshire Regiment who died on 28 April 1917, aged 33. Buried in Meza (Nikolai) Cemetery, Latvia

Born on 19 December 1883 in Macclesfield, Cheshire, the third child of John Clarkin and Jane née Cook, his father had been a Serjeant Drummer in The Prince of Wales's Own (West Yorkshire Regiment), although at the time of William's birth he was the Bandmaster of 2nd The Earl of Chester's Regiment of Yeomanry Cavalry. He died in Macclesfield in 1891.

William was admitted to the school on 26 May 1893 (Petition No. 10471) and was discharged on 10 January 1898, enlisting into The Lincolnshire Regiment as a Bandsman. His service record is no longer available, so his career until the outbreak of war is unknown, although the 1911 Census records him as a Drummer in the 1st Battalion, serving in Aden.

At the outbreak of war, the battalion was stationed in Portsmouth, Hampshire, quickly mobilised, and landed at Le Havre on 14 August 1914, where it participated in the early battles of the war. It was during the Battle of Mons that William was captured, on 24 August 1914, spending the remainder of his life as a Prisoner of War.

Records show that William died of illness in a Prisoner of War camp in Mitau, the German name for Jelgava, in Russia[167] on 28 April 1917 and he was buried in the Russian cemetery in the town. He is one of 36 British soldiers and sailors buried in Meza (Nikolai) Cemetery, four of whom are unidentified. Most died as prisoners in 1917.

Herbert Leonard William FREEMAN
Private, 22433, 1st Battalion, The Lincolnshire Regiment who died on 20 September 1917, aged 23. Commemorated on the Tyne Cot Memorial, West-Vlaanderen, Belgium

Born on 16 September 1894 in Aldershot, Hampshire, the second of four children of Sidney Herbert Freeman and his second wife, Caroline Jane née Lacey, his father had been a Corporal in The Lincolnshire Regiment and had been discharged to pension on 04 May 1904. His mother died in Secunderabad, India, on 12 September 1903.

Herbert was admitted to the school on 07 October 1904 (Petition No. 12023) and was discharged on 25 September 1908, enlisting into 16th (The Queen's) Lancers, serving with this regiment for six years, before being appointed as a Trumpeter and posted to the 8th Reserve Cavalry, stationed in Newbridge, County Kildare, on 15 August 1914, eleven days after the start of the war.

He spent almost six months in Ireland, prior to being posted to the 17th (Duke of Cambridge's Own) Lancers, which had arrived in France from India in November 1914, joining them on 16 February 1915.

The nature of the conflict meant that the regiment barely moved 20 miles from Amiens between 1914 and 1917, generally in reserve and used to plug gaps and relieve infantry battalions. Just over a year after arriving in France, Herbert transferred to his father's old regiment, joining 1st Battalion, The Lincolnshire Regiment, on 26 March 1916.

---

[167] Latvia was still part of the Russian Empire at this time, although it had been occupied by the Germans since the summer of 1915

The battalion was in reserve on 01 July, the start of the Somme Offensive and although called forward during the day, it did not suffer the casualties that many others did, but was in action by 03 July and remained in this sector for the remainder of the year.

The following year saw the battalion spending the vast majority of its time in Flanders, participating in the Battle of Messines, as well as the Third Battle of Ypres, which commenced on 31 July 1917. It was in action during the Battle of the Menin Road Ridge, which commenced on 20 September and it was on this day that Herbert was killed. His body was never recovered and he is commemorated on the Tyne Cot Memorial.

Herbert had three brothers and one stepbrother, and although none were at the school, all served during the war. His younger brother, Gordon Cecil James Freeman, was killed on 26 September 1916 and is commemorated on the Thiepval Memorial, Somme, France.

John Thomas NOKES
Private, 7843, 1st Battalion, The Lincolnshire Regiment who died on 03 July 1916 aged 31. Buried in Gordon Dump Cemetery, Ovillers-La Boiselle, Somme, France

Born on 12 April 1885 in Birmingham, Warwickshire, the fifth of six children of William Nokes and Sarah Eliza née Duckett, his father had been a Colour Serjeant in The Prince Consort's Own (Rifle Brigade) who had been discharged on 22 January 1884. He died in Birmingham on 06 March 1894.

John was admitted to the school on 04 January 1895 (Petition No. 10691) with his younger brother, James Walter Nokes, joining him on 03 June 1898 (Petition No. 11171). John was discharged from the school on 10 May 1900 and enlisted into the Royal Garrison Artillery, however he only served for five years, all of these in Britain, before he was discharged at Woolwich, *"services no longer required"*, on 19 June 1905.

It appears that following his discharge, John re-enlisted into the army, joining The Lincolnshire Regiment, and although his service record has not survived, his service number suggests an enlistment date of late-1906.

At the outbreak of war, John would have been stationed in Portsmouth, Hampshire, as part of the 9th Brigade, 3rd Division, and having been joined by a contingent of 2 officers and 125 other ranks from The Bermuda Rifle Volunteer Corps[168], it landed at Le

---

[168] Created in 1894 as a reserve for the Regular Army component of the Bermuda Garrison

Havre on 14 August 1914, going into action for the first time at Mons nine days later, at which time Dukie William Clarkin was captured. However, according to his medal index card, John did not enter theatre until two days after this first action, on 25 August.

The battalion then took part in the Retreat from Mons, fighting at Le Cateau, as well as the Battles of the Marne and the Aisne, La Bassée and the First Battle of Ypres. It did not participate in the Christmas Truce, as it had been relieved in the trenches on 24 December by 1st Battalion, The Royal Irish Rifles, spending the festive period in billets in Locre, Belgium.

The battalion was involved in the winter operations and during 1915 also participated in the Battles of Bellewaarde and Hooge, before transferring to the 62nd Brigade, 21st Division in November of that year, the formation with which it was still serving in June 1916.

The Somme Offensive commenced on 01 July 1916, considered to be the blackest day in the history of the British Army, but on that day the battalion was in reserve, although it was called forward north of Fricourt later in the day and captured Crucifix Trench and the Sunken Road, with relatively light casualties of around 100 men.

Two days later, it received orders to attack and capture Birch Tree Wood and Shelter Wood. Despite a heavy bombardment and stout defence by the Germans, the attack was successful, with 700 prisoners taken. However, the battalion war diary[169] records 243 casualties, including 34 other ranks killed, one of whom was John.

Unlike so many of the casualties that fell in the first days of the Somme Offensive, John's body was recovered and he has a marked grave. However, he is another of the "Lost Boys" whose name has been omitted from the memorial tablets in the school chapel.

James was discharged from the school *"To mother"* on 13 September 1902. The 1911 Census records him as an Assistant Caretaker for the London County Council Education Department and living in Battersea, London. However, he later enlisted in the Royal Field Artillery, achieving the rank of Serjeant by the end of the war. He died in Lambeth, London, in 1952.

---

[169] WO 95/2154/1: 1 Battalion Lincolnshire Regiment, 1915 Nov. - 1919 Mar., The National Archives, Kew

William Henry STROHM
Serjeant, 8310, 2nd Battalion, The Lincolnshire Regiment who died on 29 September 1918, aged 24. Buried in Villers Hill British Cemetery, Villers-Guislain, Nord, France

Born on 26 November 1893 in Woolwich, London, the only child of William Strohm and Mary Anne née Poole, his father was a Private in the Army Service Corps who died in Sterkstroom, South Africa, on 04 February 1900, whilst serving in the Second Boer War.

William was admitted to the school on 13 August 1903 (Petition No. 11849) and discharged to The Lincolnshire Regiment on 19 December 1907. His service record is no longer available, but the 1911 Census records him as a Boy serving with the 2nd Battalion and stationed in Victoria Barracks, Portsmouth, Hampshire.

At the outbreak of war, the battalion was stationed in Bermuda, West Indies, moving to Halifax, Nova Scotia, before returning to Britain on 03 November. After being made up to strength, it embarked at Southampton, Hampshire, on 05 November and landed at Le Havre on 06 November 1914.

Its first major action was during the Battle of Neuve Chapelle in March 1915 and it was again in action during the Battle of Aubers two months later, remaining on the Western Front throughout the war, including during the Somme Offensive in 1916 and the Third Battle of Ypres in 1917.

Following the failed German offensive in the Spring of 1918, the tide turned and the Allied armies began pursuing the Germans and, by September, the battalion was in the area of Gouzeaucourt where, on 29 September, it was ordered to attack Gonnelieu.

The attack commenced with an artillery barrage on the German positions at 0330hrs, but due to the late arrival of orders, the battalion was late in forming up and unable to get close to the barrage. Despite this, it advanced through Gouzeaucourt, being gas shelled as it did so and even though there was a good initial advance, it came under heavy machine-gun fire which halted the advance 300 yards west of the objective. Just after dusk, it was subjected to a heavy German barrage and was forced to retire to trenches north of the Gouzeaucourt to Gonnelieu road.

The partially successful attack resulted in relatively light casualties, with only 29 members of the battalion being killed on that day, one of whom was William. He is buried in Villers Hill British Cemetery, half a mile south of the village of Villers-Guislain and two miles south of the objective of 29 September 1918. Although he is commemorated on the memorial tablets in the school chapel, he is recorded as W Strohm.

William Henry Percival TOOMEY
Corporal, 7770, 2nd Battalion, The Lincolnshire Regiment who died on 10 March 1915, aged 22. Commemorated on the Le Touret Memorial, Pas de Calais, France

Born on 16 June 1892 in Hounslow, Middlesex, the fifth of six children of Michael Toomey and Caroline née Regan, his father had served in the 77th (East Middlesex) Regiment of Foot and had been discharged from the army on 05 April 1881.

William was admitted to the school on 11 September 1903 (Petition No. 11882), joining his older brother, Harold Hector Toomey, who had been at the school since 08 December 1899 (Petition No. 11380). William was discharged on 30 June 1906, enlisting straight into The Lincolnshire Regiment and although his service record is no longer available, he is shown in the 1911 Census as a Private in the 2nd Battalion, stationed in Victoria Barracks in Portsmouth.

Following the outbreak of war, William's experience would have been the same as that of William Strohm and he landed at Le Havre on 06 November 1914, the battalion's first experience of the trenches being ten days later, but it had a *"quiet time"*[170] during this period.

It spent the early part of 1915 in the area of Laventie, but at the start of March it moved into trenches opposite Neuve Chapelle, in preparation for the attack that was to be launched on 10 March. On the night before the attack, it was still in these trenches when the preparatory bombardment commenced at 0730hrs, this lifting 35 minutes later, when the battalion went "over the top".

The first trench was captured in a very short time, with the loss of just 20 men, before the blocking parties cleared the trenches. It then assaulted and captured the second German trench, although it lost its Commanding Officer in the process after a "friendly" shell had blown off his leg. The attack on the third line of trenches was held up by a water obstacle and then checked by fire from British artillery, which resulted in the battalion having to retire to the second line of trenches.

William was one of 83 soldiers killed during this attack on the 10 March 1915. He is commemorated, along with 66 of his colleagues also killed that day, on the Le Touret Memorial and has no known grave.

Harold also joined the army when he was discharged from the school on 04 June 1904, enlisting into The Duke of Cambridge's Own (Middlesex Regiment). Although discharged as medically unfit

---

[170] WO 95/1730/1: 2 Battalion Lincolnshire Regiment, 1914 Nov. - 1918 Jan., The National Archives, Kew

in 1911, he was recalled as a Special Reservist in September 1914. Suffering from nephritis, he was admitted to No. 5 General Hospital in Rouen, where he died from renal failure on 17 June 1915 and was buried in St. Sever Cemetery, Rouen. He is one of the "Lost Boys" whose name has been omitted from the memorial tablets in the school chapel and is documented later in this book.

Albert Alfred WHITE
Serjeant, 5309, 2nd Battalion, The Lincolnshire Regiment who died on 13 March 1915, aged 29. Buried in Canadian Cemetery No.2, Neuville-St. Vaast, Pas De Calais, France

Born on 19 March 1885 in Newbridge, County Kildare, the fourth of six children of Thomas White and Emily Jane née Chisnell, his father was a Colour Serjeant in The Lincolnshire Regiment.

Albert was admitted to the school on 30 August 1895 (Petition No. 10795) and discharged to his father's old regiment on 14 March 1899. Although his service record is no longer available, so his pre-war postings are unknown, he appears in the medal rolls of 2nd Battalion, The Lincolnshire Regiment, as having served in the Second Boer War.

Albert's experience at the start of the war would have been the same as both William Strohm and William Toomey, and he was present during the Battle of Neuve Chapelle, which commenced on 10 March.

The battalion was in support of The Royal Irish Rifles during 11 March, moving forward as the Royal Irish did, but had returned to its previous position in an old German trench the following morning. On the night of the 12-13 March, a shrapnel shell burst over this location that mortally wounded one officer and ten other ranks, Alfred being one of those other ranks mortally wounded.

The cemetery in which Albert is interred was established by the Canadian Corps after the capture of Vimy Ridge on 09 April 1917, so it is likely that his was one of the isolated graves moved to this location in the years after the Armistice.

Although he is commemorated on the memorial tablets in the school chapel, he is incorrectly recorded as K A White.

The Devonshire Regiment

Norman John BATTERS
Serjeant, 7642, 2nd Battalion, The Devonshire Regiment who died on 31 July 1917, aged 27. Commemorated on the Ypres (Menin Gate) Memorial, West-Vlaanderen, Belgium

Born on 27 February 1890 in Devonport, Devonshire, the third of four children of Joseph Batters and Mary Ann née Swallow, his father had been a Private in The Devonshire Regiment who had been discharged from the army on 24 June 1884, six years before Norman's birth.

The family remained in Devonport and unusually for a lot of the boys that entered the school at the time, it appears that both of Norman's parents were still alive when he was admitted on 05 October 1900 (Petition No. 11480), joining his older brother, William James Batters, who had been admitted on 05 November 1898 (Petition No. 11232). Norman was discharged from the school on 05 March 1904, enlisting into his father's old regiment, the 1911 Census recording that he was a Drummer in the 2nd Battalion and stationed in St. George's Barracks, Malta.

When war broke out, the battalion was stationed in Egypt, but quickly returned to Britain, arriving on 01 October, where it absorbed drafts of Reservists before being deployed to France a month later, landing at Le Havre on 06 November 1914.

It was to spend the rest of the war in France and Flanders, fighting in many of the battles of 1914-16, including going "over the top" on 01 July 1916 on the first day of the Somme Offensive, suffering 431 casualties killed and wounded. The battalion spent much of the rest of that year in the Somme sector and in early-1917 it followed up the German retreat to the Hindenburg Line.

In June 1917, it moved north to the area of Ypres and prepared for an offensive due to start on 31 July, the Third Battle of Ypres, or Passchendaele, as it was to become known. At 0350hrs on the 31 July 1917, the battalion attacked from Railway Wood and that morning their Colonel was killed, in addition to 12 of its 20 officers, with 230 of its men being killed or wounded, including Norman. He is commemorated on the Menin Gate, one of 45 Devonshire

Regiment soldiers who were killed on 31 July 1917 and have no known grave.

William also enlisted in The Devonshire Regiment when he was discharged from the school on 08 November 1902. It is known that he survived the war and was living with his wife, Mabel, in Surrey in 1939, where he died in 1955.

The youngest, non-Dukie brother, Frederick Thomas Batters, a Stoker 1st Class on HMS *Indefatigable*, was killed in action at the Battle of Jutland on 31 May 1916.

Walter Frederick James CARR
Drummer, 9150, 2nd Battalion, The Devonshire Regiment who died on 01 July 1916, aged 19. Buried in Ovillers Military Cemetery, Somme, France

Born on 13 August 1896 in Exeter, Devonshire, the second of four children of Albert Edward Carr and his second wife Jessie Ellen née Dibben, his father was a Serjeant in The Devonshire Regiment who was wounded at Tugela Heights during the Second Boer War and subsequently died of these wounds on 25 February 1900. However, it appears that Albert may have served previously under the name of Capon, in The Commissariat and Transport Corps, and was facing disciplinary action as, despite being married to his first wife and having a child when he had enlisted, he had claimed to be single. He was discharged following a period of being absent.

Walter was admitted to the school on 05 October 1906 (Petition No. 12282), joining his older brother, Albert Edward Carr, who had been admitted on 07 October 1904 (Petition No. 12011). Having moved from Chelsea to Guston, Walter was discharged to his father's old regiment on 06 September 1910.

The following year, Walter was recorded in the 1911 Census as a Boy in the 1st Battalion and stationed in Lucknow Barracks, Tidworth, Wiltshire. It is not clear when Walter was posted to the 2nd Battalion, as his service record is no longer available, but it is likely that he was serving with that battalion in Egypt alongside Dukie Norman Batters, as his medal index card records him disembarking in France on 06 November 1914.

Walter's battalion moved into trenches on 29 June 1916 and on the 01 July, during the last seven to ten minutes of the bombardment that preceded the opening of the Somme Offensive and which had reached its climax at 0635hrs, it advanced to within 100 yards of the enemy trenches.

The bombardment lifted from the front line onto the German second line at 0730hrs, with the battalion immediately advancing and coming under intense machine-gun fire from its front and flank that mowed down many of the troops. The fighting remained confused with very few of the Devonshires unscathed and at the end of the day it had failed to take its objective between Ovillers and La Boiselle, suffering 50 officers and other ranks killed, 200 wounded and 181 missing.

Walter was one of those killed on 01 July 1916, but unlike many, his body was recovered and he is buried in Ovillers Military Cemetery. Although commemorated on the tablets in the school chapel, he is incorrectly recorded as W T Carr.

Albert was discharged from the school on 15 December 1908 to Alexandra, Princess of Wales's Own (Yorkshire Regiment). He was discharged from the army on 10 November 1917 due to disability and died in Pontypool, Monmouthshire, in 1969.

James Henry ELLIS

Drummer, 9260, 1st Battalion, The Devonshire Regiment who died on 14 January 1915, aged 17. Commemorated on the Ypres (Menin Gate) Memorial, West-Vlaanderen, Belgium

Born on 19 January 1897 in Pembroke Dock, Pembrokeshire, the second of four children of William Henry Ellis and Lavinia Grace née Harvey, his father had been a Private in The Devonshire Regiment who was discharged as *"medically unfit for further service"* on 12 September 1899 and died in Pembroke Dock on 16 November 1903.

James was admitted to the school on 31 August 1907 (Petition No. 12416), joining his older brother, George Adolphus Ellis, who had been admitted on 14 April 1905 (Petition No. 12097). James made the transition from Chelsea to Guston and was discharged into his father's old regiment on 11 February 1911, joining the 1st Battalion at Lucknow Barracks in Tidworth, Wiltshire.

At the outbreak of war, the battalion was stationed in Jersey, Channel Islands, and landed at Le Havre on 21 August 1914, although James's medal index card states that he did not arrive in theatre until 28 August. The battalion first saw action during the Battle of La Bassée in October 1914, where it helped in the capture of Givenchy Ridge, followed by the First Battle of Ypres, where it, in common with most of the rest of the British Regular Army, sustained very heavy casualties.

It appears that James witnessed these battles and the battalion was still in the vicinity of the town of Ypres at the start of the next year, moving into trenches at Wulverghem on 11 January 1915, where it was subjected to regular shelling. This shelling was particularly heavy on 14 January 1915, with James being among the one officer and nine other ranks who were killed on that day. He has no known grave and is commemorated on the Menin Gate Memorial. Despite the Commonwealth War Graves Commission commemorating James as being eighteen at the time of his death, he was actually only seventeen, killed five days prior to his eighteenth birthday.

George had a more chequered military career. He also made the transition from Chelsea to Guston when the school relocated in 1909 and having joined The South Staffordshire Regiment when he was discharged from the school on 12 January 1910, he was Courts Martialled for *"stealing from officers"* [171] and discharged from the army, *"Services No Longer Required"*, on 14 January 1914.

However, in August 1914, he did re-enlist, into The Devonshire Regiment, in Exeter, Devonshire. He did not admit to his previous service nor his attendance at the school, although he did enlist under his real name. The front of this service record was later annotated with, *"I believe this man has previously served 3 years. He will be discharged with all convenient speed"*[172]. On 20 October 1914, George was *"Discharged medically unfit for further military service para 392(iii) King's Regulations"*[173]. Nothing is known of him following his discharge.

Beluchistan Thomas SMITH

Private, 74000, 2nd Battalion, The Devonshire Regiment who died on 31 May 1918, aged 18. Commemorated on the Soissons Memorial, Aisne, France

Born on 28 July 1899 in Devizes, Wiltshire, the youngest of three sons of James Smith and Evelyn Lavinia Mary née Leak, his father had been a Serjeant in The Duke of Edinburgh's (Wiltshire Regiment) and had died whilst serving in Quetta, India, on 30 January 1899.

Beluchistan was admitted to the school on 09 October 1908 (Petition No. 12564), joining his older brother, Charles Cecil Stanley Smith, who had been admitted six months earlier on 23 April 1908 (Petition No. 12509). Beluchistan made the transition from Chelsea to Guston and was discharged to The Duke of Edinburgh's (Wiltshire Regiment) on 24 July 1914, but as his service record is no longer available, it is not possible to ascertain when he transferred to The Devonshire Regiment, nor what his movements were prior to 1918. However, it is not likely that he arrived in France until after he turned

---

[171] WO 363: War Office: Soldiers' Documents, First World War 'Burnt Documents' (Microfilm Copies), 1914-1920, The National Archives, Kew - First World War Service Records 'Burnt Documents'

[172] Ibid.

[173] *"Not being likely to become an efficient soldier"*

18 in 1917 at the earliest, but his medal index card does not include the date he disembarked.

At the time of his death, 2nd Battalion, The Devonshire Regiment was assigned to the 23rd Brigade, 8th Division. It had been posted with four other Commonwealth divisions to a quiet sector on the River Aisne, to refit and reorganise under French command, after suffering heavy losses in the spring fighting following the German offensive.

On the morning of 27 May 1918, a massive barrage began against the front of XI Corps, with the battalion positioned approximately 1200 yards behind the front line as Brigade Reserve on Bois des Buttes, a wooded sandstone hill which had been fortified by both sides over the previous years. The frontline battalions were quickly overwhelmed by German Stormtroops and the Devonshires subsequently made them fight for every inch of the wood, with 552 men of the battalion killed or taken prisoner during six hours of fighting.

Like many of his comrades, Beluchistan's body was not recovered and relatively few deaths at this time were pinpointed to a specific date, with the Registers of Soldiers' Effects[174] stating Beluchistan to be, *"presumed dead, 26-31 May 1918"*. He is also another of the "Lost Boys" whose name has been omitted from the memorial tablets in the school chapel.

Charles also made the transition from Chelsea to Guston before he was discharged from the school on 20 December 1911, enlisting into The Duke of Edinburgh's (Wiltshire Regiment). He served during the war, but was discharged following the loss of a foot. Charles married Florence Elsie Lindsay on 12 August 1926, but sadly, the day after they returned from honeymoon in Normandy, France, on 31 August 1926, he hanged himself in the RAF Drawing Office in Farnborough, where he was employed as an Engraver. The coroner returned a verdict of *"Suicide during temporary insanity"*[175].

---

[174] UK, Army Registers of Soldiers' Effects, 1901-1929, 1914-1915, Exeter, 943001-944500
[175] *Reading Standard*, Saturday 04 September 1926

The Suffolk Regiment

Thomas Alfred COLEMAN

Private, 265811, 11th (Service) Battalion (Cambridgeshire), The Suffolk Regiment who died on 06 July 1918, aged 21. Buried in Les Baraques Military Cemetery, Sangatte, Pas de Calais, France

Born on 13 February 1897 in Shoreham, Sussex, the second of five children of James Coleman and Elizabeth née Wicks, his father had been a Private in The Dorsetshire Regiment, who was discharged from the army on 12 February 1896 and died in Chichester, Sussex, on 31 May 1905. His mother remarried in 1907, to Charles Gray.

Thomas was admitted to the school on 11 May 1905 (Petition No. 12231) and was discharged to *"Civil Life"* on 26 February 1912, following which, very little is known about him.

In addition, his service record is no longer available so it is unknown at what point he enlisted into the army, although it would appear that he initially enlisted in the Territorial Force as records show that he had served in 1/6th (Cyclist) Battalion, The Suffolk Regiment. This unit had been formed in August 1914 in Ipswich, Suffolk, joining the 1st Mounted Division and remaining in Britain throughout the war.

The battalion with which Thomas served in France, the 11th (Service) Battalion (Cambridgeshire), was formed in September 1914 and after coming under the command of the 101st Brigade, 34th Division in May 1915 and moving to various locations in England, it landed at Boulogne on 09 January 1916, although it is unknown at what point Thomas disembarked in France, as his medal index card has no disembarkation date. It is known that he was serving with the battalion in the summer of 1918.

Thomas died on 06 July 1918 in one of the three General Hospitals, or the Red Cross Hospital, located in Sangatte, his cause of death being tuberculosis. He was buried in Les Baraques Military Cemetery, which had been started in September 1917, replacing Calais Southern Cemetery as the place of burial for the men who died in the hospitals. He is another "Lost Boy" whose name was omitted from the memorial tablets in the school chapel.

Robert DEAN (served as Robert SCARR)

Private, 3/10216, 1st Battalion, The Suffolk Regiment who died on 08 May 1915, aged 38. Commemorated on the Ypres (Menin Gate) Memorial, West-Vlaanderen, Belgium

Born on 29 October 1876 in Great Shelford, Cambridgeshire, the second of seven children of Frederick Dean and Ellen née Flynn, his father had been a Private in the 43rd (Monmouthshire) Regiment of Foot (Light Infantry)[176] who was discharged from the army on 08 February 1876 and died in Chesterton, Cambridgeshire, on 08 April 1888.

Robert was admitted to the school on 09 March 1888 (Petition No. 9626) and was discharged on 22 November 1890, enlisting into The Gordon Highlanders. Just over a year after Robert's discharge, on 26 February 1892, his younger brother, Frederick Dean, was admitted to the school (Petition No. 10291).

Robert was posted to the 2nd Battalion, but less than three years later, on 04 April 1893, he was tried and convicted of theft by District Courts Martial, being sentenced to 84 days' confinement in civil prison. A month into his sentence, and whilst still imprisoned, he was discharged from the army, *"His services being no longer required"*.

Despite this discharge, on 07 January 1896 Robert re-enlisted into the army, joining The Suffolk Regiment, changing his date of birth to February 1877 and giving his name as Robert Scarr, likely due to the nature of his previous discharge.

Robert was posted to the 1st Battalion and spent the first year of this period of service in Britain until he was posted to Malta on 10 April 1897, although ten months later he was transferred to the 2nd Battalion and posted to India, on 15 February 1898. He was appointed as a Lance Corporal on 19 June 1900, although he reverted back to Private at his own request on 21 September 1901.

Eight months later, Robert was posted back to Britain, joining the 9th Provisional Battalion on 10 May 1902, although he was only with that battalion for five months before being posted to the 1st Battalion on 01 October 1902. He was then discharged as medically unfit on 31 October 1902.

There is little information about Robert following this second discharge, but it is known that his eldest son, Henry Charles Dean, was born in Ashdon, Essex, on 01 February 1906. He married Henry's mother, Eliza Annie Maria Cornell, in Saffron Walden, Essex, on 16 December 1907 using his real surname, Dean.

---

[176] Amalgamated with the 52nd (Oxfordshire) Regiment of Foot (Light Infantry) on 10 July 1881 to become The Oxfordshire Light Infantry, renamed The Oxfordshire and Buckinghamshire Light Infantry on 16 October 1908

Robert was recorded in the 1911 Census as living in Great Thurlow, Suffolk, with Eliza, Henry and two more sons, Frank Dean, born in 1908 and Frederick Dean, born in 1910. Robert's occupation is given as Farm Labourer. Their fourth child, Philip Dean, was born in 1912.

It is not known whether Robert was recalled to the Colours or if he volunteered following the outbreak of war, but he did re-join The Suffolk Regiment as Robert Scarr. When the war broke out, 1st Battalion, The Suffolk Regiment, was the garrison battalion in Khartoum, Sudan, but returned to Britain on 23 October 1914. Having come under the command of 84th Brigade, 28th Division, on 17 November 1914, it landed at Le Havre on 18 January 1915. Robert's medal index card shows that he arrived in theatre just over a month later, on 23 February 1915, likely as a replacement.

By the end of April 1915, the battalion was in the Ypres sector of the Western Front during the Second Battle of Ypres. However, the movements and actions in which the battalion was involved are unknown, as following the entry in the battalion war diary[177] dated 09 April 1915, there is not another entry until 09 May 1915. It is likely that Robert was killed in action during the hard fighting at this time, his body not being recovered explaining why he is commemorated on the Menin Gate. In addition, likely because he served as Robert Scarr, he is another "Lost Boy" whose name was omitted from the memorial tablets in the school chapel.

Frederick was discharged from the school on 21 October 1896 and apprenticed to a Mr Marfleet, Harness Maker, in Great Shelford, Cambridgeshire. He is recorded in the 1901 Census as living with his mother and sister in Great Shelford, employed as a Saddler. However, it appears that he subsequently joined the army, as he is recorded in the 1911 Census as a Corporal Saddler and living in Aldershot, Hampshire, with his wife and son, although his regiment is not given. No record of wartime service could be found, but in the 1939 England and Wales Register he is recorded as an Auxiliary Postman and living with his wife in Chesterton, Cambridgeshire. He died in Cambridge, Cambridgeshire, in 1951.

---

[177] WO 95/2277/3: 1 Battalion Suffolk Regiment, 1914 Oct - 1915 Oct, The National Archives, Kew

Francis Edward Charles HALL
Second Lieutenant, 2nd Battalion, The Suffolk Regiment who died on 16 August 1916, aged 24. Commemorated on the Thiepval Memorial, Somme, France

Born on 18 April 1892 in Wellington, India, the eldest son of Francis Marshall Hall and Jessie Ada née Johnson, his father had served for five years in The Suffolk Regiment before transferring to The Cameronians (Scottish Rifles). He was a Pioneer Serjeant in that regiment when he died on active service in Elandslaagte, South Africa, on 20 March 1900, during the Second Boer War.

Francis was admitted to the school on 07 June 1901 (Petition No. 11558) and was joined by his younger brother, Marshall Arthur Collin Hall, on 15 November 1901 (Petition No. 11626). Francis was discharged to The Suffolk Regiment on 31 October 1907, three months before his youngest brother, Bernard Louis William Hall, was admitted to the school on 20 January 1908 (Petition No. 12460).

Francis's service record is no longer available, but it is possible that, at the outbreak of war, he was serving with the 1st Battalion, stationed in Khartoum, Sudan, returning to Britain on 23 October 1914 and landing at Le Havre on 18 January 1915, although his medal index card shows his date of entry into theatre as 15 February 1915.

In July 1916, he was serving with the 2nd Battalion in the Somme sector, and although the battalion did participate in the offensive, its war diary[178] states that it did not enter the line until 08 July, moving out again on 25 July. In August, it was back in the line in Méricourt. According to his medal index card, Francis was Commissioned on 15 August 1916, although this does not appear to have been Gazetted and the following day the battalion launched an attack on the German trenches.

The attack, which lasted four days, cost the battalion 40 officers and other ranks killed, 159 wounded and 81 missing. Francis was one of those missing, recorded as killed in action on 16 August 1916, although his name is not recorded in the war diary, as would normally happen for officers, but this is possibly because he had only been Commissioned the day before his death. The Registers of Soldiers' Effects[179] also records him as a Company Serjeant Major, although this is crossed through and annotated with the words *"Cancelled. See Officers 22742 vol XX"*. He has no known grave.

---

[178] WO 95/1437/1: 2 Battalion Suffolk Regiment, 1915 Nov. - 1919 Apr., The National Archives, Kew
[179] UK, Army Registers of Soldiers' Effects, 1901-1929, 1914-1915, Warley, 563501-565000

Marshall was discharged from the school *"To Student"* on 21 August 1908 and then served in the Corps of Army Schoolmasters. He survived the war, and is recorded as a Civil Servant (War Office) in 1939. He died in Croydon, Surrey, in 1957.

Bernard also enlisted into The Suffolk Regiment when he was discharged from the school on 05 September 1911, having made the transition from Chelsea to Guston, and served in the same battalion as Francis. He also survived the war, remaining in the army. He was a Major serving in the Indian General Service Corps during the Second World War when he died in Burma on 27 November 1942 and is commemorated on the Rangoon Memorial. He is one of the "Lost Boys" from the Second World War whose name has been omitted from the memorial tablets in the school chapel and will be covered in Volume Two.

Walter Louis HARDY
Boy, 9750, Depot, The Suffolk Regiment who died on 24 July 1918, aged 16. Buried in Bury St. Edmunds Cemetery, Suffolk, United Kingdom

Born on 11 January 1902 in Ipswich, Suffolk, the youngest of nine children of James Henry Hardy and Mary Anne née Hughes, his father was a Serjeant in The Northumberland Fusiliers, but had been discharged from the army as medically unfit on 18 June 1888.

Walter was admitted to the school on 06 January 1912 (Petition No. 12951), moving to Hutton, Essex, when the school was evacuated at the end of 1914, before he was discharged to The Suffolk Regiment on 02 May 1916.

Walter was posted to the Regimental Depot in Bury St. Edmunds, Suffolk, and was a member of the regimental band, when, in September 1917, he and another Band Boy were fined ten shillings for stealing apples from the grounds of Sexton Hall.

At some point in 1918, the year that his father died in a lunatic asylum, Walter became ill himself. The cause of his illness is not recorded, but he was admitted to Ampton Hall Military Hospital in Bury St. Edmunds, where he died on 24 July 1918. He was buried with full military honours in Bury St. Edmunds Cemetery on 27 July 1918.

Lawrence Carmon HILL
Drummer, 8189, 2nd Battalion, The Suffolk Regiment who died on 26 August 1914, aged 17. Commemorated on the La Ferte-Sous-Jouarre Memorial, Seine-et-Marne, France

Born on 14 January 1897 in Aldershot, Hampshire, one of five children of John Hill and Fanny née Turner, his father had been a

Corporal in The Suffolk Regiment who died on 23 January 1902 in Quetta, India. His mother died ten months later, on 08 November 1902, in Bombay, India, leaving the children as orphans.

Lawrence was admitted to the school on 16 February 1906 (Petition No. 12197), his Petition Document having been completed by his aunt, Mrs F. Harris. His older brother, Jack Harold Hill, had been discharged from the school by the time that Lawrence arrived, having been admitted on 30 December 1902 (Petition No. 11777) and having made the move from Chelsea to Guston, when the school relocated in 1909, Lawrence was discharged to The Suffolk Regiment on 24 January 1911.

Although his service record is no longer available, it is known that at the outbreak of war, 2nd Battalion, The Suffolk Regiment, was stationed in Newbridge, County Kildare. After mobilising and being made up to strength with Reservists, it sailed from Dublin on the SSs *Lanfranc* and *Poland* on 12 and 13 August, landing at Le Havre on 14 August 1914.

On 21 August the battalion arrived in Saint Vaast, east of Mons, moving to Hamin the following day. It was reported that on 23 August that guns were heard all morning, with two companies taking up positions along the Mons-Conde Canal and suffering the battalion's first casualties of the war when three men were killed. That evening a retirement was ordered.

The battalion retired for the next two days, until 0400hrs on 26 August when it took up front line positions facing Le Cateau. At 0730hrs it came under *"most effective"*[180] shrapnel fire, before, at 1230hrs it came under extremely heavy shell fire and was enfiladed from the left of its position, which led, at 1600hrs, to a general retirement of the division.

Lawrence was not part of this retirement, however, having been killed during the Battle of Le Cateau as the action of that day became known. His body was not recovered and he is commemorated on the La Ferte-Sous-Jouarre Memorial. He is also commemorated on the memorial tablets in the school chapel, but is incorrectly recorded as L E Hill.

Jack was discharged from the school to The Suffolk Regiment on 21 January 1905 and was a Serjeant in the same battalion as Lawrence at the time of the Battle of Le Cateau, where he was taken prisoner. He survived the war, having risen to the rank of Company Serjeant Major and although it is known that he married Eileen Ermentreude Dorothea Barnett in 1920, after this nothing of his life

---

[180] WO 95/1437/1: 2 Battalion Suffolk Regiment, 1915 Nov. - 1919 Apr., The National Archives, Kew

is definitely known, although it is likely that he died in Tavistock, Devonshire, in 1962.

Prince Albert's (Somerset Light Infantry)

Frederick Charles SPIERS
Serjeant, 7972, 1st Battalion, Prince Albert's (Somerset Light Infantry) who died on 14 December 1914, aged 22. Commemorated on the Ploegsteert Memorial, Hainaut, Belgium

Born on 24 April 1892 in Aldershot, Hampshire, the youngest of six children of William Henry Spiers and Mary Ann née Kendall, his father had been a Private in Prince Albert's (Somersetshire Light Infantry) who was discharged from the army after 24 years' service on 21 July 1891 and died in Hounslow, Middlesex, on 19 July 1898.

Frederick was admitted to the school on 12 July 1902 (Petition No. 11715), five months after his older brother, Edward John Kendall Spiers, who had been admitted on 13 January 1899 (Petition No. 11250), had been discharged. Frederick was discharged from the school to Prince Albert's (Somerset Light Infantry) on 03 May 1905 and although his service record is no longer available, the 1911 Census records him as a Bugler with the 1st Battalion, stationed in Verne Citadel, Portland, Dorsetshire.

At the outbreak of war, the battalion was stationed in Colchester, Essex, moving to Harrow, Middlesex, on 17 August and embarking at Southampton, Hampshire, on 22 August, before landing at Le Havre on 23 August 1914. It then moved to the area of Le Cateau on 24 August and participated in that battle as well as the Battles of the Marne, of the Aisne and Messines.

At 0900hrs on 14 December 1914, the battalion attacked Wytschaete, but little progress was made, although it suffered only three men killed, one of whom was Frederick. Either his body was not recovered, or if it was, his grave was subsequently lost, so he is commemorated on the Ploegsteert Memorial, along with the other two casualties from his battalion who died that day.

Although Frederick is commemorated on the memorial tablets in the school chapel his name is incorrectly recorded as J Spiers.

Edward was discharged from the school on 08 March 1902, enlisting into The Black Watch (Royal Highlanders) as a Bandsman. He survived the war and died in Melton Mowbray, Leicestershire, in 1944.

Frederick and Edward's older, non-Dukie brother, William Henry Spiers, also lost his life during the war. He was a Stoker 1st Class in the Royal Navy who was killed when his ship, HMS *Triumph*, was in action against a submarine off the coast of Gallipoli on 25 May 1915.

Walter Edward WHALL MC
Captain, 7th (Service) Battalion, Prince Albert's (Somerset Light Infantry) attached 11th Battalion, The Royal Welch Fusiliers who died on 06 May 1918, age 43. Buried in Doiran Military Cemetery, Greece

Born on 30 October 1874 in Isleworth, Middlesex, the second of five children of Joseph Whall and his second wife, Elizabeth Ann née Barnes, his father had retired from the army on 20 July 1867 after 21 years' service in the 1st, or The Royal Regiment of Foot, during which he *"went through the siege of Sebastopol, and with the English and French expedition to China in 1860, took part in the capture of the Taku Forts and Pekin"*[181]. Following his discharge, he became a Scripture Reader, and died in Brentford, Middlesex, on 12 May 1883.

Walter was admitted to the school on 06 February 1885 (Petition No. 9138) and discharged to Prince Albert's (Somersetshire Light Infantry) on 24 November 1888, joining the 1st Battalion and spending the first three years of his service in Britain.

On 10 November 1891, Walter was posted to Gibraltar, by this time having been appointed as a Bugler. He spent two years here before, on 19 December 1893, he was posted to India, where he spent eleven years and was appointed as a Lance Corporal in November 1896 and promoted to Corporal in August 1897. During his time here, he was awarded the India Medal with the clasp *Punjab Frontier 1897-98*, before he returned to Britain on 08 March 1904, having been appointed as a Lance Serjeant in March 1901 and promoted to Serjeant in April 1902.

He was only to spend six months in Britain, during which time he was awarded the Long Service and Good Conduct Medal, before he returned to India on 07 September 1904, where he was to spend the next four years of his career. During this time in India, he married Annie Mary Field in the Roman Catholic Church in Cawnpore on 10 May 1905.

He returned to Britain on 30 October 1908, was promoted to Colour Serjeant on 16 August 1912 and appointed as a Company Quartermaster Serjeant just over a year later, on 01 October 1913.

---

[181] *Middlesex Chronicle*, Saturday 26 September 1914

Having given three months' notice, he was discharged from the army on 21 July 1914.

Fourteen days after Walter had retired from the army and joined the Corps of Commissionaires[182], Britain was at war. He immediately volunteered to re-join his old regiment, but was instead, on 19 September 1914, appointed as Quartermaster, with the honorary rank of Lieutenant[183], to the 7th (Service) Battalion, Prince Albert's (Somerset Light Infantry), stationed in Woking, Surrey. This battalion had been formed at Taunton, Somerset, in September 1914 as part of K2 and landed at Boulogne on 24 July 1915, Walter landing with them, having been appointed as a Temporary Captain on 10 February 1915[184].

He remained with this battalion, being appointed as Second-in-Command and promoted to Temporary Major whilst holding this appointment between 02 May 1916 and 05 July 1916[185], a position that he was in during the Somme Offensive, where he was later wounded in the jaw on 16 September, possibly during the Battle of Flers–Courcelette and was also awarded the Military Cross[186].

Although there is no *London Gazette* record for when it occurred, Walter transferred to 11th (Service) Battalion, The Royal Welsh Fusiliers, possibly following his recuperation from the wound that he had received in September 1916. This battalion had been formed in Wrexham, Denbighshire, on 18 October 1914 as part of K3. Having moved to various locations around Britain in the year following its formation, it landed in France in early-September 1915, although by 05 November 1915, it had been relocated to Salonika.

The battalion was still in Salonika when Walter joined it, and it appears that he again served with distinction. He was killed whilst commanding a trench raid on 06 May 1918 and buried in Doiran Military Cemetery. However, he is another of the "Lost Boys" whose name has been omitted from the memorial tablets in the school chapel.

---

[182] A global movement of societies intended to create meaningful employment for armed forces veterans; in the UK it is now organized as a private security company
[183] *The London Gazette*: 18 September 1914, Issue:28906
[184] *The London Gazette*: 19 February 1915, Issue:29077
[185] *The London Gazette*: 1 August 1916, Supplement:29693
[186] *The London Gazette*: 14 November 1916, Supplement:29824: *"Temp. Capt. Walter Edward Whall, Som. L.I, For conspicuous gallantry in action. He led the advanced companies in the attack with great ability, and rendered every assistance to his C.O., who was wounded and unable to get about. Later, he took over command of the battalion"*

The Prince of Wales's Own (West Yorkshire Regiment)

Thomas James BARCLAY

Lance Corporal, 8183, 2nd Battalion, The Prince of Wales's Own (West Yorkshire Regiment) who died on 21 November 1914, aged 23. Buried in Cabaret-Rouge British Cemetery, Souchez, Pas de Calais, France

Born on 19 August 1891 in York, Yorkshire North Riding, the youngest of eight children of William George Barclay and Elizabeth Sarah née Debroy, his father had been a Serjeant in in the 100th (or Prince of Wales's Royal Canadian) Regiment of Foot who had been discharged to pension on 18 August 1879. He died in York on 21 April 1902.

Thomas was admitted to the school on 10 October 1902 (Petition No. 11747), remaining there until he was discharged on 21 August 1906, when he enlisted into The Prince of Wales's Own (West Yorkshire Regiment). Although his service record is no longer available, he is recorded in the 1911 Census as a Musician with the 2nd Battalion, stationed in Sobraon Barracks, Colchester, Essex.

At the outbreak of war, the battalion was stationed in Malta, but returned to Southampton, Hampshire, on 25 September, where it became part of the 23rd Brigade, 8th Division, landing at Le Havre on 05 November 1914 and entering the trenches for the first time on 13 November.

On 18 November, the unit relieved 2nd Battalion, The East Lancashire Regiment in the trenches, remaining there until 21 November. The battalion war diary[187] entry for 21 November states, *"In trenches. All quiet. Very cold. Relieved by 2 Middx R in the evening and marched into billets at LAVENTIE. Casualties: 1 killed & 2 wounded"*.

The soldier killed on that day was Thomas. He is one of nearly 3,000 British soldiers, 25 from the West Yorkshire Regiment, buried in Cabaret-Rouge British Cemetery in Souchez, a small commune in the Pas de Calais Department, eight miles from Arras. A month

---

[187] WO 95/1714/1: 23 Infantry Brigade: 2 Battalion West Yorkshire Regiment, 1914 Nov 1 - 1916 July 31, The National Archives, Kew

later, on 19 December 1914, his non-Dukie brother, Sydney Herbert Barclay, who was serving in the same battalion, was also killed.

He is also commemorated on the memorial tablets in the school chapel, but is incorrectly recorded as J. Barclay.

Herbert BOOTH

Second Lieutenant, 12th (Service) Battalion, The Prince of Wales's Own (West Yorkshire Regiment) who died on 03 May 1917, aged 22. Buried in Faubourg d'Amiens Cemetery, Arras, Pas de Calais, France

Born on 04 December 1894 in Lichfield, Staffordshire, the eldest of five children of Herbert Booth and Martha née Wainwright, his father was a Colour Serjeant in The South Staffordshire Regiment and was still serving when he died in Hightown, Lancashire, on 29 May 1905. Anthony Clarke Booth, Herbert's grandfather, had been awarded the Victoria Cross in 1879 for his actions at the Battle of Intombe during the Anglo-Zulu War[188].

Herbert was admitted to the school on 10 November 1905 (Petition No. 12163) and was joined by his younger brother, Harold Stanley Booth, on 22 August 1906 (Petition No. 12258). Having made the transition from Chelsea to Guston, Herbert was discharged from the school *"To Student"* on 02 September 1912, although it appears that he did not travel far, becoming a Student at the school.

On 07 October 1914, Herbert enlisted into the Corps of Army Schoolmasters as a Schoolmaster on Probation, being posted to 10th Battalion, The York and Lancaster Regiment and five months later, on 15 March 1915, to the depot of The Essex Regiment in West Ham, London. He spent seven months there, before being transferred to his old school, now located in Hutton, Essex, where it had been evacuated for the duration of the war. At this time, he was still a Schoolmaster on Probation, although he only remained at the school for a month before he was discharged from the army at his own request.

On 09 February 1916, Herbert enlisted into The Prince of Wales's Own (West Yorkshire Regiment), although he remained in Britain and by 21 March 1916, he was a Serjeant. Seven months later he was discharged having been granted a Commission as a Temporary Second Lieutenant[189].

---

[188] *The London Gazette*, 24 February 1880, Issue:24814: *"Colour-Sergeant Anthony Booth, For hie gallant conduct on the 12th March, 1879, during the Zulu attack on. the Intombi River, in having, when' considerably outnumbered by the enemy, rallied a few men on the south bank of the river, and covered the retreat of fifty soldiers and others for a distance of three miles. The Officer Commanding 80th Regiment reports that, had it not been for the coolness displayed by this Non-commissioned Officer, not one man would have escaped"*

[189] *The London Gazette*, 10 November 1916, Issue:29818

His first posting as an officer was to the 12th (Service) Battalion which had been formed in York on 16 September 1914 as part of K2 and had landed at Le Havre in September 1915. Herbert joined the battalion on 30 December 1916.

On 01 May 1917, the battalion received orders that it was to attack Bois-du-Sart near Arras on 03 May and having occupied trenches near Tilloy on 02 May, it then moved to occupy its assembly trenches that evening, but came under a heavy barrage of high-explosive and gas shells, which disrupted this. However, the attack was launched at 0345hrs on 03 May, but *"owing to the darkness, mist, strong concentration of hostile MGs, prompt heavy hostile barrage and alertness of the enemy, the attack made very little progress and soon became more or less disorganised"*[190].

Herbert was one of three officers killed during this failed attack and is buried in Faubourg d'Amiens Cemetery. He is commemorated on the memorial tablets in the school chapel, along with his younger brother Harold.

Harold had been withdrawn from the school on 22 July 1910 and was serving as a Second Lieutenant in The York and Lancaster Regiment when he was killed ten months before Herbert, on the first day of the Somme Offensive.

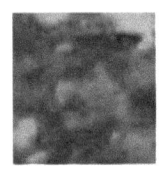

Clifford PYE

Private, 4925, 2nd Battalion, The Prince of Wales's Own (West Yorkshire Regiment) who died on 09 April 1917, aged 32. Buried in Portland (St. George) Churchyard, Dorset, United Kingdom

Born on 30 May 1884 in Castlebar, County Mayo, the third of four children of Francis William Pye and Mary Ann Moore née Skinner, his father was the Serjeant Master Tailor in 1st Battalion, The Prince of Wales's Own (West Yorkshire Regiment) and was still serving when he died of enteric fever in Dublin Royal Infirmary, on 17 December 1886. His mother remarried, to Richard Lane Pearce, in Weymouth, Dorsetshire, in 1893.

Clifford was admitted to the school on 03 September 1894 (Petition No. 10643), joining his older brother, Frank Pye, who had been admitted on 27 May 1892 (Petition No. 10341). Clifford was discharged to his father's old regiment on 31 May 1898 and although his service record is no longer available, it is known that he served in South Africa during the Second Boer War and he is recorded in the

---

[190] WO 95/1432/2: 12 Battalion West Yorkshire Regiment, 1915 Sept - 1918 Jan, The National Archives, Kew

1911 Census as a Serjeant Instructor in the regiment, boarding in Bradford, Yorkshire West Riding.

At the outbreak of war, Clifford would have been serving alongside fellow Dukie Thomas Barclay and would have had the same history until November 1914.

During 1915, the battalion was involved in the Battles of Neuve Chapelle and Loos and in 1916 was on the Somme, participating in the attack on the first day of that offensive. On 01 July 1916, the battalion was to support The Devonshire Regiment and The Duke of Cambridge's Own (Middlesex Regiment) in their assault, with a special task to capture and consolidate the village of Pozières. Although it had some success, the attack was ultimately unsuccessful, the battalion losing sixteen of its officers killed or wounded, but other rank casualties were not recorded.

During the early months of 1917, January to March, the British attempted to consolidate the positions taken during the Battle of the Ancre in late-1916, with the battalion involved in these Operations on the Ancre. It is possible that Clifford was wounded during these operations as, by April, he had been admitted to No. 1 Southern General Hospital, which was located in the University of Birmingham, Warwickshire, where he died on 09 April 1917 from consumption[191]. He was buried four days later in Portland, Dorsetshire, where his mother and stepfather had settled.

Frank was discharged from the school on 24 October 1896, also enlisting into his father's old regiment. As well as serving in Britain, he also served in South Africa, during the Second Boer War and India, from where he was invalided home and discharged as medically unfit on 27 December 1904. He is recorded in the 1911 Census as a General Labourer (Army Pensioner) and living with his mother and stepfather in Portland, although he married Annie Louisa Pilkington in 1912. They had five children before Frank died in Weymouth, Dorsetshire, on 19 January 1963.

William Swift WADE
Serjeant, 4523719, 1st Battalion, The Prince of Wales's Own (West Yorkshire Regiment) who died on 27 August 1921, aged 41. Buried in Walton-on-the-Naze (All Saints) Churchyard Extension, Essex, United Kingdom

Born on 18 October 1879 in Sheerness, Kent, the third of four children of John William Swift Wade and Hannah Frances née Webb, his father had been a Superintending Clerk Warrant Officer in the Royal Engineers who died in Malta on 05 January 1887. His

---

[191] Tuberculosis

mother remarried, to George Rose, in Alverstoke, Hampshire, in 1891.

William was admitted to the school on 23 March 1890 (Petition No. 9999), the same day as his twin brother, Frederick James Wade (Petition No. 9998) and was discharged to The Princess Charlotte of Wales's (Royal Berkshire Regiment) on 31 January 1894. Little is known of William's military career, as his service record has not survived, but it is known that he married Lizzie Cook in Keynsham, Somerset, in 1908 and that he was a Lance Corporal at the time.

As his service record is not available, it is not known when William transferred to The Prince of Wales's Own (West Yorkshire Regiment), although he is recorded in the 1911 Census as a Serjeant Tailor with that regiment, stationed in Colchester, Essex, and at the outbreak of war, he was serving with the 2nd Battalion, stationed in Malta.

Although that battalion landed in France on 05 November 1914, there is no date of disembarkation on William's medal index card, nor did he qualify for the award of the 1914-15 Star, although he was awarded the British War Medal, suggesting that he may have served overseas at some point.

William was admitted to the Military Hospital in Cork, County Cork, in June 1921, where he died from cirrhosis of the liver on 27 August 1921. Lizzie had pre-deceased him, although it is not known when, as his death notification records that he was a widower and the Registers of Soldiers' Effects[192] records his sister-in-law, Alice Cook, as his beneficiary.

Although commemorated by the Commonwealth War Graves Commission, William is another "Lost Boy" whose name has been omitted from the memorial tablets in the school chapel. Had he died five days later, on 01 September 1921, he would also have been outside the dates for commemoration by the Commonwealth War Graves Commission as a casualty of the First World War.

Frederick was discharged from the school on the same day as his brother and like William, he enlisted into The Royal Berkshire Regiment. He was still serving with this regiment in 1911, as the Census of that year records him as a Lance Corporal in the 1st Battalion. However, at some point prior to 1919, he transferred to the Army Service Corps[193], appearing in the medal roll for that corps. He died in Colchester, Essex in 1960.

---

[192] UK, Army Registers of Soldiers' Effects, 1901-1929, 1921-1922, 980501-982000
[193] Royal Army Service Corps from 1918

The East Yorkshire Regiment

James William KAVENEY
Lance Corporal, 8321, 1st Battalion, The East Yorkshire Regiment who died on 28 October 1914, aged 22. Commemorated on the Ploegsteert Memorial, Hainaut, Belgium

Born on 22 April 1892 in Beverley, Yorkshire East Riding, the youngest of four children of Terence Patrick Kaveney and Eliza Jane née Chatterton, his father had been a Quartermaster Serjeant in The East Yorkshire Regiment who had been discharged after 21 years' service on 31 July 1894. He died in York, Yorkshire North Riding, on 31 January 1901.

James was admitted to the school on 12 September 1901 (Petition No. 11596) and was discharged to his father's old regiment on 03 May 1906. His service record is no longer available, so it is unknown where he served prior to the war. However, at the outbreak of war, 1st Battalion, The East Yorkshire Regiment was stationed in York. It moved to Edinburgh, Midlothian, on 08 August, and, six days later, to Cambridge, Cambridgeshire, where it remained until September, moving to Southampton, Hampshire, and embarking on the SS *Cawdor Castle* on 08 September, landing at St. Nazaire on 10 September 1914.

The battalion had its first experiences of the trenches near Bourg on 19 September, suffering its first casualty when a man was killed by shellfire.

In October, it was in the area of Ypres at the commencement of the First Battle of Ypres, with the opposing forces advancing toward each other near Langemarck, which was captured by the Germans on 22 October. It then moved into trenches near La Vesée on 24 October and was still there four days later when, at 0530hrs, it was heavily shelled, followed by a determined German attack that managed to get into the trenches next to it, which had been manned by The Durham Light Infantry. "C" Company and two platoons from "A" Company were sent to expel the Germans, eventually being successful, but the battalion was then shelled almost continuously for the remainder of the day.

Whether it was as a result of the attack, or as a result of the shelling, James Kaveney was killed in action on 28 October 1914. His body was either not recovered or his grave was lost in the subsequent fighting and so he is commemorated on the Ploegsteert Memorial. He is also commemorated on the memorial tablets in the school chapel, but his name is misspelled as *Kaveny*.

Samuel Charles LARKIN
Private, 19417, 12th (Service) Battalion (3rd Hull), The East Yorkshire Regiment, who died on 03 May 1917, aged 37. Commemorated on the Arras Memorial, Pas de Calais, France

Born on 10 March 1880 in Salisbury, Wiltshire, the youngest of eight children of William Larkin and Sarah née Marshall, his father had been a Corporal in the 67th (the South Hampshire) Regiment of Foot who had been discharged from the army after 22 years' service on 24 November 1869. His mother died in Fisherton Anger, Wiltshire, on 30 May 1884.

Samuel was admitted to the school on 24 April 1891 (Petition No. 10153) and discharged on 10 March 1894, enlisting into The East Yorkshire Regiment. He was initially posted to the 2nd Battalion, but a year later, on 28 February 1895, he was transferred to the 1st Battalion, and was posted to Egypt the following day. After eight months, Samuel was then posted to India, on 21 November 1895, where he was appointed as a Drummer on 03 November 1896.

Three years later, on 22 February 1899, Samuel reverted to Private, although only for three months before he was appointed as a Bandsman, on 22 May 1899. During his time in India, Samuel also re-engaged to complete 21 years' service, on 09 April 1904, and was posted back to Britain on 20 February 1906.

However, three months after returning to Britain, Samuel was awarded fourteen days' detention by his Commanding Officer and reverted to Private, although the offence for which this was awarded is not recorded in his service record. He returned to duty on 11 June 1906 and, seven months later, was discharged from the army having completed 12 years' service.

Following his discharge, there is little known about Samuel until he married Elizabeth Wootton in Westminster, London, on 06 June 1909, at which time he was employed as a Butler, which was still his employment at the time of the 1911 Census, living with Elizabeth in Marylebone, London. Samuel and Elizabeth's first child, Gwendoline Florence Larkin, was born in Marylebone in 1912 and their second daughter, Irene Betty Larkin, was also born in Marylebone two years later.

At the outbreak of war, Samuel was still living with his family in Marylebone employed as a Butler and it was not until 05 June 1915 that he re-enlisted into his old regiment, initially being posted to the Regimental Depot at Victoria Barracks, Beverley, Yorkshire East Riding, before he was posted on 12 June 1915 to the 3rd (Reserve) Battalion, which was stationed in Hedon, Yorkshire East Riding, as the Humber Garrison.

Having been appointed as a Lance Corporal on 19 August 1915, Samuel remained with the 3rd Battalion when it moved to Withernsea, Yorkshire East Riding, in April 1916 and was still there when he was *"Deprived of his stripe for refusing to obey an order"* on 07 February 1917.

A month later, on 16 March 1917, Samuel landed at Boulogne, having been posted to the 1st Battalion. However, on 05 April 1917, Samuel was transferred to 12th (Service) Battalion (3rd Hull), which was training near Robecq. This battalion had been formed in Hull, Yorkshire East Riding, on 11 August 1914 and was also known as the Hull Sportsmen's Battalion. It had moved to Egypt in December 1915 before it arrived in France in March 1916.

On 03 May 1917, the 'Hull Pals', a brigade of four battalions of The East Yorkshire Regiment, attacked the Germans at Oppy Wood, a fortified defensive position, north-east of Arras. This was a diversionary attack to draw German resources away from the main offensive planned for Messines in June 1917 and in fierce fighting around the village, the city of Hull lost more men than any other. The attack failed, with around 40% of the attacking force becoming casualties, including Samuel, whose death was officially accepted on that date with no known grave.

Samuel is commemorated on the Arras Memorial and is another of the "Lost Boys" whose name has been omitted from the memorial tablets in the school chapel.

John Edward WOOD DCM
Serjeant, 8286, 1st Battalion, The East Yorkshire Regiment who died 09 August 1915, aged 23. Commemorated on the Ypres (Menin Gate) Memorial, West-Vlaanderen, Belgium

Born on 29 January 1892 in Barbados, West Indies, the only son of Joe Edward Wood and Effie Amelia née Daubin, his father had been a Colour Serjeant in The Duke of Wellington's (West Riding Regiment) and was serving in Pietermaritzburg, South Africa, when he died on 04 April 1896.

John was admitted to the school on 11 December 1902 (Petition No. 11768) and was discharged to The East Yorkshire Regiment on 08 February 1906. Although his service record is no longer available, the 1911 Census records him as a Private in the 1st Battalion, stationed in Salamanca Barracks, Wellington Lines, Aldershot, Hampshire.

At the outbreak of war, John would have been serving alongside James Kaveney and would have had the same experience, including the battalion's first period in the trenches on 19 September, when it relieved The Royal Sussex Regiment near the Aisne. The following day, some Germans advanced on The Prince of Wales's Own (West Yorkshire Regiment) under a white flag, which they discarded when approached and captured two companies of that regiment. 1st Battalion, The East Yorkshire Regiment, along with The Durham Light Infantry, launched a counterattack in order to free their comrades.

The battalion also participated in the Battle of Armentières the following month and remained in that area for the remainder of the year, although by the spring of 1915 it was in the Ypres sector and took part in the fighting of the Second Battle of Ypres. As a result of his actions during this fighting, John was recommended for the award of the Distinguished Conduct Medal[194].

In August 1915, the battalion was still in the area of Hooge, participating in the attack on the German positions that was launched at 0245hrs on 09 August. The attack was a success and the battalion was able to hold the captured positions, despite a heavy bombardment from the Germans that lasted for fifteen hours, before it was relieved by The West Yorkshire Regiment at 2300hrs and returned to billets in Ypres.

During the course of the attack, John attempted to rescue a wounded officer from his battalion. He was unsuccessful and was killed during this gallant attempt. His body was never recovered and he is one of 58 soldiers from his battalion who died on that day and who are commemorated on the Menin Gate Memorial.

---

[194] *The London Gazette*, 22 June 1915 Supplement:29202, and *The Edinburgh Gazette*, 9 July 1915, Issue:12828 *"For conspicuous and consistent zeal and devotion to duty displayed as a Platoon Commander"*

The Bedfordshire Regiment

Whilst almost all of the Dukies who served in The Bedfordshire Regiment and died during the First World War are commemorated on the memorial tablets in the school chapel, their regiment is incorrectly recorded as The Bedfordshire and Hertfordshire Regiment.

The Bedfordshire Regiment came into existence on 01 July 1881 as part of the Cardwell Reforms[195] when the 16th (the Bedfordshire) Regiment of Foot was renamed. Although the regiment was later renamed The Bedfordshire and Hertfordshire Regiment, in recognition of the contribution of men from Hertfordshire during the First World War, this did not occur until 29 July 1919, and therefore was not in use at the time that the Dukies named below were serving.

George Albert BIGSBY
Drummer, 4/6321, 4th (Extra Reserve) Battalion, The Bedfordshire Regiment who died on 16 September 1915, aged 34. Buried in Kingston-Upon-Thames Cemetery, Surrey, United Kingdom

Born on 23 November 1880 in Westminster, Middlesex, a son of George Baker alias Bigsby and Constance née Cooper, his father had been a Private in the 43rd (Monmouthshire) Regiment of Foot (Light Infantry) who had been discharged from the army on 29 October 1878.

George was admitted to the school on 30 October 1891 (Petition No. 10210) and was discharged on 24 November 1894, enlisting into The Prince of Wales's Own (West Yorkshire Regiment). George travelled the world during the 12 years that he spent with this regiment, serving in Gibraltar, Hong Kong, Singapore and India, being appointed paid Lance Corporal on 21 December 1905, before returning to Britain on 09 December 1906 and discharged from the army as a Private at the end of his first period of engagement.

It is not known what George did for the next four years, but in 1909 he married Alice Mary le Petit and on 13 May 1910 he re-

---

[195] A series of reforms of the British Army between 1868 and 1874 undertaken by Edward Cardwell, the Secretary of State for War during William Gladstone's Liberal Government of 1868-1874 and implemented during Gladstone's second Premiership 1880-1885

enlisted into the army, joining The Bedfordshire Regiment. As his service record is no longer available for this second period of service, his postings prior to the war are unknown.

It would appear that George did not serve abroad during the war, despite requests to do so and this may have led to a depression that caused him to take his own life on 16 September 1915. It was reported as follows[196]:

"SOLDIER'S SUICIDE AT SURBITON.

FOUND HANGING FROM A FENCE.

A soldier's strange and touching letter of farewell to his wife was read at the inquest held by Dr. Taylor, Coroner, at Surbiton, on Monday on the body of Drummer George Albert Bigsby, 4th Bedfordshire Regt., who was found hanging from a fence behind some bushes in Ditton-road, Surbiton, the previous Thursday.

The widow, Mrs Mary Bigsby, of 3 Wye—road, Camberwell, said her husband was 34 years of age and had been 12 years in the West Yorkshire Regiment before joining the band of the 4th Bedfordshire Regt., in which he was for four years. He was called up on the reserve at the outbreak of the war, but had not been to the front. After being home on leave he was due to return to his regiment at Dovercourt on the 12th inst., and left on that day, but on the 14th she received a letter from him. This the Coroner read, as follows:-

> *My own darling Lallie,*
> *I have now the greatest of pleasure in writing these few lines to you, to your own sweet self, love. I hope this letter will find yourself and the dear children in the best of health and spirits, but I cannot say it leaves me the same. Well, darling, this will be the last time that you, love, will hear from me. I cannot stand the pains in my head, so good-bye and God bless you and the children always. P.S. Well, farewell Lallie. You have been a good one ever since I knew you. So darling I trust you will not think bad of me for doing this.*
> *Your ever loving husband,*
> *George.*

...An officer from the deceased's regiment said Bigsby had suffered from fits of depression, and had been at times strange in his manner. He had never been on active service, but had tried several times to get out to the front. During the South African war he was in India..."

In the aftermath of this, his records show that his pension was initially denied to his widow, but there is a note that says it was granted on reconsideration and someone had added next to suicide

---

[196] *Surrey Advertiser*, Saturday 25 September 1915

"whilst temporarily insane due to active service", despite this not being true. Although he has been commemorated by the Commonwealth War Graves Commission, he is a "Lost Boy" whose name has been omitted from the memorial tablets in the school chapel.

James Elias David CANEY
Private, 10773, 2nd Battalion, The Bedfordshire Regiment who died on 16 June 1915, aged 18. Commemorated on the Le Touret Memorial, Pas de Calais, France

Born on 24 December 1896 in Frimley, Surrey, the third of six children of James Elias Caney and Eliza née Harris, his father was a Dukie, having been admitted to the Royal Military Asylum on 18 June 1880 (Petition No. 8509) and discharged to The Commissariat and Transport Corps on 03 July 1882. He was a Serjeant Master Tailor in the Army Service Corps when he was discharged from the army after 21 years' service on 02 July 1903. He died in Wandsworth, London, on 09 November 1904.

James was admitted to the school on 03 October 1907 (Petition No. 12428) and having transitioned from Chelsea to Guston, he was discharged on 25 January 1911, enlisting into the Army Service Corps. He is recorded in the 1911 Census as a Boy serving in that corps, stationed in Buller Barracks, Stanhope Lines, Aldershot, Hampshire.

According to James's service record for this period of service, he served in the Army Service Corps for just over two years before he was discharged on 26 March 1913, *"His services being no longer required"*, although no reason for this is given.

Following the outbreak of war, James re-enlisted into the army, joining The Bedfordshire Regiment and although his service record for this period of service is no longer available, his service number suggests that this enlistment was between 02 November 1914 and 12 December 1914.

At the outbreak of war, the battalion to which James was later posted was stationed in Roberts' Heights, Pretoria, South Africa, but was quickly returned to Britain, landing at Southampton, Hampshire, on 19 September and becoming part of the 7th Division. Following a refit for conflict in Europe, the battalion embarked on the SS *Winifredian* at Southampton on 05 October and disembarked at Zeebrugge on 07 October 1914.

James's medal index card records that he disembarked in theatre on 08 June 1915 and it is likely that he was one of the 100 other rank reinforcements that arrived at the battalion on 13 June 1915 when it was in the vicinity of Givenchy, moving into assembly dug outs the following day in preparation for what became known as The Second Action of Givenchy.

This battle lasted from 15 until 17 June 1915 and during its course, the battalion suffered 7 officers and 117 other ranks killed, wounded and missing, including James. He had been in theatre for eight days and likely with the battalion for only three days at the time of his death. It is also possible that he was one of the missing, as he is commemorated on the Le Touret Memorial rather than having a marked grave. In addition, James is another "Lost Boy" whose name has been omitted from the memorial tablets in the school chapel.

George CARTER
Serjeant, 6677, 2nd Battalion, The Bedfordshire Regiment who died on 30 July 1916, aged 30. Commemorated on the Thiepval Memorial, Somme, France

Born on 28 November 1885 in Greenwich, Kent, the youngest child of David Carter and Elizabeth née Legg, his father was a Serjeant in The Bedfordshire Regiment who was discharged from the army on 13 May 1884 and died in Northampton, Northamptonshire, on 10 October 1892.

George was admitted to the school on 31 January 1896 (Petition No. 10852) and discharged on 02 December 1899, enlisting into his father's old regiment, the 1911 Census recording him as a Drummer serving with the 2nd Battalion, stationed in Prospect Barracks, Bermuda, West Indies.

At the outbreak of war, the battalion was stationed in Pretoria, South Africa, but quickly returned to Britain, where it landed at Southampton, Hampshire, on 19 September. It then re-embarked at Southampton on the SS *Winifredian* on 05 October, landing at Zeebrugge on 07 October 1914.

During 1914 the unit participated in the First Battle of Ypres in October and November, and on Christmas Day 1914 it was in trenches. Whilst there was a brief truce to allow both sides to bury their dead and, according to the battalion war diary[197], enable the British to gather intelligence on the troops that they were facing, as well as the state of the German trenches, there was not the fraternisation seen in other parts of the line.

During 1915, the battalion was in action for much of the year, participating in the Battle of Neuve Chapelle in March, the Battle of Festubert in May, the Second Action at Givenchy in June and the Battle of Loos in September.

---

[197] WO 95/2333/1: 89 Infantry Brigade: 2 Battalion Bedfordshire Regiment, 1916 Jan 1 - 1916 July 31, The National Archives, Kew

The following year, it participated in several phases of the Somme Offensive. It went "over the top" during the Battle of Albert on the opening day, when its division broke the German lines, and was involved in the assault on Trônes Wood on 11 July. On 29 July, it received orders that it, along with a French company, was to attack Maltz Horn Farm in order to clear the way for a general advance. The attack was launched on at 0445hrs on 30 July and met with complete success, although the battalion suffered 6 officers and 186 other ranks killed, wounded and missing, George being one of those killed during this attack. His body was not recovered and he is commemorated on the Thiepval Memorial.

William Benjamin DICKS
Private, 33184, 2nd Battalion, The Bedfordshire Regiment who died on 01 July 1918, aged 20. Commemorated on the Pozieres Memorial, Somme, France

Born on 07 September 1897 in Portsmouth, Hampshire, the only child of Benjamin Dicks and Henrietta Jane née Hoare, his mother died three weeks after William's birth, on 28 September 1897. His father had been a Driver in the Royal Artillery, but had been discharged from the Regular Army and was serving in the Army Reserve when he died in Portsmouth on 25 October 1899. The 1901 Census records William as living with his grandmother, Elizabeth McCormack, in Portsmouth.

William was admitted to the school on 22 February 1907 (Petition No. 12336) and having moved from Chelsea to Guston, he was discharged to The Bedfordshire Regiment on 18 September 1911.

As his service record is no longer available, it is not known what his postings were prior to the war, or when he was posted to the 2nd Battalion. It is also not known exactly when William entered theatre, as this is not recorded on his medal index card. However, the fact that he did not qualify for the award of the 1914-15 Star suggests that he did not do so until 1916 at the earliest, possibly in the September of that when he turned nineteen.

At the end of June 1918, the battalion was in the vicinity of the town of Albert and was engaged north-west of the town in an attempt to capture and hold the German front line system, the attack being launched on 30 June. The assault continued the following day, and by 1200hrs, it had suffered 55 other ranks killed, wounded and missing. William was either one of those killed, and his body never recovered, or is the one missing soldier from that day of the attack. He died on 01 July 1918 and has no known grave, being commemorated on the Pozieres Memorial.

The Leicestershire Regiment

William Edmund DAYMOND
Serjeant, 7303, 6th (Service) Battalion, The Leicestershire Regiment who died on 02 August 1916, aged 27. Buried in Exeter Higher Cemetery, Devon, United Kingdom

Born on 06 March 1889 in Rawalpindi, India, the eldest of three children of William Daymond and Ellen née Connors, his father was a Serjeant in The Devonshire Regiment, but was medically discharged on 06 June 1899, the family settling in Exeter. By the time of William's petition, it appears that his father was completely unable to work and his mother was unable to do anything but look after her husband and their children.

William was admitted to the school on 12 July 1900 (Petition No. 11445), remaining at the school until he was discharged on 19 March 1904, enlisting into The Leicestershire Regiment in Guernsey, Channel Islands, on the same day. He was posted to the 2nd Battalion, which embarked for India on 20 September 1906, the 1911 Census recording William as a Lance Corporal and stationed in Fort St. George, Madras, India.

At the outbreak of war, the Battalion was in Ranikhet, India as part of the 20th (Garhwal) Infantry Brigade, 7th (Meerut) Division of the Indian Army, but was quickly embarked for the Western Front, landing at Marseille on 12 October 1914. By the time the battalion left India, William was a Corporal, being promoted to Lance Serjeant during the passage and then appointed as Acting Serjeant eight days after arriving in France.

It is unlikely that William saw action in the early battles of the war as he was posted to the Regimental Depot at Glen Parva Barracks in Wigston, South Leicestershire, on 12 November 1914, although he was there for less than two months before being promoted to Sergeant and posted to the 3rd (Reserve) Battalion, which was a training battalion in Leicester, Leicestershire, on 06 January 1915.

He was then posted to the 6th (Service) Battalion, which had been formed in Leicester in August 1914 as part of K1, when it deployed to France, landing on 29 July 1915. However, it appears that the battalion was not involved in any major actions until almost a year after its arrival in theatre, when it participated in the Somme Offensive, although not until after the offensive was under way.

The battalion participated in the Battle of Bazentin Ridge on 14 July 1916 and it is likely that it was during this action that William was wounded. He was evacuated back to Britain the following day, likely because the medical services in theatre were completely overwhelmed by the casualties that had been caused on 01 July and after. He was hospitalised in Exeter, where his widowed mother was still living, William's father having died passed in 1902 and he died as a result of his wounds on 02 August 1916. He is buried in the Higher Cemetery in the centre of the city.

Raymond Fox FERGUSON
Private, 9277, 2nd Battalion, The Leicestershire Regiment who died on 13 March 1915, aged 18. Commemorated on the Le Touret Memorial, Pas de Calais, France

Born on 15 April 1896 in Woolwich, London, the sixth of eight children of James Ferguson and Rosina Mary née Fox, his father had been a Quartermaster Serjeant in The Leicestershire Regiment, but had been discharged from the army on 05 December 1890 and died in Woolwich on 23 May 1902.

Raymond was admitted to the school on 01 September 1905 (Petition No. 12133), making the transition from Chelsea to Guston, before being discharged to his father's old regiment on 30 June 1911. He was initially stationed in Aldershot, Hampshire, but only for two months before embarking for India, arriving in Madras on 24 December 1911 and serving alongside Dukie William Daymond. He spent the next three years shuttling between Bareilly and Ranikhet, before being transferred back to Europe following the outbreak of war, landing at Marseille on 12 October 1914.

In March 1915, the battalion was located in the Artois region of France and participated in the Battle of Neuve Chapelle, an attack which was intended to cause a rupture in the German lines and which would then be exploited with a rush to the Aubers Ridge and possibly Lille.

The battle commenced on 10 March and lasted for three days. On the last day, the battalion reported that it had been subjected to shelling and that snipers had been very active. It is not recorded whether it was as a result of the shelling, or as a result of a sniper, but Raymond was killed on 13 March 1915. He has no known grave and is commemorated on the Le Touret Memorial along with 71 soldiers from his battalion who had also been killed during the battle.

Raymond's younger, non-Dukie brother, Vaughan Joseph Fox Ferguson, also fell during the war, aged 18. He died in Tanzania in 1917, whilst serving as a Private in the 7th Regiment, South African Infantry.

John Frederick Charles KIFFORD
Private, 12346, 2nd Battalion, The Leicestershire Regiment who died on 25 September 1915, aged 37. Commemorated on the Loos Memorial, Pas de Calais, France

Born on 06 September 1878 in Halifax, Yorkshire West Riding, the fourth of seven children of Charles Kifford and Sarah née Martin, his father had been a Colour Sergeant in the 33rd (The Duke of Wellington's) Regiment of Foot[198] and was still serving when he died in Southowram, Yorkshire West Riding, on 13 March 1886. He had been awarded the Distinguished Conduct Medal *'For services at the Assault on Magdala, Abyssinia'* in 1868.

John was admitted to the school on 30 November 1888 (Petition No. 9716) and discharged to The Duke of Wellington's (West Riding Regiment) on 10 September 1892, spending the first three years of his service in Britain, before being posted to Malta with the 1st Battalion on 30 September 1895.

After three years in Malta, he was then posted back to Britain for just over a year, being appointed a Lance Corporal on 04 July 1899, prior to being posted to South Africa on 23 October 1899 during the Second Boer War, where he was awarded both the Queen's and King's South Africa Medals, and was promoted to Corporal before returning to Britain on 05 October 1902.

After five months in Britain, John was then posted to India with the 2nd Battalion. However, his time here was not without incident, as on 14 March 1904 he was tried by Regimental Courts Martial for being absent without leave and breaking out of barracks, being sentenced to be reduced to the rank of Private.

John returned to Britain on 27 November 1905 and was in no further trouble for the three years prior to his discharge after 15 years' service on 07 March 1908, being attested into the Section D Reserve[199] on 01 July 1908, from which he was discharged on 30 June 1912.

---

[198] Amalgamated with the 76th Regiment of Foot on 10 July 1881 to become The Duke of Wellington's (West Riding Regiment)

[199] Section D Reserves consisted of those men who had not only completed their term of Regular service, but who had also completed their time as a Section B Reserve. Section D Reserves could only be called upon in the event of a general mobilisation

Following his discharge from the army, it appears that he was working as a Coal Miner when he was recalled as a Special Reservist on 02 September 1914. He disembarked in France on 26 January 1915 as a Corporal in 2nd Battalion, The Leicestershire Regiment. However, on 22 February 1915, he was reduced to the ranks for breaking out of camp and drunkenness on active service, as he had been in India in 1904.

On 17 May 1915, John was admitted to No. 13 General Hospital, Boulogne, with a gunshot wound to his shoulder and it was not until 24 July 1915 that he re-joined the battalion. It is likely that he was wounded at the Battle of Festubert, which took place between 15 and 27 May, and that he had previously fought at the Battle of Neuve Chapelle, between 10 and 13 March, when his battalion lost 77 men.

On 25 September 1915, the battalion attacked in the Battle of Loos, the first time that chlorine gas was used by the British on the Western Front. The battalion war diary[200] records 72 other ranks killed, 217 wounded, 42 gassed and 96 missing. It is likely that John was one of the missing from the unsuccessful attack, as his body was not recovered and so he is commemorated on the Loos Memorial. He is also another "Lost Boy" whose name has been omitted from the memorial tablets in the school chapel.

James William TALO
Drummer, 8193, 2nd Battalion, The Leicestershire Regiment who died on 29 October 1916, aged 23. Buried in Basra War Cemetery, Iraq

Born 23 May 1893 in Aldershot, Hampshire, the youngest of two children of William Talo and Abina née Sheehan, his father was a Bugler in The Cameronians (Scottish Rifles). His mother died in Shahjahanpur, India, on 11 November 1895.

James was admitted to the school on 14 August 1903 (Petition No. 11854) and was discharged to The Leicestershire Regiment on 18 July 1907, being posted to Shorncliffe, Kent, and stationed there for fifteen months before embarking on the SS *Plassey* and arriving in India in October 1908, where he would have served alongside Dukies William Daymond and Raymond Ferguson. For the next six years, James remained in India, posted to various towns in the country, recorded as serving in Fort St. George, Madras in the 1911 Census.

At the outbreak of war, his battalion was transferred back to Europe and took part in many of the early battles in of the war, including Neuve Chapelle in March 1915.

---

[200] WO 95/3945/2: 2 Battalion Leicestershire Regiment, 1914 Aug. - 1915 Nov., The National Archives, Kew

In late-1915, the battalion was transferred to the 28th Indian Brigade, arriving in Egypt in the November, but was only there for a month before re-joining the 7th (Meerut) Division and landing at Basra, Mesopotamia, in December, being in action within a month, taking part in the battle of Shaikh Saad in January 1916 and the siege of Kut al Amara in the spring.

On the 11 March, James was hospitalised after being wounded in action, suffering a severe gunshot wound to his left shoulder, but he had recovered sufficiently to return to duty in Amara by the beginning of April.

However, by October, James had become unwell and on 20 October 1916, he was admitted from Amara to No. 3 British General Hospital in Basra with *"evident signs of a failing heart – legs and thighs and back oedematous – ascites and congestion of the lungs"*[201]. Six days later, he was reported as dangerously ill and despite the best efforts of the medical staff in the hospital, he continued to deteriorate, dying at 0230 on 28 October 1916. Post-mortem examination showed *"old vegetations in the aortic valves with hugely dilated left heart and flabby right heart dilated"*[202], with the cause of death given as disease contracted on active service.

James was buried in Basra War Cemetery, incorrectly commemorated as W J Talo, which was under the care of the Commonwealth War Graves Commission until 2007, when the security situation in Iraq worsened. Sadly, in 2013, it was reported that the cemetery had been completely destroyed, with all 4,000 headstones knocked down and broken by looters and vandals.

---

[201] WO 363: War Office: Soldiers' Documents, First World War 'Burnt Documents' (Microfilm Copies), 1914-1920, The National Archives, Kew - First World War Service Records 'Burnt Documents'
[202] Ibid.

The Royal Irish Regiment

Joseph Robert CHRISTIE
Corporal, 10560, 6th (Service) Battalion, The Royal Irish Regiment who died on 09 September 1916, aged 22. Commemorated on the Thiepval Memorial, Somme, France

Born on 12 August 1894 in Lucknow, India, the youngest of two children of Joseph Charles Christie and Mary Jane née Higgs, his father was a Sergeant in The Royal Irish Regiment who died on active service at Kushulgarh, India, on 15 September 1897, whilst engaged in operations against the Afridi tribesmen who had captured strategically important forts along the Khyber Pass on India's North-West Frontier.

Joseph was admitted to the school on 05 February 1904 (Petition No. 11933), joining his older brother, George Charles Christie, who had been admitted to the school on 13 November 1903 (Petition No. 11907). Joseph was *"withdrawn by mother"* on 30 November 1906. Little is known about Joseph following his withdrawal from the school, although he is recorded in the 1911 Census living in Wandsworth, London, with his mother, stepfather and half-sister and employed as a Boy Labourer, Flour Depot.

At some point after 1911, Joseph enlisted into the army at Stratford, Essex. His service record is no longer available, but his service number suggests that this could have been sometime between 17 October 1912 and 17 February 1913. It is known that at the outbreak of war, he was stationed in Devonport, Devonshire, serving in 2nd Battalion, The Royal Irish Regiment.

The battalion quickly mobilised once war was declared, landing at Boulogne on 13 August 1914, Joseph's medal index card showing that he disembarked in theatre the following day. Due to the lack of service record, it is not possible to follow Joseph's movements during the first eighteen months of the war, nor is it possible to establish when he was posted to the 6th (Service) Battalion of the regiment.

In early September 1916, the battalion was located near Carnoy, moving into positions in the sunken road and relieving 8th (Service) Battalion, The Royal Inniskilling Fusiliers, on 08 September. The following morning the battalion, along with the remainder of the

47th Brigade, made their second attack in a week to capture the village of Ginchy. However, the Germans were found to be well-prepared, with their trenches apparently untouched by the bombardment prior to the attack, which resulted in the battalion suffering heavy casualties. Thirteen officers and 184 other ranks were killed, wounded or missing, including the Commanding Officer and Adjutant, both of whom were killed, and Joseph, who was likely one of the missing, as he is commemorated on the Thiepval memorial. He is also another "Lost Boy" who has been omitted from the memorial tablets in the school chapel.

George was discharged from the school on 30 December 1906 *"to civil life"*, although he later enlisted into the army, his service number suggesting that this was sometime between 03 March 1910 and 15 January 1911. He is recorded in the 1911 Census as a Private in 2nd Battalion, The Royal Irish Regiment and stationed in Fort George, Guernsey, Channel Islands. He disembarked in France on the same day as his brother and on 11 July 1916 he transferred to the Royal Engineers. He survived the war and died in Peterborough, Huntingdonshire, in 1961.

James Thomas TOOHEY
Temporary Second Lieutenant, 6th (Service) Battalion, The Royal Irish Regiment who died on 18 January 1917, aged 35. Buried in Pond Farm Cemetery, West-Vlaanderen, Belgium

Born on 10 January 1882 in Lincoln, Lincolnshire, the oldest child of Thomas Toohey and Betsy née Carlill, his father had been a Private in The Lincolnshire Regiment, who was discharged to a pension on 09 May 1882. He died in Chichester, Sussex, on 18 June 1887.

James was admitted to the school on 25 February 1893 (Petition No. 10440) and was joined by his younger brother, Michael Toohey, three years later, on 31 January 1896 (Petition No. 10856). James was discharged from the school on 06 November 1897, enlisting into the 7th (Queen's Own) Hussars, although six months after enlisting, on 10 May 1898, he transferred to the 10th (Prince of Wales's Own Royal) Hussars. His time with this regiment was short, as seven months later, on 07 February 1899, he transferred back to the 7th Hussars and was appointed as a Bandsman eight months later, on 07 October 1899.

Thomas was posted to South Africa during the Second Boer War, on 30 November 1901, where he was appointed as a Lance Corporal on 11 January 1902 and then promoted to Corporal on 01 April after he was mentioned in Lord Kitchener's Despatches, *"For good service and capture of two prisoners"*[203]. The 7th Hussars had supported the 2nd Dragoon Guards (Queen's Bays) at Leeuwkop in severe fighting on 01 April 1902, which was when James had captured the two prisoners.

After being appointed as a Lance Serjeant on 13 August 1903, and promoted to Serjeant on 28 November 1903, Thomas returned to Britain on 06 December 1905, re-engaging in order to complete 21 years' service on 25 February 1907, although he was discharged from the army as no longer medically fit for military service on 09 June 1911. By the time that he was discharged from the army, Thomas had married Margaret Lilian Grehan in Norwich, Norfolk, in April 1910. They had two daughters, Kathleen Lillian Toohey, born in Hounslow, Middlesex, in 1911 and Mary Grehan Toohey, born in Lincoln in 1912.

At the outbreak of war, James re-enlisted, although it is not known whether he was recalled from the Reserve or whether he was a Kitchener volunteer, as his officer's service record for the second period of service is not easily accessible. His medal index card shows that he disembarked in theatre on 18 October 1915, as a Serjeant in the 3rd (King's Own) Hussars, by which time this regiment had been in theatre for more than a year, having landed at Rouen on 17 August 1914.

Again, little is known about James once he did arrive in theatre and the cavalry at this time was employed either as working parties or alongside their infantry colleagues in the trenches. What is known is that in September 1916, James was commissioned as a Temporary Second Lieutenant[204] and transferred to The Royal Irish Regiment, joining the 6th (Service) Battalion.

This battalion had been formed in Fermoy, County Cork, on 06 September 1914 as part of K2. After moving to various locations in Ireland and mainland Britain, and being joined by a company of the Guernsey Militia, it landed at Le Havre on 18 December 1915. During the Somme Offensive, it had participated in the Battle of Guillemont between 03 and 06 September 1916, the 47th Brigade, of which it was part, capturing the village. It also participated in the Battle of Ginchy on 09 September.

In January 1917, the battalion was on the front line at Cooker Farm, near Ypres, and on 18 January 1917, the battalion war diary

---

[203] *The London Gazette*, 18 July 1902, Issue:27455
[204] *The London Gazette*, 24 October 1916, Supplement:29803

records *"2Lt Toohey killed by a sniper"*[205]. The incident was also mentioned in Thomas Burke's book *Messines to Carrick Hill*[206].

Whilst there is a J T Toohey commemorated on the memorial tablets in the school chapel, the regiment given for him is "Australian Light Infantry". This is almost certainly an error, as there was no Australian regiment of that name and the only James Toohey who died serving in the Australian forces during the First World War, in the 56th Infantry Battalion, Australian Imperial Force, had been born in Broadfield, County Clare, in September 1883, enlisting at Liverpool, New South Wales, and clearly is not the fallen James Toohey who was a Dukie.

Michael was discharged from the school three years after his brother, on 15 December 1900, enlisting into 1st (King's) Dragoon Guards as a Musician. However, after serving for just over six years, he was discharged at his own request on 15 April 1907, although it then appears that he enlisted into the Royal Marine Light Infantry, as the 1911 Census records him as living with his widowed mother in Gosport, Hampshire, as a Musician in that corps. He died in Kensington, London, in 1946.

Albert Arthur Ernest WILLIAMS
Serjeant, 6651, 2nd Battalion, The Royal Irish Regiment who died on 09 November 1918, aged 34. Buried in South Cerney (All Hallows) Churchyard, Gloucestershire, United Kingdom

Born on 28 September 1884 in Dublin, County Dublin, the youngest of nine children of John Williams and Sarah Anne née Lyons, his father had been a Serjeant in the 18th (The Royal Irish) Regiment of Foot[207], but was discharged from the army on 12 March 1862. His mother died in Dublin on 16 January 1890.

Albert was admitted to the school on 24 November 1893 (Petition No. 10546) and discharged on 07 July 1899, enlisting into The Royal Irish Regiment. However, his service record is no longer available and so his pre-war postings are unknown, although he is recorded in the 1911 Census as being a Band Serjeant in that regiment and stationed in Alderney, Channel Islands. It is also known that he married Winifred Agnes Guille in Guernsey, Channel Islands, in 1913 and his daughter, Barbara Eileen Williams was born in Devonport, Devonshire, on 23 February 1914.

At the outbreak of war, the 2nd Battalion was still stationed in Devonport, as part of the 13th Brigade, 3rd Division. It quickly

---

[205] WO 95/1970/3: 6 Battalion Royal Irish Regiment, 1915 Dec. - 1918 Feb., The National Archives, Kew
[206] Burke, T. (2017). *Messines to Carrick Hill: writing home from the Great War*. Cork: Mercier Press
[207] Renamed The Royal Irish Regiment on 01 July 1881

mobilised and landed at Boulogne on 13 August 1914, the disembarkation date that appears on Albert's medal index card. The battalion participated in the Battle of Mons and the subsequent retreat, before going back onto the offensive as the tide turned in favour of the Allied Armies, although during the Battle of La Bassée, fought between 10 October and 02 November 1914, the battalion was virtually destroyed near Le Pilly.

However, the International Committee of the Red Cross records of Prisoners of War[208] show that by this time, Albert was already a prisoner of war, having been captured at Bertry on 03 October, likely having been wounded in action.

How long Albert was a prisoner for is not known, but he was repatriated, possibly due to the extent of his wounds, which resulted in his discharge from the army on 28 May 1918. It is likely that the repatriation took place in early-1917, as his son, John Walter Williams, was born on 15 February 1918.

According to his pension record, Albert died from *"Influenza, Pneumonia"* on 9 November 1918, with his widow dying twelve days later, on 23 November 1918. It is believed that his widow had travelled from Guernsey for the funeral and died on the way back, but it is not known why they were not living together, nor why the Red Cross record of his capture states his next of kin to have been a Mrs Eva Bannister of Englefield Green, Surrey. Their children, Barbara and John, were brought up by separate family members in Kent and Guernsey.

Albert is also another of the "Lost Boys" whose name has been omitted from the memorial tablets in the school chapel.

---

[208] 1914-1918 Prisoners of the First World War ICRC Historical Archives: PA 765

Alexandra, Princess of Wales's Own (Yorkshire Regiment)

Only one Dukie who served in Alexandra, Princess of Wales's Own (Yorkshire Regiment) and died during the First World War is commemorated on the memorial tablets in the school chapel. The regiment is incorrectly recorded as The Green Howards.

The Green Howards came into being in 1744, during the War of the Austrian Succession, at a time when the regiments were known by the name of their Colonels. At that time, there were two regiments commanded by a Howard, the 19th Regiment of Foot[209], commanded by the Honourable Sir Charles Howard, and the 3rd Regiment of Foot[210], commanded by Thomas Howard. In order to avoid confusion, as there would have been two Howard's Regiment of Foot, each regiment was known by the colour of the facings of their uniforms, the 19th Regiment becoming the Green Howards and the 3rd Regiment becoming Howard's Buffs.

Although the 19th Regiment was unofficially known as the Green Howards from this time on, it was not until 01 January 1921, more than five years after Dukie James Page died in late 1915, that the regiment was renamed The Green Howards (Alexandra, Princess of Wales's Own Yorkshire Regiment).

James Percival PAGE
Private, 9516, 6th (Service) Battalion, Alexandra, Princess of Wales's Own (Yorkshire Regiment) who died on 19 November 1915, aged 19. Commemorated on the Helles Memorial, Turkey

Born on 15 July 1896 in Richmond, Yorkshire North Riding, the third of seven children of John Thomas Page and Ann née Nodding, his father was a Serjeant in The Princess of Wales's Own (Yorkshire Regiment) who had been discharged to pension after 29 years' service

---

[209] Renamed the 19th (The 1st Yorkshire North Riding) Regiment of Foot on 31 August 1782, further renamed the 19th (The 1st Yorkshire North Riding - Princess of Wales's Own) Regiment of Foot on 29 October 1875, The Princess of Wales's Own (Yorkshire Regiment) on 01 July 1881 and lastly, Alexandra, Princess of Wales's Own (Yorkshire Regiment) in 1902

[210] Renamed the 3rd (the East Kent) Regiment of Foot on 31 August 1782, and then The Buffs (East Kent Regiment) on 01 July 1881

on 30 June 1901 and died in Northallerton, Yorkshire North Riding, on 12 June 1907.

James was admitted to the school on 31 August 1907 (Petition No. 12394) and having made the move from Chelsea to Guston, he was discharged to his father's old regiment on 27 July 1910. His service record is no longer available, so his pre-war career is unknown. However, the battalion with which he was serving at the time of his death, 6th (Service) Battalion, was formed at Richmond on 25 August 1914 as part of K1.

Soon after formation, it moved to Belton Park near Grantham, Lincolnshire, before, in April 1915, it moved to Witley Camp near Godalming in Surrey. From there, on 03 July 1915 the unit embarked at Liverpool, Lancashire, and sailed for the Dardanelles where, after a stopover at Mudros, it then sailed to Suvla Bay, landing on 06 August 1915, participating in the Battle of Sari Bair.

According to his medal index card, James did not qualify for the award of the 1914-1915 Star until 28 September, so it is likely that it was not until that date that he entered theatre. The battalion was involved in various actions on the Gallipoli Peninsula during 1915 and at some point, James was wounded and evacuated to HMHS[211] *Nevasa*. He died of wounds on 19 November 1915 and as a result of having died on a hospital ship, was buried at sea, which explains why he has no known grave and is commemorated on the Helles Memorial. He is also commemorated on the memorial tablets in the school chapel, but his regiment is incorrectly recorded as The Green Howards.

Richard WEBB
Corporal, 6693, 2nd Battalion, Alexandra, Princess of Wales's Own (Yorkshire Regiment) who died on 15 June 1915, aged 27. Commemorated on the Le Touret Memorial, Pas de Calais, France

Born on 17 September 1887 in Richmond, Yorkshire North Riding, the fourth of six children of James Webb and Annie née Taylor, his father had been a Private in Alexandra, Princess of Wales's Own (Yorkshire Regiment) who died whilst serving in Richmond on 13 April 1892.

Richard was admitted to the school on 04 February 1898 (Petition No. 11121), joining his older brothers, William Webb, who had been admitted on 28 July 1893 (Petition No. 10504) and Frederick James Webb, who had been admitted on 07 June 1895 (Petition No. 10758). His oldest brother, Herbert Edward Webb, had already been discharged from the school, having been admitted on 30 December

---
[211] His Majesty's Hospital Ship

1892 (Petition No. 10416), prior to Richard's admission. Richard was joined at the school by his younger brother, Oliver Webb, on 10 August 1900 (Petition No. 11459). Richard was discharged from the school on 21 September 1901 and enlisted into his father's old regiment.

Richard's service record is no longer available, so his movements pre-war are not known, but he is recorded in the 1911 Census as a Bandsman in 1st Battalion, Alexandra, Princess of Wales's Own (Yorkshire Regiment) stationed in the British Barracks, Khartoum, Sudan. It is also not known at what point he was posted to the 2nd Battalion.

At the outbreak of war, the 2nd Battalion was stationed in Guernsey, Channel Islands, but quickly returned to the mainland, landing at Southampton, Hampshire, on 28 August 1914 joining the 21st Brigade, 7th Division, and then landing at Zeebrugge on 05 October 1914, the date shown on Richard's medal index card for his entry into theatre. The battalion arrived in Ypres eight days later, participating in the First Battle of Ypres and holding the Menin crossroads for sixteen days, but suffering heavy casualties in doing so and was not in action for the remainder of the year whilst it reformed.

On 14 June 1915 the battalion moved into trenches near Givenchy ready to launch the assault that became known as The Second Action of Givenchy the following day. At about 1500hrs on 15 June, "A" and "B" Companies moved into position, lining the British parapet. Following a heavy bombardment of the German trenches, at 1800hrs the companies climbed over the parapet to advance. However, "B" Company came under very heavy shell fire as it was climbing the parapet and suffered a large number of casualties. The battalion war diary reports that elements did get into the enemy positions, but were unable to advance further. It also reported that "A" Company *"lost very heavily; out of 5 officers and 170 Rank and File who went into action, no officers and only about 40 Rank and File came back"*[212]. Richard is one of the 126 officers and other ranks from the battalion killed during the assault and his body was not recovered. He is also a "Lost Boy" whose name has been omitted from the memorial tablets in the school chapel, despite being one of five Dukies.

Herbert was discharged from the school on 11 April 1896 and enlisted into The Alexandra, Princess of Wales's Own (Yorkshire Regiment) and served in South Africa. He is recorded in the 1911 Census as a Colour Serjeant in the 1st Battalion, stationed with

---

[212] WO 95/1659/4: 2 Battalion Yorkshire Regiment, 1914 Oct. - 1915 Dec., The National Archives, Kew

Richard in Khartoum. By the outbreak of war, he was a Company Serjeant Major, but in May 1916, was attached to 5th Battalion, The Northumberland Fusiliers as the Acting Regimental Serjeant Major in order to improve discipline. During his time with this battalion, he was Mentioned in Despatches[213], although by the time that this was Gazetted, he had been Commissioned for service in the field, and had joined 4th Battalion, The Yorkshire Regiment. He ended the war as a Captain and died in York, Yorkshire North Riding, in 1954.

William was discharged from the school on 12 November 1898 and also enlisted into Alexandra, Princess of Wales's Own (Yorkshire Regiment). He is also recorded in the 1911 Census as a Bandsman in the 1st Battalion in Khartoum. He served in India throughout the war, returning to Britain on 26 December 1919, being discharged from the army a month later on 24 January 1920. Nothing more is known of him after his discharge.

Frederick was discharged from the school on 04 February 1901 and enlisted into Alexandra, Princess of Wales's Own (Yorkshire Regiment). He is recorded in the 1911 Census as a Lance Serjeant in the band of the 1st Battalion alongside his brothers. Like William, it appears that he remained with 1st Battalion. After this, nothing more is known of him for certain, although he may have married in Bradford in 1926, his occupation given as Conductor City Tramways.

Oliver was discharged from the school on 25 May 1905 and *"Returned to civil life – unfit"*. Despite this, it appears that he also enlisted into Alexandra, Princess of Wales's Own (Yorkshire Regiment) on 05 January 1910. He arrived on the Western Front on 06 October, so it is likely that he was serving in the 2nd Battalion alongside Richard. It is also recorded that he deserted on 15 January 1915, as he initially forfeited his medals, but this cannot be confirmed as his service record is no longer available. However, he did return to his regiment, was promoted to Lance Corporal and was discharged from the army on 05 June 1918, the pension records stating that he had a disability, possibly as a result of being wounded. Following his discharge from the army, nothing more is known of him either.

---

[213] *The London Gazette*, 14 December 1917, Supplement:30434

The Lancashire Fusiliers

Walter Frederick BOND
Corporal, 7710, 2nd Battalion, The Lancashire Fusiliers who died on 09 April 1915, aged 29. Buried in Tancrez Farm Cemetery, Hainaut, Belgium

Born on 18 December 1885 in Chatham, Kent, the second of five children of George Bond and Alice née O'Shea, his father was a Corporal and had served for eighteen years in The Lancashire Fusiliers when he died in Exeter in August 1893.

Walter was admitted to the school on 05 February 1896 (Petition No. 10863) and was discharged to his father's old regiment on 10 January 1900, but because his service record is no longer available, his pre-war postings are largely unknown, although the 1911 Census records him as a Corporal in the 1st Battalion, stationed in India.

It would appear that by the time that war was declared, Walter had left the army, possibly having completed his 12 years' service and was recalled to the Colours as a Special Reservist on 08 August 1914. He disembarked in France on 17 December 1914 and is likely to have been a replacement from either the 3rd (Reserve) Battalion or the 4th (Extra Reserve) Battalion, which were both training men for the Regular battalions at that time.

An account of Walter's death is recorded in a regimental history[214]. The battalion was located at Le Touquet when, on 09 April 1915, a German counter-mine was blown in the area of the town it still held, causing heavy casualties:

> *"Reprisals came in the form of heavy shelling, one 5.9 shell coming through the battalion guard room when it was full of men, but the total casualties during the day were one man killed and 17 wounded, most of the latter being hit by bricks thrown up by the explosion of the mine".*

The Commonwealth War Graves Commission records no other deaths from 2nd Battalion, The Lancashire Fusiliers on that day, so it is almost certain that Walter was the one man killed. He is also

---

[214] Latter, J. C. (1949). *The History of the Lancashire Fusiliers 1914-1918, Volume 1.* Aldershot: Gale and Polden Limited

another "Lost Boy" whose name has been omitted from the memorial tablets in the school chapel.

William George BROWN
Private, 5651, 1st Battalion, The Lancashire Fusiliers who died on 21 June 1915, aged 39. Commemorated in Pink Farm Cemetery, Helles, Turkey

Born on 14 November 1875 in Pembroke Dock, Pembrokeshire, the eldest of three children of Henry Brown and Martha Anne née Gibbs, his father was a Serjeant in the 9th (the East Norfolk) Regiment of Foot[215]. William's Petition Document is no longer available at the school, so it is not known if or when his father was discharged from the army, or if his father was still alive at the time of his admission, but it is known that his mother died in Pembroke Dock in 1882.

William was admitted to the school on 17 September 1886 (Petition No. 9411) and discharged on 11 November 1889, enlisting into The Lancashire Fusiliers. Following his attestation, William was posted to the 1st Battalion and was to spend the first ten years of his service in Britain, during which he was appointed as a Drummer on 24 November 1889 and as a Lance Corporal on 21 November 1894. However, he reverted to Private on 05 October 1896, which was three months after he had married Catharine Madden in Athlone, County Westmeath. Their first child, Lillie Catherine Brown, was born in Athlone on 10 February 1897.

Two years later, on 13 July 1898, William was again appointed as a Lance Corporal, his second child, Thomas Henry Brown, born in Aldershot, Hampshire, four months later. On 08 August 1899, William was promoted to Corporal, nine days before he was posted to Malta. However, a month later, he was posted to Crete as part of the occupation, during which time his third child, William Brown, was born in Gozo on 09 October 1900, although he died less than three weeks later.

After ten months in Crete, William was posted back to Malta, remaining there for a year before he was posted back to Britain on 05 July 1901, joining the 4th (Extra Reserve) Battalion that was stationed in the Regimental Depot in Wellington Barracks, Bury, Lancashire. He was discharged from the army at the end of his first period of service two days later.

William was a civilian for a year before he re-enlisted into the army on 19 September 1902, serving again in The Lancashire Fusiliers, but reverting to the rank of Drummer and posted to the 2nd Battalion. He spent this entire second period of service in Britain,

---

[215] Renamed The Norfolk Regiment on 01 July 1881

during which time he and Catharine had three more children, Harry Brown, born in Bury in 1903, Archibald Brown, born in Bury in 1908 and James Alexander Brown, born in Chorlton, Lancashire, in 1910.

William remained as a Drummer and was discharged from the army for the second time, this time at his own request, on 31 January 1910, his seventh child, George Brown, being born later that year. Following his discharge from the army, it appears that the family settled in Radcliffe, Lancashire, as this is where they are recorded living in the 1911 Census, William employed as a Labourer in a cotton spinning mill. His last child, Maud Brown, was born in November of that year.

Following the outbreak of war, it is not known whether William was a Kitchener volunteer or if he was recalled to the Colours from the reserve, as his service record for this period of service is no longer available.

The 1st Battalion, with which William was to serve, had not returned to Britain until January 1915 following the outbreak of war and had then sailed for the Dardanelles two months later, landing at Gallipoli on 25 April 1915. However, according to William's medal index card, he did not disembark until two months later, on 20 June 1915, joining the battalion in bivouacs on West Gully Beach. The following day he was believed killed by shrapnel and is now commemorated with a special memorial, with the actual grave location lost, but nearby to the headstone.

William is also a "Lost Boy" whose name has been omitted from the memorial tablets in the school chapel.

Edward Reginald HUMPHREY
Corporal, 2451, 11th (Service) Battalion, The Lancashire Fusiliers who died on 22 March 1918, aged 20. Commemorated on the Arras Memorial, Pas de Calais, France

Born on 12 October 1897 in Woolwich, London, the second of six children of Robert John Humphrey and Rose Hannah née Elliott, his father had served in the Royal Artillery and been a Drummer in The Duke of Cambridge's Own (Middlesex Regiment), before he was discharged from the army as medically unfit on 28 February 1907.

Edward was admitted to the school on 08 September 1908 (Petition No. 12539), making the transition from Chelsea to Guston and being discharged on 28 October 1911, enlisting into The Lancashire Fusiliers.

Although his service record is no longer available to confirm details, it is likely that Edward was initially posted to one of the Regular battalions, 1st or 2nd, but due to his age at the outbreak of war, he may have been transferred to the 3rd (Reserve) Battalion, which was initially in Bury, Lancashire, but transferred to Hull, Yorkshire East Riding, and finally stationed in Withernsea, Yorkshire East Riding. This assumption has been made as it appears that Edward did not deploy to the Western Front until at least 1916, when he was nineteen, as his medal index card states that he was ineligible for the award of the 1914-15 Star.

It is known that in 1918, Edward was serving with the 11th (Service) Battalion and was an Acting Corporal. This battalion had been raised as part of K3 at Codford, Wiltshire, and had landed at Boulogne in 1915, fighting during the Somme Offensive in 1916, where possibly its most famous member, Second Lieutenant J. R. R. Tolkien[216] contracted trench fever, which resulted in his being evacuated home.

It also participated in both the Battle of Messines and the Battle of Pilckem Ridge, part of the Third Battle of Ypres, in 1917, but by March 1918 it was in Buchanan Camp, Achiet le Petit, spending the first two weeks in training and the next week providing working parties. However, on 21 March, the Germans launched its Spring Offensive, the battalion being ordered to take up positions behind its corps line, south of the Bapaume to Cambrai road, but it was not to be until the afternoon of the following day that it was in action, being ordered to move and meet the German attack that was advancing up the Morchies valley.

During the course of the day and night, the battalion fought hard to resist the German attack, experiencing some success, but at the cost of one officer and fifteen other ranks killed in action, one of which was Edward, who was killed on 22 March 1918. The heavy attack by the Germans on the 23 March, which caused the battalion to withdraw, is the likely reason that his body was not recovered and why he has no known grave, but is commemorated on the Arras Memorial.

William MUDDLE

Serjeant, 7864, 2nd Battalion, The Lancashire Fusiliers who died on 02 November 1914, aged 30. Buried in Strand Military Cemetery, Ploegsteert, Hainaut, Belgium

Born on 29 July 1884 in Gosport, Hampshire, the fourth of five children of Isaac Muddle and Harriet née Rowe, his father had been a Private in the 43rd (Monmouthshire) Regiment of Foot, but had been discharged from the army on 31 August 1869. He died in

---

[216] English writer, poet and academic, best known as the author of *The Hobbit* and *The Lord of the Rings*

Portsmouth, Hampshire, on 15 January 1887, William's mother dying four years later in Southsea, Hampshire, on 07 May 1891.

William was admitted to the school on 23 February 1894 (Petition No. 10585), almost five years after his elder brother, James George Muddle, had been admitted on 21 June 1889 (Petition No. 9869) and seven years after their oldest brother, Isaac Henry Muddle, had been admitted on 14 January 1887 (Petition No. 9463). William was discharged on 07 July 1900 and enlisted into The Lancashire Fusiliers. His service record is no longer available, but the 1901 Census records him as a Private in the Infantry, stationed in Chatham Barracks, Kent, and ten years later the 1911 Census records he was a Serjeant Drummer in 2nd Battalion, The Lancashire Fusiliers, stationed in Assaye Barracks, Tidworth, Wiltshire.

At some point between then and the outbreak of war, William undertook the Student Bandmaster course at the Royal Military School of Music, Kneller Hall, in Whitton, Middlesex, but was back with his battalion in August 1914, which was stationed in Dover, Kent, when it deployed to France, landing at Boulogne on 23 August 1914. It came into action for the first time on 25 August, but then participated in the long "Retreat from Mons" participating in the Battle of Le Cateau and then the Battles of the Marne and the Aisne, the latter two after the Germans had been forced onto the retreat.

In mid-October, it was moved to the Ypres Salient, arriving at Hazebrouck on 13 October, the day after what became the Battle of Messines had commenced and spending the rest of the month rotating through the trenches.

At the start of November, it is reported that two companies of the battalion pushed forward on the Messines Road, whilst the remainder were in reserve at Ploegsteert. The following day, a company was moved into the fire trenches at St. Yves to support The Somerset Light Infantry, suffering one officer and four other ranks killed, with nineteen other ranks wounded. William was one of the other ranks killed, on 02 November 1914. He was a very talented musician and according to his obituary, he had *"received the notification of his appointment as Bandmaster on the very day he was killed"*[217]. Major General Latter's previously cited Regimental history states that:

> *"One of those killed was Serjeant W. Muddle, an old Duke of York's School boy, a football player of the 4th and 2nd Battalions and a skilled musician; he was hit as he was reading a letter ordering him to return to England on promotion to Bandmaster".*

---

[217] *Middlesex Chronicle*, Saturday 09 January 1915

He is buried in Strand Military Cemetery, just outside the village of Ploegsteert.

Both of William's brothers also served during the war, joining their father's old regiment, The Oxfordshire Light Infantry, when they were discharged from the school on 11 November 1890 in Isaac's case and 13 May 1893 in James's. Both survived the conflict, Isaac dying in Oxford in 1953 and James dying in Gosport in 1940.

George Edward SIMPSON
Regimental Serjeant Major, 4486, 1st Battalion, Lancashire Fusiliers who died 21 August 1915, aged 36. Commemorated on the Helles Memorial, Turkey

Born on 06 June 1879 in Bermuda, West Indies, the third of four sons of Henry Simpson and Elizabeth née Cox, his father was a Private in the 19th (The 1st Yorkshire North Riding – Princess of Wales's Own) Regiment of Foot and died in Bermuda the year that George was born.

George was admitted to the school on 25 July 1890 (Petition No. 10043), joining his older brother, Francis John Simpson, who had been admitted on 25 November 1887 (Petition No. 9582) and soon after their eldest brother, Henry William Simpson, who had been admitted on 30 October 1885 (Petition No. 9281), had been discharged. George was discharged from the school and enlisted in The Lancashire Fusiliers on 10 June 1893, joining Francis in that regiment and although his service record is no longer available, he served in South Africa during the Second Boer War according to medal records and may have been posted to Gibraltar in 1903.

At the outbreak of war, the battalion was stationed in Karachi, India, but was then posted to Aden, Yemen, remaining there until December 1914, before returning to Britain on 02 January 1915.

Soon after arriving back from India, George married Ellen Mary Ford in Portsmouth, Hampshire, and two months later, on 16 March 1915, he left his new bride, who was pregnant and embarked for Gallipoli, landing at "W" Beach on 25 April 1915. This action was to become famous as it saw the battalion awarded *"six VCs before breakfast"* and resulted in "W" Beach being renamed *"Lancashire Landing"*.

The battalion was then involved in many of the battles in the area of Cape Helles before, on 19 August, it was transported to Suvla Bay to support The Royal Munster Fusiliers attack on Hill 112, also known as Chocolate Hill.

The attack was planned to commence on the afternoon of 21 August 1915, the timing being decided so that the defending Turks would have the sun in their eyes. However, on the day the sun was obscured by clouds and The Royal Munster Fusiliers' attack stalled, necessitating The Lancashire Fusiliers to continue the assault. The ground was rough and scrubby, the scrub catching fire in places due to the shelling and bullets. The Lancashire Fusiliers assault was also a failure and by 1930hrs it had lost 12 officers wounded and 222 other ranks killed, wounded or missing, among them George, who died on 21 August 1915. His body was never recovered and he is commemorated on the Helles Memorial. His daughter, Georgina, was born four months after his death, but died in childhood in 1922.

George's brothers both survived the war. Francis, who was discharged from the school on 23 August 1890 into The Lancashire Fusiliers, died in Portsmouth, Hampshire, in 1920. However, the fact that he has no Commonwealth War Graves Commission commemoration suggests that the cause of death was unrelated to his military service.

Henry was discharged on 15 March 1890 into the 6th Dragoon Guards (Carabiniers). In 1918, it is known that he was the Bandmaster of that regiment, although nothing more is known of him after this.

The Royal Scots Fusiliers

Stuart Coutts WALKER MM

Serjeant, 10651, 1st Battalion, The Royal Scots Fusiliers who died on 02 September 1918, aged 21. Commemorated on the Vis-En-Artois Memorial, Pas de Calais, France

Born on 02 May 1897 in Murree, India, the second of four children of Stuart Walker and Sophia Mary née Simpson, his father was a Serjeant in The Royal Scots Fusiliers who died whilst serving in Bareilly, India, on 24 April 1906.

Stuart was admitted to the school on 11 January 1907 (Petition No. 12312) and having moved with the school from Chelsea to Guston, he was discharged to his father's old regiment on 25 June 1912.

His service record is no longer available, but at the outbreak of war, 1st Battalion, The Royal Scots Fusiliers, was stationed in Gosport, Hampshire. After mobilising, it embarked at Southampton, Hampshire, on 13 August and landed at Le Havre on 14 August 1914, first going into action during the Battle of Mons. However, Stuart's medal index card shows that he was not eligible for the award of the 1914-15 Star, suggesting that he did not enter theatre until 1916 at the earliest, probably due to his age.

Between the beginning of 1916 and September 1918, the battalion was involved in some of the heaviest fighting on the Western Front, including the Battle of Albert during the Somme Offensive and the Battles of the Menin Road and Polygon Wood during the Third Battle of Ypres in 1917.

Although in Brigade Reserve at the start of the German Spring Offensive in March 1918, it did participate in the battles that finally put an end to the German advance, before advancing itself as the Allies began to pursue the German Armies.

On 01 September, the battalion moved from Havlincourt to an assembly area in preparation for an attack to be launched the following day, and at 0330hrs the following morning, it moved forward, the attack being launched at 0530hrs. Although it encountered heavy resistance from German machine-guns and artillery, and was held up on several occasions, it was able to establish and hold a position close to Noreuil, with the Welsh Guards continuing the advance on 03 September.

The fighting of 02 September 1918 cost the battalion 15 officers killed and wounded as well as 180 other ranks killed, wounded and missing. One of those killed and whose body was never recovered, was Stuart Walker, who is commemorated on the Vis-En-Artois Memorial.

Four months after his death, Stuart was awarded the Military Medal[218], although the reason for the award is not known and whilst he is commemorated on the memorial tablets in the school chapel, the award of his Military Medal is not recorded. It is also not recorded on the Honours Board that is located within the Adjutant General's Room in the school.

---

[218] *The London Gazette*, 21 January 1919, Supplement:31142

The Cheshire Regiment

William Henry GRANT
Lance Corporal, 12217, 2nd Battalion, The Cheshire Regiment who died on 08 May 1915, aged 38. Commemorated on the Ypres (Menin Gate) Memorial, West-Vlaanderen, Belgium

Born on 28 October 1876 in Colombo, Ceylon, the eldest of five children of James Grant and Elizabeth née Bourne, his father was a Serjeant in the Royal Artillery. His mother died in Hong Kong, China, on 05 December 1886.

William was admitted to the school on 27 January 1888 (Petition No. 9611) and was discharged on 08 November 1890, enlisting into The Cheshire Regiment. He was posted to the 2nd Battalion and spent the first nine years of his service in Britain, before he was posted to South Africa on 07 January 1900 during the Second Boer War. However, William was only to spend six months there before he was posted back to Britain on 06 July 1900.

Seven months after this return, William was again posted to South Africa, on 06 February 1901, spending eighteen months there, during which time he re-engaged to complete 21 years' service. He returned to Britain on 27 October 1902. Almost two years later, on 20 September 1904, William was posted to India, remaining there for five years before he returned to Britain on 04 November 1909, where he was discharged from the army at his own request on 17 November 1909.

Little is known about William after he was discharged from the army, but he is recorded in the 1911 Census as living with his uncle, Samuel Bourne, in Sandbach, Cheshire and employed as a Collier Labourer, the employment that was given when he re-enlisted into the army in Chester, Cheshire, on 21 October 1914, following the outbreak of war.

When war did break out, 2nd Battalion, The Cheshire Regiment, was stationed in Jubbulpore, India. It quickly returned to Britain, landing at Devonport, Devonshire, on 24 December 1914. Having come under the orders of the 84th Brigade, 28th Division, it landed at Le Havre on 17 January 1915, although William's medal index card states that he arrived four days earlier, on 13 January 1915.

The battalion was located in the Ypres sector after landing and was still in this area when the Second Battle of Ypres commenced on 22 April 1915, part of the force within the Ypres Salient that was withdrawn to a fresh line of trenches that left the salient less pronounced.

On 07 May 1915, two companies of the battalion took over trenches near Verlorenhoek, a hamlet four miles north-east of Ypres, where, at daybreak the following morning, the Germans commenced a heavy bombardment of these trenches. This was followed by a fierce infantry assault, including the use of gas, which resulted in a position held by one of the companies being surrounded and captured, with all of the defenders being killed or wounded.

William was one of those defenders that was killed during that attack and has no known grave. He is also a "Lost Boy" whose name has been omitted from the memorial tablets in the school chapel, the first Dukie from The Cheshire Regiment now known to have been killed in the First World War.

The Royal Welsh Fusiliers

Albert George BOOTH
Lance Corporal, 44395, 13th (Service) Battalion (1st North Wales), The Royal Welsh Fusiliers who died on 26 August 1918, aged 19. Buried in Delville Wood Cemetery, Longueval, Somme, France

Born on 06 September 1898 in Devonport, Devonshire, the youngest of three sons of Thomas Booth and Agnes Eleanor née Heath, his father was a Colour Serjeant in The Royal Welsh Fusiliers who died whilst serving in Devonport on 14 December 1901.

Albert was admitted to the school on 20 January 1908 (Petition No. 12464), joining his older brother, Robert Alfred Booth, who had been admitted on 07 March 1902 (Petition No. 11672). After moving from Chelsea to Guston, Albert was discharged *"To student"* on 21 August 1915, the June 1916 School *Chronicle* recording him as such, so it is likely that he remained at the school prior to being mobilised.

Almost a year after leaving the school, Albert enlisted into The Royal Welsh Fusiliers. He was mobilised from the Reserve on 06 September 1916 and appointed Lance Corporal on 09 March 1917 whilst training and serving in 3rd (Reserve) Battalion. He was deployed to France on 13 March 1918 and joined the 13th (Service) Battalion a week later. This battalion had been formed at Rhyl on 03 September 1914 by the Denbigh and Flint Territorial Force Associations and after moving to Winchester, Hampshire, in August 1915, it had landed in France in December 1915.

A month after joining this battalion, on 13 April 1918, Albert was admitted to hospital suffering from measles and he did not re-join his battalion until 21 May 1918.

He was killed in action three months later, on 26 August 1918, when the battalion attacked Bazentin Le Grand Wood and village at 0400hrs. The war diary[219] records that it was *"held up for considerable time by MG fire. The wood + village were eventually carried + line advanced to E of village... 4 Ors killed, 27 wounded, 5 missing, 2 gassed"*. Robert wrote

---
[219] WO 95/2555/1: 13 Battalion Royal Welsh Fusiliers, 1915 Dec. - 1919 Apr., The National Archives, Kew

to inform the school of his brother's death on 04 November 1918, the letter being published in the School *Chronicle*:

"Dear Sir,
It is with deep regret that I write to inform you of the death of my brother, George, (late Monitor and Student).
He was killed in action on August 26th last, at Delville Wood[220]*. From details gathered he met his death whilst working his Lewis Gun and was shot through the head by a Boche machine-gun bullet.*
He was only out in France five months, and had twice been recommended for a commission, but unfortunately he did not live to attain commissioned rank.
The following extract is taken from his O. C.'s letter.
..."During the recent fighting the behaviour of your gallant son was magnificent. Unfortunately he fell during the attack on Delville Wood on August 26th, 1918.
It is hard for me to adequately express my sympathy, but it may be some consolation to you in your great trouble to know that death was instantaneous, and that your son died doing his duty. Brave and fearless to the end he was a good soldier, and was always ready to take his part in the work. . . . .
With deepest sympathies,
(Sd.) A. I. Williams, Captain,
Royal Welsh Fusiliers."

It is likely that the fact that Albert was referred to in his brother's letter as George is the reason that although he is commemorated on the memorial tablets in the school chapel, he is incorrectly recorded as G Booth.

Robert also made the move from Chelsea to Guston, being discharged from the school *"To Student"* on 31 August 1909. It seems that he also remained at the school as a Student Teacher, as he is recorded there in the 1911 Census as such and it appears that he went to serve in the Corps of Army Schoolmasters from 1913 until 1934. Following his discharge from the army, nothing more is known about him other than that he died in Kettering, Northamptonshire in 1975.

Albert and Robert also had another brother, Thomas Booth, who was admitted to the Royal Hibernian Military School in Dublin on 11 August 1903. When he was discharged from that school, he enlisted into The Royal Welsh Fusiliers as a Drummer and was killed in action on 05 June 1915, aged 20. He is buried in Bois-Grenier Communal Cemetery, Nord, France.

---

[220] Bazentin Le Grand Wood and village being part of the overall battle of Delville Wood

George Woodbourne HOWELL
Second Lieutenant, 2nd Battalion attached 17th (Service) Battalion (2nd North Wales), The Royal Welsh Fusiliers who died on 22 June 1918, aged 26. Buried in Acheux British Cemetery, Somme, France

Born on 07 September 1891 in Aldershot, Hampshire, the second of six children of William James Howell and Jane née Leavey, his father was a Serjeant in The Royal Welsh Fusiliers who died whilst serving in Hong Kong, China, on 16 December 1900.

George was admitted to the school a year after his father's death, on 06 December 1901 (Petition No. 11636). His younger brother, Reginald Woodbourne Howell attended the Royal Hibernia Military School and is recorded in the January 1913 edition of *Hibernia*, their school magazine, as also enlisting into The Royal Welsh Fusiliers.

George was discharged to his father's old regiment on 12 September 1907 and although his officer's service record is not easily accessible, the 1911 Census records him as a Lance Corporal serving in the 2nd Battalion, stationed in Quetta, India.

However, by the outbreak of war, that battalion was back in Britain, stationed in Portland, Dorsetshire, and it was from here that it mobilised, landing at Rouen on 11 August 1914 as Lines of Communication Troops. George's medal index card shows that he disembarked in France two days later, on 13 August, by which time he was a Lance Serjeant.

Due to his service record not being easily accessed, it is not possible to confirm George's actions during the next two years. What is known is that he was attached to the 5th Entrenching Battalion in late-1916 and early-1917 as this was documented when he was awarded the Meritorious Service Medal[221]. These formations consisted of reinforcements who worked on rear defence works and did not get involved in offensive actions.

Towards the end of 1917, George was on leave in Britain, where he married Ada Mary Magawly in Portland, Dorsetshire, on 03 December. The marriage registers records that at this time he was an Officer Cadet, but he was soon Commissioned as a Second Lieutenant[222]. It is likely that he was attached to the 17th Battalion of the regiment, which had been formed at Llandudno on 02 February 1915 and had landed in France in December 1915, at that point.

George was killed in action six months after he was married, on 22 June 1918. The battalion war diary[223] for that day records that,

---
[221] *The London Gazette*, 29 December 1916, Supplement:29886
[222] *The London Gazette*, 8 January 1918, Supplement:30467
[223] WO 95/2561/2: 17 Battalion Royal Welsh Fusiliers, 1915 Dec. - 1919 Apr., The National Archives, Kew

"Battn. Relieved 16th Battn. RWF in MESNIL-LEFT SECTOR. A, C & D Coys in the line, B Coy in Support…Relief reported complete at 12.45 am. Casualties 2/Lt G W Howell killed, 10 OR killed & 8 OR wounded". He is also a "Lost Boy" whose name has been omitted from the memorial tablets in the school chapel, although his award of the Meritorious Service Medal is recorded on the Honours Board that is located within the Adjutant General's Room in the school.

The South Wales Borderers

Francis William Henry BLANE
Lance Corporal, 25046, 2nd Battalion, The South Wales Borderers who died on 01 July 1916, aged 23. Commemorated on the Thiepval Memorial, Somme, France

Born on 27 September 1892 in Lambeth, London, the eldest of the five children of James Francis Henry Blane and Amy née White, his father was a Staff Quartermaster Sergeant in the 5th (Princess Charlotte of Wales's) Dragoon Guards who died whilst serving in York on 22 July 1901.

Following his father's death, Francis was admitted to school on 07 November 1902 (Petition No. 11754) and was discharged on 31 January 1907 *"Returned to mother – unfit for army"*. His younger brother, Edward Ernest Blane was also a Dukie, admitted to the school on 31 March 1908 (Petition No. 12501) after his brother had been discharged. Francis's service record is no longer available, but at some point, he enlisted into The South Wales Borderers, possibly at the outbreak of war.

In August 1914, 2nd Battalion, The South Wales Borderers, was in Tientsin, China, landing at Lao Shan Bay for operations against the German territory of Tsingtao on 23 September and it was not until December that it embarked at Hong Kong, China, landing at Plymouth, Devonshire, on 12 January 1915 and moving to Rugby, Warwickshire.

Two months later, the battalion embarked at Avonmouth, Gloucestershire, for operations at Gallipoli, landing at Cape Helles on 25 April 1915, although Francis's medal index card shows that he did not disembark in Gallipoli until 06 September. The battalion remained on the Peninsula until January 1916, when it was then transported to Egypt, landing at Alexandria on 13 January 1915 and moving to Suez. After two months in Egypt, the battalion was again on the move, departing Alexandria on 10 March for France, arriving at Marseille on 15 March and spending the next year in France and Flanders.

On 01 July 1916, the first day of the Somme Offensive, the battalion was in the line opposite Beaumont Hamel and attacked on the Ancre, where it suffered very heavy casualties, including Francis, one of the 129 officers and men from the battalion to die on 01 July 1916. He has no known grave and is commemorated on the Thiepval Memorial.

Edward was discharged to the 6th Dragoon Guards (Carabiniers), on 21 December 1910. His First World War service record is not available, although the medal rolls for British War Medal and Victory Medal record him as serving with both 1st Battalion, The Royal Welsh Fusiliers and the 6th Dragoon Guards (Carabiniers). He also served during the Second World War in the Royal Army Ordnance Corps. He died in India on 15 October 1946 and is buried in Calcutta (Bhowanipore) Cemetery.

Although Edward appears in the Commonwealth War Graves Commission register, his name has been omitted from the memorial tablets for the Second World War in the school chapel and is one of the "Lost Boys" from that conflict that we will documented in Volume Two.

Arthur John HUMPHRIES

Regimental Serjeant Major, 3927, 2nd Battalion, The South Wales Borderers who died on 04 October 1918, aged 40. Buried in Joncourt British Cemetery, Aisne, France

Born on 05 February 1878 in Woolwich, Kent, the sixth child of Edmund Humphries and Mary Ann née Brown, his father had been a Gunner in the Royal Horse Artillery who was discharged from the army on 12 June 1880 and died on 22 June 1883 in Holborn, Middlesex.

Arthur was admitted to the school on 07 May 1889 (Petition No. 9798) and was discharged three years later on 13 February 1892, enlisting into The South Wales Borderers as a Drummer. He was posted to the 1st Battalion, spending the first 12 years of his career overseas, having been posted to Egypt in 1892, Gibraltar in 1895 and India in 1897. It was not until January 1904 that he returned to Britain, when he was posted to the Regimental Depot in Brecon, Breconshire. During this time, Arthur had risen through the ranks and arrived at the Depot as a Lance Serjeant.

After two years at the Depot, Arthur was posted to the 2nd Battalion in January 1906 and promoted to Serjeant two months later. Whilst there, he married Ada Beatrice Starr, his daughter, Ada Christina Alice Humphries, being born in Aldershot, Hampshire, nine months later.

On 23 July 1909, Arthur was again posted, as Permanent Staff to 1/1st Monmouthshire Regiment, a Territorial Force battalion, promoted to Colour Serjeant two years later, on 01 May 1911 and was immediately appointed as Acting Company Serjeant Major, a rank that was made substantive on 05 May 1914. It was during his time here that his son, Arthur Courtney William Humphries, was born in Newport, Monmouthshire, in 1910.

The Monmouth Regiment was an entirely Territorial Force regiment with the 1/1st Battalion located in Newport and it landed in France on 13 February 1915. Following the Second Battle of Ypres, during which all three of the regiment's battalions suffered heavy casualties, they amalgamated, resuming their separate identities on 11 August 1915, a month before 1/1st Battalion became the Pioneer Battalion to the 46th (North Midland) Division, Arthur being promoted to Regimental Serjeant Major in May 1917.

As a Pioneer Battalion, it had not participated in the "front-line" actions of 1916, 1917 and early-1918. However, in October 1918, a month before the Armistice, the unit was in the area of Montbrehain. On 04 October it was ordered to dispatch a platoon-strength patrol into the town under cover of a bombardment, but was driven off by concentrated German machine-gun fire, only three of the patrol returning unwounded. Arthur was one of those wounded and died later that day.

He is buried in Joncourt British Cemetery, in a "double grave" with Sapper William Garvie Calder of the Royal Engineers, suggesting that Arthur and William had been buried elsewhere and moved to Joncourt, but that it had been impossible to identify which man was which, so both are commemorated on the same grave marker.

Arthur's son did not attend the school, but did enlist in the Royal Navy and served during the Second World War. He was to lose his life on board HMS *Fiji* on 23 May 1941 when the ship was sunk by a bomb from a German fighter bomber during the battle of Crete.

Arthur James THURSTON
Private, 3902697, 2nd Battalion, The South Wales Borderers who died on 07 June 1921, aged 34. Buried in Jhansi Cantonment Cemetery, India

Born on 19 May 1887 in Shoeburyness, Essex, the fourth of five children of Henry Charles Thurston and Jane née Kelly, his father had been a Driver in the Royal Artillery who had been discharged from the army on 23 August 1887 and died on 24 March 1891 in Rochford, Essex. Arthur's mother re-married, to Frederick James Barker, who was a Gunner in the Royal Artillery, but she also died, on 28 May 1895 and so it was Arthur's stepfather who completed his Petition Document.

Arthur was admitted to the school on 28 August 1896 (Petition No. 10928), joining his older brother, William Gatwood Thurston, who had been admitted on 27 September 1895 (Petition No. 10810). Their youngest brother, Joseph Thurston, attended the Royal Hibernian Military School and their sister, Alice Emma Thurston, went to the Soldiers' Daughters' Home in Hampstead, Middlesex. Arthur was discharged from the school on 18 May 1901 and enlisted into The South Wales Borderers.

Arthur spent the first eighteen months of his service in Britain, initially with the 2nd Battalion before he was posted to the 1st Battalion on 14 October 1902. However, he was only with this battalion for a month before he was posted back to the 2nd Battalion which departed for South Africa on 08 November 1902. He was to spend eighteen months here before returning to Britain on 09 June 1904.

Having been appointed as a Private following his eighteenth birthday, Arthur was then posted to the 1st Battalion and departed for India on 18 October 1907, spending just over three years there before returning to Britain on 23 December 1910. Almost three years later, on 17 May 1913, he was discharged from the army having completed his first term of service.

Following the outbreak of war, it appears that Arthur re-enlisted, although his service record for this period of service is no longer available, joining the 5th Battalion of his old regiment. 5th (Service) Battalion (Pioneers), The South Wales Borderers, had been formed at Brecon on 12 September 1914 as part of K2, becoming part of the 58th Brigade, 19th (Western) Division. It moved initially to Park House Camp, Tidworth, Wiltshire, but by December 1914 it was billeted in Basingstoke, Hampshire. After converting to a Pioneer Battalion in January 1915, it moved to Burnham, Somerset, two months later moving to Bulford, Wiltshire, and finally, in April 1915, to Perham Down, Wiltshire. The battalion landed at Le Havre on 16 July 1915, Arthur's medal index card showing that he disembarked the following day, spending the rest of the war in this theatre.

Following the end of the war, Arthur re-enlisted into the Regular Army on 29 May 1919 and was posted to the 2nd Battalion, which was posted to Jhansi, India, in November the same year. It is not known of what cause, although it is likely to have been disease, but Arthur died in Jhansi on 07 June 1921 and he is another of the "Lost Boys" whose name has been omitted from the memorial tablets in the school chapel, despite being commemorated by the Commonwealth War Graves Commission.

William was discharged from the school on 29 July 1899, enlisting into The South Wales Borderers. He spent much of his service in the same battalions as Arthur and was discharged at the end of his first period of service on 28 July 1911. It is not known if he also served during the war, but if he did, he survived, appearing in the electoral rolls throughout the 1930s and he died in Uckfield, Sussex, in 1958.

Joseph enlisted into the Royal Garrison Artillery on discharge from the Royal Hibernian Military School in 1902, but served for only 8 months. He re-enlisted into the Middlesex Regiment in August 1914 and was discharged due to sickness in November 1918. He died in Islington, London, in 1935.

The King's Own Scottish Borderers

John Henry ROBERTS
Private, 10402, 2nd Battalion, The King's Own Scottish Borderers who died on 27 July 1916, aged 21. Buried in Lockerbie (Dryfesdale) Cemetery, Dumfriesshire, United Kingdom.

Born on 14 March 1895 in Lockerbie, Dumfries-shire, the third of five children of James Roberts and Kate née Mayes, his father had been a Colour Serjeant in The King's Own Scottish Borderers who had been discharged to pension after almost 24 years' service on 21 March 1894 and who died in Lockerbie on 30 December 1902.

John was admitted to the school on 13 January 1905 (Petition No. 12056) and was joined by his younger brother, Frederick Roberts, nine months later, on 13 October 1905 (Petition No. 12150). John was discharged from the school on 26 March 1909, enlisting into his father's old regiment as a Musician the same day.

At the outbreak of war, 2nd Battalion, The King's Own Scottish Borderers, was stationed in Dublin, but quickly mobilised and landed at Le Havre on 15 August 1914, taking part in the early battles of the war at Mons, Le Cateau and on the Aisne.

On 02 November, John was wounded during the First Battle of Ypres, when he sustained a gunshot wound to his left thigh which caused a compound fracture of the femur. He was also captured following this wound and was discharged from a German hospital into a prison camp on 03 February 1915, where in March 1915 he took ill. He was repatriated in the first exchange of wounded prisoners and spent time in a London hospital in July 1915, where he was diagnosed with tuberculosis. He was subsequently discharged from the army on 29 August 1915 as physically unfit.

John never recovered from his ill-health and he died eleven months later in Lockerbie. His obituary in the local newspapers stated, *"During his confinement he suffered terrible privations at the hands of the Huns. He was fortunate being amongst the first lot of prisoners to be exchanged, but his condition was so serious that any hopes of his recovery were small"*[224].

John is another "Lost Boy" whose name has been omitted from the memorial tablets in the school chapel and is also the first known

---
[224] *Dumfries and Galloway Standard*, Saturday 29 July 1916

Dukie to have lost his life serving with The King's Own Scottish Borderers in the First World War. He was also not commemorated by the Commonwealth War Graves Commission, as he did not have one of their grave markers, but on his commemoration record is the note, *"Recent research has shown that Private Roberts is buried here. The Commission is in the process of producing a headstone to mark his grave"*.

Frederick moved with the school from Chelsea to Guston and was discharged on 06 September 1910, recorded as enlisting into The Bedfordshire Regiment. The 1911 Census recorded a Frederick Roberts, born in Lockerbie in 1895, as a Boy in the 16th Lancers in Norwich, Norfolk, and he later served as a Trumpeter with that regiment throughout the war. However, other than that, it has not been possible to gather any other information about him.

The Cameronians (Scottish Rifles)

William Falconer FROST
Private, 7802, 2nd Battalion, The Cameronians (Scottish Rifles) who died on 03 April 1917, aged 28. Buried in Bray Military Cemetery, Somme, France

Born on 31 March 1889 in Kinsale, County Cork, the eldest child of William Edward Frost and Mary née Falconer, his father was a Private in The Cameronians (Scottish Rifles) who was killed in action at Spion Kop on 24 January 1900, during the Second Boer War.

William was admitted to the school seven months after his father's death, on 10 August 1900 (Petition No. 11464), remaining there for three years until discharged to the army on 14 April 1903, enlisting into his father's old regiment. The 1911 Census records William as being a Private in the 2nd Battalion and stationed in Meeanee Barracks, Colchester, Essex. This battalion was posted to Malta the following year, disembarking on the island on 17 September 1912.

When war broke out, it was still stationed in Malta, but arrived back in Britain on 22 September, deploying to France and landing at Le Havre on 05 November 1914. It was to remain on the Western Front for the duration of the war.

In March 1915, the battalion participated in the Battle of Neuve Chapelle, during which it suffered such high casualties that it was almost wiped out. However, it was reinforced and went on to participate in the Battle of Aubers Ridge in May and the action at Bois-Grenier in September, an area that was, until then, considered a quiet sector.

Although in reserve for the opening stages of the Somme Offensive in 1916, the battalion was transferred to this area and spent much of the latter part of the year in this sector of the Western Front.

In early-1917, the Allied armies were preparing for the first all-arms assault against the German positions near Arras, the town which was to give its name to the battle. However, William did not live to see the commencement of this action on 09 April. He had been hospitalised prior to then and was reported as having died of bronchitis on 03 April 1917. He was buried in Bray Military Cemetery, located in Bray-sur-Somme.

Alexander John Ralston McKAY

Private, 23285, 2nd Battalion, The Cameronians (Scottish Rifles) who died on 30 July 1916, aged 18. Commemorated on the Loos Memorial, Pas de Calais, France

Born on 04 November 1897 in Dover, Kent, the third of four children of Alexander Robert McKay and Annie Ellen née Whiting, his father had been a Corporal in The Highland Light Infantry who died at Springfontein, South Africa, on 22 May 1900 whilst serving as a Corporal in Roberts' Horse[225] during the Second Boer War.

Alexander was admitted to the school on 18 April 1907 (Petition No. 12360) and having made the transition from Chelsea to Guston, was discharged *"To Civil Life"* on 11 November 1911.

Following his discharge from the school, nothing is known of Alexander prior to the outbreak of war, although it appears that he enlisted once the war had commenced, although the date of enlistment is not known as his service record is no longer available.

Although Alexander's medal index card is available, there is no date of disembarkation date recorded, but the fact that he was not entitled to the award of the 1914-15 Star suggests that he did not arrive in theatre until 1916.

During July 1916, the battalion was in the vicinity of the La Bassée Canal moving into the support line on 26 July. Overnight on 29/30 July, two SOS messages were received from the front-line trenches, both of which were cancelled with two hours of being sent, and the battalion was relieved by 1st Battalion, The Sherwood Foresters (Nottinghamshire and Derbyshire Regiment) at 2000hrs on 30 July.

Although no casualties are recorded in the battalion diary[226], the Registers of Soldiers' Effects[227] records that Alexander was presumed killed on 30 July 1916.

His body was not recovered, so he is commemorated on the Loos Memorial. He is also another "Lost Boy" whose name has been omitted from the memorial tablets in the school chapel.

---

[225] This was corps of irregular cavalry that had been raised in South Africa during the Second Boer War.
[226] WO 95/1715/1: 2 Battalion Cameronians (Scottish Rifles), 1914 Nov. - 1918 Jan., The National Archives, Kew
[227] UK, Army Registers of Soldiers' Effects, 1901-1929, 1914-1915, Hamilton, 542501-544000

The Royal Inniskilling Fusiliers

Frank ADCOCK
Lance Serjeant, 42280, 2nd Battalion, The Royal Inniskilling Fusiliers who died on 21 March 1918, aged 29. Commemorated on the Pozieres Memorial, Somme, France

Born on 09 December 1888 in Canterbury, Kent, the eldest of two children of George Adcock and Emily née Wood, his father was a Troop Serjeant Major in the 1st (King's) Dragoon Guards who shot himself whilst serving in Canterbury on 14 February 1892.

Frank was admitted to the school on 07 April 1899 (Petition No. 11281) and was joined by his younger brother, George Adcock, on 11 January 1900 (Petition No. 11382). Frank was discharged from the school *"To mother"* on 18 December 1902 and little is known about him after that, other than being recorded in the 1911 Census as living with his mother in Kemptown, Brighton, and employed as a Paper Ruler (Machine).

It is unknown at what point he joined the army, but it appears that, according to his service number, it was after the outbreak of war. He enlisted into the Army Ordnance Corps, reaching the rank of Corporal prior to transferring to The Royal Inniskilling Fusiliers. It would also appear that he did not enter theatre until 1916 at the earliest, as although his medal index card has no date of disembarkation, it does show that he was not entitled to the award of the 1914-15 Star.

In March 1918, Frank was a Lance Sergeant and serving with 2nd Battalion, The Royal Inniskilling Fusiliers. On the morning of 21 March, it was in trenches near Artemps, when the Germans launched an artillery bombardment at 0430hrs, signalling the start of the Spring Offensive.

It is not recorded whether it was as a result of the bombardment, or as a result of the follow-up attack, but Frank was killed on that day. His body was not recovered and he is commemorated on the Pozieres Memorial. He is also another "Lost Boy" whose name has been omitted from the memorial tablets in the school chapel.

George was discharged from the school on 10 September 1904, enlisting into the Army Service Corps. He served throughout the war and was discharged from the army on 31 March 1920. Nothing more is known about him following his discharge.

George William DURHAM
Lance Corporal, 9747, 1st Battalion, The Royal Inniskilling Fusiliers who died on 05 June 1915, aged 26. Commemorated in Twelve Tree Copse Cemetery, Gallipoli

Born on 22 March 1889 in Pimlico, Middlesex, the third of nine children of William Durham and Emma née Waller, his father had served for eight years in The King's Royal Rifle Corps before serving for seven years in the Scots Guards. He was transferred to the Reserve on 04 February 1891.

George was admitted to the school on 06 April 1900 (Petition No. 11425) and was discharged *"To mother"* on 28 March 1903. However, he did enlist into the army and although his service record is no longer available to confirm when this was, his service number suggests that it was sometime between April 1909 and February 1910. He is recorded in the 1911 Census as a Private in 1st Battalion, The Royal Inniskilling Fusiliers, stationed in Peking[228], China.

At the outbreak of war, the battalion was stationed in Trimulgherry, India, but was recalled to Britain and arrived on 10 January 1915, coming under the command of the 87th Brigade, 29th Division and moved to Rugby, Warwickshire. Two months later, the battalion re-embarked and sailed for the Mediterranean. After a brief stop in Egypt, it landed at "X" Beach, Cape Helles, Gallipoli on 25 April 1915.

Once it had landed, the battalion was in action almost continuously, taking part in all three of the Battles of Krithia, the third of which was launched on 04 June 1915, with the objective of capturing the villages of Krithia and the heights of Achi Baba, something that the Allies had been attempting to do since the initial landings in April.

The plan of attack on this day was a more limited advance than the previous attacks, this time 800 yards. However, the shortage of artillery and grenades still made this a difficult task. Although the attack by the 127th and the 88th Brigades went well, with the enemy trenches being captured, the attacks on the flanks were not as successful.

Rather than sending the reserves to bolster the success in the centre, the Divisional Commander, Lieutenant-General Sir Aylmer Gould Hunter-Weston, sent them to the flanks where there was a risk that they would be cut off, forcing them to withdraw.

---

[228] Modern-day Beijing

George's battalion was in support of 1st Battalion, The Lancashire Fusiliers, attacking the left of the line, where the artillery bombardment had not been adequate, leaving the Ottoman defences largely undamaged. By the afternoon, the battalion was back at its starting position, the assault having been repulsed with almost 300 soldiers of the battalion having been killed, including George.

He has no known grave and is commemorated on the Special Memorial within Twelve Tree Copse Cemetery on the Peninsula. He is also another "Lost Boy" whose name has been omitted from the memorial tablets in the school chapel.

James MELVILLE

Serjeant, 9609, 2nd Battalion, The Royal Inniskilling Fusiliers who died on 14 July 1916, aged 21. Commemorated on the Thiepval Memorial, Somme, France

Born on 03 February 1895 in Woolwich, London, the youngest of five children of Robert Melville and his second wife Emma née Prentice, his father had been a Private in the 27th (Inniskilling) Regiment of Foot[229] who had been discharged from the army on 26 November 1878 after 20 years' service, serving for a further ten months in the Fermanagh Militia.

Despite Robert having five sons from his two marriages, James was the only one to attend the school, being admitted on 17 March 1905 (Petition No. 12092), eighteen months after his father had died in the Horton Asylum, Epsom, Surrey, on 26 November 1903. James was discharged on 11 February 1909, enlisting into The Royal Inniskilling Fusiliers from school, the 1911 Census recording him as a Boy, serving with the 1st Battalion and stationed in Tientsin, China.

By the time war broke out, it would appear that James had been posted to the 2nd Battalion, stationed in Dover, Kent, as the 1st Battalion was still in India and did not enter theatre until it landed on Gallipoli in March 1915. James's medal index card shows that he entered theatre on 23 August 1914, the day after the 2nd Battalion landed at Le Havre.

The battalion fought in the early battles of the war, being particularly heavily engaged and suffering high casualties during the Battle of Le Cateau, which led to it spending the remainder of the year in reserve. By February 1915, it was back in the line in the area of Festubert, moving to Cuinchy in early March and providing covering fire for the Battle of Neuve Chapelle.

Although the battalion spent much of the remainder of 1915 and early-1916 in and out of the frontline, it was not until July that it was

---

[229] Amalgamated with 108th Regiment of Foot (Madras Infantry) on 01 July 1881 to become The Royal Inniskilling Fusiliers

next involved in a major battle. Although it was in reserve for the initial assault of the Somme Offensive on 01 July, two companies were ordered to attack just before midday in order to attempt to turn the German position at Thiepval.

It was next in action on 10 July when it was attached to the 14th Infantry Brigade and attacked in order to extend the trench line to the left of Ovillers. Although the attack was successful, the battalion was subjected to a strong counterattack in the early hours of the following day.

For the next three days, it held the line that it had taken, with considerable bombing activity by both sides, as well as attacking in order to extend the trenches further. Despite a successful attack on 12 July, the loss of officers meant that the battalion advanced too far and was subsequently forced to retire to its start line. It was relieved at 1800hrs on 14 July by 2nd Battalion, The Manchester Regiment, having suffered 7 officers killed or wounded and 233 other ranks killed, wounded or missing during those four days. James was one of the missing, presumed killed, on 14 July 1916, his body never recovered and he is now commemorated on the Thiepval Memorial.

The Gloucestershire Regiment

James Clifford CASE
Serjeant, 22628, 12th (Service) Battalion (Bristol), The Gloucestershire Regiment who died on 04 October 1917, aged 36. Commemorated on the Tyne Cot Memorial, West-Vlaanderen, Belgium

Born on 01 May 1881 in Horfield, Gloucestershire, the second of five children of James Case and Eliza née Lott, his father had been a Quartermaster Sergeant in The Gloucestershire Regiment, having previously served in the Grenadier Guards.

James was admitted to the school on 26 February 1892 (Petition No. 10292) and discharged on 10 August 1895, enlisting into the Grenadier Guards, in which he served 12 years, most of his time in Britain, although he did spend fifteen months in Gibraltar. He was discharged from the Grenadier Guards as a Drummer on 09 August 1907.

Following his discharge from the army, James's life is a mystery, although it is possible that he is the James Case who was recorded in the 1911 Census of Wales serving as a Police Constable in Rhondda, Glamorgan. However, following the outbreak of war, he was a Kitchener volunteer, enlisting into The Gloucestershire Regiment, although his service record for this period of service is no longer available.

It is known that James arrived in France on 24 December 1915, one month after the battalion with which he was to serve had arrived, although the medal rolls state that he served in both the 8th (Service) Battalion and the 12th (Service) Battalion (Bristol), which could explain his "late" arrival. The 8th (Service) Battalion had been formed in Bristol, Gloucestershire, in September 1914 as part of K2 and landed in France on 18 July 1915. The 12th (Service) Battalion (Bristol), also known as "Bristol's Own", had been formed in Bristol on 30 August 1914 by the Citizens Recruiting Committee and landed in France on 25 November 1915.

The 12th Battalion first saw combat on 29 July 1916 at Longueval on the Somme and by the end of the battle it was said by their Commanding Officer that of the 950 who entered the battle, 736 became casualties.

On 08 May 1917, during the Battle of Arras, the battalion was practically annihilated, but James managed to survive this battle and it is known that he was back in Britain in 1917, whether on leave or recuperating from a wound is not known, as he married Minnie Howell in Woolwich.

However, James's luck was to finally run out at the Battle of Broodseinde Ridge on 04 October 1917, in Belgium. On that day, his battalion was in reserve and suffered badly from a German counter-barrage whilst in the attacking battalion's trenches. During the period 01-12 October 1917, The Gloucestershire Regiment lost 359 casualties, 150 from gas, without actually attacking, with James among the dead. His body was not recovered and he is commemorated on the Tyne Cot Memorial, along with 644 other soldiers of The Gloucestershire Regiment killed in this locale between 28 July 1917 and 30 April 1918. He is also another "Lost Boy" whose name has been omitted from the memorial tablets in the school chapel.

William Ewart FOX

Lance Corporal, 9210, 1st Battalion, The Gloucestershire Regiment who died on 04 November 1918, aged 23. Buried in Cross Roads Cemetery, Fontaine-Au-Bois, Nord, France

Born on 09 June 1895 in Coleford, Gloucestershire, the eldest son of Benjamin William Fox and Fanny née Joynes, his father had been a Private in The Gloucestershire Regiment and died in Bloemfontein, South Africa, on 12 July 1900, during the Second Boer War.

William was admitted to the school on 04 November 1904 (Petition No. 12036) and was discharged on 08 July 1909, enlisting into his father's old regiment, and although his service record is no longer available, the 1911 Census records him as a Boy in the 2nd Battalion, stationed in Verdala Barracks in Malta.

By the start of the war, the battalion was stationed in Tientsin, China, but was quickly returned to Britain, landing at Southampton, Hampshire, on 08 November before being deployed to France and landing at Le Havre 18 December 1914. It participated in the Second Battle of Ypres and in late November 1915 it was transferred to the Macedonian Front.

William landed in France with the 2nd Battalion, but was subsequently posted to the 1st Battalion, which had been on the Western Front since 13 August 1914. This battalion had participated in almost all of the major Western Front battles of the war, the last action in which it was involved being the Second Battle of the Sambre in 1918.

This was the last large-scale action in which the British Expeditionary Force was involved, commencing on 04 November, the battalion objectives being to capture the town of Catillon. The attack commenced at 0545hrs and was a complete success, with all of the objectives being achieved. It also suffered relatively few casualties, with 2 officers and 36 other ranks wounded and 4 other ranks killed, William being one of those killed on the first day of the battle. He is one of the nine soldiers from his battalion that is buried in Cross Roads Cemetery, Fontaine-Au-Bois.

Thomas George GOLDING
Private, 9227, 2nd Battalion, The Gloucestershire Regiment who died on 06 May 1915, aged 19. Commemorated on the Ypres (Menin Gate) Memorial, West-Vlaanderen, Belgium

Born on 30 August 1895 in Gibraltar, the third of four children of Frederick Charles Golding and Margaret née Maxwell, his father was a Gunner in the Royal Artillery and had spent ten years stationed in Gibraltar before he died on 02 July 1897. In 1901, the family were back in England, living in Eastleach Martin, Gloucestershire, where Thomas's mother remarried in 1902, to Walter Stone.

Thomas was admitted to the school on 21 September 1906 (Petition No. 12277), which was seven months after his brother, Frederick Arthur Golding, who had been admitted on 07 June 1901 (Petition No. 11562), had been discharged. Thomas was discharged from the school on 13 September 1909, just two months after the school had relocated from Chelsea to Guston, enlisting into The Gloucestershire Regiment. The 1911 Census recorded him as a Musician stationed with the 2nd Battalion in Verdala Barracks, Malta, where he would have been serving with a contemporary from the school, William Fox. He would also have been serving in China at the start of the war, before returning to Britain and then landing at Le Havre on 18 December 1914.

The battalion spent the first months of its deployment in the Ypres sector, its first significant action coming in May 1915 during the Second Battle of Ypres. It had moved into positions at Sanctuary Wood, to the east of Ypres, at the end of April and was still there at the beginning of the following month. On 06 May, it reported that it had been subjected to artillery bombardments both in the morning and again in the early afternoon. It also reported that German sniping was much more active, *"probably because they have finished digging themselves in"*[230].

It is not recorded whether it was as a result of the shelling or the sniping, but Thomas died on 06 May 1915. His body was never recovered and he is commemorated, along with 94 other soldiers of The Gloucestershire Regiment, on the Menin Gate Memorial.

Frederick also joined the army when he was discharged from the school on 15 February 1906, enlisting into the Royal Garrison Artillery. He survived the war, married and had five children, before dying in Poplar, London, at the age of only 43 in 1935.

Beresford John GRAY MM
Serjeant, 8015, 1st Battalion, The Gloucestershire Regiment who died on 08 September 1916, aged 25. Buried in Caterpillar Valley Cemetery, Longueval, Somme, France

Born on 17 July 1891 in Stratton, Gloucestershire, the second child of Beresford Gray and Mary Jane née Dillon, his father was a Serjeant Major in The Gloucestershire Regiment who had died of pneumonia on 19 December 1899 at Ladysmith, South Africa, during the Second Boer War.

Beresford was admitted to the school on 07 September 1900 (Petition No. 11477), and discharged on 24 August 1905, enlisting into his father's old regiment. His service record is no longer available, but the 1911 Census records him as a Private in the 1st Battalion, stationed in Cambridge Barracks, Portsmouth, Hampshire.

At the start of the war, the battalion was stationed in Bordon, Hampshire, deploying to France and landing at Le Havre on 13 August 1914 and suffering its first casualties on 26 August during the retreat from Mons, where it fought a rear-guard action in the vicinity of Landrecies.

By October, the unit was in Flanders and occupied a salient around the village of Langemarck, from where it participated in the First Battle of Ypres, and by December it was in positions near Festubert, remaining there for the rest of the month.

At the beginning of 1915, the battalion was in trenches near Givenchy, suffering heavy casualties during the Battle of Aubers Ridge in May and September saw it participating in the Battle of Loos, where it again suffered heavy casualties, but held its positions.

---

[230] WO 95/2264/4: 2 Battalion Gloucestershire Regiment, 1914 Nov. - 1915 Oct., The National Archives, Kew

It is likely that it was a result of these actions that led to Beresford being Mentioned in Despatches[231].

In July 1916, the 1st Battalion, along with eight other battalions of The Gloucestershire Regiment, was in the Somme sector and participated in the offensive. It spent a week in the line near High Wood at the end of August, during which it endured the most intense shelling it had experienced in the whole war. After three days the trenches were practically obliterated, forcing the men into the shell holes in front of these and by the time the unit was relieved on 28 August it had again suffered high casualties.

On 08 September the battalion joined 2nd Battalion, The Welsh Regiment, and 9th Battalion, The Black Watch (Royal Highlanders), in an attack which carried the German second line in High Wood, but a lack of reinforcements forced it to withdraw. The attack cost the battalion five officers and 84 other ranks killed, one of whom was Beresford, killed four days before his award of the Military Medal for gallantry in the field was Gazetted[232].

Beresford is buried in Caterpillar Valley Cemetery, Longueval, but it is likely that he was originally buried elsewhere, as when the cemetery was initially made in August 1918, it contained 25 graves. After the Armistice, the cemetery increased when the graves of more than 5,500 soldiers were *"brought in"* from other cemeteries on the Somme battlefields, most of whom had died in the autumn of 1916.

Arthur Frederick MERRIOTT

Private, 9226, 1st Battalion, The Gloucestershire Regiment who died on 23 December 1914, aged 19. Commemorated on the Le Touret Memorial, Pas de Calais, France

Born on 07 September 1895 in Southsea, Hampshire, the fifth of ten children of John Henry Merriott and Agnes Mary née Hayward, his father had been a Colour Serjeant in The Manchester Regiment who had been discharged from the army on 24 August 1891.

Arthur was the first son to attend the school, being admitted on 21 September 1906 (Petition No. 12275). His two younger brothers also attended the school, Albert Edward Merriott admitted on 20 March 1913 (Petition No. 13102) and George Hayward Merriott on 18 April 1918 (Petition No. 13740). Arthur was discharged on 13 September 1909, having made the move from Chelsea to Guston, enlisting straight into The Gloucestershire Regiment. Although his service record is no longer available, he is recorded in the 1911 Census as serving with the 1st Battalion, stationed in Cambridge

---

[231] *The London Gazette*, 13 June 1916, Supplement:29623
[232] *The London Gazette*, 12 September 1916, Supplement:29749

Barracks, Portsmouth, Hampshire, serving alongside fellow Dukie Beresford Gray and following the outbreak of the war, landing at Le Havre on 13 August 1914.

On 24 August, the battalion was at Haulchin, 25 miles south-west of Mons when, in the early hours, it heard a good deal of rifle fire. Having been initially told to hold its ground at all costs, at 0500hrs it was ordered to retire along with the rest of the British Expeditionary Force, a retirement that was to last until 06 September when the British went back onto the offensive. By the middle of October, the battalion was located in the Ypres Salient and participated in the First Battle of Ypres, remaining in this area until early December, although by the middle of the month it had crossed the border back into France and was located in the area of Béthune.

On 21 December, it was ordered to attack and retake trenches that had been lost by the Indian Corps at Festubert. By dark that evening, it had only gained about 500 yards and therefore spent the next two days entrenching and improving the positions where it found itself. The attack had cost 16 killed, 86 wounded and 94 missing, including Arthur, who was reported as having died on 23 December 1914, although the battalion war diary[233] does not record any casualties for that day. It is likely that he was one of the missing, who was not presumed dead until two days after the attack, particularly as he has no known grave and is commemorated on the Le Touret Memorial.

Arthur's younger brothers were too young to serve in the war, Albert being discharged from the school to *"Civil Life"* on 12 March 1918 and considered unfit for army service. He died in Portsmouth, Hampshire, in 1972. George was discharged on 11 July 1923, but there is no record as to what happened to him. He also died in Portsmouth, but in 1956.

Their older brother, Charles, who was not a Dukie, did serve as a Rifleman in 1/8th Battalion, The Hampshire Regiment. He was killed in the Middle East on 19 April 1917 and is commemorated on the Jerusalem Memorial, with no known grave.

Stephen MERRITT

Corporal, 4848, 1st Battalion, The Gloucestershire Regiment who died on 21 December 1914, aged 32. Buried in Brown's Road Military Cemetery, Festubert, Pas de Calais, France

Born on 14 August 1882 in Windsor, Berkshire, a son of Stephen Merritt and Ellen née Neighbour, his father was a Serjeant in the

---

[233] WO 95/1278/1: 3 Infantry Brigade: 1 Battalion Gloucestershire Regiment, 1914 Aug 1 - 1914 Dec 31, The National Archives, Kew

Scots Guards, who died whilst serving in Feltham, Middlesex, on 30 August 1890. His mother had died in Pimlico, Middlesex, on 14 January 1885 and his father remarried, in August 1886, to Annie Elizabeth née Wangford.

Stephen was admitted to the school on 26 November 1891 (Petition No. 10232), being joined by his younger brother, George William Walter Merritt, on 07 June 1895 (Petition No. 10759). Eight months after his discharge, his half-brother, William Percy Merritt, who was the son of Stephen and Annie, was admitted to the school, on 05 February 1897 (Petition No. 10990).

Stephen was discharged to The Gloucestershire Regiment on 11 August 1896 and although his service record is no longer available, the 1911 Census records him stationed in Clarence Barracks, Portsmouth, Hampshire. This was the same year that he married the widow of another soldier, Alice Amelia Griffiths. Alice had two children from her marriage to George Miles and she and Stephen also had two children together, Stephen Milton Merritt, born on 03 October 1912 and Vera Ellen Merritt, born in June 1914.

At the outbreak of war, Stephen would have been serving with Beresford Gray and Arthur Merriott, landing at Le Havre on 13 August 1914. He also would have been serving alongside his fellow Dukies when the battalion paraded at 0330hrs on the morning of the 21 December 1914, in the area of Outersteene, before marching to Béthune and then entering the trenches at Festubert at 1230hrs in order to recapture the trenches that had been lost by the Indian Corps, the attack commencing at 1500hrs. During this attack, in which Arthur Merriott was killed, Stephen also lost his life.

Although Stephen is commemorated on the memorial tablets in the school chapel, he is incorrectly recorded as S *Merriott*, the confusion with his name possibly being because of the fact that he died alongside Arthur Merriott.

George was discharged from the school to the Oxfordshire Light Infantry on 12 November 1898. He served throughout the war in the renamed Oxfordshire and Buckinghamshire Light Infantry and by 1917 he was a Company Serjeant Major having been awarded the Meritorious Service Medal[234]. He survived the war and having married two years after his brother, had three children. He died in Banbury, Oxfordshire, in January 1961.

William was discharged from the school on 27 July 1901 and enlisted into The Essex Regiment, serving 12 years before he was discharged on 15 November 1913. He was either recalled to the Colours or re-enlisted at the outbreak of war, serving in The Royal

---

[234] *The London Gazette*, 14 December 1917, Supplement:30431

Fusiliers (City of London Regiment), joining the Metropolitan Police once he had been discharged after the war. He is recorded in the 1939 England and Wales Register as a retired Police Officer and living in Twickenham, Middlesex. He died in Samford, Suffolk, in 1967.

Stephen's son, Stephen Milton Merritt was also a Dukie. He was admitted to the school on 23 November 1922 (Petition No. 14192) and discharged on 22 December 1927, enlisting into The Gloucestershire Regiment. Nothing is known of him after he joined the army, except that he died on the Isle of Wight in 2002.

The Worcestershire Regiment

John Walter FORREST DCM
Serjeant, 12361, 3rd Battalion, The Worcestershire Regiment who died on 10 June 1917, aged 21. Buried in Bailleul Communal Cemetery Extension, Nord, France

Born on 18 September 1895 in Macclesfield, Cheshire, the eldest of seven children of Samuel Forrest and Mary Ann née Massey, his father was a Serjeant in The Cheshire Regiment who was discharged to pension as medically unfit on 14 November 1900.

John was admitted to the school on 29 September 1905 (Petition No. 12144) and made the transition to Guston, before he was discharged from the school on 24 January 1911, enlisting into The Worcestershire Regiment and although his service record is no longer available, the 1911 Census records him as a Boy in the 3rd Battalion, stationed in Shaft Barracks, Western Heights, Dover, Kent.

When the war commenced, the 3rd Battalion had been posted to Tidworth, Wiltshire, as part of the 7th Brigade, 3rd Division, and it was from here that it deployed, landing at Rouen on 16 August 1914. The battalion was to spend all of its time on the Western Front, participating in the early battles of the war at Mons, including the rear-guard action at Solesmes, as well as those battles that ultimately led to the first Battle of Ypres.

During the winter of 1914-15, it was also heavily engaged, participating in the first attack at Bellewaarde and the attack at Hooge, and in the summer of 1916 it was on the Somme, suffering heavily during the Battle of Pozières.

Having survived all of these actions, in June 1917, John was a 21-year-old Serjeant in positions opposite Messines Ridge. His battalion took up positions in the front line on 07 June and at 0310hrs, following the detonation of the British mines, it advanced swiftly, although the advance was checked by German machine-gunners. After a bitter, but short, hand-to-hand engagement, the unit continued its advance, taking many prisoners. John was subsequently decorated with the Distinguished Conduct Medal[235] for his actions during this attack, but he would have been unaware of this award as he was to die of the wounds that he sustained on 10 June 1917 and was buried in Bailleul Communal Cemetery Extension, having been evacuated to that town after being wounded.

Two months after his death, and one week after his Distinguished Conduct Medal was Gazetted, John's younger brother, William Edward Forrest, was admitted to the school, on 23 August 1917 (Petition No. 13644). He was discharged to *"Civil Life"*, although the date is unknown, and died in Manchester, Lancashire, in 1926.

A third brother, Frederick James Forrest, was also a Dukie. He was admitted to the school on 07 January 1921 (Petition No. 14036) and was also discharged to *"Civil Life"* on 01 December 1924. He died in Plymouth, Devon, in 1975.

Charles Edward JELLEY
Private, 6059, 3rd Battalion, The Worcestershire Regiment who died on 04 December 1914, aged 28. Commemorated on the Ypres (Menin Gate) Memorial, West-Vlaanderen, Belgium

Born on 09 September 1886 in Fulham, Middlesex, the youngest of four children of John Robert Jelley and Elizabeth née Mead, his father had been a Private in the 18th Hussars who had been discharged after 12 years' service on 09 December 1875. He died in Fulham when Charles was only a baby, on 10 April 1887 and Charles's mother died in Fulham on 29 January 1892.

Charles was admitted to the school on 27 November 1896 (Petition No. 10951), his Petition Document having been completed by his oldest brother, also John Robert Jelley. His older brother, William Henry Jelley, had been admitted to the school on 30 September 1892 (Petition No. 10369), but had been discharged by the time that Charles was admitted. Charles was discharged from the school on 15 September 1900 and enlisted into The Worcestershire Regiment.

Although Charles's service record is no longer available, so his early career is unknown, he is recorded in the 1911 Census as a Private in the 3rd Battalion and stationed alongside Dukie John Forrest in Shaft Barracks, Western Heights, Dover, Kent.

When war broke out, he would have been stationed in Tidworth, Wiltshire, and although the battalion landed at Rouen on 16 August 1914, Charles's medal index card records that he did not disembark

---

[235] *The London Gazette*, 14 August 1917, Supplement:30234: *"12361 Sjt. J. W. Forrest, Worc. R. For conspicuous gallantry and devotion to duty. During an attack he led his platoon with great courage and ability to the objective. Immediately on reaching it he reorganised the company, all other Serjeants having become casualties, and did most valuable work throughout until severely wounded on the following day"*

in France until 11 September 1914, although the reason for this delay is unknown. At the time that he joined the battalion, it was located at Vailly-sur-Aisne, but following the commencement of the First Battle of Ypres on 19 October 1914, it moved into Belgium on 31 October with the rest of the 7th Brigade, although it was attached to the 8th Brigade from 17 November.

On 02 December, three companies of the battalion marched from their billets in Locre to relieve The Duke of Cambridge's Own (Middlesex Regiment) in trenches north of Kemmel. The battalion then re-joined the 7th Brigade on 03 December and so the companies that were manning the trenches were relieved by troops from the 8th Brigade. It would appear that sometime during this relief, Charles was killed, although there is no record of any casualties being suffered within the battalion war diary[236]. However, the Registers of Soldiers' Effects[237] records that Charles was killed in action on 04 December and buried near Ploegsteert Wood. It appears that his grave was subsequently lost, as he is now one of the missing who is commemorated on the Menin Gate. He is also another "Lost Boy" whose name has been omitted from the memorial tablets in the school chapel.

William was discharged from the school on 01 January 1896 and enlisted into The Gloucestershire Regiment. He served in South Africa during the Second Boer War and was discharged from the army after completing 12 years' service in December 1907. He became a Postman, re-joining his regiment in the early days of the war and later served in the Labour Corps. He returned to work as a Postman after the Armistice, but died in Harrow Cottage Hospital, Middlesex, on 21 January 1924, at the age of 42, having been knocked off his bicycle by a car[238].

---

[236] WO 95/1415/3: 3 Battalion Worcestershire Regiment, 1914 Aug. - 1915 Oct., The National Archives, Kew
[237] UK, Army Registers of Soldiers' Effects, 1914-1915, Exeter, Preston, Shrewsbury, Warwick, Winchester 142501-144500
[238] *Uxbridge & W. Drayton Gazette*, 01 February 1924

The East Lancashire Regiment

Sidney BRIGHTMORE

Private, 8268, 6th (Service) Battalion, The East Lancashire Regiment who died on 30 April 1917, aged 27. Commemorated on the Basra Memorial, Iraq

Born on 03 December 1890 in Vauxhall, London, the fourth of six children of Walter Brightmore and Annie Elizabeth née Carter, his father had been a Private in The East Lancashire Regiment and was discharged to pension after 21 years' service on 10 October 1888.

Sidney was admitted to the school on 06 December 1901 (Petition No. 11643) and discharged on 10 December 1904, enlisting into his father's old regiment, the 1911 Census recording him as a Drummer in the 1st Battalion, stationed in Inkerman Barracks, Knaphill, Woking, Surrey.

At the outbreak of war, the battalion was stationed in Colchester, Essex, moving to Harrow, Middlesex, on 18 August before landing at Le Havre on 22 August 1914. It then spent the remainder of the war serving on the Western Front.

According to Sidney's medal records, he did not deploy overseas until 1916 and by 1917 he was serving in the 6th (Service) Battalion. This battalion had been formed at Preston, Lancashire, in August 1914 before moving to Tidworth, Wiltshire, although by January 1915 it was in billets in Winchester, Hampshire. A month later, it moved to Aldershot, Hampshire, and four months after that, on 16 June, it sailed from Avonmouth, Gloucestershire, landing on Gallipoli on 07 July 1915.

In December 1915 the unit was evacuated from Gallipoli, arriving in Egypt in January 1916, which is possibly where Sidney joined it. However, the battalion was only to spend a month there before moving to Mesopotamia in February, where it participated in the failed relief of the Siege of Kut.

Following this failure, there was a revision of training under the new commander, General Stanley Maude, when he assumed command in July 1916 and by December the army in Mesopotamia was believed to be ready to move onto the offensive again, which it did, recapturing Kut al Amara in February 1917 and Baghdad a month later.

Once Baghdad was captured, the British then launched the Samarrah Offensive toward the Euphrates and Diyala Rivers, with Sidney's battalion being heavily involved in forcing a crossing of the latter in April 1917. It is likely that Sidney was killed during one of the attempts to cross this river on 30 April 1917.

He has no known grave and is commemorated on the Basra Memorial, which is located 20 miles along the road to Nasiriyah, in the middle of what was a major battleground during the Gulf War[239]. It was moved here in 1997 from its original location on the main quay of the naval dockyard at Maqil, which is located about 5 miles north of Basra, on the west bank of the Shatt-al-Arab.

Andrew Charles Archibald RICHMOND

Private, 13800, Depot, The East Lancashire Regiment who died on 20 August 1917, aged 43. Commemorated in Burnley Cemetery, Lancashire, United Kingdom

Born on 21 June 1874 in Sunderland, County Durham, the third of five children of Andrew Richmond and Sarah née Malone, his father was a Serjeant in the 68th (Durham) Regiment of Foot (Light Infantry)[240], serving in New Zealand and India before he was discharged on 10 December 1878. He died in Blackburn, Lancashire, on 04 January 1885, three months after Andrew's mother, who had also died there on 06 October 1884.

Andrew was admitted to the school on 20 November 1885 (Petition No. 9288) and discharged to The East Lancashire Regiment on 28 July 1887, serving for thirteen years in Britain before he was discharged as a Drummer on 27 July 1901, having lost his Good Conduct Pay twice and with 11 offences recorded.

When war broke out, he was employed as a Railway Goods Checker, but re-enlisted on 07 September 1914 and was posted to 6th (Service) Battalion, The East Lancashire Regiment, the same battalion that Dukie Sidney Brightmore was to serve with.

Andrew spent the first nine months of this second period of service in Britain before his battalion sailed from Avonmouth, Gloucestershire, on 16 June 1915, landing at Gallipoli three weeks later on 07 July.

---

[239] Referred to as Operation Granby in Britain and Operation Desert Storm in the United States and fought between 17 January – 28 February 1991
[240] Amalgamated with the 106th Regiment of Foot (Bombay Light Infantry) on 01 July 1881 to become The Durham Light Infantry

He served in Gallipoli until the battalion was evacuated in December 1915 and it is likely that he took part in the Battles of Sari Bair, Russell's Top and Hill 60 in August 1915, the final attempt by the British to capture the Gallipoli Peninsula. His battalion suffered heavy casualties in the August Offensive, which is evident in his promotion from Lance Corporal on 10 August 1915 to Acting Company Quartermaster Serjeant on 09 September 1915.

The battalion arrived in Egypt in January 1916 and it was not long before Andrew was again in trouble, as he was reduced to the ranks for drunkenness when the battalion was holding forward posts on the Suez Canal. After a month in Egypt, the unit was sent to Mesopotamia to join the Tigris Corps and was in action in the unsuccessful attempts to relieve Kut al Amara, with Andrew receiving a gunshot wound to the wrist on 09 April 1916.

Almost a year later, he was evacuated to Britain, on 16 January 1917, suffering from malaria and he was later discharged from the army on 05 March 1917 due to sickness. Six months after he was discharged, Andrew succumbed to the tuberculosis that he had contracted whilst on active service and died in Burnley, Lancashire, on 20 August 1917. He is commemorated by the Commonwealth War Graves Commission and another of the "Lost Boys" whose name has been omitted from the memorial tablets in the school chapel.

The East Surrey Regiment

Albert Terence DONNELLY
Private, 8101, 9th (Service) Battalion, The East Surrey Regiment who died on 25 January 1917, aged 27. Buried in Philosophe British Cemetery, Mazingarbe, Pas de Calais, France

Born on 12 July 1889 in Ealing, Middlesex, the second of three children of Lewis Donnelly and Justina née Howell, his father had been a Private in The East Surrey Regiment who had been discharged after 16 years' service on 27 November 1883.

Albert was admitted to the school on 02 September 1898 (Petition No. 11216) and was discharged to the Royal Engineers on 23 January 1904, attested as a Boy and promoted to Bugler ten months later in November 1904. However, his time in the army was not happy and he was discharged on 15 January 1906, *"His services no longer required"* King's Regulations para 1805 (xxv)[241], following a theft.

It is not known for certain what he did after leaving the army, but the 1911 Census records him as a Hotel Porter in Margate, Kent. Ironically, at this time, the rest of his family were living in the Duke of York's School in Guston, Kent, where his father was employed as a Pioneer (General Labourer). In 1913, Albert married Emma Timmings, a widow who had three children and their son, Albert Henry Donnelly, was born in the December.

On 28 January 1915, Albert enlisted into his father's old regiment, joining the 10th (Reserve) Battalion, which had been formed at Dover, Kent, on 26 October 1914 as part of K4. Unsurprisingly, when he did enlist, he did not admit to his previous military service.

After seven months with this battalion, Albert was posted to the 8th (Service) Battalion, which had been in France since July 1915, joining them on 11 August. The battalion was involved in the Battle of Loos, the next major battle in which it was involved being during the Somme Offensive, for which the unit is most famous.

---

[241] WO 363: War Office: Soldiers' Documents, First World War 'Burnt Documents' (Microfilm Copies), 1914-1920, The National Archives, Kew - First World War Service Records 'Burnt Documents'

On the first day of the battle, 01 July 1916, "B" Company went into the attack dribbling two footballs. It was one of the few battalions to reach and hold its objective, although Albert was not unscathed, being admitted to No. 21 Casualty Clearing Station with a gunshot wound to his left hand, that resulted in his being evacuated to Britain. Once out of hospital, Albert spent some time at the Regimental Depot in Kingston, Surrey, before being posted to the 9th (Service) Battalion in France on 12 November 1916.

In January 1917, this battalion was in trenches near Hulluch, four miles from Lens. On 25 January, three officers and 50 other ranks launched a *"successful"*[242] trench raid on the German lines, although Albert was one of the three soldiers killed in No Man's Land as the raiding party was retiring, his and the body of another soldier being later recovered and buried in Philosophe British Cemetery, three miles from where they died. The third soldier was not recovered and is commemorated on the Loos Memorial.

John Thomas EDGAR
Serjeant, 79, 7th (Service) Battalion, The East Surrey Regiment who died on 24 August 1914, aged 41. Buried in Wandsworth (Earlsfield) Cemetery, London, United Kingdom

Born on 12 June 1873 in Kamptee, India, only son of James Edgar and Hannah née O'Loughlin, his father had been Private in the 44th (East Essex) Regiment of Foot who was discharged from the army on 14 June 1881. His mother had died in Madras, India, on 19 November 1880.

John was admitted to the school on 17 January 1884 (Petition No. 9046) and was discharged on 18 June 1887, enlisting into Prince Albert's (Somersetshire Light Infantry) on the same day. He spent the first two years of his service in Britain before he was posted to India on 14 October 1889. He was appointed as a Bugler on 22 August 1890, but was in trouble a year later when he was tried by the Civil Power on 15 September 1891 and fined for *"dishonestly receiving and assisting in the disposal of stolen property"*.

A month after his conviction, on 13 October 1891 and on the recommendation of the Medical Officer, John reverted from Bugler to Private, and seven months later he transferred to The Hampshire Regiment. John remained in India for a further 12 years, being appointed as a Lance Corporal on 13 March 1897 and promoted to Corporal on 05 March 1901, before he was posted to Aden on 03 February 1903. However, he must have had some home leave prior

---

[242] WO 95/2215/1: 9 Battalion East Surrey Regiment, 1915 Aug. - 1919 Mar., The National Archives, Kew

to this posting, as he married Isabella Ellen Smith in Earlsfield, Surrey, in January 1902 and his eldest son, also John Edgar, was born in Wandsworth, Surrey, in 1903.

John returned to Britain on 19 May 1904, being posted to the Regimental Depot in Winchester, Hampshire. Having been appointed as a Lance Serjeant on 06 September 1904, he was then promoted to Serjeant on 12 December 1905 and posted to the 1st Battalion and was still serving with that battalion when he completed 21 years' service in 1908. However, John was permitted to continue service beyond this time and was then attached to the 3rd (Reserve) Battalion on 01 October 1909, before he was discharged from the army on 30 June 1910.

A year after his discharge, John was recorded in the 1911 Census as living in Tooting Junction, London, with his wife and four sons, and employed as an Insurance Clerk. However, twelve days after war broke out, on 16 August 1914, John re-enlisted into The East Surrey Regiment as a Private, but promoted to his previous rank of Serjeant on 20 August 1914. Four days after this promotion, John died from apoplexy[243] in Colchester, Essex, his body being returned home for burial. Dying on 24 August 1914 means that John, along with James Ellard, are the first Dukies to die during the war to be commemorated by the Commonwealth War Graves Commission, but John is also another of the "Lost Boys" whose name has been omitted from the memorial tablets in the school chapel.

Two of his sons were also Dukies. Arthur William Edgar was admitted to the school on 28 October 1914 (Petition No. 13331), being discharged to the Royal Engineers on 11 July 1919. The 1939 England and Wales Register records him living in Wandsworth, London, and employed as a Certificated Nurse, likely at Springfield Mental Hospital in Tooting, London. He died in Basingstoke, Hampshire, in 1974.

Five months after Arthur was discharged from the school, his younger brother, Reginald Alfred Edgar, was admitted, on 30 December 1919 (Petition No. 13950). He was discharged on 24 September 1924 and also joined the Royal Engineers. He was a Warrant Officer Class II in the Royal Engineers when he died in a motor accident in New Malden, Surrey, on 24 November 1946 and like his father, he is also a "Lost Boy", his name being omitted from the Second World War memorial tablets in the school chapel. He will be included in Volume Two and barring further discoveries for the latter conflict, father and son may prove to be the first and last

---

[243] A stroke

James William ROBINSON

Private, 23993, 13th (Service) Battalion (Wandsworth), The East Surrey Regiment who died on 24 April 1917, aged 32. Commemorated on the Thiepval Memorial, Somme, France

Born on 31 December 1884 in Rotherhithe, Surrey, the eldest of two children of James William Robinson and Alice Mary née Towner. His mother died in Rotherhithe, Surrey, on 20 April 1886. His father, who had served in the Royal Artillery, had then joined the permanent staff of 3rd Battalion, The East Surrey Regiment, when he was discharged from the Regular Army. He was murdered by a soldier whom he had earlier punished, on Hilsea Ranges, Hampshire, on 27 June 1893. It was reported that:

> *"After only three minutes' deliberation a coroner's jury at Portsmouth returned a verdict of "Wilful Murder" against George Mason, a private of the 3rd East Surrey Militia. Evidence was given that Sergeant James Robertson [sic.], of the same corps, had borne testimony against Mason, the result of which was that Mason was ordered three days confinement to barracks for neglecting duty for refusing to clean mess tins. Mason was marched to Hilsea Rifle Ranges with the other men of the corps. And was served with 14 rounds of ammunition. While the sergeant was standing at the firing point Mason, who was behind, brought his rifle to the "present", and observing to a comrade, "Here's a good mark", shot the sergeant dead, exclaiming "That's level now. He ran me this morning. Now I have run him". After the crime Mason threw his rifle under his coat, and when arrested another cartridge was found in his sleeve, with which, he said, he meant to kill a colour-sergeant whom he named. On the way back to the fort Mason said to the escort, "I shot him in the small of the back. I meant to kill him".*[244]

George Mason was subsequently tried for killing James Robinson, his defence being one of hereditary insanity. However, he was found guilty of murder and hanged on 06 December 1893.

James was admitted to the school on 29 December 1893 (Petition No. 10553) and discharged on 25 January 1898, enlisting into The East Surrey Regiment three days later. He was posted to the 2nd Battalion, appointed as a Drummer on 01 July 1902 and posted with that battalion to India on 09 December 1902. He then became a Private the day after his eighteenth birthday, on 01 January 1903, although he remained in the appointment of Drummer until he

---

[244] *South Wales Echo*, 04 July 1893

reverted at his own request to Private in one of the rifle companies on 01 June 1909. However, on 01 March 1910, he was again appointed as a Drummer.

He returned from India to Britain a year later on 17 March 1911 and discharged from the army, having completed his first term of service, on the same day. Following his discharge, it appears that James did not work, as he is recorded as unemployed in the 1911 Census and a boarder living in Walworth, London, his profession given as Ex-Soldier.

Prior to the outbreak of war, on 08 March 1914, George married Jane Susan Beaven in Southwark, London, and it then appears that following the outbreak of war, he was either recalled to the Colours or was a Kitchener volunteer, but it has not been possible to establish which is true as the record for this second period of service is no longer available, although it is likely that the latter is the case.

The battalion with he served, 13th (Service) Battalion (Wandsworth), was formed in Wandsworth, London, by the Mayor and Borough on 16 June 1915. It was adopted by the War Office on 28 August 1915, moving to Witley, Surrey, in September where it came under the orders of the 41st Division.

In October 1915, the battalion transferred to the 118th Brigade, 39th Division, located in Barossa Barracks, Aldershot, Hampshire, moving back to Witley in November 1915. Finally, on 23 February 1916, the battalion moved to Blackdown, Surrey, transferring to the 120th Brigade, 40th Division, landing at Le Havre on 04 June 1916 and taking part in some of the battles of the Somme Offensive.

It is likely that James landed with the battalion on this day, although there is no disembarkation date recorded in his medal index card, but he did not qualify for the 1914-15 Star, suggesting that he did not arrive in theatre until 1916 at the earliest.

During the German retreat to the Hindenburg Line, the battalion was in the front line at Gouzeaucourt Wood. On 24 April 1917, 40th Division was ordered to assault the villages of Villers Plouich and Beauchamp in order to gain a footing on the heights on which these villages stood. It was during this action that Corporal Edward Foster of the battalion was awarded the Victoria Cross[245].

During the assault, the battalion suffered three officers and 26 other ranks killed, with ten other ranks missing, one of these being

---

[245] *The London Gazette*, 26 June 1917, Supplement:30154: *"No. 13290 Cpl. Edward Foster, E. Surr. R. For most conspicuous bravery and initiative. During an attack the advance was held up in a portion of a village by two enemy machine guns, which were entrenched and strongly covered by wire entanglements. Cpl. Foster, who was in charge of two Lewis guns, succeeded in entering the trench and engaged the enemy guns. One of the Lewis guns was lost, but Cpl. Foster, with reckless courage, rushed forward and bombed the enemy, thereby recovering the gun. Then getting his two guns into action, he killed the enemy gun team and captured their guns, thereby enabling the advance to continue successfully"*

James. His body was never recovered and he is commemorated on the Thiepval Memorial. He is also a "Lost Boy" whose name has been omitted from the memorial tablets in the school chapel.

The school was clearly unaware of the fate of James Robinson, as within his Petition Document is a letter, received from the daughter of his father's former Commanding Officer. The letter was received by the school in 1928 and explains that following his father's death, his Commanding Officer had raised a sum of money to assist the boy. However, this money had never been passed to James and the man who raised it had now died. The letter was asking the school if they had any information on James so that it could be passed to him before it was donated to charity. The school had responded that following his discharge from the school, he had enlisted into the army and had then been discharged in 1911, but that it was no longer aware of his whereabouts.

James SPARKS

Serjeant, 1145, 12th (Service) Battalion (Bermondsey), The East Surrey Regiment who died on 03 February 1919, aged 45. Buried in Cologne Southern Cemetery, Nordrhein-Westfalen, Germany

Born on 11 November 1873 in Dublin, County Dublin, the youngest of three children of James Sparks and Margaret née Hefaram, his father had served for five years in the 5th Regiment of Foot (Northumberland Fusiliers)[246], before transferring to the Scots Fusilier Guards[247], from which he was discharged as a Private on 31 July 1883 and died of consumption in The Brompton Hospital, London, on 02 September 1883. His mother died as the result of infection three days after James was born, on 14 November 1873 and his father had remarried in Windsor, Berkshire, in April 1875.

James was admitted to the school on 11 January 1884 (Petition No. 9043) and was discharged on 14 November 1887, enlisting into the Scots Guards. He spent his entire service in the Scots Guards in Britain, having been posted to the 2nd Battalion on enlistment and where he was appointed as a Lance Corporal on 05 November 1894 and promoted to Corporal on 01 April 1897. This was the same year that he re-engaged to complete 21 years' service and also the year in which he married Adelaide Ellen Turner in Lambeth, London.

Two years after his last promotion, on 01 December 1899, James was posted to the 3rd Battalion, promoted to Serjeant and appointed as the battalion's Serjeant Master Tailor, holding this position until 01 June 1906, when he was removed from this appointment. The

---

[246] Renamed The Northumberland Fusiliers on 01 July 1881
[247] Renamed Scots Guards on 03 April 1877

following month, on 31 July 1906, he was discharged from the army at his own request.

Following his discharge from the army it appears that James and Adeleide remained in London, as they are recorded in the 1911 Census living in Lambeth, with James employed as a Civil and Military Tailor. Following the outbreak of war, James re-enlisted into the army, although his service record for this period of service is no longer available. He joined The East Surrey Regiment and was posted to the 12th (Service) Battalion (Bermondsey).

This battalion had been formed at Bermondsey, London, on 14 May 1915 by the Mayor and Borough. In October 1915, it moved to Witley, Surrey, and came under the orders of the 122nd Brigade, 41st Division, before moving to Marlborough Lines in Aldershot, Hampshire, in February 1916, from where it landed at Le Havre on 02 May 1916.

Although James's medal index card is still available, there is no disembarkation date recorded in this, but the fact that he did not qualify for the award of the 1914-15 Star indicates that he did not arrive in theatre until 1916 or later. His later medical records from January 1919 state he had been overseas for 2 years and 6 months, so it is likely he went to France in May 1916 with his battalion.

The battalion fought at the Battles of Flers-Courcelette and of the Transloy Ridges during the Somme Offensive as well as the Battles of Messines, Pilckem Ridge, Menin Road and the Operations on the Flanders Coast during the Third Battle of Ypres, before it was transferred to Mantua on the Italian Front in November 1917.

The battalion returned to the Western Front in March 1918, in time to resist the German Spring Offensive, with James celebrating his 45th birthday south of Audenarde in Belgium on the day of the Armistice. The battalion then remained in Belgium until 07 January 1919, when it was transferred to Germany as part of the occupying forces, being located in the vicinity of the town of Marialinden.

Following his arrival in Germany, James became unwell and died of influenza on 03 February 1919. He was buried in Cologne Southern Cemetery and commemorated by the Commonwealth War Graves Commission, but he is another "Lost Boy" whose name has been omitted from the memorial tablets in the school chapel.

Albert Arthur TAYLOR

Bandsman, 5436, 1st Battalion, The East Surrey Regiment who died on 27 September 1914, aged 31. Buried in St. Nazaire (Toutes-Aides) Cemetery, Loire-Atlantique, France

Born on 02 October 1882 in Battersea, Surrey, the third of five children of Joseph William Taylor and Mary Ann née Wilkinson, his father had been a Colour Serjeant in the 53rd (Shropshire) Regiment of Foot[248]. He had been discharged to pension on 05 July 1879 and died in Hanwell Lunatic Asylum, Middlesex, on 16 October 1890.

Albert was admitted to the school on 26 November 1891 (Petition No. 10227), joined by his younger brother, John James Taylor, three years later on 31 August 1894 (Petition No. 10639). Albert was discharged from the school on 02 October 1897 and enlisted into The East Surrey Regiment as a Musician. His service record is no longer available, so his career until the outbreak of war is unknown, but when war did break out, Albert was a Bandsman in the 1st Battalion, stationed in Dublin, the battalion embarking on the SS *Botanist* on 13 August and landing at Le Havre on 15 August 1914.

By 22 August, the battalion was in positions along the Mons Canal, where it came under attack the following day. On 24 August, it went into reserve, but soon found itself acting as flank guard for the retirement of the 5th Division, a retirement that was to last until early September, including its participation in the Battle of Le Cateau on 26 August.

On 08 September, the battalion began advancing toward the Germans, crossing the River Marne the following day and remaining in action whilst advancing, for the next four days. On 13 September, it was able to rest briefly whilst Royal Engineers prepared rafts to enable it to cross the River Aisne, the crossing being carried out later in the day.

It seems likely that it was on this day that Albert was among the eight other ranks wounded during the crossing of the river. He was evacuated through the casualty chain, eventually being admitted to No. 10 General Hospital in St. Nazaire, where he died of wounds on 27 September 1914. He is buried in the Toutes-Aides Cemetery in the middle of the town.

John joined the Royal Army Medical Corps when he was discharged from the school on 24 February 1902. He was discharged from the army in 1915, but re-enlisted into his old corps in 1916,

---

[248] Amalgamated with the 85th (King's Light Infantry) Regiment of Foot on 01 July 1881 to become The King's Light Infantry (Shropshire Regiment), renamed The King's (Shropshire Light Infantry) on 10 March 1882

serving a further four years before being demobilized in 1920. Nothing more is known of John after this.

Charles Frederick Arthur WEST
Second Lieutenant, 1st Battalion, The East Surrey Regiment who died on 04 October 1917, aged 31. Commemorated on the Tyne Cot Memorial, West-Vlaanderen, Belgium

Born on 16 April 1886 in Kingston, Surrey, the third of six children of Edmund Edward West and Louisa Mary née Cotterell, his father had been Colour Serjeant in The East Surrey Regiment who had died whilst serving in Malta on 12 September 1894.

Charles was admitted to the school on 30 August 1895 (Petition No. 10783) and was joined by his younger brother, Henry Victor Joseph West, on 20 August 1897 (Petition No. 11065). Charles was discharged from the school to *"Civil Life"* on 18 April 1900, but he enlisted into his father's old regiment in Kingston in 1903, giving his occupation as a Plumbers Labourer

Charles married Florence Elizabeth Smith in Jersey, Channel Islands, on 31 October 1907 and it appears that at the outbreak of war he was serving with the 2nd Battalion, which was stationed in Chaubattia, India. He returned to Britain ahead of the regiment in order to train the recruits of the Kitchener Battalions in Kingston, the 7th, 8th, and 9th (Service) Battalions all being formed in the town in August and September 1914.

Charles remained in Kingston until June 1916, when he was promoted to Warrant Officer Class II and deployed to France as the Company Sergeant Major of the 7th (Service) Battalion, which had been in France since 02 June 1915 and had taken part in the Battle of Loos in September of that year.

The battalion was in reserve on the first day of the Somme Offensive, but did participate in the Battle of Albert, which lasted from 01 July until 13 July. However, Charles was only to remain with the battalion for almost a year before he returned to Britain and was Commissioned[249].

The newly Commissioned Second Lieutenant West was then posted to the 1st Battalion, arriving at that unit on 20 September, at a time when it was engaged in fighting during the Third Battle of Ypres. Fourteen days after his arrival, Charles was in positions just south of Polygon Wood and heavily involved in the fighting to dislodge the Germans from this feature. The battalion war diary[250]

---
[249] *The London Gazette*, 21 August 1917, Supplement:30242
[250] WO 95/1579/1: 1 Battalion East Surrey Regiment, 1916 Jan - 1917 Nov, The National

records that he was one of the three officers who was killed during the fighting on this day.

His obituary appeared in a local newspaper two weeks after his death, although the date given for his death is incorrect:

> "SURREY OFFICER KILLED.
>
> *Sec.-Lieut. Charles Frederick Arthur West, East Surrey Regt, whose wife lives at 90, Canbury-avenue, Kingston, was killed in action Oct. 5. Deceased, who had only returned to the front three weeks, was formerly regimental-sergeant-major of a battalion the East Surrey Regt., and had served 14 years. He was in India when war broke out, and was one of six N.C.O.'s selected to be sent home as instructors to Kitchener's Army, Subsequently promoted the rank of sergeant-major, he went to the Western front in June, 1916, to a battalion of the East Surrey's, and was later recommended for a commission. His father served as colour-sergeant in the same, regiment; Sec.- Lieut. West leaves three young children, and has three brothers serving."*[251]

Although the obituary refers to three children, there was to be a fourth child, a son, also named Charles Frederick Arthur West. He was born six months after his father's death, on 17 April 1918.

Charles is also another of the "Lost Boys" whose name has been omitted from the memorial tablets in the school chapel.

Henry was discharged from the school on 24 January 1903 and according to school records, enlisted into the Army Service Corps. He served during the war in both The Hampshire Regiment and The East Surrey Regiment, the latter in the 1st Battalion along with his brother. He ended the war as a Serjeant and died in Winchester, Hampshire in 1964.

Archives, Kew
[251] *Surrey Advertiser*, Wednesday 17 October 1917

The Duke of Cornwall's light Infantry

William FITZGERALD
Private, 7607, 2nd Battalion, The Duke of Cornwall's Light Infantry who died on 21 January 1919, aged 34. Buried in Taranto Town Cemetery Extension, Italy

Born on 07 February 1884 in Gosport, Hampshire, the youngest of eight children of John Fitzgerald and Ann née Clapperton, his father had been a Corporal in the Army Hospital Corps[252] who was discharged from the army on 10 April 1877. He died in Portsmouth, Hampshire on 25 June 1886, two years after William's mother had died in Poplar, Middlesex, on 24 November 1884.

William was admitted to the school on 25 January 1895 (Petition No. 10704) and was discharged on 19 February 1895, enlisting into the Army Medical Staff Corps[253], although it seems that William may possibly have struggled with the medical training, as there is no evidence of wrongdoing, but he was discharged on 12 February 1902 as *"not being likely to become an efficient soldier"*[254].

However, at some point he re-enlisted, joining The Duke of Cornwall's Light Infantry, the 1911 Census recording him as a Private in the 2nd Battalion, stationed in Harrismith, South Africa, although there is no service record available for this second enlistment.

At the outbreak of war, the battalion was stationed in Hong Kong, China, but was transferred back to Britain, arriving in November, and moving to Winchester, Hampshire, before deploying to France and landing at Le Havre on 21 December 1914.

It participated in The Action of St. Eloi and the Second Battle of Ypres during 1915, but in November was transferred to the Macedonian Front, landing at Salonika on 05 December, following the defeat of the Serbian Army at the hands of the German, Austro-Hungarian and Bulgarian Armies in the October. Although there was initial success by the Allies, these were quickly reversed, forcing

---

[252] Amalgamated with the Army Medical Staff on 01 August 1884, renamed Royal Army Medical Corps on 01 July 1898
[253] Renamed Royal Army Medical Corps on 01 July 1898
[254] WO 97: Chelsea Pensioners British Army Service Records 1760-1913

a retreat back to Salonika, where, fearful of a Bulgarian assault on Salonika and uncertain of neutral Greece, the Allies spent the first half of 1916 constructing a fortified line known as 'The Birdcage' in the hills around the city.

This theatre soon resembled every other, with the opposing forces entrenched opposite each other, but with the added discomfort of heat and disease. Owing to the prevalence of diseases like malaria, which alone caused 160,000 British casualties during the campaign, both sides evacuated the Struma Valley, the main British area of operations, during the summer.

It seems that William succumbed to disease, being evacuated from Salonika to Taranto in Italy, which had been established as a Royal Navy base when Italy entered the war in 1915 and became the home of No. 79 General and No. 6 Labour Hospitals. He died of malaria on 21 January 1919, two months after the end of the war and is one of 448 British and Indian soldiers, sailors and airmen buried in Taranto Town Cemetery Extension.

Charles Guy PEARCE
Serjeant, 9287, 6th (Service) Battalion, The Duke of Cornwall's Light Infantry who died on 18 August 1916, aged 20. Commemorated on the Thiepval Memorial, Somme, France

Born on 18 September 1895 in Callington, Cornwall, the youngest of three children of John Pearce and Alice Ada née Parker, his father had been a Serjeant in The Royal Irish Rifles who had been discharged as an invalid on 06 December 1887 and died in London on 22 October 1899.

Charles was admitted to the school on 21 September 1906 (Petition No. 12273), almost a year after his older brother, Osmond Parker Pearce, had been discharged, having been admitted on 18 January 1901 (Petition No. 11565). It is likely that Charles made the transition from Chelsea to Guston, as he was discharged to The Duke of Cornwall's Light Infantry on 07 October 1910 and although his service record is no longer available, he is recorded in the 1911 Census as a Boy serving with the 1st Battalion, stationed in Gravesend Barracks, Kent.

It appears that at the outbreak of war, Charles was posted to the 6th (Service) Battalion, which had been formed at Bodmin, Cornwall, in August 1914 as part of K1 and which landed at Boulogne on 22 May 1915, the qualifying date for the 1914-1915 Star shown in his medal index card. The battalion was located in the Ypres Salient from its arrival in theatre, participating in the Action at Hooge and the Battle of Bellewaarde, both of which were part of the Second Battle of Ypres.

In February 1916 the unit was transported by train from the Ypres Salient to the Somme sector, arriving in the suburbs of Amiens on 22 February, where it was to remain in preparation for the forthcoming offensive. When the Somme Offensive was launched on 01 July 1916, the battalion, although in the trenches, did not participate in the attack. However, at the beginning of August, it was transported to Albert and following a period of training, went into the support trenches before moving into the front-line trenches at Delville Wood on 15 August.

At 0600hrs on 18 August 1916 a bombardment commenced on the German positions opposite the battalion, which lasted until 1450hrs. The attack was then launched, but due to the casualties suffered, the reserve company had to be committed just ten minutes later. Although approximately 150 German prisoners were taken, it is reported that the battalion suffered *"heavy casualties in officers and other ranks"*[255], totalling six officers and 105 other ranks, one of whom was Charles. His body was never recovered and he is commemorated on the Thiepval Memorial.

Osmond joined the Army Service Corps when he was discharged from the school on 26 October 1905, serving throughout the war. He survived, dying in Bodmin, Cornwall in 1981 at the age of 91.

Stephen George SAUNDERS

Private, 8915, 1st Battalion, The Duke of Cornwall's Light Infantry who died on 09 September 1914, aged 21. Commemorated on the La Ferte-Sous-Jouarre Memorial, Seine-et-Marne, France

Born on 14 August 1893 in Mandalay, Burma, the eldest son of William George Saunders and his first wife, Mary Elfrida née Hogan, his father had been a Serjeant in The Duke of Cornwall's Light Infantry, but had been discharged as medically unfit on 12 September 1899. Stephen's mother had died in Madras, India, on 11 July 1897.

Stephen was admitted to the school on 10 September 1903 (Petition No. 11874) and was discharged to his father's old regiment on 31 October 1907. However, his service record has not survived, so his pre-war postings are not known, but at the outbreak of war, the 1st Battalion was stationed at Newbridge, County Kildare. Following mobilisation, the battalion landed at Le Havre on 15

---

[255] WO 95/1908/2: 6 Battalion Duke of Cornwall's Light Infantry, 1915 May - 1918 Feb, The National Archives, Kew

August 1914, although, according to his medal index card, Stephen did not arrive in theatre until five days later.

Once the battalion had landed, it participated in The Battle of Mons and subsequent retreat, including participation in The Battle of Le Cateau and the Affair of Crépy-en-Valois, before it took part in the Battle of the Marne, which commenced on 06 September, and during which the Allied forces had begun advancing against the German Forces that had pursued them from Belgium.

On 09 September, the advance continued with the battalion acting as the advanced guard with The East Surrey Regiment. The Duke of Cornwall's Light Infantry located the position of the German artillery and also discovered that the area over which it intended to advance was open and easily viewed from these artillery positions, so the axis of the advance was changed, although it then came under enemy small-arms fire. Despite this, the advance was successful and, despite the Germans making a *"half-hearted"*[256] counterattack, the battalion was able to maintain its position.

It suffered 28 soldiers killed during this advance on 09 September 1914, one of whom was Stephen. His body was either never recovered or his grave was subsequently lost and so he is commemorated on the La Ferte-Sous-Jouarre Memorial, and whilst he is commemorated on the memorial tablets in the school chapel, he is incorrectly commemorated as S *Sanders*.

---

[256] WO 95/1564/1: 1 Battalion Duke of Cornwall's Light Infantry, 1914 Aug. - 1915 Dec. The National Archives, Kew

The Duke of Wellington's (West Riding Regiment)

Ernest William CHURCH
Serjeant, 5910, 2nd Battalion, The Duke of Wellington's (West Riding Regiment) who died on 23 October 1914, aged 29. Buried in Brown's Road Military Cemetery, Festubert, Pas de Calais, France

Born on 01 July 1885 in Oxford, Oxfordshire, the youngest son of Frederick Church and Ellen née Wale, his father had been a Quartermaster Sergeant in The Duke of Wellington's (West Riding Regiment) who had been discharged from the army on 03 September 1889 and died in South Stoneham, Hampshire, on 18 February 1890.

Ernest was admitted to the school on 29 September 1894 (Petition No. 10663), joining his older brother, Harry Charles Church, who had been admitted on 08 January 1892 (Petition No. 10265). Ernest was discharged to the army on 29 July 1899, enlisting into his father's old regiment and initially being posted to the 1st Battalion to train as a Tailor. He reached the age of eighteen in July 1903 and was appointed Lance Corporal in December 1904, being posted to the 2nd Battalion a year later.

On 06 April 1911, just prior to his original term of service ending, Ernest re-engaged and was promoted to Corporal, two months later transferring to 1st Battalion, The Gloucestershire Regiment, with a view to being appointed as the Serjeant Master Tailor. However, he only remained with this regiment for six months, before returning to 2nd Battalion, The Duke of Wellington's Regiment, on 05 February 1912.

He was next posted to the Regimental Depot in Halifax, Yorkshire West Riding, before being posted to the 3rd (Reserve) Battalion, where he was promoted to Serjeant just prior to being posted back to the 2nd Battalion on 15 April 1914, four months before the start of the war.

At the outbreak of war, the battalion with which Ernest was serving was stationed in Dublin, but it was quickly deployed to France, landing at Le Havre as part of 13th Brigade on 16 August 1914 and going into action for the first time at the Battle of Mons. It fought in almost all of the early battles of the war and in October 1914 participated in the Battle of La Bassée, as part of the "Race to the Sea".

At about 0800hrs on 23 October, the battalion was in trenches along the Festubert to Givenchy road, when the enemy appeared through the trees and houses opposite its position. Because the trenches were only partially dug, this meant that the heavy rifle and artillery fire that the British troops were subjected to resulted in it suffering seven other ranks killed, one officer and thirteen other ranks wounded and two other ranks missing, Ernest being one of the other ranks killed.

Harry was discharged from the school on 15 October 1896, being returned home as unfit for army service. The 1901 Census records him as a Kitchen Porter and a visitor to a family in St. Pancras, London. In 1911, he was recorded as a Chef living in Bath, Somerset. It appears that he did not serve in the military, but he did marry in 1925. The 1939 England and Wales Register records him as a Cook and living in Oxford, Oxfordshire, before he died in Weston-Super-Mare, Somerset, in 1949.

William Alexander SPRINGETT

Private, 33232, 1/4th Battalion, The Duke of Wellington's (West Riding Regiment) who died on 23 June 1919, aged 22. Buried in Kingston-upon-Thames Cemetery, Surrey, United Kingdom

Born on 18 August 1896 in Kensington, London, the third of five children of Arthur William Springett and Annie Sarah née Beadle, his father had been a Sergeant Drummer in The Queen's (Royal West Surrey Regiment) who was discharged from the army after 21 years' service on 11 February 1890.

William was admitted to the school on 31 August 1907 (Petition No. 12399) and was discharged on 16 September 1910, enlisting into the Army Service Corps. Although William's service record is no longer available, he is recorded in the 1911 Census as a Boy in the Army Service Corps, stationed in the Army Service Corps Barracks in Woolwich, London, his trade given as Saddler.

Following the outbreak of war, William spent the next year in Britain and on 04 July 1915, he married Ellen Frith. Although he was 18 years old at the time, he gave his age as 21, possibly because he would have had to have parental consent to marry in 1915 if below that age.

Two months after his marriage, on 09 September 1915, William disembarked in France. However, his missing service record means that his movements following his deployment are unknown, although he must have had leave in Britain during 1916, as his eldest daughter, Jessie Springett, was born in Woolwich on 04 May 1917.

It is known that in 1917 a group of men were transferred from the Army Service Corps to other regiments, providing reinforcements to under-strength infantry battalions and it is likely that this was when William was posted to 1/4th Battalion, The Duke of Wellington's (West Riding Regiment), the regiment with which he was recorded as serving by the Commonwealth War Graves Commission. However, there is no mention of this regiment on his medal index card, although he is recorded as serving in the Labour Corps, with a further service number, the formation of which was authorised by a Royal Warrant issued as Army Order 85 published on 22 February 1917.

Again, the remainder of William's war remains a mystery, but it would appear that by the end of 1918, he had returned to Britain. Sometime before or during June 1919, he was admitted to the Kingston, Surbiton & District Red Cross Hospital, located in New Malden, Surrey, where he died on 23 June 1919. The cause of his admission and death is not known, but he was buried in the nearby Kingston-upon-Thames Cemetery. His second daughter, Joyce Springett, was born almost three months after his death, on 11 September 1919.

William is also another of the "Lost Boys" whose name has been omitted from the memorial tablets in the school chapel.

The Royal Sussex Regiment

Archibald Thomas CLEARE
Serjeant, L/8672, 2nd Battalion, The Royal Sussex Regiment who died on 25 September 1915, aged 22. Buried in St. Mary's A.D.S. Cemetery, Haisnes, Pas de Calais, France

Born on 31 January 1893 in Chichester, Sussex, the youngest of seven children of William Cleare and his first wife, Annie née Cullen, his father was a Quartermaster Serjeant in The Royal Sussex Regiment who had been discharged from the army on 26 January 1886. His mother died in Chichester on 24 October 1895.

Archibald was admitted to the school on 05 September 1902 (Petition No. 11726), entering the school just over a year after his older brother, Francis Alfred Cleare, had been discharged. He had been admitted on 05 January 1897 (Petition No. 10971). Archibald was discharged on 14 February 1907, joining both Francis and their oldest brother William, who was not a Dukie, in their father's old regiment, joining the 2nd Battalion.

Archibald spent all of his pre-war career in Britain, appointed as a Lance Corporal in 1911, promoted to Corporal in 1912 and promoted to Lance Sergeant four days after war was declared, whilst the battalion was stationed in Woking, Surrey.

The battalion embarked on the SSs *Olympia* and *Agapenor* at Southampton, Hampshire, on 12 August, landing at Le Havre on 13 August 1914, before participating in the Battle of Mons and the subsequent retreat, and then fighting during the Battle of the Marne, during which Archibald's oldest brother, Regimental Serjeant Major William Cleare was killed as the battalion captured the village of Priez. It then took part in the Battle of the Aisne and the First Battle of Ypres, by which stage Archibald had been promoted to Transport Serjeant.

The battalion also participated in the Battle of Aubers in May 1915, before it was engaged later in the year during the Battle of Loos, which commenced on 25 September. It had moved into the trenches the day before the attack, one which saw the first use of poison gas by the British. However, the engineers manning the gas cylinders warned that these should not be used because of the weakness and unpredictability of the wind. When overruled by General Sir Hubert Gough, the gas was released, which drifted back into the British lines and caused more British than German casualties.

One of those casualties was Archibald, who died of gas poisoning on 25 September 1915 near Hulluch. It appears that he was initially unidentified and it was only in 1921, when his brother was able to identify a watch found on an unknown soldier as Archibald's, that he was identified and buried in a named grave. He is commemorated on the memorial tablets in the school chapel, but his surname is misspelt as *Clear*. His Commonwealth War Graves Commission certificate also states that his mother was Harriett Louisa, however, Harriett Louisa, née Stubbs, was his stepmother, having married William Cleare in 1903, eight years after the death of Annie.

Francis who had been discharged from the school on 13 July 1901, was also at Hulluch the day his brother died, but survived the war and was discharged from the army in 1920, settling in Chichester. He married in 1921 and had four children, naming his two sons William and Archibald after his fallen brothers. He died in Chichester, aged 50, in 1937.

Samuel George MERRITT
Lance Corporal, L/10239, 7th (Service) Battalion, The Royal Sussex Regiment attached 7th Battalion, The Queen's (Royal West Surrey Regiment) who died on 28 August 1918, aged 18. Buried in Becourt Military Cemetery, Somme, France

Born on 08 September 1899 in Storrington, Sussex, the youngest of two sons of George Merritt and Mary née Carter, his father had been a Private in The Royal Sussex Regiment killed in action on 10 May 1900, in the Battle of Zand River in South Africa, during the Second Boer War.

Samuel was admitted to the school on 29 September 1909 (Petition No. 12649) and was discharged to his father's old regiment on 28 November 1911. Although his service record is no longer available, his medal index card shows that he was initially posted to the 2nd Battalion, which at the outbreak of war was stationed in Woking, Surrey, and landed in France in August 1914.

However, possibly due to his age, Samuel appears not to have deployed with that battalion, as although his medal index card has no date of entry into theatre, he did not qualify for the award of the 1914-15 Star. He was posted to the 7th (Service) Battalion, which was formed in Chichester, Sussex, as part of K1, landing in Boulogne on 01 June 1915 and participating in the Battle of Loos. However, again it is not known when Samuel was posted to this battalion.

At some point, Samuel was attached to 7th Battalion, The Queen's (Royal West Surrey Regiment), which in August 1918 was in the area of Albert, on the Somme. On 25 August, it was ordered to move to the area of Bécourt, which it did, continuing to advance and taking up positions 400 yards west of Bernafay Wood on 27 August. It was then subjected to heavy shelling following its arrival in this position, which continued into the following day. However, this resulted in few casualties, a total of one killed, four wounded, one gassed and one "NYDN"[257] on 27 August and two killed, seven wounded on 28 August, Samuel being one of those killed on the latter date. He was buried in Becourt Military Cemetery, four miles from where he fell, and whilst he is commemorated on the memorial tablets in the school chapel, he is incorrectly commemorated as S G *Merriott*.

---

[257] Not Yet Diagnosed – Nerves

The Hampshire Regiment

Frederick BROOKER
Private, 7656, 2nd Battalion, The Hampshire Regiment who died on 08 May 1915, aged 22. Commemorated on the Helles Memorial, Turkey

Born on 27 July 1892 in Christchurch, Hampshire, the second of three children of Thomas Brooker and Emily née Flaherty, his father had been a Colour Serjeant in The Hampshire Regiment, but had been discharged from the army on 23 November 1902 and died in Christchurch on 20 January 1903.

Frederick was admitted to the school on 05 March 1903 (Petition No. 11803) and was discharged to The Hampshire Regiment on 21 August 1906. His service record has not survived, but the 1911 Census records him as a Drummer in the 1st Battalion, stationed in Badajoz Barracks, Wellington Lines, Aldershot, Hampshire.

It is uncertain at what point Frederick was posted to the 2nd Battalion, but at the start of the war, this battalion was stationed in Mhow, India. It returned to Britain, leaving India on 16 November and landing at Plymouth, Devonshire, on 22 December 1914, before moving to Romsey, Hampshire.

On 13 February 1915, the battalion moved again, initially to Stratford-upon-Avon, Warwickshire, and then Warwick, before embarking at Avonmouth, Gloucestershire, on 29 March, bound for Gallipoli. It landed at Alexandria, Egypt, on 02 April 1915, before embarking again ten days later and landing at Mudros, which was to be the advanced base for operations on the Gallipoli Peninsula, on 13 April.

It actually landed on the Peninsula at Cape Helles from HMT *River Clyde* on 25 April 1915, participating in the First Battle of Krithia, the objective of this battle being to capture the village of Krithia and the nearby hill of Achi Baba, both of which were virtually undefended. However, when the troops landed, they were without instructions and made no attempt to either advance or dig in, resulting in neither of the objectives being achieved.

After enduring Ottoman counterattacks on 01 and 04 May, the Second Battle of Krithia was launched on 06 May, with the British advancing on Fir Tree Spur and capturing Fir Tree Wood. During this battle, the assaulting troops never got closer than 400 yards to the Ottoman positions. The battle was to last until 08 May with approximately one third of the soldiers involved becoming a casualty.

Frederick Brooker was one of those casualties, killed on 08 May 1915. His body was never recovered and he is commemorated on the Helles Memorial.

Harry Arthur Frederick EADE

Private, 9593, 2nd Battalion, The Hampshire Regiment who died on 09 May 1918, aged 19. Buried in Pernes British Cemetery, Pas de Calais, France

Born on 11 November 1898 in Winchester, Hampshire, the second of four children of William James Eade and Mary Jane née Martin, his father had been a Serjeant in The Hampshire Regiment who was discharged from the army on 30 April 1902.

Harry was admitted to the school on 09 December 1909 (Petition No. 12714) and discharged on 11 November 1912 *"To civil life (educationally unfit)"*. Despite his status on leaving the school, Harry enlisted into the army, joining his father's old regiment, his service number suggesting an enlistment date sometime in mid-1914.

His service record has not survived, so it is not possible to follow his movements in the early part of the war, although it is likely that it was due to the fact that was 16 when the war broke out that he did not deploy with the regiment in 1914. Although there is no disembarkation date recorded in his medal index card, he was not entitled to the award of the 1914-15 Star, suggesting that he did not arrive in theatre until 1916 at the very earliest, possibly a battle casualty replacement after the Somme Offensive.

At the start of the German Spring Offensive in March 1918, the battalion was located in Poperinghe, Belgium, but as the offensive progressed, it was re-located on 10 April 1918 to a point between Bailleul and Nieppe in France, to meet the advance of the Germans from Steenwerck and remaining in positions around this area for the rest of the month.

At the beginning of May 1918, the battalion was located in Grand Hasard Camp, south-west of Hazebrouck, France, providing working parties to dig the reserve line around La Motte and was still engaged in this task on 09 May. The battalion war diary[258] on that day reports that it suffered one other rank wounded and two sick to

---

[258] WO 95/2308/3: 2 Battalion Hampshire Regiment, 1916 Mar. - 1919 Feb., The National Archives, Kew

hospital. It is likely that the wounded man was Harry, as the Registers of Soldiers' Effects[259] records that he was *"killed accidentally"* on that day, although there is no further information about the circumstances available.

Harry was buried in Pernes British Cemetery, joining fellow Dukie Albert Trickey, who had died eleven days before him whilst serving in the King's Royal Rifle Corps. Like Albert, Harry is also a "Lost Boy" whose name has been omitted from the memorial tablets in the school chapel.

William Bowley LATHAM

Private, 5015, 1st Battalion, The Hampshire Regiment who died on 13 October 1915, aged 32. Buried in St. Sever Cemetery, Rouen, Seine-Maritime, France

Born on 11 May 1883 in Guernsey, Channel Islands, the younger son of Hamlet William Latham and Sarah Ann née Ellis, his father had been a Sapper in the Royal Engineers who was discharged from the army on 15 May 1885 and died on 06 October 1885. William's mother died on 11 April 1891, so his Petition Document was completed by his maternal uncle, Thomas Ellis.

William was admitted to the school on 30 September 1892 (Petition No. 10374), joining his older brother, Alfred Ernest Latham, who had been admitted on 28 November 1890 (Petition No. 10096). William was discharged to The Hampshire Regiment on 15 May 1895, but as his service record is not available, it is not possible to follow his pre-war career. However, he is recorded in the 1901 Census as a Boy in the Provisional Battalion, stationed in Maida Barracks, Stanhope Lines, Aldershot, Hampshire, and is recorded in the 1911 Census stationed in Lynberg, South Africa, with the 2nd Battalion.

It is also not known when William was posted to the 1st Battalion, but at the outbreak of war it was stationed in Colchester, Essex, before moving to Harrow, Middlesex, and then landing at Le Havre on 23 August 1914, its first action being at Le Cateau, although it also fought at the Marne, the Aisne and the Battle of Messines during the rest of the first year of the war.

During 1915, it fought during the Second Battle of Ypres in April and May, and by October of that year, it was located near Mesnil, moving into Hamel Trench on the evening of the 07 October. Although the Germans shelled the trenches intermittently, the tour was relatively peaceful until 12 October when the battalion was subjected to an intense bombardment from trench mortars and aerial

---

[259] UK, Army Registers of Soldiers' Effects, 1901-1929, 1914-1915, Exeter, 724001-725500

torpedoes, receiving *"something like"*[260] 140 rounds in 30 minutes. Although a lot of damage was done, casualties were *"exceptionally small"*[261].

It would appear that one of the *"exceptionally small"* number of casualties was William, who died of wounds the day after this attack, on 13 October 1915. He is buried in Rouen, the town that it is likely that he was evacuated to following his wounding. Although he is commemorated on the memorial tablets in the school chapel, his surname is misspelled as *Lathom*.

Little is known about Alfred other than the fact that he was discharged from the school to The Hampshire Regiment on 31 December 1892. He survived the war and died in Burnley, Lancashire, in 1962.

John William LEWIS
Lance Corporal, 6691, 1st Battalion, The Hampshire Regiment who died 31 October 1914, aged 25. Commemorated on the Ploegsteert Memorial, Hainaut, Belgium

Born on 14 November 1888 in Kingston-upon-Thames, Surrey, with his twin brother, Charles Henry Lewis, two of the three sons of John Lewis and Annie née Chilman, their father had been a Corporal in The Prince Consort's Own (Rifle Brigade), but had been discharged from the army on 05 May 1883 and at the time of his sons' birth was a Postman. He died in Kingston-upon-Thames on 07 January 1899, just over a year after their mother had died on 07 November 1897, also in Kingston-upon-Thames.

John and Charles were both admitted to the school on 14 July 1899 (John's Petition No. 11307, Charles's Petition No. 11308), their petitions having been completed by their uncle, Henry Lewis. Both brothers were discharged on 01 December 1902 and each enlisted into The Hampshire Regiment. Although neither of their service records has survived, both boys are recorded in the 1911 Census serving with the 2nd Battalion and stationed in Lynberg, Cape of Good Hope, South Africa, John a Drummer and Charles a Lance Corporal. Between 1911 and 1913, John was posted to the 1st Battalion, which was stationed in Britain and in 1913 he married Ada Sarah Mabel née (confusingly!) Lewis in Kingston-upon-Thames.

When war broke out, John would have been serving alongside fellow Dukie William Latham and would have landed with him at Le Havre on 23 August 1914, experiencing his baptism of fire just three

---

[260] WO 95/1495/2: 11 Infantry Brigade: 1 Battalion Hampshire Regiment., 1915 Jan 1 - 1915 Dec 31, The National Archives, Kew
[261] Ibid.

days later, near Ligny, when the battalion came under both artillery and machine-gun fire, suffering its first casualties of the war. The battalion took part in the Great Retreat, turning to face the enemy during the Battle of Le Cateau, before it finally ceased retreating and turned to attack the Germans as they retreated, the latter having overstretched their supply lines in early-September.

By the end of October, the battalion was in trenches near Ploegsteert and engaged in what became the First Battle of Ypres. On 30 October it experienced a ten-hour bombardment before the enemy attacked and was repulsed. However, the following day, the battalion's positions were again bombarded from dawn until 1600hrs, when another German attack was launched. On this occasion the Germans succeeded in gaining a trench which was being held by the battalion's No. 10 Platoon, with one man, an orderly who had been sent back, the sole survivor.

It is likely that it was during this attack on 31 October 1914 that John was killed. He may have had a grave, but if so, due to the fighting in this area for the remainder of the war, it was likely lost, which is why he is remembered on the Ploegsteert Memorial.

John's twin, Charles, survived the war, moving to Norfolk in the aftermath, where he died in King's Lynn in 1977.

John Douglas Holland MARLOW
Private, 280459, 1st Battalion, The Hampshire Regiment who died on 29 May 1918, aged 19. Buried in Portsmouth (Milton) Cemetery, Hampshire, United Kingdom

Born on 13 September 1898 in Galle, Ceylon, the youngest of two children of William John Marlow and Helen née Ware, his father was a Dukie, having been admitted to the school on 16 August 1878 (Petition No. 8249) and discharged on 05 June 1882, enlisting into the Royal Artillery. He reached the rank of Serjeant and died on 20 September 1899, while serving in Ceylon.

John was admitted to the school on 30 June 1909 (Petition No. 12620), at the time that the school was transitioning from its site in Chelsea to Guston and was discharged to *"Civil Life"* on 21 May 1913.

It is not known at what point John enlisted in the army, but it is possible that he was a Kitchener volunteer, as there is some evidence that he had served in the 11th (Service) Battalion (Pioneers), The Hampshire Regiment. This battalion had been formed at Winchester, Hampshire, in September 1914 as part of K2, moving immediately to Dublin, as Army Troops to the 16th (Irish) Division and then Mullingar, County Westmeath, before becoming a Pioneer

Battalion in December 1914. It landed at Le Havre a year later, on 18 December 1915. It is also not known if John landed with the battalion, as he would still have been only 17, or whether he was posted to another battalion until he was old enough to be posted to the 1st Battalion, the latter being more likely.

What is known is that he was serving with this battalion in the early months of 1918 and that he was wounded, although it is not known when he received his wounds or where the action took place, but it is likely to be either during, or subsequent to, the Battle of the Lys, which took place between 07-28 April 1918, part of the German Spring Offensive. His battalion was known to be involved in some of a series of British defensive actions that took place and it suffered heavy casualties.

It would seem likely that John was evacuated back to Britain and to one of the hospitals located in the Portsmouth area, where he succumbed to his wounds on 29 May 1918, being buried in Portsmouth (Milton) Cemetery. He is also another "Lost Boy" whose name has been omitted from the memorial tablets in the school chapel.

Henry George MARQUISS
Private, 3/5331, 1st Battalion, The Hampshire Regiment who died on 26 April 1915, aged 37. Commemorated on the Ypres (Menin Gate) Memorial, West-Vlaanderen, Belgium

Born on 24 September 1877 in Gosport, Hampshire, the youngest of three children of George Nation Marquiss and Celia née O'Donnell, his father had been a Private in the 67th (South Hampshire) Regiment of Foot who died in 1878 and his mother later re-married.

Henry was admitted to the school on 24 May 1889 (Petition No. 9861) and discharged on 03 October 1891, enlisting into The Hampshire Regiment, serving for 12 years in Britain, before he was discharged at the end of his service on 02 October 1903. His older brother, George Henry Marquiss, was admitted to the Royal Hibernian Military School in Dublin and also joined The Hampshire Regiment when he was discharged.

Following his discharge, little is known of Henry, but he is recorded in the 1911 Census living in Gosport and employed in Military Tailoring as a Tailor's Presser. He is also described as a lodger and living with a woman called Clara Piele, who was to receive his pension after he was killed as his "unmarried wife".

It is also uncertain at what point Henry re-enlisted, although he may have been recalled as a Reservist. His medal index card shows that he landed in France on 27 December 1914 and it is likely that he was a replacement following the heavy casualties suffered by 1st Battalion, The Hampshire Regiment, during the 1914 battles, particularly at Le Cateau.

Henry was killed four months after his arrival in theatre, during the Second Battle of Ypres. This had commenced on 22 April 1915 and the battalion had been ordered forward to relieve the scattered detachments defending against the German attack. It is likely he was killed somewhere between St. Julien and Berlin Wood. The battalion had moved into position in the dark and once the mist rose on the morning of 26 April, the Germans began a bombardment where the guns did not cease for eight days and nights. On the first day alone, 59 men were killed and missing, possibly buried, including Henry, with over 100 more wounded. His body was never recovered and he is commemorated on the Menin Gate Memorial. However, his name has been omitted from the memorial tablets in the school chapel, and he is therefore another "Lost Boy".

George Walter MARSHALL
Serjeant, 23993, 2nd Battalion, The Hampshire Regiment who died on 13 March 1918, aged 34. Buried in Nine Elms British Cemetery, West-Vlaanderen, Belgium

Born on 15 November 1883 in Aldershot, Hampshire, the fourth of six children of William Alfred Marshall and Cordelia née Blackburn, his father had been a Private in Princess Victoria's (Royal Irish Fusiliers), although he had been discharged from the army and was employed as a Carpenter in Portsmouth Dockyard at the time of his death in Portsmouth, Hampshire, on 15 August 1892.

George was admitted to the school on 30 March 1894 (Petition No. 10591) and was *"Detained on pass"* on 21 August 1898, after which little is known about him other than that he married Henrietta Jane Smith in 1906 and that they had a daughter, Gladys Marshall, born in Raynes Park, Surrey, in 1908. However, George is recorded in the 1911 Census living with his wife and daughter in Portsmouth and employed as a Grocer Shop Assistant.

Following the outbreak of war, it would appear that George enlisted into The Hampshire Regiment. However, there is again limited information available as his service record is no longer available. It is unlikely that he was posted directly to the 2nd Battalion, as in August 1914 this battalion was stationed in Mhow, India, and did not return to Britain until 22 December 1914. Following a period of training, it then saw service at Gallipoli, before moving to Egypt in January 1916 and landing at Marseille for service in France on 20 March 1916.

Although George's medal index card is available, there is no date of disembarkation recorded, but the fact that he was not awarded the 1914-15 Star suggests that he did not enter theatre until 1916 at the earliest, by which time he was a Corporal. The lack of service record means that it is not possible to follow George's wartime career, but if he was serving with the 2nd Battalion in 1916, it is likely that he would have participated in the Somme Offensive.

In March 1918, the battalion was located at Bellevue, Belgium. The battalion diary reports that:

> *"About 9.0am, the enemy opened a gas shell bombardment on Bn. H.Q. at Bellevue. One shell pierced 8 feet of earth which was protecting the entrance to the fill-box and wounded the gas sentry. He apparently crawled into the H.Q. dug-out taking with him some of the liquid gas on his clothes etc. The passage outside was sprayed with the liquid. No effect seemed to take place at first but towards one o'clock everyone was sore about the eyes and felt ill. By 6pm, the whole of Battalion Headquarters had been removed to the dressing station suffering from poison gas. The C.O., Adjutant, Intelligence Officer, Medical Officer & Signalling Officer, the Regimental Sergeant Major, Signalling Sergeant, Orderly Room Cpl, all the runners, signallers, officers servants and medical aid staff"*[262]

Of those other ranks affected by the bombardment, one was classed as killed in action with five subsequently dying of wounds, one of those killed being George. Although buried in a named grave, he is another of the "Lost Boys" whose name has been omitted from the memorial tablets in the school chapel.

George's youngest brother, Albert Frank Marshall, who was not a Dukie, was also killed. He was serving as a Private in 2/5th Battalion, The Gloucestershire Regiment, when he was killed on 22 August 1917. He is commemorated on the Tyne Cot Memorial in Belgium.

---

[262] WO 95/2308/3: 2 Battalion Hampshire Regiment, 1916 Mar. - 1919 Feb., The National Archives, Kew

The South Staffordshire Regiment

Harold Bernard EDNEY

Drummer, 8886, 1st Battalion, The South Staffordshire Regiment who died on 03 November 1914, aged 18. Buried in Messines Ridge British Cemetery, West-Vlaanderen, Belgium

Born on 28 April 1896 in Harpenden, Hertfordshire, the only child of James Edney and Gertrude née Cook, his father had been a Serjeant in The Queen's (Royal West Surrey Regiment), who had been discharged from the army on 03 June 1895 and died in Harpenden on 12 February 1896, two months before Harold's birth.

Harold was admitted to the school on 13 October 1905 (Petition No. 12153) and would have participated in the move of the school from Chelsea to Guston, as he was not discharged until 17 October 1910, enlisting into The South Staffordshire Regiment. When Harold joined the 1st Battalion, it was stationed in Britain, but was then posted to Gibraltar in 1911, new Colours being presented to the battalion by King George V on 31 January 1912.

The following year, 1913, the battalion was posted to South Africa and at the outbreak of war was stationed in Pietermaritzburg, although it was rapidly returned to Britain, embarking on HMT *Briton* at Cape Town on 24 August and landing in Southampton, Hampshire, on 19 September. After being made up to full strength, it re-embarked at Southampton on 05 October, landing at Zeebrugge on 07 October 1914.

The battalion then fought in the First Battle of Ypres, which commenced on 19 October 1914 and during the various battles that were fought as part of this campaign, it was reported that the battalion suffered *"substantial casualties"*[263], 453 officers and other ranks being killed, wounded and captured, including Harold.

Although the Commonwealth War Graves Commission records Harold's death as 03 November 1914, the International Committee of the Red Cross records of Prisoners of War[264] shows him being wounded and taken prisoner on 07 November 1914. Despite the

---

[263] WO 95/1664/2: 1 Battalion South Staffordshire Regiment, 1914 Aug. – 1915 Dec., The National Archives, Kew
[264] 1914-1918 Prisoners of the First World War ICRC Historical Archives: PA 4608

discrepancy in dates, Harold died as a Prisoner of War and is buried in Messines Ridge British Cemetery, which was made after the Armistice when graves were "brought in" from the battlefield around Messines. In Harold's case it was likely that he was originally buried in Bousbecques East German Cemetery, on the south side of the village, where four British soldiers were buried by a German Field Hospital in November 1914.

The Dorsetshire Regiment

Edward Walter CATHCART
Lance Corporal, 3/8482, 1st Battalion, The Dorsetshire Regiment who died on 13 April 1915, aged 22. Buried in Wimereux Communal Cemetery, Pas de Calais, France

Born on 05 June 1892 in Sandhurst, Berkshire, the eldest of five children of Daniel David Cathcart and Emily Agnes née Harrison, his father was a Staff Serjeant in the Army Pay Corps and he and his family were to spend much of their time at the Duke of York's Royal Military School, both in Chelsea and Guston. Daniel himself was a Dukie, having been admitted on 09 April 1875 (Petition No. 7858), spending six years in the school before being discharged to the Band of the Royal Military College at Sandhurst on 26 August 1881. He transferred to the Army Pay Corps *"at his own request"*[265] on 01 April 1893.

By 1901, the family was living in Chelsea, London, with Daniel employed as a Clerk at the Duke of York's, to which Edward was admitted on 09 May 1902 (Petition No. 11692). Surprisingly, despite having two younger brothers, he was the only one to attend the school. Edward was discharged from the school on 21 June 1906, enlisting into the Army Ordnance Corps. His service record for that time is not available, but his later service record from when he re-enlisted in 1914, shows that he had been discharged from the army as medically unfit, although the reason for discharge was not given.

In 1911, he and the family were back at the Duke of York's, now in Guston, Kent, where his father was a civilian Clerk, having been discharged from the army on 30 September 1907. Edward was recorded in the 1911 Census employed as a Sewing Machine Salesman.

After war broke out, Edward re-enlisted on 29 September 1914 in Dover, Kent, his enlistment papers showing that at this time his civilian employment was as a Chauffeur. He enlisted into The Dorsetshire Regiment, able to do so despite his declaration that he had previously been discharged from the army as medically unfit.

---

[265] WO 364: Soldiers' Documents from Pension Claims, First World War (Microfilm Copies), 1914-1920, The National Archives, Kew

Following his attestation, Edward was posted to the regiment's depot in Wyke Regis, Dorsetshire, being appointed Acting Lance Corporal (Unpaid) on 15 November 1914.

In August 1914, 1st Battalion, The Dorsetshire Regiment, had been stationed in Belfast, County Antrim, returning to the mainland and then landing at Le Havre on 16 August 1914, with Edward posted to the battalion in France on 18 February 1915. The battalion had spent the winter months of 1914-15 near Wulverghem in the Ypres Salient prior to Edward's arrival. However, he was only to spend two months in France before succumbing to disease.

A month after arrival in theatre, on 30 March 1915, Edward was admitted to No. 13 General Hospital in Wimereux, just north of Boulogne, suffering from enteric fever. The day after being admitted to the General Hospital, he was transferred to No. 14 Stationary Hospital, located in The Grand Hotel in Wimereux. This was an isolation hospital that only accepted soldiers with infectious diseases and it was here that Edward died two weeks later, on 13 April 1915. He is one of the 3,000 British and Allied soldiers buried in Wimereux Communal Cemetery.

Frederick George CLARKE
Serjeant, 3/8345, 1st Battalion, The Dorsetshire Regiment who died on 03 May 1915, aged 36. Buried in Bailleul Communal Cemetery Extension, Nord, France

Born on 20 March 1879 in Canford Magna, Dorsetshire, the sixth of eight children of John Clarke and Mary née Hakesly, his father had been a Private in the 107th Regiment of Foot (Bengal Light Infantry)[266] who died whilst serving on 02 October 1889.

Frederick was admitted to the school on 25 July 1890 (Petition No. 10042) and discharged on 30 March 1893, enlisting into The Royal Welsh Fusiliers. He was posted to the 2nd Battalion on attestation and spent the first three years of service in Britain, during which time he was appointed as a Drummer, on 23 February 1894.

Frederick was then posted to Malta, on 08 July 1896, where he spent a year before he was posted to Crete on 31 July 1897 as part of the occupation. After just over a year on the island, Frederick spent a month in Egypt, from 03 August 1898 until 10 September 1898, before returning to Crete. It is possible that he had been evacuated to Egypt due to disease, as this was rife on Crete at that time, but if this was the case, there is nothing recorded in his service record.

---

[266] Amalgamated with the 35th Royal Sussex Regiment of Foot on 01 July 1881 to become The Royal Sussex Regiment

Three months after he returned to Crete, Frederick was on the move again when he was posted to China on 14 December 1898. He was appointed as a Lance Corporal on 23 October 1899 and as such he took part in the Battle of Peking during the Boxer Rebellion, that was recognised with the award of the *Relief of Pekin* clasp to the China War Medal 1900. Frederick spent a further two years in China, reverting to Private at his own request on 12 March 1902, before he was posted to India on 10 November 1902.

Just over a year after arriving in India, Frederick was posted to the 1st Battalion, returning to Britain on 14 January 1904 and remaining here until he was discharged from the army at the end of his first period of service on 29 March 1905.

A year after his discharge, Frederick was living in Longfleet, Dorsetshire and employed as a Tram Conductor, when he married Emily White, and by the time of the 1911 Census, he and Emily were living in Rampisham, Dorsetshire, having had two sons and Frederick being employed as a Postman.

At the outbreak of war, Frederick was still employed as a Postman, but was also part of the National Reserve and so re-enlisted into the army on 11 September 1914, joining The Dorsetshire Regiment, where he was posted to the 1st Battalion, which arrived in France on 28 December 1914. Once in theatre, Frederick took part in the battles of early-1915, being appointed as an Acting Corporal on 02 March 1915 and an Acting Sergeant on 08 April 1915.

At the end of April 1915, the battalion was in the vicinity of Ypres, and on 01 May 1915 it was in trenches at Hill 60, where it came under attack from shelling and gas, although other than some bomb-throwers moving up a communication trench to bring their bombs to bear on the British trenches, there was no further attack. The battalion was relieved by a battalion of The Devonshire Regiment the following day and took up residence in dugouts in support of the relieving Devonshires.

It would appear that Frederick became a casualty on 02 May 1915 as medical records show him being transferred to the 15 Field Ambulance on that date, where he died the following day, his death recorded as *"In action. Poison gas"* [267].

Although Frederick has a marked grave in the cemetery close to where the field ambulance to which he was evacuated was located, he is another of the "Lost Boys" whose name has been omitted from the memorial tablets in the school chapel.

---

[267] UK, Army Registers of Soldiers' Effects, 1901-1929, 1914-1915, Exeter, 173501-175000

John William Montague CROSS
Private, 9061, 1st Battalion, The Dorsetshire Regiment who died on 22 October 1914, aged 24. Commemorated on the Le Touret Memorial, Pas de Calais, France

Born on 31 May 1890 in Sialkot, India, the eldest child of John Thomas Cross and Sarah Lily née Collis, his father was a Farrier Serjeant in the Royal Artillery who had died at sea on 02 February 1900 during passage to South Africa.

John was admitted to the school on 13 July 1900 (Petition No. 11452) and was joined by his younger brother, Leslie Cuthbert Frederick Cross, on 06 March 1902 (Petition No. 11664). John was discharged from the school to *"Civil Life"* on 31 March 1904 and it appears that he worked as a Gardener for the next six years. However, on 26 August 1910, he enlisted into 3rd Battalion, The Dorsetshire Regiment, a Territorial Force battalion, although he was only "effective" until January 1911 when he enlisted into the Regular Army, joining 1st Battalion, The Dorsetshire Regiment, stationed in Alma Barracks, Blackdown, Surrey, where he was appointed as a Lance Corporal ten months later.

On 11 January 1913, the battalion was posted to Belfast, County Antrim. However, on 08 June 1913, John was charged for disobeying Standing Orders for leaving camp whilst Orderly Corporal and lost his tape, reverting to Private. On 26 August 1913, he was transferred to the Reserve having reached the end of his first term of service, although it would appear that less than a year later, he was back with the battalion following the outbreak of war, probably as a recalled Reservist.

In August 1914 the battalion was still stationed in Belfast, but was quickly deployed to France, landing at Le Havre on 16 August 1914 and going into action for the first time at the Battle of Mons on 23 August, before forming part of the rear-guard in the long British retreat. On the move for sixteen consecutive days, it marched 220 miles, reaching the town of Gagny, south of the River Marne, on 04 September as the Allies managed to halt the German advance. Two days later, the unit went onto the offensive.

The Battle of La Bassée commenced on 07 September 1914, lasting until 17 October and saw the British and French take the fight to the Germans. However, commencing on 20 October, the Germans counter attacked. At 0550hrs on 22 October, the Germans attacked and captured trenches that were being held by The Cheshire Regiment, with 1st Battalion, The Dorsetshire Regiment, participating in the battle to retake these, which lasted all day, before it was withdrawn to Festubert at 2000hrs, having suffered heavily, including 101 missing.

John is likely one of the missing, recorded as having been killed on 22 October 1914. He has no known grave and is one of 121 Dorsetshire Regiment soldiers commemorated on the Le Touret Memorial.

Leslie also served during the war, having enlisted in the Royal Horse Artillery when he was discharged from the school on 05 April 1906 and Commissioned in wartime. He too was killed and both brothers are commemorated on the memorial tablets in the school chapel. He is documented earlier in this book.

Frederick Thomas HARNETT
Corporal, 6903, 2nd Battalion, The Dorsetshire Regiment who died on 16 April 1915, aged 26. Buried in Basra War Cemetery, Iraq

Born on 07 January 1889 in Dorchester, Dorsetshire, the seventh of nine children of Michael William Harnett and Catherine née Pitman, his father had been a Private in The Dorsetshire Regiment who had been discharged to pension on 26 February 1891 and died in Aldershot, Hampshire, on 06 December 1893.

Frederick was admitted to the school on 12 August 1898 (Petition No. 11207), joining his older brother, Sidney Charles John Harnett, who had been admitted on 26 October 1894 (Petition No. 10664). Frederick was discharged on 22 August 1903, joining his older brother in The Dorsetshire Regiment.

Frederick was posted to the 2nd Battalion on 01 April 1906, prior to being posted to India on 10 October the same year, where he was to remain for six years before returning to Britain on 30 October 1912, having been appointed a Lance Corporal on 04 December 1911, whilst still stationed in Wanowrie Lines, Poona, India. Frederick was only home for two years before he returned to India on 05 March 1913 and was stationed back in Poona, which was where he was when war broke out on 04 August. He was promoted to Corporal the following day.

The battalion departed from Bombay Docks on 12 October and arrived at Bahrain eleven days later, where it carried out training before departing on 02 November, landing at Fao, Mesopotamia, on 06 November 1914. It came into action five days later, having moved up the Shatt-al-Arab, when the positions that it occupied were attacked by the Turks. The British force had some success in Basra in November, and again at Qurna in the December, before moving to the area of Shaiba, the battalion arriving there in the middle of February.

On 14 April, it was ordered to capture the South Mound, a position close to Shaiba, which was done by 1030hrs. It was then ordered to advance on a watch tower, coming under fire as it did so. Despite being ordered not to become seriously engaged in this fight, it already was, suffering severe casualties in the process, as the Ottomans' smokeless cartridges made their positions difficult to ascertain. It was not until 1700hrs that the position was taken at bayonet point, with the battalion suffering sixteen officers and 152 other ranks killed and wounded.

Although Frederick survived the battle, he was severely wounded and died as a result of these wounds in Shaiba two days later, on 16 April 1915. He was buried in the British cemetery in Basra. He is also commemorated on the tablets in the school chapel, but he is incorrectly recorded as *Harnet*.

Sidney was discharged from the school to The Dorsetshire Regiment as a Bandsman on 29 July 1899, spending the first seven years of his service in Britain, before being posted to India on 03 October 1906. However, three years later, he was invalided back to Britain, on 27 November 1909 and was discharged from the army a month later, on 28 December, as medically unfit for further service, although the reason for this is not given. Sidney did not live to see the war, as he died in Farnham, Surrey, in September 1910.

William Raitt JAMES

Serjeant, 6334, 2nd Battalion, The Dorsetshire Regiment who died on 14 April 1915, aged 27. Buried in Basra War Cemetery, Iraq

Born on 03 May 1887 in Newbridge, County Kildare, the second of four children of Robert William Frederick James and Arabella née Ellis, his father had been a Staff Serjeant Major[268] in the Army Service Corps and was still serving when he died in Portsmouth, Hampshire, on 19 January 1896.

William was admitted to the school on 06 January 1897 (Petition No. 10979) and was discharged to The Dorsetshire Regiment on 18 August 1901. He appears in the 1911 Census as a Musician, serving with the 2nd Battalion and stationed in Wanowrie Lines, Poona, India.

When the war broke out, he would have been serving alongside Dukie Frederick Harnett in Poona, the battalion being part of the 16th Indian Brigade, although following mobilisation, it landed at Fao, Mesopotamia, on 06 November 1914 as part of Indian Expeditionary Force "D", which had been tasked with ensuring the safety of the Persian oilfields, the main source of fuel for the Royal

---

[268] Warrant Officer Class I

Navy. Although the landings were unopposed, the battalion was involved in fierce fighting as it advanced on Basra, expelling the Ottoman Army from Saihan on 15 November, this being its first taste of action. Basra was reached by the end of the month.

Other than patrols and some raids, the majority of the battalion remained in Basra until February 1915, when it advanced on Shaiba, nine miles to the south-west and where it was faced with difficult conditions, including having to wade knee-deep through the flooding of the Tigris and Euphrates rivers, although it was not until a month later, on 03 March, that it came into action against the Ottoman forces. It was again engaged by the Ottomans between 12 and 14 April 1915, the latter action now known as the Battle of Shaiba.

The battalion suffered 35 men killed during this second battle, William being one of these. He was buried in Basra War Cemetery alongside 33 other soldiers from his battalion, including fellow Dukie, Frederick Harnett. The last of the 35 is commemorated on the Basra Memorial, possibly as his body was never recovered.

Sadly, the cemetery has proved difficult to maintain due to the security situation in Iraq. In the early-2000s, many of the grave markers were vandalised, but it is being renovated by the Commonwealth War Graves Commission.

Edward George MASSIE
Lance Corporal, 8977, 1st Battalion, The Dorsetshire Regiment who died on 27 March 1916, aged 19. Buried in Millencourt Communal Cemetery Extension, Somme, France

Born on 09 June 1896 in Shorncliffe, Kent, the youngest son of Edward Massie and Louisa Celina née White, his father was a Serjeant Major in the Army Medical Staff Corps who died in Shorncliffe on 11 March 1896.

Edward was admitted to the school on 14 March 1907 (Petition No. 12346) and having made the transition from Chelsea to Guston, was discharged to The Dorsetshire Regiment on 06 September 1910. A year later, he was recorded in the 1911 Census as a Boy in the 1st Battalion and stationed in Alma Barracks, Blackdown, Surrey.

When war broke out, Edward was stationed in Belfast, County Antrim, departing the city on 14 August on board the SS *Anthony* and landing at Le Havre on 16 August 1914, before moving to Belgium where he would have participated in the Battle of Mons, spending the next sixteen days retreating 220 miles to Gagny, before the tide turned and the British went back onto the offensive.

The battalion spent the latter part of 1914 and the early part of 1915 in the Ypres Salient prior to moving to the Somme sector, which in the summer of 1915 was considered to be a relatively quiet area. It remained in this "quiet sector" for the remainder of the year and was still there at the start of 1916.

The battalion war diary[269] reports during early March that the situation remained *"quiet"*, but that there was more enemy activity from the middle of the month, including shelling the town of Albert, in which it was billeted when not in the trenches. The battalion moved back into the trenches on the evening of 21 March, reporting that, other than routine patrolling by themselves and occasional shelling by the Germans, all seemed quiet.

On 26 March, the unit was subjected to heavy shelling, but this had died down by the evening. In the early hours of the 27 March, a mine was detonated under the German positions which was a signal for a raiding party of almost 100 soldiers to attack German positions in order to capture prisoners. However, whilst one half of the raiding party was entirely successful, the other half had not advanced as far as expected due to German resistance when the signal to retire was given. This resulted in one officer wounded and missing, three other ranks killed and seventeen other ranks wounded, Edward being one of the three killed. The soldiers from the battalion worked until dawn to bring in the dead and wounded, and recovered Edward's body, as he is buried in Millencourt Communal Cemetery Extension.

Although Edward had two older brothers, neither of these were Dukies. However, one of them, 2nd Corporal William Massie, Royal Engineers, was killed on 01 August 1917 and is buried in Gwalia Cemetery, Belgium.

Albert Edward MOFFATT

Private, 9489, 6th (Service) Battalion, The Dorsetshire Regiment who died on 23 March 1918, aged 19. Commemorated on the Arras Memorial, Pas de Calais, France

Born on 16 December 1898 in Gosport, Hampshire, the eleventh of fourteen children of William Henry Moffatt and Alice Louise née Lewry, his father had served as a Private in The East Lancashire Regiment who was discharged to pension after 22 years' service on 22 February 1887.

Albert was not the first of the family to be admitted to the school. His older brother James Moffatt had been admitted on 08 January 1904 (Petition No. 11928), joined by Alfred Stanley Moffatt on 08 April 1904 (Petition No. 11963), but both had been discharged by the time that Albert was admitted on 12 April 1910 (Petition No.

---

[269] WO 95/2392/1, 1 Battalion Dorsetshire Regiment, 1916 Jan. - 1919 Mar., The National Archives, Kew

12742). Albert was discharged to The Dorsetshire Regiment on 20 December 1912, almost a year before his younger brother, Horace Claude Moffatt, was admitted to the school on 02 December 1913 (Petition No. 13185).

Albert's service record is no longer available, but it is unlikely that he was deployed to France at the outbreak of war due to his age and although his medal index card has no date for his entry into theatre, it does show that he was not eligible for the award of the 1914-15 Star, suggesting deployment during 1916 at the earliest.

6th (Service) Battalion, The Dorsetshire Regiment, was formed in Dorchester, Dorsetshire, on 06 September 1914, but did not enter theatre until July 1915, initially serving in the Ypres Salient before moving to the Somme sector in 1916, participating in the Battle of Albert in the opening stages of that offensive. However, it is possible that Albert did not enter theatre until after his eighteenth birthday in December 1917, by which time the battalion was located in the area of Flesquières and Havrincourt, and was still there towards the end of March 1918.

On 09 March, it moved into trenches near Havrincourt, remaining there for an extended period due to an anticipated German attack. On 21 March 1918, the Germans launched their Spring Offensive, which was preceded by *"an extensive and intensive bombardment"*[270]. The attack led to the battalions on the right of the Dorsetshires losing ground, but this was all recaptured.

Despite this, during the night of the 21-22 March, the battalion withdrew with the remainder of the British forces and occupied a line between Hermies and Havrincourt, where on the morning of 23 March the Germans advanced on its positions with the assistance of *"flammenwerfer"*[271], but were beaten back by the intense rifle fire. It then withdrew through the 63rd (Royal Naval) Division, taking up new positions near Villers-au-Flos. Albert was killed during the German attack on 23 March 1918 and his body was not recovered, so now he is commemorated on the Arras Memorial.

James was discharged from the school on 07 February 1907 to *"Civil life – educationally unfit for the army"*. However, it would seem that he did enlist prior to the outbreak of war, the 1911 Census recording him as a Signaller in the 2nd Battalion, Grenadier Guards, although it appears that he later transferred, as he deployed to France with 1st Battalion, The Dorsetshire Regiment, on 16 August 1914. It is known that he survived the war, but nothing more is known about him other than that.

---

[270] WO 95/2001/1: 50 Infantry Brigade: 6 Battalion Dorsetshire Regiment., 1918 Jan 1 - 1918 Mar 31, The National Archives, Kew
[271] Flamethrowers

Alfred was discharged from the school on 08 July 1909 and enlisted into the 8th (King's Royal Irish) Hussars. He is recorded in the 1911 Census as a Musician in that regiment and stationed in Campbell Barracks, Lucknow, India. His medal index card shows that, following the outbreak of war, he landed in France on 11 November 1914 when the regiment arrived from where it was stationed in Ambala, India. He also survived the war, dying in York, Yorkshire North Riding, in March 1967.

The last of the Dukie brothers, Horace, was discharged from the school to *"Civil Life"* on 13 October 1916. He is recorded in the 1939 England and Wales Register as living at his mother's home in Gosport and employed as a Builder's Labourer. It is not known if he served during the Second World War, but if he did, he survived, dying in Gosport in March 1974.

Edgar Blyton TRISTRAM

Private, 3/8448, 6th (Service) Battalion, The Dorsetshire Regiment who died on 13 April 1917, aged 46. Commemorated on the Arras Memorial, Pas de Calais, France

Born on 26 May 1870 in Dublin, County Dublin, the eldest of three children of Blyton Valentine Tristram and Helen Fanny née Grout, his father had served for thirteen years in the 48th (the Northamptonshire) Regiment of Foot, before transferring to the Commissariat Staff Corps[272], from which he was discharged as a Serjeant on 26 September 1876. He died in Fareham, Hampshire, on 25 October 1881.

Edgar was admitted to the school on 10 March 1882 (Petition No. 8739) and was joined by his younger brother, George Thomas Tristram, on 14 September 1883 (Petition No. 8996). Edgar was discharged from the school on 07 June 1884 and enlisted into The Dorsetshire Regiment.

Edgar spent the first year of his service in Britain, appointed as a Drummer on 15 November 1884, before he was posted to the Mediterranean on 04 March 1885 and although his service record does not specify the location to which he was posted, it is likely to have been Malta. However, on 18 December 1885, he was posted to Egypt, spending nine months there before he was posted back to Britain on 09 August 1886.

Eighteen months later, on 08 February 1888, Edgar was again posted to the Mediterranean, before he was again posted to Egypt on 18 July 1889, remaining there for four years before he was posted to India on 27 September 1893. Three years later, Edgar returned to

---

[272] Renamed Army Service Corps in 1870

Britain, on 04 July 1896 and was discharged from the army at the end of his first period of service two days later.

However, four years later, Edgar enlisted into the Royal Southern Reserve Regiment, a precursor of the Royal Garrison Regiment[273], on 30 March 1900, although he only served for one year before he was discharged on 29 March 1901, a month after he had married Elizabeth Butcher in Holborn, London. This was three months after the birth of their first child, Elizabeth Fanny Tristram, on 17 December 1900 and she is recorded in the 1901 Census which shows the family living in Clerkenwell, London, Edgar employed as a Porter for the General Post Office. Elizabeth died in November 1901, a month short of her first birthday.

Two months after his second discharge, Edgar again re-enlisted, this time into the Royal Garrison Regiment, on 08 May 1901, serving for two years before he was discharged on 07 May 1903, although on 15 May 1903 he was attested into the Dorsetshire Regiment Militia.

Although it is not known what he was employed as, it appears that Edgar and Elizabeth remained in Clerkenwell as their next four children were born there, Edgar Tristram in 1904, Harold Tristram in 1905, Beatrice Tristram in 1907 and Edward Tristram in 1910. Edgar was discharged from the Militia to pension on 12 December 1908 and the family were still living in Clerkenwell at the time of the 1911 Census, Edgar recorded as a Porter for the London & North Western Railway. Edgar and Elizabeth's youngest child, Charles William Tristram, was born in Holborn the following year.

Following the outbreak of war, Edgar re-enlisted into The Dorsetshire Regiment on 08 September 1914 and was posted to the 6th (Service) Battalion on 19 September 1914. Having been formed at Dorchester, Dorsetshire, on 06 September 1914 as part of K2, it moved to Wareham, Dorsetshire, attached to the 17th (Northern) Division as Army Troops before it was transferred to the division's 50th Brigade in March 1915. The battalion then moved to Romsey, Hampshire, in May 1915, before it landed at Boulogne on 13 July 1915, the date shown on Edgar's medal index card for his arrival in theatre.

The battalion was initially located in the Ypres sector of the Western Front, but the following year it was moved to France in anticipation of the start of the Somme Offensive. Although it did not go "over the top" on the first day of the offensive, it did get ordered into the line at 1600hrs on 01 July 1916 in order to relieve the 7th

---

[273] Formed in 1901, this regiment was sent to relieve regular infantry battalions in overseas garrisons in order to allow the regular battalions in these garrisons to be sent on active service in South Africa. The five battalions were disbanded 1906-07 and the regiment was disbanded in 1908

Battalion, Alexandra, Princess of Wales's Own (Yorkshire Regiment), which had suffered very heavy casualties that morning on its attack on Fricourt.

By March the following year, the battalion was in the vicinity of Ivergny ahead of the start of what would become the Second Battle of Arras, which was launched on 09 April 1917. The battalion war diary for the first eighteen days of April 1917 appears to have been lost, but it is known that it participated in the First Battle of the Scarpe which lasted between 09 April and 14 April 1917, and it was during this period that Edgar was killed in action.

Edgar's body was not recovered after his death, being commemorated on the Arras Memorial and he is also a "Lost Boy" whose name has been omitted from the memorial tablets in the school chapel.

George was discharged from the school on 28 July 1888 and enlisted into the 10th (Prince of Wales's Own Royal) Hussars as a Musician. However, on 03 October 1901, he transferred to the Royal Marine Artillery as a Musician. The 1911 Census shows that he, his wife and five children were living in Portsmouth, Hampshire, and he continued to serve until he was discharged on 19 February 1917. George and his wife are also recorded in the 1939 England and Wales Register, both of them retired and living in Ealing, Middlesex. He died in Harrow, Middlesex, in 1962.

The Prince of Wales's Volunteers (South Lancashire Regiment)

Charles Henry BLUNDELL
Serjeant Drummer, 8474, 2nd Battalion, The Prince of Wales's Volunteers (South Lancashire Regiment) who died on 19 February 1917, aged 38. Buried in St. Sever Cemetery Extension, Rouen, Seine-Maritime, France

Born on 24 May 1879 in Westminster, Middlesex, the youngest child of Charles James Blundell and Margaret née Haywood, his father had been a Private in the Coldstream Guards and was a veteran of the Crimean War. He had been discharged from the army on 18 May 1880 and died in Pimlico, Middlesex, on 01 April 1886.

Charles was admitted to the school on 31 January 1890 (Petition No. 9969) and was discharged on 14 July 1894. Although there is no service record available for him, the school admission record shows him apprenticed to The Lincolnshire Regiment. However, he appears on the 1901 Census stationed in Chelsea Barracks serving in his father's old regiment, the Coldstream Guards, with whom he had served in the Second Boer War as a Drummer, alongside his oldest brother Alfred George Blundell, a Serjeant Drummer.

At some point during the next ten years, Charles transferred to The South Lancashire Regiment, as when he married Isabella Maybury on 28 February 1911 in Cork, County Cork, he was a Corporal in that regiment and stationed in Buttevant, County Cork. In 1912, the battalion was posted to Newbridge, County Kildare, before returning to the mainland in 1913 and being stationed in Tidworth, Wiltshire, from where it deployed on the outbreak of war, landing at Le Havre on 14 August 1914.

The battalion was to remain on the Western Front for the duration of the war and was involved in almost all of the major battles and offensives from the initial battles around Mons at the very outset. However, Charles's medal index card shows that he did not enter theatre until 05 December 1915. It also appears that Charles' demise was not as a result of enemy action, as the Registers of Soldiers'

Effects[274] records his death, on 19 February 1917, as being due to nephritis.

He is buried in St. Sever Cemetery Extension, on the outskirts of Rouen. For almost the entire duration of the war, there were fourteen hospitals of various types stationed in and around Rouen, the majority of the casualties buried in the cemetery originating from these. Charles is one of 35 South Lancashire Regiment soldiers who died between 25 October 1916 and 25 November 1918 and who are buried here.

Hugh GREGSON
Company Quartermaster Serjeant, 4358, 3rd (Reserve) Battalion, The Prince of Wales's Volunteers (South Lancashire Regiment) who died on 11 June 1919, aged 39. Buried in Warrington Cemetery, Cheshire, United Kingdom

Born on 10 May 1880 in Farnham, Surrey, the third child of Hugh Gregson and Annie Louisa née Hanger, his father was, at the time of his son's birth, a Gunner in the Royal Artillery. As his Petition Document is no longer available, it is not possible to establish when or if Hugh's father was discharged from the army, but it is likely that he died in Weymouth, Dorsetshire in 1885, with Hugh's mother also dying there in 1888.

Hugh was admitted to the school on 27 December 1889 (Petition No. 9950) and appears on the 1891 Census, recorded as *Greyson*. He enlisted into 1st Battalion, The South Lancashire Regiment, on 12 May 1894, the day that he was discharged from the school and was appointed as a Drummer two years later. In November 1899, Hugh was posted to South Africa during the Second Boer War and from there, in January 1903, he was posted to India, where he married Kathleen Josephine Morrison, in Bombay on 16 April 1904.

Hugh was to remain in India until 1907, posted to the 2nd Battalion, his son being born there in 1906. He was then stationed in Britain for the next ten years, being posted between the 3rd (Reserve) Battalion and the Regimental Depot, located in Peninsula Barracks, Warrington, Lancashire, as well as having two daughters, the eldest born in Blackdown, Surrey, in 1908 and the youngest in Newbridge, County Kildare, in 1912.

During this time, Hugh also rose through the ranks from Private to Acting Company Sergeant Major, which was the rank that he held when he was deployed to France on 02 May 1917, serving initially with the 2nd Battalion and then the 7th (Service) Battalion. This

---

[274] UK, Army Registers of Soldiers' Effects, 1901-1929, 1914-1915, Shrewsbury, 410501-412000

latter battalion had been formed in Warrington, in September 1914 as part of K2 and had been in France since 18 July 1915.

One month after the 7th Battalion had been disbanded in France, on 22 February 1918, Hugh was posted back to the Regimental Depot having broken his leg on 08 February 1918, spending three months here before he was posted to the 3rd Battalion, stationed in Barrow in Furness, Cumbria, as the Company Quartermaster Serjeant. It was from here that Hugh was discharged to civilian life, having completed his term of service, on 12 March 1919.

Although there is no record of any illness or disease in his service record, Hugh died three months after discharge on 11 June 1919 and is buried in Warrington Cemetery. He is commemorated by the Commonwealth War Graves Commission, but there is no evidence available to confirm he died as a result of his service.

Thomas Edward PETT (served as Thomas PARKER)
Private 8036, 2nd Battalion, The Prince of Wales's Volunteers (South Lancashire Regiment) who died on 24 October 1914, aged 26. Commemorated on the Le Touret Memorial, Pas de Calais, France

Born on 24 April 1888 in Upper Holloway, Middlesex, the tenth of fourteen children of Alfred Pett and Elizabeth née Reynolds, his father had been a 2nd Class Staff Sergeant in the Army Service Corps who had been discharged from the army as medically unfit on 23 December 1884. He died in Holloway on 21 March 1896.

Thomas was admitted to the school on 04 November 1898 (Petition No. 11224) and was discharged on 03 May 1902, enlisting into the Army Service Corps, but was discharged just over a year later, on 13 May 1903, *"His services being no longer required"*[275].

Following his discharge, little is known of Thomas, although based upon his service number, it would appear that he re-enlisted into the army in either 1905 or 1906. The fact that he had previously been discharged may account for the fact that he enlisted using the name Parker, however, much of this is speculation as there is no surviving service record for this second period of engagement.

At the outbreak of war, Thomas would have been serving alongside Dukie Charles Blundell, and although his battalion landed at Le Havre on 14 August, according to his medal index card, Thomas did not arrive in theatre until eight days later, on 22 August 1914. The battalion took part in the Battle of Mons and the long retreat, also participating in the Battles of Le Cateau, of the Marne and of the Aisne. By October, it was located in the Ypres sector and

---

[275] WO 97: Chelsea Pensioners British Army Service Records 1760-1913

took part in the Battle of La Bassée, which lasted from 10 October until 02 November 1914.

On 17 October 1914, the Battalion moved up into the line in front of Illies, where it remained for four days, during which the Germans launched a number of heavy attacks, recorded in a Regimental history[276] as follows:

> *"By the 20th however, the advent of fresh German divisions on this part of the front brought the advance to a standstill and the enemy opened a severe offensive, the brunt of which fell on the 3rd Division. When this phase of the battle began, the battalion [2/South Lancs] was holding water-logged trenches on the right of the 7th Infantry Brigade...*
>
> *During the afternoon the enemy launched a determined attack on the trenches occupied by these companies and fierce fighting ensued before the attack was repulsed. In this action the casualties of 'A' and 'C' Companies were severe...*
>
> *The entire period saw the battalion involved in severe fighting with 200 casualties on 21st October. After that day, the battalion was withdrawn into rest billets with a strength of 10 officers and 300 men."*

Although the pension record for Thomas states that his date of death was 20 October 1914, the Commonwealth War Graves Commission has recorded it as 24 October 1914. This discrepancy is likely due to the fact that the latter date was the first opportunity that the battalion had to make an official casualty list during this action. He is also another of the "Lost Boys" whose name has been omitted from the memorial tablets in the school chapel, likely due to his serving under an alias.

His younger brother, Cecil Ernest Pett, who was not a Dukie, died of disease on 07 July 1918 whilst serving with the 8th Signal Company, Royal Engineers.

---

[276] Mullaly, Colonel B. R. (1955). *The South Lancashire Regiment: The Prince of Wales's Volunteers.* Bristol: White Swan Press

The Welsh Regiment

Whilst almost all of the Dukies who served in The Welsh Regiment and died during the First World War are commemorated on the memorial tablets in the school chapel, their regiment is incorrectly recorded as The Welch Regiment.

The Welsh Regiment came into existence on 01 July 1881 as part of the Cardwell Reforms when the 41st (The Welsh) Regiment of Foot and the 69th (South Lincolnshire) Regiment of Foot were amalgamated, the 41st becoming 1st Battalion, The Welsh Regiment, the 69th becoming 2nd Battalion, The Welsh Regiment. Although the regiment was later renamed The Welch[277] Regiment, this did not occur until 01 January 1921 and therefore was not in use at the time that the fallen Dukies named below were serving.

Edward James ANDREWS
Private, 54810, 15th (Service) Battalion (Carmarthenshire), The Welsh Regiment who died on 27 July 1917, aged 20. Buried in Bard Cottage Cemetery, West-Vlaanderen, Belgium

Born on 05 May 1897 in Aldershot, Hampshire, the youngest of four children of George Andrews and Annie Wilhelmina Elizabeth née Brown, his father had been a Corporal in the Royal Engineers who had been discharged after 21 years' service on 16 July 1899 and died in Cholsey, Berkshire, on 08 March 1901.

Edward was admitted to the school on 30 March 1908 (Petition No. 12483), which was four months after his older brother, Alec George Andrews, who had been admitted on 07 November 1902 (Petition No. 11753) had been discharged. Edward would have made the transition from Chelsea to Guston before he was discharged on 29 June 1911, having been joined by his younger brother, Leslie John Andrews, who had been admitted on 26 January 1911 (Petition No. 12839).

According to the school records, Edward was discharged to The Queen's (Royal West Surrey Regiment), but there is no surviving service record available for him. However, his medal index card records him as serving in that regiment, but it is likely that he transferred to The Welsh Regiment prior to deploying overseas.

---

[277] The archaic spelling of Welsh

The battalion with which he was serving in 1917, the 15th (Service) Battalion, was formed by the Carmarthenshire County Committee in October 1914. On 04 December 1915 it embarked at Folkestone, Kent, and landed at Boulogne the same day, entering the trenches for the first time to receive instruction near Rincq nine days later and suffering its first casualties the following day. Although the battalion did not attack on the first day of the Somme Offensive, it was part of the attack on Mametz Wood from 10 to 12 July 1916, suffering 228 killed, wounded and missing.

In July of 1917, the unit was in the Zwaanhof sector near Ypres and on 27 July it was aggressively patrolling to ascertain the strength with which the Germans were holding the front line. However, the patrols had been observed advancing by German aircraft and were met with strong opposition, forcing them to retire, prior to their positions coming under heavy fire from the Germans. During the day, the battalion suffered six officers killed and wounded and 82 other ranks killed, wounded and missing, one of whom was Edward. He is buried in Bard Cottage Cemetery, barely a mile from where he died.

Alec was discharged to the Royal Engineers on 31 October 1907. He survived the war, although he was only 38 when he died in South Tidworth, Wiltshire, in 1930.

Leslie was also discharged to the Royal Engineers on 22 December 1913. It is likely that due to his age he did not see service overseas during the war, but it has not been possible to confirm this, as nothing can be found about him following his discharge from the school.

James Adventure COLLINS

Company Serjeant Major, 31311, 23rd (Service) Battalion (Welsh Pioneers), The Welsh Regiment who died on 27 December 1918, aged 56. Buried in Hendon Cemetery and Crematorium, Middlesex, United Kingdom

Born on 02 May 1862 whilst at sea during passage to Canada, his birth being registered in Frederickton, New Brunswick, he was the second son of Michael Collins and his wife Mary, and his father was a Serjeant in the 15th (the Yorkshire East Riding) Regiment of Foot[278].

James was admitted to the school on 29 September 1869 (Petition No. 7369) and discharged to the Royal Engineers on 01 May 1877. He was appointed as a Bugler on 01 October 1878 and as a Sapper six months later, on 01 April 1879. After six years, on 31 May 1885, he was transferred to his father's old regiment, joining his older

---

[278] Renamed The East Yorkshire Regiment on 01 July 1881

brother, William Collins, who was a Serjeant in that regiment. However, four months after transferring, on 25 August 1885, James paid the sum of £9 and left the army.

It appears that he then made his living as a Musician and married Alice Jane Collins in Fulham, London, in 1898. They had two children, George Louis Collins, born in 1898 and Stanley Clifford Michael Collins, born in 1901.

Following the outbreak of war James re-enlisted on 07 December 1914, at the age of 50, in the London Welsh Battalion, 15th (Service) Battalion (1st London Welsh), The Royal Welsh Fusiliers, as a Musician, being promoted to Serjeant three days later. This battalion had been formed on 20 October 1914.

On 11 May 1915 James transferred to 19th (Service) Battalion (Glamorgan Pioneers), The Welsh Regiment, appointed as Regimental Quartermaster Serjeant the following day. This battalion had been formed at Colwyn Bay, Denbighshire, in February 1915 as a Pioneer Battalion and landed at Le Havre in December 1915. However, two months prior to this, on 16 October 1915, James was posted to the 23rd (Service) Battalion (Welsh Pioneers) as a Colour Serjeant. He was then promoted to Company Serjeant Major on 20 October 1915.

This last battalion had been formed at Porthcawl, Glamorganshire, in September 1915, moving to Aldershot, Hampshire, in March 1916. It was then stationed in Thetford, Norfolk between May and June 1916, before it embarked at Devonport, Devonshire, on 13 July and moved to Salonika, arriving on 11 August 1916 and becoming the Pioneer Battalion to the 28th Division.

Not long after arriving in Salonika, James contracted malaria, which caused a facial paralysis, resulting in his being evacuated back to Britain on 06 November 1916 and being discharged from the army on 17 January 1917, medically unfit due to his service in Salonika. James's medical records also show that he had some evidence of heart disease.

James was followed up regularly by the army following his discharge, however, on 27 December 1918 he died and was buried in Hendon, Middlesex. Although commemorated on the memorial tablets in the school chapel, his regiment is incorrectly recorded as Royal Welsh Fusiliers.

Hughie Job HAYES

Company Serjeant Major, 5019, 2nd Battalion, The Welsh Regiment who died on 21 January 1915, aged 32. Buried in Bethune Town Cemetery, Pas de Calais, France

Born on 13 July 1882 in Hounslow, Middlesex, the second of three children of Edward Hayes and Mary née Strange, his father had been a Colour Serjeant in 57th (West Middlesex) Regiment of Foot who had been discharged from the army on 26 April 1881 and died in Hounslow on 12 May 1887.

Hughie was admitted to the school on 29 July 1892 (Petition No. 10345), the same day as his older brother, Edward Timothy Hayes (Petition No. 10344). Hughie was discharged to The Welsh Regiment on 08 August 1896. There is a limited amount of Hughie's service record remaining, but it is known that he saw service during the Second Boer War, serving in South Africa for more than seven years, India for almost two years and Egypt for three years.

At the outbreak of war, 2nd Battalion, The Welsh Regiment, was stationed in Bordon, Hampshire, and Hughie's second term of service, eighteen years in total, was reached on 08 August. He was a Serjeant at this stage and requested to be discharged, however due to mobilisation, this was cancelled and he landed with the battalion at Le Havre on 13 August 1914.

The battalion participated in the Battle of Mons and the subsequent retreat, as well as the Battles of the Marne, of the Aisne and the First Battle of Ypres. By January 1915, it was in the area of Béthune and engaged in digging second line trenches. On 20 January Hughie was shot by two drunken soldiers from his regiment, Lance Corporal William Price and Private Richard Morgan, after being mistaken during a snowstorm for a Serjeant whom they considered a bully and whom they later claimed regularly had them punished for crimes they did not commit. Both men immediately confessed to the Battalion Adjutant and Hughie was evacuated to No.1 Casualty Clearing Station in Béthune, where he died the following day, 21 January 1915, being buried in the town cemetery.

Price and Morgan were tried for murder by General Courts Martial on 06 February. They were both found guilty and executed by firing squad on 15 February 1915, being also buried in Bethune Town Cemetery. The incident is mentioned in Robert Graves's 1929 book *"Good-Bye To All That"*[279], although he is likely to have heard the story second-hand, as he did not join the battalion until May 1915.

---

[279] Graves, R. (1929). *Good-Bye to All That*. London: Jonathan Cape

Although Hughie is commemorated on the memorial tablets in the school chapel he is incorrectly recorded as H E J Hayes.

Edward also enlisted when discharged from the school on 30 March 1895, joining The Bedfordshire Regiment. He was discharged in 1904, but re-enlisted into The Suffolk Regiment, before being discharged as medically unfit in 1917 and transferred to the Royal Defence Corps, which the Commonwealth War Graves Commission recorded as his regiment when he died on 11 September 1919, although his grave marker shows the badge of The Suffolk Regiment. He is another "Lost Boy" whose name was omitted from the memorial tablets in the school chapel and he is documented later in this book.

George Ernest JOHNSTON

Private, 11277, 1st Battalion, The Welsh Regiment who died on 17 February 1915, aged 21. Commemorated on the Ypres (Menin Gate) Memorial, West-Vlaanderen, Belgium

Born on 24 November 1893 in Cardiff, Glamorganshire, the youngest son of William Johnston and Catherine née Thomas, his father was a Colour Serjeant in The Welsh Regiment and died whilst serving in Monkton, Pembrokeshire, on 16 July 1899.

George was admitted to the school on 14 August 1903 (Petition No. 11860), joining his older brother, Hubert William Richard Johnston, who had been admitted on 07 February 1902 (Petition No. 11653). George was discharged to *"Civil Life"* on 28 November 1907 and is recorded in the 1911 Census as a Junior Clerk, working in the Boy Scouts' Headquarters and living in Croydon, Surrey, with Hubert, their mother and stepfather, Thomas Henry Thomas. It is not known at what point George enlisted in the army, as there is no longer a service record available for him, although it is likely that it was after the outbreak of war, which is also suggested by his service number.

At the outbreak of war, 1st Battalion, The Welsh Regiment, was stationed in Chakrata, India, but embarked at Karachi and landed at Plymouth, Devonshire, on 24 November 1914. After being made up to strength, it then embarked at Southampton, Hampshire, on 16 January and landed at Le Havre on 18 January 1915, the same date of disembarkation recorded for George, moving into the trenches for the first time on 02 February. On 05 February, it moved into trenches north of the Ypres to Lille railway line, remaining in this locality for the next ten days.

At 0330hrs on the morning of the 15 February, the battalion was ordered out and marched to positions south of the town of Ypres. Throughout this tour of the trenches, it was subjected to enfilade fire from the nearby German positions, and on 16 February, one Dukie serving with the battalion, Frederick Peoples, was killed.

The following day, 17 February, it was relieved by 2nd Battalion, The Cheshire Regiment, but not without suffering eighteen soldiers killed and 31 wounded, George being one of those killed. It is not known whether George's body was not recovered or if his grave was lost during the subsequent fighting in this area, but he has no known grave and is commemorated on the Menin Gate Memorial. He is also commemorated on the memorial tablets in the school chapel, but is incorrectly recorded as G E *Johnson*.

Hubert was discharged to *"Civil Life"* on 01 June 1906. He is recorded in the 1911 Census employed as a Civil Servant in the Post Office and served in the Royal Engineers during the war. Unlike his brother, he survived, the 1939 England and Wales Register recording him employed as a Manager, Timber Merchants and living in Croydon, Surrey, the town where he died in 1947.

Charles Lionel PALMER
Private, 10578, 1st Battalion, The Welsh Regiment who died on 08 October 1918, aged 21. Buried in Mikra British Cemetery, Kalamaria, Greece

Born on 29 July 1897 in Pembroke, Pembrokeshire, the eldest of five children of Charles Palmer and Norah née Toomey, his father had been a Serjeant in The Devonshire Regiment and was killed in action on 24 February 1900 near Colenso, at the Battle of the Tugela Heights, during the Second Boer War.

Charles was admitted to the school on 07 September 1908 (Petition No. 12535) and having moved from Chelsea to Guston, was discharged to The Welsh Regiment on 05 September 1911. His service record is no longer available, so his movements are unknown both pre-war and during the early part of the war, but records show that he was not awarded the 1914-15 Star, suggesting that it was not until 1916 at the earliest that he entered theatre.

After spending the first year of the war fighting on the Western Front, on 24 November 1915 the 1st Battalion embarked at Marseille and sailed to Egypt prior to sailing for Salonika. During 1916 and 1917 it was involved in numerous actions against the Bulgarians, including the occupation of Mazirko, the capture of Barakli Jum'a, the capture of Ferdie and Essex Trenches, and the capture of Barakli and Kumli.

In the final year of the war, the unit participated in the Battle of Doiran and the pursuit to the Strumica valley, and when the Bulgarians surrendered on 30 September 1918, it was located north of Lake Doiran, Macedonia.

At this time, Charles was attached to the Headquarters of 84th Brigade, but succumbed to illness, likely pneumonia, and was admitted to hospital. He died of disease in the 28th General Hospital in Kalamaria, Thessaloniki, on 08 October 1918 and was buried in the cemetery close to where the hospital was located.

Albert Walter PAYNE
Private, 38489, 2nd Battalion, The Welsh Regiment who died on 17 September 1916, aged 22. Buried in St. Sever Cemetery, Rouen, Seine-Maritime, France

Born on 06 June 1894 in Pembroke Dock, Pembrokeshire, the third of four children of Edward George Payne and Mary Anne née Battersby, his father was a Serjeant in The Welsh Regiment. His mother died on 22 March 1902 in Cardiff, Glamorganshire.

Albert was admitted to the school on 03 June 1904 (Petition No. 11979) and was *"returned to civil life-dirty habits"*[280] on 30 April 1908. Following Albert's discharge from the school, little is known about him and he could not be found in the 1911 Census, but it is known that at some point following the outbreak of war, he enlisted into the army, joining his father's old regiment.

The exact date of his enlistment is not known, as his service record is no longer available, however it appears that, based on the surviving records of the soldiers with the service numbers surrounding Albert's, he enlisted in July 1915 and his medal index card records his date of disembarkation in theatre as 16 December 1915. The battalion to which Albert was posted, 2nd Battalion, likely as a battle casualty replacement in the aftermath of the Battle of Loos, had been on the Western Front since 13 August 1914.

During the Somme Offensive, the battalion did not participate in the fighting until 15 July when it moved into positions at Mametz Wood and by 20 August it was in positions between Bazentin-le-Petit and High Wood. During its tour of duty in the line, which ended on 28 August, the battalion suffered one officer and 41 other ranks killed, three officers and 170 other ranks wounded, 46 other ranks who left the battalion due to shock and four other ranks posted as missing.

It is likely that Albert was one of the other ranks that was wounded during this period and evacuated to one of the hospitals that was

---

[280] Enuresis

located in Rouen, as following its time in the trenches, the battalion had a period of rest and refit until 18 September.

Albert died of wounds on 17 September 1916 and was buried in St. Sever Cemetery in Rouen. He is also another "Lost Boy" whose name has been omitted from the memorial tablets in the school chapel.

Frederick Samuel PEOPLES
Corporal, 8957, 1st Battalion, The Welsh Regiment who died on 16 February 1915, aged 23. Buried in Godezonne Farm Cemetery, West-Vlaanderen, Belgium

Born on 10 April 1891 in Hythe, Kent, the seventh of nine children of James Peoples and Annie Maria née Howell, his father had been a Serjeant in The Oxfordshire Light Infantry who had been discharged from the army on 31 December 1889 and died in Shorncliffe, Kent, on 09 April 1894.

Frederick was admitted to the school on 18 July 1901 (Petition No. 11568). Records show that he was initially going to be admitted to the Royal Hibernian Military School in Dublin, his older brother, Alfred Peoples, having attended this school before he was withdrawn. Frederick was discharged from the Duke of York's to The Welsh Regiment on 26 April 1906. His service record is no longer available, but he is recorded in the 1911 Census as a Private in the 1st Battalion and stationed in Main Barracks, Abbassia, Cairo, Egypt, alongside elder brothers Alfred and Albert.

At the outbreak of war, Frederick would have landed at Le Havre on 18 January 1915, having his first experience in the trenches on 02 February, when half of the battalion supported The Northumberland Fusiliers at Zillebeke and the other half supported The Cheshire Regiment at Blauwpoort Farm, the entire battalion taking over the front-line trenches from The Northumberland Fusiliers two days later.

At 0330hrs on the morning of the 15 February, the battalion was ordered out and marched to positions south of the town of Ypres. Part of the position that it occupied had been a strong point, but was now only partially held. Throughout its occupation of these positions, the partially held trench was subjected to enfilade fire, which led to approximately 30 yards of it having to be evacuated. The casualties for that day were ten officers and sixteen other ranks killed and wounded, Frederick being one of the other ranks killed on 16 February 1915. He is buried in Godezonne Farm Cemetery.

William Amos SPONG

Serjeant, 21478, Depot, The Welsh Regiment who died on 10 March 1918, aged 35. Buried in Port Talbot (Holy Cross) Churchyard, Glamorganshire, United Kingdom

Born on 07 March 1883 in Port Talbot, Glamorganshire, the fifth of seven children of Henry Spong and Charlotte Maria née Hamer, his father had been a Serjeant in the 69th (South Lincolnshire) Regiment of Foot[281] who had been discharged from the army on 22 November 1879 and died in Port Talbot on 01 July 1891.

William was admitted to the school on 29 December 1893 (Petition No. 10562) and was joined by his younger brother, Alfred Lloyd Spong, on 29 October 1894 (Petition No. 10671). William was discharged *"To mother"* on 19 December 1896.

Following his discharge from school his life is somewhat of a mystery. It would appear that he did not enlist, but what is known is that he married Mary Ann Dawe in Neath, Glamorganshire, in 1910 and he is recorded in the 1911 Census living in Port Talbot with his wife and brother and employed as a Baker. His eldest son, Harold Henry Spong, was born a week after the census, on 09 April 1911.

Three months after war was declared, on 09 November 1914, William enlisted into 10th (Service) Battalion (1st Rhondda), The Welsh Regiment, his employment being given as Fuelworker. By this time, he had a second child, Florence Mabel Spong, who had been born in March 1913. It was also from this surviving enlistment record that the assumption was made that he had not previously enlisted, as he denied having any previous military service.

This battalion had been formed in the Rhondda Valley, Glamorganshire, in late September 1914 by David Watts Morgan, a Justice of the Peace and Rhondda miners' agent, and landed at Le Havre fourteen months later, on 03 December 1915. By the time that the battalion arrived in France, William had been appointed as a Lance Corporal and left a pregnant wife, their third child, William Alfred Charles Verdun Spong, being born in February 1916. The first month of the deployment was spent training, the battalion's initial experience of the trenches being near La Croix Barbe on 22 January 1916.

William was promoted to Corporal on 27 May 1916 and appointed as a Lance Serjeant on 29 June, and although the battalion did not participate on the first day of the Somme Offensive, it did take part in the 38th (Welsh) Division's famous fight at Mametz Wood. Commonwealth War Graves Commission information states

---

[281] Amalgamated with the 41st (The Welsh) Regiment of Foot on 01 July 1881 to become The Welsh Regiment

that he was *"made King's Serjt. At the Battle of Mametz Wood"* and his service record confirms a promotion to that rank on 10 July 1916. In just five days of combat, the largely Welsh (Pals) Battalions suffered over 4000 casualties in capturing and then holding the wood against battle-hardened Prussian troops. What is even more notable, is that William had tuberculosis that had started in June 1916, according to his medical records, meaning he took part in the heavy fighting with a debilitating cough.

This tuberculosis was to lead to his discharge from the army on 10 March 1917 and his medical records state that it was *"aggravated by active service"*. He died from the disease a year to the day after he was discharged and was buried in his hometown. He is also a "Lost Boy", as he has not been commemorated on the memorial tablets in the school chapel.

Alfred was discharged from the school on 14 August 1898 having been *"Detained off leave"*. Like his brother, little is known of his life until 1911 when he is recorded in the census of that year. It is known that he enlisted in the army during the war and was a Driver in the Army Service Corps, although he was discharged due to sickness on 03 October 1917. He died in Over Wallop, Hampshire, in 1940.

The Black Watch (Royal Highlanders)

Samuel Henry BISHOP
Corporal, 2376, 1st Battalion, The Black Watch (Royal Highlanders) who died on 21 August 1916, aged 19. Buried in Heilly Station Cemetery, Méricourt-L'Abbé, Somme, France

Born on 01 April 1897 in Winchester, Hampshire, the second of three children of Samuel Benjamin Bishop and Sarah Ann née Hannan, his father was a Lance Corporal in The Hampshire Regiment who deployed to South Africa in 1899 during the Second Boer War. He was wounded on 4 March 1900 in Koedoesrand, and evacuated to Kimberly, where he died on 4 April from enteric fever.

Samuel was admitted to the school on 05 October 1906 (Petition No. 12285), being joined by his younger brother, George Bishop, on 30 September 1909 (Petition No. 12671), after the school had made the transition from Chelsea to Guston. Samuel was discharged from the school on 25 June 1912, enlisting into The Black Watch (Royal Highlanders).

At the outbreak of war, 1st Battalion, The Black Watch, was stationed in Aldershot, Hampshire, but was quickly mobilised and landed at Le Havre on 14 August 1914. However, according to his medal index card, Samuel did not land in France until 12 October.

The battalion was then involved in all of the early battles of the war, as well as the major offensives of 1915, including Loos, and by August 1916 Samuel was a Corporal and stationed on the Somme, in trenches near Mametz Wood. He was wounded during an enemy air raid, dying of his wounds on 21 August 1916 and is one of nearly 2,400 British soldiers, 37 from The Black Watch, buried in Heilly Station Cemetery in the small commune of Méricourt-L'Abbé in the north of France. He is buried in a shared grave with Ernest Alfred Valentine, 2nd Battalion, The Suffolk Regiment.

Heilly Station Cemetery was begun in May 1916 and used by three medical units until April 1917. The burials in this cemetery were carried out under extreme pressure and many of the graves are either too close together to be marked individually, or they contain multiple burials, which explains why Samuel and Ernest have a shared grave marker.

George was discharged from the school on 17 March 1913, enlisting in the Royal Field Artillery, later transferring to the Royal Garrison Artillery in wartime. He remained in the army post-war and died in Portsmouth, Hampshire, in 1953.

George Alexander JOSEPH
Lance Corporal, 660, 1st Battalion, The Black Watch (Royal Highlanders) who died on 14 November 1914, aged 22. Buried in Chelmsford (Writtle Road) Cemetery, Essex, United Kingdom

Born on 02 July 1892 in Kennington, London, the fourth of five children of William Richard Joseph and Frances Elizabeth née Webb, his father had been a Private in the Prince of Wales's Own (West Yorkshire Regiment) who had been discharged to pension on 28 February 1888 and died in the Workhouse Infirmary in Lambeth, London, on 28 January 1898.

George was admitted to the school on 12 July 1902 (Petition No. 11707), joining his older brother, Albert John Joseph, who had been admitted on 10 August 1899 (Petition No. 11313). George was discharged on 13 July 1906, enlisting into The Black Watch (Royal Highlanders). Although his service record is no longer available, so his pre-war postings are unknown, it is likely that he was stationed in Castle Barracks, Limerick, County Limerick, in 1911, as that is where his brother, who was in the same regiment, was stationed when he married Rose Anna Anderson in that year, George being one of the witnesses at the wedding.

At the outbreak of war, George would have been serving alongside Dukie Samuel Bishop and would have landed at Le Havre on 14 August 1914. When the initial German assault came, on 24 August, the battalion was located at Merbes-Saint-Marie, 12 miles south-east of Mons, but was forced to withdraw before noon. It then took part in the retreat from Mons and fought during the Battles of the Marne and the Aisne and was involved in the "Race to the Sea", although the details of its participation are scant, as the battalion diary from mid-September to November is *'deficient'*[282].

What is known is that it was located near Ypres on 27 September 1914 when it came under heavy shellfire, during which George was severely wounded by shrapnel. He was evacuated to Britain and admitted to Hylands Auxiliary Military Hospital near Chelmsford, Essex. However, his condition deteriorated whilst in hospital and he

---

[282] WO 95/1263/3: 1 Battalion Black Watch (Royal Highlanders), 1914 Aug. - 1919 Mar., The National Archives, Kew

died on the evening of 14 November 1914 and was buried in the town's Writtle Road Cemetery with full military honours five days later, on 19 November 1914. Although he is commemorated on the memorial tablets in the school chapel, he is incorrectly recorded as J G Joseph.

Albert had also enlisted into The Black Watch (Royal Highlanders) when he was discharged from the school on 26 March 1904 and served in the 1st Battalion, although he was not posted to that battalion until 24 November 1914, ten days after his brother's death. He survived the war, dying in Bournemouth, Dorsetshire, on 17 November 1954.

Charles MELDRUM
Lance Corporal, 7849, 2nd Battalion, The Black Watch (Royal Highlanders) who died on 08 February 1915, aged 28. Buried in Le Touret Military Cemetery, Richebourg-L'avoue, Pas De Calais, France

Born on 17 June 1886 in Llangollen, Denbighshire, the fifth of six children of William Tindall Meldrum and Harriet Ann née Kent, his father had been a Troop Serjeant Major in the 16th (or Queen's) Lancers who had been discharged from the Regular Army on 03 August 1886 and was employed as Permanent Staff with the Denbighshire Hussars, a Yeomanry Regiment. He died on 05 September 1890 in Rhosllanerchrugog, Denbighshire.

Charles was admitted to the school on 03 January 1896 (Petition No. 10838) and was discharged to The Black Watch (Royal Highlanders) on 18 June 1900, and although his service record is no longer available, he is recorded in the 1911 Census as a Private with the 2nd Battalion, stationed in Sialkot, India.

At the outbreak of the war, the battalion was stationed in Bareilly, India, but returned to Europe, leaving on 21 September and landing at Marseille on 12 October 1914. During that year, it participated in the Battles of La Bassée, Messines, Armentières and Givenchy.

By February 1915, it was in the area of Richebourg-L'avoué, moving into the trenches on 01 February. During the course of the next week, the battalion suffered a small number of casualties each day, including on 08 February, three men wounded, one of whom later died of wounds. The soldier who died of wounds on 08 February 1915 was Charles Meldrum, who was buried in Le Touret Military Cemetery, close to where he fell. Although he is commemorated on the memorial tablets in the school chapel, he is incorrectly recorded as C *Meldum*.

Charles John ROBERTSON
Second Lieutenant, 1/6th (Perthshire) Battalion, The Black Watch (Royal Highlanders) who died on 22 March 1917, aged 34. Buried in Maroeuil British Cemetery, Pas de Calais, France

Born on 11 February 1883 in Colchester, Essex, the second of three children of Charles John Robertson and Julia Maynard née Rabett, his father had been a Quartermaster Sergeant in The Royal Inniskilling Fusiliers who had been discharged from the army on 27 July 1887 and died in Colchester, Essex, on 07 May 1891.

Charles was admitted to the school on 25 March 1892 (Petition No. 10302) and discharged on 13 February 1897, enlisting into The Black Watch (Royal Highlanders), although he was only serving for a month, before he was *"discharged on payment of £10 within 3 months of his attestation"* on 27 March 1897.

Following his discharge, the next fourteen years of his life are a mystery, although he is recorded in the 1901 Census living with his uncle in Westminster, London and employed as a Clerk, and he is also recorded as a Traveller (Twine) in the 1911 Census, now living with his older sister and her family in Balham, London. Two years later, he married Hilda Maud Smart in Wandsworth, London, their only son, Charles John Robertson, being born on 15 March 1914.

Following the outbreak of war, it appears that Charles re-enlisted into the army, joining the Seaforth Highlanders (Ross-shire Buffs, The Duke of Albany's). However, his service record for this period of service is not easily accessible as an officer, but his medal index card does state that he disembarked in France on 01 May 1915, the medal roll for the award of British War and Victory medals showing that he was serving in the 1/6th (Morayshire) Battalion, a Territorial Force battalion, which arrived in France on that date.

It is not possible to know all of Charles's movements, but according to the medal roll, he was an Acting Serjeant when he was Commissioned as a Second Lieutenant on 09 January 1917, although the London Gazette entry for this cannot be found. He was then posted to 1/6th (Perthshire) Battalion, The Black Watch (Royal Highlanders), another Territorial Force battalion that had landed in France at the same time as the 1/6th Seaforth Highlanders, Charles joining it on 10 January 1917.

In March 1917, the battalion was in the area of Maroeuil in France, moving into the trenches on 16 March. The tour of duty lasted six days and seems to have been a relatively quiet time. However, the battalion war diary reports that, on 22 March 1917, *"Battn. relieved by 1/7th Black Watch and moved to billets in MAROEUIL.*

Two O.R. slightly wounded; 2nd Lt C. .J. ROBERTSON killed while leading his platoon out after relief"[283].

Charles was buried in the village close to where he was killed, but he is another "Lost Boy" whose name has been omitted from the memorial tablets in the school chapel.

---

[283] WO 95/2876/2: 153 Infantry Brigade: 6 Battalion Black Watch (Royal Highlanders). 1917 Jan 1 - 1917 Aug 31, The National Archives, Kew

The Oxfordshire and Buckinghamshire Light Infantry

William Charles CRITCHER
Serjeant, 9573, 8th (Service) Battalion (Pioneers), The Oxfordshire and Buckinghamshire Light Infantry who died on 02 October 1915, aged 44. Buried in Etaples Military Cemetery, Pas de Calais, France

Born on 04 February 1871 in Malta, the eldest of three children of Charles Critcher and Eliza née Bennett, his father had been a Private in the 31st (Huntingdonshire) Regiment of Foot[284] who had been discharged from the army on 28 July 1874. His mother died in Bangor, Caernarvonshire, on 22 January 1879 and his father had remarried to Hannah Jones by the time of the 1881 Census, the family living in Bangor.

William was admitted to the school on 02 March 1883 (Petition No. 8912) and was *"Detained on pass"* on 11 August 1884. Within William's Petition Document, there is a letter from his father, dated August 1884, requesting that William be released from the school as his father had found him employment in Bangor.

On 16 December 1890, William enlisted in the Oxfordshire Light Infantry Militia, although his place of birth is recorded as Gibraltar[285] and he gave his name as Charles William Critcher, before he enlisted into the regular Oxfordshire Light Infantry on 29 January 1891. He was recorded in the 1891 Census serving in the 1st Battalion and stationed in New Barracks, Alverstoke, Hampshire.

Nine months after joining the regular army, William was posted to the 2nd Battalion and then to India on 09 October 1891, although he was only in this country for a month before he was posted to Burma on 16 November 1891. William spent seven years in Burma, during which time he was part of the Mohmand Field Force that was engaged in operations against the Hadda Mulla and Mohmand tribe on the North-West Frontier of India between 07 August and 01

---

[284] Amalgamated with the 70th (Surrey) Regiment of Foot on 01 July 1881 to become The East Surrey Regiment
[285] His father was posted to Gibraltar from Malta and there is no evidence of a Charles William Critcher being born in Gibraltar in 1871

October 1897, before he was posted back to Britain on 29 December 1898.

A year later, William was posted to South Africa during the Second Boer War, earning the Queen's South Africa medal with the clasps *Paardeberg*, *Driefontein* and the *Relief of Kimberley*, before he was posted back to Britain on 17 August 1902 and discharged from the army on 28 January 1903.

Soon after his discharge from the army, William married a widow named Edith Annie Franklin née Vickery and he, Edith, their two children and Edith's two children from her first marriage were then recorded in the 1911 Census living in Islington, London, with William employed as a Horse Helper for the London & North Western Railway.

It appears that following the outbreak of war, William re-enlisted into the army, joining the 8th (Service) Battalion (Pioneers) of his old regiment, although the exact date of his enlistment is not known as his service record for this period of service is no longer available.

The battalion that he joined had been formed at Oxford in September 1914 as part of K3 and was attached as Army Troops to the 26th Division, becoming a Pioneer Battalion in the division on 25 January 1915 and landing at Le Havre on 18 September 1915, the date shown on William's medal index card for his arrival in theatre.

William was in theatre for less than a month before he became unwell and was admitted to the 23rd General Hospital in Étaples, where he died of pleurisy on 02 October 1915. He was buried in the cemetery in the town, although he is commemorated by the Commonwealth War Graves Commission as Charles William Critcher and he is another "Lost Boy" whose name has been omitted from the memorial tablets in the school chapel.

Percy HAWKINS
Serjeant, 6765, 2/4th Battalion, The Oxfordshire and Buckinghamshire Light Infantry who died on 21 March 1918, aged 31. Commemorated on the Pozieres Memorial, Somme, France

Born on 15 January 1887 in Portsmouth, Hampshire, the youngest of three children of Henry Hawkins and Isabella née Ryan, his father had been a Serjeant in the 43rd (Monmouthshire) Regiment of Foot (Light Infantry) who had been discharged after 21 years' service on 11 August 1874 and who died in Portsmouth, Hampshire, on 09 April 1890.

Percy was admitted to the school on 13 July 1897 (Petition No. 11037), which was sixteen months after his older brother, Walter Richard Hawkins, who had been admitted to the school on 25

February 1893 (Petition No. 10448), had been discharged. Percy was discharged from the school on 26 January 1901 and enlisted into The Oxfordshire Light Infantry.

Percy's service record is no longer available, so his movements after he enlisted are mostly unknown, however, he is recorded in the 1911 Census as a Lance Corporal in the 1st Battalion of the regiment, by now named The Oxfordshire and Buckinghamshire Light Infantry, stationed in Wellington, India.

By the outbreak of war, it would appear that Percy had been posted to the 2nd Battalion, stationed in Aldershot as part of the 5th Brigade, 2nd Division, as the 1st Battalion was still stationed in India. He disembarked in France on 13 August 1914, which was when the 2nd Battalion arrived in theatre. Again, his movements during the first years of the war are unknown because his service record has not survived, but it is known that by March 1918 he was a Serjeant and serving with the 2/4th Battalion.

This battalion had been formed in September 1914 as a second line unit, moving to Northampton, Northamptonshire, in January 1915 where it was attached to the 184th Brigade, 61st (2nd South Midland) Division. It then moved to Writtle, Essex, before moving to Broomfield, Essex, in April 1915. In January 1916, the battalion moved to Parkhouse Camp on Salisbury Plain, Wiltshire, before landing in France four months later, on 24 May 1916.

When the German Army launched its Spring Offensive on 21 March 1918, the battalion was located at Fayet, Aisne. The battalion war diary[286] reports that there was a severe bombardment of high-explosive and gas shells that commenced at 0430hrs, which was followed at 0900hrs, by a strong German attack which penetrated the battalion's forward positions and surrounded the Enghien Redoubt, which was held by "D" Company and the Battalion Headquarters. Although this force was able to resist until 1600hrs, it was eventually forced to withdraw, the remainder of the battalion joining up with 2/5th Battalion, The Gloucestershire Regiment.

During the course of that day's fighting, the battalion lost 581 officers and other ranks killed, wounded and missing, including Percy. His body was never recovered, so he is commemorated on the Pozieres Memorial. He is also a "Lost Boy" whose name has been omitted from the memorial tablets in the school chapel.

When Walter was discharged from the school on 21 March 1896, he enlisted into the Royal Artillery. He was discharged after 12 years' service in 1908, but appears to have either been recalled to the

---

[286] WO 95/3067/1: 2/4 Battalion Oxfordshire and Buckinghamshire Light Infantry, 1915 Sept. - 1919 Mar., The National Archives, Kew

Colours or re-enlisted following the outbreak of war. It appears that he survived the war, but nothing more is known of him after that.

John James PEGRAM
Lance Corporal, 7567, 2nd Battalion, The Oxfordshire and Buckinghamshire Light Infantry who died on 12 November 1914, aged 26. Commemorated on the Ypres (Menin Gate) Memorial, West-Vlaanderen, Belgium

Born on 13 June 1888 in Oxford, Oxfordshire, the fourth of eight children of George Pegram and Priscilla May née North, his father was a Private in The Oxfordshire Light Infantry who died whilst still serving in Oxford on 26 November 1896.

John was admitted to the school on 05 November 1897 (Petition No. 11093), joining his older brother, Edward Richard Pegram, who had been admitted on 19 August 1898 (Petition No. 11055). He was also joined by his younger brother, Henry Reginald Pegram, on 18 July 1901 (Petition No. 11567) and John was then discharged from the school on 16 July 1903.

According to the school records, when he was discharged, John enlisted into the 2nd Dragoon Guards (Queen's Bays), but as his service record is no longer available this cannot be confirmed, but it is known that at some point he either transferred or enlisted into his father's old regiment, which was renamed The Oxfordshire and Buckinghamshire Light Infantry on 16 October 1908, and his service number suggests a 1904 enlistment.

At the outbreak of war, John was a Lance Corporal in the 2nd Battalion, which at that time was stationed in Aldershot, Hampshire. However, it quickly mobilised, embarking at Southampton, Hampshire, on 13 August and landing at Boulogne on 14 August 1914, initially moving to Wassigny, before marching north and crossing the Belgian frontier on 23 August.

On 24 August, it dug trenches at La Bouverie, five miles south-west of Mons, as a rear-guard position for the forward troops. However, by 0730hrs, it received news that the division to its right had had its flank turned and that the battalion was to retire, a retirement that would last until 08 September, when it participated in the First Battle of the Marne.

After the "Race to the Sea", the battalion was located in the Ypres Salient, taking part in the First Battle of Ypres. On 11 November it was ordered to an area north of the Ypres-Menin road in support of the Guards Brigade, which was experiencing heavy attacks and ordered to clear the Germans from Nonne Bosschen Wood, entrenching that evening to the left of Polygon Wood, where, the following day, it suffered several casualties due to German shelling.

401

Whether John was one of the seven other ranks killed, or whether he was the soldier posted as missing is not known, but he was reported as killed on 12 November 1914. He has no known grave and is one of the 54,607 casualties commemorated on the Menin Gate Memorial.

Edward was discharged from the school to The Oxfordshire Light Infantry on 12 May 1900 and Henry was *"Struck off Absent"* on 03 February 1905, although he enlisted into the Royal Artillery in June 1918.

Both of John's brothers served during the war and survived, Edward dying in Gosport, Hampshire in 1967 and Henry in Leeds, Yorkshire West Riding, in 1970.

William Henry SMITH

Bandsman, 8283, 2nd Battalion, The Oxfordshire and Buckinghamshire Light Infantry who died 09 February 1915, aged 22. Buried in Cowley (St. James) Churchyard, Oxfordshire, United Kingdom

Born on 18 August 1892 in Cowley, Oxfordshire, the youngest son of Samuel James Smith and Mary Louisa née Skinner, his father had been a Colour Serjeant in The Prince Consort's Own (Rifle Brigade). He died whilst still serving in Mullingar, County Westmeath, on 29 June 1901.

William was admitted to the school on 09 October 1902 (Petition No. 11740). This was six months after his mother had also died, in Oxford, on 16 April. He was discharged to The Oxfordshire Light Infantry on 30 August 1906.

William's service record is no longer available, but at the outbreak of war, he was a Bandsman in the 2nd Battalion, serving alongside Dukie John Pegram in Aldershot, Hampshire, landing at Boulogne on 14 August 1914 and fighting in the early battles of the war, prior to joining the long retreat from Mons, although he was back in Belgium for the subsidiary battles during the First Battle of Ypres, during which John was killed.

By early 1915 the battalion was in the area of Essars, north-east of Béthune. The month of January proved relatively quiet, the battalion suffering two casualties killed and three wounded. It would appear that William was one of those wounded, as he was reported as such in the *Birmingham Daily Post* on 06 February 1915, suggesting that he was probably one of the casualties sustained on 20 January. He was evacuated to No. 5 Southern General Hospital in Portsmouth, Hampshire, where he died of his wounds on 09 February 1915. He was interred in his hometown four days later.

The Essex Regiment

Ernest Philip Tower FIGG
Lance Serjeant, 5552, 1st Battalion, The Essex Regiment who died on 25 April 1915, aged 29. Commemorated on the Helles Memorial, Turkey

Born on 18 July 1885 in Colchester, Essex, the third of six children of Richard Figg and Charlotte née Fallowdown, his father had been a Colour Serjeant in The Essex Regiment who had been discharged to pension on 10 December 1891 and died in Newington, London, on 23 December 1894.

Ernest was admitted to the school on 25 January 1895 (Petition No. 10705) and was joined by his younger brother, Charles Figg, on 05 November 1897 (Petition No. 11083). Ernest was discharged to his father's old regiment on 28 September 1899 and although his service record is no longer available, so his pre-war career is unknown, at the outbreak of war, the 1st Battalion was stationed in Mauritius, but quickly returned to Britain, arriving in December 1914.

After a move to Banbury, Oxfordshire, on 18 January 1915, it then embarked at Avonmouth, Gloucestershire, on 21 March, travelling via Alexandria, Egypt, and Mudros before landing on the Gallipoli Peninsula on 25 April, the date shown on Ernest's medal index card as his first date in theatre. By this time, he was a Lance Sergeant.

The battalion was landed 0930hrs at Cape Helles, which began the land phase of the Gallipoli Campaign and was immediately under fire. By 1400hrs it had managed to make a small foothold by taking Hill 138 and the first enemy defensive fortification at the cost of three officers and fifteen other ranks killed, with eight officers and 87 other ranks injured, Ernest being one of the other ranks who died during the landing. He and all of the other Essex Regiment casualties killed that first day of the landings are commemorated on the Helles Memorial. He is also commemorated on the memorial tablets in the school chapel, but incorrectly recorded as E P F Figg.

Charles joined him in The Essex Regiment when he was discharged from the school on 12 February 1902. He survived the war, living until his eighties and dying in Plymouth, Devonshire, in 1970.

John Charles ONN
Serjeant, 2512, 6th Battalion, The Essex Regiment who died on 03 December 1914, aged 57. Buried in Colchester Cemetery, Essex, United Kingdom.

Born on 10 April 1857 in Chatham, Kent, the third of five children of Edmund Thompson Onn and Sarah Ann Terry née Daniel, his father had been a Colour Serjeant in the Royal Engineers who had served for 27 years before he was discharged on 26 October 1858. He died on 03 August 1867 in Dover, Kent.

John was admitted to the school on 02 January 1867 (Petition No. 7243), seemingly the only of the three sons to do so. He was recorded in the 1871 Census at the school in Chelsea and was discharged to the Royal Engineers on 18 April 1871.

He was to spend the first year of his service at the School of Military Engineering at Chatham, being appointed Bugler on 01 June 1872 and posted to the ranks as a Sapper on 01 May 1874. He proceeded to Bermuda with 10 Company, Royal Engineers on 24 January 1876 and remained there until the company was posted to Gibraltar on 18 November 1878.

He had been appointed Lance Corporal on 24 May 1876 and promoted to 2nd Corporal on 15 May 1879, when on 31 October 1880 he was tried by Regimental Courts Martial "for absence", being reduced to the ranks on 03 November 1880. However, the following day his sentence was remitted and he reverted to his former rank.

He served at Gibraltar until 19 June 1882, being promoted to Corporal on 01 December 1881, when he was posted to Halifax, Nova Scotia, where he served until 29 October 1884, having re-engaged for a second term of enlistment on 02 April 1884 and been promoted to Serjeant on 01 September 1884. He then returned home, before being posted to Egypt on 13 March 1885 with 10 Company, Royal Engineers for service in the Egyptian Campaign of 1885, later receiving the Egypt Medal with *Suakin 1885* clasp. He remained in Egypt until 07 July 1885, being then posted home.

On 24 July 1885 he was in trouble for absence once again and was reduced to the rank of Corporal via District Courts Martial in Portsmouth, Hampshire. He took his discharge at that rank on 31 May 1886 and had married Mary Josephine O'Sullivan in Portsmouth in April of that year. It is not known when she died, or if they divorced, but having been a civilian for fourteen years and married to a widow, Alice Ann Pearce on 23 February 1899 in Farnham, Surrey, he re-enlisted at Aldershot, Hampshire, on 31

March 1900, giving his occupation as Carpenter. It is possible that he had re-enlisted for service in the Second Boer War, but he remained at duty in Colchester, Essex, and was discharged as a Corporal on 26 February 1901, son John Charles Onn being born in the town on 07 June 1901.

This second discharge may have been procedural, as he re-enlisted the following day for a period of four years and resumed his service as a Corporal in Colchester, where his family had made their home. He served in South Africa from 23 December 1904 to 26 March 1905 with 55th Field Company, Royal Engineers, was discharged on the latter date in Pretoria and re-enlisted once more the following day, the reason for this procedure unknown. On 09 February 1906, he left South Africa and was discharged at Gosport, Hampshire, on 06 March 1906, having served for a total of twenty-one years.

John was recorded in the 1911 Census as living in Colchester with his wife and step-daughter-in-law, and employed as Store Clark (Army Pensioner), although his son John was not recorded. His final service record has not survived, but following the outbreak of war he enlisted for a fifth time, this time into The Essex Regiment and seemingly quickly promoted to Serjeant. He died from bronchitis and pneumonia on 03 December 1914 in Colchester and was buried in the town. He was commemorated by the Commonwealth War Graves Commission, but is another of the "Lost Boys" whose name has been omitted from the memorial tablets in the school chapel.

His stepson Albert Edward Pearce, was also a Dukie, being admitted to the school on 13 July 1897 and discharged to The Manchester Regiment on 19 January 1901 (Petition No. 11034). He was to serve until 1933, including spending most of the First World War on the Western Front, without ever being wounded, although two of his brothers fell in the war and another had died in the Second Boer War. He was Mentioned in Despatches in 1917, awarded the Belgian Croix de Guerre in 1918, appointed a Member of the British Empire in 1930 and finally awarded the Meritorious Service Medal on his retirement from the army. He died on 23 December 1958.

Joannes Leo SOUGHAN
Bandsman, 7737, 2nd Battalion, The Essex Regiment who died on 29 December 1914, aged 25. Buried in Calvaire (Essex) Military Cemetery, Hainaut, Belgium

Born Joannes[287] Leo Soughan on 11 December 1889 in Sheffield, Yorkshire West Riding, it appears that although named Joannes, he

---
[287] Latin for John

was always known by his second name, Leo. He was the fifth of six children of Thomas Patrick Soughan and Eliza née Barber and his father had been a Lance Corporal in The King's Own Light Infantry (South Yorkshire Regiment)[288], but was discharged from the army after 21 years' service on 19 May 1884, although he had abandoned his family in 1881.

Leo was admitted to the school on 04 January 1901 (Petition No. 11505) and was joined by his younger brother William Henry Soughan on 09 April 1903 (Petition No. 11827), eight months before he was discharged from the school to The Essex Regiment on 30 December 1903. His service record is no longer available, so his pre-war postings are unknown, but at the outbreak of war, the 2nd Battalion was stationed in Chatham, Kent. Over the next three weeks it moved to Cromer, Norfolk, and then Harrow, Middlesex, before landing at Le Havre on 24 August 1914.

After arrival in theatre, it came into action for the first time two days later, on 26 August, in the locality of Longsart, before participating in the long retreat and taking part in the Battles of Le Cateau and the Marne. In December the battalion moved into the trenches on the evening of Christmas Day, relieving 2nd Battalion, The Monmouthshire Regiment[289], so took no part in the fraternisation that was seen on the Western Front, but for the next three days had a *"peaceful"*[290] tour, suffering only three wounded up until 28 December.

On 29 December, the battalion was subjected to heavy German artillery fire during the day. One of the shells hit a house near the front-line that contained the Maxim gun detachment, killing three and wounding one, one of those killed being Leo, who was buried in Calvaire (Essex) Military Cemetery, so called because it had been started in November 1914 by 2nd Battalion, The Essex Regiment and 2nd Battalion, The Monmouthshire Regiment. Although Leo is commemorated on the memorial tablets in the school chapel, he is recorded as J Soughan.

William also enlisted into The Essex Regiment when he was discharged from the school on 26 April 1906. He is recorded in the 1911 Census as a Bandsman serving with the 1st Battalion in Quetta, India. However, it would appear that at some point in the next two years, he transferred to The Royal Warwickshire Regiment, as it was this regiment with which he was serving when he was discharged

---

[288] Renamed The King's Own Yorkshire Light Infantry in 1887 and The King's Own (Yorkshire Light Infantry) in 1902
[289] A Territorial Force Battalion that was part of the corps of The South Wales Borderers
[290] WO 95/1505/1: 2 Battalion Essex Regiment, 1914 Aug. - 1919 Feb., The National Archives, Kew

from the army as medically unfit for further service on 03 May 1913. He died in Colchester, Essex in 1968.

Leo and William had three older brothers, none of whom were Dukies. Their eldest brother, Thomas, was serving in The Essex Regiment when he was killed in action on 10 March 1900 at Driefontein, South Africa, during the Second Boer War and another of their brothers, Frank, was a Corporal in 1st Battalion, The Royal Warwickshire Regiment who was killed in action on 26 August 1914, in France.

William James TIPPER
Private, 19372, 1st Battalion, The Essex Regiment who died on 12 October 1916, aged 29. Commemorated on the Thiepval Memorial, Somme, France

Born on 12 July 1887 in Whittington, Staffordshire, the eldest of three children of William Benjamin Tipper and Alice née Gatcum, his father had been a Colour Serjeant in The Essex Regiment, but had been invalided out of the army after 17 years' service on 21 February 1896. He died six months later, on 15 August 1896 in Kingsholme, Gloucestershire. William's mother had pre-deceased his father by three years, dying on 26 September 1893 in Warley, Essex.

William was admitted to the school on 28 November 1896 (Petition No. 10963) and was discharged to his father's old regiment on 20 July 1901, spending the first year of his service in the Regimental Depot in Warley, before being transferred to the 1st Battalion and posted to India, where he was appointed as a Bandsman on 12 July 1905.

Having spent just over four years in India, William was then posted to Burma, on 13 December 1906 and two years later was posted back to India, on 12 December 1908. He was to spend the next five years here, being posted back to Britain on 12 November 1913 and discharged from the army at the end of his first period of service three days later.

It seems likely that he was recalled as a Special Reservist at the outbreak of war, although his service record has not survived for this second period of service, but it is known from medal records that he disembarked in the Egyptian theatre on 04 November 1915. His battalion was on the Gallipoli Peninsula at the time and it is likely that he joined as a replacement, before it was evacuated to Egypt on 08 January 1916 and subsequently moved to France in March of that year.

It is also likely that he went "over the top" on 1 July 1916 at the start of the Somme Offensive, when the battalion suffered over 200 casualties, including 35 dead, having been in reserve, but attacking at 1050hrs.

On 12 October 1916, the battalion was near to Gueudecourt and attacked Hilt Trench with The Newfoundland Regiment during the Battle of Le Transloy, which was fought between 01 and 18 October 1916. The initial objective was quickly captured and the battalion advanced to its final objective, Grease Trench, but a sharp German counterattack drove it back to the outskirts of Gueudecourt and the Newfoundlanders were forced to hold Hilt Trench with their flank exposed until being relieved that night.

The battalion suffered 88 killed that day, including William, and like him, 65 others have no known grave. His name is also omitted from the memorial tablets in the school chapel and he is therefore another of the "Lost Boys".

His brother, George Henry Tipper, who was not a Dukie, was a Sergeant in the 1st Battalion, Canadian Infantry and died of wounds from an accidental explosion on 20 July 1918 at Seaford, Sussex.

Alma Cecil VILE
Lance Corporal, 18862, 2nd Battalion, The Essex Regiment who died on 19 June 1917, aged 34. Buried in Brown's Copse Cemetery, Roeux, Pas de Calais, France

Born on 25 July 1882 in Chelsea, Middlesex, the youngest of seven children of Thomas Vile and Mary Ann née Challis, his father was a Private in the Scots Guards.

Alma was admitted to the school on 27 October 1893 (Petition No. 10537) and discharged to his father's old regiment on 25 July 1896. His brother, George Stephen Vile, had previously attended the school, having been admitted on 16 December 1887 (Petition No. 9594). Alma served in the Scots Guards for 12 years, spending the first two years of his service in the 1st Battalion and the remaining ten years being posted between the 2nd and 3rd Battalions. He was discharged from the army at the end of his first period of engagement on 24 July 1908.

After he left the army, Alma married Florence Gertrude Briston in Clapton, London, on 01 May 1910 and he is recorded in the 1911 Census, living with Florence and their one-month-old daughter, Gladys Winifred Vile, in Stoke Newington, London, with Alma being employed as a Grocer's Porter.

It is not known exactly when he re-enlisted following the outbreak of war, as there is no service record for this period of service, but it is known that he did so in Hackney, London, and that he enlisted into The Essex Regiment, suggesting that he was not recalled to the

Colours by his old regiment. It is also not known when he entered theatre, as there is no disembarkation date in his medal index card, but it is likely to have been 1916 at the earliest, as he did not qualify for the award of the 1914-15 Star.

The battalion to which he was posted, the 2nd Battalion, had been in France and Flanders since 28 August 1914, but because his service record is not available for that time, Alma's movements and which actions he participated in are not known.

In June 1917, his battalion was in the line at Roeux, east of Arras, when he was reported killed in action on 19 June 1917. The battalion war diary[291] records that *"one support line got rather badly shelled"*, with two other ranks being evacuated to the field ambulance and one missing. It is likely that Alma was one of the two evacuated as he was buried alongside a Private from the same battalion with the same date of death and was originally buried on the battlefield.

Although not recorded by the Commonwealth War Graves Commission, according to his medal records, at the time of his death he was an Acting Serjeant. He is also another "Lost Boy" whose name has been omitted from the memorial tablets in the school chapel.

George was discharged from the school on 06 February 1892 and enlisted into the 2nd Dragoon Guards (Queen's Bays) as a Musician. He had been discharged from the army on 05 February 1913, but it appears that he re-enlisted following the outbreak of war, serving with 1/5th Battalion, The Duke of Wellington's (West Riding Regiment), which landed at Boulogne on 14 April 1915. George was to spend a year with this battalion before being discharged for a second time on 14 July 1916. He died in Huddersfield, Yorkshire West Riding, in 1940.

Edward John WISE
Private, 13004, 10th (Service) Battalion, The Essex Regiment who died on 20 July 1916, aged 37. Commemorated on the Thiepval Memorial, Somme, France

Born on 21 October 1878 in Bethnal Green, Middlesex, the eldest of four children of John Wise and Frances née Blackford, his father had been a Sergeant in the 82nd (The Prince of Wales's Volunteers) Regiment of Foot[292] who had been discharged from the army on 12 September 1876.

Edward was admitted to the school on 22 February 1889 (Petition No. 9763) and was joined by his younger brother, Harry Roland

---

[291] WO 95/1505/1: 2 Battalion Essex Regiment, 1914 Aug. - 1919 Feb., The National Archives, Kew
[292] Amalgamated with 40th (2nd Somersetshire) Regiment of Foot on 01 July 1881 to become The Prince of Wales's Volunteers (South Lancashire Regiment)

Wise, on 29 November 1889 (Petition No. 9938). Edward was discharged from the school *"To mother"* on 22 October 1892.

Little is known about Edward in the ten years following his discharge, but it is known that he married Edith Sophia Priest in Bethnal Green, London, on 03 June 1899, with his occupation given as Wax House Man. He is also recorded in the 1901 Census as living in Bethnal Green with Sophia and employed as a Packer, Drapery. It is also known that their only daughter, Ethel Edith Wise, was born in 1901, but that she died in infancy.

By the time of the 1911 Census, Edward was living in Hackney, London. He had been widowed in 1908 and his father had died in 1911, so he was now living with his mother and still employed as a Draper's Porter. It appears that following the outbreak of war, Edward was a Kitchener volunteer, his service number suggesting that he joined the army between 24 August and 30 September 1914, enlisting into 10th (Service) Battalion, The Essex Regiment.

This battalion had been formed at Warley, Essex, in September 1914 as part of K2 and coming under the orders of the 53rd Brigade, 12th (Eastern) Division. It first moved to Shorncliffe, Kent, and then to Colchester, Essex, before finally moving to Codford St. Mary, Wiltshire, in May 1915 and landing at Boulogne on 26 July 1915. However, Edward's medal index card shows that he did not arrive in theatre until 02 September 1915.

The battalion remained in Brigade Reserve for two months after its arrival in France and it was not until 05 September 1915 that it had its first experience in the trenches, when it relieved 6th (Service) Battalion, The Princess Charlotte of Wales's (Royal Berkshire Regiment) near Bray.

By the following summer, the battalion were old hands of the front-line and on 30 June 1916, it moved into trenches which were part of the Carnoy defences on the Somme, going "over the top" at 0730hrs on the morning of 01 July 1916. Unlike many of the other battalions, it appears that the men of 10th Battalion met with some success in their assault and suffered only 30 men killed.

Almost three weeks later, on 20 July 1916, the battalion was in trenches in and around Delville Wood. That evening, all bar one company of the battalion was relieved by 4th Battalion, The Royal Fusiliers (City of London Regiment), but as it was making its way to Carnoy Valley, the Germans shelled all of the roads, resulting in the battalion suffering *"about a dozen casualties"*[293] and it is likely that Edward was one of these.

---

[293] WO 95/2038/2: 53 Infantry Brigade: 10 Battalion Essex Regiment, 1916 Jan 1 - 1916 July 31, The National Archives, Kew

Edward has no known grave, being commemorated on the Thiepval Memorial, but is also a "Lost Boy" whose name has been omitted from the memorial tablets in the school chapel.

Harry was discharged from the school *"To mother"* on 13 July 1894. He was recorded in the 1901 Census living in Shoreditch, London, with his wife, Eliza, and employed as an Umbrella Maker. He is then recorded in the 1911 Census living with Eliza and their four children in Shepherds Bush, London, and employed as a Motor Bus Conductor. No evidence could be found that he had served during the war, but he is recorded in the 1939 England and Wales Register as living with Eliza in Wandsworth, London, and employed as a Motor Car Washer. He died in Wandsworth in 1957.

The Sherwood Foresters
(Nottinghamshire and Derbyshire Regiment)

Thomas ENNIS
Serjeant Drummer, 5552, 1st Battalion, The Sherwood Foresters (Nottinghamshire and Derbyshire Regiment) who died on 08 July 1916, aged 33. Commemorated on the Thiepval Memorial, Somme, France

Born on 19 January 1883 in Portland, Dorsetshire, the eldest son of Thomas Ennis and Ellen née Callanan, his father had served in the 86th (Royal County Down) Regiment of Foot[294], the 83rd (County of Dublin) Regiment of Foot and was a Bombardier in the Royal Artillery when discharged to pension on 06 August 1878. He died in Portsmouth, Hampshire on 30 December 1892, two years after Thomas's mother had died in Portland, on 02 December 1890.

Thomas was admitted to the school on 24 February 1893 (Petition No. 10431) and was discharged on 30 January 1897, enlisting into The Sherwood Foresters (Derbyshire Regiment)[295]. Eleven months after Thomas was discharged from the school, his brother, Patrick James Ennis, was admitted on 03 December 1897 (Petition No. 11102).

On enlistment, Thomas joined the 1st Battalion and was posted to Malta eighteen months later. He was posted back to Britain in 1902 and stationed in Cork, County Cork, being appointed Lance Corporal in 1904 and Corporal in 1906. The following year, in February 1907, he married the daughter of a Private from his regiment, Annie Lillian Howard. Thomas was also re-engaged by the army in 1907 and posted to India in January 1909, where he was promoted to Serjeant Drummer a year later and where his two children, Cyril Stanley Ennis and Lillian Noeleen Ennis, were born.

At the outbreak of war, the 1st Battalion was stationed in Bombay, but quickly returned to Britain, landing at Plymouth, Devonshire, on 02 October 1914, before moving to Hursley Park in Hampshire. It was from here that it deployed to France, landing at Le Havre on 05 November 1914.

---

[294] Amalgamated with the 83rd (County of Dublin) Regiment of Foot on 01 July 1881 to become The Royal Irish Rifles
[295] Renamed The Sherwood Foresters (Nottinghamshire and Derbyshire Regiment) in 1902

The battalion participated in most of the battles of 1915, although it appears that Thomas was not with it for some of this time, as he had spent some time in hospital in early-1915, although the reason for this is unknown. In August 1915 he was granted six days home leave and it appears that he was then attached to the Divisional Train from his return, until re-joining the battalion in January 1916.

By July 1916 the battalion was stationed on the Somme. However, it was in reserve on the first day of the offensive, although it did participate in the opening battle, the Battle of Albert. Thomas was one of 529 soldiers from his regiment killed during the Battle of Albert, Thomas killed on 08 July 1916 and with no known grave.

When Thomas' brother Patrick was discharged from the school on 11 February 1902, he enlisted in the Army Service Corps. He survived the war and died in Greenwich, London, in 1975.

Herbert NEYNOE
Lance Serjeant, 5837, 2nd Battalion, The Sherwood Foresters (Nottinghamshire and Derbyshire Regiment) who died on 09 August 1915, aged 31. Commemorated on the Ypres (Menin Gate) Memorial, West-Vlaanderen, Belgium

Born on 02 February 1884 in Shardlow, Nottinghamshire, the fifth of eight children of Michael Neynoe and Mary Ellen née Campbell, his father had been a Colour Serjeant in The Sherwood Foresters (Derbyshire Regiment), who died in Salford, Lancashire, on 07 July 1893.

Herbert was admitted to the school on 31 August 1894 (Petition No. 10634) and discharged to his father's old regiment on 19 February 1898. Two of Herbert's four brothers, Percival Neynoe and George Neynoe, were admitted to the Royal Hibernian Military School, both joining their father's old regiment on discharge.

After spending seven months in the Regimental Depot at Normanton Barracks, Derby, Derbyshire, Herbert was posted to Malta with the 2nd Battalion, before being posted back to the Depot in December 1899. After five years there, he was posted to the Straits Settlements[296] and then to India for five years in 1906. In the 1911 Census he was serving with the 1st Battalion in Gough Barracks, Deccan, India.

In November 1911, he was posted back to the 2nd Battalion in Britain, which, at the outbreak of war was stationed in Sheffield, Yorkshire West Riding, moving first to Edinburgh, Midlothian, on 08 August, and then Cambridge, Cambridgeshire, on 15 August, before embarking at Southampton, Hampshire, on 08 September

---

[296] Penang, Province Wellesley, Singapore, Malacca and Dindings in South East Asia

and landing at St. Nazaire on 10 September 1914. It then went straight into action during the actions on the Aisne Heights, Herbert being appointed as a Lance Corporal in the wake of this action on 21 September.

In January 1915, Herbert was promoted to Corporal and was with the battalion when it was involved in the Second Battle of Ypres. It was still in the area of Ypres when Herbert suffered a gunshot wound to his right arm on 26 June, which was treated at 16 Field Ambulance, before he returned to duty a week later.

On 23 July, he was appointed as a Lance Serjeant and in August the battalion moved to Poperinghe, ready to attack at Hooge and moving into Sanctuary Wood by 0230hrs on 09 August, beginning its advance at 0310hrs.

Although the attack was successful, the battalion suffered eight officers and 337 other ranks killed, wounded and missing believed killed, one of those being Herbert Neynoe. His body was never recovered and he is one of 108 soldiers from his battalion who died that day and are commemorated on the Menin Gate Memorial. Although Herbert is also commemorated on the memorial tablets in the school chapel, he is incorrectly recorded as H *Meynoe*.

Percival was medically discharged from the army in 1911 and died in Salford, Lancashire in 1912. George served in the same battalion as Herbert during the war, which he survived. He died in Salford, Lancashire, in 1971.

Charles Deschamps RANDALL DCM
Captain, 9th (Service) Battalion, The Sherwood Foresters (Nottinghamshire and Derbyshire Regiment) who died on 09 August 1915, aged 39. Commemorated on the Helles Memorial, Turkey.

Born on 07 May 1876 in Bangalore, India, the second of five children of Charles Randall and his first wife, Julie née Channing, his father was a Colour Serjeant in the 35th (Royal Sussex) Regiment of Foot[297], but also seems to have served in the 107th (Bengal Infantry) Regiment of Foot and the 45th (Nottinghamshire) (Sherwood Foresters) Regiment of Foot[298]. He retired from the army on 05 May 1891, which was almost five years after Charles's mother had died on 04 December 1886.

Charles was admitted to the school on 01 June 1888 (Petition No. 9664) and discharged into The Sherwood Foresters (Derbyshire

---

[297] Amalgamated with the 107th Regiment of Foot (Bengal Light Infantry) on 01 July 1881 to become The Royal Sussex Regiment

[298] Amalgamated with the 95th (Derbyshire) Regiment of Foot on 01 July 1881 to become The Sherwood Foresters (Derbyshire Regiment)

Regiment) on 12 July 1890 and although his service record is no longer available, the 1891 Census records him serving with the 1st Battalion in Tregantle Fort, Cornwall. This was also the year before his younger brother, Sydney William Randall, was admitted to the school on 30 September 1892 (Petition No. 10372).

Charles served with the regiment in South Africa during the Second Boer War, by which time he was a Colour Serjeant. He was Mentioned in Despatches[299] and was also awarded the Distinguished Conduct Medal[300].

It appears that Charles later retired from the army as a Serjeant Major, becoming a Pensioner on 23 November 1911 and establishing a firm of Insurance Brokers, but at the outbreak of war, he re-enlisted into his old regiment in the same rank, although he was quickly Commissioned as a Temporary Lieutenant in the 9th (Service) Battalion on 16 November 1914[301]. This battalion had been formed as part of K1 in Derby, Derbyshire, in August 1914, and was initially located in Grantham, Lincolnshire. In April 1915 it was moved to Frensham, Surrey, Charles by this time having been promoted to Captain[302].

In early July, the battalion sailed from Liverpool, Lancashire, and landed at Cape Helles, Gallipoli on 21 July 1915, suffering its first casualty three days later, on 24 July, when Major Fielding, "C" Company Commander, was killed, with Charles then assuming command of this company.

Charles described the conditions to a Miss Fielding in a letter that was published in a local newspaper[303] after his death:

"There has been a dust storm blowing all day. We each of us are a mass of flies, and these factors, together with the excessive heat and most abominable stench, turn one from food, drink, sleep, and concentration of purpose. We have not had many casualties during our ten days in the trenches, but the exceptional conditions which prevail are much worse than actual fighting. The front line of trenches is nothing but a huge graveyard, and many hundreds of bodies still lie unburied. As these are a month old they make their presence felt in many respects. We were putting out wire entanglements a few nights ago, and to do so had to crawl through countless bodies, but contact with these was infinitely preferable to exposing oneself to a Turkish bullet. There is no "off time" on the Peninsula, and the firing goes on for ever. I am pleased to say the men are splendid, although they have not been put to a very severe test of fighting

---

[299] *The London Gazette*, 10 September 1901, Issue:27353
[300] *The London Gazette*, 27 September 1901, Issue:27359
[301] *The London Gazette*, 13 November 1914, Issue:28976
[302] *The London Gazette*, 5 January 1915, Issue:29030
[303] *Mansfield Reporter*, Friday 10 September 1915

yet. We have earned a great deal of praise from the powers that be. I am in command of C Company now, Major Fielding being killed the second day whilst talking to me. Our next period will, I think, be hell, so I must ask you to notice the casualty lists'.

The battalion was relieved by the French on 01 August and sailed for Suvla Bay, landing on 07 August 1915. Two days after landing, it moved to take up the line close to Damak Jelik Bair and proceeded to make several unsuccessful attempts to rush and capture the Turkish trenches opposite, until it was withdrawn on 10 August and relieved by 5th Battalion, The Northumberland Fusiliers at 1600hrs. It is likely that Charles was killed during one of the attacks on 09 August 1915. His body was never recovered and he is one of the 20,905 soldiers commemorated on the Helles Memorial.

Sydney enlisted into The Devonshire Regiment when he was discharged from the school on 05 September 1896 and also served during the war. As an Acting Serjeant Major in the 2nd Battalion, he was awarded the Meritorious Service Medal[304], dying in Salisbury, Wiltshire, in 1951.

---

[304] *The London Gazette*, 17 January 1919, Supplement:31132

The Loyal North Lancashire Regiment

George Patrick DARCEY
Lance Corporal, 3914, 1st Battalion, The Loyal North Lancashire Regiment who died on 27 September 1915, aged 24. Buried in Gosnay Communal Cemetery, Pas De Calais, France

Born on 03 March 1880 in Chatham, Kent, the seventh of ten children of Patrick Darcey and Jane née Cahill, his father was the Bandmaster of The Loyal North Lancashire Regiment who died in 1886.

George was admitted to the school on 25 July 1890 (Petition No. 10034), joining his older brother, Charles Patrick Darcey, who had been admitted on 24 August 1888 (Petition No. 9682). He was joined by his younger brother, William Leonard Darcey, on 27 October 1893 (Petition No. 10535). George was discharged to his father's old regiment on 03 March 1894 and was then posted in 1895 with the 1st Battalion to the East Indies, spending a year there, before being posted to Ceylon in February 1896. After three years there, he was posted to South Africa during the Second Boer War on 11 February 1899, where he was awarded both the Queen's and King's South Africa medals, with three clasps for the former and two for the latter, before he was posted back to Britain on 18 September 1902. It appears that he was then stationed in Ireland, as he married Annie Farren in Kinsale, County Cork, in September 1906.

The 1911 Census records George stationed in Bhurtpore Barracks, Tidworth, Wiltshire, and still serving with the 1st Battalion, although it appears that the battalion had returned to Kinsale by the end of the year, where George was widowed on 29 December 1911.

At the outbreak of war, the battalion was stationed in North Camp, Aldershot, Hampshire, embarking at Southampton, Hampshire, on 12 August and landing at Le Havre on 13 August 1914, crossing the frontier into Belgium ten days later and coming into action for the first time on 24 August during the Battle of Mons. It was then involved in the subsequent retreat from Mons, before again fighting during the Battles of the Marne, of the Aisne and the First Battle of Ypres.

In May of 1915, it participated in the Battle of Aubers and then, in September, the Battle of Loos. On the morning of the 25 September, the attack began with the release of gas, but as soon as this was released the wind blew it back onto the battalion's trenches. It appears that George was wounded on this day, though whether he was one of the 55 victims of the gas, or received another wound is not known, but it is known that he died of his wounds on 27 September 1915 in Gosnay. Although commemorated on the memorial tablets in the school chapel, his name is incorrectly recorded as *Darcy*.

Charles was discharged from the school to The Loyal North Lancashire Regiment on 02 January 1892, serving with the 2nd Battalion during the war. He survived the conflict and died in 1941.

William was discharged *"To Mother"* on 26 February 1898, and died the following year, aged only sixteen.

The Northamptonshire Regiment

Enas Jonathan Harry Collier BROMWICH
Lance Corporal, 9148, 1st Battalion, The Northamptonshire Regiment who died on 18 July 1916, aged 20. Buried in Contalmaison Chateau Cemetery, Somme, France

Born on 24 March 1896 in Rugby, Warwickshire, the second of four children of Jonathan Bromwich and Rose Annie née Collier, his father was a Private serving in 2nd Battalion, The Northamptonshire Regiment, who died of disease on 12 October 1900 at Kroonstad, South Africa, during the Second Boer War.

Enas was admitted to the school on 15 February 1907 (Petition No. 12331) and would have made the move from Chelsea to Guston before he was discharged on 27 May 1910, enlisting into his father's old regiment. He was initially posted to the 2nd Battalion and spent the first year of his service in Britain, having been posted to the 1st Battalion on 14 March 1911, before re-joining the 2nd Battalion and being posted to Malta on 08 September 1911.

In January 1914, this battalion was posted to Egypt, and stationed in Alexandria, but returned to Britain in October and landed at Le Havre on 05 November 1914. It remained on the Western Front, participating in the Second Battle of Ypres in 1915 and, on 09 May, it participated in the Battle of Aubers, during which Enas was wounded, sustaining a gunshot wound to the right heel and right upper arm. This resulted in him being evacuated back to Britain and treated in Lewisham Military Hospital, London.

After recuperating for nine months, he returned to France on 18 February 1916, although he was then admitted to No. 6 Stationary Hospital in Le Havre on 02 March, suffering from influenza. He was discharged ten days later to the Convalescent Depot, spending seventeen days there prior to being posted to the 1st Battalion.

Although the battalion did not participate in the main attack on 01 July 1916, it did participate in the later battles of the Somme Offensive and on 18 July it was located in trenches north-east of Contalmaison where it was subjected to heavy artillery fire in the village line, suffering one officer and twelve other ranks killed, with 25 wounded, one of those killed being Enas. He was buried in

Contalmaison Chateau Cemetery along with seven other Northamptonshire Regiment soldiers killed on the same day.

Although commemorated on the memorial tablets in the school chapel, his regiment is incorrectly recorded as The Duke of Cambridge's Own (Middlesex Regiment).

George Alexander HAYMAN

Private, 9212, 2nd Battalion, The Northamptonshire Regiment who died on 09 May 1915, aged 21. Commemorated on the Ploegsteert Memorial, Hainaut, Belgium

Born on 22 January 1894 in Wigston, Leicestershire, the fourth of five children of Robert Hayman and Clara née Blayney, his father had been a Private in The Northamptonshire Regiment who had been discharged from the army on 28 January 1889 and died in Leicester, Leicestershire, on 09 September 1904.

George was admitted to the school on 11 February 1905 (Petition No. 12086) and, after making the transition from Chelsea to Guston, was discharged to The Northamptonshire Regiment on 16 September 1910. Although his service record is no longer available, he is recorded in the 1911 Census serving in Malta with the 2nd Battalion.

When war broke out, the battalion was in Alexandria, Egypt, but returned to Britain, landing at Liverpool, Lancashire, on 16 October. After a brief stay at Hursley Park near Winchester, Hampshire, it then landed at Le Havre on 05 November 1914, entering trenches for the first time south of the Pont Logy to Fleurbaix road on 14 November.

It was in trenches on Christmas Day 1914 and the battalion war diary reports that soldiers from the battalion met with their German counterparts in "No-Man's Land", although it was also documented that the friendly advances from the Germans were designed to lull the British into a false sense of security prior to an attack.

It then spent much of the early months of 1915 in the trenches, participating in the Battle of Neuve Chapelle in March, during which it suffered seven officers and 102 other ranks killed.

At the end of April, it was still in trenches near Neuve Chapelle where, on 25 April, it received news of the *"Germans opposite French north of Ypres were using asphyxiating gases"*[305], the battalion being issued masks to *"counteract the effect of noxious gases"*[306] on 02 May 1915, prior to being relieved by The Sherwood Foresters the following day.

---

[305] WO 95/1722/1: 24 Infantry Brigade: 2 Battalion Northamptonshire Regiment, 1914 Aug 1 - 1915 Sept 30, The National Archives, Kew
[306] Ibid.

It was only to be out of the line for five days before it was again moved into trenches near Sailly on 08 May in preparation for the offensive action that would become known as the Battle of Aubers Ridge, which was to commence on 09 May.

The offensive was not a success for the British, with the battalion failing to capture any of its objectives. George was one of the twelve officers and 414 other ranks that were killed, wounded or reported missing from the battalion on the day of the attack. His body was never recovered and he is commemorated on the Ploegsteert Memorial.

Herbert Eric Charles KENDALL
Lance Serjeant, 8777, 2nd Battalion, The Northamptonshire Regiment who died on 14 March 1915, aged 23. Commemorated on the Le Touret Memorial, Pas de Calais, France

Born on 10 October 1891 in Cawnpore, India, the eldest of three children of Charles Kendall and Anne Helena Maude née Mullane, his father had served for 17 years in The Lincolnshire Regiment, before transferring to the Indian Ordnance Department. His mother died in Poona, India, on 19 October 1900, after which his father remarried, on 04 March 1902 in Northampton, Northamptonshire, to Mary Watts. Following the outbreak of war, his father re-enlisted in December 1914 into the Army Ordnance Corps. He served in France for three months in late 1915, before being invalided to Britain with myalgia. He died of tuberculosis three days after his discharge, on 02 March 1917, being commemorated by the Commonwealth War Graves Commission in Northampton (Towcester Road) Cemetery, Northamptonshire.

Herbert was admitted to the school on 08 May 1902 (Petition No. 11688) and was joined by his younger brother, Percy Hamilton Kendall, eighteen months later on 04 December 1903 (Petition No. 11914). Herbert was discharged from the school on 19 October 1905 and enlisted into the Army Service Corps.

Herbert's time in this corps was short-lived, as he was discharged on 11 September 1906 *"Services no longer required"*. However, it then appears that he re-enlisted, this time joining The Northamptonshire Regiment, his service number suggesting an enlistment sometime between 06 February 1908 and 21 January 1909, although there is no service record available for this second period of service. However, he is recorded in the 1911 Census as a Private in 2nd Battalion, The Northamptonshire Regiment, stationed in Floriana Barracks, Malta, where he would have served alongside Dukies Enas Bromwich, George Hayman and Stephen Lennon. He would also have been stationed in Egypt when war broke out, returning to Britain briefly, before landing in France on 06 November 1914.

Herbert's first four months in theatre, from November 1914, would have been the same as those of George Hayman and in March 1915 the battalion participated in the Battle of Neuve Chapelle, suffering heavy casualties, particularly among the officers, with just three of the 22 officers who had been with the battalion on the day before the battle commenced, on 10 March 1915, still with the battalion three days later.

Among the 161 casualties that the battalion suffered during the battle was Herbert, who was reported to have died on the 14 March 1915, although it is likely that he had died during the fighting of the previous three days and had not been reported as such until the first available day that it was possible to do so, the battalion being in billets on 14 March. It appears that his body was never recovered, as he is commemorated on the Le Touret Memorial. He is also another of the "Lost Boys" whose name has been omitted from the memorial tablets in the school chapel.

Percy was discharged from the school on 14 February 1907 and enlisted into the Royal Field Artillery. He served throughout the war, marrying in 1916. He is recorded in the 1939 England and Wales Register as living in Exeter, Devonshire, employed as a College Groundsman. He died in Exeter in 1960.

Stephen William LENNON

Lance Corporal, 8440, 2nd Battalion, The Northamptonshire Regiment who died on 27 May 1918, aged 25. Commemorated on the Soissons Memorial, Aisne, France

Born on 14 February 1893 in Bangalore, India, the eldest of three sons of Stephen Lennon and Margaret Ellen née Underhill, his father had been a Serjeant in The Northamptonshire Regiment who was discharged from the army on 22 February 1899 and died in Leicester, Leicestershire, seven months later, on 14 September 1899.

Stephen was admitted to the school on 05 September 1902 (Petition No. 11730) and was joined by his younger brother, James Richard Lennon, on 09 February 1906 (Petition No. 12189). A third brother, John Lennon, was also a Dukie, admitted to the school on 01 September 1909 (Petition No. 12643), by which time both of his older brothers had already been discharged. Stephen was discharged on 01 March 1907 and enlisted into his father's old regiment. Although his service record is no longer available, he is recorded in the 1911 Census stationed in Floriana Barracks, Malta, and a Private in the 2nd Battalion.

When war broke out, Stephen was serving alongside George Hayman in Alexandria, Egypt, from where he departed aboard HMT *Deseado* on 26 September and after a period of training in Britain, he landed at Le Havre on 05 November 1914.

The battalion was in the trenches south of Fleurbaix eight days later, where it experienced heavy shelling on 15 November and suffered its first man killed. For the next three years, it was involved in many of the well-known battles on the Western Front, including the Battle of Albert, during the early stages of the Somme Offensive, and the Battle of Langemarck during the Third Battle of Ypres.

Having survived this long, Stephen was with his battalion in trenches opposite Juvincourt, where, on 27 May 1918, it was subjected to a four-hour bombardment of high-explosive and gas shells, commencing at 0100hrs. This was followed by a surprise attack by the Germans that resulted in the battalion being completely surrounded. However, it was able to extricate itself from this situation, but not without suffering heavy casualties, Stephen being one of the men who died on 27 May 1918. His body was not recovered and he is commemorated on the Soissons Memorial.

James was discharged from the school on 04 March 1909 enlisting into The Royal Fusiliers (City of London Regiment) and his brother John was discharged on 24 July 1914, enlisting into the 5th (Royal Irish) Lancers. Both brothers served during the war and both emigrated to the United States, each dying in 1970, James in Cleveland, Ohio and John in New York.

The Princess Charlotte of Wales's (Royal Berkshire Regiment)

Walter BRINDLE
Corporal, 9772, 1st Battalion, The Princess Charlotte of Wales's (Royal Berkshire Regiment) who died on 25 August 1914, aged 21. Buried in Maroilles Communal Cemetery, Nord, France

Born on 11 February 1893 in Castle Eaton, Wiltshire, the sixth of seven sons of Joseph Brindle and Mary nee Tuckwell, his father had been a Lance Corporal in The Duke of Edinburgh's (Wiltshire Regiment), who was discharged from the army after 16 years' service on 27 March 1894. He died in Marlborough, Wiltshire, on 29 December 1901.

Walter was admitted to the school on 04 March 1904 (Petition No. 11947), joining his older brother, Leonard Brindle, who had been admitted on 14 October 1902 (Petition No. 11748). Walter was discharged on 21 February 1907, enlisting into The Princess Charlotte of Wales's (Royal Berkshire Regiment), although there is no service record available to confirm this and to follow his pre-war career. Two years after his discharge from the school, his younger brother, Frank Brindle, was admitted on 28 August 1909 (Petition No. 12595).

When the war commenced, 1st Battalion, The Royal Berkshire Regiment, was stationed in Aldershot, Hampshire, but following mobilisation it embarked at Southampton, Hampshire, on 12 August and landed at Rouen on 13 August 1914. It crossed the Belgian frontier ten days later, taking up positions south-east of Mons, from where it could hear battle taking place in the town of Mons itself. The following day it received orders to retire, which it did with the remainder of the British Expeditionary Force and on 25 August it was in the area of Bavai where it stood to at 0430hrs and was in action as the brigade rear-guard, soon arriving in Maroilles, where it was located close to the southern end of the bridge in the town. During the action in which the battalion was engaged it was reported that:

"Tragically, many of the wounded fell down the steep banks and drowned. Drummer Henry Savage was one of those who was floundering in deep

water and was rescued by Corporal Walter Brindle. 'Several men could not swim', Savage later told the Berkshire Gazette, 'and were drowning when Corporal Brindle under heavy fire, plunged in and rescued a number of men. He had just completed his task and was emerging from the water when a shell struck him, killing him on the spot'."[307]

Although Walter is commemorated on the memorial tablets in the school chapel, his name is incorrectly recorded as *Brindall*.

Leonard was discharged from the school on 23 March 1905, enlisting into the Royal Army Medical Corps. He served during the war, being awarded the Meritorious Service Medal[308] and was Commissioned into the Territorial Army in 1930. He was appointed as a Member of the Most Excellent Order of the British Empire (MBE) in 1938[309] and served throughout the Second World War, being awarded the Territorial Army Efficiency Decoration in 1945[310]. Although his awards are recognised by inclusion on the Honours Board in the Adjutant General's room in the school, like his brother he is incorrectly recorded as Brindall. He died in Stepney, London, in 1968.

Frank was discharged from the school on 09 July 1912 and also enlisted into the Royal Army Medical Corps. He survived the war and remained in the medical field following his discharge from the army, recorded as a "Mental Nurse" in the 1939 England and Wales Register, living in Devizes, Wiltshire, the town in which he died at the age of 64 in 1962.

Walter also had another older brother, Henry Joseph Brindle, who was not a Dukie, but who also died during the war. He was a Private in 6th Battalion, The Princess Charlotte of Wales's (Royal Berkshire Regiment), when he died of wounds on 31 July 1917. He is buried in Lijssenthoek Military Cemetery in Belgium.

Bertie KNIGHT
Private, 7868, 2nd Battalion, The Princess Charlotte of Wales's (Royal Berkshire Regiment) who died on 25 September 1915, aged 24. Commemorated on the Ploegsteert Memorial, Hainaut, Belgium

Born on 17 December 1890 in Templemore, County Tipperary, the eldest of five children of James Horace Knight and Martha née Dale, his father had been a Serjeant in The Princess Charlotte of

---

[307] Cooksey, J. & Murland, J. (2014). *The Retreat from Mons 1914: North: Casteau to Le Cateau, The Western Front by Car by Bike and on Foot*. Barnsley: Pen and Sword
[308] *The London Gazette*, 30 May 1919, Issue:31370
[309] *The London Gazette*, 30 December 1938, Supplement:34585
[310] *The London Gazette*, 12 June 1945, Supplement:37129

Wales's (Royal Berkshire Regiment), but had died whilst serving in South Africa on 10 September 1899.

Bertie was admitted to the school on 04 May 1900 (Petition No. 11433), remaining there for four years before being discharged on 27 December 1904 and enlisting in his father's old regiment. Although his service record is no longer available to confirm his pre-war postings, the 1911 Census records him as a Private in the 2nd Battalion, stationed in Meerut, India.

At the outbreak of war, the battalion was still stationed in India, although it had moved to Jhansi, but it quickly returned to Britain, landing in Liverpool, Lancashire, on 12 October, before moving to Hursley Park Camp, Winchester, Hampshire, and then embarking at Southampton, Hampshire, twelve days later and landing at Le Havre on 05 November 1914. It moved into the trenches near Fauqissart nine days after landing and suffered its first casualties during the four days in which it occupied these positions.

It was also in the front line on Christmas Day, when it is documented, that men got up on the parapet and advanced halfway to the German trenches *"and in some cases conversed with them"*[311], until orders were given at 1100hrs prohibiting men from going beyond the parapet.

The battalion spent much of early-1915 in the same locale, but on 09 March it took up positions for the attack on Neuve Chapelle, an attack that led to casualties great enough for it to require drafts from Britain in order to reform.

Despite this, it remained on the Western Front throughout the summer, and in September it was back in action. On 24 September it moved into trenches near Bois-Grenier ready for an assault on the German lines the following day, part of the diversionary attacks supporting the Battle of Loos.

The assault was launched the following morning with the battalion suffering seven officers killed and five wounded, although it suffered many more casualties among the other ranks, 32 killed, 216 wounded and 143 missing, one of those missing being Bertie, who died during that attack on 25 September 1915. His body was never recovered and he is commemorated on the Ploegsteert Memorial.

---

[311] WO 95/1729/1: 2 Battalion Royal Berkshire Regiment, 1914 Oct. - 1919 Apr., The National Archives, Kew

Arthur Henry MAIN
Private, 37913, 1/4th Battalion, The Princess Charlotte of Wales's (Royal Berkshire Regiment) who died on 07 August 1917, aged 29. Commemorated on the Ypres (Menin Gate) Memorial, West-Vlaanderen, Belgium

Born on 21 January 1888 in Gibraltar, the youngest of two children of Alexander Dehors Main and Julia née Sweeney, his father had been a Colour Serjeant in The Queen's Own (Royal West Kent Regiment), who had been discharged after 22 years' service on 02 April 1894. He died in Hampstead, London, on 10 April 1897.

Arthur was admitted to the school on 07 January 1898 (Petition No. 11120) and was *"Returned to mother"* on 22 January 1902. Little is known about his life after he was discharged from the school, although he married Constance Emily Benham in Kilburn, London, in 1910 and was recorded in the 1911 Census as a Gas Fitter living with his wife in Kentish Town, London.

Because his service record is no longer available, it can be surmised that a married man of his age, with seemingly no prior service, joined the army after the Military Service Act came into force on 02 March 1916.

His date of disembarkation is not recorded in the medal records and as he was not awarded the 1914-15 Star, he was not in France & Flanders until 1916 at the earliest, although 1/4th Battalion, The Royal Berkshire Regiment, a Territorial Force battalion that was located in Reading at the outbreak of war, had landed at Boulogne on 31 March 1915.

Although the battalion did not attack on the first day of the Somme Offensive, it was in action at Pozières two weeks later, and it is possible that Arthur participated in this attack, which saw his battalion suffer more than 230 casualties in six days. It was also engaged in pursuing the German Army as it retreated to the prepared positions at the Hindenburg Line in 1917.

The next major action for the battalion was during the offensive that was launched on 31 July 1917, which became known as the Third Battle of Ypres. A great storm on 31 July 1917 heralded a month of unprecedented rain, with the battalion moving up on 05 August 1917 to relieve 183rd Brigade south of St. Julien. It remained in flooded trenches under incessant shellfire for four days, suffering 11 killed and 31 wounded, including Arthur, who was killed two days after arriving in these positions. He has no known grave and is commemorated on the Menin Gate Memorial. His name has also been omitted from the memorial tablets in the school chapel and he is therefore another "Lost Boy".

William Kennedy RYAN

Company Serjeant Major, 10397, 8th (Service) Battalion, The Princess Charlotte of Wales's (Royal Berkshire Regiment) who died on 25 September 1915, aged 42. Commemorated on the Loos Memorial, Pas de Calais, France

Born on 17 February 1873 in Calcutta, India, a son of Jeremiah Ryan and Teresa née O'Brien, his father was a Serjeant Major in the 107th Regiment of Foot (Bengal Light Infantry) who died whilst serving in Calcutta on 28 June 1873. William's mother remarried to William Lemmon, a Serjeant in the 66th (Berkshire) Regiment of Foot[312], but died in Karachi, India, on 23 October 1880. It was therefore William's stepfather who completed his Petition Document.

William was admitted to the school on 04 May 1883 (Petition No. 8948) and was discharged at the age of 12 on 11 April 1885, his uncle, who had served in the 14th (Buckinghamshire – The Prince of Wales's Own) Regiment of Foot[313] becoming his next of kin. Three weeks after his fourteenth birthday, on 12 March 1887, William enlisted in The Princess Charlotte of Wales's (Royal Berkshire Regiment). He was appointed as a Drummer in June 1887, before being appointed a Lance Corporal in 1895 and promoted to Corporal in 1897.

He was then posted with his battalion to South Africa on 13 February 1898, where he was appointed as a Lance Serjeant two months later. During his time in South Africa, the second Boer War commenced and he earned the Queen's South Africa Medal with the clasps *Cape Colony*, *Orange Free State* and *Transvaal*, as well as the King's South Africa Medal with the clasp *South Africa 1901* before returning home in April 1901. However, he was only home for five months before returning to South Africa for another year, earning the *South Africa 1902* clasp.

His next posting was to Egypt in 1902, where he spent four years before returning home in 1906 and being discharged from the army in Newbridge, County Kildare, on 11 March 1908, at the end of his period of service.

In 1910, William married Jane Barry and was recorded in the 1911 Census living in Upton Park, Essex, working as a Night Watchman at the Bryant and May match factory. Their son, also William Ryan, was born in 1915.

---

[312] Amalgamated with the 49th (Princess Charlotte of Wales's) (Hertfordshire) Regiment of Foot on 01 July 1881 to become The Princess Charlotte of Wales's (Berkshire Regiment)
[313] Renamed The Prince of Wales's Own (West Yorkshire Regiment) on 01 July 1881

William re-enlisted after the war commenced, although this service record is no longer available, joining the 8th (Service) Battalion of his old regiment. This battalion was formed at Reading, Berkshire, in September 1914 as part of K3 and embarked at Southampton, Hampshire, on 07 August 1915, landing at Le Havre the following day. Its first experience of the front line was on 18 September, when it supplied a working party to carry cylinders of chlorine gas to the front-line trenches in preparation for the offensive that was about to be launched at Loos.

On 23 September, it moved into the trenches at Sailly-Labourse and two days later, at 0550hrs, the German positions were bombarded and the gas was released. At 0628hrs, the gas ceased and smoke bombs were thrown to mask the assault, which commenced two minutes later. However, it was discovered that the German wire had been scarcely damaged and the delay here, plus the wind blowing the gas back onto the assaulting troops, caused heavy casualties to the battalion, including William, who died on 25 September 1915. His body was never recovered and he is commemorated on the Loos Memorial.

James Edward SMITH
Private, 45986, 8th (Service) Battalion, The Princess Charlotte of Wales's (Royal Berkshire Regiment) who died on 05 September 1918, aged 18. Buried in Mericourt-l'Abbe Communal Cemetery Extension, Somme, France

Born on 06 August 1900 in Portsmouth, Hampshire, the youngest of two sons of James Edward Smith and Cecilia Blanche Adelaide née Farncombe, his father was a Lance Corporal in the Army Service Corps, who died in Portsmouth whilst still serving, on 06 August 1902.

James was admitted to the school on 31 October 1911 (Petition No. 12924) and discharged on 16 March 1914, enlisting into the Army Service Corps as a Clerk. James was still serving at the outbreak of war in August 1914, but two months later, on 05 October 1914, he was discharged, *"services no longer required"*, although the reason for this is not recorded in his service record.

Following his discharge, James later re-enlisted in Winchester, Hampshire, likely conscripted, first joining The Devonshire Regiment and then going overseas with The Princess Charlotte of Wales's (Royal Berkshire Regiment), however there is little information for his second period of service as this service record has not survived.

What is known is that the battalion to which he was posted, 8th (Service) Battalion, had been formed at Reading, Berkshire, in

September 1914 as part of K3 and was attached as Army Troops to the 26th Division. It initially moved to billets on Salisbury Plain, Wiltshire, returning to Reading in November 1914, before moving to Sutton Veny, Wiltshire, in May 1915. On 08 August 1915, the battalion landed at Le Havre, transferring to the 1st Brigade, 1st Division, before, on 02 February 1918, it transferred to 53rd Brigade, 18th (Eastern) Division.

However, due to his age, it is unlikely that James joined the battalion until 1918, although there is no disembarkation date recorded in his medal index card.

James was killed on 05 September 1918 at Méricourt, one of 56 casualties from a draft of 176 men destined for the battalion who became casualties when a shell accidentally exploded at the railway station in the town, whilst they were in transit.

James was buried along with the other casualties from that accident in the town of Méricourt, but he is a "Lost Boy" whose name has been omitted from the memorial tablets in the school chapel.

Frederick Henry WAY
Lieutenant, 2nd Battalion, The Princess Charlotte of Wales's (Royal Berkshire Regiment) who died on 11 September 1915, aged 30. Buried in White City Cemetery, Bois-Grenier, Nord, France

Born on 16 July 1885 in Chichester, Sussex, the second of four sons of George Way and Ellen née Smith, his father had been a Private in The Princess Charlotte of Wales's (Royal Berkshire Regiment), but had been discharged from the army on 05 May 1885. He died in Hawkhurst, Kent, on 01 July 1889, Frederick's mother dying in Farnborough, Kent, six years later, on 06 March 1895.

Frederick was admitted to the school on 02 August 1895 (Petition No. 10774), joining his older brother, George Reuben Way, who had been admitted on 29 December 1893 (Petition No. 10561). He was joined by his younger brother, Alexander William Way, on 28 August 1896 (Petition No. 10929), the last of the brothers, Albert Edward Way, being admitted on 03 June 1898 (Petition No. 11176).

Frederick was discharged on 17 July 1899, enlisting into his father's old regiment. His service record is not readily available as an officer, so his pre-war career is a bit of a mystery. However, he is recorded in the 1911 Census as a Lance Sergeant with the 1st Battalion, stationed in Fort Burgoyne, Dover, Kent. In fact, in 1911, three of the brothers were serving in the regiment, although Alexander was with the 2nd Battalion in India and Albert was a Drummer in the 1st Battalion, stationed in Dover Castle.

At the outbreak of war, Frederick would have been serving alongside Dukie Walter Brindle in Aldershot, Hampshire, landing at Rouen on 13 August 1914, before participating in the Battle of Mons, the Marne and during the First Battle of Ypres. On 24 November 1914, Frederick was a Serjeant and was Commissioned as a Second Lieutenant in The Royal Munster Fusiliers[314], but was only with that regiment for nineteen days before re-joining The Royal Berkshire Regiment[315].

He joined the 2nd Battalion on 25 May 1915 and by September 1915 was located in northern France, west of Lille. On 10 September the battalion relieved 2nd Battalion, The Lincolnshire Regiment, in trenches near Bois-Grenier, Frederick being killed the following day with the battalion war diary[316] simply recording, *"In trenches near BOIS GRENIER. 2nd LIEUT F. WAY killed. 5 men to hospital. 1 man from hospital"*. He was buried close to the area where he was killed, in White City Cemetery, which was used between October 1914 and December 1915.

George was discharged from the school on 04 September 1897, enlisting into The Royal Berkshire Regiment. Having served in South Africa during the Second Boer War, he was discharged from the army as medically unfit on 22 March 1902. Following his discharge, nothing further is known of him.

Alexander was discharged from the school on 13 July 1901, the school records stating that he enlisted into the 7th (The Princess Royal's) Dragoon Guards. However, he appears to have transferred to The Royal Berkshire Regiment by 1911, as this is the regiment in which he is recorded in the census of that year. He survived the war and died in Eton, Berkshire in 1959.

Albert was discharged from the school on 14 April 1903, following Frederick into their father's old regiment. He also survived the war and died in Wokingham, Berkshire, in 1924, aged only thirty-five.

---

[314] *The London Gazette*, 22 December 1914, Issue:29015
[315] *The London Gazette*, 9 March 1915, Issue:29094
[316] WO 95/1729/1: 2 Battalion Royal Berkshire Regiment, 1914 Oct. - 1919 Apr., The National Archives, Kew

The Queen's Own (Royal West Kent Regiment)

Thomas Millar CROFT
Private, G/21081, 1st Battalion, The Queen's Own (Royal West Kent Regiment) who died on 11 September 1916, aged 23. Buried in Combles Communal Cemetery Extension, Somme, France

Born on 29 December 1892 in Edinburgh, Midlothian, the eldest of five children of George Croft and Emma Mary née Savory, his father was a 2nd Corporal in the Army Ordnance Corps who died on 03 September 1901 in Pietermaritzburg, South Africa, whilst on active service during the Second Boer War. Three years after her husband's death, Emma married Herbert Charles Bloyce, who was a Corporal in the Royal Garrison Artillery.

Thomas was admitted to the school on 06 March 1902 (Petition No. 11667) and a year later, on 07 November 1903, his younger brother, George Croft, was admitted to the Royal Hibernian Military School in Dublin. Thomas was discharged from the school on 21 February 1907, enlisting into the Army Ordnance Corps. Two years after Thomas's discharge, on 25 February 1909, his youngest brother, Robert Frederick Croft, was admitted to the school (Petition No. 12567).

Almost a year after enlisting, on 18 January 1908, Thomas was appointed as a Bugler, although he reverted to Boy on 21 October 1910, prior to being transferred to the ranks as a Private on 21 January 1911, once he had turned eighteen. A year later, on 30 January 1912, Thomas was posted to South Africa, being appointed as an unpaid Lance Corporal on 24 December 1913.

When war broke out, Thomas was still serving in South Africa, but returned to Britain on 21 September 1914, a month after he had been deprived of the appointment of Lance Corporal on 18 August 1914, although the reason for this occurring is not given.

Thomas was in Britain for four days before he was deployed to France on 26 September 1914, but it seems that his time serving with the Expeditionary Force was somewhat troubled, the first time that he was in trouble being on 07 May 1915 when he was awarded 14 days' Field Punishment No. 1[317], although the offence for which this is awarded is not recorded.

Seven months later, on 02 December 1915, Thomas was under arrest and awaiting trial by Field General Courts Martial, this taking place on 10 December 1915 at Calais. He was convicted of, whilst on active service, firstly breaking out of camp on 01 December 1915 and secondly breaking out of camp when under open arrest on 02 December 1915. He was sentenced to 84 days' Field Punishment No. 1, although 28 days was remitted by order of the Calais Base Commandant.

However, in addition to his field punishment, once this was completed, Thomas was compulsorily transferred to 1st Battalion, The Queen's Own (Royal West Kent Regiment), arriving with that unit on 02 September 1916. On 09 September 1916, the battalion was ordered to take over the front-line trenches located in Leuze Wood, near Ginchy. It had initially been expected that the battalion would be launching an attack on a German trench that had been captured by 16th (County of London) Battalion, The London Regiment (Queen's Westminsters), but which could not be held and the attack was then cancelled.

During the afternoon of 11 September, the battalion's positions were subjected to an intense artillery bombardment and it was believed that an infantry attack would follow, although this did not materialise and the battalion, less "A" Company, was relieved by 3rd Battalion, The London Regiment, "A" Company moving back from the front line and becoming part of a composite battalion under the command of The Royal Warwickshire Regiment.

The battalion war diary[318] for this period reported that it suffered three officers wounded and seven other ranks killed, with 58 wounded and missing. Thomas was initially reported as missing and it was not until 22 September 1916 that it was confirmed that he had been killed in action.

Although buried in Combles Communal Cemetery Extension, he is another "Lost Boy" whose name has been omitted from the memorial tablets in the school chapel.

George also enlisted into the Army Ordnance Corps when he was discharged from the Royal Hibernian Military School. He also served throughout the war and died in 1925 from illness.

When Robert was discharged from the school on 22 December 1912, he also enlisted into the Army Ordnance Corps, although it

---

[317] The soldier being punished was placed in fetters and handcuffs and attached to a fixed object, such as a gun wheel or a fence post, for up to two hours per day

[318] WO 95/1554: 13 Infantry Brigade: 1 Battalion Queen's Own (Royal West Kent Regiment), 1916 May 1 - 1917 June 30, The National Archives, Kew

433

appears that he later transferred to The Northumberland Fusiliers. At the end of the war, he was an Acting Colour Sergeant, but there is also nothing known about him after this.

Their mother Emma was re-married to Herbert Charles Bloyce in 1904, a half-brother also named Herbert Charles Bloyce being born in 1905. Emma was to die in 1912 and Herbert was admitted to the school on 13 January 1916 (Petition No. 13463), like his two half-brothers before him. He was a Warrant Office Class II in the Royal Artillery when he died in Japanese captivity on 16 July 1942 in Singapore and is a "Lost Boy" from the Second World War, who will be documented in Volume Two.

John Louis Herbert FALKNER

Private, L/10230, 7th (Service) Battalion, The Queen's Own (Royal West Kent Regiment) who died on 04 August 1918, aged 31. Buried in St. Sever Cemetery Extension, Rouen, Seine-Maritime, France

Born on 16 January 1887 in Maidstone, Kent, the third of four children of Robert James Falkner and Sarah Ann née Godfrey, his father was a Quartermaster Serjeant in The Queen's Own (Royal West Kent Regiment), who died whilst still serving in Maidstone on 06 March 1889.

John was admitted to the school on 27 November 1896 (Petition No. 10959), the same day as his older brother, Robert George Godfrey Falkner (Petition No. 10960) and was discharged to his father's old regiment on 19 January 1901. A year after enlisting into the 2nd Battalion, he was posted to Ceylon, spending two years there before a posting to Hong Kong, China. On 28 November 1906, he was posted for two years to Singapore, before, on 07 November 1908, he was posted to India, where he was to spend almost five years, during which time he was appointed as a Musician on 13 October 1909. In the 1911 Census, both he and Robert are recorded stationed in Roberts Barracks, Peshawar.

John returned to Britain on 26 February 1913 and was discharged from the army the following day, having completed his 12-year period of service. However, it then seems likely that he was recalled to the Colours when war broke out, although there is no service record available for this period of service.

The battalion in which he was serving, the 7th (Service) Battalion, was formed in Maidstone as part of K2, moving to Colchester, Essex, in April 1915, Salisbury Plain, Wiltshire, in May 1915 and embarking on the SS *Monas Queen* at Southampton, Hampshire, on 26 July, landing at Le Havre on 27 July 1915, and having its first experience of the trenches on 08 August. However, it is likely that John did not join the battalion until 1916, as he did not qualify for the award of the 1914-15 Star.

On 01 July 1916, the first day of the Somme Offensive, the battalion was not in the first wave, but was called forward when reports were received that although the attack was going well, there was more resistance than expected. It was involved in heavy hand-to-hand fighting near Carnoy, suffering many casualties. It then went on to participate in many of the Western Front battles during the next two years, but John must have had some home leave, because he married Mabel Tilston in Maidstone in March 1917.

At the beginning of August 1918, the battalion was in reserve in the location of La Houssaye, but it seems likely that John had been wounded before this, although there is no record in the war diary of when he may have happened. He died of wounds on 04 August 1918, likely in hospital in Rouen, close to where he is buried. Although he is commemorated on the memorial tablets in the school chapel, he is incorrectly commemorated as L J H Falkner.

Robert George Godfrey FALKNER
Serjeant, L/10229, 1st Battalion, The Queen's Own (Royal West Kent Regiment) who died on 26 October 1917, aged 31. Commemorated on the Tyne Cot Memorial, West-Vlaanderen, Belgium

Born on 10 January 1886 in Maidstone, Kent, the second of four children of Robert James Falkner and Sarah Ann née Godfrey and older brother of John Falkner. His father was a Quartermaster Serjeant in The Queen's Own (Royal West Kent Regiment), who died whilst still serving in Maidstone on 06 March 1889.

Robert was admitted to the school on 27 November 1896, the same day as his younger brother, John Louis Herbert Falkner (Petition No. 10959) and was discharged from the school to his father's old regiment on 10 May 1901. However, other than his enlistment and some pre-war documents, very little of Robert's service record remains, although it is known that he served with the 2nd Battalion in Ceylon, Hong Kong, Singapore and India, proof of the last posting being that both he and John appear in the 1911 Census, stationed in Roberts Barracks, Peshawar.

Robert was discharged from the army at the end of his 12-year period of service on 15 November 1913, but re-enlisted on 02 December, as there was difficulty in recruiting men to be Drummers in the 3rd (Reserve) Battalion. He remained with this battalion, stationed in Maidstone, until posted to the 1st Battalion on 26 February 1917, although his medal index card shows that he first entered theatre on 27 November 1914 and qualified for the award of the 1914-1915 Star. Robert was appointed a Lance Corporal on 01 April 1915, appointed Acting Corporal on 20 August the same year and made substantive on 22 November, which was the rank that he held when posted to the 1st Battalion.

During 1916, Robert and John had been together in Maidstone, as John was one of the witnesses when Robert married Beatrice Lilly Prior on 31 May. Whether Robert ever saw his daughter, Barbara Ethel Falkner, who was born on 29 May 1917, is not known.

During 1917, the battalion was involved in numerous battles, Robert being appointed as a Lance Serjeant on 16 May 1917 in the aftermath of the Battle of Arras and appointed an Acting Serjeant on 11 October 1917.

During the Third Battle of Ypres, the battalion attacked on the first day of the Second Battle of Passchendaele, 26 October 1917, suffering twelve officers and 235 other ranks killed, wounded and missing, including Robert, who was reported as missing presumed dead, on 26 October 1917. His body was never recovered and he is one of the 117 soldiers from his battalion to be killed on that day who are commemorated on the Tyne Cot Memorial. Like his brother, he is commemorated on the memorial tablets in the school chapel but, like his brother, he is incorrectly recorded, as L G Falkner.

Enos Patrick RYAN

Private, L/7667, 1st Battalion, The Queen's Own (Royal West Kent Regiment) who died on 26 October 1914, aged 29. Commemorated on the Le Touret Memorial, Pas de Calais, France

Born on 17 December 1884 in Campbeltown, Argyllshire, the youngest of three children of Patrick Ryan and Elizabeth née Hooper, his father was a Battery Serjeant Major in the Royal Garrison Artillery, who committed suicide on 10 May 1890 in Campbeltown.

Enos was admitted to the school on 29 November 1895 and was *"Returned to mother"* on 20 December 1898, although he enlisted into the army two years later, on 27 July 1900, joining the Royal Field Artillery. However, he was discharged four months later, on 08 November 1900, having been *'Irregularly enlisted'*[319].

It appears that Enos then enlisted again into the army, although it is not known when, as there is no service record for this enlistment, although it would appear that any enlistment occurred after 1911, as he is recorded in the 1911 Census as a Labourer, Government Worker, living in Woolwich, London. At that time, he was a boarder

---

[319] WO 97: Chelsea Pensioners British Army Service Records 1760-1913

with his in-laws and wife, having married Adelaide Edith Huxstep in October 1910. They were to have two daughters, Margaret Catherine Ryan, born in 1911, and Edith Elizabeth Ryan, born in 1914. It is also likely that he was a pre-war Regular, as he disembarked in France on 15 August 1914 with the 1st Battalion and the prefix 'L' in his service number suggests a Regular enlistment in this regiment.

His battalion was amongst the first British troops to land in France and it saw action at Mons, Le Cateau, the Marne and Neuve Chapelle, where it suffered 450 casualties, including all but two officers. Enos's death was presumed on 26 October 1914, according to his medal index card, and the Regimental history records events on that day:

> *"On the 26th shelling opened about 7 o'clock and continued with increased vehemence all day, reaching an intensity not yet experienced. Both to the right and left of the battalion, the German infantry attacked, but not until late in the day did it get the satisfaction of having good targets to shoot at. When the attack came it was directed mainly against D Company on the right, who had been getting the worst of the bombardment and had lost Captain Tulloch, badly concussed by a shell bursting close to him. But D, unshaken by the shelling shot steadily and straight at the advancing enemy, met with the bayonet the few Germans who reached the parapet and maintained its line triumphantly."*[320]

Enos is another of the Dukies who fell in the First World War whose name is omitted from the memorial tablets in the school chapel and is therefore another "Lost Boy".

---

[320] Atkinson, C. T. (1924). *The Queen's Own Royal West Kent Regiment - 1914-1919*. London: Simpkin, Marshall, Hamilton, Kent

The Duke of Cambridge's Own
(Middlesex Regiment)

Henry John ALLEN
Private, SR/7508, 13th (Service) Battalion, The Duke of Cambridge's Own (Middlesex Regiment) who died on 30 April 1916, aged 22. Buried in Ration Farm (La Plus Douve) Annexe, Hainaut, Belgium

Born on 01 July 1893 in Camberwell, London, the third of six children of Henry Allen and Annie Elizabeth née Farrant, his father had been a Sergeant Instructor of Musketry in The Leicestershire Regiment, but had been discharged from the army on 11 January 1887 and was then employed as a Bus Conductor. Henry's mother died in Camberwell on 19 October 1900.

Henry was admitted to the school on his 11th birthday, 01 July 1904 (Petition No. 11990) and was discharged *"To civil life (unfit)"* on 20 July 1907. He was recorded four years later in the 1911 Census as living in Peckham Rye, London, with his father, and two sisters, and employed as a Shop Assistant Drapery.

Following the outbreak of war, it appears that Henry enlisted in January 1915, joining The Duke of Cambridge's Own (Middlesex Regiment), although his service record in no longer available, initially serving with one of the two Regular battalions, before he was posted.

The battalion with which he served, 13th (Service) Battalion, had been formed at Mill Hill, London, in September 1914 as part of K3 and came under the command of the 73rd Brigade, 24th Division. Following its formation, it moved to the South Downs, going into billets at Hove, Sussex, in December 1914 before moving to Shoreham, Sussex in May 1915 and then to Pirbright, Surrey, in June 1915. The battalion landed at Boulogne on 02 September 1915, although Henry did not disembark until 05 October 1915, according to his medal index card.

The battalion had its first experience of coming under enemy fire on 25 September near Vermelles, when it occupied the old British support trenches which were, in places, full of water up to the men's knees. The following day, it experienced its first combat when it advanced toward No. 8 Fosse where it was subjected to bombardment and German attacks on the trenches that it held.

By April 1916, the battalion had moved to Belgium and on the night of the 29-30 April 1916 it was in trenches near Messines, where it was subjected to a gas attack. The battalion diary reported that:

"The night was very dark, the enemy fired machine guns which swept our parapet in order that the hissing of the gas leaving the cylinders should not be heard and also to keep the sentries heads down."[321]

During the attack, the battalion suffered nine other ranks killed, one officer and 26 other ranks wounded and two officers and 40 other ranks gassed. One of those killed was Henry Allen. Although he has a named grave in Ration Farm (La Plus Douve) Annexe, he is another "Lost Boy" whose name has been omitted from the memorial tablets in the school chapel.

Frederick Albert John GREEN

Serjeant, 7632, 4th Battalion, The Duke of Cambridge's Own (Middlesex Regiment) who died on 31 December 1915, aged 28. Buried in Chapelle-d'Armentieres New Military Cemetery, Nord, France

Born on 25 October 1887 in Hounslow, Middlesex, the fifth of eight children of Joseph Green and Sarah née Williams, his father had been a Serjeant in the 77th (East Middlesex, Duke of Cambridge's Own) Regiment of Foot who had been discharged to pension on 30 March 1880.

Frederick was admitted to the school on 05 February 1897 (Petition No. 10987), being joined by his younger brother, Claude Augustus Green, on 03 February 1899 (Petition No. 11265). Frederick was discharged to his father's old regiment on 26 October 1901. Although his service record is no longer available, he is recorded in the 1911 Census as a Private in the 3rd Battalion and stationed in India, but by the start of the war, he had been posted to the 4th Battalion.

This battalion was stationed in Devonport, Devonshire, but quickly mobilised, embarking on the SS *Mombasa* on 13 August and landing at Boulogne on 14 August 1914, the date shown on Frederick's medal index card for his entry into theatre. During 1914, it participated in the Battle of Mons, during which the unit suffered fifteen officers and 467 other ranks killed, wounded, missing or captured, a casualty rate of 56% among the officers and 48% among the other ranks. It then, subsequently, took part in the retreat, fighting in the rear-guard action of Solesmes, as well as at the Battles of Le Cateau, of the Marne, of the Aisne, La Bassée, Messines and

---

[321] WO 95/2219/1: 13 Battalion Middlesex Regiment, 1915 Aug. - 1919 Nov., The National Archives, Kew

the First Battle of Ypres. The casualties inflicted on it during these actions led to the battalion having to be withdrawn from the line and reformed during 1915.

Frederick is recorded by the Commonwealth War Graves Commission as having died on 31 December 1915, but the circumstances of his death are unclear. No casualties are recorded in the battalion war diary on that day, but there was a soldier who was wounded on Christmas Day, with the only other casualties recorded in December being earlier in the month. It is possible that the Christmas Day casualty was Frederick, who died of his wounds six days later. However, the Germans also shelled the trenches at 0200hrs on 01 January 1916, causing the deaths of five men and the wounding of 30, and it is also possible that Frederick was one of these casualties, with the date of his death recorded incorrectly.

He is buried in the village of Chapelle-d'Armentieres, which was the location of the Field Ambulances that would have received casualties from the area of the front in which the battalion was located. He is also commemorated on the memorial tablets in the school chapel, but he is incorrectly recorded as T A J Green.

Claude was discharged from the school on 07 November 1903 and also enlisted into The Middlesex Regiment, although it seems that he and his brother were in different battalions. He survived the war, was Commissioned into The York and Lancaster Regiment and was a Captain in The King's Own Yorkshire Light Infantry when he died in Cleethorpes, Lincolnshire on 14 December 1940. He is a "Lost Boy" from the Second World War and will be documented in Volume Two.

Samuel William HALLETT

Lieutenant, 1st Battalion, The Duke of Cambridge's Own (Middlesex Regiment) who died on 15 July 1916, aged 34. Commemorated on the Thiepval Memorial, Somme, France

Born on 28 May 1882 in Shorncliffe, Kent, the second child of Edwin James Thomas Hallett and Ellen née Howard, his father was a Company Serjeant Major in the Royal Engineers who died whilst serving at Wadi Halfa, Egypt, on 18 April 1886.

Samuel was admitted to the school on 30 December 1892 (Petition No. 10409), and was discharged on 28 May 1896, enlisting into the Royal Engineers. Although his service record is not readily available, there are documents from a Board of Enquiry when another Boy had his leg broken during a football match at Fort Pitt in Chatham, Kent, in 1898 at which Samuel was a witness, showing that he was serving in that corps at the time.

Little is known of Samuel's pre-war career, but he is recorded in the 1901 Census as a Sapper with 60 Company, Royal Engineers, stationed in Longmoor Barracks, Hampshire, and that he married Ethel Rashbrook in Medway, Kent, in 1909. The 1911 Census, carried out a year after his son, Howard Samuel Hallett, was born records him as a 2nd Corporal in 55 Field Company, Royal Engineers, stationed in Roberts Heights, Transvaal, South Africa.

When war was declared, Samuel was a Corporal, but on 01 October 1914 he was Commissioned as a Second Lieutenant[322] in The Duke of Cambridge's Own (Middlesex Regiment) and posted to the 1st Battalion, which had deployed to France from its barracks in Woolwich, London, landing at Le Havre on 11 August 1914.

The battalion fought in France and Flanders throughout 1915, participating in the Battle of Loos in the autumn and by mid-1916, it was in the Somme sector, although on the first day of the offensive it was in billets in Béthune and it was not until 03 July that it moved into trenches in Cuinchy, reporting bad weather and that the enemy was quiet until it was relieved on 07 July. Following this, the battalion then moved south over the next week to Becordel and on the evening of 14 July it was located on the edge of Mametz Wood, setting off on the morning of 15 July to take the German trenches near the village of Bazentin-le-Petit. However, as it deployed, it came under heavy rifle and machine-gun fire from the north corner of the village, and it was then subjected to artillery fire, along with further enemy machine-gun fire from High Wood, which it had believed was in British hands.

Although the battalion attempted to dig in, the weight of fire was too great and it was forced to retire, six officers and 44 other ranks dying during this action, one of the officers killed during that failed attack on 15 July 1916 being Samuel. His body was never recovered and he is commemorated on the Thiepval Memorial.

Harold Hector TOOMEY

Private, G/841, 2nd Battalion, The Duke of Cambridge's Own (Middlesex Regiment) who died on 17 June 1915, aged 25. Buried in St. Sever Cemetery, Rouen, Seine-Maritime, France

Born on 16 May 1890 in Hounslow, Middlesex, the fourth of six children of Michael Toomey and Caroline née Regan, his father had been a Serjeant in the 77th (East Middlesex) Regiment of Foot and had been discharged from the army on 05 April 1881.

Harold was admitted to the school on 08 December 1899 (Petition No. 11380) and was joined by his younger brother, William Henry

---

[322] *The London Gazette*, 13 November 1914, Issue:28973

Percival Toomey, who was admitted on 11 September 1903 (Petition No. 11882). Harold was discharged from the school on 04 June 1904 and enlisted into The Duke of Cambridge's Own (Middlesex Regiment), serving in the regiment for seven years, all of them in Britain, before he was discharged on 20 March 1911, medically unfit for further service, although the cause is not given.

However, following the outbreak of war, Harold was recalled to the Colours, enlisting back into his old regiment in Tottenham, London, on 01 September 1914 and being posted initially to the Regimental Depot at Inglis Barracks, Mill Hill, London. Eleven days later, he was posted to the 13th (Service) Battalion, which had been formed at Mill Hill in September 1914 as part of K3 and where he was briefly appointed as a Lance Corporal on 13 October, before reverting to Private on 11 November.

Harold had a chequered career during this period of service, with seven days' Field Punishment No. 2[323] awarded on 13 February 1915, before he went absent without leave on 20 February 1915. This was followed by ten days' detention from 24 February 1915 and, after six months with the 13th Battalion, Harold was then posted to the 5th (Reserve) Battalion, stationed in Rochester, Kent, on 04 March 1915, remaining here for a week before being posted to the 2nd Battalion and arriving in France on 11 March 1915.

On 30 April 1915, Harold was again in trouble, being awarded ten days' Field Punishment No. 2 and it is possible that this would have been interrupted by the Battle of Aubers Ridge on 9 May 1915, in which his brigade was involved.

He was to only spend three months in theatre. Having been treated for a septic left leg between 23 and 26 May, he was admitted to No. 5 General Hospital, Rouen, where he died from nephritis on 17 June 1915. He is also a "Lost Boy" whose name has been omitted from the memorial tablets in the school chapel.

William was discharged from the school on 30 June 1906, enlisting into The Lincolnshire Regiment and was killed in action the day before Harold arrived in theatre, on 10 March 1915. Unlike Harold, he is commemorated on the memorial tablets in the school chapel and is documented earlier in this book.

---

[323] The soldier being punished was placed in fetters and handcuffs but was not attached to a fixed object and was still able to march with his unit

William Thomas VAUSE DCM
Company Serjeant Major, L/7674, 4th Battalion, The Duke of Cambridge's Own (Middlesex Regiment) who died on 02 February 1916, aged 28. Buried in Bailleul Communal Cemetery Extension, Nord, France

Born on 07 November 1887 in Limerick, County Limerick, the youngest of four sons of Charles Vause and Mary née Dermon, his father was a Quartermaster Serjeant in the Grenadier Guards before transferring to the Barracks Department. He died suddenly in St. George's Barracks, Bermuda, West Indies, on 05 August 1890.

William was admitted to the school on 05 March 1897 (Petition No. 11002), following in the footsteps of his older brother, Albert Edward Vause, who had been admitted on 26 June 1891 (Petition No. 10170). William was discharged on 30 November 1901, enlisting into The Duke of Cambridge's Own (Middlesex Regiment) and although his service record is no longer available, the 1911 Census records him as a Corporal in the 3rd Battalion in India. Thereafter, he was likely posted to the 1st Battalion, stationed in Woolwich, London, as in 1913 he married Ivy Elizabeth Easter in Plumstead, Kent, and their first child, Ivy Doris Vause, was born in June 1914, when the family were living in Finchley, London. At this time, the 4th Battalion, was stationed in Devonshire.

It is also unknown when he was posted to the 4th Battalion, as he arrived in theatre on 12 September 1914 according to his medal index card, by which time both the 1st and 4th Battalions had been in theatre for a month. It is possible that William was a battle casualty replacement to the 4th Battalion due to it suffering around 400 men killed during the Battle of Mons. During the remainder of 1914, the battalion participated in the various battles of that year, including the First Battle of Ypres, remaining in the Ypres sector into the early part of 1915.

During 1915, William was Mentioned in Despatches[324] and also awarded the Distinguished Conduct Medal, although the action that led to this recommendation does not get mentioned in the battalion war diary[325].

However, William's wounding is reported in the diary, the entry for 02 February 1916 stating that it was *"A bright morning & the enemy shelled our front-line trenches with 7.7s, Lieut A S Jackson, Coy Serjt*

---

[324] *The London Gazette*, 18 June 1915, Supplement:29200
[325] *The London Gazette*, 11 January 1916, Supplement: 29438, citation *"For conspicuous gallantry; he crawled to within 20 yards of the enemy trench to reconnoitre, a distance of 250 yards. Next afternoon he crawled out again in broad daylight, and brought back useful information about the wire. His fine example has had a great effect among the men. He has since been wounded"* published *The London Gazette*, 10 March 1916, Supplement:29503

Maj VAUSE and two others being wounded thereby[326]. He subsequently died of those wounds on 02 February 1916 and is buried in Bailleul Communal Cemetery Extension. His second child, Vera Emily Vause, was born four months later on 10 June 1916.

Albert was discharged from the school on 28 January 1897 to be a Pupil Teacher. He subsequently served as a Warrant Officer in the Corps of Army Schoolmasters, dying in Billericay, Essex, in 1931.

---

[326] WO 95/2158/2, 4 Battalion Middlesex Regiment, 1915 Nov. - 1916 June, The National Archives, Kew

The King's Royal Rifle Corps

Horace Henry ADSHEAD
Lance Corporal, 8109, 3rd Battalion, The King's Royal Rifle Corps who died on 07 May 1915, aged 22. Commemorated on the Ypres (Menin Gate) Memorial, West-Vlaanderen, Belgium

Born on 21 May 1892 in Portsmouth, Hampshire, the fifth of seven children of Frederick Thomas Adshead and Mary Ann née Stone, his father had been the Sergeant Master Tailor in The Princess of Wales's Own (Yorkshire Regiment), but had left the army on 31 January 1894, becoming a Publican. He died in Balham, London, on 21 April 1900.

Horace was admitted to the school on 13 September 1901 (Petition No. 11604) and was joined by his brother, Cyrus Adshead, on 06 March 1903 (Petition No. 11819). On 04 December that year, the brothers were joined by their cousin, George Albert Adshead (Petition No. 11913). On 18 March 1905, Horace's mother died in Brixton, London, and the third of the Adshead brothers to attend the school, Bertrand John Adshead, was admitted nine months later, on 01 December 1905 (Petition No. 12130).

Horace was discharged from the school on 29 May 1907, enlisting into The King's Royal Rifle Corps and although his service record is no longer available, he is recorded in the 1911 Census serving in the 1st Battalion and stationed in Alverstoke, Hampshire. By the outbreak of war, he had been posted to the 3rd Battalion, which was stationed in Meerut, India. However, it was quickly returned to Britain, arriving in November 1914 and briefly stationed at Winchester, Hampshire, prior to landing at Le Havre on 21 December, spending the end of the year moving between Aire and Hazebrouck.

When the German attack that was to become the Second Battle of Ypres was launched on 22 April 1915, the battalion was in the Ypres sector of the front, and was to remain there throughout the battle. At the beginning of May, it was in positions close to the dam on Bellewaarde Lake, where it was subjected to regular shelling by the Germans, including experiencing a *"terrific though short bombardment* which as usual broke down all telephone communications"[327] at 0215hrs on 07 May, which was followed by a German attempt *"to advance in small parties, but failed to do so in the face of our fire"*[328].

It would seem that there were no further attacks during the rest of the day and the battalion was relieved in the trenches by the 4th Battalion at 2300hrs that evening. However, Horace was one of the two soldiers killed as a result of the earlier German attacks and because he has no known grave, he is commemorated on the Menin Gate Memorial.

Cyrus also enlisted into The King's Royal Rifle Corps when he was discharged from the school on 23 July 1908, serving in the same battalion as his brother during the war. He was discharged from the army due to wounds on 02 August 1916 and died in Lewisham, London, in 1931.

Bertrand was discharged from the school, having moved from Chelsea to Guston, on 21 October 1909. He enlisted in Princess Louise's (Argyll and Sutherland Highlanders), survived the war and emigrated to Australia. It appears that he was Commissioned in the Australian Army during the Second World War and died in Brisbane in 1963.

Their cousin George, was discharged from the school on 23 July 1908, enlisting into the Army Ordnance Corps. He also survived the war, but died in Portsmouth, Hampshire in 1931.

William Joseph HARMAN

Lance Corporal, R/7894, 7th (Service) Battalion, The King's Royal Rifle Corps who died on 05 December 1917, aged 36. Commemorated in Streatham Cemetery, London, United Kingdom

Born on 11 December 1880 in Sheffield, Yorkshire West Riding, the eldest of two children of John James Harman and Martha Ann née Jarvis, his father had been a Gunner in the Royal Artillery who was discharged from the army on 12 September 1882 and died in Marylebone, London, on 13 October 1884. His mother also died in Marylebone on 07 September 1888 and William's Petition Document was submitted by an uncle named George Greenfield.

William was admitted to the school on 28 November 1890 (Petition No. 10099) and discharged on 15 December 1894, enlisting into The King's Royal Rifle Corps, spending the first six years of his service with the 3rd Battalion. On 29 November 1900, William was posted to South Africa with the battalion during the Second Boer

---

[327] WO 95/2261/2: 80 Infantry Brigade: 3 Battalion King's Royal Rifle Corps, 1915 Mar 1 - 1915 Apr 30, The National Archives, Kew
[328] Ibid.

War, spending just over two years here before he was posted back to Britain on 22 March 1903, being appointed as a Bandsman four months later, on 25 July 1903.

A year after his return to Britain, on 16 March 1903, William was posted to Bermuda, West Indies, although he was only to serve there for eighteen months before he was again posted back to Britain on 25 October 1905. Fourteen months after returning to Britain, William was discharged from the army on the completion of his first 12 years' service on 14 December 1906. However, the day after he was discharged, William re-enlisted in the army, but joined the Royal Army Medical Corps.

Having spent the first three years of his service in Britain, on 20 October 1909, William transferred back to The King's Royal Corps, posted to the 1st Battalion as a Rifleman on the same day. It seems that he then spent the remaining four years of that period of service in Britain with the 1st Battalion, before he was discharged at his own request on 03 March 1913. Following discharge from the army, there is limited information available about him, although it is known that in October of that year he married Lillian Maud Cant in Wandsworth, London.

When war broke out, Lillian was pregnant and their only child, William Ernest Harman, was born on 16 October 1914. 12 days later, William again enlisted into the army, joining 7th (Service) Battalion, The King's Royal Rifle Corps. This battalion had been formed at Winchester on 19 August 1914, coming under the orders of 41st Brigade, 14th (Light) Division, initially moving to Aldershot, Hampshire, before it moved to Grayshott, Hampshire, in November 1914 and Bordon, Hampshire, in February 1915. A month after the move to Bordon, the battalion returned to Aldershot and then landed at Boulogne on 19 May 1915, the date shown on William's medal index card for his own arrival in theatre.

William spent more than a year in France, although his movements are unknown as his service record for this period of service is no longer available. He then appears to have been evacuated to Britain, likely with trench fever[329] and he was discharged from the army on 08 March 1917. He died nine months later, on 05 December 1917, with the cause of death given as neurasthenia after trench fever contracted on active service and he was commemorated by the Commonwealth War Graves Commission. However, he is also a "Lost Boy" whose name has been omitted from the memorial tablets in the school chapel.

---

[329] A moderately serious disease transmitted by body lice

George Alexander HOOKER

Corporal, 5576, 4th Battalion, The King's Royal Rifle Corps who died on 02 March 1915, aged 25. Buried in Voormezeele Enclosure No.3, West-Vlaanderen, Belgium

Born on 03 October 1889 in Dover, Kent, the sixth of seven children of John William Hooker and Elizabeth Ann née Sainsbury, his father had been a Colour Serjeant in The Duke of Cornwall's Light Infantry and was discharged from the army on 24 May 1882. George's mother died in Dover on 22 December 1891.

George was admitted to the school on 09 February 1900 (Petition No. 11408) and was discharged on 10 October 1903, enlisting into The King's Royal Rifle Corps on the same day. After spending two years at the Depot in Winchester, Hampshire, he was posted to the 4th Battalion in Gosport, Hampshire, moving to Colchester, Essex, in 1906 and then embarking for India in 1909. The 1911 Census records that he was a Rifleman with that battalion in Chakrata and he was promoted to Corporal on 18 November that year.

George was going to leave the army having completed his initial period of service, but the outbreak of war meant that he remained in the service and when the war did commence, his battalion was still in India, stationed in Gharial, arriving back in Britain on 18 November. After a short period in Winchester the battalion deployed to France, landing at Le Havre on 21 December 1914.

In early-1915, the battalion was in the Ypres Salient and on 27 February it marched from billets in Zevercoton to Dickebusch, moving into the trenches at night in order to repair the breastworks. However, on the evening of 01 March, it marched the three miles from its billets in Dickebusch to the line at St. Eloi, in order to carry out an attack on a supplementary German trench. When launched, the attack met with more resistance than was anticipated, the Germans having created a barricade from which the attackers came under rifle fire and were bombed. Machine-gun fire was also brought to bear from the main German trench, with all who were stood up being hit. Eventually the British were able to occupy the trench and create a new breastwork to provide a degree of protection.

George died of wounds sustained during this attack on 02 March 1915 and is buried in Voormezeele Enclosure No.3, less than a mile from the scene of his death.

Three years after his death, on 02 April 1918, George's non-Dukie older brother, John William Hooker, who was eight years his senior, not the thirteen years that the Commonwealth War Graves Commission has recorded, was killed whilst serving as a Corporal in

7th Battalion, The Duke of Cornwall's Light Infantry, their father's old regiment. He has no known grave and is commemorated on the Pozieres Memorial.

William Robert KING

Rifleman, 9491, 1st Battalion, The King's Royal Rifle Corps who died on 10 March 1915, aged 19. Commemorated on the Le Touret Memorial, Pas de Calais, France

Born on 13 November 1895 in Chelsea, London, the eldest child of William King and Annie Eliza née Willby, his father had been a Private in The King's Royal Rifle Corps, although he had served under the alias of Charles White. He had been discharged as medically unfit on 30 September 1901 and died in Chelsea on 16 June 1906.

William was admitted to the school on 08 November 1906 (Petition No. 12296) and was discharged on 06 December 1911, so he would have made the transition from Chelsea to Guston. Although William's service record is no longer available, the school records show that on discharge he enlisted into his father's old regiment.

At the outbreak of war, the 1st Battalion was stationed in Salamanca Barracks in Aldershot, Hampshire, leaving eight days later and embarking at Southampton, Hampshire, before landing at Rouen on 13 August 1914. It experienced its baptism of fire ten days later when it was shelled near Givry. The battalion then took part in the retreat from Mons, not going onto the offensive again until the German forces began retiring on 06 September, participating in the Battles of the Marne, the Aisne, as well as the First Battle of Ypres. During the latter of these, "B", "C" and "D" Companies were surrounded and overwhelmed, losing a total of 1,027 men either killed, missing or wounded in just six weeks.

By the end of February 1915, the battalion was occupying trenches in the location of Givenchy, with the four companies pairing off, two companies spending 24 hours in the trenches, before being relieved by the other two companies. On 01 March, the trenches that it was occupying were visited by the Prince of Wales.

On 10 March 1915, the battalion, along with the rest of the 6th Brigade, was ordered to assault German trenches in its sector. Following a short bombardment, at 0810hrs the unit attacked the German trenches that were 170 yards away. However, it soon came under heavy rifle and machine-gun fire, suffering many casualties. Those that survived the initial fire managed to get within 30 yards of the enemy wire before being almost annihilated and although some soldiers from the battalion did manage to occupy the German frontline trench, by 1400hrs only one Serjeant and two soldiers remained, and they were forced to crawl back to their own lines.

William was one of those killed during that attack on 10 March 1915. His body was never recovered and he is therefore remembered on the Le Touret Memorial along with 142 other soldiers from his battalion.

Frank Albert McMANUS

Corporal, R/4431, Depot, The King's Royal Rifle Corps who died on 25 December 1914, aged 37. Buried in Winchester (West Hill) Old Cemetery, Hampshire, United Kingdom

Born on 19 September 1877 in Woolwich, Kent, the youngest of two children of Thomas McManus and Louisa née Bailey, his father had been a Staff Serjeant in the Royal Engineers who was discharged from the army on 15 March 1879 and died in Woolwich on 30 June 1879.

Frank was admitted to the school on 07 May 1889 (Petition No. 9810) and discharged on 26 September 1891, enlisting into The King's Royal Rifle Corps the same day. Elder brothers Louis John McManus and Edward James McManus were both admitted to the Royal Hibernian Military School in Dublin.

Frank spent the first year of service in Britain, initially with the 2nd Battalion, before being posted to the 3rd Battalion. However, on 17 September 1892, he was posted back to the 2nd Battalion which was now stationed in Gibraltar and was appointed as a Bandsman on 21 April 1893. After less than three years in Gibraltar, Frank was then posted to Malta on 13 January 1895, but was only there for eighteen months before he was again posted, this time to South Africa, on 17 July 1896.

Six months prior to the outbreak of the Second Boer War, on 06 April 1899, Frank was posted to India, although he was only there for five months before returning to South Africa on 17 September 1899, a month prior to war breaking out.

He remained in South Africa for ten months, being awarded the Queen's South Africa Medal with the clasps *South Africa 1901*, *Defence of Ladysmith* and *Orange Free State*, before he returned to Britain on 27 July 1900, having been posted to the 4th Battalion. However, the following year, on 11 December 1901, he was again posted back to South Africa, remaining there until 28 June 1904 and being awarded the *South Africa 1902* clasp for his Queen's South Africa Medal, as well as being appointed as a Lance Corporal on 05 February 1903, although he was deprived of his Lance stripe for drunkenness five months later, on 09 October 1903.

Four months after being posted back to Britain, on 10 October 1904, Frank was again posted to the 2nd Battalion stationed in India. He was appointed as a Bandsman on 09 October 1905, Lance Corporal on 27 November 1905 and promoted to Corporal on 11 March 1908, before he returned to Britain on 01 February 1910. Frank spent the remaining four years of his service in Britain, being allowed to extend beyond 21 years' service on 10 September 1912, before he was finally discharged on 23 May 1914.

However, following the outbreak of war, Frank was recalled to the Colours, enlisting on 12 September 1914 and being returned to the rank of Corporal on the same day. He was posted to the Rifle Depot in Winchester, Hampshire, where he died of heart failure on Christmas Day 1914. Although he is commemorated by the Commonwealth War Graves Commission, he is another "Lost Boy" whose name has been omitted from the memorial tablets in the school chapel.

Arthur Victor SOMERSET

Rifleman, 10435, 12th (Service) Battalion, The King's Royal Rifle Corps who died on 16 August 1917, aged 19. Commemorated on the Tyne Cot Memorial, West-Vlaanderen, Belgium

Born on 23 October 1897 in Leicester, Leicestershire, the youngest of four children of Alfred James Somerset and Alice Emma née Greig, his father had been a Serjeant Bugler in The King's Royal Rifle Corps who was discharged from the army in April 1887 and died in Leicester on 20 May 1899. Arthur's mother died eight years later, on 10 October 1907, in Winchester, Hampshire.

Arthur was admitted to the school on 20 January 1908 (Petition No. 12467) and had an older brother, George William Somerset, who had been admitted to the Royal Hibernian Military School. Having made the transition from Chelsea to Dover, Arthur was discharged to The King's Royal Rifle Corps on 01 January 1912. However, his service record is no longer available, so it is not possible to establish with which battalion he was serving when war broke out, although his medal index card shows that he was not eligible for the award of the 1914-15 Star, suggesting that he did not enter theatre until 1916 at the earliest.

The 12th (Service) Battalion, with which Arthur did later serve, had been formed in Winchester, Hampshire, on 21 September 1914 as part of K2. Having first moved to Bisley, Surrey, it then moved in November 1914 to Blackdown, Surrey, spending three months here, before moving to Hindhead, Surrey, with its last move before deployment being to Larkhill, Wiltshire, on 10 April 1915. It landed at Boulogne three months later on 22 July 1915, its first experience in the frontline trenches being south of Laventie on 27 August, a month after arrival. During 1916, the battalion was stationed in the Ypres Salient at the start of the Somme Offensive, although by September, it had moved to that sector and participated in actions there.

By the end of July 1917, it was back in the area of Ypres, participating in the Third Battle of Ypres, where, on 16 August 1917, it was tasked with attacking and capturing Langemarck, zero hour being 0445hrs. Having advanced to within 400 yards of the remains of the town, it then halted and was subjected to very heavy machine-gun fire that caused many casualties. When the advance continued, it was held up by fire from a concrete blockhouse, which was captured, along with 45 prisoners and seven machine-guns, by Serjeant Edward Cooper, a deed for which he was subsequently awarded the Victoria Cross[330].

By 0750hrs, the battalion had captured its objective, but a German counterattack at 1630hrs almost wiped out its "B" Company, although there was no loss of ground. Arthur was killed during this attack and his body was never recovered, so he is commemorated on the Tyne Cot Memorial.

George also joined The King's Royal Rifle Corps when he was discharged from the Royal Hibernian Military School in 1905. He was killed in action on 14 September 1914 and is commemorated on the La Ferte-Sous-Jouarre Memorial.

Albert William TRICKEY (served as Albert William MERRIN)

Rifleman, R/19704, 20th (Service) Battalion (British Empire League Pioneers), The King's Royal Rifle Corps who died on 29 April 1918, aged 19. Buried in Pernes British Cemetery, Pas de Calais, France

Born of 21 September 1898 in Waltham Abbey, Essex, the oldest of three children of Albert William Trickey and Elizabeth Annie née

---

[330] *The London Gazette*, 14 September 1917, Supplement:30284 *"No. R.2794 Sjt. Edward Cooper, K.R.R.C. (Stockton). For most conspicuous bravery and initiative in attack. Enemy machine guns from a concrete blockhouse, 250 yards away, were holding up the advance of the battalion on his left, and were also causing heavy casualties to his own battalion. Sjt. Cooper, with four men, immediately rushed towards the blockhouse, though heavily fired on. About 100 yards distant he ordered his men to lie down and fire at the blockhouse. Finding this did not silence the machine guns, he immediately rushed forward straight at them and fired his revolver into an opening in the blockhouse. The machine guns ceased firing and the garrison surrendered. Seven machine guns and forty-five prisoners were captured in this blockhouse. By this magnificent act of courage he undoubtedly saved what might have been a serious check to the whole advance, at the same time saving a great number of lives."*

Lanham, his father was a Corporal in The Essex Regiment who died of wounds received at Driefontein, South Africa, on 20 March 1900, during the Second Boer War. His mother remarried, to Arthur Richard Merrin, in West Ham, Essex, on 20 January 1901.

Albert was admitted to the school on 08 September 1908 (Petition No. 12540), but was only at the school for eleven days before he was returned home on 19 September 1908 due to enuresis.

Little is known about Albert after he left the school, although he does appear in the 1911 Census, recorded living in West Ham, Essex, with his stepfather and half-brother, at school and still using the surname Trickey. However, it also appears that he adopted the surname of his stepfather, becoming Albert William Merrin and that following the outbreak of war, this was the name that he used when he enlisted at Woolwich, London, joining 20th (Service) Battalion (British Empire League Pioneers), The King's Royal Rifle Corps.

This battalion had been formed by the British Empire League[331] in London on 20 August 1915, moving to Wellingborough, Northamptonshire, in February 1916 and landing at Le Havre on 30 March 1916, coming under the orders of the 3rd Division as a Pioneer Battalion on 19 May 1916.

Albert's service record is no longer available, so his movements during the war are unknown, but his medal index card, although having no disembarkation date, does show that he was not entitled to the award of the 1914-15 Star, suggesting that he did not arrive in theatre until 1916, likely with his battalion in May of that year.

Being a Pioneer unit, the battalion did not take part in the fighting of the Somme Offensive, but was used to consolidate and shore-up gains that had been made by the assaulting Allied troops, and this appears to have been its role during the majority of its time on the Western Front.

However, following the launch of the German Spring Offensive in March 1918, all troops were required to stall the rapid advance. At the beginning of April 1918, the battalion was engaged in refresher training at Bruay, before it moved into the support trenches at Sevelingue, near Choques on 18 April 1918.

The battalion was to suffer casualties on a daily basis during this tour of duty, including Albert. It is likely that having been wounded, he was evacuated to the No. 1 Casualty Clearing Station located in Choques, dying of his wounds on 29 April.

---

[331] This had been formed by Lords Avebury, Roberts and Strathcona in London in 1895 with the aim of permanently securing unity for the British Empire. It had previously helped to mobilise troops for the Second Boer War

Although he served under the name of his stepfather, his grave marker acknowledges his biological father, as it is engraved with the words, *"Here lies a mother's only son who like his father fell"*.

Likely because he spent such a short time at the school, he is also a "Lost Boy" whose name has been omitted from the memorial tablets in the school chapel.

The Duke of Edinburgh's (Wiltshire Regiment)

Alec BABBINGTON
Private, 9036, 2nd Battalion, The Duke of Edinburgh's (Wiltshire Regiment) who died on 05 November 1918, aged 19. Buried in Cross Roads Cemetery, Fontaine-Au-Bois, Nord, France

Born on 08 May 1899 in Manchester, Lancashire, the sixth of seven children of William Babbington and Emily Augusta Flora née Cadden, his father had been a Colour Serjeant in The Lancashire Fusiliers, who had served for 17 years before being discharged on 12 October 1893. The family appears to have remained in Manchester, however by 1906 they had moved to Altrincham, Cheshire, which is where Alec's mother died on 24 October of that year.

At some point following his mother's death, Alec and his family moved to London, which was where his father was originally from and he was admitted to the school on 01 June 1910 (Petition No. 12765), a month after his 11th birthday, remaining there until 23 June 1913. His service record is no longer available, but according to school records, he enlisted into The Duke of Edinburgh's (Wiltshire Regiment) on discharge.

In 1913, the 2nd Battalion was stationed in Gibraltar, returning to Britain on 03 September 1914. After a brief stay in Lyndhurst, Hampshire, it landed at Zeebrugge on 07 October and remained in France and Flanders for the duration of the war, fighting in most of the major engagements. However, due to Alec's age and medal records, it can be surmised that he did not enter theatre until late 1917 at the earliest.

In March 1918, the 2nd Battalion, like the 1st Battalion, was almost destroyed during the German Spring Offensive, but having been reformed in April, it then took part in many of the battles that made up the Hundred Days Offensive. As the end of the war approached, it captured Haussy on 20 October, sustaining about 120 casualties, although, unfortunately, most of these were from British shells falling short.

On the 04 November, the battalion was near Jenlain and captured the high ground in front of Eth. The advance was continued the following day toward Roisin, commencing at 0626hrs after a short barrage. Patrols were then pushed out to 1000 yards east of Maison Blanche, before The Royal Welsh Fusiliers pushed through the battalion to continue the advance.

During the advance on 05 November 1918, Alec was killed in action, six days before the end of the war. He is buried in Cross Roads Cemetery, Fontaine-Au-Bois, eight kilometres north-east of Le Cateau, one of 21 soldiers from The Wiltshire Regiment buried there.

Alec had an older brother, Charles William Babington, who was not a Dukie, but who did lose his life in the war. He was an Engine Room Artificer 3rd Class on HMS *Sedgefly*, one of the gunboats that was patrolling the Tigris River in Mesopotamia. He died of disease on 07 March 1918 and is buried in Kut War Cemetery.

Edward Victor DAVIES
Serjeant, 25981, 2nd Battalion, The Duke of Edinburgh's (Wiltshire Regiment) who died on 28 March 1920, aged 22. Buried in Bath (Locksbrook) Cemetery, Somerset, United Kingdom

Born on 01 June 1897 in Bath, Somerset, the second of four children of Walter John Davies and Emily Jane née Bright, his father had been a Serjeant in Prince Albert's (Somersetshire Light Infantry), who was discharged from the army on 04 August 1898 and died in Bath on 06 May 1907.

Edward was admitted to the school on 14 November 1907 and would have moved from Chelsea to Guston, before he was discharged on 29 June 1911. The school records show him as enlisting into his father's old regiment, by now renamed as Prince Albert's (Somerset Light Infantry), but as his service record has not survived, it cannot be confirmed at which point he re-enlisted or transferred into The Duke of Edinburgh's (Wiltshire Regiment).

Medal records suggest that he did not serve overseas until 1916 at the earliest and also show that when he did deploy, he was serving with 5th (Service) Battalion, The Duke of Edinburgh's (Wiltshire Regiment). This battalion had been formed at Devizes, Wiltshire, as part of K1, becoming Army Troops for the 13th (Western) Division, moving first to Tidworth, Wiltshire, and then, in October 1914, to Chiseldon, Wiltshire. Two months later, in December 1914, it moved to Cirencester, Gloucestershire, joining the 40th Brigade of the division, moving again in February 1915 to Woking, Surrey, and then three months later to Bisley, Surrey.

On 01 July 1915, the battalion sailed from Avonmouth, Gloucestershire, to Gallipoli, where it landed on 17 July, remaining there until it was evacuated to Egypt in January 1916, a month later sailing for Mesopotamia, where it was to spend the remainder of the war and where it is likely that Edward joined.

There is scant information regarding Edward's time during the war, but it is known that in 1920 he was admitted to the military hospital in Devonport, Devonshire, where he died on 28 March, possibly as a result of disease contracted whilst he was serving in the Middle East. He is also a "Lost Boy" whose name has been omitted from the memorial tablets in the school chapel.

Wilfred John LEWIS
Lance Corporal, 8537, 2nd Battalion, The Duke of Edinburgh's (Wiltshire Regiment) who died on 13 October 1915, aged 19. Buried in Cambrin Churchyard Extension, Pas de Calais, France

Born on 23 April 1896 in Alverstoke, Hampshire, the youngest of six children of John Thomas Lewis and Elizabeth née Bowyer, his father had been a Quartermaster Serjeant in the Royal Engineers who died of apoplexy on 20 October 1896 in Gosport, Hampshire.

It appears that after John's death, the family fell on hard times. Although Wilfred's mother was still alive, both he and his older brother, Frederick, are recorded in the 1901 Census as inmates at St. David's Orphanage, Gower, Wales, but their four sisters do not appear as inmates.

Wilfred was admitted to the school on 30 March 1906 (Petition No. 12214) and would have made the transition from Chelsea to Dover, before he was discharged on 03 May 1910 into The Duke of Edinburgh's (Wiltshire Regiment) as he left the school.

At the outbreak of war, Wilfred may have been serving alongside fellow Dukie Alec Babbington in Gibraltar. However, although the battalion landed at Zeebrugge on 07 October 1914, according to Wilfred's medal index card, he did not enter theatre until 08 June 1915, so it is possible that his first action was when the battalion participated in the Battle of Aubers Ridge.

In September 1915, it participated in the Battle of Loos, which was launched on the 25 September and was designed to break through the German defences in Artois and Champagne. During this battle, which lasted until 08 October, the British captured the German strongpoint of the Hohenzollern Redoubt, but this was later recaptured by the Germans on 03 October. The British then made a concerted effort to recapture this strongpoint and launched an attack on 13 October, which lasted until 19 October. It was a complete failure and caused 3,643 casualties, mostly in the first few minutes, among which was Wilfred, who died on 13 October 1915.

Unlike many, his body was recovered and he is buried in Cambrin Churchyard Extension, less than two miles from the target of the British assault on that day.

Wilfred's brother, Frederick, is also commemorated by the Commonwealth War Graves Commission. Having emigrated to the United States before the war, he enlisted into the Canadian Army in 1918 and was posted to Britain. Having contracted, and survived, influenza in November 1918, he contracted it again in February 1919 and on admission to hospital was also discovered to have tuberculosis. He was evacuated to Canada, prior to returning to home to the United States, where he died as a result of the tuberculosis in November 1920. He is buried in Sheridan Municipal Cemetery, Big Horn, Wyoming.

William Robert McCARRAGHER
Company Serjeant Major, 5063, 1st Battalion, The Duke of Edinburgh's (Wiltshire Regiment) who died on 31 January 1915, aged 30. Buried in Kemmel Chateau Military Cemetery, West-Vlaanderen, Belgium

Born on 22 July 1884 in Devizes, Wiltshire, the second of six children of Robert James McCarragher and Elizabeth Jane née Sudweeks, his father was a Serjeant in The Duke of Edinburgh's (Wiltshire Regiment) who died at sea on 16 April 1894.

William was admitted to the school on 28 February 1896 (Petition No. 10869) and discharged to his father's old regiment on 11 August 1898. Two years after William was discharged, his younger brother, Reginald Alfred James McCarragher, was admitted on 07 September 1900 (Petition No. 11479).

William's service record is no longer available, but it is known from medal records that he served in South Africa during the Second Boer War and that he was recorded in the 1911 Census as a Serjeant stationed in Le Marchant Barracks, Devizes. He was also a father by this time, having married Elizabeth Annie Adams in 1906, their first child, William George McCarragher being born in 1909, and their daughter, Evelyn McCarragher, born in 1910. They also had another son, Charles Reginald Samuel McCarragher, born in 1912.

According to his obituary in a local newspaper[332], William had been the Officers' Mess Serjeant in the Regimental Depot in Devizes until posted to the 1st Battalion, stationed in Tidworth, Wiltshire. At the outbreak of war, this battalion was mobilised, embarking at Southampton, Hampshire on 13 August and landing at Rouen on 14 August 1914. After landing, it was involved in the Battle of Mons and the subsequent retreat, the Battles of Le Cateau, of the Marne,

---
[332] *Wiltshire Times and Trowbridge Advertiser*, Saturday 13 February 1915

of the Aisne, of La Bassée and Messines as well as the First Battle of Ypres.

However, it did not participate in the Christmas Truce, the battalion war diary reporting that although there was practically no shelling, there was a little sniping and that it lost two killed, one wounded and one missing[333].

At the end of January 1915, the battalion was in trenches near Kemmel and on 31 January 1915, the battalion diary states that the trenches were shelled slightly and that there was continuous sniping, during which one man was killed, this man being William, who according to the newspaper article cited above, was *"fatally shot in the neck"*. He was interred close to the area where he died and although he is commemorated on the memorial tablets in the school chapel, he is incorrectly named as W P McCarragher.

It is not known if Reginald served during the war. He had been *"withdrawn by mother"* on 10 June 1901 and was recorded in the 1911 Census as a Barman in the Sutton Arms in Islington, London. There also appear to be no records of any service for him. However, if he did serve, he survived, dying in Edgware, Middlesex, in 1961.

Both of William's sons were Dukies. William was admitted to the school on 12 March 1918 (Petition No. 13729), but was *"Expelled for theft"* on 13 November 1922. He died in Bristol, Avon, in 1980. Charles was admitted to the school on 29 December 1921 (Petition No. 14099). He was discharged from the school on 15 December 1926 and died in Gloucester, Gloucestershire in 1982.

---

[333] WO 95/1415/2: 1 Battalion Wiltshire Regiment, 1914 Aug. - 1915 Oct., The National Archives, Kew

The Manchester Regiment

Burton Charles Langdon JOYCE
Private, 7338, 2nd Battalion, The Manchester Regiment who died on 27 February 1918, aged 30. Commemorated on the Tyne Cot Memorial, West-Vlaanderen, Belgium

Born on 27 November 1887 in Jullundur, India, the second of three children of George Joyce and Kate née Ridgeley, his father had been a Bandsman in The Connaught Rangers, who had been discharged from the army after 26 years' service on 02 June 1891 and died in Alverstoke, Hampshire, on 24 January 1893.

Burton was admitted to the school on 27 November 1897 (Petition No. 11088) and was joined by his younger brother, Cyril Francis Joyce, on 06 October 1899 (Petition No. 11346). Burton was discharged from the school on 30 November 1901 and enlisted into The Manchester Regiment as a Musician. Having enlisted, Burton spent the first month of his service at the Regimental Depot in Ashton-under-Lyne, Lancashire, before being posted to the 3rd Battalion in December 1901 and appointed as a Drummer on 08 January 1902.

On 28 July 1902, he was posted to the island of St. Helena, in the South Atlantic, remaining there for five months, being posted to South Africa on 31 December 1902. He was to spend almost three years there, before he was posted to the 2nd Battalion and returned to Britain on 01 December 1906. The next seven years of Burton's service were spent in Britain, half with the 2nd Battalion, where he was appointed as a Lance Corporal prior to reverting to Private for drunkenness on 13 December 1909, before he was posted to the 4th Battalion on 01 November 1910, a month after the birth of his first child, who was born in Portsmouth, Hampshire, in October 1910.

Whilst serving with this battalion, Burton married Ivy Lillian Gibbs in Portsmouth on 01 January 1911, their second child being born in October 1913, a month before he was discharged from the army at the end of his first period of service on 20 November 1913.

However, on 09 March 1914, Burton re-enlisted into The Manchester Regiment, being initially posted to the 3rd (Reserve) Battalion, where he was appointed as an Acting Lance Corporal on

30 August, although he reverted to Private when he was posted to the 2nd Battalion, disembarking with that battalion on 27 October 1914.

The battalion contributed to the rear-guard actions that supported the British Expeditionary Force during its retreat in the wake of the Battle of Mons and it is possible that Burton was involved in the action that saw the award of the Victoria Cross to Second Lieutenant James Leach and Serjeant John Hogan[334] from his battalion.

On 21 May 1915, during the Second Battle of Ypres, Burton suffered a gunshot wound to his foot, which resulted in his evacuation back to Britain on 31 May 1915, although he then re-embarked for France six months later on 15 December 1915. Two weeks after arriving back in France, he was posted to the 3rd Army Trench Mortar School, joining the 81st Trench Mortar Battery three months later. However, three months after that, on 12 April 1916, he was posted as an Assistant Instructor at the 4th Army Trench Mortar School and then 5th Army Trench Mortar School on 08 November 1916. On 30 June 1917, Burton, by now a Corporal, was posted to the 14th Trench Mortar Battery, the unit with which he was to spend the remainder of his war.

However, his time with this unit was not without incident. On 12 January 1918, he was tried by Field General Courts Martial for being absent without leave and drunkenness when on active service, his sentence being that he was reduced to the rank of Private. It is possible that the catalyst for his behaviour was that he had been informed about the death of his daughter, who had been born on 12 November 1917 and died four days later.

Burton was granted leave on 29 January 1918, returning to his unit on 12 February. He was killed in action two weeks later, one of four other ranks that was killed or missing in the wake of a trench raid that was carried out on the night of 27 February.

Burton has no known grave and is commemorated on the Tyne Cot Memorial. However, he is also another "Lost Boy" whose name has been omitted from the memorial tablets in the school chapel. This is possibly because the Commonwealth War Graves Commission has recorded his first name as *Burlton*.

---

[334] *The London Gazette*, 22 December 1914, Issue:29015: *"His. Majesty the KING has been graciously pleased to approve of the grant of the Victoria Cross to Second Lieutenant James Leach, and to No. 9016 Serjeant John Hogan, 2nd Battalion, The Manchester Regiment, for their conspicuous bravery, specified below: —*
For conspicuous bravery near Festubert on 29th October, when, after their trench had been taken by the Germans, and after two attempts at recapture had failed, they voluntarily decided on the afternoon of the same day to recover the trench themselves, and, working from traverse to traverse at close quarters with great bravery, they gradually succeeded in regaining possession, killing eight of the enemy, wounding two, and making sixteen prisoners."

Cyril was discharged from the school on 29 August 1903 and enlisted into the Royal Field Artillery. He spent his entire service in Britain as a Trumpeter, paying £25 to secure his discharge from the army on 15 February 1912. He seemingly did not re-enlist during the war and was a Shell Stamper at the Hadfields Foundry when he died in Sheffield, Yorkshire West Riding, in 1916, aged only twenty-six.

Charles Joseph PEAT
Lance Corporal, 251621, 1/6th Battalion, The Manchester Regiment who died on 28 March 1918, aged 37. Commemorated on the Arras Memorial, Pas de Calais, France

Born on 24 July 1880 in Bermuda, West Indies, the eldest of four children of Joseph Charles Peat and Kate née Wilson, his father had been a Colour Sergeant in the 99th Duke of Edinburgh's (Lanarkshire) Regiment of Foot[335] who had been discharged to pension. He died in Manchester, Lancashire, on 20 February 1889.

Joseph was admitted to the school on 30 August 1889 (Petition No. 9892) and was discharged *"To mother"* on 25 July 1895. His younger brother, Samuel Peat, had been admitted to the Royal Hibernian Military School in Dublin. Joseph was recorded as a Drapery Merchants Clerk in the 1911 Census, living in Collyhurst, Manchester, and it is known that he enlisted into the army during the war, although there is no service record available for him.

By March 1918, he was a Lance Corporal serving in The Manchester Regiment. The battalion in which he was serving, 1/6th Battalion, was a Territorial Force battalion that was located in Stretford Road, Hulme, Lancashire, and was part of the Manchester Brigade, East Lancashire Division, in August 1914.

On 25 September 1914 it landed in Alexandria, Egypt, before, on 06 May 1915, it landed on Gallipoli. It remained there until it was evacuated on 28 December, moving first to Mudros and then back to Egypt. It was from here that it then landed at Marseille, France, on 02 March 1917.

It is only speculation, but it is likely that Charles arrived in France after that date. His medal index card records no disembarkation date in any theatre, nor an award of the 1914-1915 Star, so with the battalion in Gallipoli & Egypt until landing at Marseille, it is reasonable to assume that he joined the battalion after that date and may well have taken part in the Third Battle of Ypres later in 1917.

---

[335] Amalgamated with the 62nd (Wiltshire) Regiment of Foot on 10 July 1881 to become The Duke of Edinburgh's (Wiltshire Regiment)

In early-1918, the battalion was still on the Western Front and was initially held in reserve during the German Spring Offensive, but by 26 March 1918 it was in the Rossignol Wood-Bucquoy sector, under heavy shelling and attacks by the German 3rd Guards Infantry Division. The battalion war diary[336] records the following on the day of Charles's death, after mention of a local attack and raid being repelled during the day:

"Around 6.0pm our forward coys and advanced posts were subject to an intense bombardment for 50 minutes after which the shelling ceased and no further attempts were made to attack during the evening... Casualties for this day Killed 7 OR Wounded 29 OR Missing 9 OR."

It is likely that Charles was one of the nine other ranks to be declared missing, his body never being recovered and he is now commemorated on the Arras Memorial. He is also a "Lost Boy" whose name has been omitted from the memorial tablets in the school chapel.

Ralph Godfrey SMITH
Company Serjeant Major, 4370, 22nd (Service) Battalion (7th City), The Manchester Regiment who died on 03 November 1918, aged 40. Buried in Staglieno Cemetery, Genoa, Italy

Born on 24 June 1878 in Barking by the Tower, City of London, the youngest child of William John Smith and Isabel née Bateman, his father had been a Serjeant in the Royal Artillery, but was employed as a Clerk in the Pensions Office by the time that his son was born, having been discharged from the army on 14 April 1874. He died in Manchester, Lancashire, on 20 February 1889 and Ralph's mother died in Manchester in 1893.

Ralph was admitted to the school on 24 May 1889 and was discharged on 04 November 1893 *"To Sister"*. Within his school record, there is a letter dated 16 October 1893 from Ralph's brother-in-law, Colour Sergeant John Power, who was serving with The Manchester Regiment at Ashton-under-Lyne, Lancashire, and was married to Ralph's eldest sister, Isabella, stating that Ralph had been orphaned and asking why he had not been passed fit for the army. A later letter from him, dated 26 October 1893, then asks that he be sent temporarily to his youngest married sister in Tottenham, London.

Despite initially considered unfit for the army, Ralph enlisted into The Manchester Regiment on 17 October 1894, spending his first

---

[336] WO 95/2660/2: 1/6 Battalion Manchester Regiment, 1917 Mar. - 1919 Mar., The National Archives, Kew

three months in the Regimental Depot in Ladysmith Barracks, Ashton-under-Lyne, before being posted to the 4th Battalion, which was also located in Ashton-under-Lyne. After four years with that battalion, he was posted back to the Depot, appointed as a Lance Corporal in June of 1899 and as a Clerk in the July.

On 01 March 1900, Ralph was promoted to Corporal, and promoted to Sergeant two years later, before being posted to the 2nd Battalion and embarking for Singapore. After a year there, he was then posted to India, returning to Britain on 26 October 1906 after he had been appointed as a Serjeant on the Permanent Staff of the 1/6th Battalion. Ralph was promoted to Colour Serjeant on 17 January 1909, married Ada Oldham in 1914 and was still with the battalion when war broke out, spending the majority of the war with the unit, before being posted to the 22nd (Service) (7th City) Battalion on 26 January 1918, in the rank of Company Serjeant Major.

The battalion that he joined had been formed in Manchester on 21 November 1914 by the Lord Mayor and City. It had then moved to Morecambe, Lancashire, in January 1915, to Grantham, Lincolnshire, in the April and finally Larkhill, Wiltshire, in the September before landing at Boulogne in early-November 1915, where it spent two years on the Western Front before moving to Italy in November 1917 in order to bolster the Italians, who had suffered a major defeat during which the Austro-Hungarians and Germans broke out of Caporetto, forcing the Italians back.

Little information can be found regarding The Manchester Regiment's involvement in the Italian Campaign, but by November 1918, Ralph had been admitted to hospital, where he died from bronchopneumonia on 03 November 1918, eight days before the war ended.

The Prince of Wales's
(North Staffordshire Regiment)

Alfred John RUTLEDGE

Serjeant, 8404, 1st Battalion, The Prince of Wales's (North Staffordshire Regiment) who died on 19 May 1915, aged 22. Buried in Ferme Buterne Military Cemetery, Houplines, Nord, France

Born on 12 January 1893 in Dover, Kent, the second son of William Rutledge and Elizabeth née Murphy, his father was a Private in The Northumberland Fusiliers and was still serving when he died in Tynemouth, Northumberland, on 17 July 1897.

Alfred was admitted to the school on 12 July 1902 (Petition No. 11720), which was four months after his older brother William Martin Rutledge, who had been admitted on 06 January 1898 (Petition No. 11111), had been discharged. Alfred was discharged on 07 February 1907 and enlisted straight into The Prince of Wales's (North Staffordshire Regiment), although his service record is no longer available.

At the outbreak of war, the 1st Battalion was stationed in Cork, County Cork, but two days later it was in Cambridge, Cambridgeshire. It then embarked on the 07 September and landed at St. Nazaire on 12 September 1914, spending its first month in theatre in northern France, participating in the Battle of the Aisne.

In mid-October, the battalion was relocated into the Ypres Salient before crossing back over the frontier into France. On Christmas Day 1914, it was still in this location and the war diary reports, *"Not a shot fired. Germans bury their dead, our men go and help. Baccy and cigars exchanged and Germans and our men walk about in the open together!! Return to the trenches at 4pm. Peace reigns till midnight"*[337].

This peace continued the following day, the diary stating that the Germans were keen to continue the peace and that the weather had changed, to the extent that by 27 December the trenches were waist deep in water, although the battalion was relieved and returned to billets on 31 December 1914.

---

[337] WO 95/1613/3: 1 Battalion North Staffordshire Regiment, 1914 Aug. - 1915 Oct., The National Archives, Kew

By May 1915, the battalion was located at L'Epinette, south-west of Armentières, with the peace that had reigned at Christmas long forgotten. On 20 May 1915, the battalion war diary records that it was a *"lovely day"*[338], although it did suffer fifteen casualties due to lots of shelling by "Little Willie", a nickname for a German artillery piece. The diary continues *"Sjt Rutledge killed cutting long grass in front overnight"*[339]. Alfred died on the night of 19-20 May 1915 and was buried in Ferme Buterne Military Cemetery, three miles from where he was killed.

William was discharged from the school on 22 March 1902 and also served during the war, having enlisted in their father's old regiment. He was killed on 07 October 1918 and although he, like his brother, is commemorated on the memorial tablets in the school chapel, he is incorrectly commemorated as *Routledge*. He is documented earlier in the book.

---

[338] Ibid.
[339] Ibid.

The York and Lancaster Regiment

Harold Stanley BOOTH
Second Lieutenant, 11th (Reserve) Battalion attached to 8th (Service) Battalion, The York and Lancaster Regiment who died on 01 July 1916, aged 19. Commemorated on the Thiepval Memorial, Somme, France

Born on 05 November 1896 in Wellington, India, the second of five children of Herbert Booth and Martha née Wainwright, his father was a Colour Serjeant in The South Staffordshire Regiment and was still serving when he died in Hightown, Lancashire, on 29 May 1905. Harold's grandfather, Anthony Clarke Booth, had been awarded the Victoria Cross in 1879 for his actions at the Battle of Intombe during the Zulu War.

Harold was admitted to the school on 22 August 1906 (Petition No. 12258), joining his older brother, Herbert Booth, who had been admitted on 10 November 1905 (Petition No. 12163). Having moved from Chelsea to Guston, Harold was withdrawn from the school on 22 July 1910, although the reason for this withdrawal is not known. The 1911 Census records him in Bradford, Yorkshire West Riding, working as an Office Boy in a solicitor's office.

Harold's service record is not publicly available, so it is not possible to establish when he enlisted into the army, but it is known that he was Commissioned as a Temporary 2nd Lieutenant in The York and Lancaster Regiment on May 1915[340] and was previously a Corporal in The Prince of Wales's Own (West Yorkshire Regiment. The battalion to which he was originally posted, the 11th (Reserve) Battalion, was formed as a Service Battalion in September 1914 as part of K3, but transferred to K4. On 10 April 1915 it became a Reserve Battalion and moved, on 24 May, to Farnley Park at Otley, Yorkshire West Riding.

How long Harold was with this battalion is not known, but at some point, he was attached to the 8th (Service) Battalion, which had originally been formed at Pontefract, Yorkshire West Riding, in September 1914 as part of K3. It then moved to Frensham, Surrey, and on to Aldershot, Hampshire, in November, before moving to

---

[340] *The London Gazette*, 28 May 1915, Issue:29175

Hythe, Kent, in February 1915 and finally, in the May, to Bordon, Hampshire. It was then deployed to France, landing at Boulogne on 27 August 1915 and it is known that Harold entered theatre on 29 May 1916.

Once it had arrived in France, the unit participated in various engagements until July 1916, when it was one of eleven battalions of The York and Lancaster Regiment to go "over the top" on the first day of the Somme Offensive, near Ovillers. Harold was one of the 21 officers and 576 soldiers from that regiment that were killed on 01 July 1916, the fifth highest casualty figure of any battalion involved in the battle on that date. He has no known grave and is commemorated on the Thiepval Memorial on the Somme.

It also appears that his rank is incorrectly recorded by the Commonwealth War Graves Commission, as it records him as a Lieutenant. There is no evidence that he was promoted to that rank, and in fact in the Registers of Soldiers' Effects[341], the entry of his rank as "Lieut" has been annotated with "2nd" in a different hand and pen.

Herbert was discharged from the school on 02 July 1912, before becoming a Student and later a Schoolmaster on Probation. He was able to resign from his position and be Commissioned into The Prince of Wales's Own (West Yorkshire Regiment). He too was killed, on 03 May 1917, and is also commemorated on the memorial tablets in the school chapel, as well as being documented earlier in this book.

Alfred George William O'LEARY

Serjeant, 12837, 6th (Service) Battalion, The York and Lancaster Regiment who died on 09 August 1915, aged 32. Commemorated on the Helles Memorial, Turkey

Born on 05 November 1882 in Pontefract, Yorkshire West Riding, a son of Arthur O'Leary and Sarah née Wensley, his father had been a Serjeant who had served for 11 years in the 38th (1st Staffordshire) Regiment of Foot[342], for 12 years in the 34th (Cumberland) Regiment of Foot[343] and finally for 13 years on the Permanent Staff of 3rd Battalion, The York and Lancashire Regiment, a post that he still held when he died in Pontefract on 27 April 1891.

---

[341] UK, Army Registers of Soldiers' Effects, 1901-1929, 1916, Army Officers, 16601-17600D
[342] Amalgamated with the 80th (Staffordshire Volunteers) Regiment of Foot on 01 July 1881 to become The South Staffordshire Regiment
[343] Amalgamated with the 55th (Westmorland) Regiment of Foot on 01 July 1881 to become The Border Regiment

Alfred was admitted to the school on 28 October 1892 (Petition No. 10380), joining his older brother, Francis Arthur O'Leary, who had been admitted on 27 November 1891 (Petition No. 10246). Alfred was discharged from the school on 07 November 1896, enlisting into The King's Own (Royal Lancaster Regiment), being appointed as a Drummer on 29 December 1896. He spent the first three years of his service in the Regimental Depot in Bowerham Barracks, Lancaster, Lancashire, before he was posted to the 1st Battalion on 01 April 1900. It was with this battalion, that he was posted to South Africa, on 26 November 1900, during the Second Boer War and for which he was awarded the Queen's South Africa Medal.

He did not to return to Britain until 09 April 1903 and spent the remaining five years of his service at home, marrying Sarah Ann Varey in Pontefract in 1905, before he was discharged as a Drummer on 06 November 1908. Following his discharge from the army, Alfred was employed as a Surface Labourer at Featherstone Main Colliery. His eldest son, William John O'Leary, was born in 1909, with a second son, Harry Burton O'Leary, born in 1912, before Alfred was recalled to the Colours on 31 August 1914 as a Special Reservist.

By 13 September he was a Serjeant serving in 6th (Service) Battalion, The York and Lancaster Regiment. This battalion had been formed in Pontefract in August 1914 as part of K1, becoming part of 32nd Brigade, 11th (Northern) Division, moving initially to Grantham, Lincolnshire, and then Witley, Surrey, before sailing from Liverpool, Lancashire, for Gallipoli on 03 July 1915. The battalion landed at Suvla Bay, Gallipoli, on the morning of 07 August 1915 and having cleared Charak Cheshme Ridge, it advanced in the evening towards Chocolate Hill in support of the 33rd Brigade. The following day it supported the brigade attack on Scimitar Hill, with its position held against numerous counter attacks.

Ground was repeatedly gained and lost in this period, before the battalion withdrew to Lala Baba on the evening of 11 August 1915. Between 07-11 August, the regiment recorded eight officers killed, eleven wounded, one missing and 78 other ranks killed, 167 wounded, 12 missing. The dead included Alfred and it was reported that his Dukie brother Francis, a Drum Major in the same battalion, was with him when he was killed[344]. Alfred's third son, also Alfred O'Leary, was born the year that his father died.

---

[344] *Yorkshire Post and Leeds Intelligencer*, Saturday 18 September 1915

Alfred has no known grave and is commemorated on the Helles Memorial. He is also a "Lost Boy" whose name has been omitted from the memorial tablets in the school chapel.

Francis was discharged from the school on 22 November 1894 and enlisted into The York and Lancaster Regiment. He had been discharged from the army at the end of his service by the time that the war commenced, the 1911 Census recording him living in Wakefield, Yorkshire West Riding, with his wife, son and daughter and employed as a Postman. He was also recalled to the Colours in September 1914 and served as the Drum Major in the same battalion as Alfred. He survived the war and died in Wakefield in 1956.

There was a third brother, Harry Frederick O'Leary, who was not a Dukie, but who also served in The York and Lancaster Regiment. According to the local newspaper report of Alfred's death, Harry was killed on the same day as him whilst serving in France with the 2nd Battalion. However, his date of death is recorded by the Commonwealth War Graves Commission as 11 August 1915. He died of wounds, received during an attempt to retake lost trenches at Hooge.

Francis Henry George WOOLGAR
Drummer, 10029, Depot, The York and Lancaster Regiment who died on 16 June 1915, aged 17. Buried in Pontefract Cemetery, West Yorkshire, United Kingdom

Born on 17 December 1897 in Wimbledon, Surrey, the only child of George Henry Woolgar and Annie Elizabeth née Daborn, his father had been a Private in The Royal Fusiliers (City of London Regiment), but had been discharged at the end of his term of service on 31 December 1901. He died in Wimbledon on 07 February 1907.

Francis was admitted to the school on 30 March 1908 (Petition No. 12479) and having moved from Chelsea to Guston, was discharged on 04 January 1912, enlisting into The York and Lancaster Regiment. He initially joined the 2nd Battalion, which was stationed in Limerick, County Limerick, before, just over a year later on 04 March 1913, he was transferred to the 1st Battalion, stationed in Jubbulpore, India. Whilst here, he contracted malaria, spending fifteen days hospitalised in April 1914.

Following the outbreak of war, the battalion returned to Britain on 23 December 1914, undergoing training before it landed at Le Havre on 17 January 1915. However, because Francis was still a Boy, and therefore underage for deployment, he was transferred to the Regimental Depot in Pontefract, Yorkshire West Riding. He was appointed as a Drummer on 03 February 1915, but three months later he developed pneumonia and died on 16 June 1915.

Francis was buried in Pontefract, but despite being commemorated by the Commonwealth War Graves Commission, he is another of the "Lost Boys" whose name has been omitted from the memorial tablets in the school chapel.

The Durham Light Infantry

Reginald David DOUGLAS
Private, 10776, 12th (Service) Battalion, The Durham Light Infantry who died on 20 October 1917, aged 22. Commemorated on the Tyne Cot Memorial, West-Vlaanderen, Belgium

Born on 28 April 1895 in Dorchester, Dorsetshire, the second of two sons of David Douglas and Catherine Ann née Beavis, his father had been a Private in The Dorsetshire Regiment who had been discharged to pension on 30 April 1899. He died on 12 May 1904 in Dorchester, two years after Reginald's mother, who had also died there, on 24 January 1902.

Reginald was admitted to the school on 08 October 1904 (Petition No. 12026) and discharged on 08 July 1909, enlisting into The Durham Light Infantry on the same day. He was a Bandsman, and not always well behaved, his conduct sheet showing that whilst still a Boy and stationed in Hyderabad Barracks in Colchester, Essex, with the 2nd Battalion, not only was he confined to barracks for being dirty on church parade in 1911, but the following year he was admonished on two occasions, the first for *"Destroying a hat, the property of Band- Serjeant Adams"* and the second for *"Wilfully breaking window panes in the motor sheds"*[345].

Despite this, Reginald was still with the 2nd Battalion at the outbreak of war, which by this stage was stationed at Lichfield, Staffordshire, although it then moved to Dunfermline, Fife, before moving again on 13 August to Cambridge, Cambridgeshire. It landed at St. Nazaire on 10 September 1914, seeing action for the first time ten days later. On the Aisne, at Armentières, in the Ypres Salient, and especially at Hooge on 08-09 August 1915, it suffered the loss of over 50 officers and 1500 soldiers killed, wounded, or missing. By September 1915, there were few men still serving who had landed in France twelve months before.

What is left of his service record does not make it clear, but at some point, Reginald was posted to the 12th (Service) Battalion, formed at Newcastle, Northumberland, in September 1914 as part of K3. This battalion had landed at Boulogne on 26 August 1915

---
[345] WO 363: First World War Service Records 'Burnt Documents'

and although in the trenches at various times, it did not participate, other than as reserve, in the two large offensives at Loos in 1915 and the Somme in 1916.

Despite being badly damaged, his service record shows that Reginald entered France on 9 January 1917. In June 1917, the 12th Battalion participated in the assault on the German trenches following the detonation of the mines under the Messines Ridge, capturing Impartial Trench for the loss of only fifteen casualties, before taking part in the Third Battle of Ypres, fighting on the Menin Road. It is likely during Third Ypres that Reginald was killed, one of seven from his battalion recorded as such on 20 October 1917. He has no known grave and is one of the 36,000 names commemorated on the Tyne Cot Memorial at the rear of the cemetery of the same name.

Llewellyn William MONGER

Serjeant, 8884, 11th (Service) Battalion (Pioneers), The Durham Light Infantry who died on 23 March 1918, aged 27. Commemorated on the Pozieres Memorial, Somme, France

Born on 26 September 1890 in Reading, Berkshire, the seventh of eight children of Edwin Monger and Ann Kercher née Ostridge, his father had been a Serjeant in the 60th (The King's Royal Rifle Corps) Regiment of Foot, who had been discharged to pension on 28 October 1879. Following discharge from the army, it would appear that he worked in Africa, although it is not recorded in what capacity. What is recorded is that he was killed on 07 May 1898 in Freetown, Sierra Leone, during the Hut Tax War.

Llewellyn was admitted to the school on 10 August 1900 (Petition No. 11465), joining his older brother, Edwin Newton Monger, who had been admitted on 03 February 1899 (Petition No. 11264). Both he and his brother left the school on 23 August 1902, having been *"detained on pass"*.

Llewellyn's service record has not survived, so it is not possible to establish when he joined the army, but his service number suggests a 1904 enlistment. It is known that he landed in France on 08 September 1914 as a Bandsman, suggesting that at that time he was serving as a Regular soldier with 1st Battalion, The Durham Light Infantry. Little is known about his time in France, but he obviously had some home leave, as he married Margaret George in South Shields, County Durham, in October 1915.

By the beginning of 1918, Llewellyn was a Serjeant with the 11th (Service) Battalion (Pioneers). This battalion had been formed in Newcastle, Northumberland, in September 1914 as part of K2, being converted to a Pioneer Battalion in January 1915 and landing at Boulogne in July 1915. By the middle of March 1918, it was engaged in work on the Ham-Noyon railway and billeted in the town of Golancourt, receiving orders to *"man battle stations"*[346] at 0620hrs on the morning of 21 March, the start of the German Spring Offensive.

It was to spend the rest of March attempting to stem the advance of the German forces, often, it appears, fighting desperate rear-guard actions. By the end of the month, it had been forced back almost 30 miles to the location of Thennes, near Amiens.

Although the battalion war diary[347] does not record casualties by day, it summarises these at the end of the month and it appears that Llewellyn was killed on 23 March 1918, during confused fighting in fog near the village of Canizy. It is likely that he is one of the 215 soldiers reported as missing between 21 and 31 March 1918, as he has no known grave and is commemorated on the Pozieres Memorial.

Edwin also served during the war, although he served as "William Stuart". He served in the Royal Field Artillery, Commissioned in 1915 and by the end of the war had been awarded the Distinguished Service Order and reached the rank of Acting Major. He was then attached to the Indian Political Department and killed in June 1920 at Tel Afar in Mesopotamia. He was buried in Baghdad War Cemetery and commemorated by the Commonwealth War Graves Commission, but, unlike his younger brother, he is not commemorated on the memorial tablets in the school chapel. He is also documented earlier in this book.

Robert SCOTT

Private, 5642, 2nd Battalion, The Durham Light Infantry who died on 03 January 1917, aged 35. Buried in Cologne Southern Cemetery, Nordrhein-Westfalen, Germany

Born on 01 September 1881 in Shorncliffe, Kent, one of five sons of Robert Scott and Elizabeth née Ferguson, his father was a Colour Serjeant in The Cameronians (Scottish Rifles), who was serving on the Permanent Staff of 4th Battalion, The Cameronians when he died in Edinburgh, Midlothian, on 19 August 1892. His mother died in London on 24 December 1893 and so the children were brought up by an aunt.

Robert was admitted to the school on 25 November 1892 (Petition No. 10403) and was joined by his younger brother, James

---

[346] WO 95/2108/2: 11 Battalion Durham Light Infantry (Pioneers), 1915 July - 1919 June, The National Archives, Kew
[347] Ibid.

Scott, who was admitted on 28 September 1894 (Petition No. 10659). Their youngest brother, Edward Scott, also attended the school, being admitted on 09 December 1898 (Petition No. 11241). Robert was discharged to The Durham Light Infantry on 31 August 1895, initially posted to the 1st Battalion as a Bugler and Musician, remaining in Britain until October 1899, when he was posted to South Africa during the Second Boer war, although during his time there he was convicted of theft by the civil power and sentenced to one month's imprisonment.

In November 1902, he left South Africa, having been posted to the West Indies, where he remained for six years and, after briefly being attached to the 3rd Battalion, he returned to Britain in November 1908, being posted to the 2nd Battalion, the 1911 Census recording him stationed in Hyderabad Barracks, Colchester, Essex.

At the outbreak of war, the battalion was stationed in Lichfield, Staffordshire, initially moving to Dunfermline, Fife, before moving to Cambridge, Cambridgeshire, and then embarking at Southampton, Hampshire, on 08 September, landing at St. Nazaire on 09 September 1914, having its first experiences of the trenches at Troyon ten days later. It then spent the rest of September and early-October rotating through the trenches near Verdun, before moving to the west of Lille.

On 18 October, the battalion was ordered to make a *"demonstration"*[348] in order to test the enemy's strength. The attack commenced at 1545hrs and was completely successful. However, it suffered two officers wounded, four other ranks killed, 74 wounded and 29 missing, Robert being one of those reported as missing and it was not until 06 May 1915 that he was finally reported as a Prisoner of War. He was held in Friedrichsfeld, near Wesel, Germany, and in January 1917, a letter was received from the Director of the Military Hospital at Bedburg Hau, Cleve, informing the British that Robert Scott had died in the hospital from pneumonia on 03 January 1917. He was buried in Cologne Southern Cemetery.

Robert's brothers all served, although James, who was discharged *"to Uncle"* on 01 March 1899 and Edward, who was discharged *"To Grandmother; weak intellect"* on 04 March 1899, both enlisted later. Their oldest, non-Dukie brother, John, was a Private in The King's Own Scottish Borderers, who died of wounds at Gallipoli in June 1915, although James, Edward and the fifth brother, Henry, all survived the war.

---

[348] WO 95/1617/1: 2 Battalion Durham Light Infantry, 1914 Aug. - 1919 Mar., The National Archives, Kew

William SMITH
Private, 80527, 1/7th Battalion, The Durham Light Infantry who died on 13 April 1918, aged 41. Commemorated on the Ploegsteert Memorial, Hainaut, Belgium

Born on 20 March 1877 in Canterbury, Kent, the second of three children of Alexander Smith and Hannah née Henderson, his father had been a Private in the 12th (The Prince of Wales's Royal) Lancers, who had been discharged from the army on 05 July 1881 and who died in Gillingham, Kent, on 12 March 1888.

William was admitted to the school on 07 May 1889 (Petition No. 9796), the same day as his younger brother, Henry Smith (Petition No. 9797). William was discharged on 26 March 1891 and enlisted into The Prince of Wales's (North Staffordshire Regiment). Following his enlistment, William was to spend the first nine years of his service in Britain, either with the 2nd Battalion or stationed at the Regimental Depot in Whittington Barracks, Lichfield, Staffordshire. During this time, he was appointed as a Drummer on 27 July 1893, as an unpaid Lance Corporal on 13 September 1897, which became a paid rank twelve days later and promoted to Corporal on 15 October 1898.

On 14 January 1900, William was posted to South Africa during the Second Boer War, serving there for two years. He was appointed as a Lance Sergeant on 05 June 1901 and promoted to Serjeant on 24 September 1901, although later antedated to 01 September 1901. William was posted back to Britain on 09 October 1902 and five months later, on 25 March 1903, he re-engaged to complete 21 years' service.

Soon after his re-engagement, William's promotion to Sergeant was antedated to 10 March 1900 and he was then posted to India on 03 October 1903, where he spent almost four years before he returned to Britain, after he was posted to the 3rd Battalion at Lichfield on 02 May 1907 as Permanent Staff. A year after returning to Britain, on 22 August 1908, William married Florence Wain in Wilnecote, Staffordshire, their first daughter, Margaret Ethel Smith, being born in Wilnecote the following year.

William was discharged from the army following 21 years' service on 25 March 1912 and it appears that he then became the Landlord of The Hatters Arms public house in Warton, Warwickshire, his second daughter, Doris Florence Smith, being born in Tamworth, Staffordshire, the year that he was discharged.

Following the outbreak of war, William remained as a Publican, but on 01 December 1915 he re-enlisted into his old regiment at Lichfield and was posted to the 11th (Reserve) Battalion, where he was promoted to Corporal on 07 December 1915 and appointed as an Acting Sergeant on 11 December 1915.

The battalion to which William was posted had been formed in Guernsey, Channel Islands, in October 1914 as a Service Battalion and part of K4. It first moved to Alderney, Channel Islands, in February 1915 before it became a Reserve Battalion in April 1915 and moved to Darlington, County Durham. It then moved to Rugeley Camp, Cannock Chase, Staffordshire, in September 1915, and it was here that William joined.

There is correspondence within William's service record[349] that shows that when he re-enlisted, he had believed that it was for Home Service only and in fact he was considered medically fit for only that type of service, but by 05 June 1916, he was considered medically fit for General Service, which was the type of attestation that he had completed. There is then further confusion within his service record, as it appears that on 03 March 1917 he was called up for service as a Private in The Durham Light Infantry.

The battalion with which William was to serve, 1/7th Battalion, The Durham Light Infantry, had been formed at Sunderland, County Durham, as part of the Durham Light Infantry Brigade of the Northumbrian Division in August 1914. It then moved to Ravensworth Park, Gateshead, County Durham and by October 1914 was located in Newcastle, Northumberland. The battalion landed at Boulogne on 17 April 1915 and in November of that year became the Pioneer Battalion that William later joined.

Although there is no date given in William's medal index card for his entry into theatre, his service record records him being posted to the British Expeditionary Force on 31 March 1918.

Less than two weeks after arriving in theatre, William was reported as missing, likely killed during the Battle of the Lys, in which the 50th (Northumbrian) Division were heavily engaged. He has no known grave and is commemorated on the Ploegsteert Memorial. He is also a "Lost Boy" whose name has been omitted from the memorial tablets in the school chapel.

Henry was *"delivered to mother"* on 10 August 1893 and very little is known about him following his discharge. Due to having such a common name, it is not possible to establish his locations during either the 1901 or 1911 Censuses. It has also not been possible to establish whether he served during the war, nor when he died.

---

[349] WO 363: First World War Service Records 'Burnt Documents'

The Highland Light Infantry

William ANDERSON

Private, 5463, 2nd Battalion, The Highland Light Infantry who died on 07 November 1914, aged 34. Commemorated on the Ypres (Menin Gate) Memorial, West-Vlaanderen, Belgium

Born on 23 August 1880 in Partick, Lanarkshire, the son of Robert Anderson and Eliza Tullis née Young, his father was a Serjeant in the 79th (The Queen's Own Cameron Highlanders) Regiment of Foot[350], who was discharged from the army on 03 June 1879 and died in Glasgow, Lanarkshire, on 18 April 1890.

William was admitted to the school on 30 January 1891 (Petition No. 10109) and discharged to The Highland Light Infantry on 08 September 1894. Although his service record is no longer available, he is recorded in the 1901 Census serving with the 2nd Battalion and stationed in Albuhera Barracks, Aldershot, Hampshire. It is likely that he was discharged from the army at the end of his first period of service in 1906.

At the outbreak of war, the battalion was again stationed in Aldershot as part of the 2nd Division. After mobilisation and coming up to full strength, it embarked at Southampton, Hampshire, on 13 August and landed at Boulogne on 14 August 1914, participating in the Battle of Mons and the subsequent retreat, as well as the Battles of the Marne and of the Aisne. William entered theatre on 31 August 1914 and likely had been recalled to the Colours following the outbreak of war.

When the First Battle of Ypres commenced on 19 October, the battalion was heavily involved in the fighting and at the beginning of November, it was in the vicinity of Ypres, moving into trenches east of the Becelaere to Passchendaele road on 02 November.

At 0430hrs on the morning of 07 November, the Germans launched a heavy attack on the battalion's "B" Company trench. This attack had come as a surprise in an area where the trenches were as little as 50 yards apart, giving the defenders little chance to shoot at their attackers and resulted in part of the trench being occupied after fierce hand-to-hand fighting. Although the attack was

---

[350] Renamed The Queen's Own Cameron Highlanders on 01 July 1881

repelled and the enemy was forced to evacuate the trench that they had captured, they later reoccupied part of the trench, before they were all killed or captured. It was this action, along with another four days later, that led to Lieutenant Walter Lorrain Brodie of the battalion being subsequently awarded the Victoria Cross[351].

However, it was also during this action, on 07 November 1914, that William was killed. It is not known whether he was buried and his grave subsequently lost, or whether his body was never recovered after he was killed, but he is one of thirteen of the twenty Highland Light Infantry soldiers killed that day who have no known grave and who are commemorated on the Menin Gate Memorial.

James FINDLAY DCM
Serjeant, 8939, 1st Battalion, The Highland Light Infantry who died on 03 July 1917, aged 28. Buried in Amara War Cemetery, Iraq

Born on 23 May 1889 in Hamilton, Lanarkshire, the eldest of five children of James George Findlay and Mary née Keith, his father was a Serjeant in The Highland Light Infantry, who died whilst serving in Hamilton on 08 December 1898.

James was admitted to the school on 12 May 1899 (Petition No. 11293) and was discharged to The Highland Light Infantry on 17 October 1903, although his service record is no longer available, it appears that at the outbreak of war, he was serving with the 1st Battalion, which was stationed in Ambala, India. It was mobilised and posted to the Western Front, via Egypt, and consequently did not arrive at Marseille until 01 December 1914.

The battalion then participated in the Battle of Neuve Chapelle in March 1915, during which James's brother Thomas, also serving in the 1st Battalion, was killed, as well as the Battle of St. Julien in May 1915 and the Second Battle of Ypres later in May 1915, before it moved to Mesopotamia in December 1915, seeing action at the Siege of Kut in Spring 1916. Whilst serving in Mesopotamia, James was Mentioned in Despatches[352] and also awarded the Distinguished Conduct Medal[353], but this is not recorded on the memorial tablets in the school chapel.

In January 1917, the battalion was detached from the 3rd (Lahore) Division and moved to the Tigris Defences, an area that was

---

[351] *The London Gazette*, 11 December 1914, Supplement:29005: *"For conspicuous gallantry near Becelaere on the 11th November, in clearing the enemy out of a portion of our trenches which they had succeeded in occupying. Heading the charge, he bayonetted several of the enemy, and thereby relieved a dangerous situation. As a result of Lieutenant Brodie's promptitude, 80 of the enemy were killed, and 51 taken prisoners"*.

[352] *The London Gazette*, 17 October 1916, Supplement:29789

[353] *The London Gazette*, 20 October 1916, Supplement:29793: *"8939 Sjt. J. Findlay, High. L.I., For conspicuous good work and devotion to duty at all times. Throughout operations his work has been excellent"*.

being held by Kazim Bey's Ottoman XVIII Corps. James survived the various actions in which he was involved, but succumbed to enteric fever, something that was easy to contract due to the conditions in which the troops were living and fighting in Mesopotamia, dying on 03 July 1917.

James was buried in Amara War Cemetery, the town having been occupied by the Mesopotamian Expeditionary Force in June 1915, immediately becoming a hospital centre. The accommodation for medical units on both banks of the Tigris River was greatly increased during 1916 and in April 1917, seven General Hospitals and some smaller units being stationed there.

In 1933, all of the headstones were removed from Amara War Cemetery when it was discovered that salts in the soil were causing them to deteriorate. Instead, a Screen Wall was erected with the names of those buried in the cemetery engraved upon it.

John Broomfield RYAN

Private, 11592, 2nd Battalion, The Highland Light Infantry who died on 17 May 1915, aged 18. Commemorated on the Le Touret Memorial, Pas de Calais, France

Born on 27 October 1896 in Ardwick, Lancashire, the eldest of three children of James William Ryan and Jane née Mitchell, his father had been a Colour Serjeant in The Gordon Highlanders, who had been discharged from the army on 27 October 1885 and died in Didsbury, Manchester, Lancashire, on 14 May 1903.

John was admitted to the school on 08 February 1907 (Petition No. 12326) and was joined by his younger brother, James Ryan, three months later on 09 May 1907 (Petition No. 12361). Having made the transition from Chelsea to Guston, John was discharged to The Highland Light Infantry on 14 November 1910.

John's service record is no longer available, but at the outbreak of war, the 2nd Battalion, in which he may well have been serving, was stationed in Aldershot, Hampshire, and following mobilisation the *"1014 all ranks and 64 horses"*[354], landed at Boulogne on 14 August 1914, although John's medal index card records his entry into theatre as 07 April 1915. On 23 August, the battalion crossed the Belgian frontier and took up positions at Pâturages, south-west of Mons, suffering its first casualties the following day when fourteen other ranks were wounded by heavy German shelling. On the evening of 24 August, it was given orders to retire, moving continually south until 06 September, before advancing north again and participating

---

[354] WO 95/1347/2: 2 Battalion Highland Light Infantry, 1914 Aug. - 1919 Mar., The National Archives, Kew

in the Battle of the Aisne. The battalion then continued further north, taking part in the First Battle of Ypres in October 1914.

By May 1915, the battalion was in the area of Richebourg, moving into the trenches on 16 May and on the morning of the 17 May it repulsed an attack with *"heavy losses"*[355] due to flanking fire by the Germans, after which it was subjected to a heavy bombardment during the afternoon and was relieved overnight, although this was not completed by dawn and elements of two companies had to remain in the trenches. John was killed on this day, although it is not known whether it was during the German attack or the later bombardment. His body was not recovered and he is remembered on the Le Touret Memorial.

James joined him in the same battalion of The Highland Light Infantry when he was discharged from the school on 22 February 1912 and also served during the war. Although he survived, on 23 April 1917, whilst serving near Arras with the 10/11th Battalion, an amalgamation of two of the New Army battalions that had been formed in August 1914, he sustained a gunshot wound to the throat. This resulted in his having a permanent tracheostomy formed and he was no longer fit for further military service. Nothing is known of James after he was discharged from the army.

---

[355] Ibid.

Seaforth Highlanders
(Ross-shire Buffs, The Duke of Albany's)

William Robert BARRETT
Private, 744, 2nd Battalion, Seaforth Highlanders (Ross-shire Buffs, The Duke of Albany's) who died on 01 July 1916, aged 20. Buried in Sucrerie Military Cemetery, Colincamps, Somme, France

Born on 01 April 1896 in Paddington, London, the third of six children of Frederick William Barrett and Ellen née Steward, his father was an Acting Sergeant Major in The Prince Consort's Own (Rifle Brigade) on the Permanent Staff of the 18th Middlesex Rifle Volunteer Corps (Paddington Rifles)[356]. His mother died in Paddington on 19 December 1904.

William was admitted to the school on 10 July 1906 (Petition No. 12245) and moved from Chelsea to Guston, from where he was discharged on 30 June 1911, enlisting into the Seaforth Highlanders (Ross-shire Buffs, The Duke of Albany's). His younger brother, Ernest Patrick Barrett, was admitted to the school a year after he was discharged, on 27 June 1912 (Petition No. 12973).

William's service record is no longer available, so his pre-war postings are unknown, but at the outbreak of war, the 2nd Battalion, was stationed in Shorncliffe, Kent, and after moving initially to York, Yorkshire North Riding, and then Harrow, Middlesex, it embarked on the SS *Lake Michigan* at Southampton, Hampshire, on 22 August and landed at Boulogne on 23 August 1914.

The battalion was involved in the Battles of the Marne, the Aisne and of Messines during 1914 and was also in trenches on Christmas Day, although it does not seem to have fraternised as much as other units did. During 1915 it participated in the Second Battle of Ypres, which was its only major action during that year and William entered theatre on 01 September 1915, likely doing so after he had turned 19 in line with the official regulations at the time, although regiments adhered to them in differing regards.

---

[356] The Volunteer Rifle Corps was the forerunner of the Territorial Force, this unit, following the Cardwell reforms of 1881, becoming the 5th (later 4th) Volunteer Battalion of the Prince Consort's Own (Rifle Brigade), although it did not change its title

The battalion was in action again the following year and on 01 July 1916 it was in trenches near Auchonvillers, going "over the top" on the morning of the start of the Somme Offensive and coming under heavy fire from the direction of Beaumont-Hamel. Although the battalion did partially achieve its objective, it also suffered extremely high casualties in both officers and other ranks, with 133 dead. Many were never found, but the battalion diary does state that the bodies of five officers and 25 other ranks were collected and laid side by side in a large British cemetery, 200 yards north-west of Sucrerie. One of those other ranks was William and the dead from his battalion also included Dukies John Chilton and John Hume. Although he is commemorated on the memorial tablets in the school chapel, he is incorrectly recorded as W H Barrett.

Ernest did not serve in the war. Having moved with the school to Warley, Essex, when it was evacuated at the start of the war, he was discharged to *"Civil Life; medically unfit"* on 13 July 1917, when he was sixteen and joined the Great Western Railway as a Lamp Attendant on 15 April 1918. He left that employment on 07 August 1919 when he enlisted in the army, although there is no service record available to show with which regiment he served. He died in Bath, Somerset, in 1955.

John CHILTON MM
Lance Corporal, 8691, 2nd Battalion, Seaforth Highlanders (Ross-shire Buffs, The Duke of Albany's) who died on 01 July 1916, aged 26. Buried in Serre Road Cemetery No.2, Somme, France

Born on 13 January 1890 in Dublin, County Dublin, the eldest of two children of John Chilton and Emily née Gray, his father had been a Private in the Seaforth Highlanders (Ross-shire Buffs, The Duke of Albany's) and had been discharged to pension on 06 July 1891. He died in Feltham, Middlesex, on 05 December 1892.

John was admitted to the school 12 May 1899 (Petition No. 11299) and was discharged on 23 January 1904, enlisting into his father's old regiment. His service record is no longer available, so his pre-war career is unknown, but when war was declared he would have been serving in Shorncliffe, Kent, possibly alongside a number of fellow Dukies and medal records confirm he landed at Boulogne on 23 August 1914, with his battalion.

John would have participated in the Battles of the Marne, the Aisne and of Messines during 1914, and during 1915 when the unit participated in the Second Battle of Ypres. He obviously had home leave in April 1916, as he married Lucy Annie Willerton in Eastry, near Sandwich, Kent, but the marriage was to only last three months before Lucy was widowed.

Along with Dukies William Barrett, John Hume and Robert Williams, John went "over the top" on the morning of 01 July 1916, coming under heavy fire from the direction of Beaumont-Hamel, and like two of his fellow Dukies, John was one of those killed. He was originally commemorated on the Thiepval Memorial as having no known grave, but in 1929 his gravesite was uncovered by workmen excavating for foundations on the south-eastern side of Serre Road Cemetery No.2 and his partial remains were identified from his identity disc. He was then re-buried with a headstone in that cemetery and removed from the Thiepval Memorial register.

A month after his death, on 10 August 1916, John was Gazetted for the award of a Military Medal for bravery in the field[357], although the citation for this does not seem to have been published. At the time, the Military Medal could not be awarded for an action in which the man was killed, so the recommendation was made for an act prior to his death. He is also commemorated on the memorial tablets in the school chapel, although he is incorrectly recorded as W Chilton.

Albert Victor HARBER
Private, 1224, 2nd Battalion, Seaforth Highlanders (Ross-shire Buffs, The Duke of Albany's) who died on 11 April 1917, aged 20. Buried in Brown's Copse Cemetery, Roeux, Pas De Calais, France

Born on 15 December 1896 in Agra, India, the fifth of seven children of George James Harber and Emily née Mills, his father was a Colour Sergeant in The East Surrey Regiment and died as a result of a gunshot wound on 13 December 1902, although the circumstances surrounding his death are not known.

Albert was admitted to the school on 06 April 1906 (Petition No. 12219) and having moved from Chelsea to Guston, was discharged on 12 July 1913, enlisting into the Seaforth Highlanders (Ross-shire Buffs, The Duke of Albany's). He did not deploy to France with the battalion when it landed in France on 23 August 1914, almost certainly due to his age and the fact that he was not entitled to the award of the 1914-15 Star suggests that he did not enter theatre until 1916 at the earliest, meaning it is not known if he went "over the top" on the morning of 01 July 1916 with his battalion, when three fellow Dukies were killed in action on the Somme.

In early-1917, the battalion was in the Arras sector, launching an attack to tie up German forces a week ahead of a French offensive. The Battle of Arras commenced on 09 April 1917 and was an initial

---
[357] *The London Gazette*, 8 August 1916, Supplement:29701

success for the British troops, who advanced three and a half miles north of the River Scarpe in bleak and wintery weather, capturing the Point du Jour Ridge.

However, both triumph and disaster hit on 11 April. The hilltop village of Monchy-le-Preux was captured and held, and Albert's battalion, along with 1st Battalion, The Royal Irish Fusiliers, attacked towards the key positions of Greenland Hill, Roeux, as well as the Chemical Works, but came under heavy fire. The attack was a complete failure and of the 1,600 men who participated, around 1,000 men became casualties, including Albert. He is buried in Brown's Copse Cemetery, just over a mile from Greenland Hill.

John Alexander HUME
Lance Corporal, 173, 2nd Battalion, Seaforth Highlanders (Ross-shire Buffs, The Duke of Albany's) who died on 01 July 1916, aged 21. Buried in Serre Road Cemetery No.2, Somme, France

Born on 03 November 1894 in Gosport, Hampshire, the second of four sons of James Hume and Mary née McSweeney, his father had been a Serjeant in the 78th (Highlanders) Regiment of Foot (The Ross-shire Buffs) who had been discharged from the army on 02 July 1867. He died in Gosport on 20 October 1905.

John was admitted to the school on 16 February 1906 (Petition No. 12195), his younger brother, Ronald Malcolm Hume, joining him the following year on 30 May 1907 (Petition No. 12381). John was discharged from the school on 23 November 1908, enlisting into his father's old regiment, although his service record is no longer available.

At the outbreak of war, he would have been serving in Shorncliffe, Kent, and his medal index card confirms he landed at Boulogne on 23 August 1914, with fellow Dukies John Chilton and Robert Williams. His experiences would have also been the same as his fellow Dukies in the time between landing in France and the build-up to the Somme Offensive.

In June of 1916, the battalion was on the Somme, spending much of the month rehearsing for the attack scheduled for the end of the month. It moved nearer to the start point on 24 June, the day that the bombardment of the German lines commenced and suffered casualties due to German counter-battery fire. It spent the 30 June making final preparations for the attack the following day and it appears that everyone was optimistic regarding the chances of success, in their objective of capturing the ridge between Grand Court and Puisieux-au-Mont.

On 01 July, John went "over the top" with Dukies William Barrett, John Chilton and Robert Williams, and faced the same heavy fire as them. Despite having reached its third line objective by 1100hrs, the battalion had only five officers left and had suffered proportionate casualties among the other ranks, so was therefore forced to retire.

John Hume, alongside William and John, was one of the *"proportionate"*[358] number of other ranks killed that day, and is the only known occasion that three Dukies died together during the First World War. His body was recovered and he is buried in the same cemetery as John Chilton.

Ronald was discharged from the school on 29 June 1911, enlisting into the Royal Horse Artillery. He was killed on 24 March 1918, but is a "Lost Boy" who is not commemorated on the memorial tablets in the chapel. He is documented earlier in this book.

John's eldest brother, James Arthur Hume, who was not a Dukie, served in the Royal Marine Artillery from 1906 until 1916 before he was discharged as medically unfit. He died as a result of tuberculosis in May 1920 and is also commemorated by the Commonwealth War Graves Commission.

Frederick Melville USHER

Private, 9996, 1st Battalion, Seaforth Highlanders (Ross-shire Buffs, The Duke of Albany's) who died on 22 April 1916, aged 29. Commemorated on the Basra Memorial, Iraq

Born on 12 March 1887 in Hounslow, Middlesex, the fifth of eight children of Edward Samuel Usher and Catherine née Melville, his father had been a Serjeant in The Duke of Cambridge's Own (Middlesex Regiment) who had been discharged from the army after 21 years' service on 24 September 1889. He died in Walworth, London, on 10 February 1895.

Frederick was admitted to the school on 19 August 1897 (Petition No. 11052), joining his older brother, Reginald John Melville Usher, who had been admitted on 27 March 1896 (Petition No. 10879). Frederick was discharged from the school on 22 March 1902 and enlisted into the Seaforth Highlanders (Ross-shire Buffs, The Duke of Albany's).

His service record is no longer available, so it is not possible to know his movements prior to the outbreak of war, but in August 1914, the 1st Battalion was stationed in Agra, India, part of the Dehra Dun Brigade in the Meerut Division. However, it was quickly

---

[358] WO 95/1483/4: 10 Infantry Brigade: 2 Battalion Seaforth Highlanders, 1916 Jan 1 - 1916 June 30, The National Archives, Kew

mobilised and deployed to Europe, landing at Marseille in September 1914, with Frederick entering theatre himself on 12 October 1914.

It was involved in fighting on the Western Front, including the Battle of Aubers Ridge in May 1915, before it was transferred to Mesopotamia later in the year, arriving in Basra at the end of December. The unit was then involved in the Siege of Kut, as part of the unsuccessful relief force, before 1st Battalion, The Seaforth Highlanders and 2nd Battalion, The Black Watch (Royal Highlanders), formed a Composite Highland Battalion, which on 22 April 1916 was tasked with capturing the town of Sannaiyat during the First Battle of Kut.

The attack was a disaster from the start. The battalion war diary[359] records that the *"artillery preparation was disappointing"* and *"At 6.20am was informed that 21st Brigade would not attack as ordered due to water on their front, the whole operation thus falling on the Battalion with the assistance of the 92nd Punjabis about 200 strong"*. Although the first and second lines were quickly reached, these were full of water and the attack was repelled, with the 1st Battalion, Seaforth Highlanders suffering nine officers and 233 other ranks killed, wounded and missing, including Frederick.

Frederick has no known grave and is commemorated on the Basra Memorial, which until 1997 was located on the main quay of the naval dockyard at Maqil, on the west bank of the Shatt-al-Arab River. However, due to the sensitivity of the site, the memorial was moved by presidential decree and carried out by the authorities in Iraq, which involved a considerable amount of manpower, transport costs and sheer engineering on their part. The end result was that the memorial has been re-erected in its entirety and is now located along the road to Nasiriyah, in the middle of what was a major battleground during the first Gulf War.

Two names below Frederick on the Basra Memorial, is a non-Dukie soldier who was serving in the same battalion and who was killed twelve days before him, Private Joseph King Watt. He is the Great Uncle of one of the authors, who had no idea when he photographed his Great Uncle's name on the memorial in early-April 2004, that the person commemorated two names above Joseph was a Dukie.

Frederick is also commemorated on the memorial tablets in the school chapel, but he is incorrectly recorded as F M *Husher*.

---

[359] WO 95/5137/4: 19 Indian Infantry Brigade: The Highland Battalion, 1916 Apr - 1916 June, The National Archives, Kew

Reginald was discharged from the school *"To mother"* on 02 December 1899. It is possible that he was unwell at the time of his discharge, as he did not enlist in the army and died in Chelsea, London, in 1905, aged only 18.

Charles Henry WALKER
235275, Private, 9th (Service) Battalion (Pioneers), Seaforth Highlanders (Ross-shire Buffs, The Duke of Albany's) who died on 18 February 1918, aged 42. Buried in Tincourt New British Cemetery, Somme, France

Born on 16 January 1876 in Glasgow, Lanarkshire, the third of seven children of William Walker and Mary Philomena née Lequey, his father had been a Private in the 91st (Princess Louise's Argyllshire Highlanders) Regiment of Foot[360], who had been discharged from the army on 25 February 1873 and died in Glasgow on 22 May 1884.

Charles was admitted to the school on 24 February 1888 (Petition No. 9618) and was *"Returned to mother"* on 16 January 1890. He is recorded in both the 1891 and 1901 Censuses, living with his mother and siblings in Glasgow, firstly as a 15-year-old Clerk and latterly employed as a Shoemaker.

Nothing further is known of Charles for several years until he married Lily Readings in Glasgow on 26 June 1908, by which time his mother had also died. Neither Charles nor Lily could be found in the 1911 Census, but his later probate record confirmed he was still a Shoemaker and they had three daughters.

Following the outbreak of war, it appears that Charles enlisted, joining Princess Louise's (Argyll and Sutherland Highlanders), although it is not known when or which battalion he joined as his service record has not survived. However, it is known that at some point he was transferred to the 9th (Service) Battalion (Pioneers), Seaforth Highlanders, although it is again unknown when this occurred.

This battalion had been formed at Fort George, Inverness-shire, in October 1914, moving to Aldershot, Hampshire, in November 1914 and coming under the command of the 9th (Scottish) Division on 03 December 1914. In early-1915, the battalion became the Pioneer Battalion of the division and moved to Farnham, Surrey, from where it landed at Boulogne on 10 May 1915.

It is not known whether Charles joined the battalion in Britain or France, as although there is no disembarkation date recorded in his

---

[360] Amalgamated with the 93rd (Sutherland Highlanders) Regiment of Foot on 01 July 1881 to become Princess Louise's (Sutherland and Argyll Highlanders), renamed in 1882 as Princess Louise's (Argyll and Sutherland Highlanders).

medal index card, he was not entitled to the award of the 1914-15 Star, and so did not arrive in theatre until 1916 at the earliest. In February 1918, the battalion was attached to the 39th Division and was in the vicinity of Heudicourt, engaged between 03 and 10 February in digging communication trenches, widening, boarding and draining existing trenches and wiring the trenches for communication.

It would seem that during this time Charles was wounded, although the nature of his wounds is not known and he was evacuated to the Casualty Clearing Station in Tincourt. Charles died of these wounds on 08 February 1918 and was buried in the cemetery in the town. However, he is another "Lost Boy" whose name has been omitted from the memorial tablets in the school chapel.

Robert Francis WILLIAMS
Drummer, 545, 2nd Battalion, Seaforth Highlanders (Ross-shire Buffs, The Duke of Albany's) who died on 23 October 1916, aged 20. Buried in Guards' Cemetery, Lesboeufs, Pas De Calais, France

Born on 17 March 1896 in Limerick, County Limerick, the second son of William Henry Williams and Annie Sophia née Browne, his father was a Serjeant Drummer who had served for almost 21 years in The Royal Irish Regiment, when he died in Kilkenny, County Kilkenny, on 04 April 1901. This was the year after Robert's mother had died, also in Kilkenny, on 03 February 1900, with his Petition Document completed by his uncle, Francis Williams, who was a Musician at the Royal Military College, Sandhurst.

Robert was admitted to the school on 05 May 1905 (Petition No. 12099), joining his older brother, William Henry Williams, who had been admitted on 06 May 1904 (Petition No. 11967). Robert would have made the transition from Chelsea to Guston, before he was discharged from the school on 27 May 1910 and enlisted into the Seaforth Highlanders (Ross-shire Buffs, The Duke of Albany's).

Robert's service record is no longer available, but it is known that he entered theatre with the 2nd Battalion on 23 August 1914, and would have had mostly the same experience as Dukies William Barratt, John Chilton and John Hume, including going "over the top" on the first day of the Somme Offensive in July 1916, although, unlike the others, he survived.

However, on 23 October 1916, the battalion was in trenches in the vicinity of Lesboeufs, in support of the battalions attempting to take the line that the French had failed to do on 12 October. Due to a heavy mist in the morning, the attack did not commence until 1430hrs, with the battalion receiving an urgent message ten minutes later to take up positions in front of Lesboeufs immediately, which it did. Despite the area being plastered by German artillery, it suffered very few casualties, although as the battalion reached the sunken road, a shell burst among it, killing or wounding almost everyone in the vicinity. In spite of this, the Commanding Officer received a message that the battalion was to capture Dewdrop Trench, but after a conversation with the commander of the 12th Brigade, Brigadier-General James Dayrolles Crosbie, it was decided that such an attack would be *"absolute madness"*[361] and that it should withdraw back to Lesboeufs.

Robert was one of the those killed during the failed attack on 23 October 1916 and he is buried close to where he fell, in Guards' Cemetery, just outside the town of Lesboeufs.

William was discharged to on 22 July 1908 and also enlisted in the Seaforth Highlanders. Little else is known about him, but it appears that he survived the war.

* * *

Postscript

In addition to the three Dukies killed with the 2nd Seaforths on the first day of the Somme and Robert Francis Williams also going "over the top" with them that day, our research has shown that the following Dukies were with the battalion at the same time, or very likely to have been, having served with the battalion in France in the right period according to their medal records; each survived the war:

- Serjeant Major Arthur Naylor Dunton[362] (later awarded the Military Cross and Commissioned)
- Private Alfred Ansell (later Serjeant)
- Private William Patrick Murphy
- Drummer John Francis Hearn
- Bandmaster Thomas Bevan Frederick Wiltshier

Alfred Ansell, William Robert Barrett (killed in action) and William Patrick Murphy all left school on 30 June 1911 and received consecutive service numbers in the Seaforth Highlanders (745, 744 and 746 respectively).

---

[361] WO 95/1483/5: 10 Infantry Brigade: 2 Battalion Seaforth Highlanders., 1916 July 1 - 1916 Dec 31, The National Archives, Kew

[362] He was later interviewed in 1973 by the Imperial War Museum and the recording is available at: https://www.iwm.org.uk/collections/item/object/80020955

The Gordon Highlanders

Robert William ELDER
Lance Corporal, 277, 2nd Battalion, The Gordon Highlanders who died on 23 October 1914, aged 19. Commemorated on the Ypres (Menin Gate) Memorial, West-Vlaanderen, Belgium

Born on 28 February 1895 in Windsor, Berkshire, the eldest of three children of Robert Duncan Elder and Caroline née Baglow, his father had been a Colour Sergeant in the Scots Guards who was Mentioned in Despatches and awarded the Distinguished Conduct Medal during the Second Boer War. He was discharged from the army in May 1904 and died in Battersea, London, five months later, on 17 October 1904.

Robert was admitted to the school on 03 February 1905 (Petition No. 12076) and discharged on 04 March 1909, enlisting into The Gordon Highlanders. His service record is no longer available, but he is recorded in the 1911 Census serving with the 2nd Battalion and stationed in Cawnpore India, although the battalion had been posted to Cairo, Egypt, by the time that war was declared.

The battalion returned to Britain, landing at Southampton, Hampshire, on 01 October 1914, and then moving to Lyndhurst, Hampshire. However, it was only there for three days before returning to Southampton and departing for Belgium, via Dover, landing at Zeebrugge on 07 October 1914. Once it had arrived, it moved to Bruges in order to draw the Germans away from Antwerp to allow the Belgian Army to escape the siege that it was under, the battalion taking up defensive positions on the Bruges-Nieuwpoort Canal, although on 09 October it was given orders to relocate to Ghent, taking up positions to the east of the town on 10 October.

However, commencing on 11 October, it began a four-day retreat to Ypres, taking up positions between Dickebusch and Voormezeele on 15 October and remaining in these positions in and around Ypres for the next three days, where it suffered its first casualties due to shellfire on 18 October.

During 22–24 October, the battalion was subjected to several small attacks, but all were repulsed. Three other ranks were killed, all of whom are named in the war diary[363], with one Serjeant and fourteen other ranks wounded.

It is possible that Robert was one of the wounded and that he later died as a result of these wounds, as the Commonwealth War Graves Commission records his date of death as 23 October 1914, although the Registers of Soldiers' Effects records his date of death as 28 October. However, the war diary records no casualties for the latter date, so it is more likely that the 23 October is his date of death. It is very likely that he would have been buried close to where he died, but the area in which the battalion was located was fought over fiercely during the next four years, so his grave was lost. He has no known grave and is commemorated on the Menin Gate Memorial.

John William GIBBON
Private, 887, 1/4th Battalion, The Gordon Highlanders who died on 23 April 1917, aged 20. Buried in Duisans British Cemetery, Etrun, Pas de Calais, France

Born on 08 May 1897 in Sedgefield, County Durham, the eldest of two children of William Gibbon and Evelina Isabella Rennison née Spencer, his father was a Private in The Princess of Wales's Own (Yorkshire Regiment), who died of disease on active service at Springfontein, South Africa on 27 April 1900, during the Second Boer War.

John was admitted to the school on 16 May 1907 (Petition No. 12369) and was transferred two years later, on 14 June 1909, to the Queen Victoria School, Dunblane, which had been opened on 28 September 1908. He was one of two boys from the Duke of York's to be transferred to this school, the other boy being Andrew David Swan (Petition No. 12352). There were also two boys transferred from the Royal Hibernian Military School in Dublin and all four were intended to set an example to the other boys. Just over a year after John had been transferred to the Scottish school, his brother, Robert Lane Gibbon, was admitted to the Duke of York's, on 20 October 1910 (Petition No. 12815).

John was discharged from the Queen Victoria School on 17 January 1912 and enlisted into The Gordon Highlanders, and it is known that in 1917 he was serving with 1/4th Battalion of that regiment. This battalion was a Territorial Force battalion that had been located in Woolmanhill in Aberdeenshire at the outbreak of the war, as part of the Gordon Brigade of the Highland Division. It had

---

[363] WO 95/1656/2: 2 Battalion Gordon Highlanders, 1914 Oct. - 1917 Nov., The National Archives, Kew

initially moved to Bedford, Bedfordshire, prior to landing at Le Havre on 20 February 1915. No date of disembarkation is recorded in John's medal index card, so it can be surmised that he entered theatre in 1916 at the very earliest, with no award of the 1914-15 Star.

On 23 April 1917, the battalion attacked the heavily defended Chemical Factory, a sugar factory near Roeux, with 154th Brigade, 51st (Highland) Division. It suffered very heavy casualties among the officers and non-commissioned officers, resulting in it becoming disorganised early in the attack. By 2100hrs it had been ordered to withdraw to the assembly positions and it was relieved the next night with little progress having been made.

Other ranks casualties included 48 killed, 197 wounded and 64 missing. John died of wounds and his burial location suggests that he had been evacuated to No. 8 Casualty Clearing Station. He is also a "Lost Boy" whose name is omitted from the memorial tablets in the school chapel of the Duke of York's, something that should be done as he was a Dukie prior to becoming a Victorian, although he is commemorated at the latter institution.

Robert was discharged from the school on 29 April 1914 and also enlisted into The Gordon Highlanders. It is not known whether he served overseas, but it is possible that he did not due to his age. He died in Chorley, Lancashire, in 1970.

Joseph HAWTIN
Serjeant, 7919, 1st Battalion, The Gordon Highlanders who died on 18 July 1916, aged 29. Commemorated on the Thiepval Memorial, Somme, France

Born on 28 September 1887 in Cork, County Cork, the eldest of two children of Joseph Hawtin and Sarah Elizabeth née Seaton, his father had served in the Royal Artillery, but was a Staff Quartermaster Serjeant in the Army Pay Corps at the time of his death in Gosport, Hampshire, on 08 January 1896, due to tuberculosis.

Joseph was admitted to the school on 25 March 1898 (Petition No. 11157) and was joined by his younger brother, Henry Hawtin, on 06 October 1899 (Petition No. 11344). Joseph was discharged from the school on 28 September 1901 and enlisted into The Gordon Highlanders.

There is a limited amount of his service record available, so Joseph's pre-war career is not known in full, but he completed his first period of engagement, having served in India and was then employed by the Sheffield Corporation Tramways until he was recalled to the Colours in 1914. He landed in France on 04 October 1914, seeing action at Maedelstede Farm on 14 December, a well-documented encounter early in the war with high casualties for The Gordon Highlanders and a time when they were still wearing shoes rather than boots, despite the winter weather. In 1915, during a period of leave, Joseph married Emily Pryor in Ecclesall Bierlow, a suburb of Sheffield, Yorkshire West Riding, but he was soon back in France and Ypres, surviving actions around Hooge and The Bluff.

His battalion did not take part in the attack on the first day of the Somme Offensive, but it did capture the village of Longueval on 14 July 1916, being trapped in Delville Wood by machine-gun fire and artillery bombardment for eight hours, before being forced to withdraw. It held part of the line for the next week until relieved and suffered more than 350 casualties, including Joseph.

His battalion had attacked north of Longueval and the northern part of Delville Wood on 18 July and were in the Montauban area on 19 July. His medal index card states the date of his death to be 18-19 July showing the confusion in an area of particularly fierce fighting. His body was not recovered and he is commemorated on the Thiepval Memorial. For many years, he was also a "Lost Boy", however, a supplementary tablet with his name and that of John May has been added to those already in place in the school chapel in recent years.

Henry was discharged from the school on 01 July 1905 and enlisted into the Royal Engineers. He ended the war as an Acting Warrant Officer Class II, earning distinction with the tunnelling companies[364], twice Mentioned in Despatches[365][366] and also awarded the Meritorious Service Medal[367]. He served continuously until 1947, retiring as a Major (Quartermaster) and was appointed as a Member of the Most Excellent Order of the British Empire (MBE) in 1941[368]. He died in Sheffield in 1977. His son, Harry Pynor Hawtin, whilst not a Dukie, was killed in action over Italy in August 1944, as a Flight Sergeant in the Royal Air Force Volunteer Reserve.

---

[364] Royal Engineer tunnelling companies were specialist units formed to dig offensive tunnels under enemy lines, placing charges that were usually then detonated prior to an attack; later used to construct deep dugouts as the war became more mobile
[365] *The London Gazette*, 15 June 1916, Supplement: 29623
[366] *The London Gazette*, 18 May 1917, Supplement: 30077
[367] *The London Gazette*, 17 June 1918, Supplement: 30750
[368] *The London Gazette*, 01 April 1941, Supplement: n/k

Percy HYDE
Private, 10047, 1st Battalion, The Gordon Highlanders who died on 23 September 1914, aged 22. Buried in Caudry British Cemetery, Nord, France

Born on 03 November 1891 in Ashton-under-Lyne, Lancashire, the second of three sons of John Hyde and Ellen Jane née Gaynor, his father had been a Private in The Worcestershire Regiment, who was discharged from the army on 29 January 1890. In 1901 the family was living in Woolwich, London, and John died in that year.

Percy was admitted to the school on 11 December 1902 (Petition No. 11765) and remained there until 24 May 1906, when he was discharged to The Gordon Highlanders. In 1911 he was appointed as an unpaid provisional Lance Corporal whilst employed in the Tailor's shop, the trade that he had learnt at the school. At this point, he was stationed with the battalion in Goojerat Barracks, Colchester, Essex.

However, by the time that war was declared, Percy had reverted to Private and the battalion was stationed in Plymouth, Devonshire, from where it deployed to France, landing at Boulogne on 14 August 1914, the date recorded in his medal index card for his own disembarkation in France. Once landed, the battalion moved to the town of Mons and took up positions along the Mons to Beaumont road. When the Germans advanced, they were stopped 300 yards from the British line, with another German column, advancing at 1600hrs, suffering the same fate. Although the losses borne by the battalion were slight, other parts of the British line had suffered greatly and at 2100hrs it was ordered to withdraw.

Following a series of staged retreats, the battalion turned to face the Germans again at Le Cateau on 26 August. The British Expeditionary Force's superior training and rapid firing succeeded in halting the German advance for a time, but eventually the enemy's superiority in numbers began to tell and the order was given to retire again. However, this order only reached Percy's battalion some hours later, by which time the bulk of the rest of the British Army was some distance away, so when the unit attempted to follow, it ran into a strong German force on the outskirts of Bertry. After an hour's fierce fighting, the survivors of the battalion were forced to surrender on 27 August.

Percy himself was reported as missing on 26 August 1914 during the Battle of Le Cateau. According to various documents in his service record, it was during this battle that Percy was killed and although he was reported as such on 24 November 1914 by Reverend Hales of the Army Chaplains Department, this was seen as an unofficial report and not accepted, perhaps as it was believed possible that he was a Prisoner of War. It was not until 16 May 1915 that the War Office finally accepted this report and it was not until 06 September 1915 that his mother was informed that he was no longer presumed missing, but presumed to have died, on 23 September 1914. He was originally buried by the Germans and his body was exhumed in September 1920, the army issue spoon and fork embossed with his service number enabling formal identification. He is now buried in Caudry British Cemetery, the other four Gordon Highlanders alongside him with a recorded date of death of 26 August 1914, rather than 23 September 1914.

William MILNE

Second Lieutenant, 1st Battalion, The Gordon Highlanders, who died on 25 September 1915, aged 38. Commemorated on the Ypres (Menin Gate) Memorial, West-Vlaanderen, Belgium

Born on 08 November 1877 in Limerick, County Limerick, the fourth of seven children of Henry Milne and Harriet née Gregory, his father had been a Private in the 82nd (The Prince of Wales's Volunteers) Regiment of Foot, but had been discharged from the army on 25 March 1879 and died in Aberdeen, Aberdeenshire, on 01 September 1882.

William was admitted to the school on 13 April 1888 (Petition No. 9648), joining his older brother, Robert Milne, who had been admitted on 25 March 1887 (Petition No. 9497). William was discharged to The Gordon Highlanders on 21 November 1891 and although his service record is not readily available as an officer, from medal records we know he served in the Second Boer War with the 2nd Battalion and in 1910 was a Serjeant Drummer, when he was awarded the Long Service and Good Conduct Medal. He had married Elizabeth Sands in Aberdeen in 1907 and their daughter, Violet Elizabeth Milne, was born in Calcutta, India in 1908.

At the outbreak of war, 1st Battalion, The Gordon Highlanders was stationed in Plymouth, Devonshire, from where it deployed to France, landing at Boulogne on 14 August 1914. They suffered heavy losses in the 1914 fighting, particularly at Le Cateau where Dukie Percy Hyde died whilst serving in the battalion. William began the war in Britain, before he was Commissioned[369] from Company Serjeant Major on 14 May 1915 and he entered theatre for the first time on 3 June 1915.

On 25 September 1915, the battalion was still in the Ypres sector and in trenches opposite Hooge. It had been ordered to attack the German positions in order to prevent them from reinforcing their

---

[369] *The London Gazette*, 14 May 1915, Issue:29162

troops further south, where the Battle of Loos was to be launched on the same day.

The attack was a failure, with the battalion suffering high casualties and although Lieutenant-General Edmund Allenby, V Corps Commander, hailed it a success for having contained the German troops within the Ypres Salient, William was killed on 25 September 1915[370]. He has no known grave and is commemorated on the Menin Gate Memorial.

Robert was discharged from the school to The Royal Scots (Lothian Regiment) on 05 October 1889 and survived the war. However, their eldest brother, Henry, who was not a Dukie, was a Serjeant in William's battalion and was not so lucky. He was killed six months after William, on 13 March 1916, and is buried in La Clytte Military Cemetery, Belgium.

Allan David RAMSAY

Private, 281, 1st Battalion, The Gordon Highlanders, who died on 25 September 1915, aged 24. Commemorated on the Ypres (Menin Gate) Memorial, West-Vlaanderen, Belgium

Born on 01 November 1890 in Gibraltar, the second of five children of William Ambrose Ramsay and Christina Elder née Meek. William was a Dukie, having been admitted to the Royal Military Asylum on 24 March 1864 (Petition No. 6889) and discharged on 27 January 1869. He initially enlisted into the Grenadier Guards as a Drummer, before transferring to The Prince of Wales's Volunteers (South Lancashire Regiment), in which regiment he was the Bandmaster when he was discharged after just under 28 years' service on 27 April 1900. He died in Wandsworth, London, on 14 December 1900.

Allan was admitted to the school on 15 March 1901 (Petition No. 11534) and was withdrawn on 01 November 1904. Following his withdrawal, little is known about him, but he enlisted into The Gordon Highlanders, his grandfather's old regiment, with his service number suggesting that this would have been in 1909. He is also recorded in the 1911 Census as a Private in the 1st Battalion, stationed alongside fellow Dukie Percy Hyde in Goojerat Barracks, Colchester, Essex.

By the outbreak of war, Allan had been posted to the 2nd Battalion and was stationed in Cairo, Egypt, and his history would have been the same as that of Dukie Robert Elder, his medal index

---

[370] Incorrectly recorded by the Commonwealth War Graves Commission as 27 September 1915

card recording that he landed at Zeebrugge on the same day, 07 October 1914.

At some point during the following year, Allan was posted back to the 1st Battalion and in September 1915 he was with fellow Dukie William Milne, in the Ypres sector. He took part in the attack on 25 September, and like William, was also killed, with no known grave. He is commemorated on the Menin Gate Memorial, but Allan is also another "Lost Boy", whose name has been omitted from the memorial tablets in the school chapel.

Allan's older brother, Ambrose Duncan Ramsay, who was not a Dukie, was also killed during the war. He had served in The Prince Consort's Own (Rifle Brigade) before the war, then re-enlisted into the Duke of Cornwall's Light Infantry as Arthur Wynne. He was killed on 25 July 1918 and is buried in Villers Station Cemetery, Villers-au-Bois, Pas de Calais, France.

The Queen's Own Cameron Highlanders

William James PROSSER
Lance Corporal, 6866, 1st Battalion, The Queen's Own Cameron Highlanders who died on 24 October 1914, aged 28. Commemorated on the Ypres (Menin Gate) Memorial, West-Vlaanderen, Belgium

Born on 20 May 1886 in Cairo, Egypt, the eldest of three children of William James Prosser and Louisa née Clarke, his father was the Bandmaster of the 19th Hussars. He had also been a Dukie, having been admitted to the Royal Military Asylum on 04 April 1865 (Petition No. 6975) and been *"Delivered to his friends"* on 06 May 1871. His brother James Prosser, William's uncle, was also a Dukie, admitted on the same day as William's father, 04 April 1865 (Petition No. 6976) and discharged to the army on 09 August 1873. William's mother died in Bangalore, India, on 30 December 1894.

William was admitted to the school on 02 September 1895 (Petition No. 10801) and discharged, unusually for a Dukie, to the Royal Marine Light Infantry on 07 October 1901. His Royal Marine service record is difficult to read, but it appears that he served as a Bugler for three years, being discharged in October 1904.

Although his army service record is not available to confirm when, following his discharge from the Royal Marine Light Infantry he enlisted into The Queen's Own Cameron Highlanders, his regimental number suggesting that this was during 1905 and in 1911 he was recorded in the Census as a Lance Corporal with the 1st Battalion, stationed in Oudenarde Barracks, Marlborough Lines, Aldershot, Hampshire.

At the outbreak of war, the battalion was stationed in Edinburgh, Midlothian, quickly mobilising and landing at Le Havre on 14 August 1914 and although the battalion diary for August and September 1914 was lost, it is known that the unit participated in the Battle of Mons and the subsequent retreat, as well as the Battles of the Marne and of the Aisne.

By October, the battalion was back in the area of Ypres and on 21 October marched to positions in the area of Langemarck, coming under attack after dark the following evening and being forced to retreat, although the line to which it retreated was reinforced by the arrival of the Scots Guards, The Black Watch and The North Staffordshire Regiment on 23 October, launching a successful attack against the Germans later that day and night.

During this action, the battalion suffered two killed, ten wounded and 74 missing, one of the latter being William, who was presumed killed on 24 October 1914. His body was not recovered and he is therefore commemorated on the Menin Gate Memorial. Although he is also commemorated on the memorial tablets in the school chapel, he is incorrectly recorded as W G Prosser.

William Albert ROWE
Private, 7059, 1st Battalion, The Queen's Own Cameron Highlanders who died on 25 September 1914, aged 24. Commemorated on the La Ferte-Sous-Jouarre Memorial, Seine-et-Marne, France

Born on 06 October 1889 in Cork, County Cork, the youngest of five children of John Rowe and Elizabeth Ann née Morey, his father was a Quartermaster Serjeant in the Army Pay Corps and was still serving when he died in Cork on 26 February 1894.

William was admitted to the school on 07 April 1899 (Petition No. 11290), joining his older brothers, Percy Henry Rowe, who had been admitted on 29 March 1895 (Petition No. 10742) and Sidney Ernest Rowe, who had been admitted on 02 April 1897 (Petition No. 11019). His oldest brother, Edward John Rowe, had been admitted to the school on 27 July 1894 (Petition No. 10627) and was discharged a month before William's admission.

William was discharged from the school on 15 October 1904, enlisting straight into The Queen's Own Cameron Highlanders and although his service record is no longer available, it is likely that he remained in Britain from the time that he enlisted until the outbreak of war, if he was posted to and remained with the 1st Battalion.

At the outbreak of war, he would have been serving alongside fellow Dukie William Prosser in Edinburgh, Midlothian, landed at Le Havre on 14 August 1914 and been involved in the early battles of the war, the details of which are very scant, as there is an entry in the later battalion war diary stating that the diary for the period from landing until 21 September 1914 had been lost on the Aisne.

On 24 September, the battalion was in trenches in a position that it was aware was under observation by a German *"captive airship"*[371]. The following day, its positions were very heavily shelled from 0715hrs until 1200hrs. The headquarters was located in a cave, but was struck by a shell at 0730hrs, entombing the Battalion Staff and

---

[371] WO 95/1264/1: 1 Infantry Brigade: 1 Battalion Cameron Highlanders, 1914 Aug 1 - 1914 Dec 31, The National Archives, Kew

killing them instantly. It lost five officers, including their Medical Officer and 23 other ranks, one of these being William.

Although some of those from the battalion killed that day have named graves, William does not, being commemorated on the La Ferte-Sous-Jouarre Memorial, suggesting that either he could not be identified or that his grave was lost during the four years of fighting after his death.

Edward was discharged from the school on 04 March 1899 and enlisted into the Grenadier Guards. His service record has not survived and after his enlistment, nothing more is known of him.

Percy was discharged from the school *"To Mother"* on 30 October 1899. No information is available as to whether he served during the war, but it is known that he died in Camberwell, London, in 1976.

Sidney did not enlist in the army when he left the school, instead going into service at the New Victorian Club, Piccadilly, London. Whilst he may have joined up at the outbreak of war (several Sidney Ernest Rowes did) it is not possible to identify if he was one of them. If he did, he survived the war, but nothing more is known about him.

John George TAYLOR
Private, 8438, 1st Battalion, The Queen's Own Cameron Highlanders who died on 14 September 1914, aged 22. Commemorated on the La Ferte-Sous-Jouarre Memorial, Seine-et-Marne, France

Born on 21 April 1892 in Bristol, Gloucestershire, the only child of John Taylor and Sarah Jane née Geake, formerly Cove, John having two older half-sisters from his mother's first marriage. His father had been Private in The Gloucestershire Regiment, who was discharged to pension after 21 years' service on 22 June 1895 and died in Bristol on 27 July 1901.

John was admitted to the school on 07 February 1902 (Petition No. 11657) and was discharged to The Queen's Own Cameron Highlanders on 03 October 1908, and although his service record is no longer available, at the outbreak of war he would have been serving alongside fellow Dukies William Prosser and William Rowe in Edinburgh, Midlothian, and landed at Le Havre on 14 August 1914, participating in the early battles of the war.

On 14 September, the battalion left its bivouacs and marched to the area of Vendresse, deploying near the Troyon factory and coming under heavy high-explosive and shrapnel fire whilst moving into these positions. At 0720hrs, the Germans launched an attack which caused it to give ground an hour later, but a counterattack by the battalion was ultimately successful. During this fight, part of the Battle of the Aisne, it suffered nine officers and 140 other ranks killed, including John. It seems that his body was never recovered as he is commemorated on the La Ferte-Sous-Jouarre Memorial, along with 112 of his comrades who died alongside him. Although he is commemorated on the memorial tablets in the school chapel he is incorrectly recorded as W G Taylor.

The Royal Irish Rifles

Whilst both of the Dukies who served in this regiment and died during the First World War are commemorated on the memorial tablets in the school chapel, their regiment is incorrectly recorded as The Royal Ulster Rifles.

After the First World War, the War Office decided that Ulster should be represented on the Army List, as Connaught, Leinster and Munster already had their own regiments and so, in 1920, a new name was proposed for the Royal Irish Rifles. From 01 January 1921 the regiment became the Royal Ulster Rifles, but as this was more than three years after both of the Dukies named below had died, the regiment recorded for both of them was not in existence at the time that they were serving.

William Abraham Bullen CLARK
Rifleman, 9564, 1st Battalion, The Royal Irish Rifles who died on 16 August 1917, aged 20. Commemorated on the Tyne Cot Memorial, West-Vlaanderen, Belgium

Born on 17 December 1896 in Barking, London, the seventh of eight children of Daniel Clark and Elizabeth Helen née Newing, his father had served in The Royal Irish Rifles and was a Colour Serjeant in the Prince Consort's Own (Rifle Brigade), when he was discharged from the army after 25 years' service on 19 July 1895. He died in London on 22 May 1903.

According to his Petition Document, William's mother abandoned the family after Daniel's death and there is reference to a letter from the Soldiers' and Sailors' Families Association within the document, although it appears that this letter has not survived. The Petition Document was completed by William's 21-year-old sister, Ethel Clark, in 1904.

William was admitted to the school on 20 April 1906 (Petition No. 12220) and having moved from Chelsea to Guston, was discharged to The Royal Irish Rifles on 31 January 1911.

His service record is no longer available, but at the outbreak of war, 1st Battalion, The Royal Irish Rifles, was stationed in Aden, returning to Britain and landing at Liverpool, Lancashire, on 22

October. After a move to Winchester, Hampshire, it then embarked on the SS *Anglo-Canadian* at Southampton, Hampshire, on 05 November 1914, landing at Le Havre on the same day, its first experience of the trenches being ten days later near Le Tilloy. Although the battalion was in the trenches on Christmas Day, there appears to have been minimal fraternisation, although a local ceasefire was agreed, ended by one of the battalion's officers firing his pistol at midnight.

It then saw action at the Battle of Neuve Chapelle in March 1915, the Battle of Aubers Ridge in May 1915 and the Battle of Loos in September 1915, before taking part in the Somme Offensive in September 1916. No date of disembarkation was recorded for William, but due to his age and medal entitlement he likely did not go to France until the start of 1917.

In July 1917, the battalion was in Belgium for the Third Battle of Ypres and attacked at 0350hrs on 31 July, the first day of that offensive. However, the attack of that morning was unsuccessful and on 16 August, at 0445hrs, it, along with the rest of the battalions in the 8th Division, launched a further attack in attempt to gain the objectives from 31 July.

Whilst the attack was successful, the casualties that the battalion suffered on that day, ten officers and 267 other ranks killed, wounded or missing, led to it being withdrawn from the line at 2200hrs. William was one of those killed during the attack on 16 August 1917 and his body was never recovered, being one of 64 soldiers from his battalion killed on that day to be commemorated on the Tyne Cot Memorial.

Henry George Augustus RAWLINSON

Serjeant, 6/10772, 6th (Service) Battalion, The Royal Irish Rifles who died on 15 August 1915, aged 40. Buried in Alexandria (Chatby) Military and War Memorial Cemetery, Egypt

Born on 02 April 1875 in Gwalior, India, the youngest child of William Henry Rawlinson and Obhaima Helena née Downing, his father had been a Private in the 54th (West Norfolk) Regiment of Foot[372], who was discharged from the army on 03 June 1878 and died in Landport, Hampshire, on 14 October 1880. Obhaima remarried in 1881, to William Skinner, a Bombardier in the Royal Marine Artillery.

Henry was admitted to the school on 25 September 1885 (Petition No. 9264) and discharged to The Dorsetshire Regiment on 13 April

---

[372] Amalgamated with the 39th (Dorsetshire) Regiment of Foot on 01 July 1881 to become The Dorsetshire Regiment

1889. Having spent the first eighteen months of his service in the 2nd Battalion in Britain, he was then transferred to the 1st Battalion and posted to Egypt on 25 September 1890. After three years there, he was then posted to India on 27 September 1893, where he was to spend the next thirteen years until 08 December 1906.

During his time in India, Henry participated in the Tirah Expedition in 1898, earning two clasps to his India Medal, although he must have had some home leave during his time overseas, as he married Annie Bromby Thompson in Portsmouth, Hampshire, in June 1902. Their first child, born in India in 1905, died when only 11 days old. Two years after Henry returned to Britain his son, William Frederick Charles Rawlinson was born on 20 August 1908. Henry was discharged from the army as a Serjeant after 21 years' service two years later, on 12 April 1910.

The 1911 Census records Henry and family, including son Victor, living in Pimlico, London, and working as a Time Keeper and Parcel Clerk. It appears that he either re-enlisted, or was recalled to the Colours, at the outbreak of war, although there is no surviving service record available for this second period of engagement.

6th (Service) Battalion, The Royal Irish Rifles, was formed at Dublin, in August 1914 as part of K1, moving to Newbridge, County Kildare, in February 1915 and to Hackwood Park, Basingstoke, Hampshire, in May 1915, before embarking at Liverpool, Lancashire, on 07 July 1915 and sailing to Gallipoli via Mudros. It landed at Anzac Cove on 05 August 1915.

Early in the campaign, Henry was wounded and evacuated to Egypt, where he died of wounds on 15 August 1915, in the 21st General Hospital in Alexandria, being buried in the cemetery close by.

Henry's private life appears complicated, as after his death, his records show not only Annie as his wife, but also Ruby Florence Kendall as his "unmarried wife". He had two children with Ruby, Florence Kathleen Adelaide Rawlinson, born in 1912 and Winifred Rawlinson, born in 1914. However, Annie also gave birth to another son, George Dudley Rawlinson, five months after Henry's death, on 21 January 1916.

Henry's eldest son, William, was also a Dukie. He was admitted to the school on 31 October 1917 (Petition No. 13696) and discharged to the Royal Tank Corps on 20 December 1923. He died in Southampton, Hampshire, in October 1981.

The Princess Victoria's (Royal Irish Fusiliers)

Henry Edward HARDWICK
Serjeant, 9686, 1st Battalion, The Princess Victoria's (Royal Irish Fusiliers) who died on 24 June 1917, aged 24. Commemorated on the Arras Memorial, Pas-de-Calais, France

Born on 14 February 1893 in Bayswater, London, the second of six children of Robert Corbett Hardwick and Ethel Mary née Kemble, his father had been a Private in the Scots Guards, who was discharged from the army after 16 years' service on 31 August 1902. The 1901 Census records Henry living with his mother and siblings in Crowthorne, Berkshire, and although his mother is recorded in the Census as "wife of a soldier", his father does not appear. They were to divorce in 1902, with his father being employed in the Broadmoor Criminally Insane Asylum when he left the army.

Henry was admitted to the school on 04 March 1904 (Petition No. 11944) and was discharged on 07 March 1905, enlisting into The Princess Victoria's (Royal Irish Fusiliers).

His service record is no longer available, but at the outbreak of war, the 1st Battalion, Royal Irish Fusiliers, was stationed in Shorncliffe, Kent, but moved to its mobilisation area in York, Yorkshire North Riding, and finally Harrow, Middlesex, before deploying to France, where it landed at Boulogne on 23 August 1914, in time to provide infantry reinforcements during the Battle of Le Cateau. It also participated in the Battles of the Marne, the Aisne and Messines for the remainder of the year, before moving to Flanders and participating in the Second Battle of Ypres in early 1915. By the end of that year, it was the training battalion for the newly arriving troops within the 4th Division and with no date of disembarkation in Henry's medal index card, he was not overseas before 1916 at the earliest.

The following year, the battalion was part of the Irish Division and sustained heavy losses during the Somme Offensive in 1916, and by 1917 it was participating in the Battle of Arras. The initial battle in April saw spectacular success by the British forces and there was a lull in the fighting after 12 April. However, a new attack was ordered on 03 May, which did not have the success of the initial attack, the casualties reducing the strength of the battalion on 04 May to six officers and 236 other ranks.

In June, the unit was still in the Arras sector and it was here, on 24 June 1917, that Henry was presumed killed. His body was never recovered and he is one of 93 Royal Irish Fusiliers commemorated on the Arras Memorial.

It appears that there was also an error by the Commonwealth War Graves Commission when Henry's death was recorded, as it is stated that he was serving in the 12th Battalion, Royal Irish Fusiliers. However, there was no 12th Battalion and the Registers of Soldiers' Effects[373] records him as serving in the 1st Battalion. The records of Irish casualties also record him as having been serving in the 1st Battalion, as do the Service Medal and Award Rolls.

Albert KNIGHT
Lance Corporal, 29574, 1st Battalion, The Princess Victoria's (Royal Irish Fusiliers) who died on 12 April 1918, aged 18. Commemorated on the Tyne Cot Memorial, West-Vlaanderen, Belgium

Born on 19 May 1899 in Aldershot, Hampshire, the second of six children of Thomas Knight and Sarah née Hammett, his father had been a Private in The Queen's (Royal West Surrey Regiment), who had been discharged to pension after 21 years' service on 18 July 1902.

Albert was admitted to the school on 04 February 1910 (Petition No. 12725), joining his older brother, William George Thomas Knight, who had been admitted on 31 August 1907 (Petition No. 12386). Albert was discharged from the school on 12 July 1913 and followed his brother by enlisting into The Princess Victoria's (Royal Irish Fusiliers).

He was originally posted to the 1st Battalion at Shorncliffe, Kent, but probably due to his age, two days after war broke out, he was posted to the 3rd (Reserve) Battalion, the depot and training battalion stationed at Lough Swilly, County Donegal, and then Londonderry, County Londonderry. It then moved to Buncrana, County Donegal, in April 1915 and on to Clonmany, County Donegal, in November 1916.

It was not until 02 April 1918 that Albert was posted back to the 1st Battalion in France, when the unit was located at Ault-sur-Mer, having just returned from operations on the Somme, although it moved to Herzeele the day after Albert joined.

---

[373] UK, Army Registers of Soldiers' Effects, 1901-1929, 1914-1915, Dublin, 665501-667000

There then appears to be a discrepancy between the battalion war diary[374] and Albert's service record. The diary entry for 09 April states that the battalion moved by rail to Poperinghe and was shelled on arrival, with one other rank being killed. But in Albert's service record, there is a letter from a Serjeant that states that on that day, the battalion was at Messines Ridge, attacked by the Germans, and that they left their trenches to meet the attack. He goes on to say that he was within five yards of Albert when a shell landed and that they were forced to take cover behind a barn. They were then approximately ten yards apart when a shell burst next to Albert and three other soldiers. He says that whilst he was able to identify the three soldiers who had been with Albert, although one was so badly injured that it was only just possible to recognise him, he could find no trace of Albert and that, in his opinion, *"L/Cpl Knight was blown to pieces in fact I told his brother what I thought concerning this NCO"*.

This action resembles a battalion diary entry for 12 April, so it is likely that the Serjeant was mistaken about the date and rather than being killed on 09 April, as he is commemorated by the Commonwealth War Graves Commission, it is more probable that Albert Knight was killed on 12 April 1918, as his comrade recalled. As a result of the shell blast, his body was never found.

Albert is commemorated on the memorial tablets in the school chapel, but incorrectly recorded as W C T Knight. As the initials so closely resemble those of his brother, who is likely the brother referred to in the Serjeant's account, it seems that the wrong brother is commemorated at school.

William had been discharged from the school to the Royal Irish Fusiliers on 19 July 1910. He survived the war, married in 1918 and settled in West Ewell, Surrey, dying in Epsom, Surrey, on 19 November 1958, aged 62.

---

[374] WO 95/2505/1: 1 Battalion Royal Irish Fusiliers, 1918 Feb. - 1919 Feb., The National Archives, Kew

The Connaught Rangers

Francis William CORRY
Serjeant, 787, 5th (Service) Battalion, The Connaught Rangers who died on 05 June 1916, aged 30. Buried in Salonika (Lembet Road) Military Cemetery, Greece

Born on 10 July 1885 in Camberwell, Surrey, the fifth child and only son of Francis Edward Corry and Annie Maud née Willis, his father had been a Serjeant in The Essex Regiment and had been discharged from the army by the time of Francis's birth, employed as a Post Office Letter Carrier (Civil Service Messenger).

Francis was admitted to the school on 28 February 1896 (Petition No. 10867) and discharged to the army on 21 July 1899, enlisting into The Connaught Rangers in Athlone, County Westmeath, on 29 July 1899, a week after leaving the school. He was initially posted to the 1st Battalion, before being posted to the 2nd Battalion on 14 December 1900, when that battalion was posted to India. He then spent the next eight years in India, not returning to Britain until March 1908, having been appointed as a Bandsman in 1902.

On 13 May 1911, Francis reverted to Private and two months later, on 28 July 1911, he was discharged from the army having completed his 12 years' service. After leaving the army, he returned to live with his mother, now in Dulwich, London, although it is not known what he was employed as.

At the outbreak of war, it is also not known whether Francis volunteered, or whether he was recalled to the Colours, but it is known that he did re-join The Connaught Rangers, travelling to Ireland to do so. The battalion that he joined, the 5th (Service) Battalion, was formed at Dublin, in August 1914, part of K1, and came under the orders of the 29th Brigade in 10th (Irish) Division.

After several moves around Ireland, the battalion moved to mainland Britain in May 1915 and was stationed in Basingstoke, Hampshire, although this was only to be for two months, as on 09 July 1915 it embarked at Devonport, Devonshire, and sailed to Gallipoli. The battalion landed at Anzac Cove on 05 August 1915 and took part in actions at Lone Pine, Sari Bair, Hill 60 and Kabak

Kuyu. Two all out attacks on the Turks on 21 and 28 August resulted in very heavy casualties for the battalion in particular.

However, this was to be a short-lived campaign as, on 30 September 1915, the battalion re-embarked and sailed to Salonika on the Macedonian Front, where, after a month's training, it crossed the Greek frontier into Southern Serbia, but, on 07 December, it faced a huge attack by the Bulgarians, which forced it to retreat back into Greece.

The climate in this theatre was particularly inhospitable with unbearable heat and malaria in summer and ice and snow in winter. The exact circumstances of Francis's death are not known, but it is recorded that he died of "heat apoplexy"[375]. He is buried in Salonika (Lembet Road) Military Cemetery, one of more than 1,500 British troops buried there.

---

[375] Heat stroke

Princess Louise's
(Argyll and Sutherland Highlanders)

George Alfred AXON
Lance Corporal, 535, 11th (Service) Battalion, Princess Louise's (Argyll and Sutherland Highlanders) who died on 22 August 1917, aged 21. Commemorated on the Tyne Cot Memorial, West-Vlaanderen, Belgium

Born on 22 August 1896 in Gillingham, Kent, the eldest of five children of George Axon and Ellen née Bradford, his father was a private in The Royal Warwickshire Regiment, who served in South Africa during the Second Boer War, during which time George, his mother, his sister, Ellen Sophia Axon and his brother, Arthur Roberts Pretoria Axon, lived with his maternal grandparents in Leamington Spa, Warwickshire. However, following his grandfather's death in 1901, George and the family moved to Nuneaton, Warwickshire, to the home of his paternal grandparents. Unfortunately, whilst there, his mother died of enteric fever on 21 November 1902.

Following Ellen's death, George's father wrote to the army asking for his children to be taken into an army school and although re-married in Devonport, Devonshire, in 1904, to Bessie Goodman, all three children were indeed sent to army schools, George to the Duke of York's, Ellen to the Royal Soldiers' Daughters' School in Hampstead, London, and Arthur to the Royal Hibernian Military School in Dublin.

George was admitted to the school on 01 March 1907 (Petition No. 12341) and discharged three years later on 02 March 1910, enlisting into Princess Louise's (Argyll and Sutherland Highlanders). His service record is no longer available, so his pre-war and early-war postings are unknown, but he disembarked in France on 19 December 1914 with the 1st Battalion and he was later hospitalised between 05 and 08 February 1915, in the 5th Southern General Hospital, Portsmouth, Hampshire, with frostbite to his feet. However, as there was no evidence of gangrene, he was discharged.

In 1917, he was a Lance Corporal serving in the 11th (Service) Battalion, part of 15th (Scottish) Division. It was located in Flanders

511

and tasked with capturing various German strongpoints in the area of the River Steenbeck, as part of the Third Battle of Ypres.

At 0445hrs on 22 August 1917, George's battalion left its trenches with the objective of capturing the German strongpoints of Beck House and Borry Farm, to the left of the Menin Road. However, as soon as it left cover, it came under sustained fire from machine-guns, snipers and bombs, and although recognition flares were seen at Borry Farm, it is not known whether there were any further advances and the survivors were forced to retreat.

George was not among the survivors and was one of 117 men from his battalion to die on 22 August 1917, his twenty-first birthday. He has no known grave and is one of more than 36,000 British and Commonwealth soldiers commemorated on the Tyne Cot Memorial.

Herbert Thomas BUNNETT

Serjeant Major, 7179, 10th (Service) Battalion, Princess Louise's (Argyll and Sutherland Highlanders) who died on 24 November 1915, aged 30. Buried in Lijssenthoek Military Cemetery, West-Vlaanderen, Belgium

Born on 01 November 1885 in Exmouth, Devonshire, the sixth of nine children of Edward John Bunnett and Ellen née Easter, his father had been a Serjeant in The Prince Consort's Own (Rifle Brigade), but by the time of Herbert's birth, he was described as an Army Pensioner.

Herbert was admitted to the school on 27 September 1895 (Petition No. 10814), the same year that his father died and a year after his older brother, Robert James Bunnett, had also been admitted on 26 July 1895 (Petition No. 10769). Herbert was discharged from the school on 02 December 1899, enlisting into Princess Louise's (Argyll and Sutherland Highlanders), initially being posted to the 1st Battalion and then the 3rd Battalion, where he was appointed as a Drummer on 09 January 1900.

Having served in South Africa during the latter stages of the Second Boer War, Herbert returned to the 1st Battalion, where he was promoted to Private in March 1905, remaining with this battalion until 1909, by which stage he was a Corporal.

In August 1909, Herbert was promoted to Serjeant and assigned to the Army Gymnastic Staff in Aldershot, Hampshire, being posted to the depot of The Norfolk Regiment in Britannia Barracks, Norwich, where, in November 1913, he was promoted to Company Serjeant Major Instructor. He also met and married his wife, Vernon Maud Mary Gunns, in February 1912, whilst stationed here.

It was not until after the outbreak of war that he was to return to a battalion of his own regiment, when, on 01 September 1914, the newly promoted Serjeant Major Bunnett was posted to the 10th (Service) Battalion, a New Army battalion which had been formed at Stirling, Stirlingshire, in August 1914 as part of K1. After two moves in 1914 following its formation, the first to Bordon, Hampshire, and the second to New Alresford, Hampshire, in February 1915 the unit moved to Bramshott, Hampshire, before landing at Boulogne on 11 May 1915.

The battalion was in action on the Western Front, its first real test coming during the Battle of Loos between 25 September and 08 October 1915, when it lost 166 officers and men. Although Herbert survived the battle and moved to Flanders when the battalion was re-deployed there, a little over a month later he suffered a gunshot wound to the head. Despite evacuation to No. 17 Casualty Clearing Station, he died of his wounds on 24 November 1915. It is possible that it was during this final action that Herbert received a Mention in Despatches, which was posthumously Gazetted[376]. He is buried in Lijssenthoek Military Cemetery, 500 yards from the former site of the Casualty Clearing Station in which he succumbed to his injury.

Robert enlisted into The Royal Welsh Fusiliers when he was discharged from the school on 16 April 1898. He survived the war, being discharged from the army on 15 April 1919 and died in Southampton, Hampshire in 1949.

William CHUDLEY

Lance Corporal, 276, 10th (Service) Battalion, Princess Louise's (Argyll and Sutherland Highlanders) who died on 09 April 1917, aged 22. Buried in Mindel Trench British Cemetery, St. Laurent-Blangy, Pas De Calais, France

Born on 13 March 1895 in Birmingham, Warwickshire, the second of three children of John Chudley and Sarah Jane née Robinson, his father had been a Lance Serjeant in The Royal Welsh Fusiliers, although he had been discharged from the army on 25 April 1893 and died in Chatham, Kent, on 23 December 1902.

William was admitted to the school on 15 September 1905 (Petition No. 12143) and discharged to Princess Louise's (Argyll and Sutherland Highlanders) on 26 March 1909. Although William's service record is no longer available, it seems likely that he was initially serving with the 1st Battalion, as at the outbreak of war this battalion was stationed in Dinapore, India, returning to Britain and landing at Plymouth, Devonshire, before moving to Winchester, Hampshire, and embarking for France in December, landing at Le

---

[376] *The London Gazette*, 31 December 1915, Supplement:29422

Havre on 19 December 1914, the date shown on his medal index card for his entry into theatre.

During 1915, the battalion participated in the Second Battle of Ypres, before, in November 1915, it was posted to Salonika. Because there is no service record, it is unknown whether William was still with it at this point, or if not, which battalion he was serving with. What is known is that by 1917 he had been posted to the 10th (Service) Battalion, which in April 1917 was in the area of Arras, the city which gave its name to the battle which was about to commence.

The assault was launched at 0530hrs on 09 April, the task of the battalion being to follow 8th (Service) Battalion, The Black Watch (Royal Highlanders) and to "mop up" the enemy trenches once they had been captured by that battalion, then to advance behind The Black Watch to the next objective.

The attack was a complete success and the Argyll and Sutherland Highlanders casualties were actually relatively light compared to many of the battles of 1914-1916, with fourteen officers killed or wounded and 99 other ranks killed, wounded or missing, one of whom was William, dying on 09 April 1917. Due to the success of the attack, William's body was recovered and he is buried in St. Laurent-Blangy, less than a mile from the cemetery for the German casualties of this battle.

Although all of William's school and army records show his name as Chudley, the Commonwealth War Graves Commission incorrectly recorded his and his mother's names as Chudleigh.

Thomas Robert Dumfries COTCHER

Company Serjeant Major, 5353, 1/7th Battalion, Princess Louise's (Argyll and Sutherland Highlanders) who died on 02 September 1918, aged 37. Buried in Brown's Copse Cemetery, Roeux, Pas De Calais, France

Born on 08 February 1881 in Cirencester, Gloucestershire, the youngest of eight children of Henry Cotcher and Mary née Russell. Henry had served in the Crimean War in the 31st (Huntingdonshire) Regiment of Foot, but had then served as a Sergeant in the Royal North Gloucester Militia, although he died in Cirencester on 06 October 1880, three months before Thomas's birth.

Thomas was admitted to the school on 29 April 1891 (Petition No. 10164), joining his older brother, Douglas Connell Cotcher, who had been admitted on 21 June 1889 (Petition No. 9872). Another of his older brothers, Henry McClyment Cotcher, had been admitted on 25 March 1887 (Petition No. 9496), but had been discharged by the time of Thomas's admission. Thomas was discharged to Princess Louise's (Argyll and Sutherland Highlanders) on 09 February 1895, although his service record is no longer available, so it is not known with which battalions he served prior to the outbreak of war, but he had been a Corporal in the 1st Battalion during the Second Boer War, according to medal records.

At the outbreak of war, Thomas was posted to the 11th (Service) Battalion, which was formed at Stirling, Stirlingshire, in September 1914 as part of K2, landing at Boulogne on 09 July 1915. Thomas also served with the 14th (Service) Battalion, which was formed at Stirling, but in early-1915 and had landed at Le Havre in June 1916. It then appears that Thomas was posted back to the 11th Battalion, before eventually being posted to the 1/7th Battalion, a Territorial Force battalion.

At the outbreak of war, this battalion had been located in Stirling as part of the Argyll & Sutherland Highlanders Brigade in the Highland Division, landing in France on 14 December 1914 and coming under the orders of the 10th Brigade, 4th Division on 06 January 1915. On 27 May 1915, the battalion amalgamated with the 1/9th battalion and did not resume its own identity until 20 July. It then transferred to the 154th Brigade, 51st (Highland) Division, on 01 March 1916.

What is known is that Thomas did not enter theatre until 1916 at the earliest, as his medal index card shows that he did not qualify for the award of the 1914-15 Star, so it would have been at this point that he joined the battalion.

In late-1918, during the Hundred Days Offensive, the battalion was involved in the Battle of the Scarpe and although the battle ended on 30 August, it appears that during the actions in the aftermath of this battle, Thomas was killed on 02 September 1918. He is commemorated on the memorial tablets in the school chapel, but he is incorrectly named as T R R *Cotcherz*.

It is unclear whether Henry served during the war, as although he joined The King's Own (Royal Lancaster Regiment) when discharged from the school on 04 October 1890, he was discharged from the army on 27 August 1892 following a conviction for absence. In 1911 he was a Market-Gardener in Cirencester and it is not known when he died.

Douglas did serve, in the 3/5th Battalion, Princess Louise's (Argyll and Sutherland Highlanders), surviving the war. It appears that that he emigrated to Canada in 1925, although, like Henry, it has not been possible to ascertain when he died, although it appears that he was still alive and living with his wife, Margaret, in Cochrane, Ontario, in 1945.

George COUNTER
Private S/3308, 2nd Battalion, Princess Louise's (Argyll and Sutherland Highlanders) who died on 20 July 1916, aged 28. Commemorated on the Thiepval Memorial, Somme, France

Born on 13 October 1887 in Stirling, Stirlingshire, the third of nine children of George Counter and Elizabeth née McKenzie, his father was a Serjeant Major in Princess Louise's (Argyll and Sutherland Highlanders), who died three months before his sons were admitted to the school, on 29 April 1898.

George was admitted to the school on 16 July 1898 (Petition No. 11187), which was the same day that his younger brother, James Ferguson Counter, was also admitted (Petition No. 11188). George was discharged on 27 October 1902, enlisting into his father's old regiment.

George was noted as a cornet player and his service record shows that that he had served for four months in South Africa in 1903, before he was discharged from the army on 21 December 1905 as *"physically unfit for the ranks"*.

Following the outbreak of war, he re-enlisted in Stirling on 02 September 1914, giving his occupation as Waiter, but the fact that he had previously been discharged may account for the fact that he denied any previous service, the service record for this period of service having survived.

George spent the first four months of this service in the Regimental Depot before he was posted to the 2nd Battalion, arriving in France on 27 January 1915. There is no mention within his service record of any actions in which he took part, but it is known that his battalion took part in the Battle of Loos between 25 September and 16 October 1915, suffering heavy casualties in the process.

By the middle of 1916, the battalion was located on the Somme at the start of the offensive, although it was in billets for the initial attack and did not go into action until 14 July, between Bazentin-le-Petit and High Wood. In the early hours of the morning of 20 July, "D" Company of the battalion occupied trenches 300 yards to its front, meeting heavy machine-gun fire initially. This company was later joined by "A" Company guarding the right flank, before "C" Company advanced along the road to High Wood later that morning, meeting heavy machine-gun fire as it did so, halting the advance. That evening, at about 1800hrs, a German aircraft that had been damaged by French troops flew over the trenches occupied by the battalion, machine-gunning as it did so. The battalion returned fire, managing to bring the aircraft down.

At the end of the day, the battalion had suffered three officers wounded and fourteen other ranks killed, 46 wounded and ten missing, George being among them. His body was never recovered, so he is commemorated on the Thiepval Memorial. He is also a "Lost Boy" whose name has been omitted from the memorial tablets in the school chapel.

When James was discharged from the school on 21 May 1904, he also enlisted into his father's old regiment, recorded in the 1911 Census as a Bandsman in the 1st Battalion and stationed in Malta. He also served during the war, arriving in France on 19 December 1914, following which he was awarded the Distinguished Conduct Medal for his actions as a stretcher-bearer between January and March 1915[377]. Unlike George, he survived the war, dying in Cullompton, Devonshire, on 09 June 1944.

Another, non-Dukie brother, Richard Counter, died on 02 February 1919 whilst serving with 16th Battalion, The London Regiment (Queen's Westminster Rifles). He had previously served with Princess Louise's (Argyll and Sutherland Highlanders) and The Gordon Highlanders, and is believed to have succumbed to influenza.

Adrian George RATTRAY

Lance Corporal, 8967, 2nd Battalion, Princess Louise's (Argyll and Sutherland Highlanders) who died on 26 August 1914, aged 25. Commemorated on the La Ferte-Sous-Jouarre Memorial, Seine-et-Marne, France

Born on 24 October 1888 in Cairo, Egypt, the oldest child and only son of John Clements Rattray and Louisa Jeanne née Francfort, his father was a Serjeant in The King's Own Scottish Borderers and was still serving when he died in Berwick-upon-Tweed, Northumberland, on 20 April 1890.

Adrian was admitted to the school on 04 February 1898 (Petition No. 11127), the 1901 Census showing him at the Duke of York's and his sister, Clementina, at the Soldiers' Daughters' Home in Hampstead, London. He was discharged from the school on 08 November 1902 and enlisted into Princess Louise's (Argyll and Sutherland Highlanders), although his service record is no longer available.

At the outbreak of war, the 2nd Battalion was stationed in Fort George, Inverness, Inverness-shire, embarking at Southampton,

---

[377] *The London Gazette*, 22 June 1915, Supplement:29202

Hampshire, "A" & "B" Companies landing in France on 10 August, "C" & "D" Companies landing on 11 August 1914.

On 23 August, the battalion arrived at Valenciennes, before crossing the Belgian frontier and taking up positions in Quiévrain. In the early hours of 24 August, it was again ordered to move, initially taking up positions just outside the town, before the majority of the battalion crossed back over the frontier and took up positions at Eth, with one platoon being deployed to hold the railway line at St. Homme, north-east of Quiévrain. When that platoon re-joined the rest of the battalion at Eth, fifteen Non-Commissioned Officers and men were missing from the party and it is likely that Adrian was wounded during this action at St. Homme, as his entry in the Registers of Soldiers' Effects states that his presumptive date of death was 24 August, although at a later date this was corrected to state that he had died on 26 August 1914, *"while Prisoner of War"*[378].

It is also likely that he was buried by his captors, but that the subsequent fighting in this area led to his grave being lost, as he has no known grave and is, like his fellow Dukie, Lawrence Hill who was killed on the same day, commemorated on the La Ferte-Sous-Jouarre Memorial.

Alfred Ronald Richard ROBERTSON

Company Serjeant Major, 8111, 2nd Battalion, Princes Louise's (Argyll and Sutherland Highlanders) who died on 24 April 1917, aged 34. Commemorated on the Arras Memorial, Pas de Calais, France

Born on 24 April 1883 in West Ham, Essex, the oldest child of Charles John Grant Robertson and Isabel Matilda née Dean, his father had been a Serjeant in the 19th Hussars, but had been discharged from the army on 17 September 1872 and died in West Ham on 23 April 1888.

Alfred was admitted to the school on 26 January 1894 (Petition No. 10571) and was discharged to Princess Louise's (Argyll and Sutherland Highlanders) on 24 April 1897 where, after spending three years in the Depot in Stirling, Stirlingshire, he was appointed as a Drummer on 07 March 1900 and posted with the 3rd Battalion to South Africa from 01 February until 23 September 1902.

Alfred was to spend the next ten years stationed in Britain, becoming a father when Thomas Ferguson Robertson was born on 06 January 1905, Alfred marrying the mother, Alice Ferguson, seven months later on 08 August 1905. One of the witnesses at this wedding was Douglas Cotcher, fellow Dukie and older brother of Thomas Cotcher, who is also commemorated in the school chapel.

---

[378] UK, Army Registers of Soldiers' Effects, 1914-1915, Perth, 184001-185500

Alfred and Alice were to have four more children, born between 1906 and 1911, before Alfred was posted to India on 11 December 1912, by which stage he was a Serjeant. He returned from India in October 1914, was posted to the 11th (Service) Battalion and promoted to Company Quartermaster Serjeant in December. It is possible that he was serving there at the same time as fellow Dukie Thomas Cotcher.

Alfred was then posted to the 14th (Service) Battalion, where he was appointed as Acting Company Sergeant Major in June 1915, prior to being posted to the 15th (Service) Battalion in the November. Despite being promoted to Company Serjeant Major when he was posted to the battalion, during 1916 Alfred wrote to his Commanding Officer to complain that he and seven other Serjeants who had been posted to the "New Army" battalions, had all seen soldiers junior promoted above them, because they had remained with the Regular battalions, asking that his Warrant be antedated to June 1915, which it was.

In August 1916, Alfred was posted to the 3rd (Reserve) Battalion, before being transferred to 1st Garrison Battalion of The Gordon Highlanders, the following month. In January 1917, he was posted back to the 3rd Battalion of his regiment and then on 17 February 1917, he was posted to the 2nd Battalion in France.

Two months later, on 22 April, the battalion moved into trenches in order to attack the high ground overlooking Fontaine Les Croisilles and the Hindenburg Line. The attack was launched on 23 April and continued the following day, Alfred being one of those initially reported as missing, but later confirmed as having died on 24 April 1917, his thirtieth birthday. He is commemorated on the memorial tablets in the school chapel, but is incorrectly recorded as A H Robertson.

Alfred's second son, Charles Graham Grant Robertson, whilst not a Dukie, is also commemorated by the Commonwealth War Graves Commission. He had enlisted into 4th/7th Dragoon Guards, but was a Staff Sergeant in the Royal Army Ordnance Corps when he died in Italy in April 1945. He is buried in Faenza War Cemetery.

Charles William THOMAS

Private, 10199, 10th (Service) Battalion, Princess Louise's (Argyll and Sutherland Highlanders) who died on 14 July 1916, aged 23. Commemorated on the Thiepval Memorial, Somme, France

Born on 16 August 1892 in Tipperary, County Tipperary, the second of four children and only son of John Thomas and Sarah née Meering, his father had served in The Loyal North Lancashire

Regiment, but was a Serjeant in the Army Medical Staff Corps when he died in Cairo, Egypt on 14 April 1896.

Charles was admitted to the school on 13 September 1901 (Petition No. 11606) and discharged on 30 August 1906, enlisting into Princess Louise's (Argyll and Sutherland Highlanders). His service record is no longer available and he cannot be located in the 1911 Census, but we can also surmise that he was serving with the 1st Battalion at the outbreak of war, returning from Dinapore, India in August and via Plymouth, Devonshire and Winchester, Hampshire, landing at Le Havre on 19 December 1914, the disembarkation date shown in his medal index card.

The 10th (Service) Battalion landed at Boulogne on 11 May 1915, relieving the regiment's 2nd Battalion in the trenches on 20 and 21 May, although its first major action was during the Battle of Loos in September 1915. Having spent the early part of 1916 in the Ypres sector, it had then moved to the Somme sector by the start of the offensive in July, although initially it was in reserve, moving into the front line on 07 July and occupying former German trenches on the "old front line". It is probable that Charles had been wounded earlier in the war and then returned to France to serve in this battalion, but that is only speculation. What we do know is that he married Elizabeth Mary Meering in July 1915 in Southampton, Hampshire, so he must have either had home leave then or been recuperating from a wound.

On 14 July, the battalion was located in trenches near Trônes Wood and at 0325hrs an assault was launched, with the German position being quickly overrun, although it then found itself on the receiving end of its own barrage. Despite this, it was able to advance further, quickly taking the central street in the town of Longueval, although it again suffered from its own guns. Despite this success, the battalion continued to receive casualties from a concealed sniper and machine-gun position until these were eventually silenced, with Charles being one of the 24 men killed during this assault. His body was never recovered and he is commemorated on the Thiepval Memorial.

Frederick Ramsay WALKER MC
Second Lieutenant, 2nd Battalion, Princess Louise's (Argyll and Sutherland Highlanders) who died on 06 January 1917, aged 34. Buried in Edinburgh (Dalry) Cemetery, United Kingdom

Born on 27 July 1882 in Tipperary, County Tipperary, the second of three children of Thomas Walker and Mary Susanna née

Lawson, his father had been a Serjeant in The King's Own Scottish Borderers, but had been discharged from the army as medically unfit and died in St. Thomas's Hospital, London, on 24 December 1892. Frederick's mother had died in Annan, Dumfries-shire on 20 July 1887 and the boys' Petitions were completed by their stepmother, Annie.

Frederick was admitted to the school on 26 May 1893 (Petition No. 10479) and was joined by his younger brother, Louis Seymour Walker, three months later, on 25 August 1893 (Petition No. 10513). Frederick was discharged on 08 August 1896, enlisting into Princess Louise's (Argyll and Sutherland Highlanders).

He served with the 1st Battalion in South Africa during the Second Boer War, being awarded the Queen's South Africa Medal with two clasps, and at some point he was posted to the 2nd Battalion, stationed in Fort George, Inverness, Inverness-shire, where in August 1912 he married Josephine Margaret Maxwell.

At the outbreak of war, Frederick was a Company Serjeant Major and the battalion was rapidly deployed to France, landing at Boulogne on 14 August 1914, where it participated in the Retreat from Mons, as well as the Battles of Le Cateau, the Marne and the Aisne. For actions during this period, Frederick was awarded the Medaille Militaire, a French decoration awarded to other ranks for meritorious service and acts of bravery in action against an enemy force. He was also twice Mentioned in Despatches[379][380].

In late-1915, the battalion participated in the Battle of Loos and in the aftermath of this, Frederick was Mentioned in Despatches[381], the third time that he had been. This was followed up on 17 January 1916 with the award of the Military Cross[382], although the citation does not appear to have been published.

At the start of the Somme Offensive, the battalion was in reserve, entering the fray on 15 July when two companies were sent to guard the right flank following the failed attack between Bazentin-le-Petit and High Wood. It remained in this sector and whilst here, Frederick was Commissioned as a Second Lieutenant[383], although eight days later, on 17 August 1916, he was one of the casualties when the trenches that the battalion was occupying near High Wood were intermittently shelled during the day.

Frederick was evacuated home and never returned to the front. He died of syncope (likely a heart attack) in Dreghorn Camp,

---

[379] *The London Gazette*, 16 October 1914, Supplement: 28942
[380] *The London Gazette*, 20 October 1914, Issue: 28945
[381] *The London Gazette*, 31 December 1915, Supplement:29422
[382] *The Edinburgh Gazette*, 17 January 1916, Issue:12894
[383] *The London Gazette*, 8 August 1916, Supplement:29699

Edinburgh, Midlothian, on 06 January 1917 and was buried in that city. By 2017, his grave had fallen into disrepair, but a mystery benefactor paid for it to be restored in time for the centenary of his death.

Louis was discharged *"To Sister"* on 23 July 1899, but he enlisted into the Royal Navy in 1902, before joining the Merchant Navy. He died in Watford, Hertfordshire, in 1932.

Victor Harold WATERFIELD
Private, 789, 10th (Service) Battalion, Princess Louise's (Argyll and Sutherland Highlanders) who died on 30 April 1917, aged 19. Commemorated on the Arras Memorial, Pas de Calais, France

Born on 25 May 1897 in Farnborough, Hampshire, the youngest of two children of George Caborn Waterfield and Minnie née McGrotty, his father had been a Serjeant in Princess Louise's (Argyll and Sutherland Highlanders), who had been discharged from the army on 13 February 1896. His mother died in Farnborough when Victor was only three months old, on 03 July 1897.

Victor was admitted to the school on 03 October 1907 (Petition No. 12431) and having made the move from Chelsea to Guston, was discharged to his father's old regiment on 29 June 1911. He was appointed as a Drummer in the 2nd Battalion on 03 August, before reverting back to Boy on 11 September at his own request. He was then posted to the 1st Battalion on 22 November 1912 and moved with it to India, where he remained until 18 November 1914.

It seems that although the battalion landed at Le Havre in December 1914, Victor did not land with them, remaining in Britain, possibly due to his age. He was then posted to the 3rd (Reserve) Battalion, stationed in Edinburgh, Midlothian, on 25 May 1915. Whilst serving with this battalion, Victor married Eliza Monteith in Stirling, Stirlingshire, in September 1915, their son, George Waterfield, being born in March 1916, five months before Victor was posted to the 10th (Service) Battalion, on 03 August 1916.

In April 1917, the battalion was engaged in the Battle of Arras, and on 29 April, a patrol was approaching what had been a British trench and observed men occupying this. The officer in charge shouted, "Are you Seaforths?". When there was no reply, he became suspicious and fired his revolver at these men, who immediately responded with a shower of stick grenades, forcing the patrol to withdraw, but in doing so, the officer in charge was severely wounded, one Non-Commissioned Officer was killed and one other rank was also wounded, the wounded man being Victor, who died of wounds the following day. Although he is commemorated on the memorial tablets in the school chapel, he is incorrectly recorded as V H *Waterford*.

Victor's non-Dukie, half-brother, Vivian Conrad George Colnaghi Caborn-Waterfield, was a Fleet Air Arm Pilot who died of natural causes on 10 August 1944 and is commemorated by Commonwealth War Graves Commission. Vivian's son, Michael Caborn-Waterfield, was the Founder of Ann Summers!

The Prince of Wales's Leinster Regiment (Royal Canadians)

Henry Archie MILLAR
Private, 8118, 1st Battalion, The Prince of Wales's Leinster Regiment (Royal Canadians) who died on 20 April 1915, aged 22. Buried in Poperinghe Old Military Cemetery, West-Vlaanderen, Belgium

Born on 28 October 1892 in Portsmouth, Hampshire, the fourth of eight children of Andrew Millar and Maria née Mason, his father had served as a Private in the 29th (Worcestershire) Regiment of Foot[384], before transferring to The Prince of Wales's Leinster Regiment (Royal Canadians), from which he was discharged on 09 February 1884.

Henry was admitted to the school on 12 August 1903 (Petition No. 11843) and was discharged on 08 November 1906, enlisting into his father's old regiment, and although there is no surviving service record, he is recorded in the 1911 Census serving with the 2nd Battalion and stationed in Jullundur, India. It is not known when he was posted to the 1st Battalion, but he entered theatre with that unit.

At the outbreak of war, the 1st Battalion was stationed in Faizabad, India, embarking at Bombay on 16 October and landing at Plymouth, Devonshire, on 16 November, moving to Winchester, Hampshire, two days later. After being made up to full strength, it embarked on the SS *Lake Michigan* on 19 December and landed at Le Havre on 20 December 1914, having its first experience in the trenches when it relieved 2nd Battalion, The Queen's Own Cameron Highlanders in the front line on 12 January 1915.

In April, the battalion was in the vicinity of Ypres, participating in the action at St. Eloi a week prior to the launch of the campaign that became known as the Second Battle of Ypres. In preparation for the launch of this battle, it moved into the front-line trenches on 19 April, remaining there until 04 May. The battalion war diary[385] reports that during this tour, it suffered six officers and 37 other ranks

---

[384] Amalgamated with the 36th (Herefordshire) Regiment of Foot on 01 July 1881 to become The Worcestershire Regiment
[385] WO 95/2266/3: 1 Battalion Leinster Regiment, 1914 Dec. - 1915 Oct., The National Archives, Kew

killed and wounded. One of the wounded, who subsequently died from these wounds, was Henry, who died on 20 April 1915 and is buried close to where he fell. Although he is commemorated on the memorial tablets in the school chapel, he is incorrectly recorded as H A *Miller*.

The Royal Munster Fusiliers

Albert Edward DOUCH
Private, 12459, 7th (Service) Battalion, The Royal Dublin Fusiliers who died on 27 September 1915, aged 41. Commemorated on the Helles Memorial, Turkey

Born on 27 July 1874 in Waterford, County Waterford, the fourth of six children of Mark Douch and Catherine née Long, his father had been a Serjeant in the Army Hospital Corps, who had been discharged from the army on 13 July 1880. He died in Hackney, Middlesex, on 23 January 1883 and Catherine re-married, to William Heath, in Hackney in 1887.

Albert was admitted to the school on 26 February 1886 (Petition No. 9328) and was discharged *"To mother"* on 03 September 1888, although he enlisted into the Army Medical Staff Corps as a Private (3rd Class Orderly) on 22 November 1890, claiming to be 18 years old, when actually two years younger. However, within six months of enlisting, on 18 May 1891, Albert was absent without leave for six days. Despite this, on 20 March 1893, he was appointed as a 2nd Class Orderly, extending his period of service to 7 years a month later, on 27 April 1893 and was then appointed to 1st Class Orderly on 26 May 1893.

This appointment did not last long, as he reverted to 2nd Class Orderly on 02 December 1893 and to 3rd Class Orderly on 09 April 1894. Five days later, Albert was again absent without leave, this time for eleven days, being awarded fourteen days' detention by his Commanding Officer when he returned on 25 May 1894. Ten days after he was returned to duty, on 18 June 1894, he was discharged from the army for misconduct, forfeiting all service towards his pension.

Seven months after being discharged from the army, on 04 November 1894, Albert married Sarah Anne Brewster in Dublin, interestingly still giving his profession as "Soldier". Their eldest child, Mark Joseph Douch, was born two months later on 15 January 1895, although sadly he and Albert's second son, Alfred Joseph Douch, born in 1896, both died in 1898.

The 1901 Ireland Census records Albert living in Dublin and employed as a General Labourer. He was still married to Sarah and they had two daughters, Mary Ellen Douch and Christina Douch. It appears that he and Sarah had other sons, Michael Joseph Douch, was born in 1899, but died in 1901 and also Albert Edward Douch, born in 1903, but died in infancy.

There is then some confusion regarding Albert's private life, as he is recorded in the 1911 Census living in Liverpool, Lancashire, and still employed as General Labourer. However, his wife's name is given as Catherine and they have three children, Mary, Sarah and Elizabeth. However, there is no record of his first wife having died, nor any record of a divorce, although it appears that following his death, Catherine attempted to claim his pension using Albert and Sarah's marriage certificate.

Again, little is known of his life after this census until the outbreak of war, but it is surmised that when he enlisted on this occasion, he gave his age as being less than 40 to meet the requirements at the time, although his service record is no longer available to confirm this.

The battalion in which he served, 7th (Service) Battalion, The Royal Munster Fusiliers, had been formed at Tralee, County Kerry, in August 1914 as part of K1, moving initially to Newbridge, County Kildare, and then to Basingstoke, Hampshire. On 07 July 1915, the battalion embarked at Liverpool and sailed for Gallipoli, Albert's medal index card showing that he disembarked at Suvla Bay on 09 August 1915.

In the seven weeks before he was killed, he would have been involved in some intense fighting, initially on Chocolate Hill and later at Kizlar Dagh Ridge. The division in which The Royal Munster Fusiliers was serving, withdrew three days after Albert's death, having gained no ground and having suffered heavy casualties as a result of administrative blunders and a shortage of water and ammunition.

At the time of his death, the battalion was occupying trenches under Scimitar Hill and he was the last soldier to be killed before it was evacuated. The battalion war diary[386] recorded that from 1900hrs on 27 September, *"Very heavy rifle fire opened by both sides along whole line. Guns opened very heavy fire on Turkish trenches. Turkish guns also fired. Fire died down, finally ceased at 20.30. "A" Coy and 2 Platoons of "B" Coy reinforced 6th R. Dub. Fus. CASUALTIES Other Ranks, one killed, 2 wounded"*.

---

[386] WO 95/4296: 10 (Irish) Division: 30 Infantry Brigade: 7 Battalion Royal Munster Fusiliers (1915 July - Sept.), 1915 June 1 - 1915 Sept 30, The National Archives, Kew

Although Albert is commemorated on the Helles Memorial, he is a "Lost Boy" whose name has been omitted from the memorial tablets in the school chapel.

George Ernest ROBERTS
Lance Corporal Signaller, 9865, 2nd Battalion, The Royal Munster Fusiliers who died on 27 August 1914, aged 21. Buried in Etreux British Cemetery, Aisne, France

Born on 19 February 1893 in Portsmouth, Hampshire, the eighth of nine children of John William Roberts and Ann née Ryan, his father had been a Serjeant in The Worcestershire Regiment and was discharged from the army on 10 May 1886. He died in Portsmouth on 28 July 1903.

Despite being one of five boys in the family, George was the only one to attend the school, being admitted on 04 March 1904 (Petition No. 11946) and discharged on 20 March 1907, enlisting into The Dorsetshire Regiment. This service record is no longer available to confirm when he transferred to The Royal Munster Fusiliers and it is not possible to confirm his postings prior to 1911, however in the census of that year, he was recorded as a Drummer, stationed with 1st Battalion, The Dorsetshire Regiment, in Alma Barracks, Blackdown, Surrey.

By the outbreak of war in August 1914, George was serving in 2nd Battalion, The Royal Munster Fusiliers, which was stationed in Malplaquet Barracks, Aldershot, Hampshire. It is possible that he transferred when the Munsters were posted to Aldershot in 1912, as it was the battalion in which his older, non-Dukie brother, Charles James Roberts, was serving. At the outbreak of war, this battalion quickly mobilised, landing at Le Havre on 14 August 1914 and coming into action for the first time on 25 August. Having detrained at Bertry during the day, that evening near Bevillers two of its companies engaged a small party of Uhlans at 1800hrs.

The following day, the battalion was again in action near Esnes from 0805hrs until 1045hrs, and again that afternoon, from 1415hrs to 1630hrs. However, the action in the afternoon occurred whilst it was in retreat, as the two companies near Le Catelet commenced their retirement at 1130hrs, with the other two rifle companies forced to retire twenty minutes later.

On 27 August, it was still in retreat. There are no reports of action or casualties in the battalion war diary[387], but it is known that three

---

[387] WO 95/1279/1: 3 Infantry Brigade: 2 Battalion Royal Munster Fusiliers., 1914 Aug 1 - 1915 Dec 31, The National Archives, Kew

companies of the battalion halted the advance of the Germans for fourteen hours in the area of Oisny and Étreux, enabling the rest of the British Expeditionary Force to withdraw to a safe distance of 12 miles. However, the battalion was decimated during this action, with only five officers and 196 other ranks surviving.

One of the casualties on that day was George Roberts, killed on 27 August 1914. He is buried in a shared grave in Etreux British Cemetery, commemorated alongside his older brother, Charles, who was a Signal Corporal in the same battalion and was killed on the same day. The Roberts brothers are believed to be the second pair of brothers in the British Army to die on the same day in the First World War.

The Prince Consort's Own (Rifle Brigade)

John Edwin HELSON
Rifleman, 519, 22nd (Wessex & Welsh) Battalion, The Prince Consort's Own (Rifle Brigade) who died on 22 August 1916, aged 46. Buried in Pieta Military Cemetery, Malta

Born on 19 October 1869 in Newbridge, County Kildare, the second of three children of John Helson and Frances Emily née Elmes, his father was a Private in the 66th (the Berkshire) Regiment of Foot, who died whilst serving on 03 November 1875.

John was admitted to the school on 29 July 1881 (Petition No. 8662) and was discharged on 20 October 1883, enlisting into The Princess Charlotte of Wales's (Berkshire Regiment)[388], spending the first fifteen months of his service in Gosport, Hampshire, and Chatham, Kent. On 25 January 1885, John was then posted to Cairo, Egypt, before he was posted back to Reading, Berkshire, in June, being posted back to Egypt four months later on 05 October 1885. During his time in Egypt, he saw active service in the Sudan.

After six months in Egypt, John was then posted to Cyprus, where he spent eighteen months before being posted to Malta on 03 February 1888. Five years later, John was posted to Bermuda, West Indies, where he was hospitalised for ten days between 29 October and 07 November 1895 due to *"alcoholism"*, before he was posted back to Britain on 16 December and discharged from the army at the end of his first period of service on 20 December 1895.

Nothing is known of John following his discharge from the army, and he does not seem to appear in either the 1901 or 1911 Censuses, but following the outbreak of war, he re-enlisted into the army on 20 October 1914 in Newport, Monmouthshire. He gave his occupation as Tailor and it appears that he had not married, as his next of kin was given as his mother, who had remarried a Private in her late husband's regiment and was now called Frances Emily Barrington, living in Wantage, Berkshire.

---

[388] Renamed The Princess Charlotte of Wales's (Royal Berkshire Regiment) on 29 September 1885, the "Royal" accolade being granted for distinguished conduct at Tofrek during the Sudan Wars

It appears that John initially enlisted into 1/1st Battalion, The Monmouthshire Regiment. This was a Territorial Force battalion that was located in Newport as part of the Welsh Border Brigade, Welsh Division. Once mobilised, it moved to Pembroke Dock, Pembrokeshire, moving to Oswestry, Shropshire, on 10 August 1914 and then to Northampton, Northamptonshire by the end of that month. After moving to Hemmingford near Ipswich, Suffolk, by October 1914 and then to Barningham near Thetford, Norfolk, in December 1914, and finally to Cambridge, Cambridgeshire, in early-January 1915, the battalion landed in France on 13 February 1915.

However, it appears that John did not land with the battalion, as although there is no date of disembarkation recorded in his medal index card, the only unit recorded is the one to which he was transferred on 25 September 1915. His service record also shows that his first posting abroad was not until 1916.

22nd (Wessex & Welsh) Battalion, The Prince Consort's Own (Rifle Brigade), was formed in accordance with an Army Council Instruction of 29 November 1915 and consisted of supernumerary Territorial Force battalions which had been formed from National Reservists and was intended to be used in guarding vulnerable points in Britain. However, in 1916, the battalion was posted for garrison duty overseas, John being posted to Salonika via Egypt, embarking at Liverpool, Lancashire, on 03 January 1916 and arriving in Alexandria on 19 January 1916.

It is not known when John arrived in Salonika nor when he reached Malta, but he reported sick with symptoms of malaria on 31 July 1916. His condition worsened and he was admitted to the military hospital at Imtarfa, Malta, on 13 August 1916 and although he was operated on to remove pus and improve his symptoms, his condition worsened. He died from malaria, suppurative parotitis[389] and meningitis on 22 August 1916, stated to have been contracted when on active service in Greece (Salonika).

John was buried in Malta, but he is another "Lost Boy" whose name has been omitted from the memorial tablets in the school chapel. His youngest half-brother Percy Barrington, who was not a Dukie, died on 31 March 1919, post-discharge from the Royal Field Artillery and is also commemorated by the Commonwealth War Graves Commission.

---

[389] Parotitis is inflammation of the parotid salivary gland, suppurative parotitis caused most commonly by Staphylococcus aureus in patients who are debilitated, dehydrated or have poor oral hygiene, all of which were likely to in the conditions in which John was serving

Alexander George KELLY

Rifleman, 3044, 3rd Battalion, The Prince Consort's Own (Rifle Brigade) who died on 16 February 1915, aged 35. Buried in Portsmouth (Highland Road) Cemetery, Hampshire, United Kingdom

Born on 25 November 1879 in Dover, Kent, the fourth of five children of Thomas Kelly and Harriet née Earwicker, his father had been a Private in The Prince Consort's Own Rifle Brigade, but had been discharged from the army on 20 July 1880 and died in Bramley, Wiltshire, on 19 September 1886.

Alexander was admitted to the school on 25 April 1890 (Petition No. 10012), joining his older brother Thomas Kelly (Petition No. 9526). Alexander was discharged to his father's old regiment on 25 November 1893, initially posted to the 2nd Battalion, but on 22 October 1895, he was posted to the 1st Battalion and sailed for Hong Kong, China. After a year there, he was posted to Singapore, prior to returning to Britain on 13 February 1898.

Whilst still with the 1st Battalion, Alexander was then posted to South Africa on 03 August 1901 during the Second Boer War and was awarded the Queen's South Africa Medal, although he was only there for seven months before being posted to the 3rd Battalion in India. On 21 November 1904, the battalion was posted to Aden, remaining there for just over a year, before being posted back to Britain at the beginning of 1906.

At the outbreak of war, the battalion was stationed in Cork, County Cork, but moved to Cambridge, Cambridgeshire, on 18 August and then Newmarket, Suffolk, on 31 August before embarking at Southampton, Hampshire, on 08 September and landing at St. Nazaire on 12 September 1914, having its first experience of the trenches two miles north of Soupir ten days later. Alexander's medal index card confirms he disembarked with the battalion.

On 1 October 1914, the battalion were in a quiet sector of trenches on the Aisne, the battalion war diary[390] reporting 104 reinforcements joined and *"one man wounded"*. Alexander's service record states he was wounded by shrapnel in the neck and shoulder on that day, so it is presumed that he was the man referred to in the war diary. Although he was evacuated back to Britain, he died of wounds four months later, in the 5th Southern General Hospital, Portsmouth, Hampshire, on 16 February 1915 and was buried in the nearby Highland Road Cemetery. In addition, although he is

---

[390] WO 95/1613: 6 Division: 17 Infantry Brigade: 3 Battalion Rifle Brigade, 1914 Aug. - 1915 Oct., The National Archives, Kew

commemorated on the memorial tablets in the school chapel, his surname is incorrectly spelt as *Kelley*.

Thomas was discharged from the school to The Gordon Highlanders on 03 December 1890. It appears that by the time war broke out, he had left the army, as the 1911 Census records him as a Farm Labourer in Baughurst, near Basingstoke, Hampshire. It is probable that, as he would have been 38 when the war commenced, he was considered too old to serve. It is not known if he married or when he died.

Joseph William MONGER
Rifleman, 200167, 18th (London) Battalion, The Prince Consort's Own (Rifle Brigade) who died on 04 June 1919, aged 41. Buried in Tooting (St. Nicholas) Churchyard, London, United Kingdom

Born on 25 September 1877 in Hastings, Sussex, the fifth of eight children of George Monger and Mary Ann née Love, his father had been a Private in the 23rd Regiment of Foot (Royal Welsh Fuzileers)[391], who had been awarded a Victoria Cross for his actions at Lucknow, India, during the Indian Mutiny[392]. He was discharged from the army on 04 November 1868 and died from tuberculosis in St. Leonards-on-Sea, Sussex, on 09 August 1887.

Joseph was admitted to the school on 24 August 1888 (Petition No. 9685) and discharged on 03 October 1891, enlisting into The Queen's (Royal West Surrey Regiment). Three months after he was discharged, Joseph's younger brother, Ernest John Monger, was admitted to the school, on 07 January 1892 (Petition No. 10256).

Joseph had a very short army career, as following his attestation with the 1st Battalion, he was posted to the Regimental Depot in Stoughton Barracks, Guildford, Surrey, on 19 December 1891, from where, ten months later on 21 September 1892, he was discharged as medically unfit for further service.

He married Isabel Louisa Clements in Hastings, Sussex, in 1897 and is recorded in the 1901 Census living in Tooting with his wife and employed as a Labourer. Two years later their only son, George Monger, was born in Tooting. Joseph was also recorded in the 1911 Census living with his widowed sister, still in Tooting, with his wife, son, mother and two nephews, his employment being given as General Labourer (Builder).

---

[391] Renamed The Royal Welsh Fusiliers on 01 July 1881
[392] *The London Gazette*, 12 April 1859, Issue:22248: *"Private George Monger*
Date of Act of Bravery, 18th November, 1857: For daring gallantry at Secundra Bagh, Lucknow, on the 18th of November, 1857, in having volunteered to accompany Lieutenant Hackett, whom he assisted in bringing in a Corporal of the 23rd Regiment, who was lying wounded in an exposed position."

When war broke out, Joseph re-enlisted into the army on 26 November 1914, initially being posted to the 1/20th (County of London) Battalion (Blackheath and Woolwich) of The London Regiment, which had been formed in August 1914 and was located in Joseph's old school, by now The Duke of York's Headquarters.

On 05 November 1915 he was posted again, to 18th (London) Battalion, The Prince Consort's Own (Rifle Brigade), which was to be formed on 29 November in accordance with an Army Council Instruction. This battalion had been created from supernumerary Territorial Force battalions which had been formed from National Reservists and used to guard vulnerable points in Britain.

On 05 January 1916 it was posted to Port Blair, Andaman Islands, India, as the Garrison Battalion and Joseph had only been in the country for a month when he was admitted to hospital on 22 February suffering from Dengue Fever[393]. During 1916, the battalion was posted to Rangoon, Burma, and Joseph was again admitted to hospital with Dengue Fever on 11 October. His luck was not to improve, as he was injured during bayonet practice when he was struck on the head with a wooden post. When he reported sick two weeks later, he was initially diagnosed with another bout of Dengue Fever, before it was realised that he had suffered a fracture to the base of his skull.

He was initially treated in Rangoon, before being transferred to Bombay for further treatment and despite returning to Rangoon, he was again hospitalised due to his injury, which resulted in him being transferred back to Britain and admitted to the Huddersfield War Hospital, Yorkshire West Riding, on 19 August 1918.

Joseph was discharged from the army on 20 September 1918 as medically unfit for further service and died the following June. It is almost certain that his death was attributable to his war service and he was commemorated by the Commonwealth War Graves Commission. He is also another of the "Lost Boys" whose name has been omitted from the memorial tablets in the school chapel.

Ernest was discharged from the school on 08 January 1895, enlisting into his father's old regiment and served for 12 years before being discharged. He re-enlisted in 1915 and ended the war serving in The Royal Inniskilling Fusiliers, having been awarded the Military Medal[394], an award that is currently missing from the Honours Board located within the Adjutant General's Room in the school. He died in Wandsworth in 1953.

---

[393] A mosquito-borne tropical disease which causes fever, headaches, muscle and joint pains and a rash
[394] *The London Gazette*, 13 May 1919, Supplement:31338

Joseph MURPHY
Corporal, B/3008, 7th (Service) Battalion, The Prince Consort's Own (Rifle Brigade) who died on 05 January 1916, aged 37. Buried in Boulogne Eastern Cemetery, Pas de Calais, France

Born on 08 October 1878 in Exeter, Devonshire, the youngest of three children of Patrick Murphy and Susan née Brewer, his father had been a Private in the 3rd (the East Kent) Regiment of Foot, who was discharged from the army on 30 April 1878 and died in Exeter on 07 January 1886.

Joseph was admitted to the school on 07 May 1889 (Petition No. 9814) joining his older brother, John Patrick Murphy, who had been admitted on 07 May 1886 (Petition No. 9359). Joseph was discharged from the school on 12 November 1892 and joined the army, enlisting into The Prince Consort's Own (Rifle Brigade).

Joseph was posted to the 2nd Battalion of the regiment and spent the first five years of his service in Britain before he was posted to Malta on 24 September 1897. Ten months after arriving in Malta, he was then posted to Egypt, on 12 July 1898, where he took part in the Nile Expedition and was awarded the Queen's Sudan Medal and the Khedive's Sudan Medal, with the clasp *Khartoum* for participation in the Battle of Omdurman.

Three weeks after the battle, on 21 September 1898, Joseph was posted to Crete as part of the occupation, remaining there for just over a year, before he was posted to South Africa on 02 October 1899 during the Second Boer War. Joseph was in South Africa for eight months before he was posted back to Britain on 12 June 1900, but he was awarded the Queen's South Africa Medal with the clasp *Defence of Ladysmith*.

He remained in Britain for two years before he was again posted, on 19 November 1902, returning to Egypt, where he spent the final three years of this period of service, being posted back to Britain on 24 October 1905 and discharged from the army having completed 12 years' service the following day.

He is recorded in the 1911 Census as a Ward Attendant working in the Three Counties Lunatic Asylum in Arlesey, Bedfordshire, and it appears that he was still employed there when war broke out, as he gave his employment as Attendant when he re-enlisted on 01 September 1914, although the enlistment was in Huddersfield, Yorkshire West Riding.

The battalion to which Joseph was posted, 7th (Service) Battalion, The Prince Consort's Own (Rifle Brigade), had been formed at Winchester, Hampshire, on 21 August 1914 as part of K1, coming under the command of the 41st Brigade, 14th (Light) Division. It then moved to Aldershot, Hampshire, before moving to Elstead, Surrey, in November 1914, returning to Aldershot in March 1915, prior to landing at Boulogne in May 1915, Joseph's medal index card confirming that he arrived in theatre on 19 May 1915.

Having been posted to the battalion on 06 September 1914, Joseph was appointed as an Acting Corporal on 09 September, confirmed as substantive ten days' later and then appointed as an Acting Serjeant on 07 January 1915, which was made substantive on 23 March 1915. However, five months after arriving in theatre, on 14 October 1915, Joseph was tried by Field General Courts Martial for drunkenness on active service and was reduced to the rank of Corporal.

Two months later, on 28 December 1915, the battalion relieved 1/4th (Hallamshire) Battalion, The York and Lancaster Regiment in trenches at Lancashire Farm, an area not far from the Ypres-Boesinghe canal and the following day Joseph was wounded by a shell. He was evacuated to Boulogne, where he died of those wounds a week later.

Joseph was buried in the town where he died, but he is another of the "Lost Boys" whose name has been omitted from the memorial tablets in the school chapel.

John was discharged from the school on 07 December 1889 and enlisted into The Prince Consort's Own (Rifle Brigade). He served with Joseph in Egypt and South Africa, although he was discharged from the army on 24 September 1902. It is also known that John served again during the war and although there is limited information regarding his service, it is known that he survived. He died in Greenwich, London, in 1952.

James Frederick WOOD
Rifleman S/26055, 1st Battalion, The Prince Consort's Own (Rifle Brigade) who died on 22 April 1918, aged 33. Buried in Le Vertannoy British Cemetery, Hinges, Pas de Calais, France

Born on 23 September 1884 in Windsor, Berkshire, the second of three children of William Wood and Mary Ann née Byrne, his father was a Private in the Grenadier Guards, who died whilst still serving on 18 February 1887. Following his father's death, his mother re-married, to John Mason, in 1889.

James was admitted to the school on 27 September 1895 (Petition No. 10811), which was two years after his brother, Richard Wood, who had been admitted on 14 May 1889 (Petition No. 9846) had been discharged. James was discharged from the school on 10 October 1898 and enlisted into the 3rd (Prince of Wales's) Dragoon

Guards. His army career at this time was short, lasting just over a year, before he was discharged from the army at Dundalk, County Louth, on 10 November 1899, his services no longer required, although the reason for this is not known.

There is little information available about James after he was discharged from the army, although he is recorded in the 1901 Census living in Westminster, London, employed as an Errand Boy for Port Drug Stores. He was living with his mother, now widowed for the second time, his sister and his half-brother, Samuel John Mason. He also appeared in the 1911 Census, still living in Westminster, but now employed as a Motor Cab Washer. The only other pre-war information available about him is that he married Melinda Creasy in Westminster in 1913.

When war broke, it appears that James initially enlisted into The King's Royal Rifle Corps prior to serving in The Prince Consort's Own (Rifle Brigade), although the prefixes of both of his service numbers suggest that he enlisted into New Army battalions and although his service record for this second period of service is no longer available, it would seem that he did not disembark in France until 1916, as he was not entitled to the award of the 1914-15 Star.

However, the medal rolls state that he also served in 13th (Service) Battalion, The Rifle Brigade, which had been formed at Winchester, Hampshire, in October 1914 as part of K3 and landed at Boulogne on 31 July 1915. Had James been serving with this battalion at that time, he would have qualified for the award of the 1914-15 Star.

It is known that in early-1917, he was serving with the 111th Machine Gun Company, which was part of 111th Brigade, of which 13th Battalion, The Rifle Brigade, was part. During March or April of 1917, James sustained a gunshot wound to his right leg, which resulted in his being evacuated to Britain and treated in the County of Middlesex War Hospital, located in Napsbury Hospital, London Colney, Hertfordshire. His records from there state that he had been in France for ten months when he was wounded, suggesting that he deployed in May or June of 1916.

Once he recovered, James returned to France and was posted to 1st Battalion, The Rifle Brigade. He was serving with this battalion when he was killed during the Battle of the Lys, which lasted from 07-29 April 1918, one of 27 soldiers from the battalion killed securing the canal at La Pannerie, near Hinges, on 22 April 1918.

Although commemorated by the Commonwealth War Graves Commission and his first service record confirming that he was a Dukie, he is a "Lost Boy" whose name has been omitted from the memorial tablets in the school chapel.

Richard was discharged from the school on 25 July 1893, enlisting into the 4th (Royal Irish) Dragoon Guards, serving for 19 years before he was discharged to pension on 29 February 1912. It seems that he did not serve during the war and nothing is known of him after he was discharged from the army.

James's half-brother, Samuel Mason, was killed in action on 17 March 1916, whilst serving in the 4th Battalion, Grenadier Guards, and is buried in Menin Road South Military Cemetery in Belgium.

Machine Gun Corps

Alfred Ernest ANDERSON
Private, 51801, 16th Squadron, Machine Gun Corps (Cavalry) who died on 02 July 1918, aged 22. Buried in Baghdad (North Gate) War Cemetery, Iraq

Born on 13 May 1896 in Pietermaritzburg, South Africa, the sixth of eight children of John William Anderson and Alice Jane née Knight, his father had been a Private in the 7th (Queen's Own) Hussars, who had been discharged to pension after 22 years' service on 25 February 1902.

Alfred was admitted to the school on 30 May 1907 (Petition No. 12376), which was three months after his older brother, George William Anderson, who had been admitted on 08 January 1903 (Petition No. 11783) had been discharged. Having made the move from Chelsea to Guston, Alfred was discharged on 27 May 1910, joining his older brother by enlisting into the 3rd (King's Own) Hussars.

Alfred's pre-war career is unknown as his service record has not survived, but at the outbreak of war, the 3rd Hussars was stationed at Shorncliffe, Kent, landing at Rouen on 17 August 1914. The regiment then spent the remainder of the war serving on the Western Front, although according to his medal entitlement Alfred did not go overseas until 1916 at the earliest, as he was not awarded the 1914-15 Star.

It is possible that Alfred was a machine-gunner with the 3rd Hussars, these men being detached in February 1916 to form the 4th Squadron, Machine Gun Corps (Cavalry). At some point, whether because he had been wounded and was reassigned on return to duty, or whether he was transferred to backfill the squadron, Alfred found himself in the 16th Squadron, Machine Gun Corps (Cavalry). This squadron was part of the 7th (Meerut) Cavalry Brigade, which although deployed to the Western Front, arriving in December 1914, did not see any significant action due to the fact that it was held in reserve in order to exploit the expected breakthrough. However, soldiers from the brigade did man the trenches in some sectors of the front.

The brigade was reorganised in June 1916 and transferred to Mesopotamia, where it arrived in the August and formed an independent brigade within the Cavalry Division, before operating as such from April 1918 until the end of the war.

Alfred died on 02 July 1918 as a result of enteric fever, a huge killer in this theatre of war and was buried in Baghdad (North Gate) Cemetery.

In 2002 it was reported that the cemetery had been vandalised, with many of the headstones removed and that the mausoleum of General Maude, the commander of III Indian Army Corps who died of cholera in 1917, had been covered in graffiti. In 2012, the Commonwealth War Graves Commission carried out repairs to many of the headstones in the cemetery as well as the boundary wall, but sadly it was reported in 2020 that the cemetery is now neglected, with many of the graves covered in thick mud and the area littered with rubbish. The condition of Alfred's grave is not known.

George was discharged from the school on 28 February 1907. He is recorded in the 1911 Census serving as a Private in the 3rd (King's Own) Hussars and stationed in Mhow, India, the place of his birth. He served as a Bandsman throughout the war, having disembarked on 15 August 1914 and was discharged as surplus to military requirements in 1919. He died in 1963.

Harry Baughton GRAYHAM

Serjeant, 30092, 32nd Company, Machine Gun Corps (Infantry) who died on 27 September 1917, aged 41. Buried in Cement House Cemetery, West-Vlaanderen, Belgium

Born on 29 August 1876 in Maidstone, Kent, the fifth of six children of Patrick Grayham and Isabella Augusta née Marshallsey, his father had been a Brigade Serjeant Major in the Royal Horse Artillery who was discharged from the army on 20 February 1866. He was then employed as the Paymaster, West Kent Militia and died in Camberwell, Surrey, on 19 February 1885.

Harry was admitted to the school on 16 December 1887 (Petition No. 9593) and was discharged on 13 September 1890, enlisting into The Black Watch (Royal Highlanders). Harry was initially posted to the 2nd Battalion, but on 11 March 1892 he was posted to the 1st Battalion in Gibraltar, spending ten months there before he was posted to Egypt. After two months in Egypt, Harry was then posted to Mauritius, on 04 March 1893, where he was to remain for almost three years, being posted back to the 2nd Battalion and returning to Britain on 06 February 1896.

After eighteen months in Britain, Harry was again posted to the 1st Battalion on 16 September 1897 which was now stationed in India and just over a year later, was appointed as a Bandsman. However, less than two years later, on 06 July 1900, he reverted to Private at his own request. Fifteen months later, Harry was posted on 24 December 1901, this time to South Africa during the Second Boer War. He remained there until 27 October 1902, being awarded the Queen's South Africa medal with the clasps *Transvaal*, *Orange Free State*, *South Africa 1901* and *South Africa 1902*. He then returned to Britain, where he was discharged from the army at the end of his first period of service, on 03 November 1902.

Following his discharge, it seems that Harry settled in Leeds, Yorkshire West Riding, as he married Eleanor Victoria Robinson in the city in 1905, with their only child, Harry Robinson Grayham, born the same year. He was recorded in the 1911 Census living with his wife and son in the city and employed as a Labourer, Iron Foundry.

Following the outbreak of war, Harry re-enlisted into the army at Huddersfield, Yorkshire West Riding, on 05 September 1914, joining The Duke of Wellington's (West Riding Regiment). After initially being posted to the 3rd (Reserve) Battalion in Halifax, Yorkshire West Riding, on 16 November 1914 he was posted to the 11th (Reserve) Battalion, appointed as an Acting Corporal the following day. This battalion had been formed at Halifax in September 1914 as a Service Battalion of K4, coming under the command of the 89th Brigade, 30th Division.

After almost a year, during which time he was appointed Acting Sergeant on 28 November 1914, Harry was posted to the 8th (Service) Battalion, which had been formed in Halifax in August 1914 as part of K1 and which sailed from Liverpool, Lancashire, in July 1915, landing at Suvla Bay on 07 August 1915. However, it appears that Harry may have been a battle casualty replacement, as his medal index card shows that he did not arrive in theatre until 19 September 1915.

Harry was only on the Gallipoli Peninsula for one month before he was posted back to the 8th (Service) Battalion in Alexandria, Egypt, on 25 October 1915. However, once there, he found himself in trouble and was tried by Field General Courts Martial on 22 February 1916 for *"Drunkenness on active service"* and was reduced the rank of Corporal.

A month later, on 29 March 1916, he was transferred to the 32nd Brigade Machine Gun Company, formally being posted to this unit on 16 April 1916 as a Serjeant and landing at Marseille, on 03 July 1916.

Harry was to remain with this company and in September 1917 he was located at Poelcappelle, Belgium. The Commonwealth War Graves Commission gives his date of death as 27 September 1917, however this may be an error as there are no casualties recorded for that date in the company war diary[395], but the entry for 26 September 1917 states that the company suffered one other rank killed and three wounded. There is also no entry for another soldier from the 32nd Machine Gun Company being killed on 26 September 1917 in the Commonwealth War Graves Commission Register.

Harry was buried in Cement House Cemetery, but he is another "Lost Boy" whose name has been omitted from the memorial tablets in the school chapel.

Henry OLLERTON
Private, 137691, 5th Battalion, Machine Gun Corps (Infantry) who died on 21 September 1918, aged 20. Buried in Neuville-Bourjonval British Cemetery, Pas de Calais, France

Born on 27 January 1898 in Manchester, Lancashire, the eldest of four children of William Ollerton and Elizabeth née McKernan, his father had been a Lance Corporal in The Manchester Regiment, who was discharged from the army after 18 years' service on 30 April 1908 and died in Manchester on 15 November 1908.

Henry was admitted to the school on 27 May 1909 (Petition No. 12592) and was joined by his younger brother, William Ollerton, on 09 December 1909 (Petition No. 12709). Henry was discharged from the school on 27 February 1912 and enlisted into The Manchester Regiment.

Henry's service record is no longer available, but it is known that at the outbreak of war he was serving with the 2nd Battalion and stationed in Newbridge, County Kildare. The regiment quickly mobilised, coming under the orders of the 5th Division and, according to his medal index card, Henry disembarked in France on 15 August 1914.

Once it had arrived in France, the battalion participated in rearguard actions in the aftermath of the Battle of Mons before taking part in the Battles of the Marne, the Aisne and the First Battle of Ypres. It was in trenches on Christmas Day 1914, but it would appear that there was no fraternization with the Germans in the opposite trenches.

---

[395] WO 95/1809/6: Brigade Machine Gun Company, 1916 July - 1918 Feb., The National Archives, Kew

It is not known when, but at some time after arriving in France, Henry was transferred to one of the employment companies in Britain. This could have been as a result of his being wounded, although the lack of service record means that this would be speculation, but these companies were established on 23 May 1917 and Henry's medal index card records him as serving in 671 Employment Company.

Home Service Employment Companies were formed by each of the home commands and contained a variety of men who were categorised into the forms of employment for which they were best suited, such as cooks, orderlies, shoemakers, etc. The company in which Henry served had been formed by Aldershot Command. It is again not known for how long Henry served with this company, but he then transferred to the Machine Gun Corps and was posted to the 5th Battalion, Machine Gun Corps (Infantry).

This battalion moved into the line near Gouzeaucourt Wood on 14 September 1918, toward the end of The Hundred Days Offensive. The battalion war diary for 21 September 1918[396] states that the positions in which it was located were shelled at regular intervals throughout the day and in return it expended 15,000 rounds of ammunition. The diary also reports that during this period in the line, the battalion suffered sixteen other ranks killed, one of whom was Henry.

Although Henry's body was recovered and he is buried in a marked grave, he is another "Lost Boy" whose name has been omitted from the memorial tablets in the school chapel.

William was discharged from the school on 27 October 1915 and enlisted into the 5th (Royal Irish) Lancers. It is known that he survived the war and did not seem to serve overseas, likely due to his age, but other than that there is no other information available about him.

---

[396] WO 95/1539/1: 5 Battalion Machine Gun Corps, 1918 Apr. - 1919 May, The National Archives, Kew

Tank Corps

Charles Matthew MATHESON
Private, 92751, "F" Battalion, Tank Corps who died on 20 November 1917, aged 22. Commemorated on the Cambrai Memorial, Louverval, Nord, France

Born on 23 July 1895 in Preston, Lancashire, the youngest of six children of Maurice Matheson and Isabella Eliza née Matthews, his father was a Corporal in the Loyal North Lancashire Regiment who had served for 21 years before joining the Militia. He accidentally drowned at Malta in 1900.

Charles was admitted to the school on 01 January 1907 (Petition No. 12305) and discharged on 29 July 1909, enlisting into his father's old regiment, and although his service record is no longer available, he is recorded in the 1911 Census as a Boy, serving with the 2nd Battalion, stationed in Gorgui Barracks, Poona, India.

At the outbreak of war, the battalion was stationed in Bangalore, India, but embarked at Bombay on 15 October, landing at Tanga in German East Africa[397] on 03 November 1914 in an unsuccessful attempt to capture the port. By 05 November, it was obvious that the attack had failed and that the only option was re-embarkation, which occurred on 07 November, the battalion then sailing to Mombasa, British East Africa[398]. However, according to his medal index card, it was not until 16 November 1914 that Charles first entered theatre.

The battalion then remained in East Africa, fighting in both British and German East Africa, until it moved to South Africa in May 1916 due to the number of soldiers who were suffering from ill-health. In December 1916, it then moved to Egypt as part of the Suez Canal defences, remaining in that country until it was posted to France in May 1918.

However, soon after the move to Egypt, Charles transferred to the Tank Corps[399], his medal index card suggesting that he

---

[397] Now Tanzania
[398] Now Kenya
[399] Originally the Heavy Section of the Machine Gun Corps, becoming Heavy Branch, Machine Gun Corps in November 1916 and finally being retitled the Tank Corps on 28 July 1917

transferred from the Loyal North Lancashire Regiment to the Tank Corps after July 1917.

The town of Cambrai was an important supply hub for the German Hindenburg Line and on 20 November 1917 six British infantry divisions launched their attack, supported by nine battalions of the Tank Corps, with about 437 tanks, which led to the success of the attack, as they were able to pass through barbed wire defences that the Germans had considered impenetrable.

The attack was expensive for the Tank Corps in casualties, suffering 91 killed on the first day of the attack, including Charles. His body was never recovered and he is one of 51 soldiers from the Tank Corps commemorated on the Cambrai Memorial who died that day. Although he is commemorated on the memorial tablets in the school chapel, both his name and regiment are incorrect, being recorded as C N Matheson, Machine Gun Corps.

Royal Defence Corps

Charles Edward GASS
Private, 2625, Royal Defence Corps who died on 16 September 1917, aged 48. Commemorated in Lambeth Cemetery, London, United Kingdom

Born on 07 September 1869 in Newbridge, County Kildare, the eldest of two children of Charles Gass and Ellen Nora née Haydon, his father was a Sapper in the Royal Engineers who died whilst serving in Gillingham, Kent, on 17 April 1871. He also had a younger half-brother, John Gilchrist Dow, who was born in 1873 after his mother had married John Dow a year after his father's death. His mother died, also in Gillingham, on 30 March 1874.

Charles was admitted to the school on 15 October 1880 (Petition No. 8558) and was joined by his younger brother, James Joseph Gass, on 17 November 1882 (Petition No. 8847). Charles was discharged from the school on 13 October 1883 and enlisted into The Royal Welsh Fusiliers.

Charles spent this entire period of service in Britain, having been posted to the 2nd Battalion which was then stationed in Ireland. Two months after enlisting, Charles was appointed as a Drummer, although he reverted to Boy on 01 July 1885. However, he was re-appointed as a Drummer on 25 April 1886 and then was appointed as a Private when he turned eighteen, being appointed as a Drummer again on 25 September 1890.

Three years later, on 03 April 1893, he was appointed as a Lance Corporal, retaining this rank when he was transferred to the 4th Battalion which was stationed in Wrexham, Denbighshire. Charles was discharged from the army on 12 October 1895 after 12 years' service. A year after his discharge, on 17 October 1896, Charles married Margaret Mary Rackstraw in Finsbury, London, the first of their ten children, being born two years later in 1898.

Soon after the birth of his third child, on 15 March 1900 Charles enlisted into The Royal Home Counties Reserve Regiment[400] for one year, with little known of him after his discharge, although he is

---

[400] The Royal Reserve Regiments existed between 1900 and 1901 and consisted of veteran soldiers. They were formed for Home Service only in order to release more men from the Regular Army for service in South Africa during the Second Boer War

recorded in both the 1901 and 1911 Censuses as a Post Office Porter, living with his wife and eight children in Camberwell, London, in the latter.

Following the outbreak of war, on 27 October 1914, Charles again re-enlisted, joining 1/24th (County of London) Battalion (The Queen's), The London Regiment and although the battalion landed in France in March 1915, Charles did not deploy with it, possibly because he was unfit for overseas service, either due to his age or health.

Charles was transferred to the Royal Defence Corps on 29 April 1916 and a year later, on 11 June 1917, he was discharged from the army due to heart disease, which was the cause of his death three months later.

The Royal Defence Corps had been formed in March 1916 and its role was to provide troops for security and guard duties inside Britain, guarding important locations such as ports or bridges. It also provided independent companies for guarding prisoner-of-war camps.

Charles is commemorated by the Commonwealth War Graves Commission, but is another "Lost Boy" whose name has been omitted from the memorial tablets in the school chapel.

His youngest son, Reginald Albert Gass, whilst not a Dukie, died in April 1942 in Malaya, whilst serving in the Royal Army Service Corps and is buried in Kranji War Cemetery, Singapore.

Younger brother James was discharged from the school on 29 November 1884 and enlisted into the Royal Engineers, serving for 25 years before he was discharged. He re-enlisted into the Royal Engineers on 05 September 1914 and was discharged on 10 March 1919, having attained the rank of Warrant Officer Class I. He was recorded in the 1939 England and Wales Register as an Engine Driver Steam (Retired) and living in Southend-on-Sea, Essex. He died in Swansea, Glamorganshire, in 1952.

Edward Timothy HAYES
Private, 37202, 3rd Battalion, Royal Defence Corps who died on 11 September 1919, aged 38. Buried in North Sheen Cemetery, Surrey, United Kingdom

Born on 19 March 1881 in Hounslow, Middlesex, the eldest of three children of Edward Hayes and Mary née Strange, his father had been a Staff Serjeant in 57th (West Middlesex) Regiment of Foot. He was discharged from the army on 26 April 1881 and died in Hounslow on 12 May 1887.

Edward was admitted to the school on 29 July 1892 (Petition No. 10344), the same day as his younger brother, Hughie Job Hayes

(Petition No. 10345). Edward was discharged to 2nd Battalion, The Bedfordshire Regiment, on 30 March 1895, spending the first four years of his service at home, before being posted with the battalion to South Africa on 16 December 1899 during the Second Boer War. He was awarded both the Queen's and the King's South Africa Medals before he returned from South Africa on 08 April 1903 and was discharged from the army at the end of his period of service on 29 March 1904.

After his discharge, he settled into civilian life, marrying Rose Catherine King in 1910 and, according to the 1911 Census, working as a Postman and living in Weybridge, Surrey.

In December 1915, Edward re-enlisted, joining 1st Garrison Battalion, The Suffolk Regiment, although he was transferred to the Royal Defence Corps on 21 August 1916. His time with this unit does not seem to have been happy, as he was sentenced to 28 days' Field Punishment No. 2 in September 1916 and 28 days' detention a month later. On 26 October 1917, a medical board was convened and his extremely poor eyesight made Edward visually unfit for war service, which led to his discharge on 16 November 1917.

It is unknown when, but at some point after his discharge from the army, Edward was admitted to Claybury Mental Hospital in Woodford Bridge, Essex, where he died as a result of *"General Paralysis, Indefinite"*[401]. He died on 11 September 1919 and was interred in North Sheen Cemetery, Surrey, and although his last regiment had been the Royal Defence Corps, his grave marker displays his Suffolk Regiment details. He is also a "Lost Boy" whose name has been omitted from the memorial tablets in the school chapel.

Hughie is commemorated in the school chapel, albeit incorrectly as H E J Hayes. He was discharged from the school on 08 August 1896 to The Welsh Regiment and in January 1915 was a Company Serjeant Major in France when he was murdered by two soldiers from his regiment. He is documented earlier in this book.

---

[401] This is a neuropsychiatric disorder likely caused by the late stages of syphilis

Army Service Corps

Whilst almost all of the Dukies who served in the Army Service Corps and who died during the First World War are commemorated on the memorial tablets in the school chapel, their regiment is incorrectly recorded as the Royal Army Service Corps.

The Army Service Corps came into existence in December 1888 with the amalgamation of the Commissariat and Transport Staff and The Commissariat and Transport Corps. Although it was later granted the prefix "Royal", this was in recognition of its service during the war and it was not the Royal Army Service Corps until late-1918, and therefore was not in use at the time that the Dukies named below were serving.

Charles AMOS

Corporal M1/07803, 90th Mechanical Transport Company, Army Service Corps who died on 23 December 1915, aged 47. Buried in Meteren Military Cemetery, Nord, France

Born on 26 February 1868, his birth record gives his place of birth as Meean Meer, India, but when he joined the army, he gave his place of birth as "At sea", so it is possible that, like Dukie James Adventure Collins, he was born during the passage when his father had been posted to India. He was the second of four children of Charles Amos and Eliza née Povey, and his father had been a Private in the 85th, or The King's Regiment of Light Infantry (Bucks Volunteers)[402], but had been discharged from the army on 15 February 1876 and died in Earley, Berkshire, on 17 August 1878.

Charles was admitted to the school on 07 March 1879 (Petition No. 8318) and was *"Delivered to mother"* on 25 February 1882. However, he joined the army four years later, on 15 March 1886, enlisting into the 6th (Inniskilling) Dragoons at Colchester, Essex, and giving his trade as Labourer.

Charles served for 16 years, five of which were in South Africa, including during the Second Boer War, the remainder of his service

---

[402] Amalgamated with the 53rd (Shropshire) Regiment of Foot on 01 July 1881 to become The King's Light Infantry (Shropshire Regiment), renamed The King's (Shropshire Light Infantry) on 10 March 1882

being in Britain. He was discharged from the army at Newbridge, County Kildare, on 30 April 1902, medically unfit for further service.

During his service, Charles married Alice Davis in Steyning, Sussex, in 1891 and by the time he was discharged from the army they had four children. It appears that he and his family settled in Sussex, as he gave his discharge address as The Surrey Arms, New Shoreham, Sussex, and he is recorded in the 1911 Census living in Eastbourne, Sussex, with his wife, four sons and his daughter, who had been born in 1908. At that time, he was employed as a Motor Bus Driver.

Following the outbreak of the war, Charles re-enlisted in London, joining the Army Service Corps. His service record for this period of service is no longer available, but it is known that he landed in France on 22 November 1914 as a Corporal in the 89th Mechanical Transport Company, part of the 1st Indian Cavalry Division Supply Column.

Because his service record is not available, his movements are unknown once he arrived in France, but he was later posted to the 90th Mechanical Transport Company. This company had been formed in October 1914 as the 1st Omnibus Company and was located in the Second Army area. It was whilst serving with this company that Charles suffered a cerebral haemorrhage that resulted in his death on 23 December 1915. He is also another "Lost Boy" whose name has been omitted from the memorial tablets in the school chapel.

Alfred Thomas ASHTON
Private, T/328474, Army Service Corps who died on 06 July 1919, aged 32. Buried in Acton Cemetery, Middlesex, United Kingdom

Born on 09 August 1886 in Shorncliffe, Kent, the youngest of seven children of Thomas Ashton and Mary née Hartnell, his father had been a Private in the 14th (King's) Hussars and had been discharged from the army after 24 years' service on 23 June 1890. He died in Hounslow, Middlesex, on 23 May 1891.

Alfred was admitted to the school on 31 January 1896 (Petition No. 10859), joining his older brother, Francis Ashton, who had been admitted on 27 April 1894 (Petition No. 10605). Alfred was discharged from the school on 01 September 1900 and according to school records, he enlisted into The Worcestershire Regiment.

Alfred's service record from when he first enlisted is no longer available, however, it appears from later documents that he transferred to his father's old regiment, his service number within the

14th (King's) Dragoon Guards suggesting that this occurred sometime between 09 March 1901 and 12 March 1902.

Again, there is no service record available for this time, but a later record suggests that in 1910 Alfred had an accident that resulted in the amputation of the second toe of his left foot, which led to him being invalided from the army as medically unfit for further service as he was no longer able to march. He is recorded in the 1911 Census as living in Willesden, Middlesex, with his older brother, John Francis Ashton and his family, and like his brother, employed as a General Labourer for the London & North Western Railway. A year after he was recorded in the census, Alfred married Beatrice Skelton in Brentford, Middlesex, their first child, Eileen Beatrice Ashton, being born later that year.

On 24 June 1914, possibly because he could see that war was coming, Alfred re-enlisted, joining the 1st King Edward's Horse. However, the previous amputation of his toe meant that he was again classed as medically unfit for service and was discharged on 01 September. It appears that this did not deter him and a week later he enlisted in Bristol, Gloucestershire, into the 13th Reserve Cavalry Regiment, but again he was discharged, only fifteen days later on 23 September, as medically unfit for service.

Yet again, Alfred enlisted into a Reserve Cavalry Regiment, this time in Dublin, on 01 October 1914, but was again discharged as being medically unfit, two weeks later on 15 October. Alfred's next enlistment was into the Army Veterinary Corps in 1915, being able to serve in France from 25 October 1915, although he was again discharged as unfit for military service on 31 May 1916.

On 16 July 1917, a year after his second daughter, Millicent Florence Ashton, was born, he re-joined the army. This time he joined the Army Service Corps, spending all of his service in Britain, although this was not without incident, as he was punished on two occasions for being absent from his barracks in Isleworth, Middlesex, before he was again discharged as being medically unfit on 17 November 1917. Following this discharge from the army, very little is known, other than his youngest daughter, Myrtle Ashton, was born in 1918.

A year after his youngest child's birth, Alfred died in Acton Green, Middlesex. Although the cause of death is not recorded, it is likely that it was deemed to be as a result of one of his periods of service, as he is commemorated by the Commonwealth War Graves Commission. However, he is another of the "Lost Boys" whose name has been omitted from the memorial tablets in the school chapel.

Francis was discharged from the school on 16 January 1899 and enlisted into the 1st (King's) Dragoon Guards, seeing active service in the Second Boer War. He was discharged from the army on his return from South Africa, although it appears that he enlisted into the 13th Reserve Cavalry Regiment a year after the outbreak of war. There is no evidence that he saw service overseas during his second war, but if he did, he survived, dying in Willesden, London, in 1938.

Walter Herbert GOULD
Serjeant, M2/105245, Mechanical Transport, Army Service Corps attached to Corps of Royal Engineers who died on 09 February 1917, aged 36. Buried in Tanga European Cemetery, Tanzania

Born on 23 August 1880 in Dublin, County Dublin, the third of four children of Shadrach Gould and Hannah née Lawes, his father had been a Serjeant in the 2nd Dragoons (Royal Scots Greys) who was accidentally killed by an officer on 03 March 1883[403].

Walter was admitted to the school on 22 December 1889 (Petition No. 9947), joining his older brother, Alfred Henry Gould, who had been admitted on 26 July 1889 (Petition No. 9877). They were then joined by their younger brother, Percy John Gould, who was admitted on 29 April 1892 (Petition No. 10320). Walter was discharged from the school on 15 February 1896 and enlisted into his father's old regiment as a Trumpeter, although his service record for this time is no longer available. For that reason, little is known about him other than the fact that he served in South Africa during the Second Boer War, according to medal records.

By 1911, it appears that he had transferred regiments, as he is recorded in the census of that year as a Drummer serving with The Prince of Wales's Volunteers (South Lancashire Regiment) and stationed in Oxford Barracks, Warrington, Lancashire. This was also the year that he married Millicent Mabel Foster, also in Warrington, their eldest child, Walter Thomas Shadrach Gould, being born in Warrington on 31 October 1911. His second child, Evelyn Francis Violet Gould, was born in Birmingham, Warwickshire, on 03 October 1915.

Because his service record is not available, it is unknown at what point Walter transferred to the Army Service Corps and it is also not possible to ascertain if he had served overseas prior to 1917, but it is known that in early-1917 he was serving with that corps and attached to the 46th Air Line Section, Royal Engineers, in the former German

---

[403] *Dublin Daily Express*, Monday 05 March 1883. Serjeant Gould was the Provost Serjeant in Ballincollig Barracks, Cork, County Cork, and was crossing the barracks at midnight on 02 March 1883 when he spotted someone he thought was a stranger. Serjeant Gould grabbed the stranger, who was actually Lieutenant Torrens of the same regiment, by the shoulder and the pistol that Lieutenant Torrens was holding discharged, the bullet penetrating Serjeant Gould's heart and killing him instantly

East Africa. Air Line Sections were responsible for the wires along which signals, telephones etc. were transmitted and were almost exclusively in rear areas.

Walter died as a result of heatstroke on 09 February 1917 and was buried in Tanga. He is also a "Lost Boy" whose name has been omitted from the memorial tablets in the school chapel.

Alfred was discharged from the school on 26 November 1892, enlisting into the Army Ordnance Corps, serving until he was discharged as a Serjeant on 04 December 1913. It appears that he was then recalled to the Colours at the outbreak of war, re-enlisting into his old corps on 31 August 1914. He landed in France on 19 November 1915, spending the entire war with the British Expeditionary Force, before returning to Britain on 19 April 1919 and being discharged from the army three months later. He died in Muchelney, Somerset, in 1951.

Percy was discharged from the school on 17 July 1897, enlisting into the Royal Artillery. He also served throughout the war, being discharged from the army in July 1921. He died in Portsmouth, Hampshire, in 1942.

James William Henry HOWARD
Corporal, T/19479, No. 1 Horse Transport Company, Army Service Corps who died on 26 May 1917, aged 28. Buried in Hastings Cemetery, East Sussex, United Kingdom

Born on 04 July 1888 in Beaminster, Dorsetshire, the youngest of two children of James Howard and Sarah née Viant, his father had been a Serjeant in the 75th (Stirlingshire) Regiment of Foot[404], who had been discharged to pension after 21 years' service and died in Leyton, London, on 20 December 1897.

James was admitted to the school on 11 August 1899 (Petition No. 11330) and was discharged on 12 July 1902, enlisting into the Army Service Corps, where he spent the first 12 years of his service in Britain, being appointed as a Trumpeter on 12 July 1904 and, nine months after his eighteenth birthday, being appointed as a Driver on 18 April 1907.

However, the following year, James was in trouble for using threatening language toward and striking his superior officer. He was tried for the offences on 14 August 1908 and sentenced to a period of detention, returning to duty on 02 November 1908. Four years later, on 20 May 1912, James was appointed as a Lance

---

[404] Amalgamated with the 92nd (Gordon Highlanders) Regiment of Foot on 01 July 1881 to become The Gordon Highlanders

Corporal and on 26 June 1914 he re-engaged to complete 21 years' service in the army.

Following the outbreak of war, James spent the first seven months in Britain before he embarked for the Mediterranean theatre, likely to Egypt, disembarking on 22 March 1915. It appears that following the Gallipoli landings, he was also on the Peninsula, but only until 22 August 1915, when he was returned to Britain due to ill-health.

The report of the medical board of 01 November 1915 states that James had developed a cough whilst serving in the Dardanelles, as well as having to regularly spit and losing weight. It concluded that he had developed tuberculosis whilst on active service and that he was no longer fit for military duty. He was discharged from the army on 26 November 1915 and awarded a pension due to his disease a year later.

James only survived a further eighteen months following his discharge. He died on 26 May 1917[405] and was buried in Hastings, Sussex, being commemorated by the Commonwealth War Graves Commission. He is another "Lost Boy" whose name has been omitted from the memorial tablets in the school chapel.

Charles Edwin MARS
Company Quartermaster Serjeant, T/23487, Mechanical Transport Headquarters Staff, Army Service Corps who died on 08 April 1918, aged 26. Buried in Dar es Salaam War Cemetery, Tanzania

Born on 17 July 1891 in Newbridge, County Kildare, the fourth of seven children of Thomas Mars and Eleanor née Richardson, his father was a Staff Serjeant Major in the 2nd Dragoons (Royal Scots Greys) who was still serving when he died in Oldham, Lancashire, on 18 July 1897.

Charles was admitted to the school on 09 November 1900 (Petition No. 11500), joining his older brother, Alfred Thomas Mars, who was admitted on 07 May 1898 (Petition No. 11168). Charles was discharged to the Army Service Corps on 26 October 1905 and whilst his service record has not survived, he is recorded in the 1911 Census as a Lance Corporal in the Army Service Corps, stationed in Buller Barracks, Stanhope Lines, Aldershot.

His wartime career is also not known, but at some point he was posted to Africa and served in the former German East Africa, possibly alongside Dukie Walter Gould. Whilst serving here, Charles Mars contracted malaria and died of the disease in No.3 East African Stationary Hospital on 08 April 1918. He was interred initially in Dar es Salaam (Ocean Road) Cemetery, then re-buried in 1968 in

---

[405] Recorded by the Commonwealth War Graves Commission as 25 May 1917

Dar es Salaam War Cemetery, when the former cemetery had to be moved to facilitate the building of a new road.

Alfred was discharged from the school to the Royal Field Artillery on 15 February 1906. He survived the war and was later Commissioned in the Royal Artillery. He died in Epping, Essex, in 1952.

Frederick McVICAR
Serjeant, T1/SR/92, Army Service Corps who died on 19 October 1918, aged 42. Buried in Alexandria (Hadra) War Memorial Cemetery, Egypt

Born on 29 June 1876 in Parsonstown, King's County[406], the fourth of six children of Francis William McVicar and Matilda née Field, his father had been an Armourer Serjeant in the 53rd (the Shropshire) Regiment of Foot who was still serving when he died in Salford, Lancashire, on 02 May 1880.

Frederick was admitted to the school on 06 May 1887 (Petition No. 9512), joining his older brother, George Robert McVicar, who had been admitted on 12 December 1884 (Petition No. 9162). Their eldest brother, John Alexander McVicar, had also attended the school, having been admitted on 12 November 1880 (Petition No. 8568), but had been discharged by the time that his brothers were admitted. Frederick was discharged from the school on 26 July 1890, enlisting into the Army Service Corps.

Frederick spent the first nine years of his service in Britain, before he was posted to South Africa on 06 October 1899, during the Second Boer War. He was awarded both the Queen's and King's South Africa medals before he was posted back to Britain on 27 June 1903, being discharged from the army two days later.

Little is known of his post-discharge life, but he is recorded in the 1911 Census as living with his widowed mother in Pimlico, London, and employed as a Carman, Army & Navy Stores. He re-enlisted in the Army Service Corps in Fulham on 24 August 1914 and his medal index card records that he entered France on 13 November 1914. He was appointed Acting Lance Corporal on 25 November 1914, but was deprived of the Lance rank for misconduct on 29 September 1915. He continued to serve in France until 05 March 1918, mostly with the 3rd (Ambala) Cavalry Brigade Field Ambulance, fracturing the fibula in his right leg on 22 December 1917 in an accident.

By 17 March 1918, Frederick was serving in Egypt with his old brigade and was admitted to No. 17 Field Hospital in Alexandria around 10 October 1918 with bronchitis. He died suddenly whilst attempting to sit up in bed on 19 October 1918, his cause of death

---

[406] Parsonstown was re-named Birr in 1899 and King's County became County Offaly in 1898

being recorded as acute bacillary dysentery[407], toxaemia[408] and oedema. He was buried in Alexandra (Hadra) War Memorial Cemetery and is also another "Lost Boy" whose name was omitted from the memorial tablets in the school chapel.

John was discharged from the school on 20 January 1883 and enlisted into The King's Shropshire Light Infantry. He married Elizabeth Denny in West Ham, Essex, in 1897 and was recorded in the 1901 Census as living with his wife and two sons in Southend, Essex, employed as a Milk Carrier. He was also recorded in the 1911 Census as living with his wife, five sons and two daughters in East Ham, Essex, still employed as a Milk Carrier. It appears that he did not see service during the war, and died in West Ham, Essex, in 1933.

George was discharged from the school on 29 September 1887 and enlisted into The Commissariat and Transport Corps. He also served in South Africa and was discharged from the army on 28 September 1908.

He could not be found in the 1911 Census, but it is known that he enlisted into the Royal Air Force on 18 April 1918 and was discharged to the Reserve on 14 February 1919. He died in Chelsea, London, in 1929.

Henry St. John SAINTY

Company Serjeant Major, T/14004, Army Service Corps attached to Canadian Army Service Corps who died on 10 March 1916, aged 32. Buried in Aldershot Military Cemetery, Hampshire, United Kingdom

Born on 25 April 1883 in Templemore, County Tipperary, the eldest of two children of Alfred Sainty and Ellen née Dwyer, his father had served in the 54th (West Norfolk) Regiment of Foot and the 20th (the East Devonshire) Regiment of Foot[409] before becoming a Serjeant Major in the Corps of Military Staff Clerks. However, at the time that he submitted the Petition Document for Henry on 27 December 1893, he was about to be discharged from the army as unfit for further service and died in Devonport, Devonshire, on 18 June 1894.

Henry was admitted to the school on 06 July 1894 (Petition No. 10619) and was discharged as medically unfit for army service on 25 April 1898. Despite this, Henry enlisted into the Army Service Corps on 09 July 1898 in Devonport, spending the first fourteen months of his army service in Britain. He was appointed as a Trumpeter in May 1899, prior to being posted to South Africa on 06 October.

---

[407] A gastrointestinal disease caused by a bacterial infection
[408] Blood poisoning from the toxins of a local bacterial infection
[409] Renamed The Lancashire Fusiliers on 01 July 1881

Henry remained in South Africa until 10 February 1905, being awarded the Queen's South Africa Medal with three clasps and the King's South Africa Medal with two clasps, and having attained the rank of Corporal. He rose steadily through the ranks and by 1912 he was a Serjeant seconded to the Canadian Army Service Corps, arriving in Canada on 15 November of that year.

Following the outbreak of war, Henry returned to Britain on 14 October, having been promoted to Squadron Serjeant Major on 23 September and embarked for France from Avonmouth, Gloucestershire, on 17 October 1914.

He remained attached to the Canadian Expeditionary Force and was promoted to Company Sergeant Major on 14 May 1915, being transferred back to Britain and stationed in Shorncliffe, Kent. However, a month after his return to Britain, he was admitted to Springfield War Hospital in Tooting, London, with a diagnosis of neurasthenia. A medical board was convened on 14 November 1915 and recommended that he be discharged from the army as being permanently unfit.

Henry was to spend the remainder of his life in Springfield Hospital, dying as a result of General Paralysis of the Insane[410] on 10 March 1916.

Archibald Benjamin Brandbury SMITH
Lance Corporal, T/28923, 5th Divisional Train, Army Service Corps who died on 13 March 1915, aged 18. Buried in Poperinghe Communal Cemetery, West-Vlaanderen, Belgium

Born on 19 May 1896 in Aldershot, Hampshire, the eldest son of Archibald Alexander Smith and Ellen Alice née Towson, his father was a Serjeant in the Army Service Corps who died whilst serving in Chatham, Kent, on 22 June 1901. Interestingly, only the younger son, Albert Edward Smith, appears in their father's service record, but the reason for this is not known.

Archibald was admitted to the school on 06 September 1907 (Petition No. 12420) and having moved from Chelsea to Guston, was discharged to the Army Service Corps on 06 June 1910. Although his service record is no longer available, he is recorded in the 1911 Census as "At drill" with the Army Service Corps and stationed in the Army Service Corps Barracks in Woolwich, London.

At the outbreak of war, his medal index card shows that he was a Trumpeter and then a Driver in No.2 Company, 5th Divisional Train, Army Service Corps and he arrived in theatre on 24 August

---

[410] Like "General paralysis, indefinite" this was a neuropsychiatric disorder likely caused by the late stages of syphilis

1914. The divisional train provided horse-drawn transport for the formation and usually comprised a small Train Headquarters, one Headquarters Company, three other Horse Transport Companies and a contingent of other troops, all of them provided by Archibald's corps.

During 1914, 5th Division participated in The Battle of Mons and subsequent retreat, including the Action of Elouges, The Battle of Le Cateau and the Affair of Crépy-en-Valois, the Battles of the Marne, of the Aisne, La Bassée, Messines and the First Battle of Ypres.

On 13 March 1915, the Germans launched an air raid on Poperinghe, which resulted in Archibald and two Belgian soldiers being killed. The three soldiers were buried together in the cemetery in the town, although only Archibald's grave seems to remain, possibly those of the Belgians being repatriated after the war to their local graveyards.

George William WHEELHOUSE
Second Lieutenant, Army Service Corps who died on 06 July 1917, aged 42. Buried in Basra War Cemetery, Iraq

Born on 23 November 1874 in Tunbridge Wells, Kent, the youngest of two sons of Samuel Wheelhouse and Ellen née Dewar, his father had been a Private in the 13th Regiment of (Light) Dragoons[411] who had been discharged from the army on 15 December 1856. He died on 15 August 1877 in Tunbridge Wells.

George was admitted to the school on 23 January 1885 (Petition No. 9177), joining his older brother, Frederick Herbert Wheelhouse, who had been admitted on 14 April 1882 (Petition No. 8756). George was discharged to the 14th (King's) Hussars as a Musician on 30 November 1889, serving for 21 years, his entire service being in Britain. During that time, he was appointed as a Bandsman on 11 February 1892, as a Provisional Lance Corporal in April 1895, which was confirmed on 01 January 1896 and promoted to Corporal two years later, on 01 January 1898.

Although promoted to Serjeant on 01 April 1900, George reverted to Bandsman at his own request on 17 December 1901 and transferred to the Band of the Grenadier Guards, remaining with this band and at that rank, until he was discharged from the army at the end of his second period of service, on 29 November 1910. In January 1912, George married Helena Freda Sachs in Wandsworth, London, their only child, Cecelia Helena May Wheelhouse, being born in Wandsworth in December of that year.

---

[411] Renamed 13th Hussars on 04 August 1861

Following the outbreak of war, George re-enlisted, although his service record for his second period of service is not easily accessible as an officer, so it is not known when he re-joined. It is known that he was appointed as a Temporary Second Lieutenant in the Army Service Corps on 13 November 1916[412] and his medal index card shows that he then entered theatre (Mesopotamia) on 05 January 1917. It is not possible to establish George's movements once he entered theatre, or to confirm whether his demise was as a result of enemy action or disease, but George died on 06 July 1917 and was buried in Basra War Cemetery.

Frederick was discharged from the school on 06 February 1887 and enlisted into the 10th (Prince of Wales's Own Royal) Hussars. By the time of the 1911 Census, he had left the army and was living in Clapham, London, with his wife and daughter and employed as a Musician. He does not seem to have served during the war, dying in Harrow, Middlesex, where he died in 1950.

Stephenson John WILSON
Private, M2/119415, Mechanical Transport Depot (Osterley Park), Army Service Corps who died on 23 March 1916, aged 42. Buried in Heston (St. Leonard) Churchyard, Middlesex, United Kingdom

Born on 28 December 1873 in Shorncliffe, Kent, the second of four children of Matthew Wilson and Elizabeth née Bowlt, his father had been a Serjeant in the 7th (Queen's Own) Hussars, who was discharged from the army on 14 November 1876 and died on 05 January 1882. His mother remarried, to Christopher Briggs, in 1887, as a result of which, Stephenson also had four stepbrothers and one half-brother.

Stephenson was admitted to the school on 15 February 1884 (Petition No. 9059), but was at the school for just under three years before he was *"Detained on pass"* on 08 December 1886. A letter in his Petition Document from his mother, dated 01 September 1886, stated that he had consumption and was not expected to live, so would not be returning to school.

Despite this, it appears that he did recover, but after he left the school very little is known about Stephenson. He could not be found in either the 1891 or the 1901 Census, although it is known that at some point he and his mother moved to Nottingham, Nottinghamshire, and that on 02 December 1904 he enlisted into the Royal Naval Reserve, having by now shortened his first name to Stephen.

---

[412] *The London Gazette*, 21 November 1916, Supplement:29833

Stephenson undertook his naval training between 02 March and 31 May 1905 on board HMS *Royal Sovereign*, HMS *Victory* and HMS *Furious*. However, it is not known where his reserve shore establishment was located, as the first Royal Naval Reserve establishment in Nottingham, HMS *Sherwood*, was not founded until 1949.

It is known that in 1909, Stephenson was located in Barrow-in-Furness, Lancashire, where he was employed by Vickers Sons & Maxim Ltd. As a Coppersmith working on HMS *Temeraire*, Stephenson was then stationed on HMS *King Edward VII* in Portland, Dorsetshire, as an Engineering Room Artificer 1st Class when that ship was undergoing a refit, but he was discharged from the Royal Naval Reserve on 27 May 1910, *"having broken leave for 72 hours without excuse"*. At the time of the 1911 Census, Stephenson was still employed as a Coppersmith and boarding with the Billing family in Stamford, Lincolnshire, working at Blackstone Engineers in the town.

By the outbreak of war, Stephenson was living in Bedford, Bedfordshire, employed at an engineering works, although in April 1915 he left due to illness. However, he then worked briefly in an engineering works in Nottingham, before joining another firm in Peterborough, Northamptonshire and then enlisted into the army on 05 September 1915, joining the Army Service Corps and again shortening his name to Stephen.

Following his training in Grove Park, Stephenson was posted to the Mechanical Transport Depot in Osterley Park, a Georgian country estate in Middlesex. It was from here that he was admitted to the Military Hospital in Hounslow, Middlesex, where he died of pneumonia on 23 March 1916.

Stephenson was buried in Heston, Middlesex, and is commemorated by the Commonwealth War Graves Commission as Stephen John, the name that he used on enlistment. He is also a "Lost Boy" whose name has been omitted from the memorial tablets in the school chapel.

Army Ordnance Corps

Whilst almost all of the Dukies who served in the Army Ordnance Corps and who died during the First World War are commemorated on the memorial tablets in the school chapel, their regiment is incorrectly recorded as the Royal Army Ordnance Corps.

The Army Ordnance Corps came into existence in 1896 when the Ordnance Store Corps was renamed. At the same time, the Ordnance Store Department was renamed as the Army Ordnance Department. The Army Ordnance Corps and the Army Ordnance Department were amalgamated on 28 November 1918 as the Army Ordnance Corps and although it was later granted the prefix "Royal", it did not become the Royal Army Ordnance Corps until 1922, so therefore was not in use at the time that the Dukies named below were serving.

William James ADDS
Corporal, 3589, Army Ordnance Corps who died on 14 April 1916, aged 38. Buried in Woolwich Cemetery, London, United Kingdom

Born on 07 October 1877 in Woolwich, Kent, the eldest of three children of William James Adds and Elizabeth née Harvey, his father was a Bombardier in the Royal Artillery Band who died whilst serving in Woolwich in 1882.

William was admitted to the school on 25 October 1889 (Petition No. 9914) and was discharged *"To mother"* on 17 October 1891. However, just over five years later, on 10 February 1897, he enlisted into the army, joining the Army Ordnance Corps, where he spent the first two years of his service in Britain before he was posted to South Africa on 06 October 1899, at the time of the Second Boer War. He was then posted back to Britain on 28 August 1900, but was only home for seven months before being posted to China on 07 March 1901.

After spending three years in the Far East, William was again posted back to Britain, on 04 March 1904, where he remained for the next five years. During this time, he was appointed as a Lance Corporal without pay on 21 February 1907, this being the same year that he married Annie Reddy in Newbridge, County Kildare, on 17 September and their first son, William James Adds, was born in

Newbridge on 28 October. He was appointed as a paid Lance Corporal on 15 November 1908.

William and Annie's second son, Frederick Adds, was also born in Newbridge in 1909, the same year that William was posted to Bermuda, West Indies, his next two sons both being born there, George Ernest Adds in 1912 and Herbert Adds in 1913. He had been promoted to 2nd Corporal on 31 January 1911.

After four years in Bermuda, William was again posted back to Britain and stationed in Newbridge, before returning to Woolwich, which is where he was when war broke out. By this stage, he was a Corporal, having been promoted on 09 February 1914 and he was quickly mobilised, landing in France on 13 August 1914. However, he was in theatre for less than three months, during which time his fifth son, Charles Edward Adds, was born in Woolwich. William returned to Britain on 01 December 1914.

It is possible that he was returned to Britain because he was unwell, although there is no mention as to a possible cause within his service record, but on 25 November 1915 he was discharged from the army as unfit for further service. He died in Woolwich four months later, in March 1916, from dysentery, three months before the birth of his youngest son, Henry Adds. William was commemorated by the Commonwealth War Graves Commission and is another "Lost Boy" whose name has been omitted from the memorial tablets in the school chapel.

William's second son, George, was also a Dukie. He had originally attended the Royal Hibernian Military School, like elder brother Frederick, being admitted on 12 January 1921, but following that school's amalgamation with Duke of York's in 1924, George was transferred, entering the school on 04 September 1924 (Petition No. 14506). He was discharged *"To civil life"* on 30 July 1926, served in the Royal Air Force in the Second World War and died in Gravesend, Kent, in October 1990.

John Edward ELDRIDGE

Staff Serjeant Armourer, 1270, Army Ordnance Corps attached West African Regiment, West African Field Force who died on 21 October 1915, aged 21. Commemorated on the Freetown Memorial, Sierra Leone

Born on 28 September 1894 in Portsmouth, Hampshire, the fourth of eight children of Charles Eldridge and Nora née Hughes, his father had been a Quartermaster Serjeant in the Royal Artillery, who had been invalided out of the army on 27 May 1905 and died in Woolwich, London, on 01 July 1905.

John was admitted to the school on 03 November 1905 (Petition No. 12159), being joined by his younger brother, William Eldridge, on 31 August 1907 (Petition No. 12418). Two more of his brothers were also Dukies, George Eldridge being admitted on 07 September 1911 (Petition No. 12898) and James Robert Eldridge being admitted on 04 December 1913 (Petition No. 13203). John was discharged from the school to the Army Ordnance Corps on 25 September 1908 and is recorded in the 1911 Census stationed at the Army Ordnance Stores in Lathom, Lancashire.

His service record is no longer available, so it is not possible to establish when he was posted to West Africa and attached to the West African Field Force, but when war broke out, Britain ordered the invasion of German colonies in Cameroon and Togoland, using its own colonies in the region as a base. The West African Frontier Force, drawn from Sierra Leone, Ghana, Nigeria and Gambia played a key role in the campaign.

The Cameroon Campaign had been launched in September 1914 and led to the invasion of this German colony, and by October 1915 the Allies occupied Mbo, near Baré in the mountains of Cameroon. Once this was done, a strong reconnaissance was dispatched toward Dschang and encountered two parties of enemy troops, each at least 100 men strong. During the ensuing firefight, on 21 October 1915, John was killed and two Sepoys were wounded. Whether he was buried near where he fell or whether his body was never recovered is unknown, but he has no known grave and is commemorated on the memorial in the capital of Sierra Leone.

When William was discharged from the school on 12 April 1911, he enlisted in the Royal Garrison Artillery, but nothing more is known about him after this.

George was discharged to *"Civilian Life (Medically unfit)"* on 21 October 1914 and it is not known whether he served. It is believed that he emigrated to South Africa in the 1920s and died in Durban, but it is not known when.

James was discharged to the Royal Garrison Artillery on 25 July 1918. Nothing more is known about him after this.

Alan Stuart GRIEVE
Staff Serjeant Armourer, A/1216, Army Ordnance Corps attached West African Regiment, West African Field Force who died on 28 March 1915, aged 22. Commemorated on the Hollybrook Memorial, Southampton, Hampshire, United Kingdom

Born on 26 May 1892 in Westminster, London, the second of five children of Philip Kerr Grieve and Emma Rebecca née Patrick, his father had been a Pioneer Serjeant in the Scots Guards who had been discharged after 18 years' service on 17 August 1897. He died in Westminster, London, on 13 May 1902.

Alan was admitted to the school on 10 September 1902 (Petition No. 11734), which was three months after his older brother, Philip Douglas Grieve, who had been admitted to the school on 06 March 1902 (Petition No. 11668), had died in St. George's Hospital, London, on 02 June 1902. The cause of Philip's death is not recorded in his Petition Document.

Alan was discharged from the school on 12 June 1907, enlisting into the Army Ordnance Corps, nine months before his younger brother, Kenneth Patrick Grieve, was admitted to the school on 30 March 1908 (Petition No. 12489). Alan's service record is no longer available, so his pre-war career is not known, nor is his career in the early part of the war. What is known is that he was posted to West Africa, where he would have joined Dukie John Eldridge and to this end, he embarked on the SS *Falaba* at Liverpool, Lancashire, on 27 March 1915. This was a 5,000-ton British passenger-cargo ship and on 28 March was off the southern Irish coast, when U-28, commanded by Baron Freiherr Georg-Günther von Forstner, surfaced and stopped the ship.

Forstner had allowed for evacuation before sinking the ship, but when *Falaba* started sending wireless messages and distress rockets for help, Forstner cut short the time to evacuate the ship. The Germans claimed that they had allowed 23 minutes for evacuation, although the British claimed that they were only given seven. U-28 fired a single torpedo into *Falaba*, resulting in 100 deaths. The Germans also claimed that the ship's cargo contained rifle cartridges that exploded, hastening the sinking.

Alan was lost at sea during the sinking of this ship on 28 March 1915. Consequently, he has no known grave and is one of the almost 1,900 servicemen and women of the land and air forces commemorated on the Hollybrook Memorial.

Kenneth was discharged from the school on 28 November 1913, enlisting into their father's old regiment. He survived the war, dying in Staines, Middlesex in 1946.

Henry John HORNER
Staff Serjeant Armourer, A/1265, Army Ordnance Corps attached 1st Battalion, The Loyal North Lancashire Regiment who died on 09 May 1915, aged 21. Commemorated on the Le Touret Memorial, Pas de Calais, France

Born on 25 October 1893 in Sheerness, Kent, the youngest of three children of Joseph Bean Horner and Mary Ann née Lockie, his father had been an Ordnance Artificer in the Royal Artillery, before transferring and becoming a Machinery Artificer Superintendent with the rank of Quartermaster Serjeant in the Army Ordnance Corps. He had been discharged from the army as medically unfit on 18 November 1903 and died in Odiham, Hampshire, on 11 April 1904.

Henry was admitted to the school on 02 December 1904 (Petition No. 12044) and was discharged on 01 January 1908, enlisting into the Army Ordnance Corps. His service record is no longer available, so his pre-war career, as well as that during the first nine months of the war, is not known. However, he is recorded in the 1911 Census stationed in Red Barracks, Woolwich, London, and it is known that by May 1915, he was a Staff Serjeant Armourer attached to 1st Battalion, The Loyal North Lancashire Regiment.

In that May, the battalion was in the area of Vendin-lès-Béthune, moving into trenches at Les Choquaux on 08 May, ready to attack on the first day of the Battle of Aubers Ridge the following day. The bombardment commenced at 0500hrs, intensifying at 0530hrs, the battalion moving forward and arriving in the front line by 0600hrs, where it was realised that the first stage of the battle had failed. It was then ordered to make its assault at 0745hrs, but was again checked, the survivors among the assaulting troops being forced to retire to their own breastworks.

The battalion was again ordered to attack at 1440hrs, but this order was then cancelled, after which it came under German artillery fire, causing many casualties and although a further attack by The Black Watch was launched at 1600hrs, with approximately 60 men getting into the enemy trenches before they were all killed, wounded or captured, the attack again failed.

The battalion was then ordered to take over the entire front line, where it remained until relieved at 0300hrs on 10 May, suffering a total of thirteen officers and 230 other ranks killed, wounded, missing or captured during the failed attack, Henry being one of those either killed or missing on 09 May 1915. His body was not recovered and he is therefore commemorated on the Le Touret Memorial. He also received a posthumous Mention in Despatches[413], although the action which resulted in this is not known.

Thomas Richard Clarence REDFORD
Private, 6016, Depot, Army Ordnance Corps who died on 07 September 1919, aged 26. Buried in Woolwich Cemetery, London, United Kingdom

Born on 18 July 1893 in Newbridge, County Kildare, the youngest of two children of Thomas Radford and Matilda née Baker, his father had been a Corporal Collar Maker in the Royal Horse Artillery who had been discharged to pension after 21 years' service on 05 December 1894. He died in Woolwich, London, on 12 February 1898.

Thomas was admitted to the school on 07 October 1904 (Petition No. 12020) and was discharged on 18 July 1907, enlisting into the Army Ordnance Corps, spending the first seven years of his service in Britain, during which time he was posted to Pembroke Dock, Pembrokeshire, Aldershot, Hampshire and Dublin.

However, after war broke out, he was deployed to France as part of the British Expeditionary Force, landing on 08 November 1914. His service record is scant regarding his employment whilst he was deployed in France, but he was posted back to Britain on 17 May 1915. After six months back in Britain, Thomas was then posted to the Mediterranean Expeditionary Force in Cairo, Egypt, on 21 November 1915. Again, there is no information as to his employment whilst he was serving in Egypt, but it would appear that he was a skilled Saddler and Tent Mender.

After two years in Egypt, Thomas was invalided back to Britain on 05 November 1917, having been diagnosed with tuberculosis which was considered attributable to his service. He was discharged from the army a month later, on 09 December 1917, settling in Woolwich, where he died two years later as a result of the tuberculosis. He is commemorated by the Commonwealth War Graves Commission as serving in the Royal Army Ordnance Corps, although he had been discharged from the army more than year before it became a Royal Corps. He is also a "Lost Boy" whose name has been omitted from the memorial tablets in the school chapel.

---

[413] *The London Gazette*, 18 June 1915, Supplement:29200

Royal Army Medical Corps

Benjamin Disraeli CONOLLY
Captain, Royal Army Medical Corps who died on 06 February 1921, aged 39. Buried in Dover (St. James) Cemetery, Kent, United Kingdom

Born on 16 March 1881 in Doncaster, Yorkshire West Riding, the youngest of five children of Thomas Parker Conolly and Catherine née Mills, his father had been a Serjeant in the 107th Regiment of Foot (Bengal Light Infantry) who was discharged from the army on 15 March 1881. Following discharge, he joined the Permanent Staff of the Royal North Lincolnshire Militia for three months, before joining the Permanent Staff of the 10th Middlesex Rifle Volunteers.

Benjamin was admitted to the school on 30 October 1891 (Petition No. 10209), joining his older brother, William Paul Conolly, who had been admitted to the school on 14 May 1889 (Petition No. 9836). Two older brothers had also been Dukies, James Mills Conolly, who had been admitted on 05 December 1884 (Petition No. 9157) and Joseph Henry Conolly, who had been admitted on 14 January 1887 (Petition No. 9461). However, by the time that Benjamin was admitted, both of his oldest brothers had been discharged, although James was still at the school as a Pupil Teacher.

Benjamin was discharged from the school on 04 April 1895, enlisting into the Army Medical Staff Corps. Because his service record is not easily accessible as an officer, little is known about Benjamin's pre-war career, although he is recorded in the 1911 Census as a Staff Serjeant in the Royal Army Medical Corps, carrying out Corps Duties in the military hospital located in The Citadel, Cairo, Egypt.

His medal index card shows that he disembarked in the Egyptian theatre on 05 November 1915 and it is known that in April 1915 he was Commissioned as a Lieutenant and Quartermaster in the Royal Army Medical Corps[414]. Although his movements following his Commission are unknown, he survived the war, then in March 1919, he married Isabella Margaret Mary Gibbons in Camberwell, Surrey.

---

[414] *The London Gazette*, 9 April 1915, Supplement:29125

Following his marriage, it appears that Benjamin was then posted to the Station Hospital, Dover, Kent, and was still there when he died suddenly on 06 February 1921. A report in the School *Chronicle*[415] states that it was believed that he had had a seizure in his bathroom and died within half an hour. Despite being commemorated by the Commonwealth War Graves Commission and his death being reported in the *Chronicle*, he is another "Lost Boy" whose name has been omitted from the memorial tablets in the school chapel.

James was discharged from the school on 03 January 1891, but remained there as a Pupil Teacher, appearing as such in the 1891 Census. It is known that he continued to serve as an Army Schoolmaster, the 1911 Census records him as a Warrant Officer Schoolmaster stationed in Ceylon. In 1918, he was appointed as an Inspector of Army Schools and appointed to the Honorary Rank of Lieutenant, promoted to Captain in 1921. He retired from the army on 28 August 1928 and in 1939 he emigrated to Australia, dying in Belgrave, Victoria, in 1951. It is also reported in the School *Chronicle* that he was Mentioned in Despatches in the war, although the *London Gazette* entry for this could not be found.

Joseph was discharged from the school on 22 March 1890 and enlisted into the Royal Engineers. He served for 22 years before he was discharged from the army on 16 May 1912. In 1932 he emigrated to Rhodesia[416], where he died in December 1939. One of his sons, Lieutenant Thomas Conolly, Royal Navy, whilst not a Dukie, died in June 1940 when HMS *Van Dyck* was sunk off the coast of Norway.

William was discharged from the school on 12 November 1892 and enlisted into The Suffolk Regiment. However, it appears that by the time war broke out, he had transferred to the Royal Army Medical Corps, and like his brother, he too was Commissioned as a Quartermaster in 1915, retiring as a Captain in 1922. He died in Worthing, Sussex, in 1949.

Frederick Joseph Alexander CROWE

Corporal, 1855, 9 Field Ambulance, Royal Army Medical Corps who died on 11 April 1916, aged 21 Buried in Poperinghe New Military Cemetery, Belgium

Born on 09 July 1894 in Dartford, Kent, the youngest of three children of Joseph William Crowe and Charlotte Elizabeth née Turner, his father had been a Private in The King's Royal Rifle Corps who was discharged from the army on 23 November 1881. He died in Hornchurch, Essex, on 11 April 1900.

---

[415] *The Chronicle of The Duke of York's Royal Military School*, No. 19: March 1921
[416] Modern-day Zimbabwe

Frederick was admitted to the school on 08 January 1904 (Petition No. 11923), joining his older brother, William Montague Crowe, who had been admitted on 09 April 1903 (Petition No. 11830). Frederick was discharged from the school on 24 July 1908 and enlisted into the Royal Army Medical Corps. His service record has not survived, but Frederick was recorded in the 1911 Census stationed in McGrigor Barracks, Stanhope Lines, Aldershot, the Royal Army Medical Corps Depot, as was his brother. He was listed as a Tailor, his brother as a Bugler.

He disembarked in France on 20 August 1914 as a Corporal with the 7th Field Ambulance, Royal Army Medical Corps and the unit is known to have served in all the major engagements of 1914, spending the majority of 1915 in the Ypres sector. By 1916, he was Acting Serjeant and known to be serving with the 9th Field Ambulance, which had been part of the Guards Division since August 1915.

In early-1916, the Guards Division was relocated to Flanders, remaining there until September 1916 when it took part in the later battles of the Somme Offensive. However, in April the Field Ambulance was located in Poperinghe and was set up in the cellar of a partially destroyed house, which was *"considered to be more than useless as a place of protection against shellfire"*[417]. A bombardment commenced at about 1745hrs on 11 April and approximately half an hour later, a request was received for five stretchers to bring in wounded from 250 yards along the road from the dressing station.

Frederick and five stretcher bearers immediately went out to bring in these casualties. However, as they were loading the casualties onto the stretchers, a shell burst among them, killing or wounding every man in the party, including Frederick. He is buried, with two of his colleagues who were killed by the same shell, in Poperinghe New Military Cemetery, on the outskirts of the town.

William also enlisted into the Royal Army Medical Corps when he was discharged from the school on 18 July 1907. He survived the war and lived to the ripe old age of 82, dying in Battle, East Sussex, in 1975.

John Henry KAY

Corporal, 12382, 33 Company (Cairo), Royal Army Medical Corps who died on 20 October 1914, aged 29. Buried in Bootle Cemetery, Lancashire, United Kingdom

Born on 26 March 1885 in Netley, Hampshire, the eldest of three children of Frederick Kay and Elizabeth Jane née Potter, his father

---

[417] WO 95/1208/1: 9 Field Ambulance, 1915 Aug - 1919 Apr, The National Archives, Kew

was a 1st Class Staff Sergeant in the Army Medical Staff Corps. His mother died in Hong Kong, China, on 09 July 1890.

John was admitted to the school on 31 July 1896 (Petition No. 10909) and was joined by his younger brother, Frederick William Kay, on 03 September 1897 (Petition No. 11073). John was discharged from the school on 08 April 1899 and enlisted into the Royal Army Medical Corps.

Although his service record is no longer available, it is known that he served in the general hospitals as a Bugler in South Africa during the Second Boer War, being awarded the Queen's South Africa Medal with clasps for *Cape Colony* and *Orange Free State*. He was later recorded in the 1911 Census as a Lance Sergeant, undertaking Corps Duties and stationed in The Citadel, Cairo, Egypt.

By the outbreak of war, John was married, his wife living in Sligo, County Sligo, and in October 1914 he was in Liverpool, Lancashire, likely preparing to return to Egypt. The casualty record for him states that he accidentally drowned, but a newspaper report of the time[418] stated that:

"A verdict of "Accidental death" was returned at an inquest held before Mr. F. A. Jones, the deputy county coroner, at Bootle yesterday, on John Henry Kay. The deceased, who was a corporal R.A.M.C., was in charge of the gangway leading from the steamship Deseado, lying in Brocklebank Dock, on Saturday night, when he fell onto the quay and sustained fatal injuries".

It is possible that after he fell to the quay he then ended up in the dock, hence drowning being recorded as the cause of death on his casualty card. His body was taken to the military hospital in Bootle, Lancashire, and he was later buried in the town. He is also a "Lost Boy" whose name has been omitted from the memorial tablets in the school chapel.

Frederick was discharged from the school on 17 November 1900 and also enlisted into the Royal Army medical Corps. He ended the war as an Acting Warrant Officer Class I, but after that, nothing more is known about him.

---

[418] *Liverpool Daily Post*, Thursday 22 October 1914

John Charles VICKERS
Private, 5558, 72 Field Ambulance, Royal Army Medical Corps who died on 18 June 1917, aged 20. Buried in Lijssenthoek Military Cemetery, West-Vlaanderen, Belgium

Born on 06 June 1897 in Portsmouth, Hampshire, the eldest of four children of John Vickers and Grace Margaret née Scowen, his father was a Serjeant in the Royal Army Medical Corps, who died of enteric fever whilst serving in Gozo, Malta, on 11 December 1904.

John was admitted to the school on 30 March 1908 (Petition No. 12480)) and having moved from Chelsea to Guston, was discharged on 29 June 1911, enlisting into Royal Army Medical Corps.

John's service record is no longer available, so it is not possible to establish for certain the units with which he served prior to the war. However, his medal index card shows that he entered theatre on 19 August 1914 and that he served with both the 5th and 7th Field Ambulances. It is known that in June 1917 he was serving with 72 Field Ambulance in the Ypres Sector. On 17 June 1917, it was reported that all of the bearers from the Field Ambulance were in the line and it is also reported that six other ranks were killed and sixteen wounded.

John was one of those wounded and on 18 June the progress report by the Officer Commanding No. 3 Canadian Casualty Clearing Station reports that he was *"dangerously wounded"*, with gunshot wounds to his genitals, abdomen, legs, head and right hand. He died of his wounds on the same day that he was reported as dangerously wounded and is one of the nearly 11,000 British and Commonwealth casualties from June 1915 until the end of the war, that are buried in Lijssenthoek Military Cemetery.

Army Pay Corps

Charles Victor AGATE

Staff Serjeant, 1058, Army Pay Office (Perth), Army Pay Corps who died on 10 August 1918, aged 35. Buried in Torquay Cemetery and Extension, Devon, United Kingdom

Born on 01 August 1883 in Trimulgherry, India, the youngest of two children of John William Agate and Sarah Elizabeth Kate Sanders née Voyzey, his father had been a Private in The Devonshire Regiment who was discharged from the army on 15 January 1884. However, he then deserted his wife and family, and nothing had been heard of him after October 1889, prior to Charles's admission to the school.

Charles was admitted to the school on 24 February 1893 (Petition No. 10429) and discharged on 14 August 1897, enlisting into his father's old regiment, spending the first three years of his service in Britain, before being posted to South Africa, on 17 October 1900, during the Second Boer War. After six months, Charles was posted back to Britain, on 02 April 1901, transferring to the Army Pay Corps the following year, on 11 February 1902 and spending the next four years in Britain, being promoted to Corporal on 11 February 1903.

Two years after his first promotion, Charles was appointed as a Lance Serjeant, on 11 February 1905 and was then posted to South Africa again on 16 June 1906, spending three years there, including being promoted to Serjeant on 11 February 1908, before returning to Britain on 03 March 1909, where he was to spend the rest of his army career, even after the outbreak of war.

He was promoted to Staff Serjeant on 25 September 1915, but nine months later he collapsed at work and was relieved from duty for four weeks. He had developed a persistent cough by this time, which he had initially thought was hay fever, but it was diagnosed as tuberculosis, which Charles believed he had contracted from working in an office with another Serjeant who had been invalided out of the army with the disease at the end of 1914.

Charles was discharged from the army as no longer physically fit on 16 November 1916, dying nine months later and commemorated by the Commonwealth War Graves Commission. He is also a "Lost

Boy" whose name has been omitted from the memorial tablets in the school chapel.

Corps of Army Schoolmasters

Leonard John RICKWOOD
Schoolmaster 1st Class, Corps of Army Schoolmasters who died on 02 January 1919, aged 41. Buried in Gibraltar (North Front) Cemetery, Gibraltar

Born on 10 November 1877 in Gibraltar, the second child of John William Rickwood and Emily Elizabeth née Hale, his father had been a Colour Serjeant in The Prince Consort's Own Rifle Brigade, who was discharged from the army on 21 January 1879 and died in Brentford, Middlesex, on 27 May 1886.

Leonard was admitted to the school on 06 January 1888 (Petition No. 9605), joining his older brother, Herbert James Rickwood, who had been admitted on 29 October 1886 (Petition No. 9430). Leonard was discharged on 03 January 1894, becoming a Pupil Teacher. He then enlisted into the Corps of Army Schoolmasters on 01 December 1901, initially posted to Preston, Lancashire, before embarking for India, acting as Schoolmaster to the 16th (The Queen's) Lancers, 2nd Battalion, The Essex Regiment and 2nd Battalion, The Connaught Rangers.

In December 1905 he was transferred back to England, before being posted to Newbridge, County Kildare, in January 1906, where he was promoted to Warrant Officer on 01 June 1906. His next posting was to Lichfield, Staffordshire, on 06 January 1908, where he married Margaret Caroline Burgess in the town in December of that year and on 17 September 1911, was posted back to his birthplace as a Schoolmaster at the Garrison School, Gibraltar, which was where he was to spend the entire war. Both of his children were born in Gibraltar, Maurice Leonard Rickwood in 1913 and Ethel Mary Rickwood in 1915. Sadly, both of his children died in infancy, Maurice at six weeks and Ethel at two weeks.

On 06 September 1918, Leonard was appointed as a Schoolmaster 1st Class (Warrant Officer Class I). However, on 21 December 1918, he was diagnosed with tuberculosis with pneumonia, a disease from which he died on 02 January 1919. He is buried in Gibraltar and commemorated by the Commonwealth

War Graves Commission, although the reason that they give his initials as "J L W C" is unclear.

Herbert was discharged from the school on 20 July 1889 *"To Mother"*, but enlisted in 1916, serving as a Sapper in the Inland Waterways Department of the Royal Engineers. He survived the war and died in Hendon in 1929, at the age of 54.

The London Regiment

William Alfred AVIS
Private, 245592, 2/2nd (City of London) Battalion (Royal Fusiliers), The London Regiment who died on 01 September 1918 aged 18. Commemorated on the Vis-en-Artois Memorial, Pas de Calais, France

Born on 02 November 1899 in Canterbury, Kent, the youngest of three children of Arthur Avis and Rosetta née Hall, his father was a Private in the 17th (Duke of Cambridge's Own) Lancers who died at sea on 12 March 1900 whilst en route to South Africa. William also had two half-siblings born after his mother remarried, to Walter Wooderson, in 1904.

William was admitted to the school on 30 December 1910 (Petition No. 12836) and was discharged *"To civil life"* on 02 December 1913. Following his discharge from the school, William's life is a mystery, but it is known that at some point after the outbreak of war, he enlisted into the Territorial Force in Canterbury, Kent, likely joining 3/19th Battalion, The London Regiment. This battalion had been formed in March 1915 and moved to Richmond Park, Surrey, prior to again moving to Winchester, Hampshire, in January 1916. On 08 April 1916, it became the 19th (Reserve) Battalion, moving to Chiseldon, Wiltshire, in November 1917 and then to Blackdown, Surrey, in 1918.

It is not possible to know for certain when William enlisted as his service record is no longer available, but it is likely that it was in 1917, as the service number that is given in his medal index card for this battalion is one that was introduced when there was a reorganisation of the Territorial Force service numbers in that year. In addition, he would not have been seventeen until November 1916 and it is likely that he spent some time with the reserve battalion in Britain, before he was posted to the 1/19th Battalion in France on 25 May 1918, his medal records confirming this and his transfer to the 2/2nd Battalion on 27 May 1918.

This battalion had been formed as 3/2nd Battalion in Epsom, Surrey, in December 1914, joining the 3/1st London Brigade at Tadworth, Surrey, in April 1915. In May 1915, it moved to Bury St. Edmunds, Suffolk, transferring to 173rd Brigade, 58th (2/1st

London) Division. It then became 2/2nd Battalion when the original was disbanded at Rouen in June 1916 and this battalion then landed at Le Havre on 22 January 1917.

At the end of August 1918, the battalion was bivouacked in "Death Valley" on the Somme, but on 31 August it embussed on the main road near Bronfay Farm and moved to positions north-east of Hem Wood, becoming the reserve to the brigade. At 0530hrs on 01 September 1918, the battalion provided support to the 2/4th (City of London) Battalion (Royal Fusiliers) and 1/3rd (City of London) Battalion (Royal Fusiliers), The London Regiment, as these had been ordered to attack the village of Bouchavesnes. Following a creeping barrage, the attack was a complete success, with all of the final objectives being reached by the scheduled time.

Although the battalion war diary[419] does not record any casualties, the Commonwealth War Graves Commission records that it suffered two casualties, one of whom was William. Both he and the other man killed are commemorated on the Vis-en-Artois Memorial, but William is another of the "Lost Boys" whose name has been omitted from the memorial tablets in the school chapel.

Edward George GAVIN
Private, 228198, 1/1st (City of London) Battalion (Royal Fusiliers), The London Regiment (Royal Fusiliers) who died on 07 June 1917, aged 27. Commemorated on the Ypres (Menin Gate) Memorial, West-Vlaanderen, Belgium

Born on 24 November 1889 in Belfast, County Antrim, the eldest of three children of Edward Francis Gavin and Isabella née Gane, his father had been a Corporal in The Royal Irish Rifles, who had been discharged after 12 years' service on 15 June 1896 and died in Landport, Hampshire on 09 December 1896.

Edward was admitted to the school on 07 December 1900 (Petition No. 11501) and was discharged *"To Mother"* on 24 November 1904. He appears in the 1911 Census, which records him as an Invoice Clerk living in Pimlico, London, and it is known that he married Mabel Matilda Croxford at Christchurch Broadway in Westminster, London, on 25 December 1912.

His service record has not survived, but at some point after leaving the school, he enlisted into the Volunteer Force[420], joining 1st Volunteer Battalion, The Royal Fusiliers (City of London Regiment)[421], although his enlistment date is unknown. At the start

---

[419] WO 95/3001/4: 2/2 Battalion London Regiment, 1917 Jan. - 1919 Feb., The National Archives, Kew
[420] Renamed The Territorial Force in 1908
[421] Renamed the 1st (City of London) Battalion, The London Regiment (Royal Fusiliers) on 01

of the war, his battalion had its Headquarters in Bloomsbury, London, its initial task being to guard the London to Newhaven Railway, but on 04 September, it embarked at Southampton, Hampshire, and sailed to Malta, landing at Valetta on 14 September 1914, although Edward did not enter a theatre of war until 1916 at the earliest based on his medal entitlement.

The battalion then left Malta on 11 February 1915, arriving at Avonmouth, Gloucestershire, ten days later, before re-embarking at Southampton on 11 March and landing at Le Havre on 12 March 1915, its first taste of action being at Aubers Ridge on 09 May 1915, during which it had five officers and 191 other ranks killed, wounded and missing.

Although the battalion was Divisional Reserve in trenches near Hebuterne on 01 July 1916, it did participate in the later battles of the Somme Offensive, as well as capturing the village of Neuville-Vitasse in April 1917, prior to the Battle of Bullecourt.

On 26 April 1917, Edward was one of several soldiers from his battalion who were transferred to 13th (Service) Battalion (Wandsworth), The East Surrey Regiment and, two weeks later on 13 May, to 26th (Service) Battalion (Bankers), The Royal Fusiliers (City of London Regiment), both of which were Kitchener Battalions.

On 07 June 1917, the 26th Battalion, was to attack from Observatory Wood to St. Yves at 0310hrs. Despite gas and enemy fire, twelve hours later it had gained its objective, and although the casualties were relatively low, Edward was killed on that day. His body was never recovered and he is commemorated on the Menin Gate Memorial. Although he is also commemorated on the memorial tablets in the school chapel, he is incorrectly recorded as E G *Gaven*.

Martin JOYCE

Rifleman, 324448, 1/6th (City of London) Battalion (Rifles), The London Regiment who died on 12 March 1918, aged 29. Buried in Cologne Southern Cemetery, Nordrhein-Westfalen, Germany

Born on 30 January 1889 in Woolwich, Kent, the sixth of seven children of Thomas Joyce and Priscilla née Newey, his father had been a Private in The Prince Consort's Own Rifle Brigade, who was discharged from the army after 21 years' service on 15 November 1880 and died in Woolwich, London, on 22 January 1892.

April 1908 and further renamed the 1/1st (City of London) Battalion, The London Regiment (Royal Fusiliers) in March 1915

Martin was admitted to the school on 08 September 1899 (Petition No. 11344), joining his older brother, Francis Frank Joyce, who had been admitted on 06 January 1897 (Petition No. 10980), and they were joined by their younger brother, Edward, on 10 January 1902 (Petition No. 11648). Their older brother, Albert, who had been admitted on 24 November 1893 (Petition No. 10547), had been discharged by the time that Martin was admitted.

Martin was discharged from the school on 31 January 1903 to *"Civil Life"*. He is recorded in the 1911 Census as a boarder, living in Dulais Higher, Glamorganshire, and employed as a Colliery Labourer Underground. However, after the outbreak of war, it appears that Martin was back in London, as he married Ellen Rust in Woolwich, London, on 12 December 1914.

Martin's service record is no longer available, so it is not known when he enlisted into the army, but the battalion in which he was serving when he died, 1/6th[422] Battalion, The London Regiment (City of London Rifles), had been formed at Farringdon Road, London, in August 1914 as part of 2nd London Brigade, 1st London Division. On mobilisation, it moved to Bisley, Surrey, and then in September 1914, it moved to Crowborough, Sussex. Two months later, in November 1914, it moved to Watford, Hertfordshire, where it was transferred to 4th London Brigade, 2nd London Division and landed at Le Havre on 18 March 1915. However, although there is no date of disembarkation on Martin's medal index card, the medal rolls for his regiment show that he did not enter theatre until 04 August 1917.

In November 1917, the battalion was in the vicinity of Bourlon Wood on the Somme. On 20 November, the Battle of Cambrai was launched, and whilst the initial assault was a success, Bourlon Wood proved a less easy target. It appears that during the attack on the wood, Martin was wounded and captured, the International Committee of the Red Cross records of Prisoners of War[423] showing that he was captured on 29 November 1917. He subsequently died as a result of his wounds on 12 March 1918 and was buried in Cologne, Germany. He is also another of the "Lost Boys" whose name has been omitted from the memorial tablets in the school chapel.

Albert was discharged from the school on 09 June 1898 and enlisted into Princess Louise's (Argyll and Sutherland Highlanders). However, his service record has not survived and it has not been possible to find further information about him after his enlistment.

---

[422] Renamed 6th Battalion on 31 January 1918
[423] 1914-1918 Prisoners of the First World War ICRC Historical Archives: PA 24551

Francis was discharged from the school on 14 September 1901 and enlisted into the Royal Garrison Artillery. He served throughout the war and was discharged from the army in April 1919. He died in Chelmsford, Essex, in 1964.

Edward was discharged from the school on 12 January 1905 and also enlisted into the Royal Garrison Artillery. His service record is no longer available, but if he did serve during the war, he survived. The 1939 England and Wales Register records him as a Police Constable, living in West Ham, Essex, but nothing more is known of him after this.

George Samuel MATTHEWS
Private, 14047, 1/3rd (City of London) Battalion (Royal Fusiliers), The London Regiment (Royal Fusiliers) who died on 19 September 1915, aged 19. Buried in R.E. Farm Cemetery, West-Vlaanderen, Belgium

Born on 28 March 1896 in Alverstoke, Hampshire, the fourth of five children of Isaac Matthews and Winifred Ann née Burton, his father had been a Drummer in The Princess Victoria's (Royal Irish Fusiliers) who had been discharged from the army after 23 years' service on 07 February 1888. His mother died in Alverstoke on 09 August 1899.

George was admitted to the school on 21 March 1907 (Petition No. 12348), which was seven months after his older brother, Albin Matthews, who had been admitted on 13 January 1901 (Petition No. 11607), had been discharged. George, having made the move from Chelsea to Guston, was discharged from the school on 06 November 1910, enlisting into The Royal Fusiliers (City of London Regiment). However, his service record is no longer available, nor could he be found in the 1911 Census, so it is not known how long he served or whether he was discharged, later joining the Territorial Force, or if he was posted to 3rd (City of London) Battalion, The London Regiment (Royal Fusiliers)[424] in order to bring it up to strength at the start of the war.

At the outbreak of war, the battalion was located in St. Pancras, London, but sailed for Valletta, Malta, on 14 September 1914, where it remained until 02 January 1915, landing at Marseille four days later and becoming part of the Gharwal Brigade, 7th (Meerut) Division, on 10 February and then the Dehra Dun Brigade in the same division a week later.

During April and May 1915, the battalion participated in the Second Battle of Ypres and when George arrived in France on 02

---

[424] Renamed 1/3rd (City of London) Battalion, The London Regiment (Royal Fusiliers) in March 1915

June 1915, he was likely a casualty replacement. In early September, the battalion was still in the Ypres sector, in the area of Lindenhoek. The Commonwealth War Graves Commission records George Matthews as having been killed in action on 19 September 1915, but no casualties are reported in the battalion war diary for that day. However, on 11 September, there was one killed, one wounded and missing, and five wounded. It is therefore possible that George was either the missing soldier or one of the five wounded.

He is buried in R.E. Farm Cemetery, which had been started in December 1914 and was located close to the Field Ambulances that were located near Wytschaete, and although he is commemorated on the memorial tablets in the school chapel, his surname is misspelled *Mathews*.

Albin was discharged from the school to The Black Watch (Royal Highlanders) on 21 August 1906. He also has no surviving service record, but it is likely that he served during the war. He died in Portsmouth, Hampshire, on 25 April 1970.

Arthur Henry NICHOLS

Private, 445004, 2/10th (County of London) Battalion (Hackney), The London Regiment, attached 11th (Service) Battalion, The Prince Consort's Own (Rifle Brigade) who died between 22 March and 01 April 1918, aged 35. Commemorated on the Thiepval Memorial, Somme, France

Born on 07 July 1882 in Dorchester, Dorsetshire, the youngest of four children of Robert Nichols and Sarah Ann née Pepper, his father had been a Gunner in the Royal Horse Artillery, who was discharged from the army on 01 February 1881 and died in Dorchester on 22 April 1882.

Arthur was admitted to the school on 26 November 1891 (Petition No. 10219) joining his older brother, Robert George Nichols, who had been admitted on 31 January 1890 (Petition No. 9958). Arthur was discharged from the school on 25 July 1896 and enlisted into The Queen's (Royal West Surrey Regiment).

Arthur joined the 2nd Battalion of the regiment and spent the first four years of his service in Britain, before he was posted, on 17 October 1900, to South Africa during the Second Boer War. He was awarded the Queen's South Africa Medal, with the clasps *Transvaal* and *Orange Free State*, as well as the King's South Africa Medal with the clasp *1901-02*. He was posted back to Britain on 08 June 1904 and was discharged from the army as a Private at the end of his first period of service on 24 July 1908.

There is limited information available about Arthur following his discharge, but he is recorded in the 1911 Census as a Boarder living in Chelsea, London, and employed as an Assistant Postman.

Following the outbreak of war, Arthur re-enlisted into the army, although his service record for this second period of service has not survived.

However, it is known that he joined 1/15th (County of London) Battalion (Prince of Wales's Own Civil Service Rifles), The London Regiment. This battalion had been formed in August 1914 at Somerset House in London. However, it is not known how long he served with this battalion, but he later transferred to 2/10th (County of London) Battalion (Hackney), The London Regiment.

This battalion had also been formed in London in September 1914, moving in November 1914 to Crowborough, Sussex, and coming under the orders of 2/2nd London Brigade, 2/1st London Division. The battalion then moved to Ipswich, Suffolk, where the formation was retitled as 175th Brigade, 58th (2/1st London) Division. Whilst the unit was stationed here, Arthur married Marie Brenda Spurr in Chelsea, London.

Arthur is recorded in medal records as disembarking in theatre on 29 May 1917, now attached to 11th (Service) Battalion, The Prince Consort's Own (Rifle Brigade) and it is likely he only served overseas with that battalion. This battalion had been formed at Winchester, Hampshire, as part of K2 and coming under the command of 59th Brigade, 20th (Light) Division, landing at Boulogne on 21 July 1915.

By early-1918, he had been overseas for nearly 10 months and was serving with the battalion when the Germans launched their Spring Offensive, on 21 March 1918. During the desperate fighting to throw back the advancing German Army, Arthur was killed in action. Due to the confusion that existed at the time, his date of death is not known for certain and his body was never recovered. Arthur is also another of the "Lost Boys" whose name has been omitted from the memorial tablets in the school chapel.

Robert was discharged from the school on 27 July 1895 and enlisted into the 9th (Queen's Royal) Lancers. He is recorded in the 1911 Census living with his wife in Regents Park, London, and employed as an Army Musician. It is also known that he survived the war, but nothing else is known of him.

Edward Thomas WALL

Rifleman, 591141, 2/18th (County of London) Battalion (London Irish Rifles), The London Regiment who died on 09 October 1916, aged 19. Commemorated on the Arras Memorial, Pas de Calais, France

Born on 19 October 1896 in Tunbridge Wells, Kent, the eighth of nine children of Daniel Wall and Eliza née Collins, his father had served in The Leicestershire Regiment, before becoming the Permanent Staff Sergeant Major of 1st Volunteer Battalion, The Queen's Own (Royal West Kent Regiment), based in Tonbridge, Kent. He died whilst still serving on 07 August 1899 in Ryde, Isle of Wight.

Edward was admitted to the school on 08 February 1907 (Petition No. 12324), joining his older brother, Richard James Francis Wall, who had been admitted on 10 July 1906 (Petition No. 12248). Edward was withdrawn from the school on 17 February 1909 and whilst the reason is not recorded in his Petition Document, he is recorded in the 1911 Census as a boarder at the Xaverian Brothers School[425] in Mayfield, Kent. This was a Roman Catholic boys' boarding school, with a small number of fatherless boys admitted each year and corresponds with the faith recorded in his Petition Document.

Edward's service record is no longer available, so it is not known when he enlisted. However, the London Irish Rifles were part of the Territorial Force and mobilised in August 1914 at Duke of York's Headquarters, Chelsea, the former site of the school. The battalion with which Edward served, the 2/18th Battalion, had been formed in London in August 1914 and was stationed in Reigate, Surrey, by January 1915. It then moved to St. Albans, Hertfordshire, in March 1915, to Bishops Stortford, Hertfordshire, in May 1915 and finally Sutton Veny, Wiltshire, in January 1916, before landing at Le Havre on 23 June 1916, the date shown on Edward's medal index card for his entry into theatre.

Edward was reported missing four months later on 09 October 1916, after a large raid of around 100 men on the German front line that evening. The raid was met with considerable machine-gun and rifle fire, having been visible for some distance as the soldiers advanced under the moonlight, with the cloud cover having broken. The Germans were well prepared for the raid and although it was successful in penetrating the German trenches, the London Irish Rifles returned without any prisoners and suffered heavily, the battalion war diary[426] recording three officers wounded, 41 other ranks wounded and five other ranks missing, all five subsequently commemorated on the Arras Memorial, including Edward. He is also a "Lost Boy" whose name has been omitted from the memorial tablets in the school chapel.

---

[425] Now Mayfield College
[426] WO 95/3031/5: 2/18 Battalion London Regiment, 1916 June – Nov, The National Archives, Kew

Richard was discharged from the school nine months after Edward's withdrawal, on 08 November 1909, enlisting into the band of the Royal Artillery. Nothing more is known of him after this.

William James WERRY
Private, 6045, 1/20th (County of London) Battalion (Blackheath and Woolwich), The London Regiment who died on 01 October 1916, aged 20. Commemorated on the Thiepval Memorial, Somme, France

Born on 01 May 1894 in Willesden, Middlesex, the eldest of four children of William Werry and Annie Elizabeth née Mitchell. William also had two older half-siblings from his mother's first marriage. William's father had been a Corporal in The Buffs (East Kent Regiment), who had been discharged from the army after 10 years' service on 31 January 1883 and died in Willesden, London, on 11 February 1902.

William was admitted to the school on 08 April 1904 (Petition No. 11957) but was discharged home as unfit for army service on 24 July 1908. He is recorded in the 1911 Census living with his mother, brother and sister in Willesden, and employed as a Page Boy in a music hall. Following the outbreak of war, it appears that William joined the army, although his service record is no longer available to confirm when he enlisted.

The battalion in which William was serving when he died, 1/20th (County of London) Battalion (Blackheath and Woolwich), was a Territorial Force battalion that had been formed at Holly Hedge House in Blackheath, Kent, in August 1914 as part of 5th London Brigade, 2nd London Division, landing at Le Havre on 10 March 1915, William joining it over a year later with other replacements on 15 June 1916.

At the end of September 1916, the battalion was in the vicinity of Flers, on the Somme. On 30 September, bombing parties from the 20th Battalion, 1/19th (County of London) Battalion (St Pancras), The London Regiment and the ANZACs[427], following artillery preparation, rushed and captured 100 yards of the Flers line.

At 0700hrs the following morning, artillery commenced a bombardment of German-held Flers, the Flers support line and Eaucourt L'Abbaye, and at 1515hrs, the three battalions, with the 50th Division on their left and the ANZACs on their right, attacked in four waves on a four-company frontage, advancing under a creeping barrage. The first two waves, 19th and 20th Battalions, The London Regiment, both reached their final objectives and dug-in on the far side of Eaucourt L'Abbaye, with the third and fourth waves

---
[427] Australian and New Zealand Army Corps

remaining in the Flers line until they were forced back about 100 yards by a small group of German bombers.

Despite the success of the attack, the battalion suffered four officers and 103 other ranks killed during the attack, including William, whose body was not recovered. He is commemorated on the Thiepval Memorial and is also a "Lost Boy" whose name has been omitted from the memorial tablets in the school chapel.

The Cambridgeshire Regiment

Criss CRISSALL
Lance Corporal 325036, 1/1st Battalion, The Cambridgeshire Regiment who died on 15 September 1918, aged 37. Buried in Valenciennes (St. Roch) Communal Cemetery, Nord, France

Born on 30 December 1880 in Haverhill, Suffolk, the fourth of five children of James Crissall and Sarah née Russell, his father had been a Serjeant in the 82nd Regiment of Foot (Prince of Wales's Volunteers) who had been discharged from the army on 27 October 1874. His mother died in Haverhill on 12 January 1889.

Criss was admitted to the school on 30 May 1890 (Petition No. 10018) and was joined by his younger brother, John Crissall, on 27 October 1893 (Petition No. 10539). Criss was discharged from the school on 08 January 1895 and enlisted into The Prince of Wales's Volunteers (South Lancashire Regiment), spending the first seven years of his service in Britain, being appointed as a Bandsman on 27 December 1895, before being posted on 11 January 1902 to South Africa, where he was appointed as a Lance Corporal a month later, on 16 February 1902.

After spending a year in South Africa, Criss was then posted to India, remaining there for four years before he was posted back to Britain on 26 January 1907, and discharged from the army at the end of his first period of service on 28 January 1907. He is then recorded in the 1911 Census living with his sister, brother-in-law and two nieces in Cambridge, Cambridgeshire, and employed as a Cleaner in a Motor Garage. It was also during 1911 that Criss married Florence Gertrude Mabel Ellis in Cambridge, their eldest child, James Frederick Criss Crissall, being born the following year.

It is not certain at what point Criss re-enlisted, but the regiment that he joined was a Territorial Force one, part of the Corps of The Suffolk Regiment. At the outbreak of war, 1st Battalion[428], The Cambridgeshire Regiment, was part of the East Midlands Brigade, East Anglian Division and once mobilised it moved to Romford, Essex, and then to Long Melford, Suffolk, before, in September, it moved to Stowlangtoft, Suffolk, and lastly, to Bury St. Edmunds,

---
[428] Renumbered as 1/1st Battalion with the formation of 2/1st Battalion in March 1915

Suffolk, in November 1914. It landed at Le Havre on 15 February 1915.

However, it would seem that Criss was not serving with the battalion at that time as, although his medal index card has no disembarkation date, he did not qualify for the award of the 1914-15 Star, suggesting that he did not arrive in theatre until 1916 at the earliest. His service record is no longer available, but it is known from casualty records that he was recorded as wounded in August 1917, likely during the Third Battle of Ypres.

On 26 March 1918, the battalion was in a new line at Herbecourt, having made attempts to resist an attack during the German Spring Offensive. By 0715hrs the line on the right gave way and small parties from the companies became separated from their comrades, some spending several days fighting with other units before re-joining their battalion. The battalion history states, this was *"one of the most trying days experienced by the Cambridgeshires during the whole campaign"*[429].

Criss was reported missing on this day and it appears that he was captured and subsequently died from nephritis whilst a Prisoner of War. It was not until March 1919 that Florence was informed of his death, by which stage their daughter, Freda Crissall, was three months old, having been born in Cambridge in December 1918. He is also a "Lost Boy" whose name has been omitted from the memorial tablets in the school chapel.

When John was discharged from the school on 14 June 1897, he joined his older brother by enlisting into The Prince of Wales's Volunteers (South Lancashire Regiment), where they served together for a period. He was discharged from the army on 14 October 1912 after 15 years' service, but re-enlisted on 08 September 1914, joining The Suffolk Regiment. He served throughout the war and by the Armistice was Acting Regimental Serjeant Major of the 11th (Service) Battalion (Cambridgeshire) and had been awarded the Distinguished Conduct Medal[430].

---

[429] Riddell, Brig-Gen E. P. A. and Clayton, Col. M. C. (1934). *The Cambridgeshires 1914-1919*. Cambridge: Bowes and Bowes
[430] *The London Gazette*, 30 August 1918, Supplement:30879

Royal Air Force

John William Ernest WOODS

Leading Aircraftman, 125062, Royal Air Force who died on 06 February 1919, aged 25. Buried in Melton Mowbray (Thorpe Road) Cemetery, Leicestershire, United Kingdom

Born on 07 November 1893 in Bareilly, India, the fourth of six children of Thomas Milford Woods and Lydia née Glanville. Lydia had previously been married to Robert Towell, who was serving in the 17th (the Leicestershire) Regiment of Foot[431] when he died in India. John's father had been a Lance Corporal in The Prince of Wales's Own (West Yorkshire Regiment), who had been discharged from the army on 15 June 1894 and died in Melton Mowbray, Leicestershire, on 30 August 1899.

John was admitted to the school on 12 August 1903 (Petition No. 11832), joining his older brother, Walter Glanville Woods, who had been admitted on 04 May 1900 (Petition No. 11430). John was discharged on 28 November 1907 and enlisted into The Duke of Cornwall's Light Infantry.

Little is known about John's service in this regiment and his service record is no longer available, although he is recorded in the 1911 Census as a Tailor in the 1st Battalion, stationed in Gravesend Barracks, Kent. In addition, his later Royal Air Force service record gives his army service number and confirms that he was awarded the 1914-15 Star, so we know that he was serving with 1st Battalion, The Duke of Cornwall's Light Infantry at the outbreak of war.

Prior to the war, this battalion was stationed in Newbridge, County Kildare, where John would have served alongside Dukie Stephen Saunders, but after mobilisation, it landed at Le Havre on 15 August 1914, although the medal index card shows that John himself disembarked six days later, on 21 August 1914. Due to the lack of a surviving service record, it is not possible to follow John's movements, but it is known that the battalion remained on the Western Front until November 1917, when it was posted to Italy, remaining there until April 1918.

Although John's Royal Air Force record has limited information,

---

[431] Renamed The Leicestershire Regiment on 01 July 1881

it does show that he was back in France on 19 February 1918, having transferred to the Royal Flying Corps on 24 January 1918. He was still serving in the Royal Flying Corps, where he was employed as a Fabric Worker, when it amalgamated with the Royal Naval Air Service on 01 April 1918, becoming the Royal Air Force.

Again, there is very little information in this record about John's movements, but it does record that he was admitted to the 5th Northern General Hospital, which was located in the disused buildings of the Leicestershire and Rutland County Lunatic Asylum, Leicester, Leicestershire. John was admitted on 03 February 1919 and died three days later from pneumonia. He was buried in the cemetery in Melton Mowbray, where his family had settled following his father's discharge from the army. However, he is another "Lost Boy" whose name has been omitted from the memorial tablets in the school chapel.

Walter was discharged from the school on 17 December 1904 and enlisted into The Leicestershire Regiment. He was discharged from the army three months later *"not being likely to become an efficient soldier"*. However, he appears in the 1911 Census as a Private in 1st Battalion, The Duke of Cornwall's Light Infantry, alongside his brother. Walter survived the war and died in Brecknock, Powys, in 1976. His son, Sergeant Donald Walter Woods, was killed in action in July 1943 when his Lancaster was shot down over Germany.

Australian Light Horse

Frederick George HALL

Trooper, 760, 8th Australian Light Horse who died on 07 August 1915, aged 23. Commemorated on the Lone Pine Memorial, Turkey.

Born on 16 August 1891 in Portsmouth, Hampshire, the youngest child of Thomas Calcutt Hall and Harriet née Freeman, his father had been a Private in the 59th (2nd Nottinghamshire) Regiment of Foot[432], but had been discharged from the army on 06 January 1880.

Frederick was admitted to the school on 10 October 1902 (Petition No. 11741), his father dying in Portsmouth a year later in May 1903. As a result of his father's death and because Frederick was the sole support for his mother, rather than joining the army when he was discharged on 18 January 1908, he became a Student at the school and it then appears that having finished his studies, he became a civilian teacher.

Despite being his mother's sole support, in 1912 Frederick emigrated to Australia, where he was employed as a State School Teacher. However, when war broke out in August 1914, it was not just the "home country" that received the call to arms, but all the countries of the Empire, including Australia. On 05 November 1914, Frederick enlisted into the 8th Australian Light Horse Regiment, although he did not sail with the regiment when it left Australia in December 1914, landing in Egypt in February 1915.

After three months, it was sent to the Gallipoli Peninsula as reinforcements due to the large number of casualties that had been suffered by the Australian infantry units. Frederick departed Melbourne on 03 February 1915 and arrived in Gallipoli on the 3rd Reinforcement Roll, being taken on strength on 27 July 1915 and posted to "C" Squadron.

On the morning of 07 August 1915, the regiment, along with the 10th Light Horse Regiment, was assembled in a trench opposite the Ottoman line that was between 20–75 yards away in a position called

---

[432] Amalgamated with the 30th (Cambridgeshire) Regiment of Foot on 01 July 1881 to become The East Lancashire Regiment

the Nek. The troops were due to go "over the top" on the cessation of the artillery barrage at 0430hrs. However, there was no synchronisation between the artillery and the attacking infantry and the barrage ceased at 0423, allowing seven minutes for the Ottomans to reoccupy their frontline positions, so when the first wave of 150 men did go over, they were met with a hail of machine-gun and rifle fire and, within 30 seconds, were nearly all gunned down.

At this stage, the futility of the effort became clear to those in the second wave and the attack should have been called off, but the second wave followed the first, two minutes later, and met the same fate, almost all of the men being cut down by heavy rifle and machine-gun fire before they got halfway to the Ottoman trench. And yet despite this, the third and fourth waves also went to their deaths.

Frederick had been on the Gallipoli Peninsula for only eleven days when he was reported *"missing"* on 07 August, although he was reported *"killed in action"* eight days later and it is almost certain that he died in that attack. He has no known grave and is one of 139 soldiers from the 8th Light Horse Regiment to be commemorated on the Lone Pine Memorial.

Alfred Robert MATTHEWS

Sergeant, 352, 2nd Australian Light Horse who died on 09 January 1917, aged 36. Buried in Kantara War Memorial Cemetery, Egypt.

Born in December 1880 in Cockfield, Suffolk, the youngest boy of at least five children of Alfred Matthews and Elizabeth née Johnson, his father had been a Gunner in the Royal Artillery who died in 1887 in Cockfield and his mother is believed to have died in 1891, although his Petition Document is missing from the school archive.

Alfred was admitted to the school on 27 November 1891 (Petition No. 10234) and was discharged on 15 December 1894, enlisting into the Royal Artillery as a Mender. His service record has survived, although not being completely legible, but it is known that he deserted on 03 January 1900, whilst serving as a Gunner in No. 10 Company, Royal Garrison Artillery, stationed in Shoeburyness, Essex. He had been confined to barracks on four occasions for *"improper conduct"* during his army career and latterly admonished for being drunk in barracks on 26 December 1898.

Thereafter little is known of his life until he enlisted in the 2nd Australian Light Horse Regiment at Rockhampton, Queensland and no record can be found for his travel to Australia, his occupation being given as Farmer on his enlistment, with his place of birth as Croydon, Surrey and an elder sister in Croydon as his next of kin. He did claim nine years' service in the 9th Lancers, but no surviving service record exists in his name.

Alfred was to become a Saddler shortly after enlistment on 02 September 1914 and embarked for active service at Brisbane on 24 September 1914. He reached Egypt in December 1914, before disembarking on the Gallipoli Peninsula on 09 May 1915, as part of the 1st Light Horse Brigade, to hold part of the defensive live around Anzac Cove. In confused and often bitter fighting at close quarters, he was wounded in the scalp on 03 July 1915, promoted to Lance Corporal the following day, then wounded for a second time on 18 July 1915, mortar bomb wounds to his head and shoulder requiring evacuation to hospital in Malta and then three weeks in a convalescent camp. He returned to Gallipoli on 09 September 1915, promoted to Corporal on 20 September 1915 and to Sergeant on 15 December 1915, the latter promotion on the island of Mudros following the withdrawal of his brigade. He was fortunate to miss the August Offensive when his regiment suffered heavy casualties around Quinn's Post and in late December 1915 they returned to Egypt.

In January 1916 the 1st Light Horse Brigade was kept in the Middle East along with other mounted units as part of the Australian and New Zealand Mounted Division and sent to guard first the Nile and then the Suez Canal, helping to repel an Ottoman advance on the canal in August 1916 during the Battle of Romani. After a period of rest, the brigade joined the advance across the Sinai in Palestine and by January 1917, was ready to assault the remaining Turkish outpost on the frontier at Rafa and secure the Sinai Peninsula.

On 09 January 1917, the initial British and Commonwealth attack against 2000 Turkish troops defending a redoubt known as Hill 255 had begun to stall as ammunition dwindled and fears mounted of an approaching Turkish relief column. In the late afternoon, the regiments of the Australian Light Horse, including the 2nd Light Horse, supported the New Zealanders and Imperial Camel Corps with a mounted charge that succeeded in overcoming the Turkish opposition, but it was during this action at Rafa that Alfred was killed in action. He was buried near to where he fell and subsequently reinterred at Kantara. He is also a "Lost Boy" whose name has been omitted from the memorial tablets in the school chapel.

Australian Imperial Force

Bertie BOOTH
Private, 5298, 28th Battalion Australian Infantry, Australian Imperial Force who died on 26 March 1917, aged 35. Commemorated on the Villers-Bretonneux Memorial, Somme, France

Born on 10 June 1881 in Aldershot, Hampshire, the youngest of three children of Richard Booth and Jane née Luck, his father had been a Private in the Army Service Corps who died whilst still serving in Newbridge, County Kildare, on 17 December 1888.

Bertie was admitted to the school on 31 October 1890 (Petition No. 10084), joining his older brother Henry Booth, who had been admitted three months earlier, on 25 July 1890 (Petition No. 10036). Bertie was discharged from the school on 28 June 1895, enlisting into the Army Service Corps and spent the first four years of his service in Britain, being appointed as a Trumpeter on 30 January 1897. However, two years later, on 30 May 1899, he was imprisoned by his Commanding Officer for fourteen days, although the offence for which he was punished is not recorded in his service record.

He returned to duty on 13 June 1899, having spent his eighteenth birthday incarcerated, and was posted to South Africa three months later, on 16 September 1899. He was to serve in South Africa for four years, being appointed as a Driver on 23 October 1900, before he was posted to Somaliland on the 17 July 1903 in the wake of the disastrous British expedition that lasted from February until June and which resulted in a British detachment near Gumburru being annihilated[433].

A year later, Bertie was posted back to Britain, where he was to spend the rest of his British Army career, being appointed as a Lance Corporal on 16 October 1908 and promoted to Corporal on 08 July 1913, before being discharged from the army at his own request after 18 years' service on 05 February 1914. Five months after his discharge, on 17 July 1914, and possibly in an attempt to avoid the coming war in Europe, Bertie travelled to Freemantle, Western Australia, giving his occupation as Farm Hand.

---

[433] This was part of the Anglo-Somali War, also known as the Dervish War, in which the British fought against the supporters of Mohammed Abdullah Hassan, also known as the Mad Mullah

If the move to Australia had been to avoid the war, it was not successful, as he latterly enlisted into the Australian Imperial Force on 18 January 1916. He gave details of his previous service on this enlistment, which could account for his promotion to Sergeant on 24 March 1916, although the entry in his service record shows that six days later, he had reverted to Acting Corporal.

On 09 August 1916, the replacements for the battalion with which Bertie was to serve, the 28th Battalion, embarked on the SS *Miltiades* at Fremantle, arriving at Plymouth, Devonshire, a month later, on 25 September 1916. After a two month stay in Rollestone, Wiltshire, the battalion embarked on the SS *Victoria* at Folkestone, Kent, on 16 November and by 17 November, he was located in Étaples. After a week, Bertie was then taken on strength by the 28th Battalion, joining the unit on 03 December, although during his time at Étaples, he had reverted to Private at his own request.

Little is known about Bertie after he joined his battalion, but on 26 March 1917, when his battalion were known to have been attacking Lagnicourt during the advance to the Hindenburg Line, he was killed in action. His body was not recovered, so he is commemorated on the Villers-Bretonneux Memorial. However, his name was omitted from the memorial tablets in the school chapel and he is therefore another "Lost Boy".

Henry was *"returned to mother"* on 26 April 1893. However, it appears that he then enlisted in the Royal Navy, serving until he was invalided out of the service on 07 November 1902. After this, it is known that he married in 1907 and had three children, but nothing more is known of him.

Daniel Edward DOCWRA
Private, 1707, 14th Battalion Australian Infantry, Australian Imperial Force who died on 29 August 1916, aged 40. Commemorated on the Villers-Bretonneux Memorial, Somme, France

Born on 03 January 1876 in Malapuram, India, the second of five children of Daniel Docwra and Bridget née Fitzgerald, his father had been a Corporal in the 43rd (Monmouthshire) Regiment of Foot (Light Infantry), who was discharged from the army on 24 July 1876 and died in Poplar, Middlesex, on 04 December 1883.

Daniel was admitted to the school on 26 March 1886 (Petition No. 9342), joining his older brother, William Docwra, who had been admitted on 10 April 1884 (Petition No. 9074). Daniel was discharged from the school on 11 January 1890, enlisting into The Gordon Highlanders. Three years after his discharge, Daniel's younger brother, John James Docwra, was admitted, on 27 January 1893 (Petition No. 10418).

Daniel was initially posted to the 2nd Battalion, but was then posted to Ceylon on 29 December 1890, joining the 1st Battalion on 25 January 1891. He was appointed as a Drummer on 04 January 1892. After almost two years in Ceylon, Daniel was then posted to India on 17 November 1892, remaining there for six years and taking part in the Chitral Relief Expedition in 1895, the Punjab frontier disturbances and the Tirah Campaign in 1897-98. He was posted to Egypt on 19 October 1898, although he was only there for two months before he was posted back to Britain on 09 December 1898.

Daniel was then posted to South Africa on 16 December 1899 during the Second Boer War, where he was awarded both the Queen's and King's South Africa medals with the clasps *Paardeberg*, *Driefontein*, *Johannesburg*, *Belfast* and *Cape Colony* for the former of the two medals. Daniel was posted back to Britain on 13 July 1902 and was discharged from the army at the end of his first period of service on 31 July 1902.

Following his discharge from the army, very little is known about Daniel, as he does not appear in the 1911 Census, although he had emigrated to Australia at some point prior to 1914, enlisting into the Australian Imperial Force on 08 October 1914.

Having enlisted, Daniel was posted to the 14th Battalion, Australian Infantry, which had been formed in Melbourne in September 1914 and where he was promoted to Sergeant on 16 January 1915, before being posted to The Dardanelles as a battle casualty replacement, arriving on 04 May 1915 and being promoted to Company Sergeant Major. Just over two weeks later, on 19 May 1915, Lance Corporal Albert Jacka was to win the battalion's only Victoria Cross[434].

Three months later, on 03 August 1915, he was evacuated to Alexandra, Egypt, and admitted to No. 1 General Hospital suffering from nephritis, although he was discharged to a convalescent camp on 31 August 1915 and returned to duty on 08 September 1915. Following his return to duty, Daniel was in trouble for the first time when he was tried by Field General Courts Martial on 21 October 1915. The offence that led to this is not recorded, but his sentence was a reduction in rank to Corporal, the rank that he held when he returned to Gallipoli, arriving there on 13 November 1915.

---

[434] *The London Gazette*, 23 July 1915, Supplement: 29240: *"For most conspicuous bravery on the night of the 19th–20th May, 1915 at "Courtney's Post", Gallipoli Peninsula. Lance-Corporal Jacka, while holding a portion of our trench with four other men, was heavily attacked. When all except himself were killed or wounded, the trench was rushed and occupied by seven Turks. Lance-Corporal Jacka at once most gallantly attacked them single-handed, and killed the whole party, five by rifle fire and two with the bayonet.*

Two weeks after his return, he was promoted to Sergeant after his predecessor had died of wounds and nine days later, on 04 December 1915, he was promoted to Temporary Company Sergeant Major when the previous incumbent was evacuated due to sickness, although Daniel reverted to Sergeant on 01 January 1916 when that Sergeant Major re-joined the battalion at Alexandria.

A month after returning to Egypt, Daniel was in trouble once more and was again Courts Martialled on 07 February 1916, this time for absenting himself on two occasions, one for a day and one for two days. He was again reduced to the rank of Corporal, although this was short-lived and he was promoted to Sergeant on 31 March 1916.

On 01 May 1916, Daniel was sent to the 4th Training Battalion for two days before returning to the 14th Battalion, although he was then admitted to hospital on 22 May 1916, again suffering from nephritis. He was discharged on 27 May 1916 and was with his battalion when it was posted to France, landing at Marseille on 08 June 1916. However, it appears that whilst he was in hospital, Daniel had again absented himself for two days and he was Courts Martialled for a third time, the sentence on this occasion being that he was reduced to the rank of Private.

Sadly, it appears that Daniel did not learn from this, as on the 26 July 1916 he faced a fourth Courts Martial, for being absent between 1830hrs on 18 July 1916 and 1830hrs on 19 July 1916, as well as being absent between 0900hrs on 20 July 1916 and 1730hrs on 24 July 1916. On this occasion his sentence was to forfeit a total of 35 days' pay.

A month later, the battalion saw its first major engagement in Europe when it was involved in the fighting around Pozières and it was during this fighting that Daniel was killed in action by a shell, when consolidating a position. Although there is a note in Daniel's service record stating that he was buried on the extreme left of Mouquet Farm, north-east of Albert, it appears that this burial was lost, as he has no known grave. He is also a "Lost Boy" whose name has been omitted from the memorial tablets in the school chapel.

William died on 22 March 1888 whilst still at the school, although the cause of death is not known. He is buried in Old Brompton Cemetery, London.

John was discharged from the school on 26 June 1897 and enlisted into The Loyal North Lancashire Regiment, serving for almost eleven months before he was discharged. He was then employed as a Hotel Servant, the employment recorded when he re-enlisted into the army on 26 September 1914, joining The Royal Scots (Lothian Regiment) and serving until he was medically discharged as a

Sergeant Drummer in May 1917. He emigrated to the United States in 1923, where he died in Worcester, Massachusetts, in 1938.

Albert Edgar WEBBER

Private, 7321, 15th Battalion Australian Infantry, Australian Imperial Force who died on 27 February 1918, aged 32. Buried in Outtersteene Communal Cemetery Extension, Bailleul, Nord, France

Born on 12 April 1885 in Exeter, Devonshire, the fourth of five children of Albert Martin Webber and Hannah Priscilla née Johns, his father had been a Serjeant Drummer in The Devonshire Regiment who died whilst serving in Exeter on 06 November 1887.

Albert was admitted to the school on 31 August 1894 (Petition No. 10636), joining his older brother, Conrad Webber, who had been admitted on 29 April 1892 (Petition No. 10327). Albert was discharged from the school on 15 April 1899, enlisting into The Princess Victoria's (Royal Irish Fusiliers), spending the first three years of his service in Britain. He was posted to South Africa on 17 December 1902 with the 1st Battalion and appointed as a Drummer on 01 March 1903. After just over two years there, he was posted to India on 11 February 1905 and appointed as a Lance Corporal ten months later, on 12 December.

Despite reverting to Private for misconduct on 02 August 1907, Albert was again appointed as a Lance Corporal on 26 September 1909, three months before he was posted back to Britain on 21 December, where he spent the last eighteen months of his British Army career before he was discharged at the end of his first period of service, on 14 April 1911.

A year after being discharged from the army, Albert married Isabella Spencer in Exeter and, shortly afterwards, he and his wife emigrated to Australia, settling in Brisbane, Queensland, although he did maintain his links to Britain by calling his house "Devonia". His daughter, Isabel Bessie Spencer Webber, was born in 1913 and his son, Edgar Martin Spencer Webber, was born in 1916.

Following the outbreak of war, Albert was working as a Stoker, but on 28 August 1916 he enlisted into the Australian Imperial Force, being posted to the 11th Depot Battalion on 22 September, and promoted to Corporal on 30 October. On 24 January 1917, Albert embarked on HMAT[435] *Ayrshire* at Sydney, New South Wales, and sailed for the war in Europe as a replacement for the 15th Battalion, arriving at Devonport in his home county on 12 April, reverting to Private the day before arriving, although he was a Lance Corporal

---

[435] His Majesty's Australian Transport

again two days later. He was posted to the 4th Training Battalion in Codford, Wiltshire, remaining there until embarking at Southampton, Hampshire, on 16 July and landing at Le Havre on 17 July 1917, joining the 15th Battalion on 29 September.

On the 26 February 1918 he was wounded by a shell as his unit made its way to the front line near the Belgian village of Hollebeke. It is believed he was a Lewis Gunner and received serious wounds to both legs near Potsdam Farm, dying as a result of these wounds the following day at No. 2 Casualty Clearing Station. He was buried in Outtersteene Communal Cemetery Extension on 09 March 1918, but he is another of the "Lost Boys" whose name has been omitted from the memorial tablets in the school chapel.

Conrad was returned to his uncle as unfit for army service on 14 September 1896. He emigrated to the United States and was recorded in the 1910 Census living in his mother-in-law's house in Whitefish Town, Flathead, Montana, employed as a Locomotive Fireman. He died in San Diego, California, in 1962.

Canadian Mounted Rifles

Harry George Thomas ANDREWS
Private, 1443, 5th Battalion, Canadian Mounted Rifles, Canadian Expeditionary Force who died on 08 November 1918, aged 19. Buried in Quievrain Communal Cemetery, Hainaut, Belgium

Born on 23 November 1898 in Dover, Kent, the eldest son of Harry Howell Andrews and Lilian Grace née Andrews, his father had been a Trumpeter in the Royal Garrison Artillery, who had been discharged from the army after 21 years' service on 26 November 1905, although he had then served as a Drummer on the Permanent Staff of 4th Battalion, The Royal Dublin Fusiliers. He was discharged as medically unfit on 09 September 1907 and died in Chartham village, Kent, on 18 May 1908.

Harry was admitted to the school the year after his father died and just before his 11th birthday, on 04 November 1909 (Petition No. 12677). He was discharged to *"Civil Life"* on 14 July 1913. A month after his discharge from the school, fourteen-year-old Harry boarded the SS *Teutonic* in Liverpool, Lancashire, travelling with the retiring Commandant of the school, Lieutenant Colonel A. H. Morris CMG DSO and sixteen-year-old James Arthur Frederick Skeggs. James was a fellow Dukie, who had been admitted to the school on 13 October 1905 (Petition No. 12154) and had also been discharged to *"Civil Life"* on the same day as Harry, having been a Monitor. They arrived in Quebec, Canada, on 13 August 1913, less than a year before the war commenced.

Following his arrival Harry worked as a Farmer, doing so until 1916, when he joined the Canadian Army, enlisting into the 150th Battalion, Canadian Infantry, on 21 September 1916. It is notable that when he enlisted, his year of birth is given as 1897, a year earlier than it actually was. It is likely that this was a deliberate act on his part, as by that stage of the war the Canadian authorities insisted that their soldiers were nineteen before they could serve overseas.

Harry arrived back in England on the SS *Lapland* on 10 October 1916 and spent the next eighteen months there, probably training, before embarking for France. On 01 March 1918 he was posted to the 10th Canadian Reserve Battalion, followed a month later by a transfer to the Quebec Regiment. However, it was not until 19 April that he landed in France and was posted to the 5th Battalion, Canadian Mounted Rifles, although he was to spend a further week in the Canadian Corps Reinforcement Camp, prior to joining his battalion in the field.

The 5th Mounted Rifles had been formed in Canada in 1915, arriving in England later that year and in 1916, it was converted to an infantry battalion, being attached to the 8th Canadian Infantry Brigade. It participated in the Battle of Amiens, the success of which was the precursor to the Last Hundred Days campaign of the First World War.

On 08 November 1918, just three days before the Armistice, elements of the 3rd Canadian Division, of which the 8th Canadian Infantry Brigade was a part, were involved in clearing the villages of Thivencelle and St. Aybert on the Franco-Belgian border. It is likely during one of these actions, that Harry was wounded, dying as a result of those wounds later that day.

Harry is buried in Quievrain Communal Cemetery, one of 35 Canadian soldiers buried there. Lieutenant Colonel Morris wrote to the school following Harry's death, telling them in his letter that James Skeggs had also enlisted into the Canadian Expeditionary Force and was still in France. James appears to have remained in Britain post-war, marrying in 1921 and he died in Blackpool, Lancashire, in 1963.

Canadian Infantry

Peter John FORD
Sergeant, 6915, 1st Battalion (Ontario Regiment), Canadian Expeditionary Force who died on 15 June 1915, aged 40. Commemorated on the Vimy Memorial, Pas de Calais, France

Born on 29 June 1874 in Buttevant, County Cork, the eldest of three children of John Ford and Ellen Jane née Sheehan, his father had been a Private in The Lancashire Fusiliers, who was discharged from the army on 20 July 1881 and died in Aldershot, Hampshire, on 22 August 1883.

Peter was admitted to the school on 09 July 1886 (Petition No. 9386) and was discharged on 28 July 1888, enlisting into The Dorsetshire Regiment. Four months after his discharge, Peter's younger brother, William Joseph Ford, was admitted to the school on 30 November 1888 (Petition No. 9726). Peter was posted to the 2nd Battalion and spent the first nine years of his service in Britain, before he was posted to Malta on 12 January 1897.

Two years after arriving in Malta, Peter was posted back to Britain on 03 February 1899, although nine months later he was posted to South Africa during the Second Boer War, on 24 November 1899, where he was awarded the Queen's South Africa medal. Peter was posted back to the Regimental Depot at The Keep, Dorchester, Dorsetshire, on 05 July 1901 and was discharged from the army three weeks later, on 27 July 1901.

Following his discharge from The Dorsetshire Regiment, Peter enlisted into the 4th Battalion, Royal Garrison Regiment, which was stationed in Malta. He was discharged from that regiment on 21 March 1905. Two years later, he emigrated to Canada, arriving at St. John, New Brunswick, on the SS *Lake Erie* in March 1907, his employment being given as Labourer. He is then recorded in the 1911 Census of Canada as living with his brother, sister-in-law, nieces and nephews, in Sarnia, Ontario, his employment given as Railway Fireman.

Following the outbreak of war, Peter enlisted into the Canadian Army on 22 September 1914, still living in Sarnia, but no longer with

William and his family, his employment being given as Locomotive Engineer. The battalion which Peter joined had been formed on 02 September 1914 and recruited from Western Ontario. It sailed to Britain on the SS *Laurentic*, arriving on 14 October 1914. It then deployed to France and participated in the Second Battle of Ypres.

On 27 June 1915, Peter was reported as wounded near Colonne, France, this report being updated on 23 August 1915 to wounded and missing. Finally, on 28 April 1916, he was officially presumed to have died on or after 15 June 1915. His body was never recovered and so he is commemorated on the Vimy Memorial. He is also another "Lost Boy" whose name has been omitted from the memorial tablets in the school chapel.

William was discharged from the school on 19 December 1891 and enlisted into The Dorsetshire Regiment like Peter. He served for almost fifteen years, during which he was part of the Occupation of Crete and served in South Africa during the Second Boer War, before he was discharged from the army on 15 May 1906.

Three months after leaving the army, William emigrated to Canada, his family joining him in June 1908. He was a Railway Fireman like his brother and following the outbreak of war, William enlisted into 149th Battalion, Canadian Infantry, in December 1915. He served in France with the Canadian Railway Troops, returning to Canada in May 1919 and died in Sarnia in 1939.

Thomas Dudley ROUSE

Private, 10617, 49th Battalion, Canadian Infantry, Canadian Expeditionary Force who died on 28 October 1917, aged 29. Buried in Oxford Road Cemetery, West-Vlaanderen, Belgium

Born on 21 April 1888 in Ipswich, Suffolk, the youngest of five children of James Rouse and Sarah Anne née Taylor, his father had been a Private in Prince Albert's (Somersetshire Light Infantry), who had been discharged from the army after 21 years' service on 09 March 1886 and died in St. Bartholomew's Hospital, London, on 25 May 1897.

Thomas was admitted to the school on 06 September 1898 (Petition No. 11107) and discharged on 17 July 1903, returning home as he was deemed unfit for army service. Despite this, on 02 November 1903, he joined the army, enlisting into his father's old regiment. He was to spend all of his service in Britain, appointed as a Bandsman on 28 September 1905. However, on 26 June 1907, Thomas was convicted by a civil court of theft and obtaining money under false pretences, and sentenced to one months' imprisonment for each offence, which were to run concurrently. As a result of being convicted of a felony, he reverted to Private on the day of his conviction and was discharged from the army on 11 July 1907.

Once he had been discharged from the army, it appears that Thomas made his living as a Musician, but he was not able to keep out of trouble. On 04 November 1909, he was convicted in Ipswich of stealing a bicycle and sentenced to one months' imprisonment. A year later, on 22 October 1910, he was sentenced to three months' imprisonment with hard labour for again stealing a bicycle and on 08 April 1911, he was bound over in the sum of £5 for obtaining by false pretences ten shillings from one lady with intent to defraud and for obtaining five shillings by false pretences from another lady, both offences being committed on 09 March 1911.

Following this last conviction, Thomas emigrated to Canada, arriving on 18 May 1911 and intending to live in Toronto and find work in farming, according to immigration records. However, following the outbreak of war, on 22 September 1914, Thomas enlisted into the Canadian Army in Valcartier, Quebec. He initially sailed to Europe with the 4th Battalion, Canadian Infantry, which, following a period of training in England, arrived on the Western Front on 11 February 1915. However, Thomas had deserted in Britain on 24 December 1914, before a Courts Martial was due to take place on 28 January 1915. He was subsequently transferred to the band of the 9th Battalion on 04 April 1915 and his military career was punctuated by frequent absences and deductions in pay, his service record noting a total of 42 days as a prisoner. He also served with the 202nd Battalion from 26 February 1917.

He was given permission to marry on 24 May 1916 in Shorncliffe, Kent, but his subsequent will, dated 03 May 1917, has his mother, who was still living in Ipswich, as his next of kin rather than a spouse, who remains unknown.

By October 1917, Thomas was serving with the 49th Battalion when he was killed during the Third Battle of Ypres on 28 October, one of three in the battalion recorded as killed on that date. He is another "Lost Boy" whose name has been omitted from the memorial tablets in the school chapel.

New Zealand Infantry

Percy Talbot FURNISH
Lance Corporal, 27740, New Zealand Rifle Brigade who died on 11 April 1921, aged 40. Buried in Rookwood Necropolis, Sydney, New South Wales, Australia.

Born on 31 May 1880 in Kirby Cane, Norfolk, the fourth of five children of James Furnish and Eleanor Tungate née Easter, his father was a Serjeant in The Buffs (East Kent Regiment) who died whilst serving in Canterbury, Kent, on 23 February 1884.

Percy was admitted to the school on 30 July 1891 (Petition No. 10176), which was three years after his older brother, Alfred Tungate Furnish, who had been admitted on 18 December 1885 (Petition No. 9302), had been discharged. Percy was discharged from the school on 02 June 1894 and enlisted into The Buffs (East Kent Regiment).

Percy was posted to the 2nd Battalion of the regiment, but served for less than two years, all of this service in Britain, before he was discharged on 29 February 1896, *"services no longer required"*, although there is no reason given for this in his service record. Four years later, Percy re-enlisted into the army, joining the Imperial Yeomanry and giving his occupation as Barman. Three months later, on 14 April 1900, he was posted to South Africa during the Second Boer War and was awarded the Queen's South Africa Medals with the clasps *Wittebergen, Transvaal, Cape Colony, South Africa 1901* and *South Africa 1902*. He was posted back to Britain on 01 August 1901 and discharged from the army for a second time on 07 August 1901.

Two months later, Percy again enlisted into the Imperial Yeomanry, this time giving his occupation as Horse Dealer, his service record stating that he was posted "abroad" on 19 October 1901, likely returning to South Africa, where he remained until 31 August 1902, prior to again being discharged from the army on 07 September 1902.

Following his discharge, Percy found himself in trouble with the law. On 03 March 1903, he was sentenced to three months' imprisonment for fraud, using the name Percy Talbot Watson and was again in trouble on 27 November 1903, when he was sentenced to fourteen days' imprisonment for begging. Eight days after completing this sentence, on 18 December 1903, he was again sentenced for begging, this time imprisoned for one month.

Percy managed to stay out of trouble for almost a year, but on 07 November 1904, he was sentenced to two consecutive three-month sentences for stealing a watch and a purse on two occasions, and a year later, on 10 October 1905, he was sentenced to 21 days' imprisonment for stealing money, using the name Joseph Furnish. His lengthiest sentence came the following year, when he was convicted of stealing a collecting box and the sum of fifteen shillings, as well as receiving collecting boxes knowing them to be stolen, for which he was sentenced to nine months with hard labour in Wormwood Scrubs.

Despite this sentence, it was reported in a newspaper[436] that he was again convicted of fraud for passing off a ring worth sixpence as 18-carat gold and selling it for one Guinea, for which, on 06 June 1907, he was sentenced to imprisonment for one month with hard labour. This seems to have been Percy's last brush with the law and in April 1908 he married Martha Ann Gertrude Grewcock, in South Stoneham, Hampshire. He was then recorded in the 1911 Census as living in Southampton, Hampshire, and employed as a Steward in the Merchant Navy.

Percy was still employed as a Steward when war broke out, as this was the occupation that he gave when he re-enlisted on 16 September 1914, this time joining the 4th (Royal Irish) Dragoon Guards, landing in France on 11 November 1914. At the end of January 1915, Percy was out riding and took a jump. It appears that he was thrown from the horse, which then stepped on his abdomen and although he felt no ill-effects, on 13 February 1915, he began vomiting, which resulted in his being admitted to the Canadian Stationary Hospital in Boulogne, with gastritis. He spent fifteen days being treated here, prior to being returned to Britain and admitted to The London Hospital, Whitechapel, spending a week there before he was admitted to Netley Hospital, Southampton, receiving a further eight weeks treatment there. As a result of this injury, Percy was discharged from the army as permanently unfit on 13 July 1915.

However, following his discharge, Percy travelled to New Zealand, possibly having returned to his employment as a Merchant Navy Steward. However, once there, he enlisted twice into the New Zealand Army, initially into the New Zealand Military Police on 09 February 1916, with his last employer given as the Shaw, Savill & Albion Steamship Company, before he was discharged at his own

---

[436] *Portsmouth Evening News*, 10 June 1907

request on 20 May 1916. He then re-enlisted in New Zealand for a second time on 13 June 1916.

Thirteen days later, Percy boarded a transport ship and was posted to Britain, arriving at Devonport, Devonshire, on 22 August 1916. Once back in Britain, Percy spent much of the next year in various hospitals with the complaint that had led to his medical discharge from the British Army and on 19 September 1917, it also led to his medical discharge from the New Zealand Army in London.

He was recorded as having left Southampton in February 1918 by ship, but it is not known when he arrived in Australia, only that he disembarked there. Records show he re-joined the Merchant Navy as an Assistant Steward and served on the SS *Tunisian* from November 1918 to April 1919, having taken 10 years off his stated age. Martha seems to have remained at their home in Southampton, but on 11 April 1921 he died in Sydney. It is likely that his cause of death was believed to have originated with the accident that had occurred whilst he was serving in France in 1915, as he is commemorated by the Commonwealth War Graves Commission. He is a "Lost Boy" whose name has been omitted from the memorial tablets in the school chapel.

Alfred was discharged from the school on 07 September 1888 and enlisted into The Buffs (East Kent Regiment). He was a Corporal serving in the 2nd Battalion when he died of enteric fever at Bloemfontein, South Africa, on 24 April 1900, during the Second Boer War. Unlike Percy, Alfred is commemorated in the school chapel, on the tablets commemorating the Old Boys who fell during that conflict.

South African Infantry

Francis WALTERS
Sergeant, 1681, 1st Regiment, South African Infantry who died on 14 July 1916, age 50. Commemorated on the Thiepval Memorial, Somme, France

Born on 22 April 1866 in Aberdeen, Aberdeenshire, the second of three sons of Francis Walters and Ann née Wood, his father was a Colour Serjeant in the 93rd (Sutherland Highlanders) Regiment of Foot[437]. His mother died in Aldershot, Hampshire, on 11 December 1872.

Francis was admitted to the school on 17 September 1875 (Petition No. 7905) and was discharged on 08 May 1880, enlisting into The Prince Consort's Own Rifle Brigade[438]. Francis's older brother, Lewis George Walters, had attended the Royal Hibernian Military School, as did his younger brother, Alexander Walters.

There is limited information available about Francis and his service record is no longer available, but it appears that he served for 12 years in the Rifle Brigade, during which time he served in India, and then emigrated to South Africa and served in the Cape Mounted Rifles, although it is not known whether he was still serving with this unit during the Second Boer War.

Again, little information is available for Francis after his time in the Cape Mounted Rifles, but it would appear that at the outbreak of the war, by which stage he would have been 48 years old, he enlisted into the South African Infantry. The South African infantry regiments had been raised from each of the four provinces of the Union of South Africa, with the 1st Regiment consisting of men who had been recruited from the Cape Province and for that reason it was also known as "The Cape Regiment".

In 1915, the 1st Regiment was sent to Egypt to deal with the Senussi Uprising[439] occurring in that country, but following success at the Battle of Agagia in February 1916, the 1st South African Infantry Brigade, of which the 1st Regiment was a part, was

---

[437] Amalgamated with the 91st (Princess Louise's Argyllshire Highlanders) Regiment of Foot on 01 July 1881 to become Princess Louise's (Sutherland and Argyll Highlanders)
[438] Renamed The Prince Consort's Own (Rifle Brigade) on 01 July 1881
[439] A rebellion by Bedouin tribesmen against the Allies in North Africa that had been encouraged by the Ottomans

transferred to the Western Front. The regiment's first combat experience in France was during the Somme Offensive, when the 1st South African Infantry Brigade, as part of the 9th (Scottish) Division, was engaged in the assault on the village of Longueval.

The attack commenced at dawn on the morning of 14 July 1916, with the South Africans in reserve, but by 0805hrs, the intensity of the fighting meant that the 1st Regiment was brought forward and the remaining three regiments of the brigade were ordered to take Delville Wood. Both engagements led to heavy casualties, including Francis on 14 July, with the battle for Delville Wood continuing until 3 September.

The South Africans held the wood until 19 July, with losses similar to the brigades involved in the initial assault on 01 July. The fact that the assault turned into such a slog is likely the reason that Francis has no known grave and is commemorated on the Thiepval Memorial.

Although not the oldest Dukie to die during the war and be commemorated by the Commonwealth War Graves Commission, he is the oldest to have been killed in action. He is also a "Lost Boy", his name having been omitted from the memorial tablets in the school chapel.

South African Native Labour Corps

John Elijah NICHOLS
Serjeant, X502, South African Native Labour Corps who died on 12 September 1918, aged 46. Commemorated on the Hollybrook Memorial, Southampton, Hampshire, United Kingdom

Born on 27 February 1872 in Warley, Essex, the eldest of six children of Samuel Nichols and Sarah née Long, his father had been a Serjeant in the 1st, or The Royal Scots Regiment, who was discharged from the army on 19 November 1878 and died in Bury St. Edmunds, Suffolk, on 24 June 1881. John's mother remarried, to Charles William Hawes, in Ipswich, Suffolk, in 1883 and he subsequently had four stepsiblings.

John was admitted to the school on 08 December 1882 (Petition No. 8871) and was discharged on 13 March 1886. The school records state that he enlisted into The Royal Scots (Lothian Regiment), but his service record is no longer available to confirm this.

It appears that he only completed his first period of service before leaving the British Army, as he appears in Second Boer War records as serving in French's Scouts, part of the South African Protectorate Regiment Field Force, these records acknowledging *"Previous service Scot Regt."*. These records also show that John served from 13 November 1901 until 12 January 1902, when he returned to Britain.

Following this service, nothing is known about John, and he does not seem to appear in the 1911 Census, although he may have been living in South Africa, as when he enlisted during the war his next of kin was given as his wife, Mary, who was living in Johannesburg. His only child, Cecil John Rhodes Nichols was born in 1909.

The South African Native Labour Corps, into which John enlisted on 23 June 1917, had been formed in June 1916 with the raising of a battalion of 1000 black South Africans who would be employed in France. Records show that John arrived in theatre on 25 July 1917 and served there until 19 May 1918, being possible that he was wounded and returned to Britain to recover.

In September 1918 he was on board HMT *Galway Castle*, which had left London, with a stop at Plymouth, Devonshire, and was heading to Natal, South Africa, with 400 South African walking wounded on board, as well as 346 passengers and 204 crew. Two days after the ship left Plymouth, at 0730hrs on 12 September 1918, the ship was torpedoed by the German submarine U-82. The torpedo broke the ship's back, and although the ship did not sink for three days, when Royal Navy destroyers arrived to take the survivors back to Plymouth, it was discovered that 143 of those on board, including John, had drowned.

John's body was not recovered, which is why he is commemorated on the Hollybrook Memorial. He is also another "Lost Boy" whose name has been omitted from the memorial tablets in the school chapel.

John's younger brother, Horace Albert Nichols, who was not a Dukie, also lost his life during the war. He was serving as a Private in the Army Service Corps when he died at Dieppe in June 1916.

Those Recorded in Error

During the course of our research into the boys from the school who are commemorated on the memorial tablets in the school chapel, not only were 88 errors found and 181 "Lost Boys" found who had been omitted, but four names were found to have been included, that should not have been on the memorial.

Their information is listed below.

Henry BARRETT MC
Captain, Royal Field Artillery

Born on 05 November 1874 in Hyderabad, India, the third of four children of Henry Barrett and Wilhelmina née Millar, his father had been a Battery Serjeant Major in the Royal Artillery, who was discharged from the army on 10 July 1883 and died five months later on 08 December 1883.

Henry was admitted to the school on 09 October 1885 (Petition No. 9270) and discharged on 01 June 1889, enlisting into the Royal Artillery. He spent three years in the Royal Artillery Depot in Aldershot, Hampshire, where he was appointed as a Trumpeter and was then posted to Woolwich, London, from where, after eight months, he was posted to 54 Battery, Royal Field Artillery, in India, spending the next eighteen years in this country. Henry was appointed as a Gunner on 31 January 1894, Acting Bombardier on 28 October 1895, Bombardier on 12 May 1898, Corporal on 12 July 1898 and Serjeant on 29 March 1900, all whilst remaining with the same battery, although being stationed in various places in India.

On 29 September 1900, Henry married Helena Gebbie in St. John's Church, Meerut, and their first child, Florence Williamina Barrett, was born five years later, in September 1905. Henry was then posted to 11 Battery, Royal Field Artillery, spending two years with this unit before being promoted to Battery Serjeant Major and posted to 38 Battery, Royal Field Artillery. His last posting in India was to 6 "B" Reserve Brigade, Royal Field Artillery, on 14 August 1910, two years after his second child, Charles Henry Barrett, had been born, and where he was promoted to Regimental Serjeant Major on 24 November 1914.

Henry returned to Britain in February 1915, having had two further children, George Edward Barrett and Ernest Barrett, and was posted to Edinburgh, Midlothian, before being Commissioned as a

611

Second Lieutenant[440]. He was then posted to 161 Brigade, Royal Field Artillery, the unit with which he was to spend the rest of his career, appointed as the Adjutant on 13 June 1915[441], before deploying to France on 21 October 1915, remaining in France and Belgium for the rest of the war and being gassed at one point in Nieuwpoort, Belgium.

Henry returned to Britain in mid-1919, possibly for the birth of his youngest child, Lillian Frances Margaret Barrett, but returned to 161 Brigade on 17 June 1919, two weeks after the award of a Military Cross had been Gazetted[442], before he was posted back to 6 "B" Reserve Brigade, Royal Field Artillery, in Edinburgh on 20 June 1919. He retired from the army on 04 September 1919, although he remained in the Reserve of Officers.

It appears that after the war, Henry and Helena settled in Charlton Adam in Somerset, the final document in his service record being a letter from Helena to the Officer-in-Charge, Reserve of Officers, Royal Field Artillery, informing them of Captain Henry Barrett MC's death.

Although commemorated on the memorial tablets in the school chapel, Henry has no Commonwealth War Graves Commission commemoration and died in 1923, outside the scope of First World War deaths[443], so it appears that he has been included incorrectly. The images of the school memorial tablets included in this book, show that Henry Barrett's name, along with the Towells brothers and the erroneously recorded W C T Knight, likely brother Albert, are in a darker engraving and have been added out of regimental order, at an unspecified date, but certainly post-1923 when Henry died and before 1935. The latter date was when the finest history of the school was published, by Old Boy Lewis Rudd[444], which includes a transcript of the names on the tablets, with those additions named above, plus "Lost Boy" Alfred Lunn and A H Gould, Yeomanry, likely the Dukie brother of "Lost Boy" Walter Herbert Gould. These additions may well be the earliest attempt to include some missing names and was followed up in the last decade with the addition of Joseph Hawtin and John May on a supplementary tablet.

Henry's son, Ernest, was also a Dukie and this could explain his later addition. He was admitted to the school on 09 January 1924

---

[440] *The London Gazette*, 11 June 1915, Supplement:29191
[441] *The London Gazette*, 5 November 1915, Issue:29353
[442] *The Edinburgh Gazette*, 5 June 1919, Issue:13453
[443] The Commonwealth War Graves Commission commemorated those who died between 04 August 1914 and 31 August 1921, the latter date being the official end of the war
[444] Rudd, L. (1935). *The Duke of York's Royal Military School 1801-1934: Its History, Aims and Associations*. Dover: G. W. Grigg and Son, St. George's Press

(Petition No. 14307) and discharged 21 December 1928, although nothing more is known about him after he left the school.

Henry Frederick Barber CARTER
Lance Corporal, 9961, 1st Battalion, The King's Royal Rifle Corps

Born on 27 February 1895 in Portsmouth, Hampshire, the eldest of four children of Henry Alfred Carter and Ada Beatrice née Eager, his father was a Gunner in the Royal Artillery, who died whilst serving in Ceylon on 24 December 1898.

Henry was admitted to the school on 06 May 1904 (Petition No. 11975) and was joined by his brother, William Alfred Harold Carter, on 14 March 1907 (Petition No. 12345). Henry was discharged from the school, having moved from Chelsea to Guston, on 24 January 1911 and enlisted into The King's Royal Rifle Corps, the census of that year showing that he was a Private in the 1st Battalion, stationed in New Barracks, Gosport, Hampshire.

At the outbreak of war, the battalion was stationed in Salamanca Barracks, Aldershot, Hampshire, leaving Southampton, Hampshire, on the SS *Honorius* on 12 August and landing at Rouen on 13 August 1914. After landing, the unit took part in the Battle of Mons and the subsequent retreat, The Battle of the Marne, The Battle of the Aisne and the First Battle of Ypres, during which "B", "C" and "D" Companies were surrounded and overwhelmed, losing a total of 1,027 men killed, wounded or missing in just six weeks.

It is likely that Henry was one of those reported as missing during this period. In the Registers of Soldiers' Effects[445], he is reported to have died as a Prisoner of War in Güstrow, Germany, on 20 January 1915. However, this entry is later annotated, sadly undated, with the words "Man alive, Prisoner of War".

Despite the fact that Henry is commemorated on the memorial tablets in the school chapel, he actually survived captivity and was released following the Armistice. He is therefore included on the memorial in error.

In 1919 he married Sylvia May Smith, although it appears that he may have been widowed or divorced, as when he died on 11 February 1934 in Portsmouth, his spouse's first names are recorded as Evangeline Grace, although no marriage record for them can be found.

---

[445] UK, Army Registers of Soldiers' Effects, 1901-1929, 1914-1915, Winchester, 176501-178000

William was discharged from the school to the Army Ordnance Corps on 08 April 1910 and survived the war, also dying in Portsmouth, Hampshire, in 1934.

J CHILTON
Princess Louise's (Sutherland and Argyll Highlanders)

On the memorial tablets in the school chapel, there is a J Chilton, Argyll and Sutherland Highlanders, that has been added in error. The school records show that there has only ever been one John Chilton who attended the school. He was admitted in 1899 and discharged to the Seaforth Highlanders (Ross-shire Buffs, The Duke of Albany's) in 1904. He did serve during the war, being awarded a Military Medal following his death on 01 July 1916, the first day of the Somme Offensive. He is documented earlier in this book and is recorded on the memorial tablets in the school chapel with the correct regiment, the Seaforth Highlanders, but with his initial as W.

The Argyll and Sutherland Highlanders records only one Chilton having been killed during the war whilst serving with the regiment, Lieutenant Frank Chilton. He was born in New Zealand, was not the son of a soldier and did not travel to Britain until 1912, when he came to study medicine at Edinburgh University, so could not have been a Dukie. For these reasons, the assumption has been made that the name engraved on the memorial tablets is a duplication of fallen Dukie John Chilton MM, but with the incorrect regiment recorded.

W M COLLINS
Royal Field Artillery

Among those commemorated on the memorial tablets in the school chapel is W M Collins, Royal Field Artillery. The Petition Documents held by the school have been reviewed and there had never been anyone with this name who had been a Dukie. There was also no Royal Field Artillery casualty from the First World War with this name and initials.

A fallen serviceman named William Henry Collins of the Royal Field Artillery, had attended the Royal Hibernian Military School in Dublin and died of wounds in December 1915, the conclusion that has been made is that he had been incorrectly recorded on the memorial of the Duke of York's as W M Collins. He is correctly included on the war memorial of his own school and other instances of Hibs and Dukies being incorrectly claimed have been found in the respective school magazines, although this is the only incidence on either war memorial.

Burial & Memorial Locations

Australia

Rookwood Necropolis, Sydney, New South Wales

P T Furnish	New Zealand Rifle Brigade	Grave C.E. 10. 3931. (GRM/2*)

Belgium

Calvaire (Essex) Military Cemetery, Hainaut

J L Soughan	The Essex Regiment	Grave I. B. 11

Hautrage Military Cemetery, Hainaut

J S Ellard	Norfolk Regiment	Grave II. A. 8

Ploegsteert Memorial, Hainaut

E W Roake	4th Dragoon Guards	Panel 1
F C Spiers	Somerset Light Infantry	Panel 3
J W Kaveney	East Yorkshire Regiment	Panel 4
J W Lewis	Hampshire Regiment	Panel 6
G A Hayman	Northamptonshire Regiment	Panel 7
B Knight	Royal Berkshire Regiment	Panel 7 and 8
W Smith	Durham Light Infantry	Panel 8 and 9

Quievrain Communal Cemetery, Hainaut

H G T Andrews	Canadian Mounted Rifles	Grave A. 30

Ration Farm (La Plus Douve) Annexe, Hainaut

H J Allen	Middlesex Regiment	Grave II. A. 17

Strand Military Cemetery, Hainaut

W Muddle	Lancashire Fusiliers	Grave VIII. A. 7

Tancrez Farm Cemetery, Hainaut

W F Bond	Lancashire Fusiliers	Grave I. D. 14

Abeele Aerodrome Military Cemetery, West-Vlaanderen

G T Wilson	The Buffs	Grave II. C. 10

Bard Cottage Cemetery, West-Vlaanderen

E J Andrews	Welsh Regiment	Grave III. G. 26

Cement House Cemetery, West-Vlaanderen

H B Grayham	Machine Gun Corps	Grave IV. D. 29
F S Peoples	Welsh Regiment	Grave II. A. 13

Hop Store Cemetery, West-Vlaanderen

C J Corbin	Royal Garrison Artillery	Plot I. Row A. Grave 36
A R Towells	Royal Field Artillery	Plot I. Row B. Grave 46

Kemmel Chateau Military Cemetery, West-Vlaanderen

A J Carne	Royal Garrison Artillery	Grave M. 31
A T James	Royal Field Artillery	Grave O. 17
W R McCarragher	Wiltshire Regiment	Grave A. 32

Ledeghem Military Cemetery, West-Vlaanderen

J R N Pope	Queen's (Royal West Surrey Regiment)	Grave B. 21

Lijssenthoek Military Cemetery, West-Vlaanderen

H T Bunnett	Argyll and Sutherland Highlanders	Grave II. D. 10A
A H King	Royal Field Artillery	Grave XIV. B. 4A
J C Vickers	Royal Army Medical Corps	Grave XIV. E. 5

Messines Ridge British Cemetery, West-Vlaanderen

H B Edney	South Staffordshire Regiment	Grave V. C. 4

Nine Elms British Cemetery, West-Vlaanderen

G W Marshall	Hampshire Regiment	Grave X. C. 3

Oxford Road Cemetery, West-Vlaanderen

T D Rouse	Canadian Infantry	Grave I. H. 13

Pond Farm Cemetery, West-Vlaanderen

J T Toohey	Royal Irish Regiment	Grave H.4

Poperinghe Communal Cemetery, West-Vlaanderen

A B B Smith	Army Service Corps	Grave II. A. 8

Poperinghe New Military Cemetery, West-Vlaanderen

H R Summers	The Buffs	Grave I. B. 27
F J A Crowe	Royal Army Medical Corps	Grave I. G. 31

Poperinghe Old Military Cemetery, West-Vlaanderen

H A Millar	Leinster Regiment	Grave II. N. 18

R.E. Farm Cemetery, West-Vlaanderen

G S Matthews	London Regiment	Grave IV. C. 1

Spoilbank Cemetery, West-Vlaanderen

J E Maddocks	Royal Garrison Artillery	Special Memorial A. 4

Tyne Cot Memorial, West-Vlaanderen

P Potter	Royal Field Artillery	Panel 4 to 6
G P Langdon	Royal Fusiliers	Panel 28 to 30
H L W Freeman	Lincolnshire Regiment	Panel 72 to 75
J C Case	Gloucestershire Regiment	Panel 79 to 80
C F A West	East Surrey Regiment	Panel 106 to 108
R G G Falkner	Queen's Own (Royal West Kent Regiment)	Panel 115 to 119
A V Somerset	King's Royal Rifle Corps	Panel 120 to 124
B C L Joyce	Manchester Regiment	Panel 128 to 131
R D Douglas	Durham Light Infantry	Panel 133 to 140
W A B Clark	Royal Irish Rifles	Panel 133 to 140
A Knight	Royal Irish Fusiliers	Panel 141 to 143
G A Axon	Argyll and Sutherland Highlanders	Panel 141 to 143

Vlamertinghe New Military Cemetery, West-Vlaanderen

R Gwyther	Royal Garrison Artillery	Grave V. E. 31

Voormezeele Enclosure No.3, West-Vlaanderen

G A Hooker	King's Royal Rifle Corps	Grave II. B. 22

Westoutre British Cemetery, West-Vlaanderen

R B P Johnson	Royal Garrison Artillery	Grave O. 2

Ypres (Menin Gate) Memorial, West-Vlaanderen

A H W G C Scott	Royal Horse Guards	Panel 5
F D Maxted	5th Lancers	Panel 5
H W Kenney	19th Hussars	Panel 5 and 9
H McNally	Royal Field Artillery	Panel 5 and 9
R W D Winter	Northumberland Fusiliers	Panel 6 and 8
J D Lake	Queen's (Royal West Surrey Regiment)	Panel 8 and 12
R R Patterson	Royal Field Artillery	Panel 9
A Belcher	Royal Garrison Artillery	Panel 9
A Barber	Royal Engineers	Panel 11
P Pitman	Irish Guards	Panel 11 - 13 and 14
A V Hungerford	Queen's (Royal West Surrey Regiment)	Panel 11 - 13 and 14
E Jepson	King's Own (Royal Lancaster Regiment)	Panel 12
W H Grant	Cheshire Regiment	Panel 19 - 22
H W King	Royal Fusiliers	Panel 21

W E Baldwin	Lincolnshire Regiment	Panel 21
N J Batters	Devonshire Regiment	Panel 21
R Dean (served as R Scarr)	Suffolk Regiment	Panel 21
J H Ellis	Devonshire Regiment	Panel 21 and 31
J E Wood	East Yorkshire Regiment	Panel 22 and 34
T G Golding	Gloucestershire Regiment	Panel 34
C E Jelley	Worcestershire Regiment	Panel 35
H G Marquiss	Hampshire Regiment	Panel 37
G E Johnston	Welsh Regiment	Panel 37 and 39
H H Adshead	King's Royal Rifle Corps	Panel 38
W Anderson	Highland Light Infantry	Panel 38
R W Elder	Gordon Highlanders	Panel 38
W Milne	Gordon Highlanders	Panel 38
A D Ramsay	Gordon Highlanders	Panel 38 and 40
H Neynoe	Sherwood Foresters	Panel 45
A H Main	Royal Berkshire Regiment	Panel 51 and 53
W J Prosser	Queen's Own Cameron Highlanders	Panel 52
E G Gavin	London Regiment	Panel 52
J J Pegram	Oxfordshire and Buckinghamshire Light Infantry	Addenda Panel 60

Egypt

Alexandria (Chatby) Military and War Memorial Cemetery

H G A Rawlinson	Royal Irish Rifles	Grave K. 4
E Rust	Royal Horse Artillery	Grave M. 137

Alexandria (Hadra) War Memorial Cemetery

F McVicar	Army Service Corps	Grave E. 27

Ismailia War Memorial Cemetery

J C Bullen	20th Hussars	Grave C. 45

Kantara War Memorial Cemetery

A R Matthews	2nd Light Horse Regiment	Grave F. 145

France

Bellicourt British Cemetery, Aisne

P W A Haviland	2nd Dragoons	Grave VII. G. 5

Etreux British Cemetery, Aisne

G E Roberts	Royal Munster Fusiliers	Grave I. 10

Joncourt British Cemetery, Aisne

A J Humphries	South Wales Borderers	Grave B. 20

Soissons Memorial, Aisne

B T Smith	Devonshire Regiment
S W Lennon	Northamptonshire Regiment

Vailly British Cemetery, Aisne

I James	Royal Field Artillery	Grave II. B. 17

Maintenon Communal Cemetery, Eure-et-Loire

W R Hope	Royal Field Artillery	Military Row South boundary

St. Nazaire (Toutes-Aides) Cemetery, Loire-Atlantique

A A Taylor	East Surrey Regiment	Grave B. 28

Bailleul Communal Cemetery Extension, Nord

F G Clarke	Dorsetshire Regiment	Grave I. D. 23
W T Vause	Middlesex Regiment	Grave II. C. 106
J W Forrest	Worcestershire Regiment	Grave III. C. 137

Cambrai Memorial, Louverval, Nord

C M Matheson	Tank Corps	Panel 13

Caudry British Cemetery, Nord

P Hyde	Gordon Highlanders

Chapelle-d'Armentieres New Military Cemetery, Nord

F A J Green	Middlesex Regiment	Grave F.3

Cross Roads Cemetery, Fontaine-Au-Bois, Nord

A Babbington	Wiltshire Regiment	Grave II. B. 8
W E Fox	Gloucestershire Regiment	Grave II. C. 14

Écuélin Churchyard, Nord

G Cochrane	Queen's (Royal West Surrey Regiment	In South-East part

Ferme Buterne Military Cemetery, Houplines, Nord

A J Rutledge	North Staffordshire Regiment	Grave C. 11

Maroilles Communal Cemetery, Nord

W Brindle	Royal Berkshire Regiment

Merville Communal Cemetery, Nord
L C F Cross   Royal Field Artillery   Grave V. B. 21

Meteren Military Cemetery, Nord
C Amos   Army Service Corps   Grave IV. F. 716

Outtersteene Communal Cemetery Extension, Bailleul, Nord
A E Webber   Australian Infantry   Grave II. A. 30

Phalempin Communal Cemetery, Nord
J J Coughlan   The Buffs   Grave D. 2

Valenciennes (St. Roch) Communal Cemetery, Nord
C H Hargrove   16th Lancers   Grave I. C. 21
C Crissall   Cambridgeshire Regiment   Grave V. F. 6

Villers Hill British Cemetery, Villers-Guislain, Nord
W H Strohm   Lincolnshire Regiment   Grave V. A. 10

White City Cemetery, Bois-Grenier, Nord
F H Way   Royal Berkshire Regiment   Grave C. 3

Verberie French National Cemetery, Oise
E R Bates   2nd Dragoon Guards

Aire Communal Cemetery, Pas de Calais
N W Fielding   Royal Horse Artillery   Grave IV. E. 24

Arras Flying Services Memorial, Pas de Calais
J C McNamara   Royal Flying Corps

Arras Memorial, Pas de Calais
A W Ganley   Royal Garrison Artillery   Bay 2
A Carter   Queen's (Royal West Surrey Regiment)   Bay 3
J A Yorke   King's (Liverpool Regiment)   Bay 3
S C Larkin   East Yorkshire Regiment   Bay 4 and 5
F C Ellery   Royal Fusiliers   Bay 5
E R Humphrey   Lancashire Fusiliers   Bay 6
E B Tristram   Dorsetshire Regiment   Bay 6
A E Moffatt   Dorsetshire Regiment   Bay 7
C J Peat   Manchester Regiment   Bay 9
H E Hardwick   Royal Irish Fusiliers   Bay 9
A R R Robertson   Argyll and Sutherland Highlanders   Bay 9
V H Waterfield   Argyll and Sutherland Highlanders   Bay 10
E T Wall   London Regiment   Bay 10

Arras Road Cemetery, Roclincourt, Pas de Calais

F R Routley	Queen's (Royal West Surrey Regiment	Grave III. C. 14

Bethune Town Cemetery, Pas de Calais

H J Hayes	Welsh Regiment	Grave III. B. 62

Bleue-Maison Military Cemetery, Eperlecques, Pas de Calais

J W Maycock	Royal Engineers	Grave A. 4

Boulogne Eastern Cemetery, Pas de Calais

M H Scarff	Royal Engineers	Grave IV. D. 32
J Murphy	Rifle Brigade	Grave VIII. C. 77
A E Freeborn	Royal Garrison Artillery	Grave VIII. D. 139

Brown's Copse Cemetery, Roeux, Pas de Calais

A V Harber	Seaforth Highlanders	Grave III. F. 27
A C Vile	Essex Regiment	Grave IV. A. 5
T R D Cotcher	Argyll and Sutherland Highlanders	Grave VII. G. 32

Brown's Road Military Cemetery, Festubert, Pas de Calais

E W Church	Duke of Wellington's (West Riding Regiment)	Grave V. D. 10
S Merritt	Gloucestershire Regiment	Grave V. G. 10

Bucquoy Road Cemetery, Ficheux, Pas de Calais

H Gratton	Coldstream Guards	Grave VI. E. 3

Bully-Grenay Communal Cemetery, British Extension, Pas de Calais

W L Donelan	The Buffs	Grave I. D. 15

Cabaret-Rouge British Cemetery, Souchez, Pas de Calais

T J Barclay	West Yorkshire Regiment	Grave XXIII. AA. 14
D Pitman	13th Hussars	Grave XXVIII. C. 5

Cambrin Churchyard Extension, Pas de Calais

W J Lewis	Wiltshire Regiment	Grave G. 46

Canadian Cemetery No. 2, Neuville-St. Vaast, Pas de Calais

A A White	Lincolnshire Regiment	Grave 3. B. 6

Croisilles British Cemetery, Pas de Calais

H H Elwick	Coldstream Guards	Grave III. C. 6

Duisans British Cemetery, Etrun, Pas de Calais

J W Gibbon	Gordon Highlanders	Grave IV. C. 3

Etaples Military Cemetery, Pas de Calais

W C Critcher (as C W Critcher)	Oxfordshire and Buckinghamshire Light Infantry	Grave IV. D. 12A

Faubourg d'Amiens Cemetery, Pas de Calais

H Booth	West Yorkshire Regiment	Grave IV. F. 23
G E Funnell	Royal Garrison Artillery	Grave VII. D. 16

Gosnay Communal Cemetery, Pas de Calais

G P Darcey	Loyal North Lancashire Regiment	Grave 11

Guards Cemetery, Windy Corner, Cuinchy, Pas de Calais

A C Rees	Royal Engineers	Grave I. G. 4

Lapugnoy Military Cemetery, Pas de Calais

W J Burtenshaw	Royal Flying Corps	Grave IV. F. 4

Lebucquiere Communal Cemetery Extension, Pas de Calais

F T Frith	Royal Field Artillery	Grave I. F. 9

Le Touret Memorial, Pas de Calais

A W Porter	Royal Engineers	Panel 6
S D W Cooper	The Royal Fusiliers	Panel 6 to 8
S J Yates	King's (Liverpool Regiment)	Panel 8
J E D Caney	Bedfordshire Regiment	Panel 10 and 11
W H P Toomey	Lincolnshire Regiment	Panel 11
R F Ferguson	Leicestershire Regiment	Panel 12
R Webb	Yorkshire Regiment	Panel 17
A F Merriott	Gloucestershire Regiment	Panel 22 and 23
J W M Cross	Dorsetshire Regiment	Panel 22 and 23
T E Pett	South Lancashire Regiment	Panel 28 to 30
H E C Kendall	Northamptonshire Regiment	Panel 30 and 31
E P Ryan	Queen's Own (Royal West Kent Regiment)	Panel 32 and 33
W R King	King's Royal Rifle Corps	Panel 37 and 38
J B Ryan	Highland Light Infantry	Panel 47
H J Horner	Army Ordnance Corps	Panel 47

Le Touret Military Cemetery, Richebourg-L'avoue, Pas de Calais

C Meldrum	The Black Watch	Grave II. E. 4

Le Vertannoy British Cemetery, Hinges, Pas de Calais

J F Wood	Rifle Brigade	Grave A. 16

Les Baraques Military Cemetery, Sangatte, Pas de Calais

T A Coleman	Suffolk Regiment	Grave IV. C. IIA
C F Bartholomew	2nd Dragoon Guards	Grave VIII. C. 2A

Loos Memorial, Pas de Calais

H J Seymour	The Buffs	Panel 15 to 19
J F C Kifford	Leicestershire Regiment	Panel 42 to 44
A J R McKay	The Cameronians	Panel 57 to 59
W K Ryan	Royal Berkshire Regiment	Panel 93 to 95

Maroeuil British Cemetery, Pas de Calais

C J Robertson	Black Watch	Grave III. M. 14

Mindel Trench British Cemetery, St. Laurent-Blangy, Pas de Calais

W Chudley	Argyll and Sutherland Highlanders	Grave B. 26

Mory Abbey Military Cemetery, Mory, Pas de Calais

E Towells	Royal Horse Artillery	Grave IV. E. 13

Neuville-Bourjonval British Cemetery, Pas de Calais

H Ollerton	Machine Gun Corps	Grave B. 35

Noeux-Les-Mines Communal Cemetery, Pas de Calais

C J White	Royal Horse Artillery	Grave I. F. 20

Pernes British Cemetery, Pas de Calais

A W Trickey (served as A W Merrin)	King's Royal Rifle Corps	Grave II. A. 16
H A F Eade	Hampshire Regiment	Grave II. B. 20

Philosophe British Cemetery, Mazingarbe, Pas de Calais

A T Donnelly	East Surrey Regiment	Grave I. L. 29

Sailly-Sur-La-Lys Canadian Cemetery, Pas de Calais

J C Atkey	Royal Engineers	Grave II. B. 36

St. Mary's A.D.S. Cemetery, Haisnes, Pas de Calais

A T Cleare	Royal Sussex Regiment	

Terlincthun British Cemetery, Wimille, Pas de Calais

J L C Hirst	Royal Field Artillery	Grave IV. D. 38
G Webb	2nd Dragoons	Grave XV. F. 12

Tilloy British Cemetery, Tilloy-Les-Mofflaines, Pas de Calais

C H Pollard	Royal Garrison Artillery	Grave I. J. 17

Vimy Communal Cemetery, Farbus, Pas de Calais

J C Turner	Royal Field Artillery	Grave A. 11

Vimy Memorial, Pas de Calais

P J Ford	Canadian Infantry

Vis-En-Artois Memorial, Pas de Calais

S C Walker	Royal Scots Fusiliers	Panel 6
W A Avis	London Regiment	Panel 10

Wimereux Communal Cemetery, Pas de Calais

E Elliott	3rd Hussars	Grave I. A. 12
E W Cathcart	Dorsetshire Regiment	Grave I. E. 27

La Ferte-Sous-Jouarre Memorial, Seine-et-Marne

T Angell	Royal Fusiliers
H Kenny	King's (Liverpool Regiment)
L C Hill	Suffolk Regiment
S G Saunders	Duke of Cornwall's Light Infantry
A G Rattray	Argyll and Sutherland Highlanders
W A Rowe	Queen's Own Cameron Highlanders
J G Taylor	Queen's Own Cameron Highlanders

Bois-Guillaume Communal Cemetery, Seine-Maritime

C W Curling	Royal Field Artillery	Grave I. B. 16A

Bois-Guillaume Communal Cemetery Extension, Seine-Maritime

T W O'Hara	Norfolk Regiment	Grave G. 23A

Etretat Churchyard Extension, Seine-Maritime

W J Curtis	Royal Engineers	Grave II. E. 2

St. Sever Cemetery, Rouen, Seine-Maritime

H H Toomey	Middlesex Regiment	Grave A. 7. 26
W B Latham	Hampshire Regiment	Grave A. 12. 36

St. Sever Cemetery Extension, Rouen, Seine-Maritime

A W Payne	Welsh Regiment	Grave B. 22. 74
W M Rutledge	Northumberland Fusiliers	Grave S. II. I. 3
C H Blundell	South Lancashire Regiment	Grave O. V. I. 2
J L H Falkner	Queen's Own (Royal West Kent Regiment)	Grave Q. IV. J. 4

Acheux British Cemetery, Somme

G W Howell	Royal Welsh Fusiliers	Plot 1. Row E. Grave 14

A.I.F. Burial Ground, Flers, Somme

T J Briggs	Royal Engineers	Grave IV. A. 9

Bazentin-Le-Petit Military Cemetery, Somme

A W Laurie	Royal Garrison Artillery	Grave E. 15

Becourt Military Cemetery, Becordel-Becourt, Somme

S G Merritt	Royal Sussex Regiment	Grave II. A. 17

Bray Military Cemetery, Somme

J J Waring	Royal Warwickshire Regiment	Grave II. D. 49
W F Frost	Cameronians (Scottish Rifles)	Grave II. F. 20

Caterpillar Valley Cemetery, Longueval, Somme

B J Gray	Gloucestershire Regiment	Grave XII. G. 17

Combles Communal Cemetery Extension, Somme

T M Croft	Queen's Own (Royal West Kent Regiment)	Grave VII. F. 23

Contalmaison Chateau Cemetery, Somme

E J C H Bromwich	Northamptonshire Regiment	Grave II. E. 9

Delville Wood Cemetery, Longueval, Somme

A G Booth	Royal Welsh Fusiliers	Grave XXII. N. 9

Gordon Dump Cemetery, Ovillers-La Boiselle, Somme

J T Nokes	Lincolnshire Regiment	Grave IV. P. 4

Guards' Cemetery, Lesboeufs, Somme

D Hurley	Royal Field Artillery	Grave VIII. O. 8
R F Williams	Seaforth Highlanders	Grave XII. M. 6

Heilly Station Cemetery, Méricourt-L'Abbé, Somme

S H Bishop	The Black Watch	Grave III. F. 40

Mericourt-l'Abbe Communal Cemetery Extension

J E Smith	Royal Berkshire Regiment	Grave III. H. 18

Mezieres Communal Cemetery Extension, Somme

R E Sladden	17th Lancers	Grave A. 15

Millencourt Communal Cemetery Extension, Somme

E G Massie	Dorsetshire Regiment	Grave C. 45
W J Kearney	King's (Liverpool Regiment)	Grave F. 68

Ovillers Military Cemetery, Somme

W F J Carr	Devonshire Regiment	Grave VIII. I. 4

Peronne Communal Cemetery Extension, Somme

T E Cherry	Royal Field Artillery	Grave I. B. 39

Pozieres Memorial, Somme

T J Fuller	3rd Hussars	Panel 3
S E Bennett	9th Lancers	Panel 4
A G Cheshire	15th Hussars	Panel 4 and 5
A J Luton	16th Lancers	Panel 5
R M Hume	Royal Horse Artillery	Panel 7 to 10
W B Dicks	Bedfordshire Regiment	Panel 28 and 29
F Adcock	Royal Inniskilling Fusiliers	Panel 38 to 40
P Hawkins	Oxfordshire and Buckinghamshire Light Infantry	Panel 50 and 51
L W Monger	Durham Light Infantry	Panel 68 to 72
T M Ryan	Royal Garrison Artillery	Panel 98 (Addenda)

Rocquigny-Equancourt Road British Cemetery, Manancourt, Somme

H C Watsham	20th Hussars	Grave VI. C. 13

Serre Road Cemetery No. 2, Somme

J Chilton	Seaforth Highlanders	Grave XXX. J. 11
J A Hume	Seaforth Highlanders	Grave I. D. 33

Sucrerie Military Cemetery, Colincamps, Somme

C S Sinclair	Royal Field Artillery	Grave I. C. 5
W R Barrett	Seaforth Highlanders	Grave I. H. 26

Thiepval Memorial, Somme

R A Grizzell	1st (Royal) Dragoons	Pier and Face 1 A
R J S Crowe	Royal Field Artillery	Pier and Face 1 A and 8 A
F E C Hall	Suffolk Regiment	Pier and Face 1 C and 2 A
G Carter	Bedfordshire Regiment	Pier and Face 2 C
J R Christie	Royal Irish Regiment	Pier and Face 3 A
F W H Blane	South Wales Borderers	Pier and Face 4 A
F Walters	South African Infantry	Pier and Face 4 C
J Melville	Royal Inniskilling Fusiliers	Pier and Face 4 D and 5 B

C G Pearce	Duke of Cornwall's Light Infantry	Pier and Face 6 B
J W Robinson	East Surrey Regiment	Pier and Face 6 B and 6 C
A Peet	Royal Fusiliers	Pier and Face 8 C 9 A and 16 A
G T Maycock	Royal Warwickshire Regiment	Pier and Face 9 A 9 B and 10 B
A H Nichols	London Regiment	Pier and Face 9 D
W J Werry	London Regiment	Pier and Face 9 D 9 C 13 C and 12 C
T Ennis	Sherwood Foresters	Pier and Face 10 C 10 D and 11 A
W J Tipper	Essex Regiment	Pier and Face 10 D
E J Wise	Essex Regiment	Pier and Face 10 D
S W Hallett	Middlesex Regiment	Pier and Face 12 D and 13 B
J Hawtin	Gordon Highlanders	Pier and Face 15 B and 15 C
G Counter	Argyll and Sutherland Highlanders	Pier and Face 15 A and 16 C
C W Thomas	Argyll and Sutherland Highlanders	Pier and Face 15 A and 16 C
H S Booth	York and Lancaster Regiment	Addenda Panel, Pier and Face 4 C

Tincourt New British Cemetery, Somme

C H Walker	Seaforth Highlanders	Grave V. A. 7

Villers-Bretonneux Memorial, Somme

B Booth	Australian Infantry	
D E Docwra	Australian Infantry	

Gibraltar

Gibraltar (North Front) Cemetery

L J Rickwood	Corps of Army Schoolmasters	Grave B. 4296
J E E Parker	Royal Garrison Artillery	Grave B. 4786
W A McKenzie	Royal Garrison Artillery	Grave D. 4117

Germany

Cologne Southern Cemetery, Nordrhein-Westfalen

R Scott	Durham Light Infantry	Grave VIII. F. 15
J Sparks	East Surrey Regiment	Grave XII. B. 25
M Joyce	London Regiment	Grave XVII. A. 43

Greece

Doiran Military Cemetery

W E Whall	Somerset Light Infantry	Grave II. B. 33

Mikra British Cemetery, Kalamaria

C L Palmer	Welsh Regiment	Grave 537

Salonika (Lembet Road) Military Cemetery

F W Corry	Connaught Rangers	

Sarigol Military Cemetery, Kriston

H E Pack	King's Own (Royal Lancaster Regiment)	Grave C. 441

India

Delhi Memorial (India Gate)

W G Newland	Royal Garrison Artillery	Face 1
E P Sadler	Royal Garrison Artillery	Face 1

Jhansi Cantonment Cemetery

A J Thurston	South Wales Borderers	Plot I. Grave 539

Jutogh New Cemetery

F Cooney	3rd (Prince of Wales's) Dragoon Guards	Grave 122

Meerut Cantonment Cemetery

A E Stone	Royal Horse Artillery	Plot 6. Grave 53

Israel and Palestine

Jerusalem War Cemetery

J V Nicholson	Berkshire Yeomanry	Grave D. 21

Iraq

Amara War Cemetery

J Findlay	Highland Light Infantry	Grave IV. E. 16

Baghdad (North Gate) War Cemetery

B R Hungerford	Norfolk Regiment	Angora Memorial 93
W G Cowley	Royal Field Artillery	Islahie Memorial 199
A E Anderson	Machine Gun Corps	Grave XI. G. 14
E N Monger (served as B Stuart)	Royal Field Artillery	Grave XIX. K. 16
J W Butts	Royal Field Artillery	Grave XXI. B. 21
J H Brighty	Norfolk Regiment	Grave XXI. J. 33

W S Reynolds	Norfolk Regiment	Grave XXI. T. 13
A L Ragin	Royal Garrison Artillery	Grave XXI. T. 14

Basra Memorial

F M Wren	13th Hussars	Panel 1
H G Smith	Royal Horse Artillery	Panel 3 and 60
F J Hodgkins	Royal Field Artillery	Panel 3 and 60
J E Williams	Royal Field Artillery	Panel 3 and 60
S Brightmore	East Lancashire Regiment	Panel 19
F M Usher	Seaforth Highlanders	Panel 37 and 64

Basra War Cemetery

F M Graydon	Royal Engineers	Grave II. K. 9
F T Harnett	Dorsetshire Regiment	Grave III. G. 18/23
W R James	Dorsetshire Regiment	Grave III. G. 18/23
G W Wheelhouse	Army Service Corps	Grave IV. K. 10
J W Talo	Leicestershire Regiment	Grave IV. P. 10

Italy

Staglieno Cemetery, Genoa

R G Smith	Manchester Regiment	Grave I. D. 37

Taranto Town Cemetery Extension

W Fitzgerald	Duke of Cornwall's Light Infantry	Grave I. D. 5

Kenya

Nairobi South Cemetery

P D Donovan	Royal Garrison Artillery	Grave IV. C. 4

Latvia

Meza (Nikolai) Cemetery

W P Clarkin	Lincolnshire Regiment	Grave II. B. 2

Malta

Pieta Military Cemetery

J E Helson	Rifle Brigade	Grave C. XI. 3

Sierra Leone

Freetown Memorial

J E Eldridge	Army Ordnance Corps	

Tanzania

Dar es Salaam War Cemetery

C E Mars	Army Service Corps	Grave 5. G. 23

Moshi Cemetery

A Harrison	Royal Fusiliers	Grave II. B. 2

Tanga European Cemetery

W H Gould	Army Service Corps	Grave V. C. 7

Turkey (including Gallipoli)

Haidar Pasha Memorial

J R Beavers	Royal Field Artillery	Addenda Extension

Helles Memorial

J P Page	Yorkshire Regiment	Panel 55 to 58
G E Simpson	Lancashire Fusiliers	Panel 59 to 73 or 218 to 219
F Brooker	Hampshire Regiment	Panel 126-135 or 223-226 228-229 & 328
E P T Figg	Essex Regiment	Panel 146 to 151 or 229 to 233
C D Randall	Sherwood Foresters	Panel 151 to 153
A G W O'Leary	York and Lancaster Regiment	Panel 171 to 173
A E Douch	Royal Munster Fusiliers	Panel 192 to 197

Lone Pine Memorial

F G Hall	Australian Light Horse	Panel 6

Pink Farm Cemetery, Helles

W G Brown	Lancashire Fusiliers	Special Memorial 10

Twelve Tree Copse Cemetery

G W Durham	Royal Inniskilling Fusiliers	Special Memorial B. 92

United Kingdom

Bletchley Cemetery, Buckinghamshire

A Lunn	Royal Engineers	Grave OC. 113A

Exeter Higher Cemetery, Devon

W E Daymond	Leicestershire Regiment	Grave C. A. 24. 4

Heavitree (St. Michael) Churchyard Extension, Devon

A T Crouch	Royal Field Artillery	Grave R. 9. 21

Plymouth (Ford Park) Cemetery, Devon

R J Davis	Royal Engineers	General H. 25. 14
R C Duggan	Royal Garrison Artillery	General L. 26. 11

Torquay Cemetery and Extension, Devon

C V Agate	Army Pay Corps	Grave M. 2. 14961

Portland (St. George) Churchyard, Dorset

C Pye	West Yorkshire Regiment	

Lockerbie (Dryfesdale) Cemetery, Dumfriesshire

J H Roberts	King's Own Scottish Borderers	Grave 1. 1807

Hastings Cemetery, East Sussex

J W H Howard	Army Service Corps	

Edinburgh (Dalry) Cemetery, Edinburgh

F R Walker	Argyll and Sutherland Highlanders	Grave H. 128

Edinburgh (Rosebank) Cemetery, Edinburgh

G R Simpson	The Royal Scots (Lothian Regiment)	

Chelmsford (Writtle Road) Cemetery, Essex

G A Joseph	The Black Watch	Grave C. 2081

Colchester Cemetery, Essex

J C Onn	The Essex Regiment	Grave S. 7. 92

Walton-On-The-Naze (All Saints) Churchyard Extension, Essex

W S Wade	West Yorkshire Regiment	Special Memorial

Port Talbot (Holy Cross) Churchyard, Glamorganshire

W A Spong	Welsh Regiment	Grave D. 18

South Cerney (All Hallows) Churchyard, Gloucestershire

A A E Williams	Royal Irish Regiment	North-East of church

Aldershot Military Cemetery, Hampshire

S H Allen	12th Royal Lancers	Grave AF. 1721
J May	4th Reserve Cavalry Regiment	Grave AF. 2133
H St. J Sainty	Army Service Corps	Grave R. 333

Hollybrook Memorial, Southampton, Hampshire

A S Grieve	Army Ordnance Corps	

Hollybrook Memorial, Southampton, Hampshire

J E Nichols	South African Native Labour Corps	

Portsmouth (Highland Road) Cemetery, Hampshire

A G Kelly	Rifle Brigade	Grave K. 12. 10

Portsmouth (Kingston) Cemetery, Hampshire

A F Richards	Royal Marine Light Infantry	Billing's. 2. 61
V E A Stimpson	Royal Engineers	Jones'. 13-14
A F McFarlane	Royal Garrison Artillery	Taylor's. 13. 7

Portsmouth (Milton) Cemetery, Hampshire

J D H Marlow	Hampshire Regiment	Grave I. 14. 28

Portsmouth Naval Memorial, Hampshire

G H Holmes	Royal Marines	6

Southampton (Hollybrook) Cemetery, Hampshire

L A Howell	Royal Engineers	Grave L. 5. 169

Winchester (West Hill) Old Cemetery, Hampshire

F A McManus	King's Royal Rifle Corps	Grave 15910

Sandown (Christ Church) Churchyard, Isle of Wight

G Truett	Royal Garrison Artillery	

Beckenham Crematorium and Cemetery, Kent

F R P Gerkins	Royal Naval Volunteer Reserve	Screen Wall. X5. 7687

Dover (Buckland) Cemetery, Kent

R C Beeston	Royal Garrison Artillery	Grave D. 2300

Dover (St. James) Cemetery, Kent

B D Conolly	Royal Army Medical Corps	Grave P. G. 2

Fort Pitt Military Cemetery, Kent

T W Goodall	Royal Engineers	Grave 1411
F Wilson	King's (Liverpool Regiment)	Grave 1415

Gillingham (Woodlands) Cemetery, Kent

H C Caston	Royal Engineers	Special Memorial
A W Romain	Royal Engineers	Special Memorial

Lydd Cemetery, Kent

E Gascoyne	Royal Garrison Artillery	Middle of cemetery

Bootle Cemetery, Lancashire

J H Kay	Royal Army Medical Corps	Grave I. CE. 279

Burnley Cemetery, Lancashire

A C A Richmond	East Lancashire Regiment	Screen Wall. 14859

Warrington Cemetery, Lancashire

H Gregson	South Lancashire Regiment	Grave D. RC. 703

Melton Mowbray (Thorpe Road) Cemetery, Leicestershire

J W E Woods	Royal Air Force	Grave 2134

Brompton Cemetery, London

T Drake	Scots Guards	Grave N. 174638

Charlton Cemetery, Greenwich, London

A C Browning	Royal Garrison Artillery	Grave N. 168

Kensal Green (All Souls') Cemetery, London

G J L Ellis	The Royal Scots (Lothian Regiment)	Screen Wall 213. 7. 8.

Lambeth Cemetery, London

C E Gass	Royal Defence Corps	Screen Wall. W.3. 6

Nunhead (All Saints) Cemetery, London

T Brown	Lincolnshire Regiment	Screen Wall. 89. 32787

Plumstead Cemetery, London

A E Gee	Royal Garrison Artillery	Grave B. 1538
W F Quigley	12th Lancers	Grave G. 79

Streatham Cemetery, London

W Kennedy	1st King Edward's Horse	Grave M. 1051
W J Harman	King's Royal Rifle Corps	Screen Wall. D. 191

Tooting (St. Nicholas) Churchyard, London

J W Monger	Rifle Brigade	Grave C. 12

Wandsworth (Earlsfield) Cemetery, London

J T Edgar	East Surrey Regiment	Grave H. 3. 8990
L D S S Senior	6th Dragoon Guards	Screen Wall. F.B. 18. 3

West Norwood Cemetery and Crematorium, London

J A Kirtland	Royal Fusiliers	Screen Wall. 31. 8433

Woolwich Cemetery, London

W J Adds	Army Ordnance Corps	Grave 11. 420
T R C Redford	Army Ordnance Corps	Grave K. 144
C S Holmes	Royal Field Artillery	Grave K. 637

Acton Cemetery, Middlesex

A T Ashton	Army Service Corps	Section A, Row B, Grave 21

Hendon Cemetery and Crematorium, Middlesex

J A Collins	Welsh Regiment	Grave D. 0. 24666

Heston (St. Leonard) Churchyard, Middlesex

S J Wilson	Army Service Corps	Grave B. 13

Twickenham Cemetery, Middlesex

W J Pepler	Royal Fusiliers	

Cowley (St. James) Churchyard, Oxfordshire

W H Smith	Oxfordshire and Buckinghamshire Light Infantry	

Bath (Locksbrook) Cemetery, Somerset

E V Davies	Wiltshire Regiment	Western. E. 607

Cannock Chase War Cemetery, Staffordshire

A E E Urell	Royal Garrison Artillery	Grave 4. G. 13

Croydon (Mitcham Road) Cemetery, Surrey

F C Hilliard	Royal Field Artillery	N4. 10944

Guildford (Stoke) Old Cemetery, Surrey

H W Pridgeon	Royal Field Artillery	Grave I. 133

Kingston-Upon-Thames Cemetery, Surrey

W A Springett	Duke of Wellington's (West Riding Regiment)	Grave C. 3702
G A Bigsby	Bedfordshire Regiment	Grave E. 1984
A B Davis	The Buffs	Grave E. "C." 4772

North Sheen Cemetery, Surrey

E T Hayes	Royal Defence Corps	Grave AC. 446

Wallington (Bandon Hill) Cemetery, Surrey

A E R Norrington   Royal Fusiliers   Grave A. 580

Bury St. Edmunds Cemetery, Suffolk

W L Hardy   Suffolk Regiment   Grave 34. 33A

Brighton City (Bear Road) Cemetery, West Sussex

L R Lewry   8th Hussars   Grave ZHN. 62

Pontefract Cemetery, Yorkshire

F H G Woolgar   York and Lancaster Regiment   Grave M. 1014

York Cemetery, Yorkshire

R J Meredith   1st (King's) Dragoon Guards   Section A. Grave 15. 28584

Index, by Service, Regiment & Corps

Royal Naval Volunteer Reserve	Page 40
Royal Marines	Page 41
Royal Marine Light Infantry	Page 44
Royal Horse Guards (The Blues)	Page 45
Royal Horse Artillery	Page 47
1st (King's) Dragoon Guards	Page 57
2nd Dragoon Guards (Queen's Bays)	Page 59
3rd (Prince of Wales's) Dragoon Guards	Page 63
4th (Royal Irish) Dragoon Guards	Page 65
6th Dragoon Guards (Carabiniers)	Page 67
1st (Royal) Dragoons	Page 69
2nd Dragoons (Royal Scots Greys)	Page 71
3rd (The King's Own) Hussars	Page 73
8th (The King's Royal Irish) Hussars	Page 75
9th (The Queen's Royal) Lancers	Page 77
12th (The Prince of Wales's Royal) Lancers	Page 79
13th Hussars	Page 81
15th (The King's) Hussars	Page 84
16th (The Queen's) Lancers	Page 86
17th (Duke of Cambridge's Own) Lancers	Page 89
5th (Royal Irish) Lancers	Page 91
19th (Queen Alexandra's Own Royal) Hussars	Page 92
20th Hussars	Page 94
Berkshire (Hungerford) Yeomanry	Page 97
King Edward's Horse (The King's Overseas Dominions Regiment)	Page 99
The Reserve Regiments of Cavalry	Page 101
Royal Regiment of Field Artillery	Page 102
Royal Regiment of Garrison Artillery	Page 134
Corps of Royal Engineers	Page 161
Royal Flying Corps	Page 179
Coldstream Guards	Page 182
Scots Guards	Page 185
Irish Guards	Page 186
The Royal Scots (Lothian Regiment)	Page 188
The Queen's (Royal West Surrey Regiment)	Page 192
The Buffs (East Kent Regiment)	Page 199
The King's Own (Royal Lancaster Regiment)	Page 206
The Northumberland Fusiliers	Page 210
The Royal Warwickshire Regiment	Page 213
The Royal Fusiliers (City of London Regiment)	Page 216
The King's (Liverpool Regiment)	Page 229
The Norfolk Regiment	Page 235
The Lincolnshire Regiment	Page 243
The Devonshire Regiment	Page 252
The Suffolk Regiment	Page 257
Prince Albert's (Somerset Light Infantry)	Page 264
The Prince of Wales's Own (West Yorkshire	Page 267

Regiment)	
The East Yorkshire Regiment	Page 272
The Bedfordshire Regiment	Page 276
The Leicestershire Regiment	Page 281
The Royal Irish Regiment	Page 286
Alexandra, Princess of Wales's Own (Yorkshire Regiment)	Page 291
The Lancashire Fusiliers	Page 295
The Royal Scots Fusiliers	Page 302
The Cheshire Regiment	Page 304
The Royal Welsh Fusiliers	Page 306
The South Wales Borderers	Page 310
The King's Own Scottish Borderers	Page 315
The Cameronians (Scottish Rifles)	Page 317
The Royal Inniskilling Fusiliers	Page 319
The Gloucestershire Regiment	Page 323
The Worcestershire Regiment	Page 331
The East Lancashire Regiment	Page 334
The East Surrey Regiment	Page 337
The Duke of Cornwall's Light Infantry	Page 347
The Duke of Wellington's (West Riding Regiment)	Page 351
The Royal Sussex Regiment	Page 354
The Hampshire Regiment	Page 357
The South Staffordshire Regiment	Page 365
The Dorsetshire Regiment	Page 367
The Prince of Wales's Volunteers (South Lancashire Regiment)	Page 379
The Welsh Regiment	Page 383
The Black Watch (Royal Highlanders)	Page 393
The Oxfordshire and Buckinghamshire Light Infantry	Page 398
The Essex Regiment	Page 403
The Sherwood Foresters (Nottinghamshire and Derbyshire Regiment)	Page 412
The Loyal North Lancashire Regiment	Page 417
The Northamptonshire Regiment	Page 419
The Princess Charlotte of Wales's (Royal Berkshire Regiment)	Page 424
The Queen's Own (Royal West Kent Regiment)	Page 432
The Duke of Cambridge's Own (Middlesex Regiment)	Page 438
The King's Royal Rifle Corps	Page 445
The Duke of Edinburgh's (Wiltshire Regiment)	Page 455
The Manchester Regiment	Page 460
The Prince of Wales's (North Staffordshire Regiment)	Page 465
The York and Lancaster Regiment	Page 467
The Durham Light Infantry	Page 472
The Highland Light Infantry	Page 478
Seaforth Highlanders (Ross-shire Buffs, The Duke of Albany's)	Page 482

The Gordon Highlanders	Page 491
The Queen's Own Cameron Highlanders	Page 499
The Royal Irish Rifles	Page 503
The Princess Victoria's (Royal Irish Fusiliers)	Page 506
The Connaught Rangers	Page 509
Princess Louise's (Argyll and Sutherland Highlanders)	Page 511
The Prince of Wales's Leinster Regiment (Royal Canadians)	Page 524
The Royal Munster Fusiliers	Page 526
The Prince Consort's Own (Rifle Brigade)	Page 530
Machine Gun Corps	Page 539
Tank Corps	Page 544
Royal Defence Corps	Page 546
Army Service Corps	Page 549
Army Ordnance Corps	Page 561
Royal Army Medical Corps	Page 567
Army Pay Corps	Page 572
Corps of Army Schoolmasters	Page 574
The London Regiment	Page 576
The Cambridgeshire Regiment	Page 586
Royal Air Force	Page 588
Australian Light Horse	Page 590
Australian Imperial Force	Page 593
Canadian Mounted Rifles	Page 599
Canadian Infantry	Page 601
New Zealand Infantry	Page 604
South African Infantry	Page 607
South African Native Labour Corps	Page 609

Appendix I – *the unveiling of the war memorial*

The following article appeared in the *Dover Express*, 30 June 1922 and is a report of the events surround the unveiling of the school war memorial, on 27 June 1922. The sermon delivered by the Chaplain-General, John Bishop Taylor-Smith KCB CVO QHC, is reproduced here in full and it is worth noting that the memorial had been paid for by subscription, amongst units of the British Army and Old Boys themselves.

THE DUKE OF YORK'S ROYAL MILITARY SCHOOL WAR MEMORIAL.

UNVEILED BY THE DUKE OF CONNAUGHT.

On Tuesday the Duke of Connaught, the President of the Duke of York's Royal Military School unveiled the War Memorial cross at the School and inspected the boys. The Duke of Connaught, who arrived at Dover by the 12.45 Boat Train, was accompanied by General Sir N.G. Lyttleton, Lieut-General Sir. H.E. Belfield, Lieut-General Sir Francis Lloyd, who are Commissioners of the School, Major-General Rover, Colonel Gordon and Mr. G.B. Crossland. The Duke's car, which carried a Union Jack, drove through Dover and up Castle Hill. Awaiting His Royal Highness's arrival, the officers, warrant officers, the students, who were in khaki, with rifles, and the boys, under Major Thomas, were drawn up on the parade ground, and His Royal Highness was received with the Royal Salute.

THE DUKE REVIEWS THE BOYS.

The Duke of Connaught made a closer and lengthy inspect of the ranks, talking to the officers and men and boys, the latter of whom wore the badge of their father's regiment. At the conclusion of the inspection, some 100 of the Old Boys, who were drawn up in the enclosure, were inspected by the Duke. The students and the boys then marched past the Duke, in open company columns, and afterwards in close company columns; and it need not be said that the march past was a perfect example of such ceremonial. The march over, the boys formed into columns for fours and headed by the band and bugles marched to the Chapel, where the Memorial Tablets with the names of the 247 Old Boys of the School, who fell in the Great War, were to be dedicated by the Chaplain General Bishop Taylor-Smith.

DEDICATION SERVICE.

These names are engraved on alabaster tablets of beautiful design, which are placed on the walls of the Chapel. The first tablet contains the names of those who fell in the War again Napoleon, and comprises those who fell in the Peninsular and at Waterloo. Following are the names of those lost in the wars since, but none contain such a list as that of the late war. It commences on one tablet that is only partly filled and takes two more completely and partly fills another. The body of the Church was crowded with the Boys, their bright red uniforms making a striking feature in this beautiful building of red brick, with white stone mouldings. After the Boys had entered, their colours were brought to the chancel and during the service, were fixed to either side of the chancel rails. The Duke of Connaught and his staff were seated on the cross-bench on the south side of the Chapel. The Old Boys and relatives of those fallen filled almost all the remaining space. The service opened with the hymn "How bright those Glorious Spirits shine," sung with spirit by the boys. Major Dryer read the Lesson from Ecclesiastics xliv., verses 1-14. The two prayers The Lord's Prayer and the prayer, Almighty God with Whom the spirits of them who departed hence." were read by the School Chaplain, the Rev. R.G. Semple.

Bishop Taylor Smith then, from the pulpit, dedicated the tablets, saying, "To the glory of God and in loving and grateful memory of those who laid down their lives for King and country in a righteous cause I dedicate these tablets. May we all look upon them and realise the peace of sins forgiven, the joy of faithful service, and the power of the endless life to which may God vouchsafe to bring us all through Jesus Christ, our Lord."

The Bishop took his text from the 12th Chapter of St. Paul to the Hebrews, the first and part of the Second verses: "Wherefore, seeing we also are compassed about with so great a cloud of witnesses let us lay aside every weight and the sin which doth so easily beset us, and let us run with patience the race that is set before us - Looking unto Jesus."

He said, "I want to speak to you very briefly this afternoon of three great things. I want to speak of a great goodness and then of a great debt and then of a great work. I want to turn your eyes in three directions to-day. First, I want you to look upwards and thank God for his great victory. But, says someone, was it not the men who brought us victory? No, it was not the men, though they went forth, many of them never to return, and those that came back fought bravely. No, it was not the men who saved us. But was it not the money, says someone. No! People gave liberally every time until it hurt, but it was not the money that saved us? But, says another, was it not the munitions, the ships, the guns, the aeroplanes? No, it was not the munitions though we saw them piled up on the battlefield and in the dear homeland. It was God who gave us victory. To an unprepared people God was most gracious. So this afternoon I want you to lift up your eyes and lift up your hearts and thank God once again for His great goodness in giving us victory. And now I want you to look in another direction. You have looked up and put God first, now we are going to look back. We are going to think of those who died for us, especially the Old Boys of the Duke of York's School, who played the game and fought magnificently and added fresh laurels to this school. They went forth never to return that you and I might go in and out of our home in safety. They went forth, forming a living wall between our enemy and our homes and when that was not enough they laid down their lives that we might live. Do not let us think of these dear boys as dead. They are with Christ, which St. Paul said is far better. Death, then, may hide, but not divide: they are but with Christ on the other side. So we may speak of Him of them as they speak to Him, no doubt, of us. They have received great promotion. They were excused the intermediate service, for this life is only the beginning of service, and so we think of them to-day serving still, without hindrance, without temptation, without sin. And their names are not only inscribed on these beautiful tablets, but their names are inscribed on your hearts and mine. So we look back and think of those who laid down their lives that you and I might live. We owe to them a great debt which we can never repay. And the third direction I would ask you to look. Having looked upward and having looked backward, now I want you to look forward and to consider the great work that lies before us. We have built again that which has been broken down. It will require the best and the most if we are going to build well; and who is there amongst us who will hang back from the task? There are three great essentials. First, that all who look upon these names may realise that peace of sin forgiven. That is the first general essential for every soul, young and old, rich and poor - the peace which tells of pardon through the precious death of Jesus. There is no satisfaction in our work whatever that work may be, unless we realise that peace of sin forgiven. Then, boys, when you run races you strip off everything that is possible to be done without so that you may not be hindered and that you may touch the tape first. Seeing we are compassed about with such a cloud of witnesses, the angels in the heavens and men on earth, if we are going to make the most of and do the best for our country then we must get rid of everything that hinders just as we cast away our garments and put on the lightest, so we must cast aside sins that hinder, whatever those sins may be, whether lying, or stealing, or swearing, or uncleanliness, whatever it is, if we are going forward. As we look forward we must cast aside every weight and the sins that so easily best us. Racing men will tell you that a man cannot run with weight and I tell you we cannot run well with sin. The second thing we ask God to grant us all who look at the Memorial, is the joy of service. There is no joy on earth like the joy of faithful service - service for God, service for King and service for country. The joy that I am speaking of was possessed by the great soldier whose body we laid to rest yesterday afternoon in St. Paul's Cathedral, Field-Marshal Sir Henry Wilson. He knew the joy of faithful service. The very night before he was called home he was dining with the Chaplain's Department in London. He stayed by my side for two hours and a half. I think of that last dinner and the conversation we had. He was such a splendid man. I wish I had time, I know I have not, to tell you the points of his character. He was strong intellectually, he was strong physically and he was strong spiritually. He loved God and he loved men and everyone loved him in consequence. I never attended a service in St. Paul's, and I have attended many memorial service, which so impressed me as that yesterday. I saw strong men having the greatest difficulty to keep tears back. He was frank, he was fearless, and he was frisky - that is the way someone described him, and you see what a noble character was his. He had the joy of faithful service. There is one thing more we pray for and that is that we may possess, all who look upon these memorials, the power of endless life. The endless life means an indwelling Christ. It is not enough to read about Jesus Christ. It is not enough to associate with Jesus Christ in service and in sacrament; it is essential you should receive him into your hearts, and then you will be the man that England needs, and you wish to be, you will be true men, strong in the Lord and strong for the Lord, good soldiers living with a great purpose and faithful unto a glorious death. So I turn your eyes in these three directions. This day we look up and thank God for His great goodness in giving us victory. We look back and we remember our great debt to those who died for us, and we look forward to consecrating ourselves to the great work that lies before us. Seeing we are compassed about with such a great cloud of witnesses, let us lay aside every weight and the sin that does so easily beset us; let us run with patience and the race that is set before us, looking to Jesus, Leader of our Faith."

The hymn, "For all the Saints," was sung, and then "God save the King," and the Benediction concluded the service.

THE UNVEILING OF THE MEMORIAL.

The memorial cross is near the gate on the Deal Road. It is the Cross of Sacrifice to be found in all war cemeteries, with a bronze Crusader's sword, and bears the following inscription:-

"To the Glory of God and in Memory of the Old Boys of the Duke of York's Royal Military School, who gave their lives for King and County in the Great War, 1914-18.
"Sons of soldiers, they gave all for their Country:
"Sons of the Brave."
"The names and the regiment of the 247 Old Boys of the School here commemorated are inscribed on tablets in the School Chapel."
"Went the day well, we died and never knew, but well or ill, England, we died for you."

The cross stands in a triangle, and round it were grouped the boys, with the Old Boys facing the cross. In addition to the Mayor and Mayoress of Dover, there were also present Councillor Mrs. Ord, Councillors Fox, Livings, Barnes and several Corporation officers, the Lord Lieutenant of Kent, the Marquis of Camden, Lord Northbourne and Colonel-Commandant Marindin, and the officers of Dover Garrison. Before unveiling the cross, the Duke of Connaught said:- "Boys of the Duke of York's School, it affords me particular pleasure to be with you here to-day on the occasion when we are dedicating and unveiling this memorial to those who were educated at this school, and who laid down their lives for King and Country. There are no less than 247 names on the tablet, and I am sure that every boy in this school, and after he leaves the school, will ever remember with pride and grief these splendid young men who were formerly Duke of York's School Boys, who laid down their lives in this splendid way. Let the example of those who did not fear death ever live with you, and may it be an incentive to all you boys, sons of old soldiers, to emulate their spirit of devotion and bravery, to which this cross is erected. I take this opportunity of saying to the boys of the Duke of York's Royal Military School how pleased I am to see them again to-day. I have been one of their governors for many years, and have inspected them on many different occasions, but always at their former home, Chelsea. I am very pleased to come and see you here. This is a more healthy place, in the neighbourhood of the old citadel of Dover, than ever it was in the old school at Chelsea. I was very pleased with the appearance of the boys on parade and the smart manner in which they executed their march past. I feel convinced that the same spirit exists amongst you boys to-day as it has done in years gone by, which has always made the boys of the

Duke of York's School respected throughout the whole of the country. I hope that this memorial, that I am about to unveil, will increase that feeling of self-respect, and that feeling of duty, which I think, had been always one of the characteristics of the Duke of York's School. It may interest some of you to know what the record of the School was during the Great War. As I have said before, no less than 247 fell in the war. The decorations awarded were:- 1 D.S.O., 32 M.C.'s. 1 Distinguished Flying Cross, 7 O.B.E.'s, 15 M.B.E.'s, 36 D.C.M.'s, 36 M.M.'s, 42 M.S.M.'s and 22 various foreign decorations." Just as the Duke was concluding his speech the threatening rain began to fall, and the flag hiding the memorial was almost torn off by the strong gusts of wind before the Duke could pull it off. The Senior Chaplain then dedicated the memorial in the same words as in the Chapel. The "Last Post" was sounded by the buglers and, after a pause, the "Reveille."

Appendix II – *account of the death of Harold Kenney*

In our research, we have only come across one truly detailed description of the death of a Dukie in the First World War, found within an October 1965 article in *American Heritage* magazine[446]. The journalist-historian Gene Smith returned to the Western Front and visited places such as Verdun and Belleau Wood, but it is his encounter at the Menin Gate with a former comrade of Private Harold William Kenney (see p. 92), that means we have reproduced the relevant section here in entirety, the emphases in italics being added by us.

YPRES: KENNEY

...one man who came back to Ypres seemed quieter than most of the others. He was A. J. Arpal, who wore in his lapel the insignia of the Old Contemptibles Association, and who had seen it through from the very beginning. *He had never been back since the war*, but now with his grandchildren in school and his wife dead, he joined a tour which went all over the British zone, transportation, hotels, and meals provided for a week, at a price of only eighteen quid. Arpal was a cavalryman.

For Arpal the symbol of that war has always been Kenney. Years and decades have passed since Kenney died, but Arpal has never forgotten him. Kenney was a laughing boy, twenty-two or three, and always wore his cap to one side. A happy kid. Arpal has thought of him a lot in these forty years while he has turned old and grey and quiet and a grandfather and Kenney has remained young in his lost grave in Belgium. Kenney represented the spirit they had in those days. Arpal was right there when this kid died. They were moving up in file early in the war and there was a volley of shots from beside the road. Kenney was knocked out of his saddle and Arpal thought to himself, Thank God he wasn't dragged by his horse. Arpal and the others leaped into a ditch and opened fire. By next morning the Germans were gone and Kenney was still lying in the road. Arpal saw at once that it wouldn't have mattered a damn if his horse had dragged him or not, for he must have been dead before he hit the ground. *When they opened his coat to get his letters and things, they saw that sewn into his collar where it buttoned next to his throat there was a union jack.* They buried him but his grave soon disappeared in shellfire. It was for Kenney's name

---

[446] Smith, G. (1965), "Still Quite On The Western Front". *American Heritage*, Volume 16, Issue 6

that Arpal looked when he came back to Ypres and saw the giant memorial where the names of the Missing are inscribed in stone. Arpal read through the tens of thousands of names and saw all the ranks of all the familiar British regiments, and those of the strange ones like the 9th Bhopal Infantry with its ranks of Subadar, Jermadar, Havildar, Sepoy. *Finally he found Kenney's name, and all the noise and traffic faded away. He had found Kenney.* That was at the Menin Gate.

YPRES: THE MENIN GATE.

The road goes eastward, through the dreary little red-brick Belgian towns so like the industrial slums of England, and finally ends at the French border. At the road's beginning in Ypres is the Gate. They dedicated it in 1927. On the outside facing the road is inscribed, TO THE ARMIES OF THE BRITISH EMPIRE WHO STOOD HERE FROM 1914 TO 1918. Inside: HERE ARE RECORDED THE NAMES OF OFFICERS AND MEN WHO FELL IN THE YPRES SALIENT BUT TO WHOM THE FORTUNES OF WAR DENIED THE KNOWN AND HONOURED BURIAL GIVEN TO THEIR COMRADES IN DEATH. Kipling wrote the words. Underneath them are the names of the Missing.

The featured speaker on July 24, 1927, was Field Marshal Lord Plumer. Bandy-legged, with a puffy face, not looking like a soldier, he stood with the King of the Belgians before the giant audience come from England. The reporters that day wrote that most of the people were aged women, shabbily dressed. The Southern Railways ran special free trains to the coast for them – first-class carriages only. The women bore rambler roses, snap-dragons, lilies from their English gardens. They sat in the hot sun facing the Gate with their backs to the Menin Road leading out to the Salient, and six pipers of the Scots Guards standing on the shell-shattered medieval ramparts by the Gate played "The Flowers of the Fields." Buglers of the Somerset Light Infantry sounded the Last Post, and to the reporters it seemed as if in the throbbing silence when the calls faded away there must come some sound, some sign, from the Salient up the road. Lord Plumer cried, "They are not Missing; they are here," and the Mums in their funny hats and long black stockings put their hands over their faces.

After that, every night at eight in the winter and nine in the summer, Belgian buglers sounded the Last Post. In 1940 the Germans came down the Menin Road and took Ypres. For four years the buglers were silenced. But fifteen minutes after the last German was rounded up in 1944 the long slow notes of the Last Post quivered out from under the Gate. On some of the nights since then, particularly when the weather is bad, there is no one to hear the buglers except the policeman who halts traffic. At other times there will be a score or even a hundred people. Delegations come out from England, elderly men marching out of step and carrying old regimental flags. Age has shrunken most of them and made them puny, and for all that they are combat veterans of the Great War. They look somewhat foolish as they line up in ragged files. Cars and trucks rattle under the Gate as they stand waiting for the police to halt the traffic. When this is done the flag-bearers go out and stand in the road. In this silence the sound of shuffling feet mixes with the dull rumble of idling motors. Someone shouts, "Attention!" and the skinny old men square-bash to something approaching the posture they were able to attain when all, the living and Missing, were young. Belgians—sometimes soldiers, sometimes members of the Ypres Fire Department—come marching out into the street to face the flags. There are often as many as four buglers. They raise silver bugles given by the British Legion. Some of the old men salute in the British palms-out way. Others take off their hats. The beautiful trilling brings to mind hazy pictures of Indian garrisons and Sandhurst and Salisbury Plain; all the calls are sounded: Reveille, Mess Call, Defaulters' Call, the Last Post. When the final note dies the Belgians lower the bugles smartly, stand for a moment, and then wheel to the right and march to the curb. The traffic is already rolling under the Gate as the old men start to furl their flags. Some of them walk back to look at the names on the walls yet again—*Arpal[447] for one last moment lets his eye rest on KENNEY*—and then the buses pull up to the curb.

---

[447] "A. J. Arpal" is believed to be Lance Corporal, 7799 Alfred J. Arkell, 19th (Queen Alexandra's Own Royal) Hussars; he reached the rank of Serjeant, being discharged in 1919

In Memoriam – *Richard Hill Watt [1967-2022]*

Sadly, we suddenly lost our friend and lead author, Rick Watt, only a few months before publication, never to see the culmination of a near three year project. He had spent countless hours in the archives of our old school, going through each and every Petition Document to ensure we had found as many of the "Lost Boys" as was humanly possible – he looked at *thousands* of records in order to do this. The proper recording of these Dukies drove him on to complete his task and this Roll of Honour is a full and fitting testament to his unstinting efforts – the names on the wall are no longer just that, Rick has given them a poignancy that has been absent for over 100 years and future Dukies will no longer wonder who these Old Boys were that went before them.

This will always be his book.

Andy Benns, April 2023

Sons of the Brave

Sons of the Brave